LED ZEPPELIN
The Press Reports....

Compiled & Edited
by Robert Godwin

Led Zeppelin - The Press Reports.... by Robert Godwin © 1997
CG Publishing 140 Battersea Park Road London SW11 4NB UK
CG Publishing Box 62034, Burlington, Ontario, L7R 4K2 Canada
ISBN 1-896522-41-6
Front Cover Photo courtesy Rephoto, Barry Wentzell
Back Cover Photo courtesy Atlantic Records
Manufactured in Canada

Acknowledgements

Led Zeppelin - The Press Reports.... would not have been possible without the hard work and dedication of the assorted journalists who reported these stories. Accolades go to, Ritchie Yorke, Chris Welch, Lisa Robinson, Nick Kent, Caroline Boucher, Charles Shaar Murray, and the dozens of others whose efforts recorded the moment for posterity.

An extra special thank you to Jimmy Page for confirmation of anecdotes.

Major thanks to Fred Lundgren for his help translating the Scandinavian material.

Thanks also go to Rick Barrett, John Brohman, Chris Doherty, Ross Halfin, Hugh Jones, Rod Kincaid, Dave Lewis, Dorte Nielsen, Eric Sachs, Dave Schulps, Bob Walker, and Tom Zeller.

Introduction

The time is July 1968. The British beat boom is gasping it's last breath and the world has had a whole year to absorb the Beatle's Sergeant Pepper.

Jimi Hendrix has stunned the British middle class with his casual disregard for protocol, blatantly ignoring the producers of the Lulu show and blasting out a tribute to his friend Eric Clapton on live TV.

Syd Barrett's Pink Floyd has already self-destructed and is in the throes of being re-invented by Roger Waters and newcomer David Gilmour, meanwhile Fleetwood Mac have just had their first chart appearance.

Two English public school boys have just written their first full musical, 'Joseph and The Amazing Technicolor Dreamcoat' and are setting their sights on the New Testament.

The Beatles are making a film to go along with their new song 'Hey Jude'.

Woodstock is still a year away and in only four months the first men will be sent hurtling towards the moon. The big movie of the summer is Stanley Kubrick's seminal masterpiece '2001 - A Space Odyssey'.

Names such as Black Sabbath, Alice Cooper, AC/DC, Genesis, and David Bowie have no meaning.

Seemingly half the world's youth are reading a fifteen year old, 1000 page novel by an aging Oxford professor, called 'The Lord Of The Rings'.

The charts are still wide open to the likes of Englebert Humperdink, The Bee Gees, and Mary Hopkin and Carnaby Street and Haight-Ashbury are still in full-tilt-rave-mode.

A leading proponent of Britain's new blues, The Yardbirds, have just played their last gig at a college in Luton. Disillusioned by a lack of direction and an apathetic British public, singer Keith Relf and drummer Jim McCarty decide to call it quits. They leave behind rhythm guitarist-turned bassist, Chris Dreja, and bass guitarist-turned lead guitarist, Jimmy Page. At some point during the eight weeks of July and August, Dreja decides to become a photographer and Page is left with a fistful of contracts for gigs in Scandinavia, the rights to the name, and an ex-wrestler-turned manager as his confederate.

Page has spent most of the decade inside the stifling confines of London's recording studios, strumming, plucking and twanging his way through countless recording sessions for everyone from The Who to Burt Bacharach. In 1966 he had finally relented on a long-standing offer to join the Yardbirds, a well respected band with the same pedigree as The Rolling Stones.

The Yardbirds had never broken down the financial barricades to the same degree as the Stones, but they did have an unparalleled reputation for pushing the limits of the form, taking the music of the Mississippi delta and contorting it into something curious enough to gain access to white-middle class America.

After the band had spawned and orphaned two guitar legends, Jeff Beck and Eric Clapton, Page stepped forward into the spotlight and made his mark on the American club circuit. Although Page was never as eclectic as Beck or as smoothly precise as Clapton, he was a disciple of multiple styles. He had spent many of his teenage evenings jamming alongside blues giant Cyril Davis and he was close friends with both Beck and Clapton. He adored British folk-heroes Bert Jansch and Davey Graham, and he had played for years as a session man knocking off everything from Muzak to Motown. Page was just beginning to stamp his impression on the Yardbirds when the band parted company.

'Only Jimmy Left To Form The New Yardbirds' proclaimed the music paper, Melody Maker.

Moving north, we come to the black country. That's colloquial English for an area in the centre of England, encompassing Birmingham and all of it's industrial suburbs, it also describes the glorious countryside surrounding the belching epicentre of the industrial revolution. For every filthy street of post-war terraced housing there is an astonishingly beautiful acre of rolling hedge-rowed turf. History abounds all over England but no more so than in the Midlands. It is no coincidence that the landscape, that stretches from Oxford in the south to Wolverhampton in the north and from Leicester to the Welsh border, was the inspiration for Tolkien's beloved Shire as well as the traumatic hell of Mordor.

Just prior to the Yardbirds dissolution in London, two aspiring teenagers were dissolving their own musical alliance. Robert Plant and John Bonham had performed up and down the country for a couple of years, most lately in 'The Band Of Joy'. Both were from traditional working class backgrounds and both had rejected that conventional lifestyle to become musicians. Plant had been signed to CBS records as early as 1966 and had swiftly banged out a trio of singles, one under the name of his band 'Listen'. He had spent much of 1966-68 trying to introduce the stolid citizens of the black country to the increasingly daring and obscure sounds of California and found that despite his outlandish stage garb his

efforts were falling on deaf ears. Both Plant and Bonham had been together briefly in a band called The Crawling Kingsnakes, they then went on to play together in one of the several incarnations of The Band Of Joy touring the UK, in January and February of 1968, as the opening act for American folk-rock singer Tim Rose. After Rose returned to America the Band Of Joy fractured and the two again went their separate ways.

By the time that Chris Dreja had relinquished his position as bass guitarist in the new Yardbirds, word had already reached Robert Plant that the singer's job was available. On the recommendation of singer Terry Reid, Page and manager Peter Grant took a trip north to see Plant performing with his latest band Hobbstweedle.

After the show Page thought that there must be something wrong with Plant's personality for him to still be languishing in the pubs of the black country, but regardless, he invited him down to his house in Surrey.

Right around this time (probably late June or early July) Plant had also crossed paths with blues-godfather Alexis Korner. Korner and Plant had played a few gigs as a duo, banging out old blues standards, and they even recorded a handful of tracks which would finally be released years later.

On arriving at Page's home, Plant quickly learned that he and Page had similar tastes in music and a bond was formed that day which would see the two inextricably linked forever.

On June 23rd Tim Rose returned to the UK and, remembering Bonham, he decided to hire him for the tour. Their first gig was in Hastings on June 28th. By the time Rose and Bonham reached the Hampstead Country Club on July 31st,

Robert Plant had already made Page's acquaintance and convinced him to take a trip to the West End venue to see if Bonham fit the bill for the new Yardbirds. Bonham, in contrast to Plant, was seemingly a practical and pragmatic man. He knew he had to earn a living and so he had accepted the position drumming for American Tim Rose, earning a steady £40 a week. Apparently Plant and Page had to follow up on their offer with multiple telegrams due to Bonham's lack of a telephone.

Another graduate of the London session circuit was a brilliant young arranger who went by the nom-de-plume John Paul Jones. Born, John Baldwin in 1946 he was from a family of musicians and had been exposed to the world of touring musicians since he was two years old. Jones had begun his session work playing back up to ex-Shadows Jet Harris and Tony Meehan. His first love was the Motown sound, and when the house-producers of Britain's insipid chart music turned their cheesy attentions to the sounds of Detroit soul, there were few local musicians who knew anything about it. Jones was, he claims, the only one who knew the first thing about the driving bottom-end that powered the Motown sound. He was snapped up while still in his teens and swiftly graduated to arranger. From 1962 to 1968, Jones was a prerequisite on hundreds of sessions, his talents cropping up on everything from Donovan to Lulu, from Herman's Hermits to Tom Jones. Needless to say by 1968 he had run into Page numerous times and he was desperately in need of a change.

Jones contacted Page and asked if he needed a bass guitarist. Page needed little convincing, knowing full well what Jones' credentials were, and so he later informed Bonham and Plant that they would be rehearsing with a session man. Plant later stated that he had visions of 'some old guy with a pipe'!

Descending into a small basement in Soho's Wardour Street, the four proceeded to rip through a variety of songs including Garnett Mimms 'As Long As I Have You' and the Yardbirds arrangement of 'Train Kept A Rollin'. In the first week of September 1968 they departed for Denmark to play their first concert.

———

Within a year, Led Zeppelin was known around the world. In 1969 alone they sold in excess of a million and a half records, by the end of 1970 the numbers had swelled to four million with no end in sight. The impetus for this unprecedented success has been the subject of speculation for years. A lot of critics suggested that the band was a fabrication, concocted by the scheming genius of Page and Grant, a 'hype' perpetrated on a gullible public that would soon fizzle out. The truth is much more straight-forward. Led Zeppelin worked damn hard.

Those who were shattered to see Led Zeppelin II knock the almighty Beatles from the top of the charts, neglected to realise that the Beatles had given up playing in public. They had retreated into the womb-like safety of the recording studio and had outgrown their status as a mere pop group. The Beatles had become Olympians, completely inaccessible, feeding the masses their gospels through the corporate bottle-neck that was Apple Records. Meanwhile the long-haired masses desperately needed mortal heroes, a band that were prepared to blow the doors right off their creaking hinges. Led Zeppelin were good, and they were everywhere. Between September 7th 1968 and November 8th 1969, they played no less than 130 concerts. Many shows were double-headers with the band performing in the afternoon and the evening. They toured Scandinavia twice, the UK four times, the USA and Canada four times and they ventured into France twice. They wrote and recorded two albums and appeared on the radio at least six times, all in the first fourteen months. Each and every time they returned to America they made the effort to play in different towns. They traveled from the frozen wastes of Alberta to the tropical haven of Honolulu. They got snowed in playing for a college dance in Iowa and blew the hell out of a massive audience at the Bath Festival in the UK. They were *everywhere*, and it certainly paid off.

Unquestionably such a swift ascent to stardom has left it's victims in the past. Pink Floyd's Syd Barrett (amongst the most obvious) had barely begun the walk to fame only to see his genius vanquished by the pressure, and yet the four young men of Led Zeppelin never seemed to be able to catch their breath long enough to realise just how popular they had become. Constantly on the go, it wasn't until August 1973 that the pace slackened off to what might be called 'a rest'. In that first five years they recorded five albums and were never off work for more than a month at a time. The sheer frenetic pace of their lives was captured in snapshots from around the world by the tenacity of the press. The band virtually never appeared on the radio and television was an abhorrence to them (they turned down countless offers to appear on the boob tube), and so the only source of information for the fans was the press.

Initially all four of them took occasional turns talking to journalists, but it quickly became apparent that Bonham and Jones were uncomfortable spokes-

men, and talking about their roles in the rock and roll circus known as Led Zeppelin did not sit well with either of them. Robert Plant, however, took to it like the proverbial fish to water. Before 1969 was done, the 21 year old had become the champion of adolescent manhood everywhere and the cause of quite a few pairs of wet knickers. His charm and vagaries always left the readers feeling like they were privy to an 'in' joke even when he blasted off into the stratospheric realms of his own imagination with the most cryptic and anomalous references. His love of Britain (or Albion as he liked to call it), and it's attendant history and allure, is infectious, and as cocky as he sometimes seemed, he was always likable and left the interviewer firmly on his side.

On the other hand, Jimmy Page was the oracle. If you really wanted to get a reasonably straight answer about Zeppelin's 'doings' Page was the man to talk to. His exuberance and enthusiasm for the band were as infectious as Plant's, and you couldn't help but feel that he *really* believed what he was saying. If the critics said Zeppelin was just a business, Page convinced you otherwise. When a journalist called his guitar playing a 'trade' you couldn't help but empathise with his indignation, and wish you were there to box the journalist's ears. Page may have infuriated a few correspondents in his time, but you had to believe that he was committed, both to his music and his partners.

As the band passed through the glories of sold-out houses from Tokyo to Zurich and the traumas of lost loved ones, they were undeniably tempered. At the time of drummer John Bonham's unfortunate fatal accident in 1980 the band were seemingly enjoying another renaissance. They had convincingly survived the scourge of punk rock and drawn unprecedented crowds to the Knebworth Festival in 1979, and had then gone on to trample the European concert circuit into dust throughout the summer of 1980. They had seen enough and been through enough to have become experts at handling the media. With the possible exception of the Beatles and Elvis Presley, Led Zeppelin and their manager Peter Grant seemed to have an uncanny and unprecedented grasp of what the public wanted, and more importantly when they wanted it.

Led Zeppelin were clearly a product of their times. As much as their music has survived the trials of being despised (by the media and punk fans of the late 70's) or adored and over-played (by the media and the revivalist heavy fans of the late 80's) it has become clear that the chemistry that created this enduring phenomenon was a direct result of the era it was produced in. We will never see another band like this because they were a creation of the late 60's and as such will never be duplicated anymore than we can put another *first* man on the moon or capture that Glenn Miller sound for the first time. Reading the reams of journalism in chronological order it starts to become clear that although Led Zeppelin were created by the sixties blues-boom they were confronted with many of the same problems that still face new bands today.

At the beginning of their career they couldn't get arrested for an interview and the clubs wouldn't book them unless they agreed to be billed as The Yardbirds. They got paid ridiculously low fees (£75 for one night) and the press in the UK pretty much ignored them. However when they left their own country they drew immediate attention. Even their first appearance in the USA, where they

weren't even billed, got reviewed the next day. This syndrome of having to leave home to get noticed still afflicts the music industry today. However, Led Zeppelin were immediately recognised by the US press and once they finished that first tour in February 1969 they returned home and the history began.

As the first couple of years went by, their popularity grew so swiftly that they soon became easy targets for criticism. During this period a few people became staunch allies. Ritchie Yorke, an Australian by birth, worked at the Toronto Globe and Mail in Canada. The Globe is the nearest thing Canada has to a conservative and inflexible newspaper (it has that *London Times* feel to it) which makes it all the more surprising to find Yorke's zealous prose leaping off the page touting the band's talents. As the 70's progressed Yorke began to write a semi-regular column for the New Musical Express in the UK and Billboard in the USA, and he often chastised his colleagues in the press for not recognising Zeppelin's virtues. Another constant ally was Chris Welch who from his desk at London's Melody Maker brought the band's exploits to life for the English fans as he followed them around the world. One more writer who rarely disguised her enthusiasm for the band was Lisa Robinson who reported back from the 'trenches' of the New York concert halls. Robinson had a long run of easy access to the band, and she repaid this by delivering the news back to her employers in succinct and positive style. Finally, Caroline Boucher was responsible for many good interviews with the band while she worked for Disc & Music Echo. All four of these journalists seemed to gain access to the inner circle and were rewarded with the knowledge that the band were four intelligent, sometimes eccentric, professionals. As often as the tabloids would have us believe that Led Zeppelin indulged in all manner of perversions and contemptible behaviour these four writers were there to tip the scales back towards a more even-handed reality.

Criticism of Zeppelin did become more common as the years progressed. The band seemed to circle the wagons tighter as their career trundled along to it's untimely conclusion, and inevitably they became less accessible. In this book you will see how a combination of the emergence of Punk Rock and the band's own problems led to a situation where the interviews became orchestrated and less frequent.

After the ruinous ending to their tour of the United States in 1977, they seemed to lose a lot of confidence in their own fan base and abilities. However in their early years they seem to have recognised the problems that they faced with the media and often they tackled them head-on. Vigorous and swift denials always met the 'breaking-up' rumours and they also went out of their way to try and allay the British fans fears that they might desert Britain for the more lucrative stadiums of the United States.

Their handling of the media has often been portrayed as coldly calculating, but on closer inspection it seems to have had it's ups and downs, revealing more often a band who desperately wanted to do the right thing but often stumbled. If anything, the only thing which remains untarnished would seem to be Peter Grant's handling of the band's timing, which can be all important in the music business. His management skills seem to have been peerless. He knew exactly when and how to reveal the band's next move.

In this book you may notice a definite bias towards the weekly British music papers. This proved to be inescapable. During the era 1968-1980 there were very few weekly periodicals in the United States that concerned themselves with rock music. Rolling Stone is the obvious candidate, but for whatever reason it's editors chose to barely acknowledge that the band even existed until 1975. In many of the conventional daily papers of the USA, if the band was mentioned it was often in an off-the-wire reprint of articles from Melody Maker or New Musical Express. Glossy magazines like Circus and Creem infrequently revealed anything new about the band, concentrating mainly on the pictures rather than the news. In Australia the magazines like Go-Set also reprinted articles from the British weeklies and so the core of the information comes from New Musical Express, Disc & Music Echo, Melody Maker, Sounds, and Record Mirror all of which originated in London England.

There are no doubt numerous articles out there which were not exhumed. Many of them are probably important and relevant, but please note that this is not just the positive critiques. Basically everything that was found was included. This revealed one quite remarkable detail. In many histories written about Led Zeppelin and indeed in many interviews with the band there are an abundance of references to how cruelly they were treated by the media. There are in fact so many references to this unjust bias that it has become a truism. However, when you start to actually examine the evidence, as presented in this book, you will find that for the most part the press were quite generous. For every slagging there seems to have been numerous articles extolling the band.

Foreword.

The following articles are mostly paraphrased by myself. Unfortunately it would be impossible to just reprint the originals. The copyright laws are quite specific about that. I have therefore endeavoured to capture the salient points from the original stories and to abbreviate them to the best of my ability. Often this may have led to my own somewhat mangled prose filling in for the handiwork of the many professionals who originally related these stories. I hope that the original points still come across clearly enough and that the originators forgive me. I have made no effort to correct any of the errors found in their articles. Consequently you may find inconsistencies, especially in the concert itineraries, but I thought it of more interest to note what was *thought* to be happening at the time rather than what *did*. In some instances I have criticised articles (if it seemed appropriate), after all in some cases the original reporters were just so far off-base I couldn't let it slip by. In other cases I have just mixed my observations in amongst the text.

I hope as you read this you might begin to detect some of the same insights that revealed themselves to me. Once again the history of the phenomenon is fascinating, and I think this compilation of observations from around the world sheds a unique light on that phenomenon.

Robert Godwin

LED ZEPPELIN
The Press Reports....

1968

June 1968

29 **Melody Maker reports....** Yardbirds Split?.... earliest article reporting the Yardbirds demise. It speculates that they will disband on returning from America, and cites one Ren Grevatt as the source in New York. It continues detailing that Page will reform with a new singer and drummer to replace Relf and McCarty....

July 1968

20 **Melody Maker reports....** Yardbirds Split.... Confirmation that the band have split into two groups. Page and Dreja going one way and Relf and McCarty going another. The name of Relf and McCarty's new group will be Together. A group spokesman states, *"There were no personal differences among the boys. It is just that Keith and Jim are following an entirely different musical line from Jimmy and Chris.".....* Review of Tim Rose concert by Tony Wilson at Blaises Club in London. The review reads, 'Foggy Mountain Breakdown gave a chance for drummer John Bonham and bass guitarist Steve Dalon to take solos.'....

August 1968

3 **Melody Maker reports....** Tim Rose has postponed his American tour from August back to November. (This may have been due to him losing his drummer, John Bonham.... R.G.)..

September 1968

4 **Glostrup Handelsblat reports....** Advert reads — Brondby Pop Club Saturday 7 Sept, at 19.30 The Yardbirds with Jimmy Page - The Day Of Phonix -

The Eyes - Ham Norregards-Hallen....

7 **Copenhagen Berlingske Tidende reports....** Advert reads — Teen Clubs Box 45, Gladsaxe 19.30 Welcomes Yardbirds, Fourways, Bodies, Tickets 5.00 and 7.00 crowns (This was almost certainly Led Zeppelin's first public concert)....

9 **Roskilde Tidende reports....** Review of the show at the Roskilde Hall accompanied by a picture of the Ladybirds (topless and sporting guitars)....

11 **Glostrup Handelsblat reports....** Review of the show at Brondy Pop Club under the heading — Superloves Million Dollar Bash — Barnegråd, Yardbirds and Super Love is a great mix and made up this seasons first pop-fest in Nörregårdshall. Expectation is the best thing said Sören Kierkegård. When you start a new season you always try to make the opening night a little better than you need to.The "little better" this time was the fan-

Brøndby Pop-Club

Lørdag den 7. sept. kl. 19.30

VI starter sæsonen med

THE YARDBIRDS med JIMMY PAGE

The Day Of Phønix

The EYES

HAM

Entré kr. 8,00

Medlemskort 1968—69 kr. 4,00

NØRREGÅRDS-HALLEN - Stolpevej 36

ved Brøndbyøster S.Station

Yardbirds i Brøndby Pop-club

Startskuddet for genåbningen af Brøndby Pop-club lyder den 7. september

tastic Yardbirds in a whole new line-up, Day of Phonix, the Eyes and Ham. Let me start from the top. With the "Ham". This band would entertain the audience between the sets. They did this so well and with such intensity that Bisgaard couldn't make the band notice that it was time for the Yardbirds to play and time to end their set. "Day of Phonix", with their imported westcoast-style and Cy Niclio(?) at the mike, reached into the young people's hearts. This mix of folk music and beat will definitely catch the audience interest and Day of Phonix deserves this. Super Love celebrated their 1-year birthday (hurray hurray), and what a birthday. The house-band the Eye was in on building a psychedelic light-show and showed a movie. The Yardbirds however, requires a closer examination. Jimmy Page has again put a new band together. The music is the same, only better than ever. The new members are: Robert Planto (sic) vocals, John Paul Jones,bass-guitar, John Bonham, drums and of course Jimmy Page on solo-guitar. Robert Planto should face some small criticism

and a lot of praise for an excellent performance. There is no doubt that he is a good singer but he doesn't have to twist his body like he's having a ruptured appendix, or does he? Musically the band is super-great. Their hard disciplined beat is amazing. Of course it was foremost Jimmy Page that was responsible for this but the drummer should also be mentioned; a drum solo so wild and good is hard to find. It was so good that one almost wished that John Bonham wouldn't stop. All in all, the start couldn't be better and if the many new English bands that Bisgaard and Lycirsen have contacted come here, I would almost think that this season will be the best so far.....

12 **Stockholm Express reports.... & Stockholm Daily News reports....** Advert reads — Grönalund Stockholm Tivoli, Big popfinal! English Yardbirds on the big stage at 8 o'clock (tonight)....

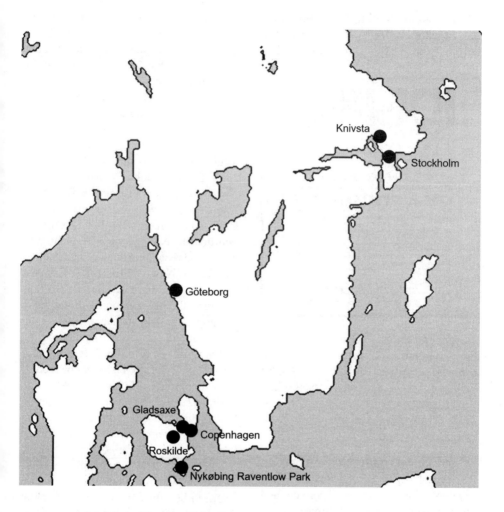

Scandinavian Tour Fall 1968

September 7th, 1968 Teen Clubs Box 45 Gladsaxe
September 7th, 1968 Brondby Pop Club Norregard Hallen Copenhagen
September 8th, 1968 Fjordvilla Roskilde
September 8th, 1968 Nykøbing Raventlow Park Falster Island
September 12th, 1968 Gronalund Tivoli Stockholm
September 13th, 1968 Inside Club Stockholm
September 14th, 1968 Angby Parkdans Show, Knivsta
September 15th, 1968 Liseburg Amusement Park Göteborg

13 **Stockholm Evening Press reports....**
& Stockholm Daily News reports....
Advert reads — Stockholm Inside Club

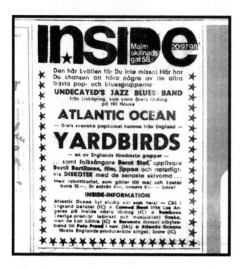

Tonight Yardbirds - One of England's Finest Groups.... **Uppsala New Paper reports....** Advert reads — Angby Parkdans Show, Knivsta. Season Final Sat. 14 September From The Scene at 23.00 (11pm) The Yardbirds. Dans 20.30 - 01.00....

14 **Stockholm Daily News reports....** Review of show at the Inside Club. Yardbird Hurts.... 'It has been up and down for the Yardbirds. A couple of years ago, they were on top. For a while, a lot of people thought that the Yardbirds would lead the developing English pop, but their efforts led nowhere. The members changed and the Yardbirds currently touring Sweden have very little in common with the original line-up. It is not only the line-up that has changed. The style of music is different, as is the quality. Only the name is the same. Friday night they played the Inside. They were so loud it almost hurt. Sometimes playing loud has

an important role in pop, but here it was just a superficial effect.'.... **Uppsala New Paper reports....** Headline reads, Blues group From England....Yardbirds are a well known band that are guests in Sweden right now. Those who want to hear the youngsters get an opportunity in Angby Park on Saturday night. Yardbirds perform with a new line-up this season. Jimmy Page, guitar and violin (!), has banded with three new qualified musicians. Drummer John Bonham has earlier played with American singer Tim Rose. John Paul Jones, bass, was in on Donovan's three latest LP recordings. Fourth man is singer Robert Plant who has a good reputation on the English blues scene.... **New Musical Express reports....** Yardbirds re-shaped.... article outlining the new personnel in the band. "Jimmy Page and manager Peter Grant have formed a new company called Super-Hyp (sic) recording." It goes on to say that the band will no longer be recording with producer Mickie Most. Attention is drawn to the fact that the new group will probably not be with EMI and that four major companies are bidding for the band. "Led Zeppelin are currently touring Scandinavia"...it then goes on to outline how the band has already been invited to return to Scandinavia in January and that "the band will depart to tour America on November 14th to play a series of one-nighters and college dates." The article then speculates that the band will likely record for Warner-Reprise....

15 **Göteborg Evening News reports....** Advert reads — Star Scene at 20.00 Yardbirds pop band Liseberg Amusement Park. Tickets 10.00 crowns....

21 **Melody Maker reports....** "Three of the four Yardbirds have quit to be replaced

MUSIKPAVILJONGEN
KL. 17
Jazzkonsert av Gunnar Lind-
groms The Opposite Corner

STORA SCENEN KL. 19
THORE SKOGMAN
och elefanten
TANYA

STJÄRNSCENEN KL. 20
YARDBIRDS popband

STJÄRNSCENEN KL. 22
Ossie Noble
Peggy Gill
Noy and Rey

STORT FESTFYRVERKERI
avbrännes från Stora Scenen
kl. 21
I DAG ÖPPET 13–23

OBS! Nåst sista söndagen för säsongen!
Blommiad öppnar redan kl. 10!

Liseberg

Hela nöjet till halva priset
med Lisebergs rabatthäfte!

Vuxna 16:—
Tonåringar 7:50
Barn 5:—

---

by Robert Plant, John Paul Jones and John Bonham".... Page to produce future discs.... management negotiating with record companies.... first British date to be the Marquee on October 18th.... "group leaves for the USA on November 14th". This was later proven to be inaccurate as they didn't arrive in the USA until Christmas....

October 1968

12 **DISC reports....** PJ Proby's new single Merry Hoppkins Never Had Days Like These (which featured all four members of Led Zeppelin playing back up) is a spoof of the popular singer recorded by Proby and some of his friends, it has been cut down from twelve minutes to seven and a half... **Melody Maker reports....** Only Jimmy Left To Form the New Yardbirds... after the demise of the Yardbirds last incarnation, Page conducts a short interview with Chris Welch. Led Zeppelin are referred to as a "..welcome

piece of fire power to the armoury of British Groups..." In reference to the Yardbirds, Page, *"We didn't do any gigs in England for two years, so no wonder we lost popularity. But just before we split we did a couple of colleges that were really fantastic. I was really knocked out. We were a happy group and used to get on well socially until we got on stage and Keith lost all enthusiasm. I used to say; 'Come on let's make an effort', but it had all gone. When they split, I don't think Jim wanted to leave, but Keith was depressed. I think it did us all a favour because the new chaps are all 19 and full of enthusiasm. It was getting a bit of a trial in the old group."*

On the new band's sound, *"It's blues basically, but not Fleetwood Mac style. I hate that phrase progressive blues. It sounds like a hype, but that's more or less what the Yardbirds were playing at the end, but nobody knew about it because they never saw us."*

On the new album, *"We've start-*

It goes on to say that the band have just completed their debut album and a single will be released in December.... this was later proven wrong as no single was released in the UK from this album, it reached promo stage but was withdrawn.... **New Musical Express reports....** "The Yardbirds will make their farewell London appearance at the Marquee Friday." The article goes on to announce that the new group Led Zeppelin will make its debut in late October and that the band has already cut it's first LP to be released in December. It then says that they have been signed by Harold Davison, presumably an agent...

26 **DISC reports....** The Yardbirds provided the backing music for PJ Proby's new single The Day Lorraine Came Down.... **Melody Maker reports....** Led Zeppelin Debut.... article outlining the band's debut performance with the new name. It states, ".... make their debut at Surrey University tomorrow (Friday) (25th)." It goes on to state (incorrectly) that the band will debut their American tour on November 16th....

ed working on an LP and we're going to the States in early November. I'm hoping the Marquee will be a good scene. Robert can get up and sing against anybody. He gets up and sings against Terry Reid! Those two are like brothers together."

In conclusion, *"It's refreshing to know that today you can go out and form a group to play the music you like and people will listen. It's what musicians have been waiting for for twenty years."*

19 **DISC reports....** "The Yardbirds are to change their name to Lead (sic) Zeppelin courtesy of the Who's drummer Keith Moon".... **Melody Maker reports....** Article reads, "The Yardbirds to perform two farewell performances at the Marquee Friday 18th and Liverpool University Saturday 19th.... from Sunday group is to be known as Led Zeppelin.".

November 1968

2 **DISC reports....** Remnants of the Yardbirds will reform under Jimmy Page who is an amazing guitarist. He is to be backed by three other equally worthy musicians. The band could be very good indeed....

9 **Melody Maker reports....** Letter to the editor asking about Page's guitar playing, Page's answer, *"The sustain is achieved by volume combined with the use of a Tone Bender. It is virtually a standard model, but with a few modifications car-*

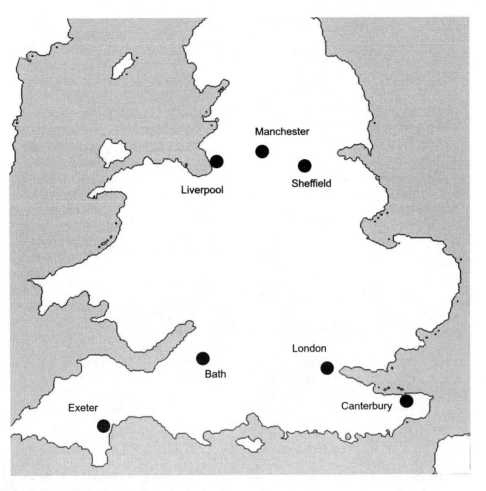

UK Tour Winter 1968

October 18th, 1968 London Marquee
October 19th, 1968 Liverpool University
October 25th, 1968 London Surrey University
November 9th, 1968 London Chalk Farm Roundhouse
November 16th, 1968 Manchester College Of Science & Technology
November 23rd, 1968 Sheffield
November 29th, 1968 London Richmond Athletic Club
December 10th, 1968 London Marquee
December 13th, 1968 Canterbury Bridge Country Club
December 16th, 1968 Bath Pavilion
December 19th, 1968 Exeter City Hall
December 20th, 1968 London Wood Green Fishmongers Hall

ried out by it's inventor, Gary Hurst, which provide more sustain and a harmonic overtone. My guitar is a Fender Telecaster, given to me by Jeff Beck. It is a very early model and I have wired the pick-ups together, creating a different sound, which cannot be obtained on the new models. I use an ordinary violin bow on the guitar, given a little more tension on the horsehair than one would employ for violin playing, plus lots more rosin. It gives an infinite variety of sounds, ranging from violin to cello and from a whistling wind to a Boeing 707 taking off." .... Advert reads — Yardbirds now known as Led Zeppelin at the Roundhouse Chalk Farm, Saturday November 9th 10.30 - dawn, support John Lee Hooker, Deviants, John James, Tyres, Jeff Dexter, members 16/- guests 26/-....

23 **DISC reports....** In alphabetical listing of important bands 'Z is for Zeppelin' a still largely unknown quantity but due to Page's presence they can't be bad.... **Melody Maker reports....** Advert reads — Led Zeppelin to appear at the Crawdaddy Richmond Athletic Ground Friday November 29th billed as Led Zeppelin (Formerly Yardbirds)...Zeppelin debut at London's Marquee on December 10th. "They are to leave for the USA on Boxing Day. They will travel with Vanilla Fudge for one week and then spend three weeks doing club, college and concert dates" this provides the only accurate detail about the band's first tour of the USA.... "LZ I to be released in February to tie in with a six week British tour which will include 16 concerts and then selected ballroom and club gigs" this gives the only real indication of the duration of the Spring 1969 UK tour.... "Led Zeppelin will appear at the Bridge Country Club in Canterbury on December

13th".... Advert reads — Marquee Tuesday December 10th Led Zeppelin (Nee The Yardbirds)....

Official Atlantic Press release.... FOR IMMEDIATE RELEASE - From Bob Rolontz

ATLANTIC RECORDS SIGNS ENGLAND'S HOT NEW GROUP, LED ZEPPELIN IN ONE OF THE BIGGEST DEALS OF THE YEAR

Atlantic Records has signed the hot new English group, Led Zeppelin, to a long term exclusive recording contract. Although the exact terms of the deal are secret, it can be disclosed that it is one of the most substantial deals Atlantic has ever made. Agreement for the group's services was made between Jerry Wexler, Executive Vice President of Atlantic Records, and Peter Grant, manager of the group.

Led Zeppelin consists of four of the most exciting musicians performing in Britain today. They are Jimmy Page, leader of the group and lead guitarist, John Paul Jones, bassist, pianist, organist, arranger; John Bonham, drums and Robert Plant, lead vocal and harmonica.

Jimmy Page is a former member of the Yardbirds, the group that spawned the careers of two other great musicians, Eric Clapton and Jeff Beck. Page joined the Yardbirds in 1966 and stayed with the group until it disbanded in the summer of 1968. Prior to joining the Yardbirds he was one of the busiest session men in London.

John Paul Jones is considered one of England's finest arrangers as well as an outstanding bass player. He is the arranger of Donovan's 'Mellow Yellow', 'Sunshine Superman', and 'Hurdy Gurdy

Man', and of the Rolling Stones' 'She's A Rainbow.' Drummer John Bonham created a sensation with his drum solos while accompanying Tim Rose on his British tour in early 1968. Vocalist Robert Plant is considered one of England's outstanding young blues singers, and has been involved in singing blues since he was 15. All of the members of the group are in their early 20's.

The pulsations surrounding Led Zeppelin have intensified ever since the group recorded its first (and as yet unreleased) album, which was produced by Jimmy Page, just a month ago in London. Top English and American rock musicians who have heard the tracks have compared the LP to the best of Cream and Jimi Hendrix, and have called Led Zeppelin the next group to reach the heights achieved by Cream and Hendrix. This Led Zeppelin LP will be released by Atlantic early in January.

Led Zeppelin is the eighth British group to be signed by Atlantic during the past 24 months. The others are Cream, Bee Gees, Julie Driscoll-Brian Auger & The Trinity, The Crazy World of Arthur Brown, The Marbles, The Magic Lanterns, and Jimmy James & The Vagabonds....

30 **Billboard reports....** Atl. Rides $200,000 On Zeppelin, UK Act. Article outlines the details of the deal struck between Atlantic's Jerry Wexler and Peter Grant. It says the label will pay a similar amount to what they paid for the Bee Gees two years ago. It goes on to say that the band's debut album was produced the previous month in London by Jimmy Page and will be available in January....

December 1968

7 **Record Mirror reports....** Atlantic Records are reportedly paying $200,000 for Jimmy Paige's (sic) new group Led Zeppelin.... **New Musical Express reports....** June Harris reports from the USA that Led Zeppelin led by Jimmy Page will be in the USA by the end of December....

14 **Melody Maker reports....** Advert reads — Friday December 20th 7.30 pm at the Fishmongers Hall in Wood Green billed as Led Zeppelin (formerly Yardbirds)...**New Musical Express reports....** Led Month in U.S.... 'Led Zeppelin's first tour of the USA begins on Boxing Day...the band play one week opening for the Vanilla Fudge and then play three weeks of colleges and club dates. The band's debut album is complete and will be released in January by Atlantic records in the USA and in February in the UK at which point the band will play 16 dates in the UK'.... basically reiterating the MM story of the pre-

Music

'SOUNDS OF THE UNDERGROUND' — Creedence Clearwater Revival of "Suzy Q" and "I Put a Spell on You" recording fame, and Popcorn, group that changed its name from The Daily Flash, plus Retina Circus, rock concert presentation of Boyd Grafymre and KOL-AM-FM, at Eagles Auditorium, 7th and Union, Jan. 4; doors open 7 p.m., music 8 p.m.-midnight. Advance tickets: Discount Records, Campus Music, Warehouse of Music, Shoreline Music, The Factory, Bon Marche and other agencies.

VANILLA FUDGE — In concert with Led Zeppelin, 8 p.m. Dec. 27, Seattle Center Arena; Concerts West presentation. Tickets at Fidelity Lane and suburban outlets: $1, $4 and $5.

23

vious week....

16 Los Angeles Free Press reports....
January 2 Thru 5 Led Zeppelin And Alice
Cooper featuring Jimmy Page Formerly
Of The Yardbirds Whisky A Go Go
Sunset Strip, No Age Limit....

21 Melody Maker reports.... Led
Zeppelin are a very heavy group.... amp
troubles at the Marquee gig didn't help
...band was too loud...Page and Plant did
some interesting interplay during Days Of
Confusion (sic).... Bonham is a forceful
drummer.... Advert reads — Friday
December 20th 7.30 pm at the
Fishmongers Arms in Wood Green billed
as Led Zeppelin (formerly Yardbirds) supported by Closed Cell Sponge and
Explosive Spectrum.... Quiz reads, Led
Zeppelin is the name of (a) Jimmy Page's
new group, (b) A very heavy balloon or
(c) A German band leader....

22 The Sunday Denver Post reports....
Advert reads — for Spirit at the Denver
Auditorium Arena in-the-round (appear-
ing with Vanilla Fudge) ...no mention of
Led Zeppelin on the bill....

27 Seattle Post-Intelligencer reports....
Advert reads — Music Vanilla Fudge In
Concert with Led Zeppelin, 8 p.m. Dec
27, Seattle Center Arena; Concerts West
presentation. Tickets at Fidelity Lane and
suburban outlets: $3, $4 and $5....

28 DISC reports.... Led Zeppelin are to
fly out to the USA on Boxing Day (26th)
for six week tour of the USA with Vanilla
Fudge.... **Los Angeles Free Press
reports....** Advert reads — January 2 thru
5 Led Zeppelin and Alice Cooper featuring Jimmy Page formerly of the
Yardbirds...Whisky a Go Go Sunset Strip

652-4202 No Age limit.... **Billboard
reports....** Atlantic have just paid another
six figure advance for British group
Cartoone only two weeks after paying
$200,000 for Led Zeppelin....

29 The Sunday Denver Post reports....
Review of the show at the Denver
Auditorium, the band's first ever concert
in America, *"The concert was kicked off
by another British heavy, the Led
Zeppelin, making it's first U.S. tour. Blues
oriented, hyped electric, the full routine in
mainstream rock, done powerfully, uni-
fiedly, inventively and swingingly. Singer
Robert Plant a cut above average in style,
but no special appeal in sound. Guitarist
Jimmy Page of Yardbirds fame, exceptionally fine. Used a violin bow on the guitar
strings in a couple of tunes with resultant
interesting well integrated effects. Bassist
John Paul Jones, solid, involved, contributing, John Bonham a very effective
group drummer, but uninventive unsubtle
and unclimactic in an uneventful solo."*

Rolling Stone reports.... Article states
that Atlantic have signed Led Zeppelin for
a $200,000 advance. It mentions the band
members early career moves as well as
pointing out that the band's first album
will be released in January....

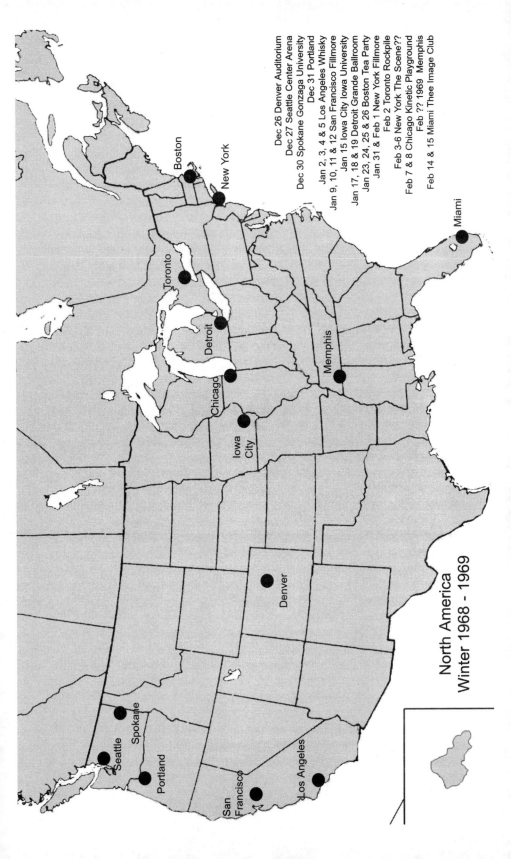

North America
Winter 1968 - 1969

Dec 26 Denver Auditorium
Dec 27 Seattle Center Arena
Dec 30 Spokane Gonzaga University
Dec 31 Portland
Jan 2, 3, 4 & 5 Los Angeles Whisky
Jan 9, 10, 11 & 12 San Francisco Fillmore
Jan 15 Iowa City Iowa University
Jan 17, 18 & 19 Detroit Grande Ballroom
Jan 23, 24, 25 & 26 Boston Tea Party
Jan 31 & Feb 1 New York Fillmore
Feb 2 Toronto Rockpile
Feb 3-6 New York The Scene??
Feb 7 & 8 Chicago Kinetic Playground
Feb ?? 1969 Memphis
Feb 14 & 15 Miami Thee Image Club

Boston
New York
Toronto
Detroit
Chicago
Memphis
Miami
Iowa City
Denver
Spokane
Seattle
Portland
San Francisco
Los Angeles

1969

January 1969

Official Atlantic Press release....
LED ZEPPELIN - THE BEGINNING

Led Zeppelin began in a small, stuffy rehearsal hall, mid London, late 1968. *"Four of us got together in this two by two room and started playing. Then we knew - we started laughing at each other. Maybe it was from relief, or maybe from the knowledge that we knew we could groove together. But that was it. That was just how well it was going."* Jimmy Page, master guitarist, former Yardbird, was watching his thoughts, his ambitions, his concealed desires as a musician, take shape in a new supergroup, Led Zeppelin. *"The statement of our first two weeks together is our album. We cut it in 15 hours, and between us wrote 8 of the tracks. Our main problem was knowing what channel to take it along musically. Everyone in the group had such a high musical content we thought each of us would be into our own thing. But it all fell in together.*

"We'll probably always be faced with the fact that individually each member could cut his own album going in his own direction and it would be great. But all those ideas in one outfit, well, that's pretty fantastic too." The formation of Led Zeppelin was no easy task. When it became generally known that Jimmy Page was putting a group together, he was inundated with calls from musicians all over the country. When the Yardbirds finally split up in the summer of 1968, Jimmy was ready to take bass player Chris Dreja with him into Led Zeppelin.

Chris eventually backed out of the arrangement, choosing instead to go into management.

"When I joined the Yardbirds, my main reason was to give myself the opportunity of playing my own music. Before that, my only interest was session work. I began to feel limited not being able to express myself. When I left, it was for almost exactly the same reasons. The group split because everyone began to feel the need to go in his own direction. The pity is, there would have still been great potential."

It was all down to Jimmy Page, alone, on a one man campaign to make himself heard. As a session guitarist he was, and still is, one of the finest in England, contributing his work to tracks by such as the Stones, Donovan, and latterly, Joe Cocker, who took the Beatles' 'With A Little Help From My Friends' to such a smash.

"I was working on the Donovan album, 'Hurdy Gurdy Man' with John Paul Jones who did some of the arrangements. He asked if I could use a bass guitarist in Led Zeppelin. John is an incredible arranger and musician. He didn't need me for a job, but he felt the need to express himself and figured we could do that together.

"Sessions are great, but you can't get into your own thing. Both myself and John felt that in order to give what we had to offer we had to have a group. He wanted to be part of a group of musicians who could lay down some good things.

"I can't put a tag to our music. Every one of us has been influenced by the blues, but it's one's interpretation of it and how you utilise it. I wish someone would invent an expression, but the closest I can get is contemporary blues.

"I want us to be raw and basic. That was the whole thing that made the Yardbirds happen. To go into your own

thing is fine, but it has to be a form of experimentation that evolves from a basic sound that everyone else knows and can relate to.

"Perhaps that's why the blues is so big. You can recognise the roots."

It took about two years for Led Zeppelin to emerge. The name was conceived by Jimmy Page when he was still with the Yardbirds and each member of the group took a shot at recording on his own. Jimmy penned "Beck's Bolero" for Jeff Beck. Today, it's a Beck standard, then, it was a track on which the Who's Keith Moon played drums. *"When we were kicking around group names, I suddenly remembered Led Zeppelin which I had come up with at that time."*

That, too, would have been a supergroup, but every musician to his own bag, and for Jimmy Page, it's John Paul Jones, John Bonham and Robert Plant to make Led Zeppelin an example of great music. And this is a group that won two standing ovations and two encores on their first date in London, with only six hours of rehearsal behind them.

It's the greatest trip any selection of musicians can take their audience on, the greatest feeling of being into a scene, one which America is ready and waiting for.
By JUNE HARRIS

LED ZEPPELIN - BACKGROUND

JIMMY PAGE, 23. Lead guitar, pedal steel guitar, acoustic guitar.
One of Europe's foremost musicians, Jimmy Page embarked on his career at the age of 15, devoting equal time to playing with various groups while studying at a London art school. His forte was to become session work, and the studio experience he gained from backing up such artists as Mick Jagger and Keith

Richard, The Kinks and Donovan, to name a few, gave him a sound knowledge of production, put to extremely good use in the first Led Zeppelin album.

Jimmy joined the Yardbirds in 1966. His first performance with them occurred in London at less than five minutes notice when Paul Samwell Smith fell ill just prior to a performance and Jimmy offered to replace him for just that one show. The Yardbirds wanted Jimmy to stay but he refused their offer, choosing instead to return to his own busy schedule which sometimes included as many as three recording sessions a day. However, when the Yardbirds offered him a U.S. tour, Jimmy reversed his decision, stating that maybe the time had come for him to start playing some of his own stuff. He played bass for that tour, and switched to lead guitar only after Jeff Beck fell out of several dates through illness.

When Jeff recovered, he and Jimmy Page played dual lead which continued after they returned to England and throughout a successful Rolling Stones tour.

Anxious to get back to his own session work, Jimmy was ready to leave the Yardbirds in 1967. But Jeff Beck quit instead and Jimmy stayed on until the entire group split to go their separate ways in the summer of 1968.

A remarkable point in Jimmy Page's career came when he produced an Eric Clapton single for Andrew Oldham's Immediate Records two and a half years ago, after Eric had left the Yardbirds. They went into the studio and cut "Witch Doctor" backed with "Telephone Blues," said to be one of the finest blues tracks ever recorded in England.

As a musician, Jimmy and Eric played together on an album titled "Blues Anytime", now a collector's item in England.

Jimmy Page, the only unmarried member of Led Zeppelin, lives in a house supported by stilts in Pangborne on the River Thames. He owns a 20 foot motor launch fully equipped with an 8 track stereo tape system and has a studio in his home where he writes and the group sometimes rehearses. His house is furnished in 17th and 18th century antiques and has a huge, four poster bed.

JOHN PAUL JONES, 22. Bass, organ, piano.

A sought after arranger of great repute in England, John Paul Jones is the former bass player with Jet Harris and Tony Meehan, who broke away from Europe's top instrumental group The Shadows, in the early 60's, and found great success on their own. Today, Tony Meehan is a producer at British Decca, and until John Paul Jones joined Led Zeppelin the pair of them continued to work together on various recording sessions.

Like Jimmy Page, John Paul Jones has arranged and played bass with several leading artists in the studio, his most memorable offerings being the arrangements on Donovan's 'Mellow Yellow', 'Sunshine Superman', 'Hurdy Gurdy Man' (both the single and different tracks on the album), and for the Stones' 'She's a Rainbow' and two tracks on 'Their Satanic Majesties Request.'

John Paul Jones played organ on the current Jeff Beck "Truth" album, and made one of his rare professional appearances playing bass for Dusty Springfield during her stint at London's Talk of the Town.

Though his brilliance as an arranger and musician brought him fame, John Paul Jones is in agreement with Jimmy Page that session work can be stultifying. The mood that he now creates in his playing, proves beyond any shadow of a doubt that he needed to make his move when he did.

JOHN BONHAM, 21. Drums.

Still too young to have an illustrious career behind him, John Bonham created a sensation with his drum solos while accompanying Tim Rose on his British tour in 1968.

In Jimmy Page's words, *"I went to see him and couldn't believe how he was living his music. He's extremely inventive, more so than any other drummer I've heard. He does his drum solo with his hands. When he gets into a trip, the audience goes with him."*

John Bonham comes from the industrial town of Birmingham. It is not the hub of British music, but in order to get his experience he played with as many groups as he could in the area and eventually joined one of the top local outfits, The Band of Joy. The Tim Rose jaunt brought John well deserved national acclaim and opened the door to the next chapter in his success story. Married, and still living in Birmingham, John is, according to Jimmy Page, *"The champion beer drinker in England."*

ROBERT PLANT, 21. Lead vocals, harmonica, occasional bass.

"Robert Plant's voice is so powerful that when the speakers broke down during our first date in Sweden, you could still hear his voice at the back of the auditorium over the entire group. When he records, we have to put screens around him."

Robert Plant has been into the blues as long as he can remember. While in his teens his roots were country blues, and then he moved on to city blues a la Otis Rush and Buddy Guy. However, his interpretation of today's blues is his own thing, totally different from anything heard before.

Like John Bonham, Robert hails from Birmingham and was a member of the Band of Joy, now defunct. He also played on several occasions with Alexis Korner, who fathered the blues revival in England. It was singer Terry Reid, a friend of Jimmy Page's, who suggested Robert for Led Zeppelin, and there was no need to look further....

2 **The Village Voice reports....** Advert reads — Bill Graham Presents In New York Friday & Saturday January 31st and February 1st Iron Butterfly, Led Zeppelin, The Move. Fillmore east Second Avenue at Sixth Street. This ad runs weekly for the next few weeks....

3 **Los Angeles Free Press reports....** Advert reads — January 2 thru 5 Led Zeppelin and Alice Cooper featuring Jimmy Page formerly of the Yardbirds...Whisky a Go Go Sunset Strip 652-4202 No Age limit....

4 **New Musical Express reports....** June Harris reports from New York that Led Zeppelin will be "whopping great big names" after the release of their debut album. She goes on to mention the band's appearance at the Fillmore East with Iron Butterfly on January 31st and February 1st....

Rolling Stone reports.... full page advert reads — Led Zeppelin, their first album is now available on Atlantic Records....

Billboard reports.... A good start to the

reviews from the music industries own trade rag, "Excellent musicianship...an excellent new British combo."....

9 **The Detroit Fifth Estate reports....** Quarter page ad reads.... 'The Grande - Led Zeptlin (sic) Linn County & Lawrence Blues Band January 17 - Target January 18 Sunday 19 Wind.' In the events calendar it reads 'Fri. Jan. 17 Grande Ballroom Led Zeptelin (sic) along with Linn County and the Lawrence Blues Band. - Sat. Jan. 18 Grande Ballroom Tonight's program includes Led Zeptelin and Target. - Sun. Jan. 19 Grande Ballroom From 7 to 11 pm tonight will be Led Zeptelin and the Wind.'

11 **New Musical Express reports....** Zeppelin beats blizzard.... June Harris reports from New York with details of the first American tour. She reveals that the band will only spend a week with the Vanilla Fudge. "Jimmy Paige's (sic) Led Zeppelin opened their first US tour after Christmas opening for the Vanilla Fudge.... in Seattle the band were subjected to blizzards which hit the city as they arrived but the weather didn't affect the attendance at their show.... immediately following their week with the Fudge the band moved in to the Whisky A Go Go in Los Angeles and then will move on to the Fillmore in San Francisco.... the debut album 'Led Zeppelin' is slated for release this week.". When Zeppelin and the Fudge parted ways Zeppelin went into the Whisky in Los Angeles while the Fudge went on to play in San Diego on the fourth. Part of the reason that they parted ways would seem to be that the Fudge and Spirit, who also shared the bill with Zeppelin, were to play Los Angeles at the Shrine on the 11th while Zeppelin played the Fillmore...

A curious shot of Jimmy Page and backdrop on stage at Iowa University

15 **Daily Iowan reports....** Led Zeppelin in concert Main Lounge IMU January 15 - 8 pm Tickets on sale now Box Office IMU $2.50 reserved, $2.00 General Admission. Also appearing Mother Blues.... The pulsations surrounding Led Zeppelin have intensified ever since the group recorded it's first (and as yet unreleased) album, which was produced by Jimmy Page, just a month ago in London. Top English and American rock musicians who have heard the tracks have compared the LP to the best of Cream and Jimi Hendrix, and have called Led Zeppelin the next group to reach the heights achieved by Cream and Hendrix. This Led Zeppelin LP will be released by Atlantic early in January....

Robert Plant on stage at Iowa University

23 **The Boston Globe reports....** What's Going On? Led Zeppelin, The Boston Tea Party, Berkeley St. through Saturday only, Admission $3.50.... **The Village Voice reports....** Advert reads — Dancing - Blues - Concert. Feb 3 - Feb 6 Lead (sic) Zeppelin. Steve Paul's Scene 301 West 46th St. (The band may not have played this engagement.)....

25 **Record Mirror reports....** Both Cartoon (sic) and Led Zeppelin are getting $200,000 advances from Atlantic Records.... **New Musical Express reports....** Zeppelin are new Cream hails June Harris from New York.... calling the band "the biggest happening of the 1969 heavy rock scene" she then conducts a short interview with Jimmy Page from the band's gig at Iowa University.... the band were completely surrounded by bad weather.... Page, *"Yeah really it's been incredible. We're all so knocked out. All the kids keep telling us they've heard the album and how quickly can they get it and all that. And we haven't even done half the tour yet!"....* an Atlantic rep says that he could sell 50,000 copies of the album if he could get it.... **Billboard reports....** Rock Pile's Acts Listed. Article mentions that Toronto's only underground venue has booked Led Zeppelin, Iron Butterfly, The Mothers, John Mayall and others for February and March....Advert reads — Led Zeppelin One, The Heavy Sounds

Are On Atlantic-Atco....

30 **The Village Voice reports....** Advert reads — The Heavy Sounds On Atlantic - Atco Records. Iron Butterfly & Led Zeppelin Appearing at The Fillmore East Fri., Jan. 31st & Sat., Feb. 1st....Advert Reads - Dancing - Blues - Concert Mon Feb 3 Thru Thur. Feb 6 Jimmy Paige (sic) and England's Most Exciting New Group Led Zeppelin. Joining Led Zeppelin on Tuesday Feb 4 The Very Special Voices & Being Of Betty Carter & Her Trio. Steve Paul's Scene 301 West 46th St. (The band didn't play this engagement.)....

31 **New York Times reports....** Fillmore East, Bill Graham Presents in New York tonight and tomorrow night Iron Butterfly - Led Zeppelin - Porter's Popular Preachers.... **Fillmore East Programme reports....** Bill Graham Presents In New York Iron Butterfly, Led Zeppelin, Porter's Popular Preachers, Joshua Light Show, Fillmore East January 31 - February 1, 1969. Biography of the band and comments by Page, *"We'll probably always be faced with the fact that individually each member could cut his own album going in his own direction and it would be great. But all those ideas in one outfit, well that's pretty fantastic too."*

Iowa State University "Hawkeye" 1969 yearbook reports.... The Led Zeppelin appeared Jan. 15 with a local group, The Mother Blues. Led Zeppelin specialised in acid rock music....

February 1969

1 **Billboard reports....** Ritchie Yorke reports from Toronto that Led Zeppelin

The Heavy Sounds On Atlantic-Atco Records

IRON BUTTERFLY
BALL
Atco SD 33-280

LED ZEPPELIN
Atlantic SD 8216

IRON BUTTERFLY & LED ZEPPELIN
Appearing at The Fillmore East
Fri., Jan. 31st & Sat., Feb. 1st

will be playing the Rockpile on Feb 2 the same night as Iron Butterfly play Massey Hall. He mentions that Atlantic will be heavily promoting the band's new album....

3 **Toronto Globe & Mail reports....** Ritchie Yorke reviews the previous night's show at the Toronto Rockpile. Yorke had in fact introduced the band on stage the previous night and his enthusiasm shows

through in his exuberant review, *".... one visual image stood out. It was the sight of Led Zeppelin's hero-worshipped lead guitarist Jimmy Page - resplendent in avocado velvet suit, bent over as if in agony to the audience, his fingers working like a touch typist's his foot thumping like a kangaroo's tail, the sounds as clear and as piercing as a bedside phone in the stillness of 3 am.... several critics, myself included, had suggested Led Zeppelin just might be the next so called supergroup.... Advance airplay and reviews brought over 1200 people to the Rockpile. They expected a lot and few were disappointed."*

5 **Boston After Dark reports....** Jimmy Page after the Yardbirds.... review of the Tea Party shows and an interview with Page backstage after the show on Thursday the 23rd. When asked if Zep were just another blues band, Page, *"We're trying ideas with each other. I love Jeff Beck, he's basically Chicago Blues - a different concept. All of these musicians - jazz and all that - we're basically rock and roll musicians."* Page goes on to mention that he likes being with Atlantic records because, *"When we went to San Francisco they knew us and the numbers by the band."* He goes on to mention that the band had just played a state college in Iowa, Detroit and the Whisky in New York (sic). From Boston they go on to New York, Toronto, Chicago, Memphis and Miami. When questioned on the differences between American guitarists and the British - Page, *"In England, the systems of living are different. Nobody cares if you drop out of school. If a guy wants to sit around and play his guitar all day, no one will stop him. There's more freedom to do what you want. Nobody pays for your schooling; there's less pressure if you drop out. This may be why people in America are late developers as musicians."* The reviewer says this of the concerts, *"For four consecutive evenings (Led Zeppelin) virtually blew an overflow Boston Tea Party crowd clear into the Charles River...if you don't want to jump dance and smile after hearing this, you must be dead!"*

THE ROCK PILE IS:

- Canada's prime showcase for the world's finest rock album performers . . .

- The only club where un-commercial musicians can groove and jam . . .

- Proof that Canadian audiences are as hip as any . . .

- Sometimes called the Fillmore of the North . . .

CHECK US OUT

Rap with

LED ZEPPELIN	SPIRIT
BLOOD, SWEAT AND TEARS	JOHN MAYALL
COUNTRY JOE	SAVOY BROWN
MOTHERS OF INVENTION	FAMILY
LIGHTHOUSE	NUCLEUS
PAUL BUTTERFIELD	ARTHUR BROWN
BRIAN AUGER	JOOLS
MUDDY WATERS	ALBERT KING
THE NICE	RHINOCEROS
CHUCK BERRY	MCS
HOWLIN WOLF	KENSINGTON MARKET
THE WHO	OTIS SPANN
MOTHER TUCKER'S YELLOW DUCK	
and many more	

THE ROCK PILE IS:
THE PLACE TO BREAK A HEAVY ACT IN CANADA
Toronto, Ontario   Call: (416) 920 1729

8 **Honolulu Star Bulletin reports....** Led Zeppelin is the most exciting group out of England in two years. Their first album shows more than just promise. It is already one of the best British hard rock LPs in release. Don't pass this one up. Cartoone is another excellent new British group which forces the question, 'Is there some sort of rock renaissance going on in Bonnie England where not much has been happening lately?' Jimmy Page who stars with Led Zeppelin is artist on this LP and his work is exciting on both albums - he's definitely a musician to watch....

```
┌────── DANCING - BLUES - CONCERT ──────┐
│ WED. JAN. 9      SAVOY BROWN          │
│ LAST NIGHT       BLUES BAND           │
│ ------------------------------------- │
│     TONIGHT THRU SUNDAY               │
│ N. R. B. Q.  •  SOFT WHITE UNDERBELLY │
│                  HAL WATERS           │
│ ------------------------------------- │
│ MON. FEB. 3        JIMMY PAIGE and England's │
│ THRU THUR. FEB. 6  most exciting new group   │
│                                       │
│        LED ZEPPELIN                   │
│ ------------------------------------- │
│    Joining LED ZEPPELIN on Tuesday, Feb 4 and │
│ staying thru March 2: The very special Voice & Being of │
│                                & Her  │
│   BETTY CARTER                Trio    │
│ ------------------------------------- │
│ FEB. 9 & 10          PENTANGLE        │
│ ------------------------------------- │
│ FEB. 24 Thru MAR. 2   FLYING BURRITO BROS. │
│ ------------------------------------- │
│ MARCH 17            JERRY LEE LEWIS   │
│                                       │
│    NEW EARLY and LATE, LATE SHOWS     │
│ Uninhibited Dancing & Listening Encouraged │
│ STEVE  SCENE  JU 2-5760               │
│ PAUL'S        301 WEST 46th ST.       │
└───────────────────────────────────────┘
```

14 Miami Herald reports.... Led Zeppelin Atlantic recording group, with Jimmy Page, a graduate of The Yardbirds, in concert appearances tonight and Saturday from 8.30 to 2, at Thee Image, 183rd St. and Collins Ave....

15 New Musical Express reports.... Article reads, "Led Zeppelin returned this week from their first tour of the USA, they soon leave for a tour of Scandinavia on March 15th.... as expected the band played an amazing set for over 90 minutes at the Fillmore East.... the band's album has sales of over 100,000 units.... drum-mer John Bonham had to return to the UK when his young son was in an accident which required stitches to his head.... Bonham returned to the USA in time for the band's gigs in Chicago."...this article reveals the true date that they finished the first tour of the USA (Mid February and not the end of January as has been often speculated) it also fills a gap in the tour by revealing Bonham's trip to the UK in mid-tour. The band were slated to play at The Scene in Manhattan but all four nights presumably were blown out. The date of March 15th for the start of the Scandinavian tour was later proven incorrect as the band played there on the 13th... **Billboard reports....** review of Iron Butterfly and Led Zeppelin at the Fillmore East in New York by Fred Kirby. He says the band will play four weekend shows and played a fine set which left Iron Butterfly with a hard act to follow. He says Page 'ranks with the top pop guitarists' and that Plant is 'a blues style screamer and wailer whose vocalizing was wild.'....review of Led Zeppelin One says, 'Britannia will continue to rule the airwaves so long as new groups like Led Zeppelin continue to come up.' It concludes that the album 'can't miss.'....

22 **New Musical Express reports....** Led Zeppelin recently returned from the USA (last weekend) the band's new album Led Zeppelin is released by Parlophone on March 1st....

OZ #19 reports.... Felix Dennis writes an incredibly perceptive review of LZ I.... "Very occasionally a long-playing record is released that defies immediate classification or description, simply because it's so obviously a turning point in rock music that only time proves capable of shifting it into eventual perspective.... the album makes you feel good.... of course as a result of this album we'll lose the group to the States, and almost certainly within months the Melody Maker letters page will headline - 'Is Page better than God?' and then the BBC will begin negotiations on a feature film.... "....the issue also features a half page advert reading "Led Zeppelin - the only way to fly."

March 1969

1 **Record Mirror reports....** Led Zeppelin are an excellent example of how the USA rewards British bands for hard work.... they are a good band and they deserve it.... **Melody Maker reports....** Led Zeppelin have been offered a second tour of the United States....

8 **Record Mirror reports....** Jimmy Page states *"We don't want to specialise in singles. In fact we don't want to do any. If the record company want to re-issue some album cuts that's OK with us, but we don't make anything we want to be released as a single."* .... Robert Plant's voice is so powerful that screens have to be put around him when they record.... **New Musical Express reports....** advert for Chrysalis agency...the ABC of Chrysalis featuring Led Zeppelin by arrangement with Peter Grant and Harold Davison.... **Melody Maker reports....** Advert reads — Friday March 7th Back From their sensational American tour Led Zeppelin - The Hornsey Wood Tavern Admission 7/6-....

11 **Stockholm Express reports....** Advert reads — Country Joe & The Fish Led Zeppelin Concert House Friday March 14 at 19.30....

13 **Copenhagen's Ekstra Bladet reports....** Advert reads — Super session, Country Joe and The Fish, Led Zeppelin, Keef Hartley Blues band at Tivolis Koncertsal Sunday 16th March.... **Uppsala New Paper reports....** Advert reads — Country Joe & The Fish Led Zeppelin Friday 14th March at 22.00 Uppsala University Aula (Hall)....

14 **Stockholm Daily News reports....** Advert reads — Country Joe & the Fish - Led Zeppelin Concert House Friday March 14 at 19.30....Article reads, Country Joe & The Fish are the main

THE ONLY WAY TO FLY

ATLANTIC

588 171

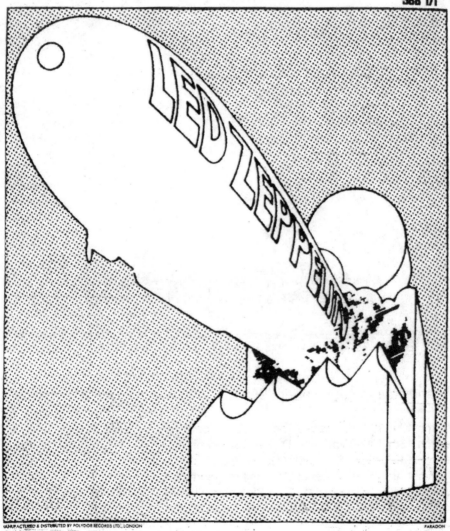

MANUFACTURED & DISTRIBUTED BY POLYDOR RECORDS LTD., LONDON

PARAGON

Scandinavian Tour Spring1969

March 13th 1969 Gladsaxe Teen Club (Copenhagen)
March 13th 1969 Gladsaxe TV-Byen (Copenhagen)
March 14th, 1969 Stockholm Concerthouse
March 14th, 1969 Uppsala University Lecture Hall
March 15th, 1969 Brondby Pop Club Norregard Hallen (Copenhagen)
March 16th, 1969 Tivolis Koncertsal Copenhagen

attraction but a lot of people will surely be there to listen to the opening act - England's Led Zeppelin. They formed late last year and have already put out an album which is being talked about. Led Zeppelin are expected to be the band filling the gap left by Cream. The leader of Led Zeppelin is named Jimmy Page and like many great English guitarists he has played with the Yardbirds, as did Eric Clapton and Jeff Beck. When the Yardbirds split up, last fall, Jimmy decided to form something new. He looked hard for the right musicians and first found John Paul Jones, who plays bass, organ and piano with Led Zeppelin. Jones is known in England mostly as the man behind the arrangements on Donovan's 'Mellow Yellow' and the Rolling Stone's 'She's A Rainbow'. John Bonham is the drummer and Robert Plant sings and plays harmonica and sometimes even bass. Jimmy Page is an excellent instrumentalist, as skillful on bass as on guitar. He played both instruments in the Yardbirds. Right after Eric Clapton left the Yardbirds, Jimmy on bass, together with Clapton made some instrumental duo-numbers. They are some of the best early English blues recordings in existence. After Stockholm, Led Zeppelin and Country Joe & the Fish play at Uppsala University Hall at 10 at night.... **Uppsala New Paper reports....** Advert reads — Country Joe & The Fish Led Zeppelin This evening at 22.00 Uppsala University Aula (Hall).... Friday's Musicians (pictured). Pop music shows are frequent these days. The long haired youngsters in the picture will be heard at the University hall tonight. They come from England and are the band Led Zeppelin, which might be called, parts of the Yardbirds. The leader Jimmy Page played with them for the last two years. He plays solo gui-

tar, pedal steel guitar and acoustic guitar. The other three are John Paul Jones, bass, organ and piano, John Bonham, drums and Robert Plant, vocals, harmonica and occasional bass. The guys in Led Zeppelin are not alone at the University Hall tonight, Country Joe & The Fish are also playing. Uppsala and Stockholm are the only places in Sweden that gets honoured by a visit....

15 Stockholm Daily News reports.... review of the show at the Concerthouse.... Double show at the concerthouse Friday night - two big acts on the same bill. English Led Zeppelin and American Country Joe & The Fish. Most pop concerts in Stockholm usually have one headliner and one or two opening bands. Instead it was two main attractions and that was good because the tickets were unusually expensive. The Concerthouse was almost sold-out. Led Zeppelin first impressed me because they played so hard and loud. Not in that typical thin English way. They had an almost American heaviness and depth to their music. But the group is just a few months old and they haven't found their place yet. The guitarist Jimmy Page is good, a skillful and imaginative soloist. His bassist was good too and the drummer was promising. The singer I didn't like. He mostly screamed and the lyrics he was screaming were banal.... **Stockholm Express reports....** Different Taste At The ConcertHouse - There were different tastes at the Concerthouse last night. First the blues band Led Zeppelin, in tight pants and explicit moves. They played the same kind of blues most English bands play today. Not much more original and definitely not the new Cream. The highlight was Jimmy Page's solo on a specially built guitar.... **Swedish Daily News**

UPPSALA UNIVERSITETS AULA

reports.... Led Zeppelin Better Than Tired Country Joe. Even though Country Joe & The Fish was the big name at Friday night's concert in Stockholm, Led Zeppelin did a much more interesting performance. If one was disappointed at Country Joe & The Fish one was happier to hear Led Zeppelin. Unfortunately some of the group's equipment was forgotten at a TV recording that day, but one could hardly notice. The band plays a very hard and intensive blues. It's music has room for much experimenting and is, to a great extent, built on an exciting dialogue between former Yardbirds guitarist Jimmy Page and singer Robert Plant. This man has a strange voice. He sings more tones than words and lets the tones and intensity stand in for the songs contents. Jimmy Page is among the really big names in English guitarists and showed his class in an unusually beautiful solo number called 'White Summer'. He experimented further with bow and guitar in the evening's finest song 'Dazed & Confused', from their LP, Led Zeppelin. Another visit from Led Zeppelin would be really welcome and for those who didn't take the opportunity last night, should really not miss seeing that.... **DISC reports....** Led

Zeppelin Most Exciting Sound Since The Cream.... feature article.... Led Zeppelin is being hailed as the most exciting thing since the early days of Jimi Hendrix or the Cream.... as a measure of their success Zeppelin will play the last night of the Newport Jazz Festival along with the jazz acts.... Page, *"I knew you could sit around as a new group for months in England and have no notice taken of you at all. For one thing there's very few places to play and then it's pretty unlikely you're going to get many radio plays. But in the States a new group can get so much more exposure. We played all the underground capitals, like San Francisco, Los Angeles, New York, Cleveland, Boston, where they have FM radio stations which play stereo progressive rock music all the time. They often play 20 minute tracks and no one gets uptight about it.*

"Although we didn't know each other at all to begin with we seemed to come together musically from the very beginning. We did maybe two takes of each number, for one we just did the one take, because we wanted as near a live sound as possible. It's pretty unheard of in these days of eight track recording. But we just did one instrument on each track, with the singer more or less live and that was it.".... BARTS II nightclub has become a hang-out for Led Zeppelin... **New Musical Express reports....** full page advert reads — The Only Way To Fly.. Led Zeppelin.... **Melody Maker reports....** Chrysalis Management Advert listing clients including Led Zeppelin by arrangement with Peter Grant and Harold Davison....

22 **Melody Maker reports....** Why Led Zeppelin took off in America and not Britain.... Chris Welch interviews Page in large feature article.

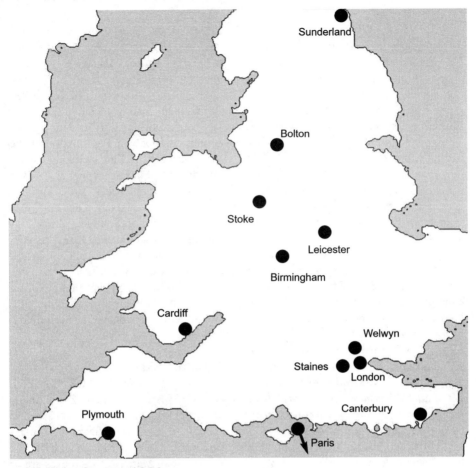

UK Tour Spring 1969

March 1st, 1969 Plymouth Van Dyke
March 3rd, 1969 London Maida Vale BBC Studios
March 5th, 1969 Cardiff
March 7th, 1969 London Hornsey Wood Tavern
March ?, 1969 Bolton
March 12th, 1969 Leicester
March 19th, 1969 London BBC Studio Session
March ??, 1969 Paris Olympia
March 21st, 1969 London 'How Late It Is' BBC TV
March 22nd, 1969 Birmingham Mother's
March 25th, 1969 Staines Super Session
March 28th, 1969 London Marquee
March 30th, 1969 London Southall Northcote Arms Farx
March 31st, 1969 London Cooks Ferry Inn
April 1st, 1969 London Hampstead Klook's Kleek
April 5th, 1969 London Dagenham Roundhouse
April 8th, 1969 Welwyn Garden City Cherry Tree
April 9th, 1969 London Tolworth Toby Jug
April 14th, 1969 Stoke
April 17th, 1969 Sunderland

Page, *"We played a date in England recently, and although we were OK, the other band with us had beer glasses thrown at them by all these yobs. And looking around, it all seems to be going back to violence with kids wearing the kicking boots and shaven heads.*

"I was really surprised when I walked around the West End last night how many more yobbos there were than two months ago. I kept running into these people with braces. I didn't have any trouble just the usual obscene yelling. It's a bloody nuisance. I hate the whole scene.

"We've been very successful in the States. We can hardly believe it! At most of the places we play we seem to get mass hysteria. In Boston I noticed all the boys in the front row were beating their heads in time.

"When we started the group, we only had enough material for fifty minutes, but this has extended to two hours. We're all feeling happy, especially about the American reaction which is more than we ever dreamed could happen.

"I'm looking forward to playing the Newport Jazz Festival. It's a great honour because there will be people like Muddy Waters and Stan Getz. What's so good about the States is they can mix so many different styles. I saw a concert with Cecil Taylor, who is as far out as you can get, on the same bill with Ritchie Havens and the Yardbirds. That's three completely different styles and they were all accepted by the audience at the Fillmore. Music is part of their life. In England a club is more of a place for kids to meet and they are not really interested in the music, which makes it hard for a new group to get off the ground."

Welch poses the question whether Led Zeppelin might turn down the volume as had been suggested in an earlier review in Melody Maker, Page, *"No - we're getting louder! Our drummer is amazingly loud. I come off stage with my ears ringing after a set."*.... Advert reads — Mothers High Street Birmingham Saturday March 22nd Adm 10/- Led Zeppelin plus ex-Jethro Mick Abrahams Blodwyn Pig.... Advert reads — Bluesville '69 Club's Grand Opening Tuesday Apr. 8th Led Zeppelin.... Advert reads — Klooks Kleek Tues, April 1st Led Zeppelin.... Advert reads — Farx Northcote Arms in Southall, March 30th Led Zeppelin and Smokey Rise sounds by Andy Dunkley 7.30 pm.... article Zeppelin Tour U.S. the tour opens April 24 at the Fillmore in San Francisco, the band have been recording their next album and play dates in Scandinavia before leaving for the USA....

26 **Official Press release....** From Rogers, Cowan & Brenner Inc. FOR IMMEDIATE RELEASE.... Led Zeppelin at Marquee.... Led Zeppelin the most talked about British group of the moment, plays London's famous Marquee Club on Friday night, March 28th. All eyes are on Led Zeppelin following the fantastic success of their first album (Atlantic 588 171), which in a matter of weeks in America climbed rapidly into the upper limits of Billboard, Cashbox and Record World charts. This album entitled simply 'Led Zeppelin' was recently released in Britain and seems destined for similar success. Led Zeppelin features two of Britain's top young musicians Jimmy Page (guitar) and John Paul Jones (bass, organ) plus drummer John Bonham and singer Robert Plant. The group returns to America for a second tour shortly, starting on April 18th when they will play New York University's Third Annual Jazz Festival, along with Dave Brubeck and

Errol Garner. Other dates so far booked on this tour are San Francisco's Fillmore (April 24, 27), Los Angeles (May 2,3), Seattle (May 9), Vancouver (May 10), Portland (May 11), Detroit (May 16,17), Minneapolis (May 18), Baltimore (May 23) and New York's Fillmore East (May 29-31). For further information contact: Chris Greenwood - Rogers Cowan and Brenner Inc....

28 International Times reports.... Farx Club Northcote Arms Southall Middlesex Sun Mar 30. Led Zeppelin and Smokey Rice, lights by Pale Green Limousine Heavy Sounds by Andy Dunkley.... Klooks Kleek Railway Hotel West Hampstead Tube, Tues. April 1 Led Zeppelin and The End....

29 DISC reports.... Led Zeppelin are to leave for a US college tour on April 18th.... they are scheduled to appear at the 3rd New York University Jazz festival with Errol Garner and Dave Brubeck.... **Record Mirror reports....** Jimmy Page was spotted at the revolution club last week watching Terry Reid.... Led Zeppelin I is bubbling under on the charts.... **Melody Maker reports....** Jimmy Page Triumphs! Led Zeppelin is a gas.... A very positive review of LZ I .... "Jimmy Page triumphs.... the legend comes to life.... technical, tasteful, turbulent and torrid.... (Plant, Jones and Bonham) are more than adequate.... production is excellent.... ".... A further article details that Led Zeppelin replaced the Flying Burrito Brothers, an American group who were to have appeared on BBC-TV's How Late It Is that Friday.... Led Zeppelin whose first album is currently in the Top 20 best selling US albums open their second US tour on April 24th at the Fillmore West San

Francisco.... The Zeppelin tour major American venues through to July.... Led Zeppelin have also been working on a second album and play dates in Scandinavia prior to their second American tour.... " This corrects the previous error which MM had reported, in which Zeppelin were to have played the New York University Jazz festival on April 18th.... Advert reads — Marquee Friday March 28th 7.30 - 11.00 Led Zeppelin, Eyes Of Blue.... Advert reads — Bluesville '69 Club's Grand Opening Tuesday Apr. 8th Led Zeppelin.... Advert reads — Klooks Kleek Tues, April 1st Led Zeppelin.... Advert reads — Monday Cooks Ferry Inn Angel Road Edmonton Led Zeppelin (This would make this date the 31st...RG).... article reviewing the Super Session in Staines by Chris Welch, nothing much revealed other than Led Zeppelin were one of the band's performing.... **Oz #20 reports....** Felix Dennis interviews Page, *"It all really began for me rehearsing with Cyril Davies. That would be around six years ago now, just after he'd split with Korner. Then I was accepted for Art College and I had to decide between painting and playing. Well, the music scene was pretty depressing around that time.... nobody was interested in Chuck Berry or Bo Diddley, all they wanted was Top Twenty & Jazz...so I went to College. Of course, about a year later everything began to happen with the Stones and Liverpool and the R 'n B scene so I took to jamming occasionally at the Marquee on Thursday nights. Somebody asked me to play on a record - can't remember what it was to tell the truth - but from that session came offers of work and suddenly there was more than I could cope with, four or five sessions a week. I began missing too many lectures & taking days off at College so I thought*

I'd better finally decide; painting or playing? It wasn't an easy decision but finally I took the plunge and chose sessions. Sometimes I wonder whether I made the right decision.

"The Yardbirds came out of getting bored with session work, which is so unpredictable. One minute you're playing with really good musicians and the next .... well.... Herman's Hermits are into their own thing no doubt, but it isn't my scene exactly. I'd known Jeff Beck in the Yardbirds for quite a long time and when Paul Samwell-Smith quit that was it. I'd never played bass before but I dug it & we left for the States shortly after I'd joined. Then Jeff was ill one time in LA and it was a case of me play lead guitar and Chris Dreja do the bass or scrub the gig. After that it worked out that the Yardbirds had two lead guitars, until Jeff left finally to form his own band. It was a shame that the Yardbirds eventually folded out. Towards the end Keith and Jim McCarty just didn't have their heart in the music. They were almost ashamed of the name Yardbirds in the finish, though I don't know why; on the last tour we were getting better reaction than we'd ever had. They were a great band, I was never ashamed of playing in the Yardbirds."

After discussing the music press, the Underground music scene, censorship, Screaming Lord Sutch, "hit" records, groupies, Dylan, and America the interview turns to Led Zeppelin.... Page, *"Well you can't really judge anything about Led Zeppelin from the album alone. The group had only been together for two and a half weeks when we recorded it. We'd had fifteen hours rehearsal before shooting over to Scandinavia for a few gigs, then straight after that we cut the album. There's very little double tracking, we were deliberately aiming at putting* down what we could actually reproduce on stage. I know that I influenced pretty heavily the content and arrangements on this first one, but that was only because we didn't have the time to discuss everything between us. The next album will almost certainly be more of a group project. The best thing about the Zeppelin is that no one's being carried. Robert and the two Johns are all excellent musicians, they all have something to say.

"John Bonham and Robert Plant were both in a group from Birmingham, 'The Band Of Joy'. I was very lucky to find two such fine musicians available at the time. John Paul Jones, well, I expect you already know quite a lot about him. He's done an awful lot of studio work; I'd say he's one of the best bass players in the country.

"I don't know how you'd bag our music.... maybe it's too early to say. Anyway we're not consciously aiming at anything or in any specific direction. Just playing together and taking it as it comes. Since recording the album we've changed a lot of the material, and the length of the numbers seems to have expanded. One thing that used to get me about The Cream was the way I thought they relied too heavily on Master Eric for the improvisations. That's not going to happen with us. Everybody's got something to say and well, that's what we'll be doing. I can't believe that we've all come together so quickly. If I'm really honest with you though it'll probably sound like I'm boasting, I'd say that I feel very confident about the direction of Led Zeppelin.".... **New Musical Express reports....** Led Zeppelin will be appearing at the new Farx Blues Club in Southall on Sunday 30th....

Chrysalis

Number   1057

An AGREEMENT made the   11th   day of   March   19   69

between   Gas Entertainments & Promotions.   hereinafter called the management of the one part

and   Superhype Ltd.   hereinafter called the Artiste of the other part

WITNESSETH that the Management hereby engages the Artiste and the Artiste accepts an engagement

to present   Led Zeppelin

appear as   Known

(or in his usual entertainment) at the Dance Hall/Theatre and from the dates for the periods and the salaries stated in the Schedule h...to

The Artiste agrees to appear at   1   Evening performances at a salary of £   75 (SEVENTY FIVE)

or Percentage Terms   60   %   which ever the greater.

Schedule   1 Day(s) at   Farx Blues Club,   on   Sunday,   19

      Day(s) at   Northcote Arms,   on   30th March,   19   69

      Day(s) at   Northcote Avenue,   on   19

      Day(s) at   Southall, Middx.   on   19

Additional Clauses

1 It is agreed that the management will provide and pay for microphone equipment and grand piano

2 Playing times to be decided by the management but it is agreed that   The Artistes   will not be required to play for more than a total of   1   hours in   2   sessions

3 Cash/Cheque Settlement   Cash with bandleader on night of engagement

4 Band or artistes to arrive by   6.30.p.m.   Equipment by

5 where musicians are booked through this Agency the Management agrees that any other band performing the Engagement(s) described in this agreement shall be composed of members of the Musicians' Union

6 The artiste shall not without the written consent of the management appear at any place of public entertainment within a radius of   miles of any of the venues mentioned herein for   weeks prior to and   weeks following this engagement

I/We the undersigned acknowledge that I/We have read the above special Clauses and agreed that they will be adhered to in detail

Signature   Address

Chrysalis Agency Limited 155-157 Oxford Street London W1   **Telephone 01 734 9233**
Licensed annually by the City of Westminster

This Agency is not responsible for any non-fulfilment of Contracts by Proprietors Managers or Artistes but every reasonable safeguard is assured

Creem reports.... Journalist Pam Brent reports back from the band's Sunday gig at the Detroit Grande Ballroom. She states that all the local Detroit music royalty are in attendance including Amboy Dukes and MC-5. She reports that Robert Plant was 'fluent and capable' and that drummer John Bonham, suffering from a headache was also 'capable'.

She states that the band played a set which included I Can't Quit You, Killing Floor, White Summer, and Communication Breakdown. Apparently the band thought their gig on Saturday was better and that their show in San Francisco was the best yet. She concludes that she wasn't very impressed but that 1969 may yet be the 'year of the Zeppelin'.

April 1969

2 **Record Retailer reports....** Led Zeppelin I is a mover....

5 **Record Mirror reports....** Led Zeppelin I has sold over a half million copies in the USA and one track has now entered the singles charts.... Led Zeppelin I is #9 in the RM chart.... **Melody Maker reports....** Letters to the editor, "Jimmy Page is very much more versatile a guitarist than either Clapton or Hendrix, just listen to the Led Zeppelin LP for proof. Turn on to Page, he makes Clapton look like a learner.".... "The BBC flattened their knockers with their new How Late It Is series. The musical content was first class, multi-instrumentalist Roland Kirk was superb and Led Zeppelin showed they are going to be a top attraction...."…. article on the band, Page, *"Turning down? No we're getting louder. Our*

drummer is amazingly loud. I come off stage with my ears singing after a set." Journalist Chris Welch goes on to state that the band are almost as loud as Captain Beefheart who "made me deaf for two days."…. Advert reads — John Peel's Midnight Court assembles every Friday at the Lyceum, Strand, London. 12.30 till Dawn from Friday April 11th onwards. Future attractions include Led Zeppelin, watch this space for further news.... Led Zeppelin Return to US.... article states that the opening gig on the US tour will be the New York University Jazz festival. Other dates include, Detroit, Seattle, Portland, Minneapolis, Baltimore, San Francisco, New York, Los Angeles.... **New Musical Express reports....** We're losing too many top groups to America Zeppelin is latest.... article reprimanding the British public for not listening to the local talent causing many to leave for America to get taken seriously. Over lunch Jimmy Page tells the interviewer, *"In America the audiences get into the music more. They are more appreciative. They will listen to the sort of patterns you are playing. In Britain all they are interested in is the way to the bar. And over there they clap you not because it is the right thing to do. They clap in the right places and it is good because if you are trying to do something and everyone in the audience is spurring you on then it really gets you at it.*

"Most places here they just go to have a dance or to have a drink. Not to listen. They don't care who's on. Of course there's more money to be made in America but the main reason is that the public is more appreciative."

He also thinks there are other reasons for why bands emigrate to the USA, *"The basic reason is the lack of exposure. There just aren't the big venues in which to play. What is needed is a club in every major city which is something between the size of the Marquee and the Roundhouse.*

"Like the Cream and Hendrix got to the stage where they needed gigantic places. They could get a 6,000 audience with ease and there was nowhere to accommodate them. Any group that plays the Albert Hall is out of their head because of the acoustics."

Page then concluded the interview and headed for a gig in Bolton.... Led Zeppelin begin their second tour of the USA...first gig is an appearance at the New York University Jazz festival on April 18th.... other dates include San Francisco Fillmore West April 24-27, Los Angeles May 2-3, Seattle May 9, Vancouver May 10, Portland May 11, Detroit May 16-17, Minneapolis May 18, Baltimore May 23, New York Fillmore East May 29-31....

9 Record Retailer reports.... Led Zeppelin I is #9....

11 International Times reports.... 'Led Zeppelin - Plant'.... interview with Robert Plant conducted on March 28th.... Having just escaped from an emergency landing on a flight in from Bremen - Plant, *"The captain came on and told us there's going to be an emergency landing and then, from being way up in the blue one minute, we're suddenly going down, but very down. My scotch went up in my face and the next thing I know there's some guy asking me to help the older cats out of the plane, and there I am doing the boy scout bit while everyone else is running away!"*

On the subject of the Band Of Joy, *"There were very few other groups around at the time doing that sort of*

thing, but eventually we were getting 60 and 75 quid a night. In the end however, I just had to give up. I thought 'Bollocks, nobody at all wants to know.'

"I met Terry Reid, who I'd played one or two gigs with in the Band Of Joy days, whilst I was down trying to get something together with Tony Secunda and he told me that the Yardbirds singer had just left and suggested that I try and get into that scene. I knew they'd done a lot of work in America, which to me meant audiences who DID want to know what I'd got to offer, so naturally I was very interested. I went down to Pangborne where Jimmy lives, it was the real desperation scene man, like I had nowhere else to go. There I was with my suitcase getting off the train and suddenly this old woman starts slapping my face and shouting about my hair. Well, I was staggered, so I called a cop and he says it was my own fault for having long hair. So much for British justice! Anyway I got to Jimmy's and we found we had exactly the same tastes in music.

"The first music that appealed to me, when I was at school even, was stuff like Dylan's 'Corinna Corinna', and when you look deeper into that sort of thing you find there's a lot of the same feelings that are in blues music, like Leadbelly's stuff and then you realise that the blues field is a very wide one. There's a lot of shit of course, all the old guys, such as Bukka White, who originally recorded in the late 20's, are suddenly being grabbed a hold of and shoved into a studio to do an ethnic blues recording. They think, 'Well it's 200 bucks, that'll keep me in firewood for the next three months', so they get into their wheelchairs, do the thing, and all the blues freaks say, 'Well man, this is the real blues', and it's really a load of bollocks'."

Later Plant is asked about the groupies in the USA, *"It's an art over there, it really is. Take the Plaster Casters in Chicago, it's the only thing they've got in the world man, because they couldn't pull a fella if the fella was blind and pissed, 'cause they're so revolting, but they can turn around and say, 'Well I've got so and so's plaster cast.' When they came round to see us they came in with the wooden case, suitably inscribed, all very ceremoniously, it was SO funny. So one of them starts this big scene, 'cause to them that's all part of their ritual, and she goes on doing it for an hour, a whole hour. All of a sudden she stops, having decided that it's just not going to work. Then she starts taking her clothes off, because she feels that she's got to do something having wasted the last forty minutes. And she's rather large, no doubt about it, she's rather well built and there she is standing there as naked as the day she was born. So then she got covered in soap from head to foot, then she got cream doughnuts and then whisky rubbed in together and there she was a moving mountain of soapy flesh. At first she dug it but soon she got rather afraid and her friend, a virgin who'd just come along for the ride, was trying very hard to disappear under the bed, like she just didn't know where it was at. Eventually she got into the shower, grabbed her clothes and split. A few days later we heard she'd quit the Plaster Casters - had enough! It's so sad that people like that exist, man. It wasn't as if it was a perversion she enjoyed, which would have been OK. It was just a ritual she had to do to get herself noticed. A very weird scene."*

After concluding the interview Plant left for the Marquee, where although Page apparently had some trouble with his guitar in the first few minutes,

they put on an "absolutely total" show.

12 **Record Mirror reports....** Cover Story.... We Could have Been A Bum Group.... interview with Page and review of the Marquee gig,.... "Jimmy Page bent double over his guitar and straining for unknown notes, listening hard because he's right there in the middle of that Led Zeppelin wall of sound, the sweat oozing torrential down his face and dripping off the ends of that long wavy hair down onto the guitar and one expects that guitar to fizz and steam because it's so near boiling point. John Bonham wild on the drams, looking over almost painful with effort at John Paul Jones laying down such a heavy bass, and through it all is the power of that Robert Plant voice. Led Zeppelin at the Marquee. Led Zeppelin anywhere, for that's how they are on stage. Powerful, heavy and very very good",.... Page, *"Led Zeppelin, we could have been a bum group. Who knows. No one ever knows until you start working together. And if you're good things start happening.*

"It's amazing, we're working every day now—but before we went to the States no one wanted to know. And it's not just London — it's all over the country. Very pleasing reaction. I still reckon the States is our main market though—it's so very big. It's not that I'm opposed to working in Britain—far from it—people got that impression with the Yardbirds as well, but it's not that. The thing is that we can get exposure in America whereas here it's all very different—it's so limited. The only radio programme, for example, is John Peel's.

"In America there's the whole of the underground press offering as much exposure as you want—it's not such a big battle to get everything in, get publicity, as it is here. It makes working much less

of a strain. It can be tough working in America though, but you have to go about it the right way. For example it's so vast that the only way to travel without completely knocking yourself out is by plane. Obviously it's more expensive than hiring a car and driving yourself all over the place—but it's worth it. It's more relaxing, and less of a hustle.

"The most strenuous time we have is when we're on stage—we go on, and it just happens. You don't realise how much you give, how much effort you put in, until you come off at the end. On stage you just put everything you've got into it.

"We've been very lucky, it's been a very rapid success— it's amazing. Atlantic had a lot to do with it—they made sure that people knew each member of the group as an individual. Also I suppose there was added interest in myself being an ex-Yardbird. A lucky combination really. There's been a barrage of groups over there from this; country—but, as I said, we've been lucky.

"There's still a lot of magic attached to the Yardbirds name, and I find it amazing. I saw that group crumble—not in popularity, but from the inside—and I couldn't believe it when someone said to me that if the Yardbirds had stayed together a bit longer it could have been the biggest group ever. But I can see that might possibly have happened—if we'd stayed together.

"But I'm pleased with the way things are going for Led Zeppelin—our album's doing well at the moment too. The only thing is that I wish we'd recorded it now instead of when we did—we hadn't been together too long, and it could have been a lot better. But it isn't bad—I don't wince when I hear it. Robert has such a nice voice—and he's very good on stage.

"Working in America pulled the group together a lot— the album is a good illustration of where we were. After we'd recorded that we had a fifty minute stage act together. But at the end of our U.S. tour that had stretched to two and a half hours—and it happened naturally. The act changes every night. At places like the Fillmore where you play encore after encore, you just have to stretch the numbers out—especially when we first went over, because we didn't have time to get new numbers together to add.

"The trouble is, of course, that now we're back in Britain the numbers are too long—and that's our main problem at the moment. Radio especially is used to short numbers—on "Top Gear" for example, we had to tailor all our songs to fit them in.

"We're working on our next album at the moment. We've got about four numbers together, and we want to get recording started before we go back to the States next. We go on April 20, and we want to finish the album as soon as we get back to have it ready for June release."

Led Zeppelin Invades...review of Led Zeppelin I.... Full of nice tastes and ideas that actually work, the album is very well done, a good first volume that must lead on to an excellent second volume in the recording career of a new and expectedly exciting group. Led Zeppelin.... Advert reads — Wednesday Toby Jug Tolworth Surrey Led Zeppelin.... Letter to the editor from the USA says Led Zeppelin are slated to appear at the Palm Springs Pop festival the letter is signed Brian Wilcox road manager of Savoy Brown....

16 **Record Retailer reports....** Led Zeppelin I is #14.... poster inside features the blue lettered album cover....

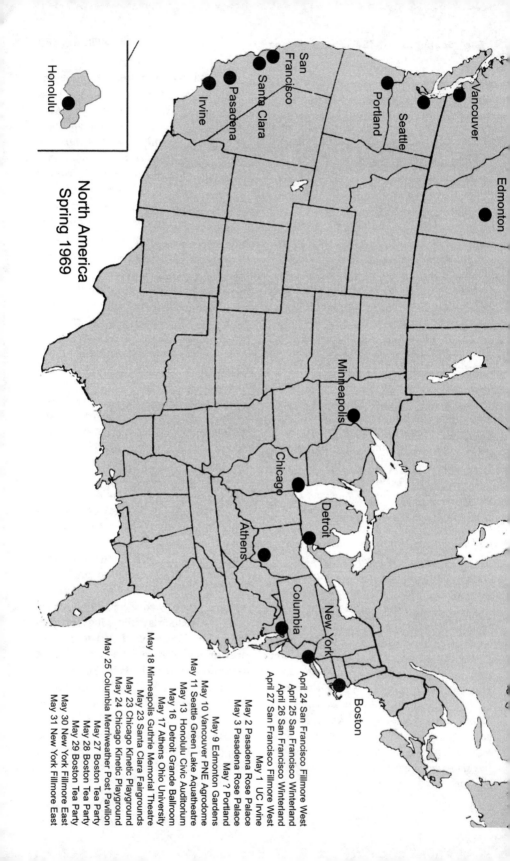

North America
Spring 1969

Honolulu

Vancouver
Edmonton
Seattle
Portland
San Francisco
Santa Clara
Pasadena
Irvine

Minneapolis
Chicago
Detroit
Athens
Columbia
New York
Boston

April 24 San Francisco Fillmore West
April 25 San Francisco Winterland
April 26 San Francisco Winterland
April 27 San Francisco Fillmore West

May 1   UC Irvine
May 2   Pasadena Rose Palace
May 3   Pasadena Rose Palace
May ?   Portland
May 9   Edmonton Gardens
May 10   Vancouver PNE Agrodome
May 11   Seattle Green Lake Aquatheatre
May 13   Honolulu Civic Auditorium
May 16   Detroit Grande Ballroom
May 17   Athens Ohio University
May 18   Minneapolis Guthrie Memorial Theatre
May 23   Santa Clara Fairgrounds
May 23   Chicago Kinetic Playground
May 24   Chicago Kinetic Playground
May 25   Columbia Merriweather Post Pavilion
May 27   Boston Tea Party
May 28   Boston Tea Party
May 29   Boston Tea Party
May 30   New York Fillmore East
May 31   New York Fillmore East

19 **DISC reports....** Led Zeppelin are to leave tomorrow (Friday) for the USA.... apparently they will be well secured on the plane. The previous week on a flight from Bremen Germany an engine on their plane caught fire and they had to make a crash landing.... **Record Mirror reports....** Tony Stratton Smith says Led Zeppelin is *"Big, but BIG. It's a nice payoff for Jimmy Page for all the years he's invested in building up a following here. His manager Peter Grant rescued me off a rain sodden street in a chauffeur driven Cadillac on West 55th St., if I have to spend this much time in the rain I may have to put up my fees!"*.... Led Zeppelin are really packing in the crowds during their British club appearances.... LZ I is #12.... **New Musical Express reports....** Led Zeppelin will be opening their latest tour of the USA at the Fillmore West in San Francisco.... **Melody Maker reports....** Letters to the editor... At last Jimmy Page is getting some of the recognition he so rightly deserves. For years now he has been the most under-rated guitarist to hail from these shores which is strange when you consider the great guitar work he did with the Yardbirds. Mick Hawksword London.... Led Zeppelin are slated to appear at the Pop Proms on June 29th at the Royal Albert Hall.... the band recently had problems when their plane returning from Germany had an engine catch fire requiring a forced landing....

22 **San Francisco Chronicle reports....** Led Zeppelin, a British band led by ex-Yardbird Jimmy Page, will perform Thursday and Sunday at the Fillmore West and Friday and Saturday at Winterland....

23 **Record Retailer reports....** Led Zeppelin I is #12....

25 **International Times reports....** Led Zeppelin go into Olympic Studios this week.... no single will be released.... the new album is an amalgam of styles says Jimmy Page and it should be out in about two months....

26 **DISC reports....** Led Zeppelin will play at the Pop Proms on June 29th.... Jimmy Page will back up Joe Cocker on his first album.... **Record Mirror reports....** Tony Colton claims that Jimmy Page used to come to the Flamingo Club to tape Albert Lee. He would then take the tapes home and practice.... LZ will appear at the Pop Proms.... Led Zeppelin are admirers of Hard Meat.... LZ I is #8.... **Melody Maker reports....** Led Zeppelin will be playing the Newport Jazz festival....

30 **Record Retailer reports....** Led Zeppelin I is #8....

May 1969

3 **Record Mirror reports....** Led Zeppelin are fans of Gypsy after a joint appearance at Klooks Kleek.... LZ I is #6.... **Melody Maker reports....** Letter to the editor from Dave Pegg of Fairport Convention, "It's nice to see young musicians from Birmingham gaining national recognition. Led Zeppelin's Robert plant's incredible voice and John Bonham's percussion have really been brought out to the full by the brilliant playing of Jimmy Page and John Paul Jones. It won't be long before the playing of many other midland musicians is also acknowledged.".... **Los Angeles Free Press....** Full page two-color Advert reads — Scenic Sounds Presents Led Zeppelin,

Brian Auger and Julie Driscoll and The Trinity, May 2 and 3 8pm to 1am Doors open 7.00pm. Lights by Thomas Edison. Sound by Black Gold. tickets $3.50 advance $4.00 at the door 835 S. Raymond The Rose Palace Pasadena.... **Billboard reports....** Led Zeppelin are expected in Hawaii....

5 **Honolulu Advertiser reports...**The hottest group from England, Led Zeppelin will be here next Tuesday May 13, at the Civic. Indicia Music Productions are the lucky promoters who got Led Zeppelin's only Hawaii date for the year. There will only be 4,500 tickets so don't miss it....

7 **Record Retailer reports....** Led Zeppelin I is #6....

9 **Vancouver Sun reports....** Music - Led Zeppelin Saturday 8.00 pm Agrodome.... **International Times reports....** An interview with Jimmy Page conducted in an office in London's Soho. When asked about Britain's music scene, Page, *"I don't think there really is one.... Over here in Britain there are a few record companies promoting things that ought to be heard but that's all. In America the big difference is that most of the cities have a couple of FM underground stations and they keep everybody informed about what's happening nationally, which groups are coming to town, and they play the records that the groups they're talking about have made. So the kids are fully aware of everything that's going on. In Britain, after we'd formed the new group, nobody wanted to book us because we weren't called the Yardbirds! That situation just wouldn't occur in the States. Of course once we'd been to the States and begun to make a name for ourselves, all the British promoters wanted to know. It's*

such a drag. At first I thought the group was going to crumble before it had started properly.

"(Radio) is very important, but over here the BBC have effectively killed the progress of 'underground' music. I know the policy down there, there's a reviewer who gives new releases one listen, just ONE listen and if it fits the Radio One concept of what a groovy record should be, it MIGHT get selected for plugging and they only plug six records per week. It's amazing that they should be allowed to do that. It's only John Peel and that other guy Pete Drummond, who can play any of the good stuff. The only producer who's really into it is Bernie Andrews.... Nightride was a show I liked. Not the sort of thing our group could be on though, but it had a lot of good things to say, presented a good variety of sounds.... if they had put it on every night you'd be falling into the same trap as Radio One does with say the Jimmy Young show. I mean think about lorry drivers going across the country every night, they'd get pissed off listening to the same stuff every night with no alternative station to switch to. There really needs to be an alternative.... I really don't understand why the British just accept everything that's laid on them without trying to resist."

On the subject of the possible expansion of progressive music, Page, *"There is nothing else, Jimmy Young and the Love Affair can't go on churning out the same rubbish forever. I hope that kids will move over to progressive stuff as they get a little bit older, rather than turn on 'Family Favourites' every week. You can't really tell, there's so many things involved. I do think that many of the important people in the business are becoming much hipper than they used to* be, so maybe they'll try and effect some changes."

The new album, Page, *"Well all the things on the album are things that just seemed to be natural for the group to do. There's no reason to stick to one style of music nowadays.... We do the same arrangements on-stage as we did on the album. As a group we don't want to be put into a category because we are bound to develop individually and therefore the group will always be changing. That was the trouble with the Yardbirds, everyone expected to see Keith playing harmonica like Sonny Boy Williamson, so he had to do it, even though he wanted to get into different scenes.... I suppose (that's why we split)...but there were so many things involved, it's never that simple. We quit when we were enormous in America and forgotten over here. It was a very strange situation to live with."*

10 **DISC reports**.... Led Zeppelin will play the Bath Festival this summer.... **Record Mirror reports**.... LZ I is #9.... **The Edmonton Journal reports**.... review of show on the 9th at the Edmonton Gardens, "Led Zeppelin is brutal. The hottest new rock band from Britain stalked on stage and let loose an earthquake of sound and frenzy.... Led Zeppelin compels excitement and involvement.... guitarist Jimmy Page, 'I can't put a tag to our music. Every one of us has been influenced by the blues, but it's one's interpretation of it and how you utilize it. I wish someone would invent an expression, but the closest I can get is contemporary blues.'.... As Led Zeppelin plays it, it's knock-down drag-out blues.".... **New Musical Express reports**.... Led Zeppelin exceed their wildest dreams.... Nick Logan conducts an interview with Jimmy Page about the

band's huge success in America.... Page grumbles about the ridiculous attitudes at the British venues, *"I was at one of those lush chandelier ballrooms and at first they wouldn't let the group in because they didn't have ties. Robert Plant and John Bonham had to call the manager to get in. If it had been me I wouldn't have had anything to do with it. Then there was a bloke who came miles to see us and they wouldn't let him in because he was wearing a cravat. Robert got him in. We'd been told we had to do an exact 45 minute spot and if we went a minute over that was it. So we cut it down and when we started the last number if we'd have been allowed to complete it we'd have over-run by six minutes. They turned on the revolving stage as we were playing and the deejay came around. The audience was whistling and booing. It was a terrible shame because all they usually get in those places are Mickey Mouse groups and I'd played Cardiff before with the Yardbirds and they were great audiences. That sort of thing is just not fair to people who come along to see you."*.... Ann Moses reports from Hollywood about the band staying in the Chateau Marmonte.... Page, *"America made us. It really did. It takes two or three years to build up a reputation in England, but we came over here as soon as we could and when we went back our success had already been heard of over there. I was anxious to get to America. We came as soon as we could. I didn't have any confidence in British audiences. No confidence at all. That's because the Yardbirds had their biggest success in America and I just assumed it would be the same with us."*...Atlantic have released Good Times Bad Times as a single in the USA, Page, *"It makes them happy they had their reasons, but singles aren't important to us. We don't want any.*

We're the kind of group that plays out. A track can go for eight minutes one night and twenty minutes the next. You have to be kind of sophisticated to do a single. You have to stick to what you've done on the record but we're not that way we like to really soar.".... **Billboard reports....** Atlantic records first quarter earnings are way up in part due to the sales of Led Zeppelin One....

11 **The Seattle Times reports....** Advert, Led Zeppelin and Three Dog Night rock concert, Green Lake Aqua Theatre today 2 to 6....

12 **The Vancouver Sun reports....** Up Up and Away With Zeppelin.... Review of the show at the Vancouver Agrodome .... "Nearly 4,000 young people accorded Led Zeppelin, a British contemporary rock blues group, a wildly cheering ovation Saturday Night in the PNE Agrodome. .... Page is a facile powerful guitarist.... Bassist Jones was a rumbling rolling mountain of foundation while Bonham's drums were alternately brilliant in solo, adept in accompaniment.... Plant's singing power and projection were amazing."

14 **Record Retailer reports....** Led Zeppelin I is #9....

15 **The Fifth Estate reports....** Events calendar reads, 'Fri. May 16 Led Zepplin (sic) and Sun Ra will appear at the Grande Ballroom, Grand River and Beverly for two shows, $5.00.'

16 **Detroit News reports....** On the rock scene this weekend, Led Zeppelin tonight only at the Grande Ballroom....

17 **Record Mirror reports....** LZ I is

#10.... **New Musical Express reports....** Led Zeppelin packed out two nights in Pasadena at the Rose Palace on May 2nd and 3rd.... **Billboard reports....** Article says Led Zeppelin will be playing three days with the New York Rock and Roll Ensemble starting on May 12th. This is somewhat confusing as the issue is dated May 17th and the band certainly didn't play this gig....

19 **Honolulu Advertiser reports....** Review of the show on the 13th at the Honolulu Civic Auditorium, "Led Zeppelin was the first major British rock group to appear in Hawaii, and I think most people at the Civic Auditorium last Tuesday night will agree that we want more. The showmanship exceeded any rock performance here to date.... I really wondered before the concert if Led Zeppelin could sound as good as their Atlantic album - they sounded better.... Local promoters want to book Led Zeppelin again in August."

21 **Record Retailer reports....** Led Zeppelin I is #10....

23 **The Old Mole reports....** Happenings.... Tuesday May 27 Rock: Led Zeppelin and Zephyr, Boston Tea Party, expensive.... Thursday May 29 Led Zeppelin etc.... **International Times reports....** Apparently Jimmy Page has been told that the safest place to be during an earthquake is in the bathtub, he has therefore banned anyone from using it, this must surely make Led Zeppelin the smelliest band in the world.... **San Diego Free Press reports....** Concerts May 23-25 Santa Clara Pop Festival, Santa Clara California - Groups include Jimi Hendrix Experience, Jefferson Airplane, Chambers Brothers, Led Zeppelin.... and

more Tickets from $3.75 to $6.50....

24 **DISC reports....** Led Zeppelin soon to start a short tour...dates to include Birmingham, Manchester, Newcastle, Bristol, Portsmouth, London.... **Record Mirror reports....** LZ I is #12.... Bill Graham brought a live octopus to the Led Zeppelin party in the USA.... **Melody Maker reports....** Letter to the editor suggests that Plant and Page should listen to 'I Wanna be Like You' from the Jungle Book soundtrack if they want to learn how to perform scat between voice and guitar.... **Billboard reports....** Advert reads — The Rockpile is Canada's prime showcase for the world's finest rock album performers. Check us out Rap with Led Zeppelin, Spirit, etc. The Rockpile is the place to break a heavy act in Canada....

Article mentions that Led Zeppelin will be playing at the Pop Proms at Royal Albert Hall.... **Billboard reports....** Record companies are delighted with strong sales in Canada of such albums as Led Zeppelin One....

28 **Record Retailer reports....** Led Zeppelin I is #12....

31 **Record Mirror reports....** Led Zeppelin are booked to play a huge outdoor pop festival called Woodstock.... The Chrysalis Agency now has Led Zeppelin for the USA.... LZ I is now #12.... **New Musical Express reports....** Golden Zeppelin, the band are awarded gold records for Led Zeppelin I at the Plaza in New York.... Jerry Wexler of Atlantic makes the presentation.... Page, *"There hasn't been a time when I can honestly say we've ever felt let down for one moment, Look at this, these watches were presented to us by the owner of the*

Kinetic Theatre in Chicago after our date there last weekend. It's just fantastic!".... The band will headline at the Fillmore East in New York the final two days in May.... Zeppelin were in New York to put down some tracks at the A&R studios.... the band return to the UK next week $150,000 richer, Page, *"It's been a fantastic tour. Over on the West Coast, it was just like the old days of rock with kids jumping on the stage and dancing while we were playing!"....* Led Zeppelin will perform a series of gigs in the UK prior to the show at The Royal Albert Hall Pop Proms on June 29th, dates are Birmingham Town Hall Jun 13, Manchester Free Trade Hall Jun 15th, Newcastle City Hall Jun 20, Bristol Colston Hall Jun 21, Portsmouth Guild Hall Jun 26.... more dates to follow.... **Billboard reports....** Article states that Atco's Led Zeppelin will be playing the Fillmore East on Friday May 30 and Saturday 31.... **Cashbox reports....** Cover story — Superb cover shot of the band. Article mentions tour dates in San Francisco, Los Angeles, Seattle, Vancouver, Portland, Detroit, Minneapolis and Baltimore and then finishing at the Fillmore in New York....

June 1969

7 **Record Mirror reports....** LZ I is #12.... Led Zeppelin is booked to play an open air gig in Central Park.... when asked about the problems of touring, Jimmy Page, *"Airlines losing equipment"*, John Paul Jones, *"Changes in altitude while flying that hurt your singing voice, LA smog which does the same and one-nighters."* John Bonham, *"Hostility towards long hair and dress from adults at hotels and airlines."* Robert Plant,

"POP PROMS"

AMEN CORNER
CHUCK BERRY
CHICKEN SHACK
DUBLINERS
THE EQUALS
FAMILY
FLEETWOOD MAC
INCREDIBLE
STRING BAND
LED ZEPPELIN
MARMALADE
JOHN PEEL
THE PENTANGLE
THE WHO

and many more!

Hope to see you at the Royal Albert Hall
June 29th-July 5th

All tickets now on sale at Royal Albert Hall, London, S.W.7
or ticket agencies.

FOR BEST RESULTS — BOOK NOW!

A News Presentation

"Large auditoriums that boom. Harder to sing.".... Led Zeppelin go down well at the Fillmore.... **New Musical Express reports....** half page advert for LZ's upcoming tour of the UK.... Advert for the Royal Albert Hall Pop Proms Sunday June 29th at 5.30 and 8.30 Led Zeppelin.... Article. Sensational Line-Up Set For Bath Blues Festival. Booked to headline, Led Zeppelin, Fleetwood Mac, Ten Years After etc. John Peel will be compere, tickets are 22/6 on the day and 16/6 for the evening only.... Who's Where, Led Zeppelin Birmingham Town Hall (13), Manchester Free Trade Hall (15).... **Melody Maker reports....** Advert reads — Bath Festival Of Blues Saturday June 28th featuring Fleetwood Mac, John Mayall, Ten Years After, Led Zeppelin, Nice, tickets in advance 18/6 on the day 22/6.... Advert reads — If You Live Around London Your Only Chance To See The Amazing Led Zeppelin is at the Royal Albert Hall Sunday June 29th 1969 at 5.30 pm and 8.30 pm tickets 5.30 5/- to 15/-, 8.30 5/- to 20/-.... Half page advert reads — Led Zeppelin Lands.... June 8th Newcastle City Hall, June 13 Birmingham Town Hall, June 22 Manchester Free Trade Hall, June 23 Bristol Colston Hall, June 27 Portsmouth Guild Hall, June 28 Bath Pavilion, June 29 London Albert Hall, Come & Take Off Levitate With The Led Zeppelin Album, Atlantic 588 171....

9 **Honolulu Advertiser reports....** Now that the July 4th weekend is shot (no Doors, no Pop Festival) look forward to the Led Zeppelin's return on August 2. The British based rock group seems to have the perfect combination of professional skill and emotion, and anyone who took in their last concert at the Civic will tell you that they are one of the best

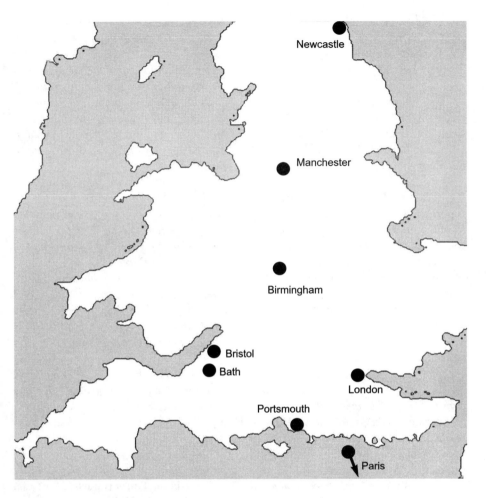

UK Tour Summer/Fall 1969

June 13th, 1969 Birmingham Town Hall
June 15th, 1969 Manchester Free Trade Hall
June 16th, 1969 London Dave Symonds Show BBC
June 20th, 1969 Newcastle City Hall
June 21st, 1969 Bristol Colston Hall
June 24th, 1969 London John Peel's Top Gear BBC
June 25th, 1969 Paris Tous En Scene TV
June 26th, 1969 Portsmouth Guild Hall
June 27th, 1969 London BBC Playhouse Theatre
June 28th, 1969 Bath Festival
June 29th, 1969 London Royal Albert Hall
October 10th, 1969 Paris Olympia
October 12th, 1969 London Lyceum Ballroom

groups ever to play in Hawaii....

11 **Record Retailer reports....** Led Zeppelin I is #28....

12 **The Village Voice reports....** Advert reads — the Schaefer Music Festival In Central Park 33 Nights Of Rock, Pop, Folk Monday July 21 7.00 & 9.30 PM Led Zeppelin/ BB King....

13 **Official UK Tour programme reports....** Jimmy Page, *"Four of us got together in this two by two room and started playing. Then we knew - we started laughing at each other. Maybe it was from relief, or maybe from the knowledge that we knew we could groove together. But that was it. That was just how well it was going.*

"The statement of our first two weeks together is our album. We cut it in 15 hours, and between us wrote eight of the tracks. Our main problem was knowing what channel to take it along musically. Everyone in the group had such a high musical content we thought each of us would be into our own thing. But it all fell together.

"We'll probably always be faced with the fact that individually each member could cut his own album going in his own direction and it would be great. But all those ideas in one outfit, that's pretty fantastic too.

"When I joined the Yardbirds, my main reason was to give myself the opportunity of playing my own music. Before that, my only interest was session work. I began to feel limited not being able to express myself. When I left, it was for almost exactly the same reasons. The group split because everyone began to feel the need to go in his own direction. The pity is, there would have still been

great potential.

"I was working on the Donovan album Hurdy Gurdy Man with John Paul Jones who did some of the arrangements. He asked if I could use a bass guitarist in Led Zeppelin. John is an incredible arranger and musician. He didn't need me for a job, but he felt the need to express himself and figured we could do that together.

"Sessions are great but you can't get into your own thing. Both myself and John felt that in order to give what we had to offer we had to have a group of musicians who could lay down good things.

"I can't put a tag to our music. Everyone of us has been influenced by the blues, but it's one's interpretation of it and how you utilize it. I wish someone would invent an expression but the closest I can get is contemporary blues.

"I want us to be raw and basic. That was the whole thing that made the Yardbirds happen. To go into your own thing is fine, but it has to be a form of experimentation that evolves from a basic sound that everyone else knows and relates to. Perhaps that's why the blues is so big. You can recognize the roots.".... **International Times reports....** full page advert for the Pop Proms....

14 **DISC reports....** BBC Radio One will depart from normal protocols and will allow Led Zeppelin to play a full hour live on June 27th...Adrian Henri from Liverpool Scene will be on hand to assist.... **Record Mirror reports....** LZ I is #18.... **New Musical Express reports....** Led Zeppelin will be appearing in a one hour BBC Radio One special.... Zep have also been offered an appearance at the Expo in Japan in August.... Led Zeppelin will be introduced by Chris Grant on Sunday's Dave Symonds show

June 22nd.... Album to be released in July by Atlantic called 'Flying High' featuring previously available track by Led Zeppelin.... Who's Where - Led Zeppelin, Liverpool Scene and Blodwyn Pig Newcastle City Hall (20) Bristol Colston Hall (21).... **Cashbox reports....** Review of the show at the Fillmore East.... 'British rock quartet Led Zeppelin made a strong return to New York at a four show concert at Fillmore East.... they have carried the British bass-drums-guitar concept to an extreme.... this quartets obsession with power volume and melodramatics leaves little room for subtlety.... the combo has forsaken their musical sense for the sheer power that entices their predominantly juvenile audience.'.... **Billboard reports....** review of the band's show at the Fillmore East. 'Led Zeppelin are the loudest group around.....Plant prances around in neo-Jagger manner providing competition with the light show....this powerful and dominating quartet had it's usual standing ovation.'....further article states that Led Zeppelin have been booked to play the Schaefer Music Festival in New York's Central Park....

15 **Manchester Guardian reports....** Advert for the Royal Albert Hall Pop Proms, A Nems Presentation Main Artistes in order of appearance Led Zeppelin, Fleetwood Mac, Pentangle etc....

18 **Record Retailer reports....** Led Zeppelin I is #29.... Led Zeppelin are recording Killing Floor in an LA studios owned by two UK guys Doug Moody and Chris Huston....

19 **The Village Voice reports....** Advert reads — On July 4th and 5th The Atlanta Raceway will be Pop City. The Atlanta International Pop Festival Performing In person Led Zeppelin etc.....

21 **DISC reports....** Tune in to Radio One this Sunday.... Dave Symonds (Symonds On Sunday) will be on holiday so Chris Grant will host Marmalade and Led Zeppelin beginning at 10.00 a.m.... Jimmy Page is to be one of the featured guitarists at a Guitar virtuoso show at the Singer Bowl in New York.... **Record Mirror reports....** LZ I is # 18.... **Melody Maker reports....** Review of Birmingham, "Led Zeppelin showed just why they have taken America by storm when they began their tour with Blodwyn Pig and Liverpool Scene at Birmingham Town Hall on Friday.".... Advert reads — Pop Proms, Led Zeppelin and many more! Hope to see you at the Royal Albert Hall June 29th - July 5th. For best results - book now!.... **New Musical Express reports....** review of Led Zeppelin's performance at the Birmingham Town Hall.... songs included Dazed & Confused, Babe I'm Gonna Leave You, White Summer and How Many More Times. The band played to a full house.... says reviewer Richard Green, "An almighty wall of sound and a huge crashing of drums signaled the start of the group's act which eventually over-ran by quite some time. The audience rose as one and cheered and clapped for several moments."....

25 **Record Retailer reports....** Led Zeppelin I is #36....

28 **Melody Maker reports....** Advert for Bath Festival.... **Billboard reports....** Atlanta Pop Festival on July 4th and 5th will include Janis Joplin and Led Zeppelin....

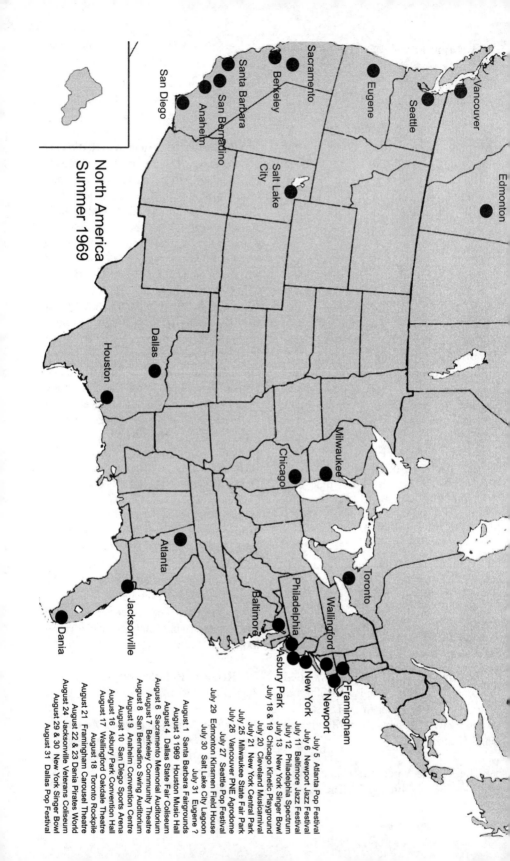

North America
Summer 1969

San Diego
Santa Barbara
Berkeley
Sacramento
Anaheim
San Bernardino
Eugene
Seattle
Vancouver
Edmonton
Salt Lake City
Dallas
Houston
Milwaukee
Chicago
Atlanta
Jacksonville
Dania
Baltimore
Asbury Park
Philadelphia
New York
Wallingford
Newport
Framingham
Toronto

July 5   Atlanta Pop Festival
July 6   Newport Jazz Festival
July 11   Baltimore Jazz Festival
July 12   New York Singer Bowl
July 13   Philadelphia Spectrum
July 18 & 19   Chicago Kinetic Playground
July 20   Cleveland Musicarnival
July 21   New York Central Park
July 25   Milwaukee State Fair Park
July 26   Vancouver PNE Agrodome
July 27   Seattle Pop Festival
July 29   Edmonton Kinsmen Field House
July 30   Salt Lake City Lagoon
July 31   Eugene ?
August 1   Santa Barbara Fairgrounds
August 3 1969   Houston Music Hall
August 4   Dallas State Fair Coliseum
August 6   Sacramento Memorial Auditorium
August 7   Berkeley Community Theatre
August 8   San Bernadino Swing Auditorium
August 9   Anaheim Convention Centre
August 10   San Diego Sports Arena
August 16   Asbury Park Convention Hall
August 17   Wallingford Oakdale Theatre
August 18   Toronto Rockpile
August 21   Framingham Carousel Theatre
August 22 & 23   Dania Pirates World
August 24   Jacksonville Veterans Coliseum
August 29 & 30   New York Singer Bowl
August 31   Dallas Pop Festival

July 1969

2 **Record Retailer reports....** Led Zeppelin I is #17....

5 **DISC reports....** Pop Proms a riotous start.... If the best of the Pop Proms carry on as explosively as they began there won't be any Albert Hall left! Not that there were any riots but the sheer exciting volume of Led Zeppelin all but precipitated a bloodless revolution.... when Led Zeppelin came on and played at a good ten times the volume of everyone else, the audience very nearly freaked completely. They stormed the stage danced in the aisles and the boxes and were screaming so hard that the band did three encores.... **Record Mirror reports....** Led Zeppelin have been invited to play the Newport, Baltimore and Philadelphia Jazz Festivals on July 6th, 11th and 12th.... **Melody Maker reports....** Zeppelin and Fleetwood take off with a roar.... review of the Sunday night Pop Proms performance at the Royal Albert Hall.... Zeppelin leave the stage after 11.00 pm.... the crowd demands more, but the band returns to a stage without power.... encore is Long Tall Sally.... Liverpool Scene's and Blodwyn Pig's saxophonists join in with Zeppelin.... other songs include Communication Breakdown, I Can't Quit You, You Shook Me, How Many More Times, and Dazed & Confused.... midnight interview with Jimmy Page on the way back from a recording session, *"We've cut tracks for this album both here and in the States. It's just a matter of time, fitting in what we can where we can. There's a lot of rocks tracks on it, it's just a matter of juggling with what we've got. We're going back to the States and we'll be there until August 3rd. This will be our*

third trip since the group started. Since we've been going we've only been here for three months at the most and that's probably why we've got a bigger name over there.

"Everywhere we played before we went over last time was really great though. We played places like the Marquee and Klooks Kleek where there were more people turned away than there were inside." On the subject of his musical preferences, Page, *"My influence? I've listened to everybody and every style of music. I appreciate all types of music, I like Bert Jansch, Joni Mitchell...Ritchie Havens, I like him, there's a lot of people.*

"The Yardbirds were very influential. The split came at the end of last summer when there was Jim, Keith and Chris Dreja and myself left. They were one of the first R&B groups and really got into the progressive thing at the end.

"I wouldn't like to be based in the States. American audiences let you know whether they like something straight away - halfway through a drum solo or something there's an uproar whereas here they really let you know at the end of the act. I was talking to Three Dog Night and they were very disturbed about the reaction they were getting here. I told them not to worry. They couldn't get used to the audience reaction at the end.

"Everywhere you play it's a new challenge. I'd like to go to Australia and Japan. You have to work just as hard wherever you go. You know, England has really produced some fantastic things in all spheres from blues groups to string bands. It really floors America. They keep on saying 'where do all those guitarists keep coming from?' They haven't really got that many - Jimi Hendrix I suppose, but even the Americans think of him as being British."

On the subject of Led Zeppelin, *"It's going really well. We've got much closer together musically during the past few months. The policy of the band is that if someone wants to go off at a tangent everyone else would follow. Now we can feel these things easier, it's much more relaxed. I'm really enjoying playing."*.... review of the Bath Festival by Chris Welch. "A Zeppelin attacked the city of Bath and gassed 120,000." .... **New Musical Express reports....** Review of the band's first appearance at the Royal Albert Hall.....Zeppelin and Fleetwood take off with a roar.... "Led Zeppelin took flight to score a massive personal triumph when they closed Sunday's first night amid incredible scenes and gave the Pop Proms the kind of start the organisers would have been brave to dream of.... promoters turned the power off and Plant came back and played harmonica until they turned it back on and the band then blew into Long Tall Sally.".....

9 **Record Retailer reports....** Led Zeppelin I is #24....

12 **DISC reports....** Toast Of America.... feature article.... (Led Zeppelin) have been the toast of America since they first appeared there some months ago.... they have been invited to play the Newport Jazz Festival.... they played an incredibly riotous first night of the Pop Proms.... Zeppelin are currently finishing their second album and are preparing a six-week trip through the USA.... Page, *"We've worked solidly since last October and we're all looking forward to a long rest. I don't know what the rest are doing but I'm going abroad somewhere, probably Morocco. Where I'll no doubt get deported!"*.... the second album is taking a lot longer than the first to record...Page, *"We*

did the first album in about a week, but that was easy because we had a repertoire of numbers all worked out and we just went in the studio and did it.".... **Record Mirror reports....** Festivals & Pop Proms.... review of Bath and Royal Albert Hall.... 40,000 raving music buffs migrated to the site on Saturday the 28th via train, plane, car and foot to see the vast line-up of acts which included Fleetwood Mac and Lep Zeppelin (sic).... Led Zeppelin and the Nice appeared to have stolen the show.... backstage the bar ran dry, Plant, *"We're not supposed to drink so the bar doesn't affect us. The only drawback to the show was the short sets. We have trouble with short bits because you can't connect as people unless everybody has a chance to do their solo. But still there were a lot of acts to go on."*....

The concept of the Pop Proms was proven stable from the first rapturous night on which Led Zeppelin, again, were topping the bill.... Zeppelin were incredible as only they can be. Robert's screeching voice was in good shape and his seaweed hair flopped in earnest. Jimmy Page played up to his legend and darted about the stage like a caged animal. Jimmy's guitar solo and John Bonham's drum solo started the ravers going in the aisles. Occasionally there was a hint of a smile from the man of steel, John Paul Jones. There were no less than three encores which ran on even after the power had been cut and Robert had to resort to using his harp.... I haven't seen a band go down so well for a long time.... LZ I is #24....

16 **Record Retailer reports....** Led Zeppelin I is #12....

18 **Chicago Tribune reports....** Advert reads — Led Zeppelin, Savoy Brown, Litter all three perform tonight and tomor-

row in the Kinetic Playground 4812 N Clark St. Tickets are $5 doors open 7.30 pm....

19 **Record Mirror reports....** LZ I is #12...**New Musical Express reports...** Great Zeppelin closed Newport, despite ban!.... Newport festival attracted some 80,000 people and panicked the local authorities who forbade Led Zeppelin from playing their set on Sunday.... promoter George Wein announced to the crowd that Zeppelin wouldn't be appearing and so the crowd began to disperse.... Jimmy Page, *"You don't blow a date like this one. Not after all that. The Newport Jazz Festival was far too important to us to just cancel out and I'm very upset about the whole thing. Wein should never have announced that one of us was ill."....* **Melody Maker reports....** Led Zeppelin Off.... article outlining the band's problems at Newport Jazz festival. It details how the city council were afraid of riots and so the festival organiser, George Wein, announced that Zeppelin wouldn't be appearing. Peter Grant, *"This announcement was given without our consent and it meant that many people who had traveled to Newport to see the group had to miss seeing them."* If this is a direct quote from Grant it must have been made while the situation was still developing because the band DID appear.... Letter to the editor suggests that Led Zeppelin have definitely displaced Cream as hard rock's champions.... **Billboard reports....** review of the troubles at Newport Jazz Festival where the band almost didn't play because promoter George Wein was troubled by the huge attendance. Peter Grant, *"George Wein panicked. It was obvious they weren't going to get everybody in. He thought there'd be about 15,000 who couldn't get*

in so they announced that one of the group was ill and they wouldn't appear. This was done without our knowledge. Actually we came over from England to do the Festival. We were very excited about it. We felt it was progressive musically and would give us a new audience. We feel this hurt the act a lot."... The article says that Grant is planning another free show for the people who didn't get in. It mentions that the band played Long Tall Sally in their final medley and that nearly 80,000 people attended....

21 **Milwaukee Journal reports....** Advert for Midwest Rock Festival State Fair Park, Milwaukee Wisconsin. July 25, 26 and 2. Friday July 25 Performance starts at 5 p.m. Led Zeppelin, Buffie Sainte Marie, First Edition, Sweetwater, Pacific Gas & Electric, SRC, Shag...tickets for each day $15....

23 **Record Retailer reports....** Led Zeppelin I is #22....

25 **Time reports....** Article outlining the summer's problem festivals, specifically Newport Jazz where it states that promoter George Wein had canceled Led Zeppelin's appearance in the interest of public safety, concluding with the news that rock has been permanently banned from Newport.... **San Diego Free Press reports....** Advert August 10th Led Zeppelin and Jethro Tull, Sports Arena, 8.00 pm Tickets $2.50 to $5.50.... **Los Angeles Free Press reports....** Advert reads — In Concert Only LA Appearance Led Zeppelin And Jethro Tull Sat Aug 9 8:00 pm Anaheim Convention Center....

26 **Record Mirror reports....** America's Superstars Are British.... feature article about UK bands in the USA.... Guests at

the Loews Motor Inn in New York include Led Zeppelin, Ten Years After, Jethro Tull, Savoy Brown.... at the Newport Festival organisers nearly destroyed Led Zeppelin's appearance because they were upset by the number of fans from nearby Boston who were arriving into the town to see Zeppelin (over 25,000 fans from Boston alone), they announced on the local radio stations that Zep would not be performing as one of the members was ill. As the day progressed and the announcements were made by the hour, thousands of fans left on the long trek home. Zep's manager Peter Grant was furious and brought the boys up to do their show. True to form they dominated the evening and had the audience screaming for more.... Back in New York the band's headquarters was an English pub called The Haymarket at 47th and 8th, Zep, Jethro and Ten Years gathered there to swap tales.... on the second night at the Philadelphia Spectrum it was the turn of Jethro and Zeppelin. Zeppelin are without a doubt the second most powerful live draw in the States. The audience went berserk. When they eventually fought their way back to the dressing room after being escorted off by armed guards the audience kept screaming and shouting and banging for more until the organisers had no choice but to bring them back for an encore for fear the fans would demolish the stadium.... A nude man appeared on stage during Led Zeppelin's Atlanta Pop appearance.... John Bonham a Jaguar enthusiast has bought five cars since December.... LZ I is #22.... **The Vancouver Sun reports....** Tonight 8.30 pm Led Zeppelin The Agrodome.... **New Musical Express reports....** "two members of Led Zeppelin have bought new cars, Jimmy Page a Rolls Royce Silver Cloud and John Bonham a Daimler

Sovereign."…. **Melody Maker reports….** Newport Rock Ban…. article states that 'any rock groups' have been banned from appearing at Newport. It says this is due to Led Zeppelin appearing despite the organiser asking them not to. It goes on to say that Grant was trying to negotiate a future appearance (probably because so many people believed they wouldn't be there and went home). Grant was apparently also flying to the USA to organise a second show at Carnegie Hall after the first sold out…. **Billboard reports….** Led Zeppelin will be playing alongside Vanilla Fudge at Vancouver's Agrodome on Saturday 26th and again at Salt Lake City's Lagoon Wednesday 30th….Article reviewing the Jeff Beck concert at the Singer Bowl on July 13th where Page, Plant and Bonham joined in a jam session. Over 7,000 people attended with a gross of $31,500 other people on stage included Jethro Tull's Glenn Cornick and Rod Stewart….

28 **The Vancouver Sun reports….** Led Zeppelin Flies Directly to the Nerve Ends…. review of show at the Agrodome, Vanilla Fudge were the opening act…. "In rock parlance Led Zeppelin is a very together group. It is made up of four individual musicians attuned to each others whims, capable of ensemble performance as well as separate forays into the jungle of lonely escapades."…. **New Musical Express….** Zeppelin Tours of Germany, UK…. Led Zeppelin who are in the USA will be returning there for a second tour in October. When the band returns to the UK in September they will begin a tour of Germany as well as appearing at the Paris Olympia in October. Zeppelin is expected to tour the UK for three weeks in December or January. Zeppelin have recently sold out all the tickets for their

show at New York's Carnegie Hall on October 26th. (This date was later changed. R.G.) The band's manager Peter Grant is now traveling to America to organise a second show at the prestigious hall….

30 **The Edmonton Journal reports….** review of show at the Edmonton Kinsmen Field House…. "Led Zeppelin were hampered by the sound system as well as having to go on stage first…. Vanilla Fudge should have opened…. the show was probably the best of the year and the turn out probably caught the promoters by surprise…. not enough chairs to go round for the 5,000 people."…Page, *"When people are no longer interested in what we do - it could be tomorrow, it could be five years - I'll go back to art."….* Plant, *"When we began, English audiences just didn't want to know us at all. We could have been around for years and years, (but in the US) the crowds began to really like what we were doing…. I don't know what it is. All I know is that I wouldn't like to stand still all night. I gotta move to be able to let it out."….* **Record Retailer reports….** Led Zeppelin I is #12….

August 1969

2 **Record Mirror reports….** Rumours that Led Zeppelin wouldn't play at Newport Jazz Festival provoke mass exodus of fans. Peter Grant has to fly up with a lawyer to assert that the band will appear…. LZ I is #12 **New Musical Express reports….** Led Zeppelin received a gold record award in New York. The award was made by Jerry Wexler of Atlantic records. The band's first album has sold over $1 million in the USA. Led Zeppelin's current tour will

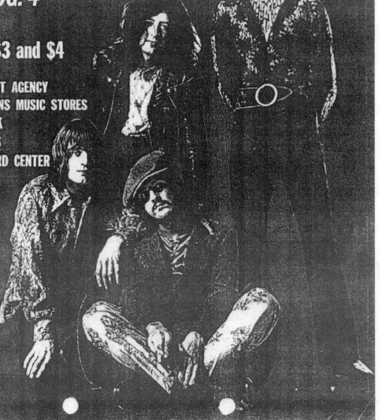

CONCERTS WEST PRESENTS
LED ZEPPELIN

**STATE FAIR
COLISEUM — FAIR PARK
MON.- AUG. 4**

TICKETS - $3 and $4

PRESTON TICKET AGENCY
COGHILL-SIMMONS MUSIC STORES
EXCHANGE PARK
NEIMAN-MARCUS
PRESTON RECORD CENTER

gross over $300,000. They are earning as much as $15,000 per night. Jimmy Page, *"There hasn't been a time when I can honestly say we've ever felt let down for one moment. These watches were presented to us by the owner of the Kinetic Theatre in Chicago after our date there last weekend. It's just fantastic! And for each of us to have gold records. We didn't tell Bonzo. He thought we were going to get one between us and we'd have to split it up, each of us getting it for three months at a time. I think he's speechless."....* Led Zeppelin are one of the acts booked for the Bilzen Jazz festival in Belgium on August 22 - 24 (This didn't happen R.G.).... **Melody Maker reports....** Letters to the editor from disgruntled Cream fans saying Led Zeppelin could never replace Cream.... **Billboard reports....** Review of Zeppelin's appearance at the Cleveland Musicarnival on July 20th. The article says the band played to a sold-out house of 2,574 fans but only played a five song set including White Summer, Communication Breakdown and Dazed & Confused. the support act was the James Gang....Further article is cover story which outlines how British bands are storming the USA most of which, including Led Zeppelin are booked by Premier Talent Booking Agency...

3 Houston Chronicle reports.... Zeppelin To Moor Here.... An English group called Led Zeppelin will be presented in concert tonight at 8 in the Music Hall by Concerts West and KILT. Tickets are available at the door....

4 Dallas News reports.... Concerts West presents Led Zeppelin Monday August 4, 8.00 State Fair Coliseum...Tickets $3 advance, $4 at door.... **Houston**

Chronicle reports.... review of the show at the Music Hall under the headline 'Page is Led Zeppelin's Helium'.... It states that the band started with an unfamiliar number called 'Sweet Baby' before turning to selections from their first album. The reviewer calls Page 'a one man, one instrument rock band'. He concludes 'The frail sensitive lead duo of the Zeppelin personifies the soul of unisex. But the music is what matters, and it's early Hell's Angel.'....

6 San Diego Free Press reports.... Promoter Terry Phillips brings Led Zeppelin and Jethro Tull for a surprise package at the Sports Arena. Zeppelin is being touted as the new Supergroup but look for Tull to prove that super is a word only in the mind of the press agent....

9 DISC reports.... Tune in to BBC Radio One this Sunday.... Led Zeppelin Live show to take up second half of Top Gear between 8 and 9 p.m.... **Record Mirror reports....** Advance orders for LZ II exceeds 250,000 units.... LZ I is #25.... **Record Retailer reports....** Led Zeppelin I is #25.... **New Musical Express reports....** Led Zeppelin win a gold album for one million dollars worth of sales in the USA. Jerry Wexler Atlantic records executive presented the award. The second Led Zeppelin album is nearly ready and has advance orders of over 200,000 units. Zeppelin have just completed the first part of their American tour which is set to earn them at least $350,000.... box office records were broken at the Cleveland Musicarnival and the Chicago Kinetic Playground.... **Melody Maker reports....** Led Zeppelin receive Gold Disc In States.... Article outlines how Jerry Wexler of Atlantic records presented the band for sales of over one million dol-

lars for Led Zeppelin I. It states that advance orders for the second album have reached 200,000 units. It then goes on to state that the tour will net the band $350,000 and that they broke the house record at the Kinetic Playground in Chicago and sold out the Cleveland Music Carnival.... **Billboard reports....** Led Zeppelin awarded gold record for $1 million in sales, meanwhile second LP is complete....

13 **Newark Star Ledger reports....** Summer Stars in Asbury Park's air-conditioned Convention Hall on the boardwalk, Sat Aug. 16th at 7.30 and 10 pm Led Zeppelin plus Joe Cocker....

14 **The Village Voice reports....** Advert reads — The Texas International Pop Festival Labor Day weekend Aug 30-31 Sept 1 Led Zeppelin Sunday etc....

15 **Newark Star Ledger reports....** British Combo To Appear. Moe Septee will promote two shows at the Convention Hall tomorrow at 7.30 and 9.45 with British group Led Zeppelin and Joe Cocker....

16 **Record Mirror reports....** LZ I is #14.... En route to Chicago Led Zeppelin's plane is caught in a 70 mph gale. The plane's tail is blown off.... **Record Retailer reports....** Led Zeppelin I is #14.... **New Musical Express reports....** Robert Plant called the NME reporter, Ann Moses, just as he was leaving to see Elvis in Vegas. Plant, *"At one time or another everyone says 'Oh Elvis is rubbish, Elvis is no good' but everybody's got to own up in the end. Really his potentiality is and was so strong. Apparently his act consists of nearly all rock and he's still moving about doing*

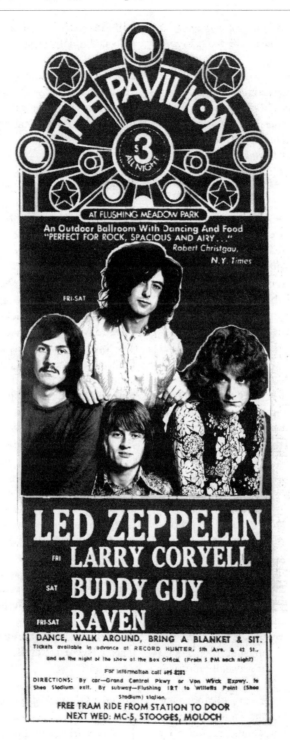

what he did before with an audience so that must be phenomenal. To me his early career is fascinating. I was talking to Jerry Wexler at Atlantic records who was around in the early days and I was really interested because Elvis early stuff was straight from the blues like 'That's Alright Mama'. Jerry told me about the time Elvis stood in for Ray Charles to a completely coloured audience and he went down a storm."...

19 Toronto Globe And Mail reports.... Ritchie Yorke writes, "Led Zeppelin soars to the pop stratosphere", he goes on, "last night's Led Zeppelin concert at the Rock Pile was the most significant pop event this year.... I doubt even Cream could have topped what Zeppelin offered.... Plant makes Morrison look like a mardi-gras parader.... he pushes sex like Colonel Sanders peddles chicken."....

20 San Diego Free Press reports.... Review of the band's concert in San Diego.... "I have been to several concerts since the last 'Tracks' writing, ranging from the Everley Brothers to the Supremes to Led Zeppelin. Most of the concerts, with the exception of the latter, were guilty of what had been previously mentioned. However, the Led Zeppelin-Jethro Tull concert, was different. All the conditions were there to make it the usual run of the mill dull concert, it took place at the super-hype Sports Arena, a large rent-a-gestapo was present, and it was a sit down affair. Both groups played extra long sets and did encores for an appreciative audience, an unusual San Diego occurrence since encores usually mean an added expense for the promoter. When the Zeppelin came on, several thousand music lovers ignored that stupid unwritten law which says you should sit perfectly

still in your numbered seat like a respectable citizen, and converged to the floor area and felt free. The two encores cost the promoters an additional couple of grand and it was with their approval that the encores were permitted. Instead of the usual 11.00 pm deadline the concert ended at 12.05."...

22 Miami Herald reports.... Led Zeppelin group specializing in "contemporary blues" appears along with three local groups at Pirates World Amusement Park, Broward County; tonight and Saturday night, concerts begin at 8. pm with Led Zeppelin on at 9.30.... **Framingham-Natick News reports....** Sell Out At Carousel. According to the review, the show was held at the Carousel Theatre with an audience of nearly 3,000. The opening band was called Orpheus. Plant announced that although they had been traveling for 18 days without stopping, he and his colleagues were willing to give a first attempt at performing a new number 'What Is And What Should Never Be' from the second and newest long playing album and the result earned them a standing ovation. The night was especially important for guitarist Jimmy Page formerly with the Yardbirds, who was featured in several challenging numbers including White Summer, but in honor of the audience was given the title White Massachusetts, and another unnamed oldie requiring strange tuning and filled with new and hidden surprises....

23 Record Mirror reports.... LZ I is #11.... **Record Retailer reports....** Led Zeppelin I is #20....

28 The Village Voice reports.... Advert reads — The Pavilion $3 all night At Flushing Meadow Park. Fri- Sat Led

Zeppelin, Fri - Larry Coryell - Sat Buddy Guy. Dance walk around bring a blanket & sit. Tickets available in advance at Record Hunter....

30 **New Musical Express reports....** "Led Zeppelin has been booked to play one week in Scandinavia and Holland beginning on October 3rd. They then return to Britain for a week before going off to the USA again for another major tour to begin on October 16th." (This turned out to be inaccurate as the tour of Scandinavia was delayed until the following February)...Jimmy Page is planning a September holiday in Spain and Morocco...June Harris reports from New York on Robert Plant's birthday party at the Haymarket Pub. Plant was presented with a cassette recorder by his agent to which he said, *"I've always wanted one of these and I'm very grateful. You can tell them all at the NME."* Led Zeppelin II is complete.... **Record Retailer reports....** Led Zeppelin I is #11....**Billboard reports....** Article states that 45-50,000 people are expected at the Texas pop Festival which will feature Led Zeppelin on Sunday 31st....further article states that Led Zeppelin, Larry Coryell and Raven will play the New York Pavilion on August 29 and 30....Further article states that the Toronto Rock Pile re-opened with style when Led Zeppelin played two shows August 18th....

September 1969

6 **Record Retailer reports....** Led Zeppelin I is #23....

13 **Melody Maker reports....** Led Zeppelin and how they made 37,000 dollars in one night.... an interview with Jimmy Page.... *"I can't see the heavy thing going out. Ever since the Underground thing started a couple of years ago, people's tastes have been broadening. You can have a group like Pentangle, who are into a light folky thing on one hand, and us on the other. The scene is broad enough to take us all in, and I don't see why that situation shouldn't continue."* In New York, 21,000 people showed up to an auditorium that held 10,000. The promoter offered the band more money to do a follow up date which the band had to refuse.... the band received a gold disc for a million dollars in sales.... LZ II has advance orders for 350,000 units.... the band are taking a months holiday.... Page, *"It was tremendous in America, we went down very well, and so did Jethro Tull, particularly on the West Coast. I think the scene is very healthy at the moment. People have all kinds of records in their collection, and that's a very good thing. Like they may have albums by Crosby Stills and Nash who are still basically a Top 40 thing, as well as us. I think that what we play is music from the stomach rather than the head, although it does come from the head too.*

"I don't get much time to listen to records in the States, but over here it's my way of relaxing. I listen mainly to guitar dominated music, naturally, and I dig all kinds of things, including flamenco. have you head Manitas De Plata? He's ridiculous. That gypsy thing is fantastic.

"Britain is one of those places where you've got to make it, but it's a lot more difficult. Over here you feel you've got to knock yourself out before the people start listening to you, but in the States they listen from the start, and if they don't like you they simply don't come to see v again. But it's far from being a wal

for British groups in the States. It's fatal for a group to go over there when it hasn't got it's internal affairs sorted out. Jeff Beck for instance, takes a new band every time he goes over there, so it's no wonder he's sick of the country.

"America couldn't be better for us at the moment. The scenes there are just incredible. The new system is to put groups on a percentage of the gate money, and we drew 37,000 dollars from one amazing gig in Los Angeles.

"When we formed the group a year ago and took it to America for the first time, I think it was my name that was the attraction, because I'd been there several times with the Yardbirds and we always did pretty well. The biggest problem with the new group was getting everyone's name across to the fans, and I think we've done that now. That's very important, and I'm happy about the situation now that there's no star name in the group - everyone's equal. I think we'll probably spend six months of the year in America in the future. That sounds a lot but people don't realise the size of the country. You can get lost there.

"I can't see this ever getting stale, because new ideas are coming up all the time. The new album is so different from the first, and the next one will probably be just as different again. John plays organ and we're going to use that on stage in future, and I play pedal steel guitar, so that opens a lot of new musical doors for us. And then Robert Plant is such a fantastic singer. Every time he sings a song, his phrasing is different, which is very stimulating. I do jam occasionally in clubs but you've got to know it's going to be good before you start, otherwise it's not worth doing. I've seen so many really boring jams.

"Atlantic put out a single from

the first album in the States, but it was never meant as a single. Jethro Tull have proved that a good single can get through, so we're going to try it. I don't see any reason why we can't cut a good 2½ minute track, and a lot of the things on the new album are quite short - about four minutes, but they're really just frameworks for our stage performances, when we really stretch out." Page is then asked if he would ever return to session work, *"Definitely not. It used to make me into a nervous wreck, and I'd enjoy perhaps one session every two months. But I do like doing things like Joe Cocker's album, where he knew just which musicians he wanted."....* **Record Retailer reports....** Led Zeppelin I is #17.... **Billboard reports....** review of Dallas Pop Festival states that Jimmy Page 'lived up to expectations' and that Robert Plant 'showed a noticeable improvement'....

20 **Record Mirror reports....** Cover story.... The Single Challenge...interview with Jimmy Page about the upcoming second album and the band's affairs in general, *"The last I heard, there were orders for over 350,000 copies. It's only got another 70,000 to go before it's a Gold Disc. And this might happen before it's officially released! I guess this has happened because people were happy with the first one.*

"Naturally I'm very pleased with the advance orders apart from having produced the album. I did the first one as well. I got into producing originally when I did a few things for Andrew Oldham and that gave me the incentive to do some more.

"The way I see it is if you're a composer and a writer, you should go into the studio when your composition is being recorded and see the whole thing through

either as a producer or to be on hand to say how it should be done. If I failed in producing for the group, then I would call someone else in.

"If you only concern yourself with your own group, it's difficult to see what is going on outside of that. The main reason (we haven't done a single) is because we have had a bit of a struggle to get the second album out. I'm going off on holiday and when I come back the group is really going to work hard and spend time on producing a single. In a way, it's going to be a bit of a challenge. Because in the past on the albums we've done long tracks so it's a question of condensing a 15 minute performance down to about three minutes.

"I think the underground has now become an established musical form. One of the groups who have helped to do this is Jethro Tull. They present their music with a great deal of excitement which is what is needed these days.

"I'm not at all happy with a lot of the BBC programme planning. One of the hang ups with the BBC as it is now is it caters for what they think is the general public. And because of this many groups who have a lot to say musically don't stand a chance of performing on it.

"We did an hour show on BBC recently with various guests and I believe it was successful. What I'd like to see is other groups who aren't recognized as single chart successes do the same thing, because otherwise there's no chance of their getting any air-play.

"Another thing I'd like to see happen is the return of commercial radio — I'm all for it. It would wake a few people's ideas up and make things competitive.

"With the music we're playing, the people in the street know what it's about but the adults don't know at all. Poor old John Peel did a lot of good. But his programme was originally on at the wrong time on a Sunday afternoon — the same time as the Sunday afternoon film and the adults were normally watching that. If the music had enough exposure so many more people would understand it.

"It's hard to say which way Led Zeppelin is going. For a start the group has changed so much over the last year, but the thing is we are each affected by the other members of the group.".... **Record Retailer reports....** Led Zeppelin I is #30.... **Melody Maker reports....** Pop poll says Led Zeppelin are 6th best album, 4th brightest hope, 3rd brightest International hope....

27 **DISC reports....** Led Zeppelin raid USA to earn home acclaim.... full page article about the band's decision to pursue their fortunes in America.... Plant, "When we got together, nobody wanted us here. Nobody wanted to dig us, they don't want to dig anybody who hasn't got a name. It was 'oh we'll have them as a favor' and all that rubbish, So we decided to go to the States. Then we came back here and everyone was raving about us. It was kind of hypocritical."

On the labeling of Zeppelin as a heavy band, "I think they've got the terms the wrong way round. To me heavy music is something like the Incredible String Band or Buffalo Springfield. They tax your mind and you have to get really into them. Light things are Creedence Clearwater, or the Who—you don't have to get into them. I think we come just in between the two at the moment. By relying on albums you get the right audience. People who buy an album that takes a bit of listening to, make a better audience.

"That's the thing about an

American audience—you find what you thought was the minority is in fact the majority. Appreciation is a lot higher, they know what to listen for. In England they flock to a concert rather than go individually.

"In England at a concert before people jump up they look round and see if everyone else is doing it. That's not the way to enjoy yourself. There are so many limitations for someone going to a concert—to appreciate a lot of the music being played in London now you can't be a bank clerk during the day and a hippy at night. How can you get your head into shape like that? I'm determined to let everyone know what we're about, because I'm sure half of them don't know."....

Melody Maker reports.... An interview with Robert Plant revealing a lot about his early roots.... "My band was breaking up and I didn't know where to go next, and then I got a call from Jimmy which changed everything!

"I was turned onto the blues by a guy named Perry Foster, who I later learned was involved with the Yardbirds in their early days before Keith Relf joined them. I played kazoo and washboard in the sort of bands which if they had been based in London instead of Birmingham, would probably have become the Rolling Stones. We used to do the whole country blues thing: Memphis Minnie, Bukka White and Skip James numbers, which at that time, about six years ago, were really deep blues - and they are now too.

"This sort of music turned my mind to the ideal that I could really express myself through the medium of the blues. I had a certain freedom, and while the other singers were copying all the pop records I could get up on stage and sing blues with any group. The Band Of Joy was really a launching pad for my ideas

and theories about music. I liked Buddy Guy very much - things like 'First Time I Met The Blues', and that rough sound, coming after Muddy Waters and Willie Dixon on those old Pye albums, really was devastating.

"Anyway slightly later my manager got me some acetates of unreleased material from the States, things like Buffalo Springfield. That made me realise that crash-bang music for want of a better word, could be combined with meaningful lyrics, and it was a big pointer for me. You know the Springfield's 'Bluebird'? That's the sort of thing I mean.

"Then everyone began boosting the Cream up as the greatest thing in the world, but I couldn't see it. I'd rather listen to the Youngbloods or Poco who maybe aren't the greatest musicians to a virtuoso like Ginger Baker.

"Then the Band Of Joy began to crumble up and all my hopes started to vanish. I worked with Alexis Korner occasionally in a band with Steve Miller on piano and had a wonderful time. Then Terry Reid told me that Keith Relf had left the Yardbirds, but although I respected them very much for their originality I didn't know that our ideas were on the same lines.

"Jimmy Page and Peter Grant our manager, came up to see me in Birmingham when I was with a group and trying to invade Smethwick with the West Coast Sound! They suggested that I go to Jimmy's house for a few days to see if we got on together, and it was fantastic because I rummaged through his record collection and every album I pulled out was something I really dug. I knew that we'd click.

"Nobody in Britain wanted to know us, but Jimmy told us it'd be different in the States. The first time we went we

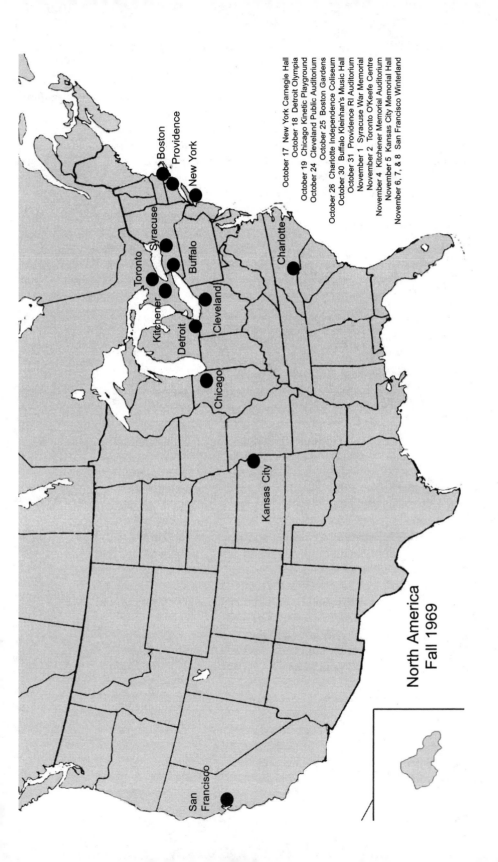

North America
Fall 1969

October 17 New York Carnegie Hall
October 18 Detroit Olympia
October 19 Chicago Kinetic Playground
October 24 Cleveland Public Auditorium
October 25 Boston Gardens
October 26 Charlotte Independence Coliseum
October 30 Buffalo Kleinhan's Music Hall
October 31 Providence RI Auditorium
November 1 Syracuse War Memorial
November 2 Toronto O'Keefe Centre
November 4 Kitchener Memorial Auditorium
November 5 Kansas City Memorial Hall
November 6, 7, & 8 San Francisco Winterland

Boston
Providence
New York
Syracuse
Toronto
Buffalo
Kitchener
Detroit
Cleveland
Charlotte
Chicago
Kansas City
San Francisco

started off right down the bill on the West coast, but by the time we got over to the East coast we were at the top.

"I was very nervous when we started off, because everything I'd done previously had more or less been a failure. The first album was done in a hurry, and we were all feeling our way around the group. Now as we get more familiar with each other better things will come.

"My voice really started developing when I was 15 and we were singing Tommy McLennan numbers and so forth, I don't really know why it's as powerful as it is. After the first album I concentrated on developing the range of my voice, and on developing it so that I can do more things.

"I'm very hung up on the songs of Moby Grape and Arthur Lee of Love. That's nice stuff, and I'm beginning to write in that sort of style. This group has really woken me up from inertia. Years and years with no success can keep you singing, but it can bring you down an awful lot.".... Led Zeppelin manager Peter Grant given a special gold disc, inscribed with his name by Atlantic to mark million dollar sales of their LP....

October 1969

Creem Volume 2 #6 reports.... Advert reads — 'Saturday Night October 18 Led Zeppelin, Lee Michaels, Magic Veil Light Show at Olympia 8:00 until? at the Eastown at Harper and Van Dyke.'

4 **Record Mirror reports....** LZ I is #17.... **Record Retailer reports....** Led Zeppelin I is #40.... **Melody Maker reports....** Zeppelin Show.... Article states that Led Zeppelin will be appearing at the Lyceum in London on October 12th pro-

moted by Tony Stratton-Smith for "The highest fee ever paid a British group in England for one concert."....

9 **Chicago Seed reports....** The Electric theatre Presents Aaron Russo's Kinetic Playground October 19th Afternoon and Evening Show Led Zeppelin Santana and Lighthouse.... **The Village Voice reports....** Advert reads — Howard Stein Presents Led Zeppelin at Carnegie Hall Next Friday Night (the 17th) at 8.30 and Midnight. Standing Room only....

11 **DISC reports....** Last chance to get tickets for Led Zeppelin show at the Lyceum Ballroom.... tickets are £1 show is 7.30 to 11.00 p.m.... **New Musical Express reports....** "Led Zeppelin will be reportedly receiving the highest amount ever paid to a single band in the UK for their appearance in October at the Lyceum Ballroom in London, the actual figure is a secret.".... Nick Logan interviews Robert Plant and asks why so many bands go to America.... Plant, *"As a group we have to go to America because the audiences there are so ultra responsive. English audiences will look around to see if others are clapping before they do. And they rely on whether the pop papers are raving over somebody before they will say they like them. They are like sheep. In the States you can be terrible musically. Take a group like Country Joe and the Fish who are not brilliant musicians. But when they play the warmth comes across."* Logan and Plant then talk about the new album about which he says, *"Jimmy does the chords and I write out the melodies and the lyrics. Ramble On is inspired by The Lord Of The Rings."* He mentions that he had to complete Bring It On Home in a shed in Vancouver. .... Plant then grum-

bles about the criticism the group takes, *"I hate the way people slam us for going to America saying that it's all for the bread. In the old days people used to leave groups if they weren't earning money. We have earned our money. We've gone for eleven months without a real break. I don't think any fair-minded person would begrudge it us."*.... **Record Retailer reports....** Led Zeppelin I is #25.... **Melody Maker reports....** advert for Led Zeppelin, Audience and Frosty Moses at the Lyceum, admission 20/- Students 16/- doors open 7.00 pm concert begins 7.30 pm.... article states Zeppelin will play the Carnegie Hall on October 17 before touring the USA for three weeks. It says they will commute directly from France to the USA after playing at the Olympia in Paris on the 12th. They are then slated to return to the UK to record their third album while the second album will be released in late October having been delayed when the sleeve art was lost. Advances for the second album are now above 400,000 and the band's first album is number one in Australia....

14 **Cleveland's Plains Dealer reports....** Audience on Chairs ordered for Led Zeppelin.... "When the Led Zeppelin music group performs at Public Hall Oct. 24 the audience will be in seats - not blankets spread around the hall's main floor.... Radio Station WIXY complains that the open floor seating arrangement has been introduced successfully at concerts all over the country.... Fire Chief said the blankets would create a fire hazard. Belkin Productions has $15,000 invested in the concert which features the popular English pop group."... Advert reads — WIXY 1260 presents in person Led Zeppelin plus Grand Funk Railroad Public Hall Tonite 8pm Tickets $4.00 -

$4.50. Belkin Productions....

16 **Detroit News reports....** Advert The Led Zeppelin, Grand Funk Railroad, MC-5, Lee Michaels, starting at 8 pm Saturday at Olympia Stadium, Tickets $6, $5, and $4.... **The Village Voice reports....** Advert reads — Led Zeppelin II is Ready On Atlantic Records and 8 Track Cartridges....

17 **Detroit Free Press reports....** Saturday Led Zepplin (sic), MC-5, Lee Michael and special guests Grand Funk Railroad will be at Olympia. You can get tickets at Hudson's and the Olympia box-office. They cost $4, $5 and $6."

18 **Record Mirror reports....** Revealing article about a badly documented period. The tour of Holland is a complete mystery, "Led Zeppelin just returned from a highly successful tour of Holland...they appear at the Paris Olympia next week and then fly to the USA on October 16th to play Carnegie Hall the next night. They play a three week tour of the USA and then return to the UK to record a single and their third album. No release date is set for LZ II for the UK. 400,000 advance units have been ordered for the USA."... **New Musical Express reports....** review of the Zeppelin show at the London Lyceum by Nick Logan.... "Over 2,000 people at £1 a head packed the famous ballroom to see Led Zeppelin." Apparently Logan didn't think the band's performance was particularly good calling it "less than inspiring".... **Billboard reports....** Article says Atlantic will release Led Zeppelin 2 to tie in with their tour of the USA. Tour dates will include Carnegie Hall Oct 17, Detroit 18, Chicago 19, Cleveland 24, Boston 25, Charlotte 26, Buffalo 30, Providence 31, Syracuse

Nov 1, Toronto 2, Kitchener 4, and Kansas City 5....Advert for Led Zeppelin 2 on the cover....

22 Boston After Dark reports.... third of a page advert reads - "Narragansett Brewing Company Proudly Presents, Led Zeppelin, with the MC-5 and extra attraction Johnny Winter, Saturday October 25 8.00 pm Boston Garden. Tickets $3.50, $4.50, $5.50.... produced by Robert Chernov.... "

24 Cleveland's Plain Dealer reports.... WIXY 1260 presents in person Led Zeppelin plus Grand Funk Railroad...public hall tonite 8.pm tickets $4 advance and $4.50 at the door.... **The Old Mole reports....** Happenings, Saturday October 25 - Music Led Zeppelin, MC-5 and Johnny Winter at Boston Garden 8 pm $$....

25 Melody Maker reports.... Cover Story.... Led Zeppelin at Carnegie Hall. Chris Welch files a two page report from the USA, where he attends the band's historic appearance at Carnegie Hall in New York City. The band meet Welch at Euston station in London, he interviews Plant en route, *"I think a lot of people in Britain have been against us for some reason. I just can't understand it, but they say we are a manufactured group because we were successful right away. But we just got together the same way all groups get together. I don't see how some magazines can call us a hype."*

"When we went over to America for the first time last Christmas we found we weren't even billed and we got a bit depressed. But Atlantic Records began pushing out LPs to the towns where we were due to play, so people heard us before we arrived. People were ready to accept us from the album and it was up to us to prove ourselves on stage."

On the subject of the new album Plant commented, *"The tracks were done all over the place, in Los Angeles, New York and London. On one number I put the vocals on a backing track that had been recorded in Atlantic studios in New York, in a hut in Vancouver. It's hard to say how different it is from the first. You can distinguish the voices and the songs are better. The band is better because we have been together longer. The excitement is still there and we also do some quieter things which can be equally effective as groups like Fairport Convention prove. They don't need crescendos all the time. On the last album the drum and guitar sound was the same on every track. This one has different sounds for different songs, which are all originals. Really we can't wait to get onto our next album."*

On arriving at the hall, John Bonham comments, *"This is it lads, Gene Krupa and Buddy Rich they've all played here. So I'd better be good tonight!"*

The band kick off at 8.30 pm to an enthusiastic reaction from the New York crowd. The band hit the stage, Plant in black, Page in white satin trousers, Bonham in a leather hat, and Jones in red. The set includes Communication Breakdown, I Can't Quit You, White Summer, Moby Dick, with an encore of Summertime Blues. Welch and engineer Eddie Kramer watch from the wings. The band turn in two separate two hour plus marathons which extend until 2.00 am. After the show Page comments: *"I never expected anything like the success we have had when we started the group. Our following here is huge - they travel miles to see us. And that's really encouraging. After doing such a long show you don't really feel like repeating it the same*

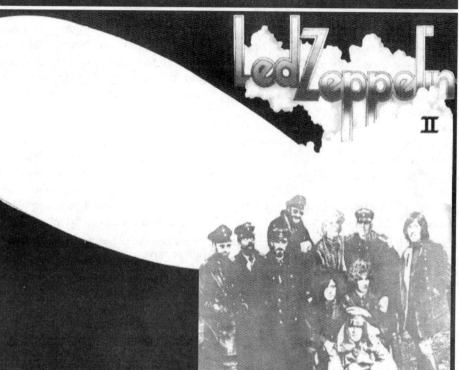

evening, especially after a long flight but nervous energy sustains you." Plant, *"You should see the kids in Boston or Detroit. You can control the audience if you are reasonable with them and don't chuck them off stage too violently!"* Jones, *"We played over three hours in Boston once. You get to the stage when you don't want to get off the stage!"*

Page comments that someone in the audience offered him a bottle of champagne after completing White Summer. The next day the band leave for Detroit.... third of a page advert appears reading "Led Zeppelin 2...now flying.".... **Record Retailer reports....** Led Zeppelin I is #24.... **Toronto Globe & Mail reports....** Advert reads — Martin Onrot Presents Led Zeppelin 2 Performances Only Sun, Nov 2. O'Keefe Centre All seats reserved. 5 pm 8.30 PM Tickets $5.50, $4.50, $3,50 Available At O'Keefe Centre Box Office and all four Sam the Record Man locations. This Show Is Rated 'H' (For Heavy)....

31 The Buffalo Evening News reports.... Kleinhans Hall - Led Zeppelin soars and the audience is loath to leave.... review of the show the night before, "Led Zeppelin sounds much more professional and pleasing in concert than on record because of the electric tension it shares with the audience.... " The concert ran a half hour longer than expected and the hall had to pull the plug on the band.

November 1969

1 DISC reports.... Led Zeppelin II is reviewed.... "album is superbly heavy, dynamic, driving and exciting.... Plant does a remarkable Leadbelly, with superb boogie harmonica, Jimmy Page's guitar

work is brilliant throughout." .... PJ Proby's album Three Week Hero is finally released and reviewed with no mention of Led Zeppelin supporting Proby.... This album is one of his best. It sizzles with excitement...this is very much a hit LP ****.... **Record Mirror reports....** Tony Stratton Smith intends to sponsor a series of Live Album concerts. He hopes to get Led Zeppelin to play all of Led Zeppelin II at their Lyceum show.... **New Musical Express reports....** June Harris reports from the USA that Led Zeppelin and the Who met for a party at Max's Kansas City. The party was thrown by Bill Graham. The Who had just performed Tommy at the Fillmore East and Zeppelin were there to witness the opening night. Zeppelin had sold out their shows at Carnegie Hall and scalpers were hawking tickets outside for twice face value.... full page advert for Led Zeppelin II.... **Record Retailer reports....** half page advert reads .... Led Zeppelin 2 Now Flying.... **Melody Maker reports....** Review of Led Zeppelin II.... it states, "This is the music of NOW, certain of itself and needing no apologies. Excitement added to fine musicianship. A fine LP.".... **Toronto Globe & Mail reports....** Advert reads — Martin Onrot Presents Led Zeppelin and Edward Bear Sun, Nov 2. O'Keefe Centre 5 pm Some Good Seats Available. 8.30 PM Sold Out. Tickets $5.50, $4.50, $3,50 Available Only At O'Keefe Centre Box Office and Sam the Record Man Yonge St. This Show Is Rated 'H' (For Heavy)....

3 Toronto Globe & Mail reports.... "Led Zeppelin the hardest rock around" says reporter Ritchie Yorke, "O'Keefe was packed to the brim with standing room only for both shows, total attendance 6,470.... the best rock concert in Toronto since their last appearance in August....

the complete 100 minute performances were staggering.... this is what pop is all about."....

5 **Record Mirror reports....** Led Zeppelin II doesn't disappoint...it's really loud and raunchy with lots of crashing guitar and sensual rhythms, it also has a really nice fold-out sleeve.... LZ II is #4.... **San Francisco Chronicle reports....** Bill Graham Presents at Winterland, Led Zeppelin, Isaac Hayes, Roland Kirk, Wolf Gang, Lights by Brotherhood Of Light Thurs, Fri, Sat Nov 6,7,8 at Winterland, Post and Steiner.... **The Kitchener Record reports....** Review of the show in Kitchener by Jim Clements. Headline reads, Page Gives Led Zeppelin Rock A Diamond Hardness. Clements says that Page's guitar, 'splits through the heavy background and Plant's frantic singing like light from a facet of a 30 carat stone.' He goes on to say that attendance was low (2,000) due to Iron Butterfly playing a gig the previous week and ticket prices being set too high. Page, *"Tonight was a very short set. I didn't do my set because of the amplifier blowing and the drummer didn't do his set because he wasn't feeling well. They were a very good audience. I mean they were really with it at the end. You could see that.*

"I guess I am pretty shy. Nobody ever gets to really know me. There's only a very few who know me well. It doesn't bother the rest of the group. I just sit back and try not to be noticed. I'd like to do less touring now. We've had to work jolly hard, as you can imagine to get the band going. It's the touring that's the worst. There's a lot of work to be done behind the scenes."....

6 **The Kansas City Star reports....** Music in Mid-America...review of the

show at the Memorial Hall in Kansas City the night before, "It is somewhat amazing though not surprising that the Led Zeppelin sounded as good as they did...considering the circumstances." The band played the entire set using the support band's equipment.... **International Times reports....** review of Led Zeppelin II.... "On first hearing, the numbers on this album seem weak plagiarisms of those on the group's first record. It's as if the band don't know what they're good at and aren't prepared to deviate in the cause of progressiveness. But getting into the cuts is wholly worthwhile and the key is in the production. Page who produced this album did so with a great deal of thought, understanding of the group and it's music and not a little gentle cunning. The vocal echo and phasing on What Is And What Should Never Be is bombshell, as is the throwing of harsh guitar chords twixt the speakers. Page uses what others regard as production gimmicks as if they were standard techniques, dead natural. His choice of engineers Eddie Kramer and Andy Johns, was obviously not a casual one either. Bob Plant is sounding really beautiful the brash Brum eroticism coming on strong. It's nice to hear him sing a love song, 'Thank You', as well as blues based material he's feeling more familiar with, such as 'The Lemon Song' and 'Bring It On Home'. John Bonham has some nice drum things going particularly on Whole Lotta Love, and John Paul Jones bass playing is suitably heavy and his organ work on 'Thank You' is tastefully decorous. Possibly the best over all example of the group's work is 'Ramble On' which darts from a crisp country chooglin' to harsh Zeppelin pounding. In essence a well proportioned album of heavy music made even more noteworthy by attentive production."....

8 Record Retailer reports.... Led Zeppelin II is #4.... Led Zeppelin II review.... "This is again another brilliant effort by Messrs Zeppelin each number is carefully and beautifully arranged so that listening is not marred by padding.... stock up now sales will be massive."...**New Musical Express reports....** review of Led Zeppelin II by Nick Logan.... "Music for the paranoiac 20th century city man, another brilliant album from the remarkable Led Zeppelin.".... **Melody Maker reports....** Robert Plant apparently bought an 18th century farmhouse for £6,000 in Worcestershire.... top three drummers in the world are Ian Paice, John Bonham and Carl Palmer....

12 Record Mirror reports.... the long awaited Supershow Movie is to premier at the Lyceum on the 14th November.... a Jimmy Page Eric Clapton album Blues Anthology is to be released on Immediate next week.... Radio One chief Douglas Muggeridge states he likes the Beatles and Led Zeppelin.... LZ II is #4....

15 New Musical Express reports.... Led Zeppelin have been invited to play the prestigious Montreux Jazz festival in Switzerland next June 6th.... **Record Retailer reports....** Led Zeppelin II is #4.... **Melody Maker reports....** The motion picture Supershow debuts at the Lyceum in London on the 16th....

19 Record Mirror reports.... LZ II is #5....

21 International Times reports.... Article about rock in general.... "The lead contenders in the heavy blues field must surely include Led Zeppelin.... I doubt if many people realised the spectacular

impact that Led Zeppelin would have in the States.... their debut album is one of the best I've heard."....

22 New Musical Express reports.... "Led Zeppelin will be releasing a new single in the UK called "Whole Lotta Woman" (sic). Reports from the USA has Led Zeppelin II outselling the Beatles Abbey Road in some areas. The album is expected to reach number one within a month...the new single will be out in the USA within a few weeks. In an interview Jimmy Page stated that he didn't think that albums and singles mixed very well." (This release of Whole Lotta Love was shelved.).... Zeppelin announced a major concert tour with a two hour show at seven separate venues.... including Birmingham Town Hall Jan 7, Bristol Colston Hall Jan 8, London Royal Albert Hall Jan 9, Portsmouth Guild Hall Jan 13, Newcastle Town Hall Jan 15, Sheffield City Hall Jan 16 and Leeds Town Hall Jan 24.... more dates may be added.... **Record Retailer reports....** Led Zeppelin II is #4....

29 Record Mirror reports.... Tour dates for January are announced.... a new single will be released of Whole Lotta Love next week.... Peter Grant is negotiating a full colour TV spectacle.... LZ II is #7.... **Rolling Stone reports....** "Led Zeppelin II is ready, on Atlantic Records and 8 track cartridges.".... **New Musical Express reports....** Led Zeppelin is number 2 in the USA, only Abbey Road is keeping it off the top spot.... **Record Retailer reports....** Led Zeppelin II is #4.... **Melody Maker reports....** Led Zeppelin January Tour.... Article states that Zeppelin will tour Britain in January performing seven shows. It goes on to say that the single "Whole Lotta Love" will be delayed in the UK. Dates include Birmingham (7), Bristol Colston Hall (8), London Royal Albert Hall (9), Portsmouth Guild Hall (13), Newcastle Town Hall (15), Sheffield City Hall (16), and Leeds University (24).... article states that Led Zeppelin are out buying mansions except Jimmy Page who is filling his with antiques....

Creem Volume 2 #7 reports.... "Terry Reid currently on the Rolling Stones tour, has acquired new management, Reid's former manager the formidable Peter Grant, ex-Yardbirds and presently Led Zepplin (sic). Reid's story concerning the management switch is all too common among today's rock and roll groups; Terry found that Peter Grant had all too little time to devote to Reid's precarious career, being committed to the Zepplin a far more profitable group." .... also featured are two separate reviews of Led Zeppelin II, one good one bad, 'Led Zeppelin is the best English superfunk band.... they're really good...I'll give it an 83 because it makes you want to shake your ass.'

' Led Zeppelin in excess of overt hipness, hypeness, hollowness.... the songs are only redone joplinshake heavybody drughendrix.... what kind of wack is this?.... nothing to write or celebrate about.'

Rolling Stone reports.... John Mendelsohn reviews Led Zeppelin II in hilarious fashion disproving that Rolling Stone had nothing good to print about the band.... "This is one fucking heavyweight album! .... Shit man, on this album (Jimmy Page) demonstrates that he could absolutely fucking shut down any white blues man alive, and with one fucking hand tied behind his back too. I listened to (the album) on some heavy Vietnamese

Weed and very nearly had my mind blown." He then points out that this may not be the most objective state of mind to be in so he tried listening while under the influence of mescaline, old Romilar, novocain and ground up Fusion. He goes on, "Plant sings some notes only dogs can hear, (and) Bonham demonstrates that he could shut down Baker even without sticks."....

Billboard reports.... Review of Led Zeppelin II. The industry bible gives the band a definite thumbs-up, "Page and his crew stormtroop through with commando precision.... the group delivers more sheer tension and power than anything previous.... the first major rock sound of the 70's."

December 1969

6 **DISC reports....** A new single from Led Zeppelin is being released against their wishes...Whole Lotta Love to come out in a truncated version of three minutes is being rush released by Atlantic against the band and their manager's wishes.... Peter Grant states the band had no intention of releasing a single but were recording a track which specially suits the singles market.... upcoming tour dates include Birmingham Town Hall (7), Bristol Colston Hall (8), London Royal Albert Hall (9), Portsmouth Guild Hall (13), Newcastle Town Hall (15), Sheffield City Hall (16), and Leeds Town Hall (24)....
Record Mirror reports.... Cover Story, interview with Robert Plant conducted at the Kentucky Palace in London, *"I get a certain amount of criticism for moving about a bit on stage when I sing but I'm not trying to put anything over on the audience that's just the way it happens.*

It's not worked out like Tom Jones who jigs about like a concrete mixer. I don't want it to look that way but if the critics expect me to come on stage with bags under the bags under my eyes looking like I've been immobilized by barbiturates and announce that everything is 'a heavy trip man' they can want.

"It's very difficult for me to gauge just how popular I am as a personality but naturally I'm grateful although I would like a little more recognition for my work as a vocalist and a lyricist on our albums. I'm not likely to get too carried away with myself while people still come up to me after the show and say 'Great great - you were great tonight Jimmy!

"I don't think anyone really saw it all coming. One week I was playing to half a dozen people at Birmingham 'Mothers' and the next there was standing room only and they were even packed into the 'bogs' to listen. I knew Zeppelin would be bigger than the Band of Joy in which I played before but I had no idea it would reach the kind of proportions that it has now in America where the cops shut off streets in areas where we are going to play because of the crowds .

"The underground scene has really boiled over and those who were involved in it initially in America have made fortunes. Bill Graham who owns Fillmore and is one of the most influential men now made a million dollars out of posters before he ever became involved in promoting. Aaron Rousseau who owns the Chicago Kinetic Playground also manages the Flock and he presented us all with gold watches after our concert there on the last trip.

"What happens now is that quite often the music is created during some improvisation on stage one night. Some of our numbers can go on for half an hour

and during that jam something might emerge which will be the riff upon which we hang a new number.

"That's really part of the beauty of today's group scene that you can hear things being created at the time on stage and so little is prefabricated. For example in Toronto we just got involved in a country and western thing which went on for 20 minutes just as a spontaneous thing. Four years ago if you had asked some guitarist to ad lib on a 12 bar blues they would have probably dropped their plectrums!

"The great thing now of course is that you don't have to go to the people so much - they come to you so there is no need to compromise your own musical standards. You do your best and the feel of what is right for your market is almost inbred into the writer - it comes quite naturally. You can sense amongst the group what is right and throw away what is not.

"Musical freedom of that kind only becomes a danger when it is abused as some of the big American groups seem to abuse it. They go on stage drugged out of their heads as though they are doing everyone a favour or simply just don't turn up. Tonight for example I was really looking forward to seeing Arthur Lee and Love but they just haven't turned up. Traffic tended to give the impression that they didn't really care whether they worked or not and you just can't afford to be that apathetic.

"When I write something I just draw from a real experience which has some value to me something from life and hope the words communicate. The kind of things we have on our second album should be a pleasant surprise to most people who dig Zeppelin. I'm striking up more of a musical sympathy with Jimmy and our styles and variations have

widened considerably." .... Plant is at present reading "The Lost Continent of Mu' by James Churchward. (This was one of the book's which led to Plant's choice of the feather for the fourth album title.).... **New Musical Express reports....** In an interview the Rolling Stones Keith Richards stated that he had listened to Led Zeppelin's album a few times but *"the guy's voice started to get on my nerves. He's a little too acrobatic, but Jimmy Page is a great guitar player and well respected."*.... three British albums are at the top of the American charts, The Beatles Abbey Road, Led Zeppelin II and Tom Jones.... Jimmy Page has been spotted around the antique markets, apparently he is quite a collector.... **Record Retailer reports....** Led Zeppelin II is #6.... **Melody Maker reports....** Zeppelin To Issue Stereo Single.... article states a specially edited version of "Whole Lotta Love" will be rush released by Atlantic on Friday. It goes on to say the decision was made due to unprecedented demand in the USA. Peter Grant, *"Led Zeppelin had no intention of issuing this track as a single as they felt it was written as part of their concept of the album. They've written a special number which they intended as their first British single which they will be recording this week."*....

13 **DISC reports....** Quarter page two colour advert announces UK tour dates.... Birmingham Jan. 7th, Bristol Jan. 8th, London Jan. 9th, Newcastle Jan. 15th, Sheffield Jan. 16th.... **Record Mirror reports....** Robert Plant is a Thelonious Monk enthusiast.... LZ II is #7.... **New Musical Express reports....** half page advert for upcoming tour dates...**Record Retailer reports....** Led Zeppelin II is #13.... **Melody Maker reports....** Platinums for Zeppelin.... article states

that the band have surpassed a million sales of each album worldwide and will be presented platinum record awards at the Savoy hotel. It goes on to say that Peter Grant had persuaded Atlantic to not release "Whole Lotta Love" as a single and the band will record a single for release in January.... Full page advert for UK tour showing Blimp in hangar says Chrysalis Presents In Person Led Zeppelin with tour dates....

20 **DISC reports....** Zeppelin is a gas, say the government.... feature article.... In just over a year (Led Zeppelin) have toured America four times, Denmark and Sweden twice, been round France and done nearly every club and town hall here. They have also managed to produce two albums clocking up more than £2 million worth of sales in America alone.... John Paul Jones, *"We're doing a tour here in the New Year before going back to America, and we're working on our third album at the moment."*...Mrs. Gwyneth Dunwoody Parliamentary Secretary to the Board Of Trade went along to a party at the Savoy Hotel to thank them for their value as exports, *"You seem to be gas rockets rather than Led Zeppelins"* said Mrs. Dunwoody. Jimmy Page didn't make it to the reception because he was involved in a car accident on the way down.... Jones, *"I don't know why we're so popular there (America). I suppose it's a combination of a good band and the time it broke. Cream had gone, other groups had an even chance of getting in, but somehow we made it."*

For three years Jones worked on sessions, *"It just turns you into a vegetable. You have to accept every session you're offered, you're either in or out. I was starving and people would actually ask me to play on their records but I'd*

never be rung up and told about it.
"We don't need to tour England in the New Year. I know everyone goes on at us about our apparent desertion of the country, but if we didn't go to America now they'd accuse us of deserting them. After all they made us what we are and they do buy an awful lot of our records. One feels an obligation to Britain in general, and after all we are a British group so why shouldn't it be a tour of Britain?"

At one time Jones was going to attend the Royal Academy Of Music but by the time he reached 17 he was touring with Jet Harris and Tony Meehan. Jones, *"One can get fed up with touring, we've done an awful lot of it lately. It's all a mass of airports, that's all you ever see. But we've always had such good receptions it's made it worth it. I don't know how we've managed to do so much in the last year. Looking back none of us know how we've done it."....* **Record Mirror reports....** Robert Plant, John Paul Jones and John Bonham are present to get a platinum disc from MP and Parliamentary Secretary to the Board Of Trade Gwyneth Dunwoody, disc is for sales of $5 million in the USA.... LZ II is #15.... **New Musical Express reports....** the band are awarded gold records at London's Savoy hotel for sales of $5m in the USA.... **Record Retailer reports....** Led Zeppelin II is #9.... **Melody Maker reports....** Achtung Led Zeppelin.... picture of the band with their platinum albums and a caption that says Page was late arriving for the ceremony due to a car accident on the M4 motorway. He will soon be buying a Rolls-Royce.... Chris Welch interviews John Bonham and Jimmy Page. Bonham, *"When we got back from the States last month we started recording again for the next album and we have only done one gig since then in Paris. We try to record a lot*

when we're not doing gigs so we don't get stale. The awards are really great — twelve months ago I didn't expect we would get one. It's been complete chaos for us recently as Robert John and I have all been buying houses and getting ready for Christmas.

"It will be the first Christmas at home for me with my son Jason (age three). Last year I was away and before that he was too young to know. He's music mad and I've bought him a great set of miniature drums. It's an absolutely perfect replica down to the bass drum pedal and hi hat. Even I can play them. They are Japanese made and I saw them in a shop window in Toronto. They weren't really for sale and were just on display. But I offered them a hundred dollars and bought them."

Welch asks why the predicted single release of 'Whole Lotta Love' didn't come about, *"There was a bit of a mix up. We never wanted to put it out in England it was only for American AM radio stations to promote the LP and that was a full-length version of the LP track. In England they pressed up an edited version and we want to release a single that we feel won't be conning the public. We don't want kids to think we are just releasing an LP track to get into the chart I'm dead against that sort of thing."*

He is asked how he feels he is progressing, *"I thought the solo played at the first Carnegie Hall concert was about the best. I try to vary the solo each night and at Boston where they had seen us twice before and my hand drum solo, I played conga drums. I really want to learn to play vibes now because I want to write a lot more and it's a bit frustrating just being able to play drums. And on the next LP I'd like to play a percussion num-*

ber with vibes and timpani rather than an ordinary drum solo. I was quite pleased with the solo on the last LP but I didn't seem to be getting anywhere. When you are playing live it's exciting when you look up and see the audience reacting. You get back and play some more! But in the studio when you look up you just see the engineer staring at you I'd rather play live dates anytime.

"I always like to try new things but in 12 months with Zeppelin we have been so busy I haven't had a chance to practice. At my house I've got a shed I am soundproofing. I've had a blow at Traffic's cottage and I've played some things there I couldn't remember to do again. It's nicer than jamming in a club with a group where the audience think you are just showing off. Jamming is great as long as it's in private."

Welch then turns to Page and asks about the new album. Page, "We did an electric and an acoustic version of the same number to see which comes out best. We've been writing a lot of new material and we should have a proper single out in January. It wouldn't be fair if we just changed our sound and said we were going to do all new things. It's a shame when groups say 'that was yesterday's music' because fans get very disappointed and brought down. They want us to play their favorite numbers and that's what we want to do — please them. It's very rash to make a complete change of style — especially if the 'new thing' doesn't work out. We have included some older numbers and we can always infiltrate new material into the old songs without making everything we've done before   obso-

lete. We're still a heavy group."....

27 **Melody Maker reports....** Cover story.... Jimmy Page reviews the new sounds in Blind Date. Page participates in a Melody Maker staple of pulling in popular musicians to review new singles. One single is by Les Paul and Mary Ford. Page, *"Les Paul - he's the man who started everything, multi-track recording, the electric guitar - he's just a genius. I think he was the first to use a four track - or was it an eight track recording machine. I met him once and apparently he started multitrack recording back in about 1945. Jeff Beck and myself have always dug him and poor old Wout Steinbus has dedicated his life to emulating Led Paul, and he'll never top him. The only trouble with these records is that Mary Ford's voice dates them a bit. It's back to early fifties and Kay Starr. Even so it's very subtle and nice. Les Paul played brilliantly at the right speed as well as finger tremolo and feedback - he did all those things years ago. Let's listen to Deep In The Blues. Blues fans probably think this is dated, but there is something there for every guitarist. He has the whole concept in his head of the straight guitar solo and the multi-tracking. The finished product is totally incredible."*
Page also reviews singles by The Peddlers, Merle Travis, Lonnie Johnson and Eddie Lang, Charlie Christian, Fairport Convention, and Bukka White.... **Record Retailer reports....** Led Zeppelin I is #9.... Plant and Bonham pictured with Phil Carson receiving a gold record for $5 million sales in the USA....

1970

Peace and Goodwill

Blodwyn Pig
Chicken Shack
Clouds
Family
Jethro Tull
King Crimson
Led Zeppelin
Liverpool Scene
Christine Perfect
Principal Edwards
    Magic Theatre
Savoy Brown
Stone the Crows
Ten Years After
Village   *together at* **Chrysalis**

January 1970

3 **DISC reports**.... Led Zeppelin's success makes their leader uneasy...feature article and interview with Jimmy Page....

"I'm doing so many things. I've just started my painting again, I'm also writing a dossier of things I've done in the past - things I've written on odd scraps of paper. It's interesting to see what I thought when I was 16 and 19 compared to now I'm 24. Sometimes there's this same line of truth that runs through all along. It's just a personal thing - most people would think it was a waste of time.

"The whole group (the Yardbirds) was a guitar precedent. Everyone was just doing what's known now as jamming on stage. Eric started the precedent and when he left Jeff felt he had to do better than Eric and when I was left

I felt I had to try hard too. So it was an excellent learning in that way.

"When the Yardbirds decided to go their different ways, it was either go back to art or start a new band. Everyone gave me the confidence to get something together, and the whole thing did - it was amazing. The trouble was I could play a lot of different styles and I didn't really know what to do. I wanted to do a hard rock thing or a Pentangle style of thing, but as soon as I heard Robert (Plant) I realised it was going to be the former.

"They never look right (lyrics) I just can't feel happy with my lyrics. Writing the music it's just a chord or a riff that inspires me and then I go on and see how it goes colourwise. The whole thing just grows like an acorn or something. I'm not a natural musician, I really have to practice damned hard to get anything out.

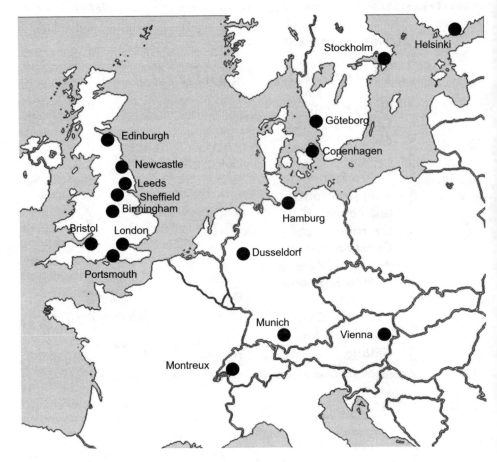

European Tour Spring 1970

January 7th, 1970 Birmingham Town Hall
January 8th, 1970 Bristol Colston Hall
January 9th, 1970 London Royal Albert Hall
January 13th, 1970 Portsmouth Guild Hall
January 15th, 1970 Newcastle City Hall
January 16th, 1970 Sheffield City Hall
January 24th, 1970 Leeds Town Hall
February 17th, 1970 Edinburgh Usher Hall
February 24th, 1970 Helsinki
February 25th, 1970 Göteborg Konserthuset
February 26th, 1970 Stockholm Konserthuset
February 28th, 1970 Copenhagen K.B.Hallen
March 7th, 1970 Montreux Casino
March 8th, 1970 Munich
March 9th, 1970 Vienna Konserthaus
March 11th, 1970 Dusseldorf
March 12th, 1970 Hamburg Musikhalle
April 26th, 1970 London Julie Felix TV Show

"I don't know what it is, when you hear something a musical work and something appeals to you in it, you say 'Well I really like that' but what is it? It's a certain magical thing about it. That's what I'm trying for in a musical way - to produce something that will reduce someone to tears, or make them very happy.

"I find an affinity with the ideals of the pre-Raphaelites. I like the way their furniture grows as if it's organic. I think I'm basically a romantic, I can't relate to this age, which is one reason I get out in the country. Everything's so enclosed there's nobody, no line in the buildings. I like something you can look at and find something in."

Whenever Zeppelin are not performing Jimmy likes to hitch around, *"It's just the great thing of a pilgrimage, traveling to the places you meet people and talk. I'm missing out on that at the moment and just because the money has come my way it's torn out this side of me that's been a part of me since goodness knows when. I find I get wanderlust and I have to suppress it. Although Zeppelin has happened and it's really great I also want to start traveling again. Life's short and there's a lot to see."*.... **Record Mirror reports....** LZ II is #19.... **New Musical Express reports....** Led Zeppelin are awarded the Cat's Whiskers award for setting the USA alight.... **Melody Maker reports....** Advert reads — Peace & Goodwill Blodwyn Pig, Chicken Shack, Led Zeppelin etc together at Chrysalis.... **Billboard reports....** Zeppelin Flies On Gold Line. Led Zeppelin have received a gold and platinum record for $2,000,000 in just over a month on sale.....

10 **DISC reports....** Led Zeppelin -A-Week...There's nothing better than a good

rave, says John.... interview with John Bonham, *"I couldn't do what Jimmy does and shut myself away in the country,"* he says apologetically. *"I like people around me all the time, parties, going out and general looning I suppose I'm a bit of a noisy person—in fact I'm probably the noisiest of the four of us.*

"When we were in New York one time we went to a party. Liverpool Scene were making their debut, and Keith Moon was there and the drummer from the Bonzos. It was mad—everyone started throwing cream cakes. I loved that, it was great."...on the subject of marriage, *"After all we've gone through, our marriage should survive anything. So the strain of me being away for so long with Zeppelin touring is nothing compared to that. Anyway, Pat prefers me being what I am to doing anything else—like when I worked on a building site for a bit once.*

"It was good from the outset because there was nobody saying 'you've got to play this or that,' and surprisingly that does matter to a drummer — some things are very uninteresting, like soul night after night. With the things Zeppelin do, I can play different things every night.

"When I got married I swore to give up drumming, but every night I'd come home and just sit down at the drums. I'm miserable if I can't.

"Otherwise I'm still the same person. I enjoy decorating and gardening, and I'm still as hotheaded as ever. I'm a bit quick tempered—I never sit down and think about things.

"We're not too close, not so that every little thing bothers us. If one of us is ill, the rest of us don't all come out in rashes too. We're close in another way.

"With musicians it doesn't matter how good you are—a lot of people still look down on you. But when you make it,

although you're not a better person or musician they suddenly respect you. They don't say 'oh you're a better drummer than you used to be.' They just unquestioningly say he must be good because he's with Led Zeppelin.".... **Record Mirror reports....** LZ II is #12.... **New Musical Express reports....** Led Zeppelin's appearance at the Royal Albert Hall is sold out.... **Billboard reports....** Atlantic president Ahmet Ertegun will travel to the UK to see Led Zeppelin in London on Friday 9th....

17 **DISC reports....** Zeppelin refuse a TV Fortune.... cover story.... Led Zeppelin currently Britain's hottest property have put a ban on TV appearances in the UK, Europe and America.... Peter Grant, *"Zeppelin won't do any TV dates anywhere until they get the right offer. We don't want to do any of these three minute guests spots on shows. They don't present them properly."*.... the band have turned down offers from 'Top Of The Pops', 'This Is Tom Jones', 'The Ed Sullivan Show', and Germany's 'Beat Club'.... Grant, *"Top of the Pops invited the group to appear any week they wished. They said they could do any track from the album if they didn't want to do the single. But they still stuck to the three minute limit. We'll do TV so the fans can see the group. But only when the right offer comes along. Zeppelin feel very strongly about this."*.... Led Zeppelin-A-Week, Robert's Rebellion against a shallow world.... Plant interview.... *"That's one thing Led Zeppelin has done for me. It's slowed me down. I can take a lot of things I wasn't able to before. Making it has made me just that much easier—I can sit down and try things I haven't tried before.*

"It's exactly what I always wanted. It gives me room to think, breathe and

live. I wake up in the morning and there are no buses, no traffic. Just tractors and the odd pheasant hooting in the next field. I was pretty fed up with humanity in the big cities. I'd been round big cities since I first left home and ran away to Walsall. You can walk round London at night and it doesn't matter whether you're the king or the Queen—you'll still have a bad time.

"Before, whenever I came to London it had a sort of big aura about it. It was frightening. Now it's a case of if you're popular, everybody wants to know you, so really to me London is a very shallow place. All those Speakeasy and Revolution club people don't want to know you if you're on the way up or down.

"Everyone tells me it's a guitar orientated world. The weekend hippies are all turned on to guitars. When I was younger I wanted to be a front man, to do exactly as I liked and tell my backing group what to do. But now I realise that would kill other musicians.

"Finally, though, I'd like to be able to play a guitar onstage. I think it gives a singer a lot of sympathy with rhythms. I can play guitar vaguely— enough to play along with the Neil Young album.".... Zeppelin Rock and Rave.... review of the Royal Albert Hall gig.... Led Zeppelin proved on Friday that inside even the coolest hip audience there's a rocker screaming to get out. At the end of 2½ hours the entire Albert Hall was on it's feet jiving, stomping and stripping.... three encores and then the old Eddie Cochran favourites.... **Record Mirror reports....** Led Zeppelin, 'We're Gonna Groove' said Robert Plant to the packed audience at Royal Albert Hall and Led Zeppelin did just that.... Jimmy Page proved he is one of the best musically equipped guitarists on the pop scene.

Hunched over his guitar he poured out a string of explosive guitar solos.... with paper planes flying around them at the end, Led Zeppelin were still flying high.... LZ II is #7.... **New Musical Express reports**.... cover story.... Zeppelin put the excitement back into Pop.... Nick Logan reviews the band's show at the Royal Albert Hall at which they played for two and a quarter hours.... the audience clapped for 35 minutes for an encore...songs included Dazed & Confused, White Summer, Moby Dick, and How Many More Times. In the audience were John Lennon, Eric Clapton and Jeff Beck.... Page is interviewed and he expresses his enthusiasm for doing longer shows without a support act. He then expounds on how he expects Led Zeppelin III to be better than anything that had gone before by the band.... **Melody Maker reports**.... review of The Royal Albert Hall show by Raymond Telford who seems less than impressed with the band's performance until they performed a rock medley during How Many More Times. He describes White Summer as boring, with Bonham's congas barely audible. He calls Since I've Been Loving You one of the best numbers of the evening and generally approved of Bonham's Moby Dick solo. He concludes, "Nearly a flop but even so I think they succeeded in sending out a few good vibes."....

24 **DISC reports**.... Led Zeppelin-A-Week...John Paul Jones Interview conducted at Bendicks restaurant.... *"I like messing about with tapes and making tracks by building things up and doing photography — there's space for a dark room in the house.*

"I'd get bored playing only bass guitar all the time. I play organ onstage a little now and I want to concentrate on that more and more. Organ was always my first love, but for sessions I found it was much easier to carry a bass guitar to work than a Hammond organ. That's all I had—guitar Hammond, table and bed in my little room.*

"I don't get bored playing onstage with the band. I don't mind being in the background. I wouldn't like to be out front playing like Jimmy. To be any sort of artist you have to be a born exhibitionist—I am, but not over anyone else in the business. I believe you should do what you have to do, and if I'm bass, rather than try to lead on bass and push myself, I prefer to put down a good solid bass line.

"I would like to think that if we have to stop actually touring we'll be in a position to make records together because this particular combination of people turned out nice things, I think. And I've been around long enough to know that few combinations of people actually work.

"What I would like to do—having got myself into a reasonable position and recognised — is to just make albums of assorted music and use the profits for something humanitarian.

"Lots of pop stars with a lot of money really aren't doing anything at all. They're selfish, plain apathetic, or too damn lazy to get it together. At the moment I'm still building up the situation from which I can work — straightening out my own backyard.".... Are Fan Clubs Out Of Date, article about the demise of the fan club.... Walking down Oxford Street with Jimmy Page last week, a shattering thing happened. It was the freak-out Tottenham Court end of the street where the hip-folk meet. As Jimmy passed the supposedly cool trendies leant

forward, knelt down to touch his coat and tap his arm. No requests for autographs, scream or assaults - just this frightening form of worship to a chorus of "Oh What, Man" and "Oh yeah Jimmy Page, what" in reverent whispers.... **Record Mirror reports**.... LZ II is #2 .... **New Musical Express reports**.... Led Zeppelin will be appearing at Leeds University for a one nighter.... European tour dates announced....

31 **Record Mirror reports**.... LZ II is #2.... LZ I is #20.... **Melody Maker reports**.... Led Zeppelin Top in U.S.... cover story...Led Zeppelin have just seized the number one slot in the major US album charts with their second LP, "Led Zeppelin II" which has toppled the Beatles Abbey Road from the top spot.... a sixth tour of America starts March 21.... Peter Grant, *"Their month long tour will earn them 800,000 dollars.... a Led Zeppelin TV spectacular has been sold to American TV, filming began at the Royal Albert Hall, a special album will be issued to coincide with the screening of the show in the States."*....

February 1970

7 **DISC reports**.... Cover story, Screaming Single By Heavy Mob.... Six of Britain's top progressive musicians have joined forces with the most colorful character in British Pop music.... Led Zeppelin's Jimmy Page and John Bonham, Jeff Beck, Noel Redding and Nicky Hopkins are all guised under the name Heavy Friends and featured on 'Cause I Love You' the first single in nearly five years by Screaming Lord Sutch.... the song was written by Sutch and Page and will be released on February 13th....

Record Mirror reports.... LZ II is #1.... LZ I is #24.... **New Musical Express reports**.... Congratulations to Led Zeppelin for knocking the Beatles off number one.... Robert Plant pictured...Plant had just discharged himself from the hospital after sustaining injuries to his face in a car crash on Saturday night. The band's concert in Edinburgh on Sunday is canceled. **Melody Maker reports**.... Article states that Robert Plant was in a car accident on Saturday returning from Mothers Club in Birmingham where he had been attending a Spirit concert. Both cars in the accident were write-offs and he was admitted to Kidderminster Hospital with facial lacerations and damaged teeth. It goes on to say that it is hoped he will recover in time to play the gig in Edinburgh on Saturday.... **Billboard reports**.... Finnish promoter Leo Helnonen will bring Led Zeppelin to Helsinki in the Spring of 1970....

14 **Record Mirror reports**.... LZ II is #2.... **Melody Maker reports**.... Cover story.... The Paganini Of The Seventies.... a feature article by Chris Welch who takes some time at Page's riverside house.... Welch and Page venture out to a local tea shop and experience quite a bit of abuse from the locals, including kids who taunt Page about his appearance...Page takes it with good humour but Welch is baffled by the way people treat the superstar...Page, *"I'm changing my telephone number. They tell me I should have done it long ago. We get about thirty or forty calls a day. I was editing tapes yesterday for the new LP and you need your wits about you for that. There were interruptions all the time which made it a day long job. I'm not ex-directory and you can't tell people you are busy. They think you are just trying to*

1969 GRAMMY AWARDS

BEST ALBUM COVER NOMINEES

AMERICA THE BEAUTIFUL—Gary McFarland

BLIND FAITH—Blind Faith

RICHARD PRYOR—Richard Pryor

LED ZEPPELIN II—Led Zeppelin

PIDGEON—Pidgeon

NARAS members are now voting for this year's Grammy Awards in 45 categories. Winners will be announced at NARAS chapter awards ceremonies on Wednesday, March 11. Many winners will be starred on the Academy's TV spectacular, "The Best on Records," over NBC on Wednesday, May 7, from 10 until 11 p.m.

These nominated covers are printed and published as an industry service by Billboard, which urges every active member of NARAS to vote very carefully and to mail his ballot so that the return envelope is postmarked on or before Wednesday, February 25, and received by the accounting firm of Haskins and Sells by February 27.

get rid of them.

"All this started within the last six months. I bought the house about two and a half years ago when I was with the Yardbirds. There hasn't been much time to decorate being away in the States so much, but you wouldn't have believed the scene when I moved in. The previous owner had great garlands of plastic flowers everywhere. She even had a barrow in the corner decorated with plastic flowers. I can't wait for the summer. Once the sun comes out we all go on the river and every day is a holiday."

Welch then tours the house and makes mention of the huge collection of Crowley's works. Roger Daltrey shows up with his girlfriend in a Corvette Stingray at which point he engages Page in a conversation about the pitfalls of being a country squire...Page, "Steve Winwood lives not far away. We often get friends dropping in. We don't exactly take part in village life."....

21   Record   Mirror   reports.... Superstar...interview with Page, "To begin with we arrived on the scene at just the right time in America as the Cream had disbanded and Hendrix was into other things — Atlantic Records were looking for a new heavy rock group to boost and we were it. There was a certain nostalgia for me from the Yardbirds and that coupled with Robert Plant's powerful stage presence was enough to get us going. In the States now they are talking about Robert as the next Mick Jagger!

"I think our initial success was due to the fact that so many of the good American groups were moving towards softer sounds which made our heavy rock approach more dramatic. Blind Faith were a disappointment to many because they expected them to lean more toward the Spencer Davis-Winwood era than an extension of Traffic which is what they were. It meant that no one was filling the gap left by the Cream and in many ways it is their audience we have captured.

"Our first album was put together in something like three weeks but we felt tremendously enthusiastic and confident about it because everything was so fresh to us. I think the excitement that we felt at the time came through on the record. A lot more planning went into the second album and I think maybe we got too close to it, so that we knew every track backwards - I was far less confident about that album although I was pleased with the variation we got into the songs.

"Now I feel that the third album on which we are working is perhaps the most significant of all. We are not changing our policy. I still feel that some so called progressive groups have gone too far with their personalised intellectualisation of beat music. I don't want our music complicated by that kind of ego trip — our music is essentially emotional like the old rock stars of the past. It's difficult to listen to those early Presley records and not feel something. We are not going out to make any kind of moral or political statement. Our music is simply us.

"I'm musically psychoid in as much as I sit around playing acoustic guitar at home and electric only on stage. I think this will come out on the next album and we intend to go in for at least one big production number that may last for at least 20 minutes or even one side of the album. We'll just let it happen like it does on stage.

"I don't read the musical papers any more. It may be professional suicide to admit it, but I don't, not unless I am shown something. If you get to looking each week for your picture and a feature *it can become a sort of religion — the papers become your bible.*

"Don't misunderstand me—I'm not saying that the press is not important or relevant to a group's success. It is just that I do not have time to become too engrossed in what they say. Making music is my concern. The only press I have ever really objected to is the pseudo intellectual underground papers who write in clichés and give rock and roll a pretension it does not need.

"I think the thing which annoys me most about mass media and popular music today is that so little attention or time is given to our music when young people are showing quite clearly by their attendance that there's an enormous demand to hear it. When are TV and radio in this country going to wake up to the fact that millions of young people want to see and listen to more music from groups like ours?" .... LZ II is #3.... **The Vancouver Express reports....** Led Zeppelin sailing out for sixth tour.... Led Zeppelin head out from London March 21 for their sixth North American Tour.... (the band) are expected to earn about $800,000 in the month long trek which will include Vancouver. Also in the works is a TV special which has been snapped up blind by an American network.... **New Musical Express reports....** Led Zeppelin nearing two million sales after 15 weeks.... **Melody Maker reports....** Cover story.... Part two of Chris Welch's interview with Jimmy Page.... *"Before they saw us in America there was a blast of publicity and they heard all about the money being advanced to us by the record company. So the reaction was 'Ah. a capitalist group.' They realised we weren't when they saw us playing a three hour non stop show every night.*

"And the reason why we played

that long was because when we started out a year ago we had worked out a one hour set and on stage this naturally expanded to an hour and a half. As we put in other numbers that became two hours. In America they wanted encores and it expanded to three hours with the extra material from the second album.

"We enjoy ourselves and that shows in our playing. If somebody wants to hype a group they only suffer in the end because people know what's going on now. People understand the economics of the bands, especially in the States where it is the fashion to ask who is getting what out of what.

"I'm sure that when Hendrix played a West Coast Festival people knew he was being paid 100,000 dollars. There were a lot of snide remarks, and afterwards he seemed to drop in popularity. If we play at a University kids say: 'Hey, you're getting a thousand pounds tonight.' So what? They think £1,000 is a lot of money but it's not in relation to the expenses of a band with road managers, air fares and hotel bills. But really money has nothing to do with it. You can tell when a band is being hyped by their manner. You can tell from the vibrations. I can tell so I'm sure everyone else can.

"The only criticism came after our Albert Hall concert in London recently. One reviewer said we got off to a slow start. Well I don't know if the guy had heard us before but the idea is to start off with recognisable Zeppelin things—then go much quieter and use acoustic guitar which is always well received. Then we build it up again. You can't possibly have a climax all the way. We like to play a cross section of styles. We're not a rabble rousing group. We are trying to play some music. One has to remember at the Albert Hall concerts all the tickets were sold out

in a day so they must have been Zeppelin people in the audience who knew what we play."

Welch asks whether he thinks the Rock revolution is being scrutinised too much by the press.

"There should be a lot more written about it because pop is going through a very revolutionary stage at the moment. I saw the Jack Bruce film on TV and I was quite amazed. He was tremendous. The whole message was—just listen to the music. That's what it's all about. Many classical people listen to pop music. They realise pop is not just a joke. Critics like Tony Palmer in the Sunday newspapers have helped it all to an incredible extent.

"It's strange but I never saw the Cream and I had never seen Jack Bruce until his Lyceum concert. I've started going to concerts because I never saw any when I was working so hard touring. You have to be quick these days to see a group before they spilt up. I never saw Hendrix or the Cream while we were working in the States or any other groups unless they were on the same bill as us. This has been my first real break in years although we are working on the third album. We have to keep working all the time. We are working on a film. I don't know if it will ever be shown really but we filmed the Albert Hall concert and it will be a documentary on what has been going on with the band.

"Everything has been slowed up with Robert's accident. That was a horrific scene. The police came banging at the door with flashlights and asked me if I knew a Mr. Robert Plant. When they advised me to call him in Kidderminster Hospital I knew it had got to be serious. I was really worried wondering if he had the baby in the car.

He's still in a bad way and we had to can-

cel some work although he said he would appear on stage in a wheel chair. He can't lift his arm above his shoulder and he has a cut over his eye.

"We've got a lot of recording to do. On the first album we were finding out about each other. On the second I really thought John Paul Jones came through strongly. We can feel each other much more. I've prepared a lot of acoustic stuff for the next album. It's just a matter of getting into a studio. They are all fully booked—its incredible. We all do a bit of writing in the group and make tape recordings of ideas for songs. I like to get a basic construction together and a number grows from that."

Welch asks what he thinks about the new Jazz rock.

"I don't like it personally. I never liked Blood Sweat And Tears. I'm all for a fusion of ideas but this is just not my cup of tea and it has not been as well accepted as classical rock.

"Jazz-rock all rests on the brass players waiting for the chance to play as fast as possible at 78 rpm. To me it represents cacophony. I like and understand Eric Dolphy and John Coltrane but when you get Fred Bloggs blowing away —it doesn't come off.

"The thing's Dick Heckstall-Smith plays with Colosseum are good and valid and they make sense. When it doesn't make sense — I can't be bothered. I was never convinced by Blood Sweat And Tears yet lots of people think it's the epitome of pop today.

"What didn't I like about them? The arrangements and the singer. I couldn't believe that singer. Everything sounds so false after one or two listens. The most progressive groups today are the Pink Floyd and Moody Blues. I've been asking myself if we were pro-

gressive. In fact I've been waiting for somebody to ask me that. I don't know. What we have done is to present rock in a different package. We are not a band like the Floyd which are really progressive. Maybe our next album will be progressive — for us. People tend to say Pink Floyd are still just a 1967 Flower Power group, but they are not. They sound fresh and beautiful.

"It's been quite a year I can hardly believe how much has happened— four tours of the States and two Platinum albums. It sounds like a lot of old bull, but I can't really believe it sometimes. It's like looking at somebody else's career. There is a very powerful astrological force at work within the band which I am sure had a lot to do with our success. Robert is a Leo which makes him a perfect leader, with two Capricorns on either side and a Gemini behind. Leo is always a leader like Ginger Baker, Keith Moon and Mick Jagger. I'm a Capricorn, which speaks for itself — very stubborn with a split personality.".... Zeppelin Farewell.... article states that the band played their last UK gig in Edinburgh and are now off to Europe and the USA. Gigs include Helsinki Feb 23, Göteborg 25, Stockholm 26, Copenhagen 28, Montreux March 8, Vienna 9, Frankfurt 10, Hamburg 11, Dusseldorf 12 before Vancouver on the 21st.... **Billboard reports....** Full page advert reads — 1969 Grammy Awards Best Album Cover Nominees (including Led Zeppelin II).... New U.S. Tour For Zeppelin. Article states the band will play the following dates: March 23 Portland Memorial Coliseum Oregon, Denver (25), Salt Lake City (26), Pittsburgh (30), Philadelphia (31), Dayton (April 3), Indianapolis (4), Baltimore (5), Charlotte NC (7), Raleigh (8), Tampa (9), Miami Beach (10), St. Louis (11), Evansville (16) and Memphis (17)....

25 Göteborg Tioningen reports.... They're Finally Here - Led Zeppelin. Article detailing the band's history to date in preparation for their show in Göteborg that night. It goes on to say that the relatives of the German inventor Von Zeppelin are outraged by the theft of their family name by a 'bunch of screaming monkeys'. The Concerthouse is sold out....

26 Göteborg Express reports.... The Hip Band Led Zeppelin In Sweden. *"In 1969 we earned over a million pounds. This year we'll probably double that. It's a hell of a lot! But compared to other pop bands, we are worth the money."* John Bonham 21, drummer in Led Zeppelin told the Express. *"Us touring Scandinavia is actually pure charity. The money here is pocket money compared to what we get in the USA."* For the tickets in Göteborg yesterday and Stockholm today Led Zeppelin gets 35000 crowns ($7,000). On top of that are first class flights from England for nine people, free hotels, free booze and so on. But that is nothing compared to what they make in the USA in one night. In a concert hall in Los Angeles the fee was $90,000, a little over 450,000 crowns. Led Zeppelin, of course, filled the Göteborg Concerthouse, that means 1,300 people. The tickets to tonight's show at the Stockholm Concerthouse are sold out. Thanks to huge record sales, 7.5 million LPs sold in 1969, Led Zeppelin are considered the world's third most popular band behind the Beatles and the Rolling Stones. What makes this success? John Bonham, *"We play hard, simple music. When we started out in the Fall of 1968 the audiences were tired of so-called experimental Pop music. They longed for basic rock and roll. Then we came along* *and played 'raw and basic pop' without anything fancy."* The members of the group are: Jimmy Page, he started the band in 1968 and was previously a member of the Yardbirds. Guitarist. He has a reputation as one of England's best studio musicians. He is 24 years old. John Bonham, 21, drummer, was picked up by Jimmy Page in his home suburb of Worcestershire where he worked in his father's construction company. John is incredibly fast and original in his drum solos. John Paul Jones, 23, from Hertfordshire, studio musician who amongst other things has backed Donovan and the Rolling Stones. He was also hand-picked by Jimmy Page. Robert Plant, 21, the band's vocalist, comes from Worcestershire like John Bonham. Has a very special way of singing. He says CSNY are his favourite band. After the Stockholm concert the band goes on to Copenhagen, after that to Switzerland, Germany and Italy. They are touring USA for all of March. The band's third LP is expected out in May.... **Swedens Daily News reports....** Advert reads — SBA-Sonet Present Led Zeppelin Concerthouse Thursday 26/2 kl 19.... **Göteborg Tioningen reports....** Whining Harmonica Fired The Zeppelin's. Tommy Randes reviews the show. He mentions at a press conference that day Page commented that communication with the audience is the key to Zeppelin's success. Page, *"It is important that the audience is into the music. If they are, we get inspired to play better and so on."* Randes mentions that the band had just arrived from Helsinki and after Göteborg they move on to Stockholm. He points out that when the band arrive in the USA they will receive two platinum record awards for a million copies sold of each album. Page also admits to playing on records by the Stones, the Beatles (!) and The Kinks but

he diplomatically points out that it is not because the band's own guitarists can't play but because they prefer to arrange. He is then asked about why Zeppelin don't include politics in their lyrics. Page, *"I'm a musician not a politician. There's a lot of guys out there today that haven't made up their minds about what they are."* Page goes on to say that he hopes the band's TV documentary will make it out but he suspects it will end up in his library at home. Randes reports that the band began their set tentatively, perhaps because of the poor acoustics. As much as the band and the audience tried, the atmosphere wasn't there. Finally after finishing 'White Summer' Page stood up and spit on a member of the audience. Randes says his behaviour was fully understandable as during the entire song this particular individual was playing a harmonica. Randes says, "It was devastating. The song was fine-tuned with oriental parts here and there, and that whining harmonica...." He concludes that the band suddenly improved when they became angry and aggressive. By the end of the show the band and audience were fully fired up....

27 **Sweden's Daily News reports....** Zeppelin Victorious. Björn Hakanson reviews the show at the Stockholm Concerthouse. The band filled the hall and played for two and a half hours. He observes that the volume was not as loud as he expected. "Jimmy Page has been in the guitar elite for many years and his presence in his latest surrounding has not weakened his position." He concludes, "The band is excellent at what they do. The music comes rushing like a freight train at the audience, you just have to grab hold and hang on."....

28 **Record Mirror reports....** LZ II is

#3.... When confronted with playing contrived music Peter Noone of Herman's Hermits states that Led Zeppelin is about as contrived as you can get.... he remembers when Jimmy Page used to play for him and when John Bonham (sic) played organ for him on a tour of Germany. He concedes that they are very good musicians.... **Melody Maker reports....** an interview with Jimmy Page.... Chris Welch confronts Page with the news that Eva Von Zeppelin is affronted by the band's use of the family name...Page, *"Then we shall call ourselves the Nobs when we go to Copenhagen, the whole thing is absurd. The first time we played we invited her backstage to meet us to see how we were nice young lads. We calmed her down but on leaving the studio she saw our LP cover of an airship in flames and exploded! I had to run and hide. She just blew her top. So—it's shrieking monkeys now. But she is quite a nice person.*

"They wanted us to fly in an airship over Montreux Switzerland one time. That's tempting fate isn't it? I told them to fly without us and say we were inside."

One newspaper ran an article calling the band Ned Zeppelin, Page *"On our next LP sleeve we were planning to print all the weird comments that have been made about us. That would have been great—Ned Zeppelin!"*

"I've been practicing three hours a day. Unfortunately there has been a great lack of practice in the last year or so. I play a long improvised solo to get fluency and then attempt a difficult phrase to see if I can pull it off. I'd like to be able to play piano. It sounds strange. I can play guitar with finger style independence but I can't play piano. I'd like to play violin but that's not as easy as it looks. When I use violin bow on guitar it's not just a gimmick like people think. It's because some great sounds come out. You can

employ legitimate bowing techniques and gain new scope and depth. The only drawback is that a guitar has a flat neck, as opposed to a violin's curved neck which is a bit limiting.

"Everyone likes to play around with different people, and it can be stimulating to do sessions with other groups. But the kind of work I was doing before proved completely stifling. Never being involved with the artist; it was like being a computer. Originally I used to jam with a group at the old Marquee when Cyril Davies was still alive. One day someone asked me if I wanted to play on a rock session — and that's how it started. At that time only Big Jim Sullivan was around and if there were three sessions, he could only do one, and the others would end up with well, no names mentioned. Without Jim they were desperate. From then on work for me escalated. I was at art school and had to leave because I couldn't do

both. When I first joined a group the scene had become completely stagnant and I lost all faith in music and myself. It was about the time the Beatles were beginning to break. I really wanted to be a fine art painter. I was sincere in that aim and when I went to college I kept quiet that I played guitar or else they would expect me to play in the lunch hour. A conflict between music and art arose and it came to the point where I had to make a decision.

"I enjoyed playing and the R&B revival restored my faith in music. The Rolling Stones were playing a lot of Muddy Waters numbers and the Beatles were doing things by the Marvelettes and the Shirelles. I just picked it up when I was at school. I had my guitar confiscated every day. They handed it back to me at 4 pm.

"I didn't have any guitar lessons because there was nobody to teach me and I couldn't get up to London. I couldn't read at all when I started session work I had to teach myself on a crash course. There was no individuality involved at all. The arranger said this is what you play and that's what I played. I got fed up. It began to be a pain in the neck. When the Yardbirds came up, that was it. I was a good friend of Jeff Beck, who had replaced Eric Clapton, I was there when Paul Samwell-Smith had a great row and left the group so I had to take over on bass. I had never played one before. Then Chris Dreja swapped from rhythm guitar to bass and the idea was for me and Jeff to get a stereo guitar sound.

"With two lead guitars it worked really well. Lots of people have done it since, but I think we must have been the first. When we went over to the States we took them by storm. The funny thing was the Yardbirds didn't mean anything as a

group in England. There was no magic attached to the name. In America it was different. The mystique formed because they liked Jeff and knew Eric had been in the group. There was the whole raver thing as well. English bands liked to loon and Hollywood went wild. Anyway it was an exciting group.

" 'The Yardbirds appeared with their cacophony of sound,' that's what an English newspaper said when they reviewed a show we did at the Albert Hall. But in those days groups used the Albert Hall's PA system and you know what that's like. The guitars were really loud— and bad! Eric had always used a little amp and that was Keith Relf's big complaint about Jeff and me. 'Eric used to play through an AC 30 and you've got 300 watts each!' He got more and more reticent, but nobody was trying to drown him out. Obviously there was a lot of tension and that's why he made two solo records. I've heard Renaissance are great and I'm pleased Keith is doing well.

"You know, it wouldn't surprise me if Eric didn't go back to the blues and form a little group. I like the Stones—they went through a lot of changes and came up with 'Jumpin' Jack Flash' and the Beatles went through 'Sgt. Pepper' and 'Get Back'. They all want to go back to their roots.

"We want to do some free concerts this year. We may be doing one at Glastonbury at the time of the Summer Solstice. But I'm not so sure about Hyde Park. I know in the States they can't have any more because of the Stones thing at Altamont. They won't grant licenses because everybody is frightened. It's a shame because this type of concert is valuable and legitimate."

As far as the rumours about the imminent demise of Led Zeppelin, "There is no *reason to split up. There is nothing in-herent musically in Led Zeppelin to harm or destroy it. There is variety, great free-dom and no restrictions on the players whatsoever. It's good from a head point of view, in our band everybody respects each other. Everybody plays something to knock each other out. I can't see any split coming. People say to us— 'Now you are established. when are you going to break up?' That's a terrible attitude."....* **New Musical Express reports....** Zeppelin become Nobs!.... "Led Zeppelin will play a concert in Copenhagen this Saturday under the name of The Nobs. Countess Eva Von Zeppelin has threatened legal action against the band if they use her family name.... Led Zeppelin's show in Frankfurt this weekend has been canceled due to riots when Jethro Tull played there last week."...

March 1970

6 Los Angeles Free Press reports.... Full page advert reads — In the Beginning God Created The Heaven And the Yardbirds.... Ad is for the new Keith Relf, Jim McCarty band Renaissance....

7 DISC reports.... Front Page News.... cover story and feature article.... Just back from a tour of Scandinavia Zeppelin start their fifth tour of the USA in two weeks, they return here on April 19th and rest until May and then they will finish their third album.... at the end of May they tour Japan and then return to America.... Zeppelin's gross earnings for 1970 will top £2,000,000.... total album sales are now over 7,000,000...the band were awarded a gold record in Sweden the only group to get one other than the Beatles.... In Hamburg the band extended their

scheduled show to two because of the line outside.... last year the band spent £24,000 on airfares.... Robert Plant bought a farm for £8,000.... Page bought a converted boathouse near Pangborne for £30,000.... Bonham has bought six or seven cars in the last year including a Rolls Royce.... the band have no fan club, Grant, *"I think they're a bit passé and phony."..* Page owns a Bentley...Plant owns a Land Rover and is buying a Jaguar.... Jones is learning to drive in a Fiat.... Zeppelin's equipment weighs about two tons.... the sound system is by WEM and is worth £4,000.... Bonham spent £1,800 on percussion.... Page plays a ten year old Les Paul which is worth about £600.... John Paul Jones Hammond Organ is worth about £800.... Led Zeppelin earn as much as 30,000 dollars per night in the USA.... at the Royal Albert Hall they came away with about £2,000 between them.... Page practices for three hours a day.... Zeppelin own their own publishing company Superhype and the sheet music is published by Steingarten, Wedeen and Weiss of New York.... In Denver Colorado the band recently sold out 12,000 tickets in two days on the strength of one newspaper advert.... they have earned a gold disc for Led Zeppelin I and a gold and Platinum for Led Zeppelin II which has sold 2,500,000 copies in America and 130,000 copies in the UK, Led Zeppelin I sold 1,800,000 copies in the USA.... **Record Mirror reports....** LZ II is #3 ...LZ I is #20.... **New Musical Express reports....** Led Zeppelin II is still number one in the USA...the new tour is expected to gross $800,000....

13 The Memphis Press Scimitar reports.... Led Zeppelin Is Heavy, Man And So's The Ticket Demand.... feature

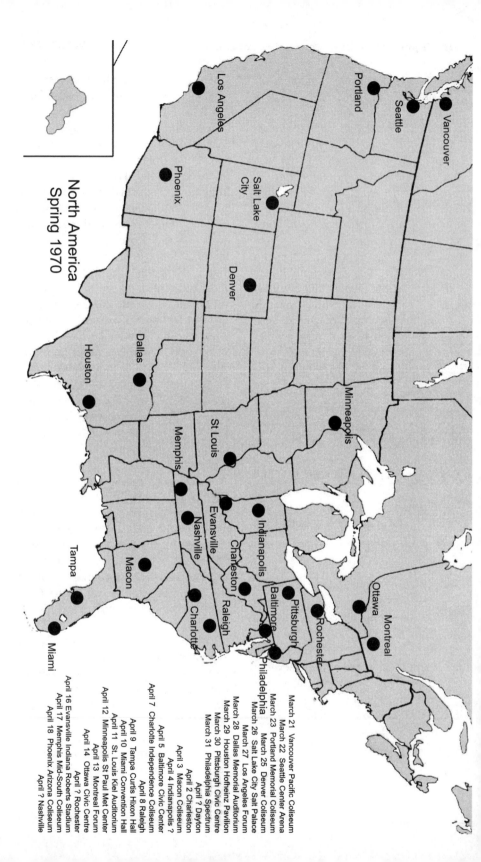

North America
Spring 1970

March 21 Vancouver Pacific Coliseum
March 22 Seattle Center Arena
March 23 Portland Memorial Coliseum
March 25 Denver Coliseum
March 26 Salt Lake City Salt Palace
March 27 Los Angeles Forum
March 28 Dallas Memorial Auditorium
March 29 Houston Hofheinz Pavilion
March 30 Pittsburgh Civic Centre
March 31 Philadelphia Spectrum
April ? Dayton
April 2 Charleston
April 3 Macon Coliseum
April 4 Indianapolis ?
April 5 Baltimore Civic Center
April 7 Charlotte Independence Coliseum
April 8 Raleigh
April 9 Tampa Curtis Hixon Hall
April 10 Miami Convention Hall
April 11 St. Louis Kiel Auditorium
April 12 Minneapolis St Paul Met Center
April 13 Montreal Forum
April 14 Ottawa Civic Centre
April ? Rochester
April 16 Evansville Indiana Roberts Stadium
April 17 Memphis Mid-South Coliseum
April 18 Phoenix Arizona Coliseum
April ? Nashville

article.... Does Johnny Cash's little brother really play lead guitar in Led Zeppelin.... Is Led Zeppelin really the Kingston Trio in disguise. No, an emphatic no in each instance. The questions are just a sampling of quack mail a guy who writes about music can receive.... Led Zeppelin is a reality and the famed London rock group whose music is electric sounding as it's name, will perform at the Mid-South Coliseum for two straight hours April 17th. Non stop and alone. Zeppelin's two albums have sold more than $2 million worth each the past 18 months. Led Zeppelin II had been on the stands only three days when it rang up a whopping $1 million in sales. Zeppelin is making a month's tour of the U.S. during April and all available tickets have been gobbled up in Los Angeles, Denver, Salt Lake City and Pittsburgh. Some 20,000 tickets offered in L.A. were gone in a matter of days.... Led Zeppelin began in a small stuffy rehearsal hall, mid-London in 1968. *"Four of us got together in this two-by-two room and started playing,"* says former Yardbird master guitarist Jimmy Page. Page is a real wild man, when he gets into a piece. He can start slow then gradually, before you know it, he'll be gyrating all over the stage and maybe playing his electric guitar with a violin bow.... Incidentally whatever did happen to the Kingston Trio?....

14 **Record Mirror reports....** LZ II is #4.... LZ I is # 16.... **New Musical Express reports....** Whole Lotta Love is number one in Germany.... **Billboard reports....** Article states that Led Zeppelin will play Munich Germany on Sunday March 8, Frankfurt (10), Hamburg (11) and Dusseldorf (12). It goes on to say that Led Zeppelin II is at the top of the Metronome sales charts....

21 **Record Mirror reports....** Cover Story reports GOLDRUSH; with Led Zeppelin pictured receiving their gold discs.... a movie filmed on their current tour is reported to be released next year.... LZ II is #6...LZ I is #15.... **The Vancouver Express reports....** One of the few groups capable of filling a hall the size of the Coliseum, Britain's Led Zeppelin looks set for another sell-out there tonight. The group starting a 30 day tour of North America, filled the Coliseum on their last visit.... **Melody Maker reports....** Led Zeppelin may be playing Le Bourget Pop festival on March 28th.... **Billboard reports....** Zeppelin Returns To North America Tour. Article states that the band will conduct a four week tour starting Vancouver on March 21 and 27 cities including, Denver, Los Angeles, Dallas, Houston, Philadelphia, Pittsburgh, Seattle, Portland, Salt Lake City, Nashville, Baltimore, Miami Beach, Phoenix and Las Vegas.... Full page advert for guitarist Deniel Edwards which mentions his association with Jimmy Page and John Bonham through the Lord Sutch album.... Led Zeppelin II is #1 in Canada....

22 **The Seattle Times reports....** Advert Led Zeppelin rock group, Seattle Center Arena 8....

24 **The Vancouver Express reports....** Zeppelin Pack 'Em In.... Review of the show at the Pacific Coliseum in Vancouver.... nearly 19,000 fans jammed the building for the group's first concert in a 19 city tour.... the show started half an hour late at 8.30 and lasted for two and a half hours.... songs played included one new song Since I've Been Loving You as well as Dazed & Confused, How Many

More Times, Heartbreaker, White Summer, Moby Dick and Whole Lotta Love...the crowd mobbed the stage at the end, *"Never before in the history of Led Zeppelin has this happened,"* joked Plant.... the show was a fitting tribute to one of the most talented rock groups in the business today....

26 **The Denver Post reports....** Review of the show of the 25th...apparently the biggest audience ever drawn in Denver attended the show with some 11,500 punters. The article notes that the band had made their debut American appearance in Denver eighteen months before. It states, 'It's hard to fault the group's performance...Led Zeppelin had the crowd soaring from the beginning.... they are skillful enough to overpower friend and foe alike with good solid rock and roll.'...

28 **DISC reports....** Jimmy Page is scheduled to appear on the Julie Felix television show on Sunday April 12th.... Page stars solo in the show with The Hollies also guesting.... LZ II is #6.... LZ I is #15.... **Melody Maker reports....** Cover story.... A letter to the mailbag from Robert Plant, *"I must disagree strongly with the comments of M. Winser (Mailbag 14/3/70) on Arthur Lee and Love, having followed their progress from the days of The Castle, etc.*

"Arthur Lee as a person and environmentally (which are the seeds, one would think of lyrics and melodies) is as different from M.Winser as he is from Lonnie Donnegan, so what appears to be pretense to our friend could be honesty to Arthur Lee.

"On the word hype, having seen them all at the Speakeasy, I would have expected to see Arthur Lee surrounded by a mammoth string section in an attempt to

attain the brilliance of *"Forever Changes".* Instead I have found a somewhat nervous band. I'm sure that accompanied by a proficient string section either á la Love Affair or even Denny Laine's Electric String Band, they would have been heralded as the *"new whatever the term is this week,"* and our friend would be singing their praises until it was time to forget them after receiving mass acclaim.

"As each musician is guilty of possessing his or her own clichés, which is only one of the properties of originality, I would dearly like to know what M. Winser thinks of the Yeah Yeahs of the Beatles, the vibrato of Neil Young, or the humour of Roy Harper.

"So perhaps the life of a musician in the hills of L.A. is not to be compared with the life of our friend in Newbury, in which case Arthur Lee as a person may or may not receive the acclaim he deserves, but no one can deny the beauty of "The Old Man" or "And More Again" and the future of a truly creative quantity. Yes." - Robert Plant (Led Zeppelin)....

Interview with Robert Plant conducted on the way to Heathrow airport in London where Plant was catching his flight to Vancouver to kick off the US tour.

"The only heavy band I really dig is the Zeppelin, apart from that I dig the mellower things - for instance I'd love to see Trader Horne make it, because they're doing beautiful things (and Judy Dyble's very pretty) and also people like the Fairport Convention. Even that Matthew's Southern Comfort album was really excellent."

When asked if he was frustrated by Zeppelin's stage mania, *"Oh no...that's something I need, that I have to* have. It's like bottling it all up, and when I go on stage I can let it all out. It's really very good for me. Jimmy's path and my path seem to criss-cross, they meet at certain points along the way, and that's where we meet and play together.

"We're really into very different things, and John Paul and Bonzo are too. In fact I suppose if we all sat down and talked about music, John Paul and Bonzo and I wouldn't agree at all."

On the subject of the second album, "Ramble On, that was my baby, and I hoped everybody would suss it out and realise that was where I want to go. But I never even heard it mentioned...I was very disappointed about that."

The third album, "We haven't prepared much material yet, but we have got a few things down. AND IT'S ALL ACOUSTIC FOLKS! You can just see it, can't you 'LED ZEPPELIN GO SOFT ON THEIR FANS' or some crap like that.

"No seriously, Jimmy and I are going to rent a little cottage near the River Dovey in Wales where we can lock ourselves away for a few weeks just to see what we can come up with when there's no one else around. The next album will probably come out of that.

"I don't think we'll go into decline. We've made people aware of us, and what we've got to do now is consolidate the position we've arrived at, so that eventually we'll be able to say what we really want to say and people will listen to it because it's us.

"That's why we're working so hard now, and I dig it because we can get through to a lot of people. And I really enjoy the raving bit, like on 'Whole Lotta Love' I really enjoy watching their faces when I start it, and sometimes I sing the most ridiculous words to it. Then I look at their faces again to see if they've sussed it

out, and if they haven't ...then I laugh all the more.

"One band I hope really makes it is Bronco, because I've known Jess Roden for a long time. When we were about 15 we were in competing groups, he was in the Shakedown Sound and I was in the Crawling King Snakes, I'm not kidding, his band could have blown the Who ten miles off stage...to say nothing of Led Zeppelin.

"I went down to hear them rehearsing and they sounded really fine. The lead guitarist was in The Band Of Joy, and I'm really longing for them to do well.

"Terry Reid, too - he's fantastic. When I started with Zeppelin I was really nervous and I didn't have it too together, but after a couple of weeks with him I realised what I should do. I went to hear him at Mother's in Birmingham some time ago, and we sang together on the stage. Man that was fantastic, after only half an hour I was really whacked out.

"Wow can you imagine it - Roden, Reid and Plant? That would be fantastic. Maybe that's the sort of way it's going to go, because I really want to work with people like that."

On the subject of other performers, "Crosby, Stills, Nash and Young - well, I spent all that concert wiping the tears off my face. Every time Neil Young did something it was all too much for me. The way he plays guitar is really indescribable. It's very simple, but it pleases my ear a lot more than some people who can play five million notes a second. It's real music.

"Arthur Lee, too, is incredible, and when you hear bands like Love or the Youngbloods on stage at somewhere like the Fillmore in San Francisco then you begin to realise where they're at and that *the vibration thing from the audience isn't just something that's talked about at the Speakeasy.*

"When I heard the Youngbloods I realise that they were doing it just how I'd always wanted to do it. Maureen and I stood there smiling all the way through their set - we simply couldn't stop smiling. So beautiful.".... **Billboard reports....** Full page advert reads — Premier Talent Associates Inc Exclusively Representing Led Zeppelin etc....Article states that Metronome in Germany released a special double Led Zeppelin album for 35 marks combining the band's biggest 'hits' to coincide with the band's German tour. It goes on to say that 'Whole Lotta Love' has sold 200,000 copies in Germany....

Beat Instrumental reports.... Cover story. 1969/70 Poll Winners. Jimmy Page #2 guitarist - Led Zeppelin #3 British group - Jimmy Page #5 recording manager - John Paul Jones #4 Bass guitarist - Robert Plant #1 Recording vocalist - Led Zeppelin #5 Song writing team - Led Zeppelin #1 Live group....

April 1970

1 **Philadelphia Evening Bulletin reports....** Review of the show. 15,800 fans attended a two and a half hour concert. The promoter apparently paid $25,000 to the band. The reviewer concludes that the show was 'top-shelf, pure and uncut'....

4 **The Montreal Gazette....** Rock's newest heavyweight champions, Led Zeppelin considered by many as the greatest group in the contemporary performing arts, will appear in concert on Monday 8.00 pm at the Montreal

Forum.... The Stones, Cream and Hendrix have all influenced Zeppelin but their own creativity and exciting showmanship have built their reputation as the most outstanding group in rock music today.... **New Musical Express reports....** Living Loving Maid is destined to become a hit for Led Zeppelin in the USA...ASK-IN with a Led Zeppelin a week...beginning of a four week series with Ritchie Yorke interviewing the band members in Toronto.... Bassist John Paul Jones... Yorke asks what Jones was doing before Led Zeppelin, *"Vegetating in studios in London mainly. Jimmy's also done his share of that. But he got out and went into the Yardbirds. Just before joining the band I had gotten into arranging and directing which was better than just sitting and being told what to do. I did a lot of Donovan's stuff. The first thing I did for him was Sunshine Superman. I happened to be on the session and I ended up arranging it. The arranger who was there really didn't know about anything. I sort of got the rhythm section together and we went from there. Mellow Yellow I did entirely on my own. I was pleased with it, it was different to what was happening in the general session scene."*

Yorke then asks him about influences on his bass playing, *"It was only recently that you could even hear the bass on records. So apart from the obvious jazz influences like every good jazz bass player in history; Mingus, Ray Brown, Scott Lafaro...I was into jazz organ for quite a while until I couldn't stand the musicians any longer and I had to get back to rock and roll. I listened to a lot of jazz bass players and that influenced my session playing and then I cannot tell a lie, the Motown bass players! You just can't get away from it. Every bass player in every rock group is still doing Motown phrases* whether he wants to admit it or not. Motown was a bass players paradise because they'd actually found a way to record it so you could hear every note. Some of the Motown records ended up sounding like a concerto for bass guitar! The Motown record that really impressed me was I Was Made To Love Her by Stevie Wonder."

Yorke asks him what he thinks of McCartney, "Well I think he's perfect. He's always been good. Everything he's done has always been right, even if he didn't do too much. He's improved so much since the early Beatles days.

"The first record that really turned me on to bass guitar was Phil Upchurch's You Can't Sit Down which had an incredible bass solo. Very simple musically but it had an incredible amount in it."

He is asked how he feels about band life, "It's a strain, but it's a different kind of strain. I much prefer it. In sessions you just vegetate and you reach a certain period where you're working a hell of a lot and that's it. You can't do anything musically and it's horrible. You become a well used session musician with no imagination. I used to be the only bass player in England that knew anything about the Motown stuff so I used to do all the cover versions. I often used to almost be in tears at the sound they'd get and the way they used to mess up the songs. Every record that's been made in England you could have been on, if they used your particular instrument, from Petula Clark to visiting Americans. I remember one day, firstly at Decca studios with the Bachelors, then Little Richard, who'd come over to do a couple of English sessions, and it was bloody awful."

Yorke asks him whether it both-ered him that people perceived Led Zeppelin as Jimmy Page's band, "Well if Jimmy had been incredibly insecure and really wanted to be a star, he would have picked lesser musicians and gone on the road and done the whole star trip. Everybody in the band recognised that at first having Jimmy's name was a great help. In fact it opened a lot of doors, and once you realised that, and because you're aware that you had a job to do, it worked out all right. I've been playing bass for ten years now. I've been on the road since I was two years old, my parents were in the business too, in variety. They had a double act, a musical comedy thing. I was in a professional band with Jet Harris and Tony Meehan. That was when I was seventeen."

Yorke then asks his opinions of the other band members, "Robert is unique. We're all unique really but Robert is really something. I can't imagine any other singer with us. Robert is Robert and there's nothing else to say. John is the find of the year as far as British drummers are concerned. I can't remember anyone like him either. It's obvious why these people have ended up in the same group. We're all the right people if anybody had to leave the group would have to split up because it wouldn't be LZ anymore. Each of us is irreplaceable in this band. For years and years I've rated Jimmy. We both come from South London and even then I can remember people saying, 'You've got to go and listen to Neil Christian and The Crusaders they've got this unbelievable guitarist!' I'd heard of him before I heard of Clapton or Beck. I've always thought Jimmy to be far superior to any of them. It sounds like a mutual admiration society, people don't believe me when I say this but I mean it.".... **Billboard reports....**

CHARLOTTE COLISEUM ★ TUES. NITE, APR. 7th ★ 8:00 P.M.
TOMORROW NIGHT
IN CONCERT — IN PERSON
LED ZEPPELIN

"Whole Lotta Love"

"Livin' Lovin' Maid"

No. 1 Album In the Country "Led Zeppelin II"

★
SEE THEM PERFORM A FULL TWO HOUR CONCERT
TICKETS: $7.00 - $6.00 - $5.00 - $4.00
GOOD SEATS STILL AVAILABLE AT ALL PRICES

TICKETS NOW ON SALE: COLISEUM BOX OFFICE, HI-FI CAMERA CENTER, ERNIES, NATIONAL HAT SHOP, MF SHRUDE HOLDING CO., CANNED HEAT, RECORD BAR COLISEUM BOX OFFICE OPEN 6 P.M. TUESDAY NIGHT

Led Zeppelin II is selling well for Warner. The band opened their fifth American tour in Vancouver and are also expected to play other Canadian dates in Montreal April 13 and Ottawa April 14....

5 **St. Petersburg Times reports....** Advert reads — Led Zeppelin Rock group Curtis Hixon Hall, 600 Ashley St. Tampa 8 pm $5.50 to $7....

6 **Charlotte News reports....** Advert reads — Charlotte Coliseum Tues Nite, Apr. 7th 8 pm Tomorrow Night In Concert In Person Led Zeppelin No. 1 Album in the Country Led Zeppelin II. See them perform a full two hour concert Tickets $7.00, $6.00, $5.00, $4.00, Good seats still available at all prices available at the Coliseum Box Office.... **Charlotte Observer reports....** Advert reads — Charlotte Coliseum Tues Nite, Apr. 7th 8 pm Tomorrow Night In Concert In Person Led Zeppelin etc....

7 **Charlotte Observer reports....** Led Zeppelin To Play At Coliseum Tonight. the Led Zeppelin will appear at 8 tonight in the Charlotte Coliseum. The British blue-hard rock group which played Friday night to a sold-out crowd of 10,000 in Macon Georgia will give a two hour plus concert. Apparently over 5,000 advance tickets were sold....

8 **Charlotte Observer reports....** Heavy Zeppelin Sailed Clouds Of Euphoria. Review of the show in Charlotte. Journalist Bob Kerr attempts to describe the gig in prosaic terms often referring to the overall warmth of the atmosphere. Over 7,500 people turned up, with some having to leave due to the band's intensely loud sound. He mentions that they per-

formed Heartbreaker. 'Those lucky enough to sit on the floor in front of the stage were orderly. Everyone was orderly. The Led Zeppelin is not the type of group to inspire mass assaults on the stage like some of their counterparts. Such action would be a violation of the mood, and the mood is beautiful.' The band played for over two hours concluding with a song called 'When Will Be The Next Time' (!)....

10 **The Miami Herald reports....** Special Events.... Led Zeppelin English underground music stars led by guitarist Jimmy Page with John Bonham, Robert Plant and John Paul Jones tonight at 8.30 Miami Convention Hall.... **The Memphis Press Scimitar reports....** This is Led Zeppelin, the hard and heavy English rock group which is well on the way to becoming in the 70's what the Beatles were in the 60's. They're currently on an American tour which brings them to the Coliseum next Friday night for a concert. Individually they are Jimmy Page, vocalist and electric guitar, Robert Plant, lead vocalist and harmonica, John Paul Jones, vocalist, bass and organ, and John James Benham (sic) vocalist and drums....

11 **DISC reports....** Pop Politics and Rock - Lord Sutch Is Back.... feature article about the Sutch album featuring Page and Bonham.... Lord David Sutch has actually made an LP, which sold 70,000 copies in America in a month and is to be released here soon.... called Lord Sutch and Heavy Friends it includes Jimmy Page and John Bonham.... Sutch and Page wrote most of the 12 tracks...reviewers compare Sutch to Robert Plant who Sutch says is, "a thousand times better than me!".... **Record Mirror reports....** Tony Burrows (pop singer) says Led Zeppelin's

Roger (sic) Plant has a limited vocal range and although he can improvise lyrics it doesn't make him a good singer.... **The Montreal Gazette reports....** Led Zeppelin are Jimmy Page: lead guitar, John Paul Jones pianist, John Bonham drummer, Robert Plant vocalist and harmonica. Their music is a mixture of intensified rock and contemporary blues, at the Forum April 13.... **New Musical Express reports....** ASK-IN with a Led Zeppelin a week.... second of a four week series with Ritchie Yorke interviewing the band members in Toronto.... singer Robert Plant.... Yorke asks what Plant was doing before Led Zeppelin, *"I was working immediately before Led Zeppelin with a group called Alexis Korner and we were in the process of recording an album with a pianist called Steve Miller, a very fluid thing, nothing definitely set up. We were going to do a few festivals in Germany things like that. Before that I hadn't done much at all. I'd cut three singles which I prefer to forget. I want to leave them in the dimmest past! John Bonham and I worked together for a total of about two and a half years. It was a period of trying to find what I wanted to do musically. So I feel my first four or five years were finding out what I wanted to do. The first year of Led Zeppelin has made me see a lot more of what I want to do. This year has been much more valuable to me than the other five. In England nobody wanted to know."*

After some discussion about the band leaning on Page's previous reputation with the Yardbirds the subject turns to taking yourself too seriously like Jim Morrison, *"We only played with the Doors once in Seattle and it seemed like he was screwed up. He was giving the impression he was into really deep things like Skip Spence of Moby Grape. You can* get into a trip of your own that you don't really realise what's going on in the outside world. Morrison went on stage and said 'Fuck you all' which didn't do anything except make a few girls scream. Then he hung on the side of the stage and nearly toppled into the audience and did all those things that I suppose were originally sexual things but as he got fatter and dirtier and more screwed up they became more bizarre. So it was really sickening to watch. My wife and I were there watching and we couldn't believe it.

"I respected the Door's albums, even though they're not brilliant musicians and as I said that doesn't matter. What Morrison was doing on record was good. The track "Cancel My Subscription" was great. He was just miles above anyone's head. It seemed that he realised that the Doors were on the way down. He went on stage with that opinion and immediately started saying all those strange things which nobody could get into. There were one or two people there crying 'You're God, you're king' and I was thinking why? And then the Youngbloods went on stage and wiped everyone out because they were so warm. We're not over here to have a bad time. We're over here to have a good time and people pay money to have a good time as well."

Yorke then turns the conversation to Plant's influences, "There was a guy called Tommy McClellan who recorded on the Bluebird label for RCA in the 30's. His rapport the way he completely expressed himself on record was great because it was saying 'To hell with you' all the time, and he was just shouting out all these lyrics with such gusto that even now you could sit there and go 'Corrr'. It's the same with Robert Johnson. His sympathy with his guitar playing. It's just

like when you have a vocalist you have to be sympathetic with the musicians you're playing with. I always respected Steve Winwood I must admit. He was to me the only guy. He had such a range in the early days when Spencer Davis became popular. They were doing things like Don't Start Crying Now by Slim Harpo and Watch Your Step and Rambling Rose Jerry Lee Lewis and the whole way. Steve was one of the first people who wasn't sticking to the normal. Like the Hollies and all those groups who has been a dot dash dot dash follow the lines and sang all the same thing every night. And along came Winwood who was only a bit older than me and started screaming out all these things and I thought 'God that's what I've been trying to do."

Yorke asks his opinion of his band mates, Jones first, "What a question. As a musician incredible. His imagination as a bass player is very good. Also as a pianist and organist because he looks at the whole thing in a completely different way to me. I mean the five lines and five spaces were never of any importance to me because I was a vocalist. You don't have to know much you just have to sing. John comes in with rhythms and the whole Stax and soul side of things to give you the back beat that you need so I appreciate that.

"Bonzo's a good sparring partner. We played together for a long time and I think this is the only band we've had any success with. If I didn't like him as a drummer I suppose he wouldn't have been the drummer because someone would have said no. So he's got to be alright."

Finally his comments on Page, "To begin with when someone comes along and says 'Come with us you're going to make a lot of money' you think he's got to be joking so you say OK. But in the beginning I held myself a long way off from him. The more you get into the bloke although he seems to be quite shy, he's not really. He's got lots of good ideas for song writing and he's proved to be a really nice guy."…. **Melody Maker reports….** Heavy Friends help the Lord's come-back…. article detailing the Heavy Friends album by Lord Sutch with an interview with Sutch. *"Jimmy Page co-produced the album with me and that's the best way to do it, to be on both sides of the box. We wrote the songs too. I made sure that we didn't make the mistake that all the other rock groups have made, including the new lot, The Wild Angels. All they do is the old songs like C'mon Everybody, Great Balls Of Fire and Blue Suede Shoes. That doesn't sell because everybody's got ten versions of it already. What we've done is modern rock and roll with the real Zeppelin sound, that driving beat with loads of excitement. That Bonham is a tremendous drummer. The album has sold 70,000 in one month in the States which is more than I did here in six years."…*

13 **The St. Louis Post Despatch reports….** Kiel Crowd Cheers British Rock Group…. review of the gig at the Kiel Auditorium…. Full of sound and fury Led Zeppelin played long and hard Saturday night and drew repeated standing ovations from a crowd of 9,000 at Kiel Convention Hall…. Led Zeppelin played for more than two hours…. (they) are dominated by the technical proficiency of Jimmy Page on guitar and the screaming vocals of Robert Plant…. a Led Zeppelin concert over-all is about as interesting musically as a long playing record of train whistles…. the things Jimmy Page can do with a guitar are astounding. He wrench-

es sound from the strings…. but his music like that of the rest of the group is a series of crescendos with no build up, no sense of space…. one longs for a BB King or Eric Clapton to break through the mass of noise and play some music…. It was interesting to watch the audience try to dance to Led Zeppelin…. the sound at the convention hall was miserable as usual….

14 **The Montreal Star reports….** Sell-out crowd greets Led Zeppelin, event of the year…. review of the show at the Montreal forum…. a scathing review from the Star makes you wonder just what the band did to the guy! "Anticipation was the name of the game before last night's Led Zeppelin show at the Forum…. it was the rock event of the year. The Led Zeppelin show was the first legitimate sell-out for rock at the Forum. But these are the big salad days for hype, and Led Zeppelin are the most hyped group of them all. To say that Led Zeppelin is awful is merely an understatement…. the volume is turned up high and each note sounds like an avalanche. False meaning is thus attached to each sound, listeners are conned into the belief that because Led Zeppelin is ridiculously loud then they must necessarily play important music…. the group is ridiculously monotonous…. there is a patent lack of rhythm in Zeppelin's noise…no need to worry about mistakes because no one knows the difference. Including the musicians (a charitable word). Imagination is wholly absent in Zeppelin's performance…. Guitar companies must be pleased with Jimmy Page's work because all he is doing is demonstrating with as much creativity as an encyclopedia salesman the range of sounds and gimmicks that can come out of an electric guitar. Listening to Page was for me about as satisfying as

watching a television picture signal. Obviously Zeppelin fans loved the show. The group gave them what they wanted to hear."...**The Ottawa Citizen reports....** Tonight The Treble Clef presents the Led Zeppelin 8.30 P.M. at the Civic Centre, tickets $4.50 at the door!....

17 **The Memphis Press Scimitar reports....** A Zeppelin that didn't go down.... interview with John Bonham on the telephone from Montreal.... The Led Zeppelin is not going down like a lead zeppelin. They're going over like the Beatles.... John James Benham (sic) Led Zeppelin's drummer described it, *"Every concert has been fantastic, four and five encores. Everybody has been going sort of mad. In Montreal the hall seats 13,800 and we drew 16,000. They sold all standing room and all the aisles.*

"It's not that we're any more popular here than in England, but the halls are smaller. The Albert Hall (in London) is one of the largest and it only seats four and a half thousand people. We sold that out about three times. The reaction is just as good but having 4,000 people leaping about and applauding is much different from 16,000.

"That first tour we were a new English group and the audiences and critics sort of gave you a big chance. There's something about American audiences. They give you a listen and see. The critics are trying to pick fault rather than trying to pick up on the good things. It's like they sit down and say, 'We know all the good points, let's find the bad ones.' But when you are in the public eye, you are open to criticism.

"Most concerts with supporting acts run late. By the time we got on, the most we could play was an hour. We can't really do in an hour what we need to do.

It takes like two hours and 15 minutes for just the tunes off both albums. Our shows run more nearly three hours.

"Say we had a couple of supporting acts. The kids don't really want to see them. They want to see us. Other groups that have back up acts are just making it so they don't have to play so long. Most don't have to do two hours like we do. There is a lot of money involved. If the kids pay $4 for a ticket, it is better to give them value than have them see two acts they never heard of before us and see us 45 minutes."

Talking from Montreal Benham and the Zeppelin had done 17 straight nights of concerts in a different town every night with him doing a 25 minute drum solo every night. *"You get on stage with the warmth from the crowd and you forget about being tired."*

Zeppelin music is often described as contemporary blues, *"Not 12 bar-blues but anything sad, anything like that expresses blues really. You could dance to a lot of the stuff, a lot is just sitting and listening. There's a good variation like semi-different things. I think underground is coming out of the ground at the moment. I don't think it is like it was. It is getting more now as though everything has got a chance if it is good.*

"We were sort of classed as underground. Anything was, except the pop manufactured record, 2½ minutes long. Anything original, different, anything that wasn't establishment was underground. The kids thought if it was underground it was good. Something on commercial stations was bad. We are playing the same but now they play us.

"Whatever is good is selling and popular now. Now the kids are looking more, looking harder, much more interested, more aware. They are much more sen-

sitive now. You can see the reaction from the audiences. They really do get involved. Something sort of very touching, they get very emotional about it, completely involved in a number. They don't just sit there and say, 'We're in the auditorium and watching.' They get completely involved in the music.

"One reason is that music is a very big outlet, really isn't it? At the moment there are a lot of bad things, Viet Nam and all these things. A large thing is that they can get to a concert, see a group they really like and forget everything. That 2½ hours they can get really involved in the music and forget everything else, let off all the steam they want to.

"In our concerts we do like a large selection from the first and second albums. They listen and applaud. Jimmy does his guitar solo, I do a drum solo. Then we go into several different rhythms, different tunes, a bit of rock, where they can all take part. They have listened to two hours of the show. Now they can get up and dance and do whatever they like. We get them to sing with us. It is sort of good. So many groups go out and try to be ultra-cool. I don't dig it. We like to put our whole heart and soul in it.

"Oh say, have you heard anything about we might get the keys to the city?" He was assured that Mayor Loeb has the keys ready and waiting for them.... **Las Vegas Sun reports....** Advert for free albums.... Dick Kanellis turns you on to an Entire Evening with Led Zeppelin, 8 pm Sunday April 19 Convention Center Rotunda.... when asked why there is no support act promoter Dick Kanellis says, "Why take up precious playing time with anyone else." ....

18 **DISC reports....** Cops Move In - and

Zeppelin walk off to stop a 'police riot'.... Full page article reviewing show in Pittsburgh Pennsylvania.... Jimmy Page, *"We couldn't play with that sort of friction so we just, stopped playing and walked away.*

"That seemed to cool the police from running round sorting out the audience, and when we went back on stage after five or ten minutes, there was no trouble. What we're finding so often on this tour of the States is that the relations between police and audience are bad from the start, so it ends up with us having to cool things down.

"The police act tough with crowds out of fear but if they just left people alone and didn't get all worked up and scared, I'm sure nothing would happen.

"I mean, you see a cop waving a stick and you get shaky —and - how can we carry on playing when the cops are roaming among an apparently peaceful audience, anticipating trouble? That's what's happening. In Boston, two people in wheelchairs who came to see the show rode down the gangway and some attendants didn't care a damn that they were incapacitated. If you're not sitting in the seats you've been allocated you can't be in this hall,' they told them. People get so nervous and worked up by anything out of the ordinary.

"A girl in Baltimore asked me if she could come backstage and watch the show from there. I thought this was the usual line from a girl just wanting to hang around with us. So I said: 'Why don't you go and sit in your seat and watch us?' She said- 'Because last time at this place, the cops tear gassed the place and I'm frightened of being out there.'

"That's the sort of tension we keep finding. There's such a lack of understanding and trust between the

audiences and the police. The warm atmosphere and reaction at the end of each concert makes it all worthwhile—unless you get a nasty scene like a dig at your long hair between the hall and the hotel room, which often happens.

"The people who dig the music are the ones who count to us, and if they take the trouble to come out and see us, we mustn't let them down just because others try to disrupt things.

"We go through a lot of changes in style during the act. Starts off quite progressive and then we do some quiet numbers featuring organ. It's the first time we've used organ over here and people like it. We're doing one number—a 12-bar progressive blues, 'Since I've Been Loving You,'—that will be featured on the next LP, which might as well be called Led Zeppelin 3. Incidentally, three quarters of the album is already done." ....

Record Mirror reports.... Led Zeppelin need bodyguards to tour the Deep South of the USA, on their 200 mile car ride it was like something out of Easy Rider...they return to the UK on April 20th and start recording their new album May 19th.... LZ II is #4.... LZ I is #23....

New Musical Express reports.... ASKIN with a Led Zeppelin a week...third of a four week series with Ritchie Yorke interviewing the band members in Toronto.... drummer John Bonham.... as usual Yorke begins with his start in the business, *"Five months before Led Zeppelin appeared I was playing with Robert Plant in the Band Of Joy. We had a tour as the supporting act with Tim Rose. Then Tim went home and we continued for a bit longer then we broke up. Tim Rose was then coming back for another tour and he remembered me from the Band Of Joy and offered me the job so I took it. Robert and I lost contact for about two or three*

months. The next time I saw him I was with Tim and he'd joined what was then the Yardbirds. He said they needed a new drummer for the group. About two weeks later he came with Jimmy Page to one of Rose's concerts, saw me playing and then I got offered the job."

Influences? *"Loads of drummers. I dig listening to drummers I know aren't half as good as perhaps I am. I can still listen to them and they still do things I don't do so therefore I can learn something. I like Vanilla Fudge's drummer. I like Frosty with Lee Michaels. I walked into that club last night (Toronto's Penny Farthing) and there was a group (Milkwood) whose drummer was great. He had such a great feel to the numbers. I was very influenced by (Baker) in the early days because when I first started Baker had a big image in England. He was the first rock guy like Gene Krupa. In the big band era a drummer was a backing musician and nothing else. And in the early American bands the drummer played with only brushes in the background. Krupa was the first drummer in a big band to be noticed. You know he came right out in front and he played drums much louder than they were ever played before and much better. Nobody took much interest in drums before that and Baker did the same thing with rock. I don't think anyone can put Baker down. Baker was more into jazz I think. He still is, he plays with a jazz influence. He does a lot of things in 5/4, 3/4. He's always been a very weird sort of bloke. You can't really get to know him he won't allow it."*

Yorke then asks about Ringo, *"The drumming on all the Beatles records is great. The actual patterns are just right for what they're doing. Some of the rhythms on the new album are really far out."*

Bonham is asked how many skins he breaks on a tour, *"None, you can hit a drum hard if you take a short stab at it and the skin will break easily. But if you let the stick just come down it looks as though you're hitting it much harder than I am. I only let it drop with the force of my arm coming down. But I've only lost one skin on this tour. That was a bass drum skin and that was because the beater came off and left the little iron spike there and it went straight through. But that snare skin has been on there for three tours. When the bass skin went we were into the last number "How Many More Times" and Robert was into his vocal thing just before we all come back in. It was a bit of a bummer."*

Asked how he started to play with his hands, *"It goes back a long time to when I first joined Robert. I saw a group years and years ago on a jazz programme do it and I think it impressed me a hell of a lot. It wasn't what you could play with your hands you just get a lovely little tone out of the drums that you don't get with sticks. I thought it would be a good thing to do so I've been doing it ever since."*

He is then asked about his band mates, *"I could talk about Robert for days because I know him so well. I think we were sixteen when we first met, which is six years ago. That's a long time, he knows me off by heart and vice versa. I think that's why we get on so well. I get on well with John, we have our differences now and then. But to me some groups get too close and the slightest thing can upset the whole group. In this group we're just close enough. I get on well with Jimmy. He's very good. He's quite shy in some ways. When I first met him he was very shy. But after 12 months at it we're all getting to know one another. That's why*

the music has improved a lot. I like Jimmy a lot. To me he's a great guitarist in so many fields. He's not just a group guitarist who plugs in and plays an electric guitar. He's got interests in so many kinds of music So many guitarists won't play anything but 12 bar blues and they think that's it." .... **Melody Maker reports....** Article states that Zeppelin have to be accompanied by Armed guards in the Deep South of the USA. It goes on to state that they will return next week to take a month off and begin recording their new album.... **Billboard reports....** Article states that Atlantic records winter sales program racked up $12 million in sales in part due to Led Zeppelin II being a best-seller around the world....

20 **Las Vegas Sun reports....** Rock Concert Never Does Get Rolling.... report of why the show in Vegas was canceled. Apparently people were protesting the price of the tickets when the show was canceled after Plant collapsed on stage in Phoenix the night before, radio promoter Randy Dormio says, *"There wasn't enough time to get a group equivalent to their caliber, so rather than offer an inferior program we canceled it."*....

25 **Record Mirror reports....** LZ II is #3.... **New Musical Express reports....** ASK-IN with a Led Zeppelin a week...fourth of a four week series with Ritchie Yorke interviewing the band members in Toronto.... guitarist Jimmy Page.... Yorke's interview with Page is more general than the previous three.... Page expresses the belief that the band's following comes from the underground club scene and that he is surprised at the band's enormous success. He acknowledges a debt to the American music scene and to band's like Arthur Lee and Love.

On the Doors, *"I was surprised after hearing a lot of advance publicity in England about how sexy Jim M. was. How virile and whatever. I was surprised to see how static he was live on stage. I admire his writing ability and when he gets it together in the studio, but on stage he's not really for me. (Robert and Morrison) are completely different. If you want to relate Robert to a sexual image and a lot of people are doing that he's all those things one would associate with it. He's good looking he's got the virile image he moves well on stage and he looks right and he sings well. As far as I could see the Morrison thing is just an embarrassment towards the audience. He would actually insult them and swear at them and his sexual thing is more of an introvert thing, it isn't so extroverted as Robert's."*

Yorke then raises the subject of the financial rewards that the band is garnering, *"We started off at less than $1,500 a night actually. We played for $200 one day but it was worth it because we didn't care we just wanted to come over and play the music. In England we had such a bad time and bookers were saying 'Led Zeppelin used to be the Yardbirds we'll book them but we'll put them as the New Yardbirds', it was just a joke in England that they wouldn't accept you. They won't accept anything new. In Boston we got $45,000 for one gig which was just incredible. The artistic side can go so far then the managers take over on the business and you start working on percentages above guarantees and it obviously depends on how big the place is."*

Yorke then moves the subject to other guitarists, Beck first, *"I think he's great. When he's having a shining night he's really fantastic. He plays things of sheer genius."*

Clapton? *"He's a very tasteful player I haven't seen him play since John Mayall days. I didn't see Cream or Blind Faith. There's a friend of mine called Joe Walsh who's got a group going around the Cleveland area called the James Gang. I heard them and they were very good. I was really listening to acoustic guitarists like Bert Jansch. He's my all time favourite. I was listening to that more than anything and that's what I play at home a lot. I still listen a lot to Otis Rush and a guy called Matt Murphy, and Buddy Guy of course. I like Johnny Winter's steel playing very much, his bottleneck Robert Johnson things he's got those off to a tee."*

The Beatles? *"They just turn it out don't they? It's always good and always sounds fresh whether it is or it isn't. It's amazing the way their guitar styles come into it."*

Yorke then moves the conversation on to Zeppelin's future directions, *"It sounds corny but we've got something we want to try out but I don't want to tell you about it in case it doesn't come off. It's an idea for a really long track on the next album. In so much as Dazed & Confused and all those things went into sections well we want to try something new with the organ and acoustic guitar building up and building up to the electric thing. It will probably be a fifteen minute track and I'm really looking forward to doing it. I can't really tell you any more about it in case it doesn't work out, but I think it will."* This is obviously a reference to Stairway and it is fascinating in so much as it predates the trip to Bron-y-Aur as well as the release of Led Zeppelin III.... **Melody Maker reports....** Review of Lord Sutch & Heavy Friends by Chris Welch. He begins, "Stand by for Led Zeppelin III! With Jimmy Page and John Bonham thundering away on several

tracks it amounts to a bonus Zeppelin album." Welch calls it a fine set and concludes, "Listen to Bonham and Page, too much!".... Article speculates that Jimmy Page, Eric Clapton and Pete Green may join the James Gang on stage in Newcastle May 23rd.... **Billboard reports....** Zeppelin II 2-mil Seller. Article states that Led Zeppelin's second LP has sold more than two million units in it's first six months of release. It was a gold record before it was released. It is only the second Atlantic-Atco album to sell two million copies along with Iron Butterfly's In- A- Gadda- Da- Vida.... Zeppelin Bests Beatles' Draw. Article claims that Led Zeppelin sold 19,000 tickets in Vancouver at the outset of their latest tour beating the Beatles 1966 show by 2,000 people. It also says it was the biggest show in Vancouver since Elvis Presley in 1957....

May 1970

2 **Record Mirror reports....** LZ II is #6.... LZ I is #27.... **New Musical Express reports....** Led Zeppelin's current tour of the USA is a huge success...the band play 26 shows grossing over $1,200,000.... most shows sold out...20,000 showed up in Los Angeles grossing $71,000 .... 19,000 in Vancouver breaking the Beatles house record.... 18,000 in Montreal.... the band return for another tour in July and August.... Page, *"The third LP will be released in July. It will have more variety than the other two albums, and there'll be more emphasis on acoustic guitar."* Plant, *"And there'll be some nice vocal harmony things."* The band stayed at the hotel in Montreal where Lennon had his famous bed-in with his wife Yoko Ono....

9 **Record Mirror reports....** LZ II is #8.... **Billboard reports....** Zeppelin Sets Forum Record. Article states that Led Zeppelin set a new attendance record at the Montreal Forum on April 13th. 17,500 people paid an astounding $93,000 to see the band. The tour was booked by Barbara Skydell of Premier Talent....

16 **DISC reports....** Led Zeppelin are to debut a new television series.... the show is planned by Granada producer Johnny Hamp, the series comprises six, thirty minute shows. Says Hamp, *"I got the idea from Led Zeppelin, who didn't want to do the usual three minute slot on TV.... most of the names are booked. But I'm still negotiating for Zeppelin."*.... **Record Mirror reports....** LZ II is #11.... **Melody Maker reports....** Cover Story, Fantastic Line Up For Bath Zeppelin, Byrds etc. with details about ticket sales and the venue....

23 **Record Mirror reports....** LZ II is #11.... **New Musical Express reports....** rumours point to Peter Green and Robert Plant jamming with the Grateful Dead.... **Melody Maker reports....** full page advertisement for Bath Festival Of Blues and Progressive Music '70 - Bath and West Showground Shepton Mallet.... Saturday 27th Sunday 28th June....

30 **Record Mirror reports....** LZ II is #12.... **Melody Maker reports....** half page advertisement for Bath Festival Of Blues and Progressive Music '70 - Bath and West Showground Shepton Mallet.... Saturday 27th Sunday 28th June.... Article speculates Led Zeppelin may be splitting up....

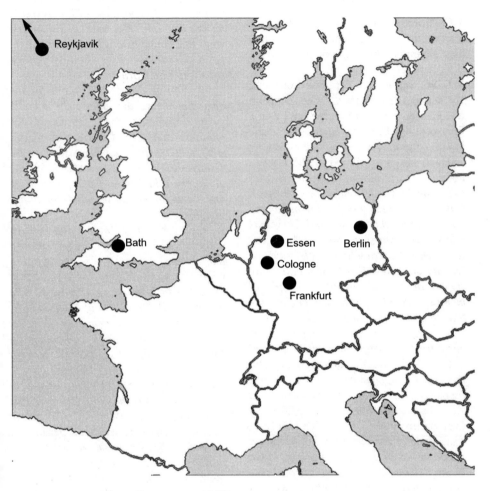

European Tour Summer 1970

June 22nd, 1970 Reykjavik Laugardalsholl Sports Center
June 28th, 1970 Bath Festival
July 16th, 1970 Cologne
July 17th, 1970 Essen Grugahalle
July 18th, 1970 Frankfurt Festhalle
July 19th, 1970 Berlin Deutschlandhalle

June 1970

3 **Cashbox reports....** Cover story.... A brief group biography and a mention that their album is riding high on the charts....

6 **DISC reports....** Zeppelin hour-long TV show.... cover story.... Led Zeppelin will be seen for the first time on TV in a film costing £25,000 financed by the group.... the movie will be one hour long and will be partly filmed in the USA.... Peter Grant, *"I haven't seen the Beatles Let It Be film but from what I've heard it'll be nothing like that. Zeppelin had the idea of doing this before last Christmas and shooting starts in January. A camera team will be traveling with them to Iceland on June 22 and the whole thing should be tied up within a couple of months. I've already had offers for the film from America and I expect it to be shown in Britain by December.... (the rumours of Zeppelin splitting are) absolute rubbish. We have bookings till the end of the summer. I can assure you there's no truth in these stories."....* Zeppelin play Bath festival June 28th and then Berlin Essen and Frankfurt July 9-11.... Grant, *"I'm currently negotiating a couple of concerts at Expo '70 in Japan on July 31 /August 1. Then the group goes back to America for a month."....* **Record Mirror reports....** LZ II is #9.... **Melody Maker reports....** Cover Story.... an interview with John Bonham at Olympic studios while recording the third album.... Bonham, *"I've got this pain in my palms and hands, I can't hold anything tight. We've got a lot of recording to do, so I'll have to see a doctor. It could be anything— and I'm getting it in the chest as well.*

"We'll be recording for the next two weeks and doing a lot of acoustic things as well as the heavy stuff. There will be better quality songs than on the first albums. I'm not sure if I'll play a solo on the new one. I've been practicing on vibes and conga drums lately, and I might do a percussion thing. Ordinary drum solos get a bit worn out.

"I've done three tracks for the next album and the vibes help a lot in writing. When I started playing I was about 15 and started to learn to read. I wish I had kept it up because it helps. Jimmy showed me a few chords on the guitar the other night. I just picked it up and started to get all these rhythm things going.

"We all see quite a lot of each other when we are not working, more so than before. We overdid working for a while and we were supposed to go back to the States in July, but we've put it back to August. We did five tours of America in 15 months. We are slackening off the pressure slightly so we can work more in England. We played six nights a week for a month and I was doing a long drum solo every night. My hands were covered in blisters. It's funny thinking back. Our first tour was terrible. We played for eleven weeks — anywhere we could get in. But we were lucky. We had an album out and that's what helped it sell. There's nothing more ridiculous than doing a tour with no album to promote. In Vancouver we broke records. The whole of the last tour was a sell-out. We had an incredible experience at Montreal when 18,000 people lit candles and held them up as peace signs. It looked fantastic and brought a tear to your eye.

"The band just goes from strength to strength. I keep thinking we're going to wake up one morning and find it's all over. Sure we've had criticism. It always happens. When we first came up, we were called a second Cream, but now

you see they call some new groups 'A second Zeppelin.' We've had a few snide things too — that we haven't appeared here enough, But there aren't many bands who work three hours a night as often as us. And we'll be around for a bit longer. We're not breaking up yet. We just keep battling on. We want to keep a good working average. I can't say how long it will last. But we'll go on as long as we can. It's a funny thing to say—but when I first joined the group I didn't know Jimmy and I felt a bit shy. He was the big star and had been around for ages with the session thing and the Yardbirds. But now the group is better than ever. And there is such a lot of scope for all of us."...

Robert Plant is asked about the upcoming election in the UK, *"Everybody should forget the election. Every aspect of the whole thing is centered on what the local candidate can do to get into parliament, he's hustling to get his seat. After they've got in so few of them uphold the promises they made prior to the election. Quite a lot of independent candidates have good ideas because they don't follow any party policy. The parties are really one of the worst things about the system, because the MPs seem to do whatever their masters tell them. It's not a people's election anymore. Until it is I say forget it."...*

13 **DISC** reports.... Zeppelin Turn Down US In Favour Of Bath.... cover story ...Zeppelin turned down an offer of 200,000 dollars for two US gigs (Boston and Yale) in preference of the Bath Festival.... Plant is renovating his farmhouse in Worcestershire.... Joe Wright former roadie for the Yardbirds is forming his own band Joe Jammer, Grant, *"Joe has been around a long time and was a general helper on tours. He got the nick-*

name Joe Jammer because he always ended up jamming with the groups. About six months ago he asked me if I could help him get to Britain and now he has formed his own group."*.... Why Bob Plant Needs The Soil.... interview with Robert Plant on his farm in Worcestershire and shopping in Carnaby Street where he attempts to buy a shirt with a check and even though the store manager recognises him and even pulls out a copy of Led Zeppelin II she won't take a check from him without ID, at which point Plant tears up the check and leaves .... Plant, *"I would go mad* (if he had to live in London), *I'd have to be the big star, or else I'd go to clubs every night and never see the sun."*

At this point he is still recovering from a car accident *and* bruised ribs due to his Aston Martin falling on his chest while he was working under it. Plant, *"The worst thing in the world is to rush. Being on the road has taught me that. All you want to do is sit back and take it easy. The farm calms me down anyway. It's got to be there. When I'm away on-stage I'm so into it that if I didn't have the farm I'd go mad. The farm is the other end of the scale for me."* Plant apparently works the farm himself he has tilled several acres and is in the process of renovating the main building. *"The local people have given me a lot of help and advice. The farmer next door came by the other day when I was digging furrows for potatoes, 'Morning Master Robert' he said, 'Digging tunnels for Turks then.' Apparently I was digging them much too deep.*

"You just pick up knowledge as you go along. Going to college I suppose is a help, but I think it's a bit like going to Grammar school to do French and then going to France. Agricultural college must be a bit like that.

123

"It's a really lazy feeling down at the farm. You pull up into the drive and there's a jeep parked half way up the bank and an Aston Martin covered in filth. Most people say 'Wow, an Aston Martin' but I never ever clean it. I could never give up singing and just do the farm full stop though. It has to be the balance for singing. I know there are rumours going round of Zeppelin breaking up but it's nonsense. I've always got to sing. Even when I go bald I'll go on singing. And it's the same with everyone in the band. there's such an intensity and there's so much happening, we're writing such incredible new things.

"It's stupid. I can't think who puts around such a rumour. And I've heard it started because people thought we'd made enough money to call it a day. That's ridiculous, I've enough money to buy two stately homes and six Rolls Royces, but I couldn't give up singing."

Page has been staying with Robert for the last few weeks since they took Jimmy's girlfriend Charlotte, Plant's wife Maureen and their daughter Carmen and dog Strider up to a cottage in North Wales to write new songs. Two roadies went along to chop wood. P&P went off to a Waterfall to write. Plant, *"I hope people who bought the records in the past will say 'great' they're going into new things. I'm trying new ways of singing. I've always been wary in the past but I'm trying straight singing. We're so close as a band now that if I sing in a certain manner the guitar will be in sympathy and then something will come along and the mood will change and you pick up on that."*

The band's upcoming appearance at Bath will be filmed and cut together with the Albert Hall footage so the songs will suddenly go from one venue to the other.... Plant, *"Bath is going to be my big thing this year. So many people together can be really wonderful. The festival feeling is something you really need, we all need it. I really hope there's no hassle so everyone enjoys themselves."*

Plant doesn't socialise much with the industry types, *"I'd hate it if lots of groups kept coming around, because they'd expect me to try and do things for them, and that's really not my scene."* His daughter is 19 months old, *"I'm quite paternal, I didn't really see her grow up at the beginning so I like to cling to her more now. But she's a bit towards her mother which is understandable I suppose."*

The band had just screened the Albert Hall footage, *"It was really funny, the expressions with me muttering between numbers, and the terrible faces we made if there was a wrong note. We were roaring with laughter, if that's a representation of us then it's the best I've seen. The film was the idea of all of us really. Nobody wanted to do telly appearances. I suppose in the end it will be about an hour and a half of film and it should be quite good."*

Despite collapsing at the end of the last US tour he denies he'll quit, *"I just don't worry about my voice ever giving out or anything. True it did at the end of that tour but we did 27 gigs. It's all psychological. If you worry it goes, if you don't it's fine."*.... **Record Mirror reports....** LZ II is #12.... **New Musical Express reports....** Led Zeppelin II is now #1 in Germany.... a general report of the band's progress. It gives the original planned starting date for their American tour. This was later delayed. The big hoopla made in the press about the band turning down Yale in favour of Bath was misguided as the band obviously just did

the date later. "Led Zeppelin will play here in Autumn...the band first play another tour of the USA opening on August 5th and playing through to a conclusion in New York on September 19th.... the band were recently offered $200,000 to play in concert at the Yale Bowl in the USA, they have declined in favour of playing the Bath festival on June 28th.... the new album will be out soon and is currently titled 'Led Zeppelin'.... a film of the band on tour is being prepared for release, it features footage from their last American tour as well as the show last January at the Royal Albert Hall."....
Melody Maker reports.... Article states Led Zeppelin have turned down $200,000 for two gigs in the USA on June 27th and 29th to keep their commitment to play the Bath festival....

20 **Record Mirror reports....** LZ II is #18.... **Melody Maker reports....** Members of Led Zeppelin were spotted at Eric Clapton's gig at the Lyceum....

21 **Reykjavik Morgunbladid reports....** Article welcoming Led Zeppelin to Iceland. The article shows a picture of the band and a picture of a huge queue around the Laugardalsholl Sports Center waiting to buy tickets....

23 **Reykjavik Morgunbladid reports....** Review of the show in Reykjavik says that over 5,000 people were in attendance....

27 **DISC reports....** Me and My Music by John Bonham.... *"I've wanted to be a drummer since I was about five. I used to use a bath salts container with wires on the bottom and a round toffee tin with a loose wire on it to give it a snare drum effect. And there was always my mum's pots and pans. She bought me a snare*

á slóðum œskunnar

Heimsókn Led Zeppelin

drum when I was ten. It's like it's always been there. You can look back and associate things like that and see that it was always there.

"When I was sixteen I joined my first group, you'll die at the name, Terry Webb and the Spiders. We used to wear purple jackets with velvet lapels. The singer wore a gold lamé jacket and we had greased hair and string ties. That was six years ago.

"It lasted about a year. Then I joined a group called A Way Of Life. I got married, most of the others got married and it broke up. Next I joined a group with Robert called the Crawling King Snakes. I happened to meet him and he needed a drummer. We played around a bit then I went back to A Way Of Life.

"I also played a couple of weeks with Steve Brett and the Mavericks. Dave

Holland was in that group and he's with Miles Davies now. Strange things happen in this business...

"Then I went back to work hod carrying. I did that sort of thing to make money to buy new equipment.

"My first real break was backing Tim Rose. Soon after that the Yardbirds split and Jimmy Page and John Paul Jones were thinking of forming a new group. They needed a drummer and Robert remembered me and he and Jimmy came along to see me with Tim Rose at the Hampstead Country Club. That was in the summer of 1968 and in October I was on a Scandinavian tour with Led Zeppelin.

"I never had any lessons. When I first started playing I used to read. I was very interested in music. But when I started playing in groups I did a silly thing and dropped it. It's great if you can write things down.

"I've always been obsessed with drums. They fascinate me. Any other instrument, nothing. But drums! I play acoustic guitar a bit. But it's always been drums first and foremost. I don't reckon on this jack-of-all-trades thing.

"I had my first full drum kit when I was 15½. My Dad bought it. It was almost prehistoric. Most of it was rust. Now I've got Ludwig. I really look after my drums. People who don't annoy me. A guitarist always looks after his guitar and drums should have the same respect.

"I decided I was going to try to be a drummer as soon as I left school. I was very determined. It really started to happen when I was with Tim Rose. I was doing OK, and I was getting offers. Joe Cocker was interested, so was Chris Farlowe, and Robert and Jimmy. It was baffling. I had to consider so much. It wasn't just a question of who had the best prospects but which was going to be the right kind of stuff.

"Farlowe was fairly established and I knew Cocker was going to make it. But I already knew what Robert liked and I knew what Jimmy was into and I decided I liked their sort of music better. And it paid off. It's absolutely marvelous.

"I just thought that playing the stuff I liked was the best idea. And I'm still happy because we're doing different things all the time. I don't consider that I'm particularly influenced by anyone or anything. But when I started playing I was influenced by early Soul. It was just that feel, that sound. And I said to myself, 'I'll get that sound.' I like drums to be big and powerful. I've never used cymbals much. I crash into a solo and crash out with them. I like the sound of drums. They sound better than cymbals.

"That's why I play with my hands. You get the absolutely true sound, there's no wood involved. It hurts at first but the skin hardens and now I can hit a drum harder with my hands than with sticks. I was always breaking heads when I started playing. Now I hardly ever break any. I don't hit them so hard, but I play much louder. It's all to do with the swing. You get much better tone with a big stroke than you do with a short stab.

"I think that feeling is a lot more important than technique. It's all very well doing a triple paradiddle, but who's going to know you've done it. And if you play technically you sound like everyone else. It's being original that counts. When I listen to drummers I like to be able to say, 'Oh! I haven't heard that before.' Being yourself is so much better than sounding like anyone else. Ginger Baker's thing is that he is himself. So it's no good trying to do what he does. It's just the same as Clapton.

"I yell out when I'm playing. I

yell like a bear to give it a boost. I like it to be like a thunderstorm. My ambition is to record the 1812 Overture. I would overdub all the rhythm sections, the bells, cannons and tymps. I'll do it one day.

"My son Jason, he plays, you know. I've got him a little Japanese drum kit, made to scale. It's got a 14" bass drum.

"He's got his mother's looks but in character he's just like me. He's always drumming. Even when we go out in the car he takes his sticks to bash on the seats. he hasn't got much technique but he's got a great sense of time. Before the end of Led Zeppelin I'm going to have him on stage with us at the Albert Hall."....

Record Mirror reports.... Long Hair Almost Got Us Shot!.... Interview with John Bonham, *"It's incredible the stuff that gets started here while we're not around. I pick up one of the music papers and read how we're due to break up or how we're going to stay and live in the States. All of this is untrue and also very annoying. The press chaps pick on a comment and it's around the whole country in a week, building up into full scale stories. We're working like fiends and there isn't ever an argument that could threaten to break us up.*

"We could go to the States and stay there six months, playing at our leisure, but instead, we stay on the road all the time, working 28 out of 30 days so we can get back home. Although I'm not really bitter, America gave us our chance. When we formed, we couldn't get a gig here worth playing. America wanted us because Jimmy came from the Yardbirds so we went there. We just had to try harder here, but this is home and it's more important to do well in your own country. In the very early days, I suppose we did

lose faith in England. After all that rehearsing, it was disarming to find you couldn't get a gig. It was the Fillmores in America that made us and the kids have been great ever since. The trouble is with the adults-the older people. Some of those scenes in 'Easy Rider'were true, but overdone. Some were true just as they were. The restaurant scene is very true in the southern parts. We've gone in for a coffee and watched everybody else in the place served as they go in and out, but no one served us. Everybody sits and looks at you, just waiting for you to explode.

"We even had a gun pulled on us in Texas. There was a guy shouting and giving us general feedback about our hair etc., so we just gave it back to him. Later after the show, we were leaving when the same guy turned up at the door. He pulled this pistol on us and said "You gonna do any shouting now?" We cleared out of there toute de suite. There's going to be a real revolution over there with the kids in an army against their parents. They just don't understand one another at all. You either find them totally for you or totally against you; never an in between, that kind of thing could never happen here. Fortunately, we don't encounter much trouble from audiences while we're on stage and if it does occur, Robert is very good at cooling them down. I know there is a lot of trouble on the outside, but when you walk into a gig, it's a whole different world. Even if you feel terrible and don't want to go on, as soon as you get on stage, everything is changed; you feel great. It works for the people watching too. We've played places where you could sense the resentment from the kids towards the armed police, but by the end of the act, the cops had put down their batons and were clapping along with everyone else. At one gig, the entire

18,000 strong audience had individual candles which they all held up at once. It was a grand sight.

"By and large, we don't play enough here, but we're out to alter that. It's so good to get home, we're going to start playing a lot more here."....

New Musical Express reports .... cover story.... Happier than ever says Zep's John Bonzo Bonham.... interview by Roy Carr with John Bonham about the band's future and the splitting up rumours.... Bonham, "I want to say here and now that it's all utter rubbish, we're all happier now than we have ever been. And I want everyone to know it. At the moment the four of us are enjoying making our third album and taking it easy at home in between sessions.

"On this album people are going to listen to each one of us. We are all writing so much better than before, and there will be much more inventiveness from the group as a whole. This time we are also doing some acoustic tracks apart from the familiar heavier stuff. At the moment we've got ten good tracks laid down, and we have yet to do a couple more. If they turn out OK then we'll stick em on the album. The way things are going it looks as though it's going to be a long one. But again it's only going to be a single album. We are not going to do the expected double album thing simply because most of these are just padded out with studio left overs. On the Zeppelin's albums we only include what we all consider to be our very best material."

Carr then shifts the topic of conversation to Lord Sutch and Bonham's appearance on his album, "Sutch is a great bloke but he used our friendship to sell his album. It started out in the middle of last year in Los Angeles. We were in this club enjoying ourselves and so was Dave Sutch. Well he came over to the table and we started talking about oldtimes. During the course of the conversation Sutch mentions how he's been in the business for years but never had the chance to cut an album. He then asked Jimmy and myself if we would do a few backing tracks for him. But on the complete understanding that under no circumstances would he mention our names. As we had a couple of days to spare we agreed. But it now seems as though he really took us in, so we did it purely as backing musicians and old friends NOT as Zeppelin. When we arrived at the studio he said he mainly wanted to do souped up versions of rock standards. So we said OK that sounds fine. What we didn't know was when Sutch came to dub on the vocals in our absence he had re-written entirely different lyrics so that 'Lucille' became 'Thumping Beat' and Roy Head's 'Treat Her Right' became 'Baby Come Back'. You've only got to play the album to spot where the other songs originated from. We didn't even notice that photographs were being taken during the sessions. Everyone did that album as a favour to Sutch and didn't want any credit. But as it turns out he deliberately used all the people's names to sell the album. So you can believe how amazed we all were when we saw our names in bold type all over the cover."

On the subject of the new Zeppelin movie, "It will probably be an hour long semi-documentary and will include footage from the Royal Albert Hall concert. One of the highlights of the film will be a sequence featuring my 4 year old son Jason playing his drums. He's got a completely scaled down replica of my kit and believe me he can play them. To put a complete end to the break-up rumours. Anyone who goes to Bath *will see and hear Led Zeppelin play as they've never heard us play before. We are really looking forward to that gig. In fact we are quite excited. It's going to be a fantastic day I can assure you."....*

July 1970

4 **DISC reports....** Hells Angels, delays, traffic chaos.... and a giant success.... article reviewing the Bath Festival.... Zeppelin manager Peter Grant disturbed at the lengthening delays, said on Saturday that he'd told the group to start out about 6 pm on Sunday. They were due on stage at 8 pm. A hasty phone call altered all that. And eventually John Paul Jones, his wife and child accompanied by Julie Felix and boyfriend arrived by helicopter and were collected from a nearby field by a Hell's Angels motorcycle cavalcade.... By Saturday sundown the audience stretching as far as the eye could see across the enormous field was around 150,000 strong. Sunday lunch time the figure had soared sensationally and when Led Zeppelin finally clambered aboard the stage, estimates reckoned around a crowd of about a quarter million.... Led Zeppelin surprisingly owned up to "butterflies" before their spot. Said John Bonham, *"I always feel uneasy particularly on British gigs like this."* He needn't have worried, despite the list of American attractions, it was Zeppelin that sold the date. The crowd just wouldn't let them leave the stage! Zeppelin even agreed to line-up for a rare group photo session and afterwards spent an amusing few minutes astride handy motorcycle track bikes. The Bath Festival and the music which created it will never be forgotten by those who attended. Without a doubt the clearest fact

to emerge was predictably that Led Zeppelin had more fans there than anyone else. Would the crowd have been so big if they hadn't been on? As soon as Zeppelin ripped into their first number the living field of people exploded. Zeppelin immediately seemed to be in top gear. But then they don't use any lower ones.... (the band) were on stage for nearly two hours. And long before the end they were in overdrive. The pitch of excitement they achieved was frightening. They did four encores but they could have played all week and most people would have stayed. The rock classics they threw in "Whole Lotta Love" "Long Tall Sally" among them might have little to do with a Blues and Progressive festival if you cared about definitions. But nobody did! The sounds that filled the Somerset air from Zeppelin's instruments, the guitars of Page and Jones, Bonham's thunderous drums and Robert Plant's voice blasted more people than any other group could have done. Zeppelin brought the festival to a peak.... Country Joe announces he is seeking out Jimmy Page to be a backing musician for his upcoming UK tour.... in answer to a letter to the editor John Bonham's education is listed as Lodge Farm County Secondary School and an agricultural school.... Zeppelin Tour.... Led Zeppelin hit of last weekend's Bath Festival leave for their next American Tour on August 6. Group tours States for four weeks, takes an 11 day holiday in Hawaii before returning to New York for two concerts at the famous Madison Square Gardens for which they are expected to gross £40,000.... **Record Mirror reports....** Led Zeppelin will receive over £30,000 for an appearance at Madison Square Gardens in New York late September. The band embarks on a tour which will include Cincinnati on

August 6th, Quebec, Atlanta, New Orleans, South Carolina, Boston, New Haven, New Mexico, San Antonio, Fort Worth, Tulsa, Winnipeg, Detroit. Then in September Seattle, Oakland, San Diego, Los Angeles and Hawaii after which they will take an eleven day holiday.... LZ II is #9.... **Melody Maker reports....** Five Encores For Zeppelin, cover story with picture of Zep on stage at the Bath Festival...Led Zeppelin stormed to huge success at the Bath Festival, about 150,000 fans rose to give them an ovation. Plant, *"We've been away a lot in America and we thought it might be a bit dodgy coming back. It's great to be home!"*...Zep play over three hours with five encores.... set included Immigration Song (sic), Since I've Been Loving You, The First Time, How Many More Times, Communication Breakdown and a medley of songs by Little Richard, Elvis Presley and Chuck Berry.... **New Musical Express reports....** Led Zeppelin will be playing the States again starting in Cincinnati on August 6th. The tour includes Canada and Hawaii where the band will take an eleven day holiday.... they are currently finishing their third album.... Julie Felix danced on stage with Led Zeppelin at their performance at the Bath festival.... Roy Carr interviews Robert Plant about his new found sex symbol status.... Plant, *"You know someone actually called me a sexual beacon. Now if you see a groovy little chick shake it one time for you that's cool! All music has a certain sexuality. Even Neil Young's coolness can turn you on. It's just a matter of approach. But let's face it it takes two to tango!"*

The conversation then turns to cars, *"We were all rehearsing for the new album at my farm in Worcestershire when one evening we decided to go boozing.*

Around closing time we became so hungry that we all decided to go to Bonzo's place and scoff all his grub. Bonzo was in his Jensen which was parked in my yard. It ended up with me having to tow him off with the Jeep. I think I'm going to get him a Centurion tank. He's had so much bad luck that I'll have to set up an army surplus dump for him."

Finally they talk about the new album, *"It will prove something of a change from the two previous ones. We are even using different instruments on some tracks. John Paul plays mandolin and Jimmy is on dulcimer. It'll be acoustic as well as electric with the emphasis on everyone in the group."* .... **New York Times reports....** Advert reads — Led Zeppelin Madison Square Garden Saturday Sept 19 2.00 and 8.00 pm Tickets $4.50 $5.50 $6.50 $7.50. Available at the Madison Square Garden Box Office seven days a week. Mail orders promptly filled. Make check payable to Madison Square Garden Center. Mail to Led Zeppelin Ticket dept., MSG Center, 4 Penn Plaza, NYC, 10001....

11 **Record Mirror reports....** LZ II is #13.... **New Musical Express reports....** rumours of the Who changing their name to Leeds Zeppelin have been squashed....

18 **DISC reports....** Festivals Fun or Fiasco...interview with John Bonham about Bath and other festivals.... Bonham, *"The atmosphere was fantastic really when you consider it was cold and windy. And even when it rained they sat through it and could still be happy.*

"I don't think you could get an atmosphere like that at a concert. But I do agree that at a lot of festivals they try to put on too many acts—because they don't

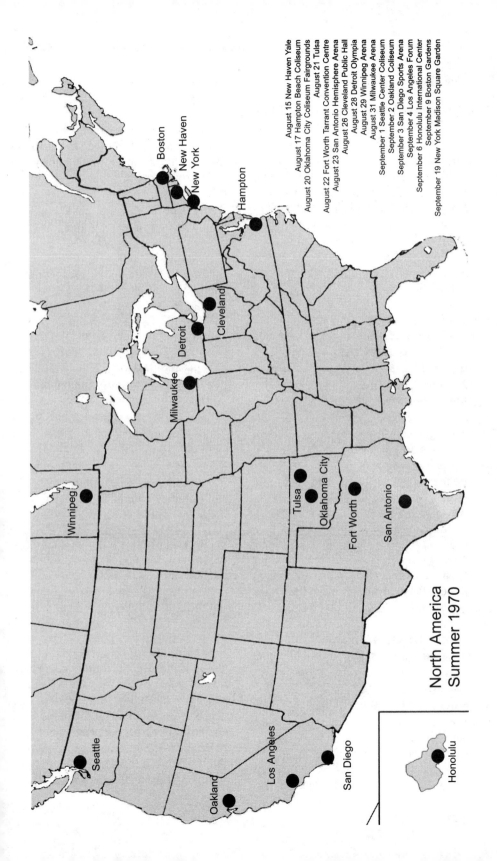

North America
Summer 1970

August 15 New Haven Yale
August 17 Hampton Beach Coliseum
August 20 Oklahoma City Coliseum Fairgrounds
August 21 Tulsa
August 22 Fort Worth Tarrant Convention Centre
August 23 San Antonio Hemisphere Arena
August 26 Cleveland Public Hall
August 28 Detroit Olympia
August 29 Winnipeg Arena
August 31 Milwaukee Arena
September 1 Seattle Center Coliseum
September 2 Oakland Coliseum
September 3 San Diego Sports Arena
September 4 Los Angeles Forum
September 6 Honolulu International Center
September 9 Boston Gardens
September 19 New York Madison Square Garden

Boston
New Haven
New York
Hampton
Cleveland
Detroit
Milwaukee
Winnipeg
Tulsa
Oklahoma City
Fort Worth
San Antonio
Seattle
Oakland
Los Angeles
San Diego
Honolulu

allow for any difficulties.
    "No, I can't see festivals replacing concert tours. The last tour we did did very well. We sold out everywhere we played —but then we did it on our own. It was just "An Evening With Led Zeppelin;" and this gives you terrific scope and you can do everything you really want to do in a concert.
    "As far as fees go—it depends what you call large sums of money. Somebody's going to make the money somewhere— and if we don't get it it's going to go into the promoter's pocket. I don't think we charge large sums of money. We just charge a fair price for concerts. We don't want to rob the fans!".... **Record Mirror reports....** LZ II is # 12.... **Melody Maker reports....** Zeppelin Split Denied.... article states that John Bonham was rumoured to be leaving Zep but the band's agents at RAK deny this vigorously. A spokesman said, *"Last week it was Robert Plant. In fact the relationship could not be better."* Apparently Bonham has bought a new house in Hagley. Bonham's wife Pat commented, *"There have been no disagreements, really. If there was anything in it, he would have told me."....* **Billboard reports....** Canada Rock Fest Aug 7 - 9. Led Zeppelin will be appearing at an outdoor festival in New Brunswick along with many other top name bands....

25 **Record Mirror reports....** LZ II is #7.... **Melody Maker reports....** Led Zeppelin in Germany...large feature article reviewing the band's tour of Europe...Chris Welch noted journalist tours from Cologne to Frankfurt with the band ...After a bumpy flight to Dusseldorf on the Thursday.... Bonham is ill...the band play well to an audience of around 4,000 while 1,000 people demand free

admission and riot when they weren't allowed in.... Plant, *"The kids don't come for trouble surely?"....* Friday, Page and Grant go in search of antiques the band then play that night at the Grugahalle in Essen.... the audience are so noisy the band give up on the acoustic set, Page, *"Christians to the lions"...*Bonham, *"noisy load of buggers."....* Plant, *"We have a problem if you are going to make this much noise we might as well go away - so shut up!"...*bottles fly at the stage.... Bonham's drum solo is 'staggering'.... Saturday they play to 11,000 at the Festival in Frankfurt...Welch joins them on stage to play timbales during Whole Lotta Love.... Sunday the band move on to the Deutschelandhalle in Berlin.... they visit the Berlin Wall.... Page is sick but still plays well...Grant is kept busy busting bootleggers.... **Billboard reports....** Article states that the Toronto Peace Festival has been canceled. It then goes on to say that a Festival will take place in New Brunswick called 'Strawberry Fields' between August 7th and 9th and will feature Led Zeppelin on the 8th. The site is 767 miles from New York City!....

Music Life reports.... Reprint of Chris Welch's Melody Maker interviews with Jimmy Page but in Japanese....

August 1970

1 **Record Mirror reports....** LZ II is #9.... **Winnipeg Tribune reports....** Advert reads — Sat Aug 29 Winnipeg Stadium 12:00 noon to 11:00 PM Led Zeppelin Iron Butterfly, Youngbloods, Euphoria etc. $5.50 per person until Aug 14 and then $6.50 Come Un Come All....

4 **Honolulu Advertiser reports....** Good

news for rock fans Led Zeppelin is calendared for Sept 6. (yes on the eve of Labor Day) at the Honolulu International Center Arena. 'Twill be a K-POI presentation....

5 The Winnipeg Tribune reports.... Zeppelin heads Man Pop Festival.... Tickets are on sale for "Man Pop the Centennial pop festival to be held on August 29 at the Winnipeg Stadium.... Tickets will be available at $6.50 each. Led Zeppelin will headline an all-star cast of musical talent.... featured along with Led Zeppelin will be Iron Butterfly, The Youngbloods, The Ides of March, and the Canadian group Chilliwack...the festival will begin at 12.00 noon and run until 11.00 pm....

6 The Village Voice reports.... Advert reads — Concerts East Presents Led Zeppelin. By themselves for a special two and a half hour concert. Saturday September 19 at 2.00 pm and 8.00 pm. Madison Square Garden. Tickets $4.50, 5.50, 6.50 and 7.50. Box office opens August 8....Advert reads — First Annual Boston College Eagle Rock Festival Friday August 14 Boston College Stadium 10.30 AM to Midnight. Led Zeppelin two hour performance. (Zep did not play this date)....

8 Record Mirror reports.... LZ II is # 7.... **Melody Maker reports....** Page Off To Finish Zeppelin III.... third album report, "Jimmy Page goes off to New York the beginning of next week to do the final mixes on the new Led Zeppelin album entitled Led Zeppelin Three. Seventeen tracks have been recorded and of these eight or nine will be selected and included. Their manager Peter Grant, told the MM that the LP will be entirely different to their past recordings. The group begins

a four week American tour this Friday, August 14, and it is possible they will do two-week trips to Japan and Australia just before Christmas.".... **New Musical Express reports....** Led Zeppelin will be doing a show in California....

11 Boston After Dark reports.... Music.... the Boston College Eagle Rock Festival on August 14th. An all day affair, it will feature Led Zeppelin, Lighthouse, The Allman Brothers, The Stooges, The MC5, Catfish, Big Brother & The Holding Company, The Amboy Dukes, The American Dream, and perhaps most important of all Junior Wells and Buddy Guy....

15 Record Mirror reports.... LZ II is #8.... **New Musical Express reports....** Zeppelin their next American Tour.... tour details, "Led Zeppelin fly to the States on Sunday and on Monday night open at Hampton Beach Virginia. They stay in America until September 20 and during that time will play the Madison Square Gardens on Sept 19. The group have completed tracks for their forthcoming Led Zeppelin 3 album and will mix and complete it in the States. In December they undertake a tour of Japan and Australia.".....

17 Honolulu Advertiser reports.... Rock fans had better get down to the HIC box office today because tickets go on sale for what should be the show of the year - Led Zeppelin. In two shows September 6. 7 and 10.30. Tickets are quite reasonable compared with their current mainland tour with tickets going for $5....

18 Boston After Dark reports.... The Eagle Rocked.... article detailing the cancellation of the Eagle Rock Pop

The Cleveland Press Tuesday August 25th 1970.

TIME CHANGE — Due to a death in the family of one of the stars, the Led Zeppelin concert — originally scheduled for 8:30 tomorrow night in Public Hall — has been changed to 5:30 p.m. tomorrow in Public Hall. If this new time is inconvenient for advance ticket holders, they can get refunds before 3 p.m. tomorrow from the locations where they purchased the tickets. Tickets at the door will be $6.50. The Led Zeppelin will fly to England immediately after the show for the funeral in the family of John Paul Jones.

Festival...On June 30th Boston College requested a permit to hold the festival which was to include Led Zeppelin and eleven other groups.... the mayor's office signed the permit but it had to be counter-signed by the police. The police requested an additional 67 officers be on site as well as the BC security force and 150 student marshals. Plans were running smoothly until August 10th when the mayor's office asked BC to move Led Zeppelin's perfor-mance to earlier in the day.... a group of influential home owners had been lobby-ing the mayor's office since the date was announced, and they had the support of the police department who were also ner-vous since a fatal shooting of a 14 year old boy...the mayor finally relented to the voice of the power elite and canceled the permit. BC then tried to secure Suffolk Downs or Harvard Stadium but was turned down by both. But on Sept 8. Led Zeppelin will appear at Boston Garden for Eagle Rock ticket holders and there will be an early show for those without tick-ets....

21 **The Los Angeles Free Press reports....** Half page advert reads — An Evening With Led Zeppelin At The Forum. Friday, September 4, 8:30 PM. Tickets $7.25, $6.25, $5.25, $4.25 Available at Forum Box Office....

22 **Record Mirror reports....** LZ II is #12.... **Billboard reports....** Led Zeppelin will return to Hawaii on September 6th courtesy of KPOI radio to play the Honolulu Civic....

25 **Cleveland Press reports....** Advert reads — Time Change. Due to a death in the family of one of the stars, the Led Zeppelin concert, originally scheduled for 8.30 tomorrow night in Public Hall, has been changed to 5.30 pm tomorrow in Public Hall. If this new time is inconve-nient for advance ticket holders, they can get refunds before 3 pm tomorrow from the locations where they purchased the tickets. Tickets at the door will be $6.50. The Led Zeppelin will fly to England immediately after the show for the funer-al in the family of John Paul Jones....

27 **Cleveland Press reports....** Review of the show — Zeppelin Thrills 7500 at hall — Dick Wootten reports, "A group like Led Zeppelin makes you realise that music is not something static. It's ever changing and ever developing. The Zeppelin floats into some pretty bizarre territory but the trip there is interesting just the same."....

28 **Detroit Free Press reports....** Advert reads — The Led Zeppelin Britain's out-standing Rock Group, appears in concert tonight at the Olympia at 8 pm. Tickets cost $4.50, $5.50, and $6.50 and can be purchased at Hudsons or Olympia.... **The Milwaukee Journal reports....** Due to a death in the family the Led Zeppelin con-cert has been postponed to Monday August 31st.... tickets on sale now at Arena ticket office and all Milwaukee area Sears stores. Concert time 8PM.... **The Winnipeg Tribune reports....** At least 12,000 people will attend Man Pop from advance sales.... featuring one of the biggest groups in the world today Led Zeppelin, The Centennial Corporation has budgeted $130,000 for the show and about $80,000 is for the entertainment. The Led Zeppelin cost $50,000, by far the biggest chunk of the performance bill.... **Los Angeles Free Press reports....** Advert reads — An Evening With Led Zeppelin at the Forum Friday September 4 8:30 pm Tickets $7.25, $6.25, $5.25,

The Led Zepplin, Britain's outstanding rock group, appears in concert tonight at the Olympia.

Music

DETROIT SYMPHONY ORCHESTRA—Valter Poole conducts Fri., and Sat., at 8:30 p.m., from the steps of the R a c k h a m Memorial Bldg., Farnsworth at Woodward. Saturday nostalgically marks the final performance of the symphony under Mr. P o o l e 's direction. Free.

OLYMPIA STADIUM—Led Zepplin plays their million dollar m u s i c at 8 p.m. Fri. Tickets cost $4.50, $5.50 and $6.50 and can be purchased at Hudsons or Olympia.

$4.25 Available at Forum Box Office Ticketron Outlets and all Mutual Agencies. Stop by your neighbourhood Thom McAn Shoe Store and register for free tickets for the Led Zeppelin concert....

29 **Record Mirror reports....** LZ II is #9....

30 **Honolulu Advertiser reports....** two shows next Sunday.... Led Zeppelin, a rock group featuring Jimmy Page, Robert Plant, John Paul Jones and John Bonham, will present two shows next Sunday at 7 and 10.30 pm at the Honolulu International Civic Arena, Tickets for the concert, at $6, $5, $4 and $3 are on sale....

31 **The Winnipeg Tribune reports....** Weird, wet wonderful and wild. That was the Man-Pop 70, a triumph for hardy Winnipeg youth.... The stadium had a picnic like atmosphere in the warm 70 degree temperatures Saturday morning.... then as the sky began to turn grey and a cool wind began to blow the crowd began to don sweaters and coats...sprinklings of rain fell until about 5 pm when the skies opened up... Centennial chairman Maitland Steinkopf finally came out at about 7 pm to announce that everything was being adjourned to the arena. The rain at that time was coming down in torrents.... the only problems occurred at about 8 pm when the doors to the arena were shut leaving hundreds of ticket holders stranded outside.... the final performers, Led Zeppelin drew as much enthusiasm as the first, and finally as the last burst of music faded away the weary music lovers faded away into the night....

Beat Instrumental reports.... Cover story. Article chronicling the band's

career to date including a small interview with John Bonham. The interview took place in London and the interviewer found Bonham to be 'open, likable and uninhibited, unaffected by the burden of superstardom'. The first question is how does he feel about selling so many records? *"Great! Led Zeppelin was the first time I ever made money from playing. Before that I used to play in a group called Robert Plant & The Band Of Joy, and I also backed Tim Rose when he was over here. I've been playing about four years now, I used to borrow from my Mum and Dad and do labouring sometimes to make a living. You just have to keep your morale up and hope when you're in that position."*

Apparently Bonham had recently bought a Rolls Royce car and had fulfilled one ambition, to play at Carnegie Hall, *"When you start playing you have things you want to reach, but by the time you've done them the thrill is gone. Once you pass that stage you're back into*

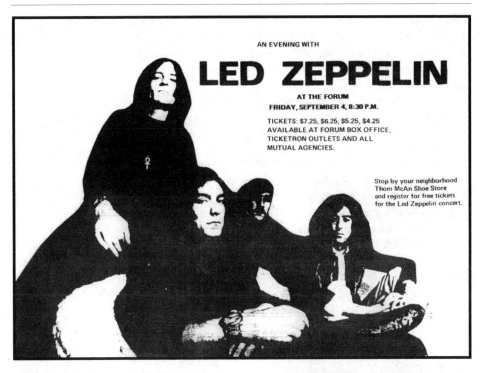

music, it's what you start from and what you get back into.

"The album is nothing without you playing to promote it. The people had a product they could go and see performed on stage, and then go and buy the next day in the record shop. Supergroups and that are getting out of hand, with all the breakups and so on. There's an audience, and you can't go on stage and play for yourself, not when you're charging admission."

Bonham talks about the rigours of touring, "Anything to do with the hotel part of touring I don't like, there are times when you sit down and say 'I wanna go home'. It's not the playing, I could do that all day. There was once in Indianapolis when there was almost a fight in the hotel bar, these blokes were taking the mick out of our long hair, calling us sissies and so on. Which is ridiculous."

The subject turns to the band's personal relationships with each other, "We're pretty easy going with each other, we don't look for trouble. I don't think that four blokes can live together on their own, like some supergroups who go to a cottage to get it together, but not every hour of the day. If they decided to enjoy each other's music and respect each other, it would work. Everyone in Led Zeppelin is completely different, and that helps. It also pays to not take what other people say about you too seriously. They say you're breaking up and so on, but it's not true. We're only just starting, we've got so much to do. We want to play in England for a start and do more concerts here, and then we may be doing a tour of Japan and Australia."

He then talks about the future of Led Zeppelin's music, "When we first formed we got branded as a second

Cream, but I don't think we sound anything like them; if people had listened to the records they'd know that. We've been recording the new album, Led Zeppelin three, which should be out soon. We can record quite quickly; a lot of the tracks we do are two or three takes. It's very difficult comparing this album with the others, there's a lot of acoustic stuff on it, and I've written a couple of heavy things by way of complete contrast. But we all contribute. If you start with a bare guitar riff you still need rhythm and so on."

The article concludes with a brief review of the performance at the Bath Festival. The crowd was some 200,000 strong and when Robert Plant announced it was good to be back in England the audience responded in kind....

September 1970

1 **The Milwaukee Journal....** Led Zeppelin a Hit With Arena Crowd.... review of the show at the Milwaukee Arena.... England's Led Zeppelin and a crowd of 6,000 became good friends in two hours Monday night.... The audience loved the acid rock group for it's musical content. There were none of the old promotional tricks, No local DJ's No local bands just the crowd and Led Zeppelin.... There was Robert Plant who looks and acts and sings like a lion, noble but warm. There was Jimmy Page who looks like an Appalachian Jug Band reject, but who has more musical talent than the Tennessee Valley has water. And John Bonham who proved again that beat is only music without melody. And John Paul Jones still a little down over his father's death last week, but sending out vibrations in his

organ solo. Led Zeppelin is so much a part of today that it can easily transform into tomorrow. It's music cannot get much louder or it's talent much better....

4 **Los Angeles Free Press....** A typical underground newspaper announcement, "This Friday night the Fabulous Forum will be the scene of yet another heavy concert, kids, featuring one of the only nine million remaining British supergroups: Led Zeppelin. Oh! I feel a wet dream coming on. Thousands of 16 year old red-freaked would-be pop stars dream they are Jimmy Page playing all over his instrument, thrilling 18,000 onlookers with multi-note runs of power-volume guitar shriek. Thousands of cuddly little bra-less 13 year old girl children dream of guitar necks ramming into their foxy boxes and frying their puberty pubic hair with ever lasting nirvana ecstasy, as they pray for a chance to ball Robert Plant and/or Page. Greed soaked crass promoters erectify over thoughts of a big money gate."

5 **Record Mirror reports....** Zep III 60,000 Advance, full colour cover story.... Advance orders have been pouring into the Atlantic offices at an alarming rate since the announcement that the album would be released soon.... no release date is set...Jimmy Page currently is mixing the tapes in the USA.... release will likely follow the bands return to the UK.... their current tour ends September 29th (sic) when the band play the Madison Square Gardens in New York, the first British band to play the venue.... LZ II is #9.... **The Honolulu Advertiser reports....** Marijuana survey at Rock show.... The 15,000 people expected to attend tomorrow's two Led Zeppelin rock concerts will be asked to tell what they think about

the use of marijuana.... Questionnaires on marijuana use will be distributed by the Committee On Marijuana Education....

6 The Honolulu Advertiser reports.... Zeppelin at HIC today. The group's second island appearance. Tickets are $6 - $3 available all day at the HIC box office....

7 The Honolulu Advertiser reports.... review of the Honolulu show.... Times have been good to Led Zeppelin. They are making both good money and good music. If their heavy sound has gotten too much for you, rejoice. It has had the same effect on them and they are back into more acoustic material. They did some material from the third album which has four or five acoustic tracks. .... Both Jimmy Page and Robert Plant are more relaxed and human now. The first concert had them being pretty much concerned with being rock stars, but that is over now. Plant seemed especially perceptive about what was going on around him. He stopped the show twice for emergencies, something which they probably would not have done the first time they were here....

Page played well, but there was a certain routine manner about his gig. Which is not to say it was bad. Page at his worst is better than most people. He plays extremely fast and accurately and has a fine sense of dynamics. He is one of the elite. So you wonder why they made John Paul Jones play that solo on the organ. Without qualification it was the worst piece of garbage I have ever heard a major group put out. He knew it and they must have known it. He is obviously learning to play which is good, but they ought to at least wait until he can use both hands. It didn't do it any good, but it could not have spoiled what was some first rate music from a group that may be just ready to start....

8 Boston After Dark reports.... What's happening...Led Zeppelin Boston Garden Sept 9. ....

12 DISC reports.... New Look - New York Zeppelin.... Led Zeppelin were in New York this week, having to cancel some concert dates due to the death of John Paul Jones father. Robert Plant and Jimmy Page both came into Max's Kansas City one night quite late.... both sporting new beards and Jimmy Page with short hair!.... **Record Mirror reports....** Polydor announces that Led Zeppelin will be featured on their new sampler album The New Age Of Atlantic.... LZ II is #9.... **Melody Maker reports....** Cover story.... excellent interview by Chris Welch with Robert Plant in which Plant reveals many details about his pre-Zeppelin career.... Welch asks whether Zeppelin's success is partly based on something more than music.... Plant, *"To begin with, apart from anything physical, the person who criticises us has to decide for himself whether in fact he likes the record or the performance that he hears. If it really gives him the feeling of a teenybopper thing, he should just say, 'I think it sounds like such and such...' But there are a lot of people who generalise and say, 'This surely must be...' and 'I think everybody's agreed that...' which is ridiculous. It's rather unfortunate because when you're up there enjoying yourself, the physical side has to come in too. When you're on stage and you're playing to people and you know that they're ready to chew on whatever you sing or say or do or even think, and to be physical as well, to jump about...well, Africans jump about, Howlin' Wolf jumps about. Mick Jagger jumps about but he can still write 'Sympathy For The Devil'. It's another thing that goes with music that can really get you up.*

"I don't think English people realise what places like the Fillmore in San Francisco are like; the people there have been into all sorts of things for a long time, and they get up and jump about and go wild. Everything that's in them comes out, and that's what entertainment's all about. It isn't something that demands that people should adhere to some strict line, that 'this is a teenybopper group'. There should be no barrier, everybody should be able to enjoy it, and at the same time we as musicians should come off at the end feeling pleased and I think that if we just went on stage and just stood there, we'd be cheating ourselves and the people we're playing to.

"But teenybopper, what does it really matter? You can acquire musical taste at any age. Young girls can go and enjoy listening to Sandy Denny and then wet their knickers over Scott Walker, there's no reason why not. But I can't really see that there's any sense in all that crap about us. If you're dancing in a club, you don't have to dance like the next person. You've just got to enjoy yourself.

"I don't think that rock and roll is any more teenybopper than Indian music anyway, and I can go home and play Elvis 'When My Blue Moon Turns To Gold' and get off on that just as much as I could get off on something from the opposite end of the spectrum, that the critics say everyone's supposed to be digging. It's all a bit mystifying."

Welch then asks him how he got started, Plant, *"There was a fellow called Terry Foster, who came from not far away from here, and he was an incredible eight string guitarist. Instead of playing it the normal way he used to play like Big Joe Williams, with it half on his lap. He was a horrible bloke at times, but he was a real white bluesman, and when I was fifteen*

immediately fell under his spell. My dad used to drop me off at the Seven Stars Blues Club in Stourbridge and we used to wail on 'Got My Mojo Workin' old Chris Wood used to play with us and Stan Webb and Andy Sylvester were in a competing band, this is going well back, and we had a residency at the Seven Stars.

"All the other guys, who didn't have residencies used to come along and sit right at the front with their arms folded. It was a real good atmosphere, a real blues club like I'd love Smitty's Corner in Chicago to be. The sound was good and everybody who saw me there six or seven years ago still remembers it. They always say 'Well you've come a long way, but the music's still the same.' And really that was the initiation. The group was called the Delta Blues Band, and when we weren't doing 'Corrina' and all those really vulgar blues, like Pettie Wheatstraw's stuff.

"I was at school at the time and it was really hard to combine the two and keep a compatible relationship with schoolmasters and parents at the same time as doing what I really wanted to do. It was great because I was having drink under age, and it was a break into a different society because you can go to a grammar school and never see the light of day again for the rest of your life. The minute you pass your 11 plus it could be all finished for you.

"So I got in with this crew which I'm afraid upset my parents a bit, and the cleft between Mum and Dad and Robert got a bit wider and a bit wider until I joined a group in Kidderminster called the Crawlin' King Snakes at the same time as old Jess Roden had his Shakedown Sound and I think the personnel of the two bands are still around now, and they've all been in bands with me or Jess since then, it's like a football team that keeps

swapping over.

"It was a little bit more commercial sound then, it was 'Daddy Rolling Stone' and hopping about the stage with the mike stand up in the air. A lot of incredible things happened and I met a lot of people who made sure that I'd carry on in the way I was going. Like the first Blues Festivals I ever went to, I always got a shiver every time I saw Sonny Boy Williamson, the way he strutted out on the stage. Finally I nicked one of those big bass mouth-harps off him, which I've still got at home.

"Sonny Boy really did it for me, that control that he had, and the tales I've heard about him since, like he always liked a bit of rabbit to eat and one time in a hotel in Birmingham the only way he could cook his rabbit was in a coffee percolator, and he fell asleep and the rabbit cooked and cooked and they had to evacuate the whole floor of the hotel, and he was still snoring away. But he had this sort of charm, he'd have a really good time yet he was really coarse and he was everything I wanted to be at the age of 70. It was people like that that made sure that it wasn't down to joining the Ivy League or even doing an Alvin Lee and backing the Ivy League.

"I never really knew where I wanted to end up; for a long time I thought I just wanted to do Country Blues, maybe only two people or a very straight blues band and the first time I heard Fleetwood Mac they were the very straight blues band that I wanted to be, that sort of Chicago tightness.

"Then I found out that I was in a rut, really I'd been with a lot of groups and written a few things myself that really didn't have the balls behind them that they should've had, and it just went round in circles until I formed the first Band Of Joy.

"This Band Of Joy, I've got to own up, every now and then there'd be a Darrell Banks number slipping out, or an Otis Clay, and living near Birmingham I got in with a lot of Jamaicans and I started to like the old Blue Beat, and the drummer in the band, Plug, who's now with Bronco, he'd got the most incredible feel for that stuff. The lead guitarist was an Anglo-Indian with long black hair and he used to bob up and down, and what with that and the drumming you'd really got to groove on it.

"It was like a poor version of those Little Milton things, and of course it was received everywhere with open arms, and I got sacked thoroughly and utterly sacked because Plug used to slow the beat down every now and then and I'd turn round and wind him up and he didn't like it. And the guitarist played a few odd chords: he never really played 'Sunny' with the same chords on any two nights, God bless him.

"But we were all still learning, we will learn for ever, there's no ending to it, and it was a good time because people were suddenly twigging that there was more to it than just Dave Dee. At last I could slip in a few blues things and they were going down as well as Darrell Banks, that's progress.

"Anyway everybody loved it, and I was sacked because the manager who was the organist's father told me I couldn't sing, 'I'm sorry Robert, but there's something about you.' he said and I said, 'Please give me a chance,' but I couldn't understand it.

"So I got the sack and formed another Band Of Joy, still with the illustrious manager, I'd gone back to him out of desperation, and this band decided to have painted faces, it was a little before

143

Arthur Brown, believe it or not. It frightened everybody to death and there was this big bass player who'd come running on and dive straight off the stage. He was so fat and wearing a caftan and bells billowing into the audience, and I howled so much that I couldn't do anything at all. It was absurd. I was driving the van and everything and I thought it was time for another Band Of Joy.

"In came this fantastic guitarist, Kevin who's also with Bronco now, and we hit it off well. We had a good bass player and John Bonham came in on drums. It was debatable whether he'd join because it was a long way to go and pick him up and we didn't know whether we would have the petrol money to get over to Redditch and back! We always laugh about that.

"It turned out to be a really good group. It was a combination of what we wrote ourselves, which wasn't incredible and rearrangements of things like 'She Has Funny Cars' and 'Plastic Fantastic Lover'."

The conversation then turns to Plant's love of the West Coast sound and early blues. He rattles off a list of people who's music was important to him, "Well I must admit that for a long time things like the Beatles had really ****ed me off, until somewhere around 'Strawberry Fields' they started to get interesting again. I remember the first time I heard Buffalo Springfield's 'Flying On The Ground Is Wrong', I thought, 'That sounds like nothing at all,' the lyrics at the time weren't astounding but there was something there. Then I got the album and it was great because it was the kind of music you could hare around to or you could sit down and dig it and I thought, 'This is what an audience wants, this is what I want to listen to.

"Then I got the first Moby Grape album, which was a knock-out the guitar playing and everything was really good, it fitted together so well. It was that spirit that I reacted to and when I finally got to San Francisco and saw the Youngbloods and the remnants of that 1966 spirit it was a cross between being in tears and giggling all the time, because I saw that air that I knew I'd see one day, and all it was was a sort of sincerity. All that music from the West Coast just went bang, and there was nothing else there after that. I love good blues, but all of a sudden I couldn't listen to any old blues anymore and say it's OK. It just tore me up, like three years before I was shuddering to listen to Sonny Boy Williamson and three years after that I was sobbing to Arthur Lee and 'Forever Changes' and I thought there must be something wrong with me! For something to get at me that much, I mean three years before Sonny Boy I was sobbing in the choir because it moved me so much.

"I've talked to you before, and probably given you the impression that I believed Zeppelin was never going to do what I wanted to do, but the new album is really getting there."

Chris Welch steers Plant on to the subject of where he was before Zeppelin, "At the time I was playing with Alexis Korner, and they said, 'Go down to Jimmy's for a week, and see how you get on.' and I looked through his records one day when he was out and I pulled out a pile to play, and somehow or other they happened to be the same ones that he was going to play when he got back, to play to me to see whether I liked them! We just giggled at each other for a bit, and it just worked from there because if you can hit it off at one stage like that, if we came together like that 20 months ago, then despite all the rows and bothers on the way up we've still got to keep coming together. So really I thought, 'It's so fresh that it's untrue. I don't know the person. Why not try it because it's something completely new'. Jimmy wasn't dominating or anything as I might have suspected; I could suggest things and the two of us rearranged 'Babe I'm Going To Leave You' although it doesn't say that because I was under contract to somebody else and when we heard it back in the studio we were shaking hands with our brains because it turned out to be nice.

"It was good to be able to hit it off like that. Had I been asked to join Jeff Beck I'd have probably gone down and seen him found out that he was a good guitarist. Needed the bread gone with him and got really off. When we got together it was almost like forming a group in your own home town like who can we get on drums and what kind of a drummer do we need? We needed one who was a good time-keeper and who laid it down and the only one I knew was the one I'd been playing with for years which was John. Now you couldn't put another drummer with us because although we're different people he's the only drummer who can sympathise with what we do.

"Nobody knew him. He'd been in the Band Of Joy up until I went off with Alexis, and he went off with Tim Rose I thought 'It's got to be John, and I got so enthusiastic after staying down there a week I hitched back from Oxford and chased after John, got him on the side and said, 'Mate, you've got to join the Yardbirds,'he said 'Well I'm all right here, aren't I?' So I had to try and persuade him, because he hadn't earned the bread before that he was earning with Tim Rose, and I had nothing to convince him with except a name that had got lost in

American pop history — the Yardbirds

"Finally I pulled him away, so that was him, and Jonesy decided that he didn't fancy sessions any more I didn't meet John Paul till the first practice and of course it sounded great. We did a Garnett Mimms thing, As Long As I Have You, which we used to do in the Band Of Joy — that was the first number Zeppelin ever rehearsed.

"The first practice well, it says it in all the publicity but it's right, you couldn't just walk away and forget it. The sound was so great. It's taken a long time to know each other properly, I think, because a lot of the time that we've spent together has been spent getting on with what's in - hand rather than with getting to know each other. We've got to know each other more through playing than we've got to the playing through knowing each other, if you see what I mean.

"But had we not had Peter behind us we could easily have gone to pieces. As much as the credit goes to us, it goes to old Peter as well, because he goes all round the States with us, everywhere we go, when he could just sit in the office in London. He's been a big part of the thing — it's a funny relationship all round, I don't think Jonesy's ever worked with anybody like me before, me not knowing any of the rudiments of music or anything like that; and not really desiring to learn them, but still hitting it off — that's been amazing.

"It was just the way it happened. The old story goes that we tried to play in England several times, trying to get billed. as Led Zeppelin, and they always put The New Yardbirds on the posters, and they'd drag along the audience who'd come four years before to hear the Yardbirds, and of course there we were doing stuff like 'Communication

Breakdown'.

"So America saved us, because they were willing to book us under our new name, everybody knowing who Jimmy was and not having to rely on the Yardbirds'name. We enjoyed it, but I think it was the biggest strain we've ever had. There must have been a big thing around us, with everybody saying, 'Well, they don't play very often, I wonder what they're really like?' We'd never done much, no TV or radio, nobody could see one of us and think, 'Ah, he's that kind of a bloke.' So we knew that it was going to be a crucial thing, we went on and we knew that the next two or three hours were going to be the ones, as far as holding our heads high. You can still go to the States and earn incredible bread, but that's not what it's all about.

"(At Bath) I think really we weren't into it until the acoustic number, when we all had a chance to sit down and take a took around. Then it was like clockwork, we looked at each other and we heard it was sounding good, and we looked down and everybody else was grooving too.

"I didn't feel guilty (about being put at the top of the bill) but the geezer had probably billed us like that because of our mystery value, not having played around much. The Byrds are like the Youngbloods, they can do anything and it'll be good. Those are the groups, the ones which have an atmosphere, and really like to think that we are one of them in our own way.

"It isn't just a teenybopper swinging - the mike around thing, there's something else going on. Like there'll be one number that we've been doing every night; for God knows how long, every night it's different. Maybe Bonzo'll start it out of the blue while everybody's having a

quick orange juice and we'll probably go through a lot of different things before we finally get into a riff of the song we're going play. I think the audience knows that it isn't all contrived things.

"That's one thing about blues you can do more or less anything, around a very vague shell, and the more of it you do, the better you get, until at the end there's very few boundaries to it at all and yet it's all very tight.

"All this jamming that's going on, it's there in a way but it never quite reaches what we get. There's been four of us together for 18 months now, and because we start going off like that the first night that we ever played, the end product was really good to listen to at the time.

"You can never say what is going to last for how long but it's so refreshing to all of us to be able to sit down and come up with these things with everybody having ideas that they've never had before. Everybody being a part of the finished article, and it's good.

"All that crap about Zeppelin splitting up, when we turn out an album like the new one, everybody's really pleased. Zeppelin'll last as long as it'll last but it's really good to know that from the first LP to the third it has been a very nice charge producing something different all the time.

"There's a lot of things that I've never tried that I'd like to do. I'd like to play more instruments, because it's confining only to be able to strum a guitar and not be a part of it. But really the type of music that I can suggest has already been verged on by Zeppelin. It's approached by everyone in a very personal way. When you're doing that you're going onto the boundaries of anything that I might want to do. The makings of it

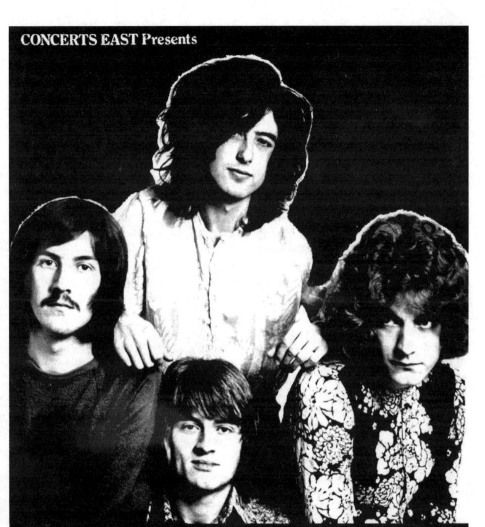

LED ZEPPELIN
By Themselves for a Special 2½ hour Concert

SATURDAY, SEPTEMBER 19
at 2:00 P.M. and 8:00 P.M.

 **madison square garden**

Pennsylvania Plaza, 7th Ave., 31st to 33rd Sts.

Tickets: $4.50, 5.50, 6.50 & 7.50. Available at the Madison Square Garden Box Office from Saturday, August 8. Mail orders promptly filled. Make check or money order payable to Madison Square Garden Center. Enclose self-addressed stamped envelope and add 25c per order for handling. Never mail cash. Mail to Led Zeppelin Ticket Dept., Madison Square Garden Center, 4 Pennsylvania Plaza, New York, N.Y. 10001. For more information call (212) 564-4400.

is all there. I don't think I've got to bother.".... apparently Carl Palmer is a big fan of Zeppelin's John Bonham.... **New Musical Express reports**.... Robert Plant pictured with his dog and goat and family on his farm in Worcestershire.... Led Zeppelin III has advance orders of over 60,000 units....

14 **Honolulu Advertiser reports**...Led Zeppelin - Just for the record the second show at 10.30 pm was far superior to the first at 7 pm. Probably the cause was that the audience didn't get it on with the group. When vocalist Robert Plant yelled, 'Say wooman', there was no response... but for the second show 'woooman' was shouted loudly back. I'm glad I went to both shows; the first featured Jimmy Page on bow, a 'Page specialty'. I had hoped he would do it on the second show but he didn't. Aside from the bow the last show featured longer solos of each member of Led Zeppelin including the best drum solo ever done in Honolulu by John Bonham.

It was also during the second show that Robert Plant stopped the show twice with his fast thinking. The first was a man having a seizure during the group's acoustic number. He called for a doctor and had the spotlight turned on the victim for more light. The second time came when a small fight broke out between ushers and spaced-out rock fans. By stopping the show, he stopped the fight.... it takes a pretty aware cat to be able to do that.

Led Zeppelin informed us that a new album called Led Zeppelin III will be out soon.... and did a few numbers from it.

After two concerts I could have gone for a third. The band was very mellow compared to last year's Civic show. The very showy stuff is almost gone, pure music is what they're into; from very heavy rock to beautiful acoustic numbers.... it was a night we'll never forget! Attention if you haven't sent in your pot ballot passed out at the LZ concert - do it now!

15 **Boston After Dark reports**.... First there was the Hindenburg...article detailing the show at Boston Gardens and the local promoter's problems with the band.... "The signs did not augur well for last week's Led Zeppelin concert. First off the skywriter made the Z backwards when he spelled the groups name in smoke.... on Sunday night three days before the concert the Garden had sold only 1,200 seats for Zep's first show. So the five o' clock show got killed and with it Zeppelin's pretensions to membership in the big league. The Stones sold out the Gardens twice, Zeppelin fell 1,400 seats short of selling it out once.... the promoter got burned, Boston College got burned and the audience got shucked.... After the first six numbers, a new song that included some licks reminiscent of Zappa's Hot Rats, a flashy Heartbreaker, during which Page simultaneously played and tuned his guitar, a dull number which featured him bowing his guitar; a new song that included some licks reminiscent of Midnight Rambler right down to the harp part, a wretched watery acoustic number that had neither a melody nor any harmonic body to it and a folky acoustic solo by Page, it became clear the show was a bomb. .... Not that Zeppelin gave an off performance. Page played with incredible speed and precision, the echo effects, the zooms and the wah-wah's all came off without a hitch. But the licks were dry and sterile and Jeff Beck had played some of them first. Rob Plant out-Janised Janis plenty of shriek and body English but nothing

you could call beautiful vocal. John Bonham did some very nice drumming. Beating the toms with his hands, he performed his ten minute solo Moby Dick which looked as if it would be tremendous fun to do but which was less than inspiring to listen to. John Paul Jones played a perfectly competent bass and organ.... Despite the slickness of the performance those of us who were not confirmed Zeppelin fans could not quite understand the prolonged applause.... we felt slightly cheated. Another person feeling cheated was Robert Chernov who promoted the concert, *"I have never seen anyone as vicious and money-minded."* he said of the group, their manager and their lawyer. *"These guys are worse than GM ever thought of being."* Specifically Zeppelin had cost Chernov $12,000 and Boston College $15,000. Zeppelin had been the headline attraction at Eagle Rock Festival which was canceled last month.... *"There was no way one show in the Garden would get anybody out of the hole,"* said Chernov. On Sunday, the group called Chernov from Hawaii and announced that American Airlines refused to ship their equipment on Labour Day. They claimed they couldn't make it in time for the first show. American Airlines told Chernov that they shipped every day of the year and didn't even charge for it. (At this point anyone would question the validity of this claim.... RG) Chernov then offered half of their promised fee of $87,000 but the group insisted on $75,000 or they wouldn't play. Eventually a deal was made for $61,000. *"They knew they had a school by the balls,"* said Chernov....

16 **The Honolulu Advertiser reports....** LZ First; Beatles 2nd.... A poll printed yesterday in Britain's most widely read music newspaper shows the Led Zeppelin have replaced the Beatles as the nation's most popular group, the first time The Beatles have not been No. 1 in eight years. The Beatles placed second in the Melody Maker poll with the Rolling Stones sinking to sixth. The Led Zeppelin's lead singer Robert Plant won top honors in the male singer category....

17 **The Village Voice reports....** Advert reads — Led Zeppelin Madison Square Garden Saturday Sept 19 8:00 Show sold out. Good seats still available for 2:00 pm show....

19 **Record Mirror reports....** LZ II is #6.... **Melody Maker reports....** Cover story Zeppelin topple Beatles.... Pop Poll Rocked.... The papers annual readers poll lists Robert Plant as #1 Male Singer, Led Zeppelin as #1 group, Led Zeppelin II as #1 album, Jimmy Page #2 guitarist (behind Clapton), John Paul Jones #2 bass guitarist (behind Jack Bruce), John Bonham as #5 drummer (behind Baker, Hiseman, Moon, and Rich), Jimmy Page as #6 producer, ... the Beatles are routed from their usual position as the world's number one group by Led Zeppelin.... Zeppelin Magic Band In The Beatle Tradition.... feature article analysing the band's success.... full page advertisement.... I II III Thank you for making us the World's No. 1 Band, from Jimmy Page, Robert Plant, John Bonham & John Paul Jones.... Band flew in from Hawaii to accept their award....

26 **Record Mirror reports....** LZ II is #8....

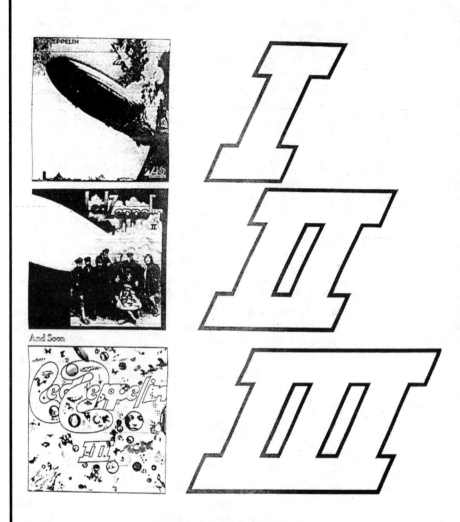

Thank you all for making us
the World's No. 1 Band

from Jimmy Page, Robert Plant, John Bonham & John Paul Jones

Management
Peter Grant

Distributor
Polydor Records Ltd.,
17/19 Stratford Place,
London, W.1.

October 1970

3 **DISC reports....** Zeppelin Play For the Tots.... review of the show in New York.... the Zeppelin certainly excited the crowd that were there.... the sound system was excellent.... the band featured songs from the forthcoming album including 'That's The Way' and 'Since I've Been Loving You' as well as a fifteen minute drum solo from Bonham.... the afternoon show was three-quarters full and sold out at night, 22,000 people.... **Melody Maker reports....** Led Zeppelin Hammer Bootlegs.... Cover story.... A London record distributor said this week that two new Led Zeppelin albums will shortly be in the shops, both unofficial, illegal bootlegs. But Zeppelin's management immediately blasted back with a denial that any tapes were in private hands, and added the threat that anyone who tries to bootleg the group will promptly be sued.... Phil Carson European General Manager of Atlantic records who handle Led Zeppelin, *"We will be taking positive legal action against anyone found pressing marketing or retailing these albums. In fact our people in Hamburg got onto it and several people are in custody awaiting trial."*.... Peter Grant, *"As far as I know there can be no tapes of Zeppelin available. After hearing some time ago that there was going to be an attempt to bootleg some tapes of the band, I flew to America. We've managed to retrieve all the tapes and we know of nothing in existence that can be issued."*.... letter to the Mailbag, "So Led Zeppelin, you are now the number one group in the world not surprisingly. But remember you are now the pacesetters. The Beatles had to step down - mainly because they refused to be a live group anymore. Don't desert us for-

ever, Zeppelin. America's where the bread is - OK - but don't leave us out altogether - as you have still got Taste knocking on your door." .... Led Zeppelin sold out two shows at Madison Square Gardens with over 12,000 people at each show. The story of them toppling the Beatles was on most American TV stations and in most newspapers.... **Billboard reports....** Talent In Action reviews Led Zeppelin at Madison Square Gardens. It says the group showed no fatigue. They sold out the second show and had a good crowd for the first show. They apparently grossed over $200,000, being the only band on the bill. The second show lasted nearly three hours, and one highlight was Bonham's solo on 'Out On The Tiles'. They also played 'Blueberry Hill' and an acoustic set....

10 **DISC reports....** Led Zeppelin concerts plan.... cover story...Led Zeppelin are lined up for a series of concerts before the end of the year, their first live appearances here since the July Bath Festival...dates are for late November early December.... Peter Grant, *"The dates are only an idea at the moment. Nothing definite has been fixed. But Zeppelin do want to do several British concerts again. There wouldn't be any other acts on the bill because of the time factor involved. Zeppelin like to give value for money."*.... Led Zeppelin III is released this week to an advance order of 50,000 copies, the album will be in a specially designed double sleeve.... Review...I,II,III.. and Zeppelin Weaken.... Led Zeppelin III is here after a year of eager anticipation and it's disappointing.... the album leaves you feeling deflated.... It is more acoustic especially on side two, and the overall effect lacks that funky exciting live feeling they captured

ATLANTIC

DISTRIBUTED BY POLYDOR RECORDS LTD

before. There's more double tracking, there are strings added on a couple of numbers. Some of the numbers 'Celebration Day', 'Out On The Tiles' have the driving funk, but the edge seems taken off them by too much loving care in the studio. There are some very pretty acoustic numbers, 'Tangerine' and 'That's The Way' which has a sort of watery effect and Plant is in fine voice throughout. 'Bon-y-Aur Stomp' (sic) (written about the cottage where they composed most of the album in Wales) has a beautiful barn danc-ish effect. But even with the michael taken out of Roy Harper with Page in bottle-neck (Hats Off To (Roy) Harper) the album seems to lack sparkle. Don't Zeppelin care anymore? *** (out of four stars).... **New Musical Express reports....** review of Led Zeppelin III.... Zeppelin Solid Gas, Solid Gold.... Nick Logan does a track by track analysis.... "One can only applaud them for sidestepping the obvious course...though it remains to be seen how far Zeppelin lovers will go along with what is a pretty drastic change in direction." Logan then concludes.... "Hats off to Zeppelin.".... article about Plant attempting to join Clapton on stage.... Robert Plant was pushed from the stage at Birmingham Town Hall by a roadie on Monday.... Plant was there to see Clapton and his new group Derek & the Dominos.... he wandered onto the stage and was promptly ushered out the door by the roadie who apparently didn't recognise him...none of Clapton's band saw the incident.... **Melody Maker reports....** review of Led Zeppelin III. Headline reads, Zeppelin III Is Pure Magic. Song by song review concludes with, *"The main quality is that indefinable Zeppelin magic. It spells another massive hit album."*.... Article headline, Bootlegs. In depth report on

bootlegging by Chris Charlesworth. Apparently Zeppelin managed to stop the importation of the imminent bootlegs (probably Blueberry Hill and Mudslide). Peter Grant comments, *"In Germany the situation is terrible, there were attempts to record us at every venue we played there, cables on the end of broomsticks hanging over hall balconies. The ideal way to try to prevent it is by warning people not to do it, because they'd be breaking the law. If equipment is still in the hall, managers should tell the police, or confiscate it themselves. Bootlegging is not only dishonest but a diabolical insult to an artist. The records sell at £4. It probably cost 2s 6d to make each copy. But people who buy the albums must be told they wear out after about 20 plays. The quality is very poor. Compare this operation with what a band like Zeppelin does for it's real albums. On Zeppelin three one track was recorded last Christmas, the rest in February, June and July sandwiched between a tour of Britain, the Continent and the States. The sleeve is very expensive and took three months to prepare. Jimmy Page did some mixing in New York and Memphis. I've often been very unpopular with engineers because I always insist that tapes come away from the studio after all our sessions. That cuts down the risk.*

"But in spite of our efforts there are still people out to illegally present recordings. It makes me very angry. We've always tried despite adverse knocks to present Zeppelin as a people's band, no single has been issued in England, and we set the pace to do long live shows. That's why we'll stamp out the bootleggers. Zeppelin will not allow themselves to be represented by an inferior product, and I feel sure, too, that the public will not buy these records which are putrid in quality."....

11   **Rock   Magazine   reports....**
Everything you always wanted to know
about Jimmy Page (but were afraid to
ask).... Interview with Page conducted
just before the band flew out to Hawaii in
September.... after shopping on
Hollywood boulevard for old Crowley
books Page agrees to be interviewed for
about 45 minutes, Allan Rinde the interviewer asked John Paul Jones to conduct
the interview but Jones passed.... Rinde
asks Page whether he expected Zeppelin
to be so successful, Page, "*No, no not at
all. I don't think anybody really expected
it to go like this, even after the first album.
We seemed to pick up a lot of popularity
when we were playing around on the first
tour. Especially when we hit San
Francisco. Prior to that we'd done some
dates with the Vanilla Fudge, supporting
them, which were our first dates, sort of.
Seattle, Portland, Oregon and those
places, where we weren't even billed and
nobody even knew who we were. We just
walked out and said, 'Well actually, we're
Led Zeppelin'. Those dates were...you can
imagine the reaction of the crowd, not
knowing who we were. They were quite
warm receptions actually, but nothing like
what happened later.*

"*Anyway we got here (Los
Angeles) and did the Whisky and I was
really, really ill. In fact the doctor said I
was insane to do the set. The first night I
did it I had a temperature of 104, but he'd
given me the shots and things so I was
able to make it. We managed to finish the
whole engagement without letting the guy
down, but of course he docked us money
because we only did one long set each
night, we couldn't do two. It's not the
greatest paying job in the world anyway,
and he knocked money off, we were all
really down about that, as you can imagine. That was our first set of dates.*

"*Then we got to San Francisco. I
was feeling better and everyone else in
the group was happy to see me better and
we really started to play from that point
on. We were playing all right before, but
from that point it was really jelling more.
The rest of the boys had gotten more
accustomed to the American audiences
they had never been to America before,
and they were able to gauge things a little
better. Everyone felt free. They felt they
could relax more on stage. That's the nice
thing about American audiences, they
don't really want to see a show or anything, they just want to see what you can
do. So, right there is when it started happening. From then on we could see that
there was some sort of reaction to us, but
still nobody ever expected it to get into a
really big thing.*".... on the subject of
musical direction, Page, "*Well, you know,
it's funny because people have been coming up to us and saying, 'Well I hear your
new album's all acoustic.' But it's not all
acoustic. In actual fact it's only about 50
percent acoustic. They also say, 'Oh
you've changed, have you, you've
changed to doing all acoustic.' Well we
haven't really changed. The first album
had two acoustic things, well three really,
because Babe I'm Gonna Leave You was
an acoustic thing and then there's the little instrumental which I did, and Your
Time Is Gonna Come although it was a
little heavier it also had acoustic on it. So
it wasn't a new thing to us to use
acoustics, but we wanted to try a different
attitude within the lyrical content so
Robert came up with some nice lyrics. So
that's probably what's changed a bit
more, the direction of the lyrics as
opposed to the music. But you haven't
heard the third album yet have you so
we're really talking in the dark.*"
Rinde has heard Gallow's Pole,

"That's not a single as you know but just to clarify, it's just a cut. But that's like a halfway house thing because it's acoustic and it gets heavier at the end. But there are much lighter things and there's also heavier things as well. The only fault I find in it is that there aren't any really long tracks. I'd like to have got one long track on it, but as it was we had fourteen tracks to choose from and to get a cross section of what we were doing at that point we had to select very carefully, and a lot of good things had to be left off because of it only being a single album. Had it been a double album we'd have been in better shape, but we'd already scheduled it as a single and the cover was already done, and so it was too late to change it into a double, which was really a shame.".... on the subject of recording at Sun Records studios, Page, *"Well, I wanted to, but old Sam Phillips wouldn't do it. It was on the first tour and I suppose he thought who the Christ are they and he wasn't really interested. It had always been a dream of mine to record at Sun. The Yardbirds had recorded there but I wasn't with them at that time, Jeff Beck was always full of praises for Sam Phillips and I really wanted to get down there and cut some things in his sort of element and see how it worked out. But it didn't."*

On the subject of enjoying the tour, Page, *"Oh, yeah. The only thing is that with the sale of the dates now, the sort of, well, the auditorium bit with seats and everything, I find that's a bit of a problem because in some places you're getting a lot of policing. You know it's 'You paid so much, you sit there and you don't come down from up there.' approach. We were talking about it amongst ourselves and I really think that on the next.... if there is a next.... next time*

we come over, which will almost certainly be next year we're gonna try and see if it's possible, of course all this power lies with the municipal people, whether it's possible to have the floor open, no chairs at all, and just the seats around the top part of it, so if people want to get right up to the stage they can do it without any fear and they can walk around just like the old Fillmore in San Francisco used to be. I feel that's the most relaxed atmosphere. When it's all sitting down in that regimental fashion, you've got your seat ticket and everything and people are policing you and shining torches when you stand up. It kills the atmosphere and makes it harder for us. It's not till the end that it really gets off the ground.

"I'd love to go back and do small clubs, I really would. Not the cellars but places like the Grande Ballroom in Detroit. That sort of club was a moderately sized place. The old Fillmore also. But you see, the problem is that if we do those places and it even happened on the third tour, it was when we did the Kinetic Playground in Chicago and the whole street was blocked they had to close the street off, because more people came than the place could hold. And that's the problem. We did the Forum last night and that was sold out. I don't know what you can do it's a vicious circle. When you know people are going to turn up and they can't get in, you just feel really bad about it. Then again, the venues are too big, they're uncomfortably large really, and it's hard to get across as we'd like to. But you just have to, it's a challenge and you just have to meet it. But reaching every person there is difficult when there's that many people.

"In Europe nobody will allow the big stadiums to be used, I don't think. The biggest legitimate venue is the Albert

Hall, which I suppose holds 5,000 people. It's a great atmosphere apart from some of the officialdom. You do run into that again. Once it goes past 11 o'clock at night they usually pull the plugs and you have to give them a few quid and they'll put the electricity back on. But it's gotten to be a very nice atmosphere considering. Every concert's a warm one. Not just us, I mean every concert, and people know it's quite a relaxed scene there."

Page had recorded a session with Britain's Screaming Lord Sutch and the album had just been released, *"Well, I've known Sutch for years and years, and he's been in the business for 12 years and he's never had an album out. Last time we were in L.A. he came to me and said, 'I wish you could help me out, I've got a chance to make an album and I've been in the business for 12 years,' and he started citing other people who had been in the business for a long time, and even died, as did one particular chap, Johnny Cato, but you wouldn't have heard of him. He was in the business for about 12 years and he got killed in a car crash, I think it was, and he didn't have an album out.*

"So, Sutch is telling me all this, saying, 'Oh dear, I must have an album out, you've got to help me,' and I said, 'Look, I'll help you if I can.' It was all fixed that I'd go down there and just do a bit, so we went down and played and I just did some backing tracks to numbers like "Good Golly Miss Molly" and "Roll Over Beethoven." You've got the picture, right? I didn't do any solos, no solos at all. I did a little bit of wah wah on one track, but I didn't do the solo in the middle, which isn't a wah wah thing, somebody else put that on.

"So, to cut a long story short, he rewrote all the tunes and he put another guitarist on over the top. But, and this is

where the criminal side of it comes in, he didn't put "Extra guitar: So and So" or "Lead guitar played by so and so"'he put "Guitar: Jimmy Page," so everybody thought, 'Oh, Jimmy Page played that heap of crap,'and it became more than an embarrassment. He also wrote me in as producer, which was very nice of him. I wasn't interested in that, I just went down to have a laugh, playing some old rock and roll, a bit of a send-up. The whole joke sort of reversed itself and became ugly."

"There is a chap called Roy Harper, who you may or may not have heard of, but we're very friendly with him and I played on his new album. That was just as a studio date, there won't be any credit on it. He's just a very nice person."

At this point the conversation turns to having to cut sets short as Harper had done the previous week at the Troubadour.

"We did when we first started out, and it's a hard thing to do when you've got a certain balance within the program that you've worked out carefully. Even if you drop certain numbers out each night and replace them with other ones, you've still got a certain balance which you rely on. To have to cut it short, maybe cut it in half, is really destroying. It ruins the whole balance of what you've been working on over a year or two years or whatever the circumstances are."

On the subject of recording new ideas outside the confines of Led Zeppelin, Page, *"I know what you mean, I know exactly what you mean. however, I've got a lot of things which we didn't even cut tracks on last time, songs that in a way I really wish had been on the album because, although they're acoustic things, they have really complicated patterns which are more advanced than those we* did. I'd like to cut something like that, but I'd still like to keep trying everything through the framework of the Zeppelin, and I think everybody feels the same way too, because everybody's got ideas and as yet we still haven't reached the full potential of what's there. John Paul Jones has especially increased his participation in the group, and that's good because he's a damn fine musician. If you've seen him, you know that. And the organ, the keyboard things he's doing now, has helped to broaden the outlook of everything.

"There was only so much we could really do with three pieces. He's got bass pedals on the organ, and it's not easy but he certainly pulls it off well. You don't miss the bass not being there. We do one of the numbers on-stage that's on the new album, "Since I've Been Loving You" . . . in fact, it was the first one that was written for this album. It was one of those things that comes out of just a day's rehearsal. Anyway, we do that on stage and he uses the organ pedals, and on the record it's the organ pedals, so that's something to look out for. He's doing it all at once. In fact, that was a whole live cut.

"All the songs on the album are original, except for two traditional tunes, "Gallow's Pole" is a traditional but we've rewritten the whole thing, except for the chorus, which is the same. But Robert rewrote all the words and I changed the chords and the whole pattern of it is different. And then there's a little country blues thing as well, which is like a traditional thing too. But the rest of the things came from us.

"We've started doing the acoustic things on stage and it's been going off well, especially here. Some places, though, it's been a bit of a shock. I relate it back to the period after we'd done the first album, but the second one hadn't come out. We always try to get new numbers going on stage, we used to do "What Is and What Should Never Be" and it didn't really happen when we first started to do it because there's no association, nobody knew what it was. The reaction was a bit cold, really. But then, once they'd heard it a little bit, it became one of the most popular ones that we do off the second album, judging from the applause anyway.

"A similar sort of thing has happened with the acoustic things, for the moment, there not being any association. The audience is hearing them fresh and there have been mixed reactions. They've always gone down okay, but in some places you just get the feeling that people prefer to hear the heavier stuff, which is a bit of a mistake because there's a lot you can give and the best thing is to show them what you can do altogether, as opposed to just expose one angle of what you can do, one facet. We started to do the new things and you'd get people shouting out, "Lemon Song," "Whole Lotta Love."

"You're obviously going to do "Whole Lotta Love," it doesn't take much to work that out, does it? They'll be yelling out on the third number in and you say, 'Look, hold your horses, we'll be playing it, but listen to the new things.' And as soon as you say "new things," then the other half of the audience is going, 'Yeah, new things.' It gets a bit raucous sometimes, those audiences, it's just like a free-for-all: 'We've paid so you play what we want,' and pay the piper sort of thing. But we always give as much as we've got to give that night. When it comes to the encores, we'll go on and on and on if they want to."

On the subject of the British music scene, Page, "The whole thing that's going on now is like a 1970's state-

ment on all of the folk rock over the last five years. Fairport Convention was always a very popular group, and then they split up into a few different groups. There's Fotheringay, Trader Horne, Matthew's Southern Comfort and one other one formed by one of the ex-bass players in the band. They've really pulled it together, all those people. It's good music, it really is. Especially Fairport, I like them and they're really good. Although I think I preferred Sandy Denny when she was with Fairport, her new group, Fotheringay, should have a very fine second album soon. So there's that.

"Apart from that, the English kids are getting a misguided view of what's going on over here and they've been hanging on to a lot of the American bands, picking up on them. You don't really see so many American bands over there. Over here, although we don't come over here quite so much now, there are bands like Savoy Brown and Jethro Tull, that always seem to be here. You don't get it like that over there. There aren't any groups that you always seem to know are going to be around. So they're a bit starved as far as the American music scene goes, except when the festivals bring them over.".... August 26th at the official opening party of Hendrix Electric Ladyland studios the press are disappointed to find that all the Zeppelin tapes have recently been removed.... review of the Detroit Olympia show.... "So Led Zeppelin know all the heavy tricks a freak psychedelic rock group has to know. Jimmy Page and Co. wowed the audience at Detroit's Olympia with their expertise in the heavy idiom: Page in particular has a way of turning down his volume to a whisper (but only for a moment at a time) that puts the crowd right on the edge of their seats. Drummer John Bonham does

the obligatory lengthy solo, as well as most rock drummers usually do it, but not any better. The crowd of course ate it up. But Led Zeppelin almost let the collective energy of their concert blow away when they put aside electric instruments to do acoustic material from their latest album. Page, playing guitar and bassist John Paul Jones on mandolin, couldn't possibly force their sound through a PA system entirely unsuited to subtlety. (Maybe I'm wrong maybe it just wasn't working.) At any rate, after two songs worth of squirming fans and frustrated musicians, Zep had to plug back in to rescue the evening, which they did with a vengeance."....

17 **Melody Maker reports....** Zeppelin Get Golds For Export Boost.... article outlining the band's award of two gold discs for their contribution to British exports. One disc was for a million sales of 'Whole Lotta Love' in the USA and one million sales of LZ2 in Europe. A spokesman from Polydor said, *"The government is recognising their contribution to exports and the money they have made for the country."* It goes on to say that LZ3 will be on sale on Friday with advance orders of over 80,000 units...Letter to the editor asks how Jimmy Page gets those effects? Page replies, *"I've got a Gibson Les Paul which I obtained in the States from Joe Walsh of the James Gang. I had a three pick-up Gibson Les Paul custom stolen recently in America. On the electric guitar I use Ernie Ball Super Slinky strings with my own set-up. My acoustic guitar is a Martin D28 with Martin bronze light-gauge strings. I've also got a Fender pedal steel guitar. My amp is a 100 watt Hiwatt with two stacks each containing 4 x 12 speakers."....*

24 **DISC reports....** Zeppelin win a 'gold' from the men at the Ministry.... HISTORY repeated itself last week when Led Zeppelin came to town. Minus John Bonham, the other three gathered in London to collect some gold discs for overseas sales of their "Zeppelin II" album from the Board of Trade—almost exactly a year after they did the same thing for "Zeppelin I." And undoubtedly next year they'll be doing the same thing for Zeppelin III.... *"And it's the best album we've done—possibly we'll ever do,"* says Robert Plant proudly.... the album was conceived in Wales ...the tapes then followed the band to Memphis where the album was mixed...Plant, *"Bron-Y-Aur Stomp'was my influence really. I love folky things, especially with a beat like that. I don't know if we'll do these numbers on-stage, I'm sure the audience wouldn't mind—it depends if they let me play guitar. I didn't play on the album, and I'm not very good, but I've been playing the odd rhythm things I mean, I could never compete with Page."*.... Plant's farm is being renovated while Page is adding to his Art Nouveaux collection, while he is also contributing to the magazine "Man, Myth and Magic."…. a bootleg was released of the band recently. *"You should hear it,"* says John Paul Jones, *"it sounds like some other band rehearsing."*

"But now we've done 'Zeppelin III' the sky's the limit," says Robert. *"It shows we can change, shows we can do these things. It means there are endless possibilities and directions for us to go in. We're not stale and this proves it."* ....
Melody Maker reports.... Cover story.... full page advertisement for The Age Of Atlantic compilation album.... Page reviews the new album.... Page, *"(IMMIGRANT SONG): That's a voice at the beginning incidentally which somebody*

said was a wailing guitar. On stage this number has already developed into a much longer thing, with a full instrumental passage. The hiss at the beginning is a tape build-up, then John Bonham comes in. It's not really tape hiss, it's echo feedback. Robert wrote the lyrics to this one. (FRIENDS): Again Robert wrote the words. He did them all except on Tangerine. The idea was to get an Indian style with the strings. The string players were not Indian however, and we had to make some on-the-spot changes. John Paul Jones wrote an incredible string arrangement for this and Robert shows his great range — incredibly high. He's got a lot of different sides to his voice which come across here. It has a menacing atmosphere. A friend came into the studio during the recording and it was bloody loud and he had to leave. He said 'You've really done something evil!' Moog synthesiser at the end and that's a bottle neck string bass with John Paul playing. (CELEBRATION DAY): The reason the voice is alone is the tape got crinkled in the studio and wouldn't go through the heads, so the end got ruined, but it worked out all right by using the idea of bringing the synthesiser down in pitch to the voice it was either that or leave the track out altogether. Why 'Celebration Day' it's saying "I'm happy," that's all.*

(SINCE I'VE BEEN LOVING YOU): This was a live track John Paul plays organ and foot bass pedals at the same time. My guitar solo? It could have been better— but, y'know. You are never satisfied with a performance, although of course there are those lucky musicians who can play it perfect every time. On these type of numbers John decides his own drum beat to play. We might occasionally suggest the use of conga drums on a particular num-

ber, but he always fixes his own beat. (OUT ON THE TILES): This is Bonzo's riff (John Bonham) Originally we had a set of lyrics to go with this relating to a night going out on the tiles. (GALLOWS POLE): A traditional song which stems from Lead Belly I first found it by Fred Gerlach. He was one of the first white people on Folkways records to get involved in Lead Belly. We have completely rearranged it and changed the verse Robert wrote a set of new lyrics. That's John Paul Jones on mandolin and bass, and I'm playing the banjo, six-string acoustic, 12-string and electric guitar. The bloke swinging on the gallow's pole is saying wait for his relatives to arrive. The drumming builds nicely. (TANGER-INE): That's commonly known as a false start. It was a tempo guide, and it seemed like a good idea to leave it in—at the time. I was trying to keep the tempo down a bit I'm not so sure, now if it was a good idea. Everybody asks what the hell is going on. I did the pedal steel guitar and that's Robert doing the harmonies as well as lead. (THAT'S THE WAY): Ah, this was written in Wales, where Robert and I stayed at a cottage it was one of those days after a long walk and we were setting back to the cottage. We had a guitar with us it was a tiring walk coming down a ravine, and we stopped and sat down I played the tune and Robert sang a verse straight off. We had a tape-recorder with us that sounds a bit strange, but it was part of the kit and we got the tune down. This wasn't recorded in Wales, if I gave that impression. The 'Los Paraguyos' bit is the mandolin. (BRON-Y-AUR STOMP) That's an acoustic bass, not a double bass- it's like an acoustic guitar with a reasonable body. John Paul took the frets out and he plays it acoustically. This has got the rattling of the kitchen sink —

we've got everything in it! We over dubbed Bonham on castanets, and spoons. (HATS OFF TO (Roy) HARPER): There's that freaky echo. The voice sounds like that because it went through a vibrato amp. This came about from a jam Robert and I had one night. There is a whole tape of us bashing different blues things. Robert had been playing harmonica through the amp, then he used it to sing through. It's supposed to be a sincere hats off to Roy because he's really a talented bloke, who's had a lot of problems."

Which was Jimmy's favourite track? "I like 'Gallows Pole.'But there are others — the point is we had seventeen tracks to choose from to put on the album. Some were written out at the cottage. Some show different stages of development. There was a lot like our early stuff—pretty powerful and John Paul Jones wrote a piece which was all piano, which would have related to what's coming up in the future. This album was to get across more versatility and use more combinations of instruments. The next one will be just one long track on one side with these combinations of instruments, mandolin, banjo and so on. It would last about 25 minutes with instrumental sections. It's still in the planning stages.

"We'll never stop doing the heavy things, because that comes out of us naturally when we play. But—there is another side to us. The new album is totally different from the others and I see that it's obviously a new direction. The fourth album should be our best, and if it isn't well, we might as well give up and retire with red faces. I haven't read any of the reviews but people have got to give the LP a reasonable hearing.

"Everybody in the band is going through some changes. There are changes in the playing and in the lyrics Robert is really getting involved in his lyric writing "It was my idea to have a revolving wheel. I remembered those old gardening catalogues. You'd turn it to 'roses' and find out what kind of manure to use. There's a lot more to see on the wheel. When you get fed-up with the LP there is the added pleasure of ripping the cover apart to find out what's on the rest of the wheel."....

The Honolulu Star Bulletin reports.... Led Zep's latest deserves Raves.... review of LZ III.... Any group that ousts the Beatles as the most popular group in England has got to be examined carefully. And the only group that's ever done it is, no not the Stones, Led Zepplelin (sic). Their third album called Led Zeppelin III (Atlantic 7201) already is a million seller and by next week should be the best selling LP in the nation. Few are likely to be disappointed. Led Zeppelin showed in the first two albums what they are capable of and LZ III is more of the same. From the almost totally undisciplined Jimmy Page (sic) shouting to the absolutely controlled balladeering "III" has it all. While I've never thought the group was as "together" as the Beatles and probably never will be, Led Zeppelin enters the so-called heavy territory where the Beatles never ventured. Of the 10 songs on the LP eight were composed by group members and two "Gallows Tree" (sic) and "Hats Off To Roy Harper" are traditional. To name a favourite is to imply that the others are inferior, which is not true, but I found "That's the Way" to my liking and also "Bron-y-Aur Stomp". But all are uniformly well done and the album with the exception of the design, which is kind of sophomoric, is totally satisfying.... **New Musical Express reports....** Led Zeppelin III is poised for #1 in the USA....

Record Mirror reports.... Zep Denies Soft Charge. Robert Plant interview about the band's third album and it's criticism by the press. *"I am a reflection of what I sing sometimes I have to get serious because the things I've been through are serious. We've been to America so much and seen so many things we don't agree with that our feelings of protest do reflect in the music. I know a lot of people do it but when you have the justification it must be done. America makes you aware of the proximity of man's fate. You see so much that is great, so much that is terrible. The rush, the hassles, the police, people may say we make bread but in some cities it's so rough at concerts the audiences are scared to come. Our manager has had a gun pulled on him and we've been threatened with arrest if we returned to the stage for an encore. The police accused us of being drug addicts, the whole bit. If you can't find anything wrong with somebody to throw at them, just throw anything, just accuse. That type of thing won't happen again. I've come around to another way of thinking now. A while back, we were upset because we didn't get much early help here at home. Times were not too good when we first started. Now I can see it a different way. I want to play more at home. Britain has so much that America doesn't. I could never move from here.*

"There's Whole Lotta Love in everything we do. If we don't say the line the feeling is still there. Music doesn't stop at one point, you don't restrict it into categories. What I want to do is combine the whole lot. There are different moods to it the same as people have different moods, sometimes they laugh, sometimes they cry. There's a physical approach to singing and then sometimes it's more pensive, but both are natural. The lighter things are not really light if you grasp the atmosphere and the intention."....

November 1970

7 Melody Maker reports.... full page advertisement for Led Zeppelin III.... Article states that John Bonham jammed with Trapeze on Sunday at Mother's in Birmingham....

12 Rolling Stone.... full page advert announcing Led Zeppelin III is here.... and after you play the album play the jacket....

14 New Musical Express reports.... Led Zeppelin has been banned from the Albert Hall. They were supposed to play four or five shows in the UK but no one will book the band for fear of riots at the shows....

21 DISC reports.... Yardbirds are to reform for a one off gig at the Chalk Farm Roundhouse negotiations are underway with Eric Clapton, Jimmy Page and Jeff Beck to all be there.... **New Musical Express reports....** Led Zeppelin's single the Immigrant Song is approaching the US top 30.... Led Zeppelin aims at January dates.... due to a dearth of available venues the tour has been pushed back to the new year. Peter Grant, *"At this moment I don't know exactly how many concerts there will be. But although some halls are known to be refusing to book rock shows. I do not anticipate too much difficulty in finalising the venues."....*

December 1970

12 DISC reports.... Cover story... Zeppelin shoots at the Gasbags.... interview with John Paul Jones...the band are recording in a crumbling mansion in Hampshire, having already been up to

Bron-y-Aur a cottage in Snowdonia.... Jones, *"The first two were written on tour, in the studio, or came about at rehearsals - but no actual time was spent on just writing.*

"It's a better idea to do it all the way we do now because you haven't got so many distractions. We've done a good deal - broken the back of it, and recording starts this month. But rather than waste a lot of studio time thinking of the riffs and lyrics in the studio, we decided this place in Hampshire was definitely the best place to get the numbers down before we went there.

"There's really no format, no set ideas. People seem to look for it but there isn't one. The amount you do makes it more difficult to select what you're going to put on the album, with so many ideas coming out. We're using acoustic things, rock things, and strange timings.... it's getting better and better - we're beginning to understand each other more.

"People don't expect groups to last long, so they put the rumours around. When people stop buying our albums we'll stop. Every group has to do like a hard graft to get in a position when they can do what they want, when they want. We can do what we want musically at all times - but it's finding the time to do it comfortably that's difficult. On the other hand you can get lazy, but if you've got a contract that says you've got to make two albums a year, then you've got that hanging over you.

"I suppose we're all capable of putting a trademark on an album, marking just one person - but none of us are so narrow-minded. That wouldn't be the group, and the group's always played what comes out and what comes out goes down. If it sounds good to everybody, then it's played. If a number calls for bass then

you play bass. I don't want to give it up because I'm bored. If you do and you play something you prefer, then the music isn't spontaneous, it's contrived.

"I don't think we can take America again for a while. We'd like to do things here because it's nice to play here. But it's getting it fitted round the recording, so it won't be until next year. But America definitely unhinges you. The knack is to hinge yourself up again when you get back.

"It's all geared to selling a product. All the hype that goes into selling doesn't go into the album though - how they sell it is none of our business. It concerns us in the end but they don't worry us while we're making it. If they don't like it they needn't sell it."....

Creem reports.... Review of Led Zeppelin III by Alexander Icenine. As you might suspect the reviewer's name says it all about this review. This guy's editor should have shot him. The entire review is an exercise in how to write like a drunken fool, concluding with, 'There are myriads of wonderful bung-mung on this here record....I really dung this requiem a lot.'....

Zigzag reports.... In a great in-depth interview with Page he talks about his early career. He is asked whether Neil Christian's Crusaders was the first professional band he was in. *"Yes, I was with them when I left school, but all the traveling to one nighter gigs made me ill—I used to get sick in the van—and so I left to go to art school. Then, when I left there, I began to do sessions bit by bit, and the work just began to escalate; at first, it was a nice scene, because there were good things to be done—around the advent of the Beatles and Stones booms—and I*

worked as a freelance and, because I was a new face on the scene, I got bookings all over the place."

ZigZig's reporter asks whether he was first spotted as a potential session man when he was playing at the Marquee, *"Yes, it was something like that I used to go up there and play in the interval spot with three other guys—we didn't really know each other outside the Marquee; we just used to meet there, and get up and play."*

One of his comrades on the stage was pianist Andy Wren, *"That's right—I wonder what happened to him he was really good. To back track a moment, when it came to the point when I wasn't going to go on with Neil Christian anymore, I was approached by Cyril Davies, who was forming a group, and I went as far as rehearsing with them before I came to the decision that there was no point in going on because I'd just get into the same situation of feeling sick during all the traveling—so I packed it in and went off to art school for about 18 months."*

He is asked whether he had any control over which sessions he played, *"Not really; you'd get the sort of situation where, say, a violinist session fixer, who didn't really know many other session musicians, would hear that there was a new guitar player around, and he'd book me for what turned out to be a ludicrous session—like muzak for supermarkets or something like that. Sometimes, I'd be asked to do a session and the fixer would say 'So and so wants you to do it' and I knew I'd be OK, that it'd be a suitable sort of job, but often I'd arrive without knowing what it was for—and as I got a little more experienced, those were the sort of things I learnt to avoid I mean, they were just a headache—things I shouldn't have been doing."*

The interviewer points out that the sessions he did with Shel Talmy at the helm are probably his most well-known, *"I was thinking about those the other day, and I was wondering why Shel Talmy got so involved with the session men he used to use, because quite often, they just weren't necessary at all. For instance, I wasn't really needed on the Who's 'Can't Explain' session, but I was there—and all I managed to do was sneak in a couple of phrases on the B side. Maybe Talmy used to have people like me standing by in case the group couldn't quite make it on some level I mean the Kinks didn't really want me around when they were recording. One aspect of being in the studio whilst potential hits were being made was the press, too many people were making a fuss about the use of session men I wasn't saying anything, obviously, but it just leaked out, and that sort of thing often led to considerable bad feeling."*

When he is told that Townshend acknowledges his contributions but the Kinks Ray Davis maintains he only played tambourine, *"That's fair enough — I didn't really do that much on the Kinks records I know I managed to get a couple of riffs in on their album, but I can't really remember —I know that he didn't really approve of my presence.*

"Suffice it to say that during the period of 1964-1967, say, I was in there, groveling around on a lot of sessions, but if I went into details, it would be a bit of a nause for the people concerned."

The interviewer mentions how a lot of guitarists were inspired to buy Les Paul guitars because of him but he is asked where he learned from, *"I chose that Les Paul Custom purely because it had three pick-ups and such a good range of sounds—it seemed to be the best all rounder at the time. The Stratocaster is* probably the best all rounder now, but at that time it was the Les Paul. But Eric (Clapton) must take the credit for establishing the 'Les Paul Sound', the sort of playing he was doing in the Bluesbreakers, for instance. You see, even though I may have been one of the first to have a Les Paul, I didn't often get the chance to get going on it. On the odd occasion, I was able to put a bit of feedback onto some record or other, but it was only after all the other musicians had gone home, because when I played like that, they just used to put their fingers in their ears. The limitations were often really frustrating — a factor which eventually led to my leaving session work — because I rarely had a chance to roar into something. The sax players and violinists used to look at me as though I were some kind of joke.*

"In most cases, they'd give you a part, which was written down and sometimes it was good, but usually you'd only play it as it was written if you wanted to be really nasty. Often, the part would be really bad, and you knew that you could do so much better if only you had the chance —you know, things that flowed and sounded better, and had more life in them. It all depended how willing the musical director was, if he accepted your suggestions, you obviously had a freer hand, but if he wanted every part to be his invention, you had to follow his instructions."

He is asked about his influences, such as James Burton and Scotty Moore, *"That's right — I've always listened to them and the Everly Brothers had a good steel player (on things like 'Lucille' and 'I'm Not angry') called Johnny Day. I asked the Everlys who that was, because everyone was saying it was Chet Atkins and I didn't think it was. But I was inter-*

ested in any of those guitarists who were bending strings — all the earthier ones.

"I went to see Bert Jansch at Les Cousins, just as his second LP was released (June 1965) and he was great— fantastic, he really was: if he was only still working as a solo now!"

What about legendary guitarist Davey Graham? "He wasn't for me; I always thought that Bert was the one with the touch ..... he was always far more adventurous and complicated in his technique, although Davey Graham, let's be fair, was the innovator of those raga things and he was really good at those. But you listen to things like 'Alice's Wonderland' and 'Finches' from the first Jansch LP — they're so complex and full of weird timings, and Davey Graham never did anything like that. So, yes Bert Jansch really impressed me very greatly — his first album particularly is just great from beginning to end. I was friendly with Jon Mark who in turn was a good friend of Davey Graham's who I've never met."

The interviewer mentions Page's early use of the sitar, "Davey Graham never had a sitar but he must take credit for working out those guitar tunings he used on his raga pieces — they had a somewhat similar tuning to the sitar, though I don't know whether it was intentional or not. I know that he'd been to Morocco and played with musicians over there but I don't know if he ever got actively interested in Indian music. Jon Mark and I got involved in Indian music, and I had a sitar sent over from India before any other people in pop ..... certainly before George Harrison, for instance. I'd been to see Ravi Shankar years before he became fashionable because the audience was nearly all adults —there were only about two young people there. I never did use it on record— because I knew what would happen when someone eventually did . . . and I wasn't wrong. To use an instrument, which has been developed over thousands of years. as a quick gimmick — well......"

The interviewer mentions the gimmicky way that the sitar had been used by Donovan and the Byrds for 'Eight Miles High', "Yes, but that was a great record. I remember that I, personally, wasn't too happy with the way George Harrison used it on 'Revolver' though everyone else seemed to think it was incredible as far as sitar playing went — it wasn't, but later on when he did 'Within You, Without You', I think that's unsurpassed to this day. So he really did good things for Eastern music and was the one who woke people up to it on mass-media level, but it was people like Davey Graham who were into it long before anyone else."

The interviewer then confronts him with the rumors about him taking a tape recorder to Albert Lee gigs, "I admit that I used to record one or two people — like Cyril Davies and Little Walter and John Lee Hooker— but that was to listen to rather than copy. No, Albert Lee's in a class of his own — country guitar, and I was never into that style."

He is then asked why he only did one solo single, "I wasn't allowed to make a second one, but that single was a joke and should anyone hear it now and have a good laugh, the only justification I can offer is that I played all the instruments myself, except the drums. The other side was instrumental featuring harmonica, because I got all interested in that around that time."

Was this why he taped Little Walter? "Oh no, that was just to listen to — to put in my personal archives, which have quite a lot of interesting stuff —

Johnny Kidd, Cliff Bennett, all sorts of people."
The conversation now turns to the legendary Immediate sessions with Page and Clapton. *"That was really a tragedy for me. I got involved with Immediate, producing various things, including John Mayall's 'Witchdoctor', 'Telephone Blues' and a couple of others (around late 1965) — and Eric and I got friendly and he came down and we did some recording at home, and Immediate found out that I had tapes of it and said they belonged to them, because I was employed by them. I argued that they couldn't put them out, because they were just variations on blues structures, and in the end we dubbed some other instruments over some of them and they came out— with liner notes attributed to me (on earlier copies) though I didn't have anything to do with writing them. I didn't get a penny out of it anyway."*

And who else played on those sessions? *"Stu from the Stones (roadie) was on piano, Mick Jagger did some harp, Bill Wyman played bass and Charlie Watts was on drums."*

And the other Immediate tracks credited to The All Stars? *"They were tapes Immediate had in their possession from a long time before ..... it was in fact, the Cyril Davies All Stars without their guitarist and they were just tracks we'd done for fun after the real session was over. It was just a case of Immediate hustling together whatever they could to fill out the albums, and I'm really embarrassed about the whole thing because everyone thought I'd instigated it, and I hadn't at all. As it was, nobody got paid for any of it and well......"*

The interview now turns to how he joined the Yardbirds, *"Paul Samwell-Smith said 'I'm leaving.' It was a great night, because it was at one of those silly ball things — either Oxford or Cambridge. I can't remember which—but everyone was dressed up in dinner jackets, and Keith Relf got totally drunk and was rolling round the stage, grappling with the mike, blowing his harmonica in all the wrong places and just singing nonsense words but it was great just fantastically suitable for the occasion. But Samwell-Smith was always after musical precision and adherence to strictly rehearsed neatness and it was more than he could take—it was the last straw he'd just had enough and decided to quit.*

"I used to go to all the gigs with them because I was really into what they were doing so he jacked it in and told the others that they'd do the same if they had any sense but they had two gigs following closely and felt they had to do them—and it was a case of me helping them out of a spot; I offered to play bass though I'd never played one in my life before. I knew their act and what they were doing and learnt enough to get through—and then they suggested that I stay on—so I did.

"Jeff (Beck who replaced Clapton) often used to say 'I wish you could join and we could play together' and I agreed that it would be good but I never took it seriously because there was this thing about five Yardbirds and to bring in a sixth would have destroyed that so my joining was never a real consideration until Samwell-Smith left and I took over on bass. The idea was that Chris Dreja who was the rhythm guitarist should learn bass and when he became proficient enough we'd switch jobs and The Yardbirds would then have two lead guitarists and that eventually manifested itself on the Stones/ Ike and Tina Turner Tour (which opened on 23rd Sept 1966) A lot of people think I never played lead

alongside Jeff but in fact we played together for several months.

"But wait a minute I think the switch was necessitated earlier than planned because of one of Jeff's collapses. We had to play this gig in San Francisco at the Carousel I believe and Jeff couldn't make it so I took over lead that night and Chris played bass it was really nerve-wracking because this was at the height of The Yardbirds reputation and I wasn't exactly ready to roar off on lead guitar but it went off alright and after that we stayed that way—so when Jeff recovered it was two lead guitars from that point on."

The interviewer says that he had heard they rehearsed Freddie King solos for the tour, "It wasn't just Freddie King. We rehearsed hard on all sorts of things especially introduction riffs to things like 'Over Under Sideways Down' which we were doing in harmonies and we had sections worked out where we'd play rehearsed phrases together it was the sort of thing that people like Wishbone Ash and Quiver have perfected, that dual lead guitar idea, of course that was all very well in theory and at rehearsal but on stage Beck would often go off into something else.

"It was never a case of trying to blow each other off because I was trying to get it working, so you had this stereo effect on the guitars. There was no point in doing battle that would've just led to a useless sound."

Did he ever consciously change the way he moved around once he began playing to audiences? "To tell the truth, I didn't even think about it. When I'd been in Neil Christian and the Crusaders I'd had to do things like arc over backwards until my head touched the stage—you know those silly things that groups used to

do—but The Yardbirds were never into choreography or anything like that it was just a case of acting naturally, I suppose."

The interviewer mentions that the only apparent recordings to survive of him with Beck were 'Happenings Ten Years Time Ago' and 'Psycho Daisies'. "I think that's right I played bass on 'Psycho Daisies' and there's a bit of a story attached to 'Happenings' we were in the studio waiting for Beck to turn up and Relfy had this little bit recorded on a tape recorder the sort of riff pattern for the song. Well, I worked on the riff and the structure of it and we'd got it all ready by the time Beck eventually showed up—and he just put some guitar on top of it and that was it but I think it turned out well. There's also a double lead on 'Stroll On'."

It is drawn to his attention the apparent leap in quality from the Yardbirds last album 'Little Games' and the first Led Zeppelin record, "Well, on half the tracks we didn't even hear the playbacks they were first takes. That's how it used to be done; we would spend time on singles, but Mickie Most thought that LPs were nothing—just something to stick out after a single."

And were the last two singles in fact session men or really the band? "No, it was us alright, but both of those tracks were a bit of a con-job it happened like this; Mickie Most would say 'Why don't we try to do 'Ha Ha Said the Clown' but in a Yardbirds style?' And we'd say 'Don't be silly'. But he'd say 'Come on, let's try it—it'd be an interesting experiment if it doesn't work, we'll scrap it.' Of course no sooner was it recorded than out it went, despite the fact that it was terrible and then, to cap it all, we fell for exactly the same line on Nilsson's 'Ten Little Indians', but at least we managed to get *one interesting effect on that one. That was the sort of thing that led to a lack of confidence within the group and it's eventual split."*

What about the withdrawn album 'Live Yardbirds with Jimmy Page'? *"If you've heard that, you'll know why it was stopped. Those sort of things are always happening in the record business. What happened was, Epic said to us 'Can we do a live LP?' and they sent down the head of their light music department to do it. The agreement was that if it was good they'd release it, but if not, they'd just file it away of course, it was terrible. The bloke had done things like hang just one mike over the drums so none of the bass drum came out, and he'd miked up a monitor cabinet on my guitar instead of the real one, through which I played all the fuzz and sustain notes—so all that was lost, and we knew it was just a joke when he did it. He assured us it would be alright. 'It's amazing what can be done electronically' he said, and then when we went to listen to the master tape there were all the bullfight cheers dubbed on it every time there was a solo and it was just awful, so they had to shelve it. They must've dragged it out of the vaults a few years later when someone realised they had some unreleased Jimmy Page stuff, and out it came. It was just too ridiculous, but it circulated and sold a few copies before we put the injunction on it. I wish people would accept it for what it is, a pathetic load of crap. We did some studio work with the same guy a little later (Goodnight Sweet Josephine/Think About It), but that was desperation, I suppose, because we were so anxious to get something done if only to prove to ourselves that we could still do it."*

The interviewer observes that the band split after a final college gig in Luton when Relf apparently wanted out. *"Yes, over the months before the break, Relf, particularly, and McCarty had been talking about starting up a new scene. To counteract the sort of stuff I was listening to, they were into very light things like Simon & Garfunkel, the Turtles and people like that, and they wrote some songs in that vein, which they wanted to go off and record. I was in favour of us keeping the group together and tried to persuade them to stay and record their songs as The Yardbirds because I knew we had the potential to pull it off—but they just wouldn't have any of it. Keith was really the instigator, I think, and he said this very weird and interesting thing that I'll always remember 'The magic went for me when Eric left'. Now I've always thought that The Yardbirds best stuff came from the Beck era, when they did all that incredible experimental stuff—but anyway they decided to go.*

"Well, I didn't want the group to break up, and I thought there was a chance that if we made it clear we were going to carry on, maybe Keith and Jim would change their minds and come back—but they went off and made their own record, produced by Paul Samwell Smith I can't recall their name at the moment."

At this point the interviewer offers an interesting line-up for the new band. Page, Dreja, Terry Reid on vocals and Paul Francis on drums. *"Almost, but I can't remember anything about Paul Francis—he must've been someone who Chris had in mind. Yes, it was going to be Terry Reid, because I'd seen what a good singer he was when we toured with him; he was in Peter Jay & the New Jay Walkers then, but by the time I got to him he'd just been signed to a solo deal with Mickie Most, and he'd got a trio together* but he recommended this bloke called Robert Plant. The drummer I had in mind was BJ Wilson but I don't think we ever actually approached him because when I went up to see Robert who I immediately knew was the one for the job, he suggested I go and check out his friend John Bonham. When I saw what a thrasher Bonzo was, I knew he'd be incredible. He was into exactly the same sort of stuff as I was."

It is suggested that by September Dreja had gone to America to go into photography and at that point Jones contacted Page, *"Yes; he got wind that I was forming a new group and phoned to see if it was true and then he asked if he could join and I said 'Great—you're in'. Chris had always been interested in photography, he'd taken some really good pictures and it had always been a toss-up whether he'd leave The Yardbirds to do photography full time I think he got a chance to go to New York to work with Irving Penn and that's what he did.... went through an apprenticeship thing. He's back here now, I think doing quite well."*

Did he know Jones from his session days? *"Yes, I knew him through sessions he even did that cello arrangement on 'Little Games'. So we dropped that name (New Yardbirds) because we felt it was working under false pretenses."*

In conclusion he is asked whether there were any rumours to a Yardbirds reunion gig at the Roundhouse in the summer of 1970, *"Yes Giorgio Gomelsky wanted us to do it, he was going to make a film and a record of the performance and, for my part, I said I'd do it if it was done chronologically— a set with Eric on lead, a set with Jeff then a set with Jeff and me, and finally a set with me, because it obviously wouldn't work with all of us on stage at once I don't know*

why it never happened—all I can assume is that somebody wouldn't agree to it. I don't know."

Rock & Folk reports.... Interview with Jimmy Page by noted journalist Philippe Paringaux.

Page is asked what was the main thing he remembered about the band's last tour of the United States, *"The main thing in the USA is the violence. When we arrive there are always a lot of police. We always play these municipal halls and you have no say. At one show our manager Peter Grant had a gun pulled on him. We were forced to hire an ex-FBI agent. In England everything is completely different. Everything is completely calm."*

Paringaux asks about his experiences with the French audiences, *"We played one time at the Olympia (in Paris) and it wasn't a good time. We got the impression that the audience was as old as the hall."*

1971

January 1971

2 **Disc and Music Echo reports....** Led Zeppelin II is the album of the year.... **Record Mirror reports....** Led Zeppelin III is #4, Led Zeppelin II is #20.... **Melody Maker reports....** Article states that Led Zeppelin II was 1970's best-selling album on the MM charts....

9 **Melody Maker reports....** Cover story.... John Paul Joans hits the charts with his single Man From Nazareth, no this is not the one from Led Zeppelin.... article states that Peter Grant has had to sign on at a health farm.... **Record Mirror reports....** Led Zeppelin III is #4, Led Zeppelin II is #27.... Can Zeppelin Keep It Up In 1971?.... back cover full page article.... biography of the band plus picture of Plant on stage at the LA Forum in September....

16 **New Musical Express reports....** Led Zeppelin are making plans to play in April or May. Manager Peter Grant is trying to set up venues.... **Record Mirror reports....** Led Zeppelin III is #4, Led Zeppelin II is #13.... Led Zeppelin will play in Holland in the first part of 1971....

23 **Record Mirror reports....** Led Zeppelin III is #4, Led Zeppelin II is #33....

30 **New Musical Express reports....** Led Zeppelin is expected to play in a large soccer stadium some time this year.... **Record Mirror reports....** Led Zeppelin III is #5, Led Zeppelin II is #32.... will Robert Plant produce the Boneheads new LP?.... cover story Jones Vs Joans in Name Row.... article outlining John Paul Jones fight with stand up comic John Paul

Joans about using his name to record a single called Man From Nazareth. Ironically both appeared at last years Bath festival without causing confusion. Joans is managed by Mickie Most who is a close associate and friend of Peter Grant manager of Led Zeppelin. Peter Grant commented, *"Our John Paul Jones and the other man John Davidge were once managed by the same man Harvey Lisberg. He told John Paul that he was knocked out with his name and would like to use it for one of his comedians. This was agreed providing Joans never interfered with Jones by making records. Now he has done it. This is a personal thing between the two men. John Paul will certainly apply for the injunction if necessary. If you welch on a bet, you expect to have it put right. This man is making some uncool remarks and people are being confused by the name. He is a northern comedian and should have used another name."*...**Melody Maker reports....** John Paul and the name game. Article which seems to contradict some of the things in the Record Mirror article. Peter Grant, *"It is some years now since John Paul Jones was asked by Harvey Lisberg, then manager of comedian Reg Gray, if he, Jones had any objection to Gray changing his name to John Paul Joans. Jones replied that he had no objections providing Joans appeared purely as a comedian and did not venture into the pop music world. So the position remained until Joans recent record success. We have now advised Joans new manager, Miss Maureen Press, that under present circumstances John Paul Jones has no option but to take whatever steps may be necessary to protect his name. Those are the plain facts!"* ....

February 1971

6 **New Musical Express reports....** John Paul Jones has now issued a writ in his battle with John Paul Joans.... **Melody Maker reports....** Zeppelin To Tour.... Cover story by Chris Welch.... Announcement of the Back to The Clubs tour. Dates will include March Dublin (5), Belfast (6), Leeds University (9), University Of Kent Canterbury (10), Southampton University (11), Bath Pavilion (13), The Place Stoke-On -Trent (14), Liverpool University (16), Mayfair Ballroom Newcastle (18), Manchester University (19), Stepmother's Birmingham (20), Nottingham Rowing Club (20), Marquee London (23).... On April 4 the group broadcast on BBC radio's Sound Of The Seventies show....

Peter Grant, *"The boys came to me after Christmas and talked about the next tour. We decided let's do the clubs.... When I rang the manager of the Marquee he refused to believe it was me offering him Led Zeppelin. So he had to call me back to be convinced! We are also planning to give a charity concert and give the entire proceeds to Release who are in trouble. I'm working it out with Caroline Coon.*

"A lot of the small clubs have disappeared because groups have charged too much in the past. We want to prove the biggest of groups can go out and play there."

Bonham, *"It'll be great because the atmosphere is always much better than a big place like the Albert Hall. We wanted to do a tour where the greatest*

The offending single by comedian John Paul Joans

number possible could come and see us, at the places that made us when we started out.".... **Record Mirror reports....** Led Zeppelin III is #5, Led Zeppelin II is #32.... John Paul Joans manager Mickie Most's office is directly across the corridor from Peter Grant's....

13 **New Musical Express reports....** Will Zeppelin split up?.... article which continues to throw gas on the 'splitting up' fire, "Rumours abound that Led Zeppelin will split up after conducting a farewell tour of the UK. Reports say the band are interested in pursuing personal projects. One rumour has one member teaming up with George Harrison. The band's manager denied the band had any intention of parting company. He also denied any rumours of tour dates yet within 48 hours the band's agency Chrysalis announced tour dates as follows: March 5th Dublin Boxing Stadium, 6th Belfast Ulster Hall, 9th Leeds University, 10th Canterbury University, 11th Southampton University, 13th Bath Pavilion, 14th Stoke Hanley Place, 16th Liverpool University, 18th Newcastle Mayfair, 19th Manchester University, 20th Birmingham Stepmothers, 21st Nottingham Rowing Club, 23rd Marquee London.". This article gives the first real details of the back to the clubs tour and gives a good clue to the towns they may have played on their first tour in 1968... John Paul Joans will now be known as "John" in the USA but will continue to be known as John Paul Joans in the UK.... Led Zeppelin IV will likely be released in April.... **Melody Maker reports....** the phone at the Marquee club has been ringing off the hook since Led Zeppelin's tour announcement.... tickets go on sale on March 1st and are limited to club members at first one ticket per member...Peter Grant says

he has received dozens of calls from clubs wanting to book the band.... **Disc and Music Echo reports....** Zeppelin Still Flying High.... interview with Robert Plant by Caroline Boucher. Plant is in London for rehearsals and takes time out to discuss the pitfalls of success, *"To go into the clubs to play and make nothing at all seems to be the only way we can go without being crucified. The being recognised thing isn't nearly so bad today, but I see now that the Beatles must have been the most pestered people in the world."* After he relates an amusing anecdote about being completely unrecognisable at the band's North Wales retreat (Bron-y-Aur) the topic shifts to the band's newest recordings which they began in November in Wales. *"This next album won't be called Led Zeppelin 4. We'll think of something else. So far we've got 14 tracks down and we did quite a bit with a mobile recording truck down in Hampshire. A studio is an immediate imposition; it's quite a limiting thing compared to sitting around a fire playing away and we've been able to experiment with drum sounds by using just one microphone and things. At times it sounds like early Presley records drumming. Then we've got Stu who plays piano for the Stones sometimes, on a couple of tracks, really earthy rock. John Paul's done a couple of things using recorders and he's been using the synthesiser very tastefully. Then there's a nice ten minute thing 'Stairway To Heaven' which starts off acoustically and just builds up. In my opinion it's one of the nicest things we've done. Then there's 'Sloppy Drunk' on which I play guitar and Jimmy plays mandolin, you can imagine it being played as people dive round the maypole. With 14 tracks we have enough for two albums, but we won't put out a double album.*

People can appreciate a single album more because there's only eight tracks as opposed to 16.".... Disc music awards.... Led Zeppelin top group in the world.... Jimmy Page #3 musician.... Robert Plant #3 singer.... Led Zeppelin III #3 album.... Led Zeppelin #4 group in the UK.... **Record Mirror reports....** Led Zeppelin III is #5, Led Zeppelin II is #32.... Led Zeppelin will release the Immigrant Song as a single in the USA the B-side Hey Hey What Can I Do is not on any album....

20 **New Musical Express reports....** All four members of Led Zeppelin deny they are splitting up says a group spokesman.... **Melody Maker reports....** Zeppelin Deny Split. Led Zeppelin spokesman Bill Harry says, *"There are no plans for Led Zeppelin to split up. And there are no plans for any member of the group to work with other artists. The group have all been joking about these rumours, but they are upset at the way they are being spread by people who claim to be close to the band. We'd like to know who these people are and where they get their information. They have been working hard on their new LP and are looking forward to the tour. Manager Peter Grant is in America this week discussing the future. People may be puzzled why they never appear on TV but their plans for a Zeppelin TV spectacular have not been shelved. Jimmy Page is working on various projects and the group which has established itself as number one in the world, on records and personal appearances alone, will be expanding into TV in the future. They have got a long way to go together yet and are all extremely happy."....* **Disc reports....** Disc Valentine Awards presentation review...First on the scene was the shy man of Led Zeppelin John Paul Jones, who hovered from foot to foot not being a man normally seen at all at such events.... within minutes Cliff Richard was engaged in deep conversation with JPJ providing a rare sight for all who think pop and progressive can't mix. The other three Zeppelin's arrived with manager Peter Grant a giant of a man in all senses of the word. It was the first time that all four had gathered in public since the Bath Festival last year.... comments overheard - Cliff Richard to JPJ, *"You used to play on some of my records."* JPJ, *"Yes, I watch you making a fool of yourself on your TV show sometimes too."* Cliff, *"Yes I always think it's a nice unpretentious little show!"*.... **Sounds reports....** Led Zeppelin hottest rock band alive by Royston Eldridge. Article chronicling the band's initial formation which reveals nothing new other than an updated list of their stage gear....

PA:
3000-watt JBL PA system
8 6 ft. x 4 ft. Wuffer speaker cabinets
4 Long-range horns
4 Medium-range horns
4 Close-range horns (all with electronic crossovers)
1 Binson echo chamber
500-watt monitor system with close-range horns
2000-watt WEM PA system (used in Europe only)
4 4 in. x 12 in. Marshall speaker cabinets, each having four 35-watt speakers in each cabinet
2 Hiwatt 100-watt amplifiers, which have been treble boosted
2 Vox echo chambers
1 Echoplex echo chamber
1 Sonic Wave (Therome)
Custom 100 Marshall amplifier
Fender Super Reverb amplifier
2 Marshall 4 in x 12 in horn cabinets

2 Marshall 100-watt amplifiers
3 Acoustic cabinets
2 Acoustic amp. tops (Preamp.)
MICROPHONES:
Shure Unidyne
GUITARS:
2 Les Paul guitars
1 Rickenbacker 12-string guitar
1 Fender Telecaster
1 Martin Jumbo 6-string acoustic guitar
1 Fender jazz bass guitar
1 Fender Telecaster bass guitar
STRINGS:
Ernie Ball Super Slinky strings
Herco (heavy gauge picks)
DRUMS:
1 Ludwig 26 in. x 15 in. bass drum
2 Ludwig 14 in x 6½ in. snare drums
1 Ludwig 18 in. x 16 in. side Tom-Tom
1 Ludwig 16 in. x 16 In. side Tom-Tom
1 Ludwig 14 in. x 10 in. side Tom-Tom
Speed King pedals
Ludwig conga drums
36 in. Gong and stand
CYMBALS:
1 Ludwig 24 in. ride cymbal
2 Ludwig 20 in. crash cymbals
2 Ludwig 14 in. Hi Hats
STICKS:
Ludwig drum sticks
ORGANS/PIANO:
1 Farfisa Duo Pro organ
1 Farfisa single manual organ
1 Hohner electric piano
OTHER INSTRUMENTS:
1 VC. 3 Moog Synthesiser
1 Martin mandolin
Ludwig tambourines
Super Vamper harmonicas
1 Revox 2-track tape recorder

27 **Record Mirror reports....** Zep come to the People...interview with Jimmy Page about the upcoming 'Back To The Clubs Tour' by Keith Altham. Page, *"The audi-*

ences were becoming bigger and bigger but moving further and further away. They became specks on the horizon and we were losing contact with people -- those people who were responsible for lifting us off the ground in the early days.

"We are playing those clubs like the London Marquee for exactly the same amount as we did in the old days as a thank you to those promoters and the audiences alike. By doing this we will be able to tour the entire of Britain and not just those cities who are fortunate enough to contain large venues.

"We will establish contact with our audience and re-energise on their reaction while they will have a chance to see a group which in the accepted tradition would be appearing only at high prices in large auditoriums.

"The only aspect which troubles me is that there will obviously be a large number of people who will be turned away on the night and I get a pang of conscience every time I see someone who has trekked miles to see us being sent away. I can only hope that the club owners will distribute tickets fairly and preferably on a first come first served basis. We have kept our price down and we expect them to do the same with their admission charges. It is my opinion that the real excitement and life's breath of progressive music comes from these small clubs we hope our appearance will give them a shot in the arm and close contact will revitalise our enthusiasm.

"If I thought about the money coming in or the money going out I would go stark raving bonkers. We have managers and accountants to take care of our business problems and leave us with what concerns us most. The music.

"My ultimate objective and challenge is to excel in all spheres as a gui-

tarist and I want to attempt all styles. Maybe it will mean I will end up as a Jack of all trades and master of none but at least I will have sampled the different sweets available. I don't want to be better than any one particular guitarist just more versatile."

Altham asks whether the press will be treated to their usual privileged seating arrangements during the tour of the clubs, *"If they expect red-carpet treatment then my advice is don't bother to come. Because they are taking up valuable space which someone who really wants to hear us would otherwise occupy. We are not playing for the sole benefit of the Press or those particular critics who we all know review most of the shows from the beer tent or the bar! There are plenty of new young faces on the musical papers now who would enjoy to come and hear us play and I hope they do. My message to the journalists looking for V.I.P. treatment is don't bother to turn up."*

The tour was to include at least one charity show in aid of a drug rehabilitation charity called Release, *"Release is the one organization which most young people would automatically turn to if they found themselves in trouble with drugs. Caroline Coon and her helpers have done more to help young people in that area than anyone else -- they do good work."*

Altham then asks bluntly how much it costs for Zeppelin to tour, *"Oh goodness knows - for a start we have to lay out £8000 for a new P.A. system because someone left our old one out in the rain! Then we have to buy a new van which will probably mean another £2000 - two roadies a tour manager and our personal manager. The only major difference is not having to worry about someone leveling a gun at your head as they do in the U.S. so there is less emphasis on securi-*

ty." Altham raises the question of people joining Zeppelin to jam, a possibility presented by the small venues.

"Let me give you an example. A year ago I went to see Howling Wolf perform in London and I was really looking forward to hearing him. I stood at the side of the stage and the whole time the management were pestering me to go on and jam. 'We can get him off now if you want to go on!' Now I hadn't come with the intention of playing and the people there had not turned up in the hope of hearing me. Howling Wolf had a lot to offer and we wanted to hear him. It's the same scene with us - we have a lot of new material and new numbers to offer. It won't be the same kind of programme that we will play in the Clubs as we have here in concert. John Paul Jones is playing a lot more piano on our forthcoming album and we intend to feature him. There will be a new sort of dynamics about our music now. There is so much potential and so many new combinations which the group has to offer that we want people to hear them before anyone else gets into the act!".... **Melody Maker reports....** Letter to the editor from B.J. Lucille in West Bromwich reads — Zeppelin's Roots. I often hear people asking 'Who are the Band Of Joy that Robert Plant and John Bonham used to play with?' As a friend of all in the old band I would like the Melody Maker to get the story in full. Kevin Gammond, the incredibly fast guitarist with Bronco, used to play lead and sometimes was known as Carlisle Egypt. Paul Lockey, now with a very good band called Bonehead, played bass, he now does a lot of writing and plays lead; Chris Brown who played organ, now spends a lot of time abroad with Life. This was not the first Band Of Joy, which had Vernon Pereira on lead, he's with Possessed now,

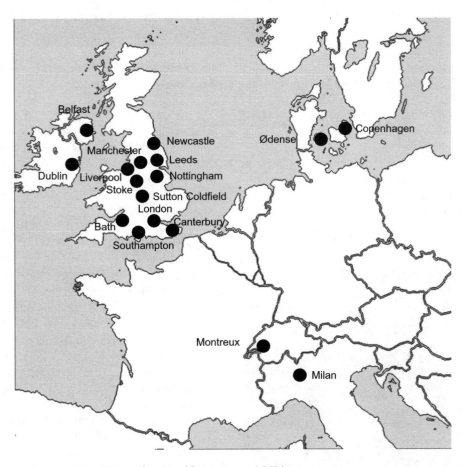

European Tour Spring/Summer 1971

March 5th, 1971 Belfast Ulster Hall
March 6th, 1971 Dublin Boxing Stadium
March 9th, 1971 Leeds University
March 10th, 1971 Canterbury University
March 11th, 1971 Southampton University
March 13th, 1971 Bath Pavilion
March 14th, 1971 Stoke Hanley Place
March 18th, 1971 Newcastle Mayfair
March 19th, 1971 Manchester University
March 20th, 1971 Sutton Coldfield Belfry
March 21st, 1971 Nottingham Rowing Club
March 23rd, 1971 Marquee London
April 1st, 1971 London BBC Paris Theatre
May 3rd, 1971 Copenhagen K.B.Hallen
May 4th, 1971 Ødense Fyns Forum
May 10th, 1971 Liverpool University
July 5th, 1971 Milan Vigorelli Stadium
August 7th & 8th 1971 Montreux Casino

a funky three piece. Plug (Peter) Robinson drummer with Bronco, Chris Brown and several bass players, including Paul Lockey, Lyddon Laney (of Laney sound equipment) and John, bass player with Velvet Fogg....

Phonograph Record Magazine reports.... Cover story with great picture of Page. Headline reads - Jimmy Page 'n Groupies. Article inside doesn't mention Zeppelin but talks about groupies in detail....

March 1971

6 **Melody Maker reports....** cover story.... Zep Away on tour.... Richard Cole says Led Zeppelin will use over 4 tons of equipment and 2000 watts of sound.... picture of Bonham in his new hot-rod, the caption states that the band are leaving this weekend to go on tour. The car is his £3,000 1923 Model T-Ford with a Chevy engine. It says he bought the car in

Boston and paid £2000 to fly it home to his house in Hagley. It says the car is capable of 0-60 mph in 3.2 seconds....

13 **Melody Maker reports....** cover story.... Chris Welch reviews the bands opening gigs in Belfast and Dublin.... The band rip into an explosive set which launches the audience in Belfast into a frenzy.... the set includes Immigrant Song, Heartbreaker, Since I've Been Loving You, Dazed & Confused, Black Dog, Stairway To Heaven, Moby Dick, Whole Lotta Love, Boogie Mama and Communication Breakdown.... on the way to Dublin Bonham accidentally drives through the Falls Road area, one of the most dangerous places in Ireland, Bonham, *"The street was covered in glass, and there were armored cars and kids chucking things. We just kept our heads down and drove right through."* In Dublin the band toss in Summertime Blues as an encore and Phil Carson (General Manager of Atlantic Records European division) joins them on stage...Page, *"I enjoyed Ireland and wish we could come back. We're not playing the great long three hour shows now, but like to give a good balanced programme, with new and old material.*

"On the new LP John Paul Jones has over tracked recorders on the introduction to Stairway To Heaven which we can't reproduce on stage, but the acoustic guitars come off well. The words are brilliant, they are the best Robert has ever written. The album is almost finished. We recorded some of it on location with a mobile truck and got a really good atmosphere. Actually the words of one song relate to earthquakes, and right after we did the number, the earthquake happened in California, which was a bit unnerving! I don't know if that song will go on the LP,

nobody wants to drop anything. All of the songs we have done hold up.

"We used the Rolling Stones mobile recording truck which we parked outside a house while we played inside. We had the drums in the hall and we sat around the fire and played our guitars. Bonzo got a big and fat drum sound. I expect you notice the sound of the drums often gets strangled in a studio.

"We have all contributed to the writing but there is no point in trying to explain all the numbers. You'll have to listen to the LP. It would be really nice to do a double album and maybe get the truck out to record some live gigs. It's really good to be back playing again. It was a kind of instant excitement on the first concert. I was wondering what it would be like. There is a danger that if the fans get too excited that you can't get the acoustic numbers across. That's all we ever want,

a chance to get all of our music across. We've got four albums of material now to choose from and I think we got a pretty good balance.".... supergig at Bumpers Club featuring Robert Plant, Jon Lord, Roger Glover and John Bonham.... **Disc and Music Echo reports....** Zeppelin get a Whole Lotta Love.... Tony Wilson reports from the band's gig in Dublin.... "The visit of a band of the stature of Led Zeppelin is rare in Dublin, so it was not surprising that last week the National Stadium, normally a venue for amateur boxing tournaments was packed with 3,000 Irish progressive music fans. Led Zeppelin were playing the second concert of their current British tour after a three month lay off for recording work, and having played a sensational concert the night before in Belfast, came south and proceeded to whip up the Dublin fans into a cheering, stamping, throbbing mass.

The standing ovation started long before the show was over, and at the end the Zeppelin had to come back for several encores before they could get away. Zeppelin are the heaviest and loudest group yet heard in Dublin, and the huge banks of amplifiers and speakers pushed out a fantastic wrap-around volume. Their performance comprised of material from their previous three albums and a preview of some of the tracks from the forthcoming album. There was a bit of confusion at the start over what they were going to play. *"We had a list on a piece of toilet paper,"* explained Robert Plant, *"but I think it's been used."* However once under way Led Zeppelin cruised through the evening without much trouble. Jimmy Page played some excellent guitar throughout, including a clever piece with a violin bow during "Dazed & Confused", and John Bonham won huge applause for his drum solo during "Moby Dick". The place really erupted when Zeppelin went into "Whole Lotta Love" which had been shouted for since the start of the show and many of the fans were standing on their seats waving their arms and cheering for the duration of the number. "Stairway To Heaven" was one of the new numbers, which starts off in a relaxed way and builds up into heavy rock. Page switched to a twin-necked guitar with six and twelve strings, and featured some nice finger style work in the introduction. Another new number from the upcoming fourth album was "Going To California" with John Paul Jones on mandolin and Page on acoustic guitar. With Plant on vocals, all three sat down for the one which provided an ear-resting contrast to the remainder of the programme. "California" showed an influence that may have come from Robin Williamson and Mike Heron and on their next album

this could become known as Led Zeppelin's Incredible String Band. The last part of the concert was given over to a mixture of old and new rock items like "Suzie Q", "Sugar Mama", "The Lemon Song", "That's Alright Mama", and "C'mon Everybody" all following in quick succession. It raised the excitement to fever pitch and the short haired grey suited officials of the National Stadium gave up trying to make the people sit down and instead ranged themselves along the front of the stage in case of a possible riot. However it all finished peacefully and 3,000 fans went off into the night more than satisfied with the tremendous concert."....

20 **Melody Maker reports....** Advert reads — Marquee Tuesday March 23rd 7.30- 11.00 Led Zeppelin Sold Out No Tickets available on night....

27 **Go-Set reports....** reprint of the reviews from Melody Maker of the shows in Dublin and Belfast by Chris Welch.... **Melody Maker reports....** letter to the editor calls Led Zeppelin's set at Canterbury self indulgent and the band's performance barely adequate.... **New Musical Express reports....** Electrifying Zeppelin...review of the band's concert at the Belfry in Sutton Coldfield.... over a thousand people witnessed the power of Led Zeppelin up close for over three hours.... songs played included Since I've Been Loving You, Communication Breakdown, Whole Lotta Love, Black Dog, Going To California, and Stairway To Heaven.... **Sounds reports....** Tony Stewart reviews the band's gig at one of their favourite haunts in Plant and Bonham's own neighbourhood. The review suggests that the date took place on March 20th. "My immediate reaction

after seeing Led Zeppelin was to throw away their albums, because they don't put across the electrifying excitement of the band, the drama of Robert Plant throwing back his golden locks and contorting his face as he throws out each word, of Jimmy bent over using a bow on his guitar, and John and Bonzo flogging away to lay the foundations. As soon as they appeared at the Belfry, Sutton Coldfield, on Saturday the dance hall was jammed, you couldn't even lift a hand to light a cigarette. The band took a lot of trouble to satisfy everybody. Zeppelin music involves you straight away. As they batter you with their intense rock you can't help but move. They certainly don't hold anything back, working through the well known numbers— 'Since I've Been Loving You', 'How Many, More Times', 'Communication Breakdown', and, their anthem 'Whole Lotta Love'. Then they played samplers from the new album — 'Black Dog', the beautiful 'Stairway To Heaven', and 'Going To California'.

The sound was loud and clear with an expert use of sound effects. Jimmy's exciting and fast playing blended well with the unpredictable bass lines. Robert has such a range that at times he seems like two vocalists. Even after three hours the applause was deafening and Zeppelin were lucky to leave the stage even then. Perhaps I'd better keep those albums — it could be a long time before they tour again."

April 1971

3 **New Musical Express reports....** Pictures showing Robert Plant live in action in Southampton.... **Disc and Music Echo reports....** tune in to Radio One for rebroadcast of Sunday's Led Zeppelin concert.... **Record Mirror reports....** Led Zeppelin III is #21, Led Zeppelin II is #10, Led Zeppelin I is #47.... advert for book called "Words the record song book" featuring   cover stars Led Zeppelin....

10 **New Musical Express reports....** Andy Fairweather-Low blames Led Zeppelin for the state of play in the singles charts, complaining that if good bands like Zep were to release singles then perhaps the charts wouldn't be so boring.... **Record Mirror reports....** Led Zeppelin II is #15....

17 **Record Mirror reports....** Led Zeppelin III is #40, Led Zeppelin II is #20....

24 **Record Mirror reports....** Led Zeppelin III is #28, Led Zeppelin II is #11.... special article on Alexis Korner outlining his involvement with the British Blues scene as well as the short tenure with Robert Plant.... "Alexis and Robert traveled the club circuit together. Jimmy Page asked Robert to join Led Zeppelin and he then left immediately for California, and was thus unable to finish an album that he and Alexis were doing with the pianist Steve Miller.... a few tracks completed are expected to be released later on an anthology album."....

May 1971

1 **Record Mirror reports....** Led Zeppelin III is #17, Led Zeppelin II is #15.... Keith Moon had a party at his pub in Chipping Norton, the Who, Led Zeppelin and the Bonzo Dog Band all in attendance, no one was hurt!....

8 **Melody Maker reports....** letter to the editor, Led Zeppelin should leave out the slow stuff.... **Disc and Music Echo reports....** Led Zeppelin play Liverpool University on the 10th at 7.30 pm tickets are 60p.... **Record Mirror reports....** Led Zeppelin III is #27, Led Zeppelin II is #10....

15 **Record Mirror reports....** Led Zeppelin III is #38, Led Zeppelin II is #18.... John Bonham and Dave Pegg jammed at the Midland Beat Revival Night at the Belfry in Sutton Coldfield near Birmingham.... **New Musical Express reports....** Led Zeppelin even better now.... review of the band's performance at the KB Hallen in Copenhagen... nearly 4,000 people packed in to Led Zeppelin play for 135 minutes.... Zeppelin played material from all three albums as well as a new number called something like "Stairways To Heaven". Other songs included Gallow's Pole, Tangerine, Dazed & Confused and Since I've Been Loving You concluding the show with Whole Lotta Love, That's Alright and Mess Of Blues.... Led Zeppelin is THE rock 'n roll band in 1971 no doubt!....

22 **Record Mirror reports....** Led Zeppelin III is #50, Led Zeppelin II is #25.... Led Zeppelin voted #4 group in poll.... CCS sold 250,000 copies of their single Whole Lotta Love in the USA....

29 **Record Mirror reports....** Led Zeppelin III is #34, Led Zeppelin II is #33.... cover story....

June 1971

5 **New Musical Express reports....** A U.S. Rock Phenomenon But Still The Media Ignores Zeppelin.... feature article by Ritchie Yorke reporting from America.... Yorke attacks the mainstream American Media for ignoring Zeppelin's enormous commercial success.... On their first US tour Zeppelin played for as little as $750 per night but their current asking price is around $50,000 per performance.... the band are currently working on their fourth album for a summer release, there are plans for tours of the USA, Europe, Japan and Australia.... **Record Mirror reports....** Led Zeppelin III is #31, Led Zeppelin II is #17...

12 **Record Mirror reports....** Led Zeppelin III is #30, Led Zeppelin II is #19...

19 **Record Mirror reports....** Led Zeppelin III is #24, Led Zeppelin II is #21...

26 **New Musical Express reports....** Led Zeppelin may play an upcoming concert for the victims of the flooding in Bangladesh.... **Sounds reports....** cover story.... Interview with Robert Plant by Steve Peacock.... The first question Peacock asks is whether the band have been recording. Plant, *"Yes, it's that long dragging out thing of mixing a lot of the tracks. The intention originally was for a double album, and then we thought 'well, not this time'— but then we've been saying 'not this time' since the second album. Jimmy (Page) - took all the material over to Sunset Sound in Los Angeles with a very famous producer who said it was THE studio, and did the mixes. We finished recording in February and the idea was to mix it there and get it out in March. But he brought the tapes back and they sounded terrible, so we had to start mix-*

ing all over again. It's a drag having to do it twice, but we're coming to the tail end of it now."

SP then asks who is producing "Well, we all discuss, the thing, but when it comes to putting it right down he's usually the one to do it. I'll be there as often as I can because I know exactly what I want, but I know that if I'm not there then we know each other well enough to know exactly what we both want. But for me it's really a case of getting to know things at the moment. I can go along there and sit for twelve hours and suggest things, but I like to be of some practical use. Still it's only three years now that I've been in a position to get accustomed to recording studios. It's growing pains that I've got now."

SP asks what is the musical style of the new record, "I don't think there's any set thing. We don't get into any mould and stay there. People might want us to, and other people might not want us to, but bollocks anyway. Most of the mood for this new album was brought about in settings that we hadn't come across before — we were living in this old falling apart mansion somewhere out in the country I can't quite remember where and we had the Stones mobile truck, so the mood was . . . bang!... like that, and we could hear the results immediately. There was no big scene about going back into the studio and doing it again because we had time to experiment, especially with drum sounds.

"We did this thing called "When the Levee Breaks" which is an old Memphis Minnie number, a Kansas Joe McCoy thing, and the drums on it sounded incredible. There was a secret to it which we just stumbled across really, which was just one microphone, just one — and the revelation of finding out that one microphone did more than about 35

in a studio set the mood really. It was enthusiasm. Out of the lot I should think there are about three or four mellow things.... they're really improved a lot — there's a thing called "Stairway To Heaven" and a thing called "Going To California", but also there's some nice strong stuff, some really . . . we don't say 'heavy' do we? Well I don't know whether we do. But it's strong stuff and exciting, and the flame is really burning higher and higher. But it's probably best that we keep out of the way and quiet, and then when the album comes out we'll wait for the torrent and the retort. But it isn't as simple as one, two, three, four and away we go— I don't think it ever has been like that, because 'Communication Breakdown' at the beginning wasn't a one, two, three, four, and we'll see you at the end. There's groups who do that who are supposed to be copyists of us and things like that, but you listen to groups who are 'copyists' of yourself and there's nothing going on. I mean, to have people coming along and saying Grand Funk are the Led Zeppelin of America and they're really knocking Zeppelin off their position— you're going well 'please stop, I think you've got it wrong'."

SP asks Plant if he enjoys doing the acoustic material, "I do, because I manage to plonk guitar on about three numbers on this album and it means so much to me to be involved more than just vocally, to know that I've been able to contribute something a little more. But they can be so good because they can start off in one vein, and when you come to do them on stage they're nearly always like a stomp type of thing, and it gets really close to the people. That's all it is really with us. I think, just saying well, 'Good evening', and if you don't laugh and if you cry, and if you don't shout, and if you don't moan, and if you don't argue, then *you haven't had your money's worth. There's no story. Everybody's getting hung up on critics and things, but if they just let people get on with it, and let audiences pay their five bob or seven and sixes, or whatever we try to keep it to, and just came out saying something and laughing, then whatever it might be, so long as people get something positive out of it then we've done our job."*

Will Plant do a solo record or will he use Zeppelin as the vehicle for future projects, *"It can be the vehicle for anything any of us want to do. John Paul's delving very deeply into electronic stuff now, which to begin with I thought was a bit harsh. But listening to him a bit more and watching him a bit more and knowing him a lot more.... it all fits in. We don't get on each other's nerves, because each time we feel as if we're going to do that we just say "See you in a week", so every time a new idea comes up it's chewed and chewed. That's why people can't expect us to keep to "Whole Lotta Love" and things like that, because somebody might arrive at a rehearsal or a session and say-'How about this?'*

"The idea of a solo album occurs obviously, to everyone, but the thing is who else could play on it apart from me? There'd only be three other people, and that's Bonzo and Jonesy and Jimmy, because they're the most accustomed to what I do—vocally and everything else. I've sung with other people, people who I've admired and things like that, but there's a thing that spurs up in me when we (Led Zeppelin) are doing something good and it gets into a good thing. I don't mean repeating "Whole Lotta Love" every night, but there may be a section in the middle which has never arisen before, and at that point everybody just looks around at each other and goes

"Right", and we go from there.

SP asks whether the band feel obliged to play the old standards, *"Well it is expected isn't it? But it isn't just "Whole Lotta Love" because that lasts on stage maybe four minutes and for the rest, the construction that comes at different parts in that four minutes, spreads it to a ten minute thing. But within that ten minute thing, there are parts where the audience are up and applauding, there are parts when they'll maybe be quiet, and there are parts where they're shouting their heads off. That's how all that started really, with things like "Dazed And Confused" and "How Many More Times". When we recorded "How Many More Times" we just didn't know what we were, going to do; we knew the basic riff, but we didn't know 'The Hunter' was going to come into it, or 'Rosie'— they come on the night, or they come at the session. I think that's why we're still together and we're not bitching at each other or anything like that, because we know that wherever it is—even if it's in Iceland — if we suddenly hit on something . . . you can feel it coming from behind—the bass and drums suddenly knit together and its like a big handshake between the two and they go off, and Jimmy and I'll stay doing something else. It's like a good jigsaw puzzle. That's why a solo album would be useless because you wouldn't get half of it together. You could bring in all the incredible musicians you liked — the Memphis Horns, anybody — but you wouldn't get such a strong buzz. I wouldn't anyway."*

Does Plant feel held back by the audience expectations? *"Well I don't think that what they want is what we have to play, because we didn't have to play "Bron-Y-Aur Stomp" or "Friends" and things like that because it wasn't expected* of us was it and we did get a bit of a knocking for it, although personally I think that album (III) is the best thing that we've done. But you see you can get upset momentarily by the remarks, and probably all the way through this interview you'll get this one coming from me, but for all the people who griped and took the trouble to write gibberish to the music papers there were a lot of people who were surprised that we'd taken that much trouble to go that much farther.

"It's been there with James from the word off really, because really it was his conception and compared to mine his alternatives were numerous. I think he probably could have started doing something like that, but that probably it wouldn't have been as largely accepted. It's nice to have an audience and to say 'Right, we want to please people' and to get the ultimate kick out of it ourselves, because really there's very little else to get kicks out of apart from music, and the arts generally. You can't really turn up one day and decide to do a completely acoustic album and write twelve acoustic numbers three minutes long. But it isn't as if it has to be acoustic . . . on this new album the electric numbers are, in my eyes a lot better than the ones before. They many not be as instantly commercial, but if you listen to them long enough I think there's a lot more thought and a lot more maturity in them."

Peacock asks whether Plant thinks of the commercial consequences when he is writing, performing or recording. "Well they are three vastly different things. Writing a song, all it is is that you're in a certain mood and something starts to come out. It might never reach an audience and there are things that haven't reached audiences. If at the end of a song it's a gas then it's on the LP, and if it's a

gas that we want to think about a bit longer then it's not, or maybe there isn't room for it on the album. Writing a song is the last place you're going to start thinking about 2 x 20,000 people in Madison Square Garden. Making an album is a case of making your own personal idea of what is perfection at that point. I mean with the third album, I shed a couple of tears because I was so happy with it, but a lot of people weren't, so there's one proof of its pudding.

"If that was the case I'd want to be on the front of the _____ every week, I've seen people, mind you, who worry about the position of their guitars before they go on stage at "Top or The Pops"— and there's another farce. Bonzo and I went there the other night, and we went into the bar, and there were record pluggers everywhere. There was nil conversation — the whole thing stank. I'm afraid we became objectionable, because the more it went on the more I was thinking 'why?', and 'When's the train to Worcestershire?', and 'How did I get in here anyway?', and I got in because I said I was Mickey Most anyway, and they didn't know I wasn't. I'm going to get shot next week now. But the whole thing typified exactly what you were saying do we think about— and we don't. You can't, because if we did I'd have done something really silly to myself by now. That is The Business."

Peacock asks whether Plant is ever tempted to shock the audience with a totally different approach. "I don't think you can decide when you go on stage. I mean, you can't deny that when you're in a position to impress then you give them all you've got — everything, everything that you've got. But the mood changes often through three hours you get knackered in some places or maybe your heads spinning round and round but there's a part, five minutes on as it's building to it that you suddenly get caught up and you go right up to it and you take off somewhere. It's just a case of light and shade really and the audience are there as a black cloth for your light and shade so you can either get off on it or please themselves. There's a premeditation, there is the fact that 'Whole Lotta Love' will come somewhere towards the end of the show, but not really otherwise.

"(We wouldn't leave out Whole Lotta Love) because a lot of people have come because they want that, and they haven't the time to get into 'Friends' or 'Celebration Day', but 'Whole Lotta Love' has to be there to suck everybody in. Ah, that's a rash statement. To get people in who wouldn't come just to hear the other things."

Peacock asks about the legendary Lemon Song lyrics, "I think that was poetry at the time. In it's original context, that Robert Johnson album 'Travelin Riverside Blues', I was playing the album the other night and I am so proud of owning it, and that line 'squeeze my lemon 'till the juice runs down my leg' was just so indicative of that person Robert Johnson. When we recorded that it was in LA and it was a time when there was a lot of looning going on—and it was one of those states of mind you get into when everything's rosy and shining, and so a lyric like that comes zooming in. It's borrowed, admittedly, but why not? I really would like to think that someone who heard that and then saw some clever critic writing about Plant living off the far superior Robert Johnson, or whatever they have to say to keep their jobs, would go and listen to Robert Johnson as a result. But I wish I'd written that, I really do. Sometimes I wish I'd been Elvis . . . or

Superman, or that fella in the San Franciscan cartoons who always ends up an alley with some chick with her legs up in the air.

"But Robert Johnson . . . just him, the sympathy between guitar and vocal, the whole atmosphere of a record that was done in some back room—you can do that with John Lee Hooker and it's 40 minutes of boredom half the time, sometimes. But this Robert Johnson thing was a complete and utter statement. He was almost the innovator of the walking bass and all that sort of thing that Tommy McClennan and Muddy Waters grew from. Tommy McClennan especially came along afterwards and said 'Well, that's it, that's the ultimate personal blues.' But "squeeze my lemon" — I wish I could think of something like that myself. But it's not cool to do that these days you realise that don't you? If I'd been Elvis Presley I could have done something like that, but he cottoned on to Arthur Crudup instead. I could have just been a Robert Johnson bloke."

Peacock asks what Plant thinks the band has accomplished, "Well I hope we've made the impression by now that nothing is the norm, that nothing need be the same next time. We haven't categorised ourselves. And I don't think we've thrown ourselves at the public as much as a lot of other people who say they haven't — we don't put ourselves in the way of glory. But three years is such a short time to start making any grand assessment. We've had the opportunity to be super-duper incredible stars, and we could have lived on that much more than we have done, but I think it's just a case of holding back all the time because if you take the reins that are given to you, you end up destroying yourself—overdoing it, over playing it, over living it, and suddenly *finding out that the things from your past don't fit in at all with what you're doing now. Therefore it's much better for me to go home and be as I have been for years and years and years, than make some new being out of myself.... I haven't set myself any sort of position, and I don't look up to myself as being this that or the other. It's easy to say you don't, and do, but I think if I just carry on like this then our success will carry on for a long time, at least I hope it will. But anyway, our ability will increase and that's the main thing. I'm not going to lose sight of dry land, I don't think, though I've seen a lot of people do that."*

Was Led Zeppelin really formed to cash in on the dissolution of the Yardbirds? *"No, not really. What happened was that Jimmy didn't want to pack up altogether but Relfy and all that lot did and the stuff that the Yardbirds were doing was exciting — the fact that it had been overlooked in England and that the Yardbirds had overlooked England also was by the by. The Yardbirds weren't the biggest thing in America but they were the innovators almost of something that smelled refreshing to the American public. The ideas that Jimmy had were his own ideas, some of which he got out in the Yardbirds, some of which he didn't. His ideas were fresh and they excited me, and the ideas that I'd got, lyrically didn't have to coincide with what he was doing — they could have been totally different, and if they had been then I imagine that the group would have been different altogether. But we came together and we had the same likes and dislikes anyway, and blah, blah, you know it all anyway because you've read it a million times. But the point was, had that fusion not been the way it was we might have been like anybody—Edmundo Ross if you like it didn't*

have to be the way it turned out, because you can't tell someone how to write a song. Had I been a different kind of person or had anybody else in the group been just fractionally different. It would have been a different kettle of fish."

SP asks whether Plant thinks Page just hired the right people just to fit a preconceived mould. *"Well you don't think Jimmy asked me to join the group before he'd seen me work, do you? I mean he didn't say 'I'll have you, now what can you do?' People have said that, and it has been said by the people who say things for us but this is where you lose the artist or the person who is directly involved. That was the case, in as much as Jimmy wanted to continue as the Yardbirds were with a powerful thing. His alternatives were great and I know that at one point he probably wanted to do something at the other end of the scale, which he'd probably have done equally as well. But it wasn't a case of filling in any gap — it was the fact that I went to Jimmy's and because of what he had written and what he was playing the group turned out the way it did. Had it been simply a gap to be filled it would have been easy to take every cliché everything from the Yardbirds everything from everybody else who was fading or messing around, and built something on it. I've seen a lot of groups do that — a lot of groups who are supposed to be Led Zeppelin copies — and you can take so much, but that doesn't make you original. And I think we were (original), despite the orientations that were there and will always be there because I have to listen to sounds and I can't avoid it. But we weren't created to fill that gap primarily. Although it was my first chance of doing anything constructive with established people, apart from Alexis (Korner) and people like that I just* *couldn't have changed after all those years of battling and saying I believed in what I was doing. I had the Band of Joy, and we couldn't get many gigs in the Midlands, and we finally made Middle Earth and things like that, so I'd been adamant that long that it would have been pointless for me just to do anything, to accept being told to do anything, just to fill that gap. It's a fine point and it would take me a long time, and I'd have to know you a long time before I could get into explaining it in the finest detail, but it is something that mustn't be just stated as a fact. It's not as simple as that.".... * **Disc and Music Echo reports....** cover story.... Led Zeppelin are interested in playing at the Edgar Broughton Pakistan Relief concert.... **Record Mirror reports....** Led Zeppelin III is #33, Led Zeppelin II is #20, Led Zeppelin I is #47...Jimmy Page has bought a retreat in Scotland....

July 1971

3 **Record Mirror reports....** Led Zeppelin III is #35, Led Zeppelin II is #19...

6 **Il Milanese reports....** Uproar as Tour Begins, Hooligans and Police Clash at Led Zeppelin Concert.... once again a pop concert transforms into a riot at Velodromo Vigorelli and in adjacent streets, shower of stones against the authorities: two police injured, two arrests.... The tour at Milan was taken as an opportunity for the ever-present hooligans of pop music to unleash an absurd affront. Groups of young people, among whom were political demonstrators, clashed with the police. Showers of stones were met by gun fire. Two officers were injured and two ruffians were arrested.

The outcome would have been worse if the police department, remembering the sad consequences of past incidents, hadn't prepared in advance for such an eventuality. From the start of the evening over two thousand policemen were placed at strategic points in the stadium. Up to 9.30 p.m. the situation was normal. The public comprised of thousands of people who came to listen to the celebrated group Led Zeppelin. Outside the stadium only a small group of people roamed about trying to gain access without tickets, as well as a group of extremists who were distributing flyers announcing a rally organized for Thursday at Citta Studi. At 9.30 p.m. a large group of about four hundred people appeared on Arona Street and began to clap their hands to the well known song "French May" and to yell out, "PS-SS". Rocks started to fly and a police division fired to disperse the crowd. However they returned ten minutes later and the deputy police chief Dr. Vittoria called in a column of Jeeps. The violence moved into Corso Sampione (where police fired tear gas) and then moved to the perimeter of the stadium. The police blocked all entrances to the stadium but the hooligans persisted. At 10.30 p.m. barricades were placed at Domodossola St. and at Giovanni Da Procida St. The police opened fire again at Arona St. and surrounded a group of ruffians and confiscated their home made bombs....

10 **New Musical Express reports....** Led Zeppelin are hit by tear gas in a major riot at their show in Milan Italy.... **Record Mirror reports....** Led Zeppelin III is #35, Led Zeppelin II is #17...

17 **Record Mirror reports....** Led Zeppelin III is #28, Led Zeppelin II is #10...

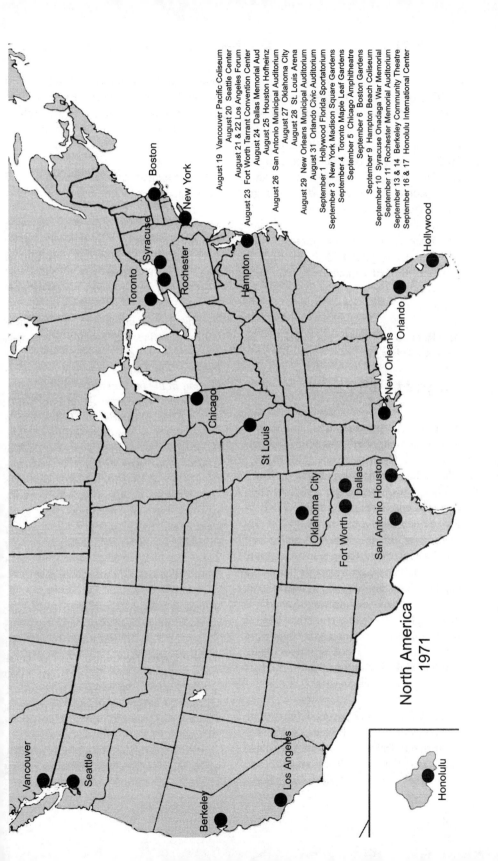

North America
1971

August 19 Vancouver Pacific Coliseum
August 20 Seattle Center
August 21 & 22 Los Angeles Forum
August 23 Fort Worth Tarrant Convention Center
August 24 Dallas Memorial Aud
August 25 Houston Hofheinz
August 26 San Antonio Municipal Auditorium
August 27 Oklahoma City
August 28 St. Louis Arena
August 29 New Orleans Municipal Auditorium
August 31 Orlando Civic Auditorium
September 1 Hollywood Florida Sportatorium
September 3 New York Madison Square Gardens
September 4 Toronto Maple Leaf Gardens
September 5 Chicago Amphitheatre
September 6 Boston Gardens
September 9 Hampton Beach Coliseum
September 10 Syracuse Onadaga War Memorial
September 11 Rochester Memorial Auditorium
September 13 & 14 Berkeley Community Theatre
September 16 & 17 Honolulu International Center

Boston
New York
Syracuse
Rochester
Toronto
Hampton
Hollywood
Orlando
New Orleans
Chicago
St Louis
Dallas
Oklahoma City
Fort Worth
San Antonio Houston
Vancouver
Seattle
Los Angeles
Berkeley
Honolulu

19 The Honolulu Advertiser reports.... Rumours are that Led Zeppelin will play here in August at the Civic. The reason for the Civic rather than the HIC is that the HIC is booked the only dates the Zep can play Honolulu. This is good news for anti-HIC people, because the dance-boogie will probably go for two shows....

24 Record Mirror reports.... Led Zeppelin III is #24, Led Zeppelin II is #21.... **Billboard reports....** Italian audiences prefer top pop acts such as Led Zeppelin and Donovan....

31 Record Mirror reports.... Led Zeppelin II is #21...

August 1971

5 Tokyo Asahi reports.... Immediate Announcement...Led Zeppelin Concert Canceled!! Contact Kyodo 417 8155.... **The Village Voice reports....** Advert reads — Concerts East Presents Led Zeppelin with Host, Scott Muni, WNEW-FM. Friday September 3 at 8:00 PM. By themselves for a special two and a half hour concert. Very few groups can create vibrations like Led Zeppelin. They've captured it on records and in concert, they bring the art of audience involvement to new heights. It's been a year since they've been in the States. Don't miss their only New York concert. Madison Square Garden. Tickets $5.50, 6.50 and 7.50. Box office opens August 5 at 10:00 am....

6 Tokyo Asahi reports.... Immediate Announcement.... Led Zeppelin Concert Confirmed! Tickets go on sale 8/9 (Mon) at all "Play Guide" outlets Contact Kyodo 417 8155.... **Los Angeles Free Press**

reports.... Advert reads — Concert West Invites You To Spend An Evening With Led Zeppelin Thursday August 19th at 8:00 PM at the Fabulous Forum. (This show was rescheduled)....

7 New Musical Express reports.... Led Zeppelin are off to America again to play a series of 18 concerts beginning in Vancouver on August 19th.... **Record Mirror reports....** Led Zeppelin III is #50, Led Zeppelin II is #25.... **Billboard reports....** UK Tour-ism Is Alive and Well in U.S.. Cover story detailing how British band's are faring well on the American tour circuit. In an interview with one of Premier Talent's agents it is revealed why Led Zeppelin didn't perform at Woodstock. *"There's a misconception in the business that from a monetary point of view festivals are successful. At the time of Woodstock, Led Zeppelin played five dates around the area at triple the money. The festival audience usually travels from 200-300 miles to make the festival scene, which usually means a 'barring clause' goes up against working the area. Zeppelin would not have been able to play those five dates if they had done Woodstock. The same is true today. I advise my acts against festivals."....* Led Zeppelin to begin an American tour....

9 The Honolulu Advertiser reports.... Led Zeppelin at the Civic. The show we rumoured as happening in August will happen instead September 16. The dance show will be one price $5 with only 4,000 tickets available. They go on sale soon.... **Honolulu Star Bulletin reports....** Tickets for the Led Zeppelin go on sale on Friday, The group's Shea Stadium concert in N.Y. is already sold out (55,000 seats) as is it's upcoming show in L.A. and appearances in Vancouver, Dallas and

Houston. A really hot rock act.... **Melody Maker reports....** Led Zeppelin are back on tour....

13 **Los Angeles Free Press reports....** Advert reads — Concert West Invites You To Spend An Evening With Led Zeppelin Saturday August 21st at 8:00 PM. By Special Request we're adding a 2nd show Sunday August 22nd at 8:00 PM At the fabulous Forum.....

14 **Record Mirror reports....** Led Zeppelin II is #16.... **Sounds reports....** Led Zeppelin From Ashes.... Article charting Zeppelin's rise from the ashes of the Yardbirds. Inevitably the band is compared to the Cream and the band's soaring success is said to have taken it's toll on their staunchest of allies. Plant remarks that he has to hold himself back a bit to prevent burn out, *"If you take up the reins that are given you, you end up destroying yourself."* The band's last album was recorded in the country on a mobile truck. A new album recorded in February should be released shortly after mixing problems are resolved.... The article then goes on to list the band's equipment.... Jimmy Page, Four 4x12 Marshall Speaker Cabinets, there are three 35 watt speakers in each cabinet, 2 Hiwatt 100 Watt Amplifiers with treble boosters, 2 Vox echo chambers, 1 Echoplex echo chamber, 1 Sonic Wave (Therome), 2 Gibson Les Paul Guitars, 1 Rickenbacker 12 string guitar, 1 Fender Telecaster, Ernie Ball Super Slinky Strings, Vox Wah Wah Pedal.... John Paul Jones, Fender Jazz Bass Guitar, Fender Telecaster Bass Guitar, 3 acoustic cabinets, 2 Acoustic Amp tops (pre amps), 2 Marshall 4 x 12 horn cabinets - 3 SW speakers, 2 Marshall 100 Watt amplifiers, 1 Farfisa Duo Pro Organ, 1 Farfisa single manual organ, 1 145 Leslie Speaker cabi-

net.... John Bonham, Drums all made by Ludwig, 1 14" x 10" side Tom Tom, 1 16" x 16" side Tom Tom, 1 18" x 16" side Tom Tom, 2 26" x 15" bass drums, 2 14" x 6½" snare drums, 1 24" ride cymbal, 2 20" crash cymbals, 2 14" Hi-hat cymbals.... Robert Plant, 3000 Watt JBL PA system, 8 6" x 4" Wuffer speaker cabinets, 4 Long range horns, 4 medium range horns, 4 close range horns all with electronic cross-overs, 1 Binson echo chamber, All instruments and drums are miked up with Shure Unidyne microphones....

17 **Boston After Dark reports....**Advert reads — Concerts East presents Led Zeppelin Boston Garden Sept. 6, 8 pm $6.50, 5.50, 4.50 On sale Monday August 16 at all Ticketron Outlets....

20 **Vancouver Sun reports....** Rock Concert noise monitor beaten up, machine broken. Article details that a $2,500 noise monitoring device was smashed and it's operator beaten when he placed it on the stage to check noise levels at a Led Zeppelin concert at the Vancouver Coliseum. The victim says he was dragged outside and beaten and his machine was returned to him smashed....

21 **New Musical Express reports....** Jimmy Page is pictured on stage in Montreux Switzerland... the band will be playing to full houses across America... **Record Mirror reports....** Led Zeppelin II is #30.... **Sounds reports....** Zep US Tour. Picture of Page with accompanying article.... LED ZEPPELIN are on another blockbusting tour. After two unusual dates at the Montreux Casino in Switzerland, where dinner jacketed diners mixed with Zeppelin fans, they leave for a mammoth tour of the United States, Canada and Japan. They open on the West

CONCERTS EAST Presents

LED ZEPPELIN

WITH HOST, SCOTT MUNI, WNEW-FM

FRIDAY, SEPTEMBER 3 AT 8:00 P.M.

By Themselves for a Special 2½ hour Concert

VERY FEW GROUPS CAN CREATE VIBRATIONS LIKE LED ZEPPELIN. THEY'VE CAPTURED IT ON RECORDS AND, IN CONCERT, THEY BRING THE ART OF AUDIENCE INVOLVEMENT TO NEW HEIGHTS. IT'S BEEN A YEAR SINCE THEY'VE BEEN IN THE STATES. DON'T MISS THEIR ONLY NEW YORK CONCERT.

 **madison square garden**

Pennsylvania Plaza, 7th Ave., 31st to 33rd Sts.

TICKETS: $5.50, 6.50, 7.50 available at Madison Square Garden box office and all TICKETRON outlets. Make check or money order payable to Madison Square Garden Center and enclose stamped, self-addressed envelope and 50¢ per order for handling. Never mail cash. Mail to Madison Square Garden Center 4 Penn Plaza N.Y.C. For information phone: (212) 564-4400 or Ticketron at (212) 644-4400.

BOX OFFICE OPENS THURSDAY, AUGUST 5 AT 10:00 A.M.

Coast of Canada at Vancouver on August 19 and the itinerary continues: Los Angeles 21 and 22, Fort Worth 23, Dallas 24, Houston 25, San Antonio 26, New Orleans 29, Orlando, Fla. 31, Miami, September 1, New York Madison Square Gardens 3, Toronto 4, Chicago 5, Boston 7, Hampton 9, Syracuse 10, Rochester 11 San Francisco 13 and 14 Honolulu 16 and 17. After that they rest and then continue with five days of gigs in Japan....

25 **Tokyo Asahi reports....** Pop Concert in Autumn.... No. 1 band in England Led Zeppelin.... This time 4 extra players bass, piano, etc, will accompany the band live on 9/6 & 7 at Koseinenkin. This is an event in the series known as "Rock Carnival" which started last year. This is the 7th "Rock Carnival" presentation. Other Bands in the series included Chicago and Grand Funk. Now Led Zeppelin will play Japan.

28 **Record Mirror reports....** Led Zeppelin II is #39...

29 **The Miami Herald reports....** Special Events.... Led Zeppelin - Popular heavy rock group plays one-nighter at Miami Jai

Alai Fronton at 8 pm Wednesday.... **New Orleans Times Picayune....** Advert reads — It's What's Happening Today Led Zeppelin 8 pm Municipal Auditorium....

September 1971

1 **The Miami Herald reports....** Rock Concert Site Changed.... The concert by the rock group Led Zeppelin scheduled for 8 pm tonight at Miami Jai Alai fronton will be staged instead at the Hollywood Sportatorium....

2 **Honolulu Advertiser reports....** Led Zeppelin's Hawaii bound again with two instead of one night at the Civic.... the band will perform Friday as well...Show time both nights will be 8 pm....

4 **Disc and Music Echo reports....** Led Zeppelin sold out two nights at the LA forum...36,000 people. The band then went to the Rocking L Ranch in Texas for a rest.... **Record Mirror reports....** Led Zeppelin II is #39.... **New Musical Express reports....** Led Zeppelin cause plenty of action in audience as well as on stage!.... article chronicling the legendary event when Peter Grant smashed the equipment of a Canadian government scientist. "Zeppelin is in the middle of an American tour, last weekend in Vancouver the band played in the hockey arena which houses over 13,000 people but it wasn't enough and nearly 3,000 didn't get in. Inevitably the police clashed with the punters outside.... During the show a group of government scientists were checking sound levels but their equipment was mistaken for bootlegging gear. Their equipment was summarily destroyed. The local police are looking for the band's manager for questioning....

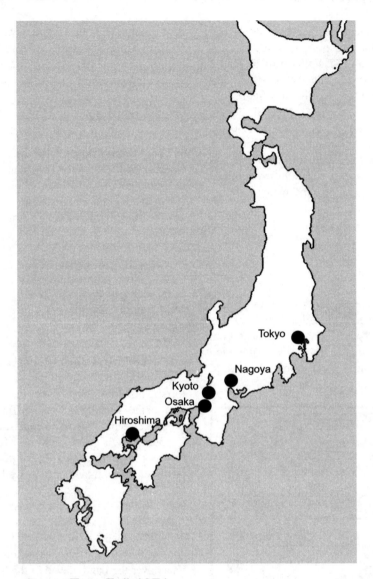

Japan Tour Fall 1971
September 23rd & 24th 1971 Tokyo Budokan Hall
September 27th, 1971 Hiroshima Shiei Taiikukan
September 28th & 29th 1971 Osaka Festival Hall

Japan Tour Fall 1972
October 2nd & 3rd 1972 Tokyo Budokan Hall
October 4th, 1972 Osaka Festival Hall
October 5th, 1972 Nagoyashi Kokaido
October 9th, 1972 Osaka Festival Hall
October 10th, 1972 Kyoto Kaikan #1 Hall

the band's upcoming show at Toronto's 18,000 seat Maple Leaf Garden's is expected to sell out.".... **Billboard reports....** Zeppelin Rocks On To Hawaii. Article outlines American tour dates. It says the band's upcoming show at New York's Madison Square Gardens on September 3rd sold out in a few hours. Further tour dates are said to be, Orlando Civic Auditorium Tuesday August 31, Maimi's Jai Alai Fronton Wednesday (1), Madison Square Garden (3), Toronto's Maple Leaf Garden (4), Chicago's Amphitheater (5), Boston Garden (7), Hampton Roads Coliseum Virginia (9), Syracuse War Memorial (10), Rochester War Memorial (11), San Francisco Berkeley Community Theatre (13 & 14), and Honolulu Civic Auditorium (16 & 17).... **Toronto Globe & Mail reports....** Advert reads — Some Tickets Still Left. Hurry! Tonight at 8.00 pm. Concerts East Presents Led Zeppelin Only Eastern Canadian Appearance. Led Zeppelin drew 17,500 in Vancouver last week 3,000 were turned away. Tickets at the Gardens Box Office. A Maple Leaf Gardens 40th Anniversary attraction....

11 **Record Mirror reports....** Led Zeppelin II is #27...

17 **Honolulu Star Bulletin reports....** Led Zeppelin is Shot Down.... review of the show in Honolulu.... The real irony of Led Zeppelin's two hour performance last night was that they played their own review in their last number, "Communication Breakdown". The show itself was marred by a generally sloppy performance on the part of the group, rather noisy behaviour on the part of some of the 4,000 people in attendance, and a hot and sweaty atmosphere on the part of the good ol' poorly ventilated Civic Auditorium.... the music was limp and uneven during all but a small part of the evening.... they started with Immigrant Song and from the first note it was obvious that these guys were not into what they were doing. Rhythms were off, Plante's (sic) vocals were relatively impotent and the overall group cohesion and enthusiasm was missing.... throughout Since I've Been Loving You, Celebration Day, Dazed & Confused, I Can't Quit You, Black Dog, and Stairway To Heaven you couldn't help but get the impression that these guys were tired and looking forward to the end of the evening.... the only bright spot came with a crisp drum solo by John Bonham and a romping version of Whole Lotta Love which featured a number of old rock 'n' roll songs including 'Hello Mary Lou'.... Aside from someone yanking down the microphone and yelling into it, another clown jumped up on the stage and started yelling some four letter gems into the mike. The band should be commended for their ability to put up with such obstacles.... **Honolulu Advertiser reports....** Advert reads — KPOI Presents an Evening with Led Zeppelin Civic Auditorium 8 pm Sept 16 and 17 Civic Auditorium Tonight....

18 **New Musical Express reports....** Led Zeppelin will be part of a film festival at the National Film theatre.... **Sounds reports....** Atlantic will release the new Led Zeppelin album in the next few weeks.... **Record Mirror reports....** Led Zeppelin II is #50...

25 **New Musical Express reports....** Zeppelin Now.... cover story.... Led Zeppelin currently on a record breaking tour of America return to this country early next month to plan the release of their new album and forthcoming British

tour which it is hoped will take place before Christmas.... Jimmy Page is mixing the album but no release date is set.... the band plan a trip to India before their British tour.... Ritchie Yorke reviews the band's gig at Maple Leaf Garden's in Toronto Canada.... the band flew in from New York for the show, they played for over two hours and then went straight on to Chicago. The tour is only 20 shows long and is expected to gross over $1 million.... songs at the Toronto show included You Shook Me, Communication Breakdown, Dazed & Confused and Whole Lotta Love.... the band sold out New York's Madison Square Gardens in record time.... the band's fourth album continues to be delayed.... rumours of the band's break up were denied by Page, *"We just hadn't had any time to sit down and get a balance on things. Now it's much more together. We'd been touring so much earlier this year and I think everything tended to lose proportion. It was rough for a little while. But we now plan on doing a lot more things than previously."* .... **Record Mirror reports....** Led Zeppelin II is #37...

October 1971

2 **Melody Maker reports....** Cover story Led Zeppelin fly in.... the cover of the new album is completely wordless and it should be out in five weeks.... **Record Mirror reports....** Led Zeppelin II is #37.... **New Musical Express reports....** Page's Rages.... In the second part of his interview with Jimmy Page, journalist Ritchie Yorke begins with the subject of Grand Funk Railroad who at the time were being compared favourably with Zeppelin. Page, *"I've never heard anything by them. I know it sounds outra-*

geous to admit that but it is true. I've only ever seen them doing a small segment on a BBC TV show I watched in England. It was at the time when they were just starting to get big in the States. It was difficult to judge from that."

Yorke mentions Grand Funk had recently drawn 50,000 people to Shea Stadium. *"Yes that's true but we heard that Humble Pie went down better with the kids at that gig."*

Yorke observes that Black Sabbath are now drawing big crowds in America, *"Really? That's the first time we've heard that. They've done quite well in England but I didn't know they were drawing big crowds in North America."*

At this point Yorke switches to the overall American music scene and Page's impressions, *"It's hard to say really. The sort of scene I'd like to see is where all the different facets of the arts in the musical sphere are accepted readily by the media and the public. As it stands at the moment and it's because of the press there has to be one particular thing in vogue at any one time. And soon as that one thing becomes really popular, that's it; you've got to find something else, something new. And then as soon as that is exposed and everybody knows about it. It's time to find something new again. It's the old esoteric thing. Unfortunately the whole thing that is happening with us is the same as the James Taylor thing — but a complete opposite, suddenly people are starting to say, 'Hang on he's a damn good lyricist and a good songwriter but on stage he sounds very samey after about 40 minutes.' And now of course all the people that were waving the flag are sort of crapping themselves a bit.*

"I blame the press for the whole stagnancy that frequently comes over the music business. It's totally because of the

press. Just let the musicians and the people get on with it, which is all the people ask for. Then everything would be accepted and there's so much happening in the music scene when you think about it. Many critics seem to let their personal tastes jade what they're seeing and hearing. It's that whole thing of being put in a bag. Unfortunately people are so trendy, that's the terror of it all really. There always seems to have to be a trend to follow. And if what you sing on that stage doesn't comply with what they consider should be the particular trend they tear it apart. Of course these people should not be allowed anywhere near a pen or a typewriter or the press because what they're saying and doing is just totally the opposite of what's going on in the scene and what's going down. I mean it's like me going along and trying to write up a report on well.... I don't know."

Yorke briefly discusses the fact that the critics, especially in America don't seem to have much respect for talent in general. Page, *"We're not asking for their respect I mean, criticism can be great, valid criticism that is. I said it before and I'll say it again— if I play badly I know that I've played badly, and when I play well, I know I've played well. According to my own capabilities. People shouldn't go along expecting an enigma when they see this bloke on the stage, and expect to see the epitome of what they consider to be the best rock guitarist.*

"They should realise the bloke is only a human being — another struggling musician trying, trying, trying to better himself. That's why there's always this big race about who's the best. There's nobody who's the best—nobody's the best. There's always somebody who's got a particular field who's better than the bloke who's claimed to be the best. That's

what's so good for me—that's what makes the whole scene for me but for these others who always have to classify everything."

Yorke points out that Eric Clapton probably quit the scene due to the media and their expectations of him. Page, *"Well I dunno. I went through what I think Eric may have gone through. It's just the fact that suddenly everything you pick up seems to go sour. Everything you read. You know, you're trying your hardest and everyone is just saying, well you know, putting you down every time you try something. I think for everybody who is really trying their hardest and is reasonably sensitive into the bargain it's gonna do a lot of damage, and I think it certainly did a lot of damage to Eric. I know another person it did do a lot of damage to, about three or four years ago, and that was George Harrison, who could hardly pick up a guitar because he just felt that everyone thought he was a joke. It was obviously totally untrue as far as the public went, but as far as the press went, there were these snide comments and all that sort of thing. He made a friendship with Eric and he went through the sitar thing, which was pretty valid and he did some good things on that. But as soon as he got with Eric, he became a guitar man, and he tried and he tried and he tried. Now he's having a go and he's won through which is good for him if he's got the strength and, the will to persevere, but for some people, it could shatter them totally. But it's funny that since their split, you can see how important it was when the four of them were together. I met Paul McCartney in New York recently and he was talking to me about the album he was doing — the second one, 'Ram'. He said you can't believe how hard it is when you've worked with people for that amount of time—the same four people working together — and you come up with a song. And you just say, 'All right, here it is,' and everybody just fits their bit in and it's there I know exactly what Paul means, because it's like that with us. He said it was so difficult to get it together with all fresh studio people. And I can sympathise with him. I know what it was like when I was playing sessions in London. The blokes would come in with their song and every session musician would have to try and do his best. Obviously it wasn't as good as the bloke's own group but some A & R man was saying 'well there's got to be the session man, the group don't match up to the quality we require."*

Apparently soft-rock had been dominating the radio of the time, Yorke mentions this. *"Oh really I can tell you one thing — whenever a good rock 'n'roll single comes out in England, it goes to No 1 every time without fail. All the old schmaltz will start happening and you've only got the radio stations to blame for that. I am going to repeat myself time and time again because I think this is so important — radio stations and rock writers should give an overall picture of what's going on, without all these jaded opinions that come in. All that 'this is what's happening man — forget everyone else —put them down because this is happening.' It's so wrong man. But I know what my personal record collection consists of, and it's got just about everything from ethnic folk music of the aborigines, to Mahler. It's all part of it."*

Yorke asks Page what he listens to at home. *"All sorts of different things. Bert Jansch is often on. Paderewski. No, that hasn't been on for a while. Lots of early rock.... lots of that. All the Sun stuff, it still sends shivers up my spine. It really*

does. You put on something like the early Presley records and you hear the phrasing, you hear the excitement, and everyone's really into it. At the end of 'Mystery Train,' you hear them laughing— it's fantastic. And I can still get into those records because I know the excitement and the feeling that was there in those early days when they really knew that they were breaking into something, a new form of music. It has become a bit of a vogue. Unfortunately too. I personally feel people like Elton John should leave it well alone. It's very hard. His albums are really really good. For what he's doing. I wouldn't fault them. For his bag. But when he stands up and in some sort of yellow jacket, pink suit and pink trousers and silver shoes, then kicks over the stool which I thought was an incredible sendup of Jerry Lee Lewis. I thought it was great humour and then suddenly you realise that he's serious and it's a bit of a comedown after watching all that other stuff."

Is there anyone that Page rates on the current British scene, *"Yes quite frankly there are (some) but my head's spinning at the moment and I can't bring anything to mind. If you asked me about American bands I couldn't even answer right now."*

Yorke persists with Grand Funk. Page, *"That wasn't a put down on the band, it's just that in England they don't get played. I've heard reports about them, but nothing that would send me to a record shop to buy them on the off chance that they are good. I'll never do that again anyway with a record. And I advise everybody else to do the same. Never buy a record until you know it's good. I just seriously and honestly haven't heard a Grand Funk Railroad record. I don't know what they're up to or anything."*

Page is asked what he will be up

to in the near future, *"I think home recording studios are going to be a big step towards better things. I hope for myself anyway. We've been recording on and off for a year. Not constantly for a year, but every now and again we said, 'all right let's go in and see what we can do'. Every sort of thing seems to be a relative statement of where you are at that point, you know what you're up to then. It's a relative statement for the time. And what you've got to think of all the time is that the next one will be better, better, better. That's all you can do really. We had a big discussion amongst ourselves, and the idea was to just keep working, doing a couple of dates a week around England so that we're never rusty. Because sometimes we'd really knock ourselves out doing five days a week and all that in America, and then going back knackered. Then when it came to do a date, you'd be rusty, but now the idea is to just keep it ticking over nicely."*

Yorke continues by asking what happened at the band's recent catastrophic concert in Milan Italy. Page, *"The policing of the people was what initially ruined it. It wasn't until the brave few rushed forward that things started to happen. But I'll give you the whole rundown on it. We were playing on the grass in a huge football ground. There were five or six groups before us, and it was sort of a festival thing which had been apparently organised and sponsored by the government. We went out on stage and started playing, and suddenly there was loads of smoke coming from the back of the oval. The promoter came out and said tell them to stop lighting fires. So like twits we said into the mikes, 'Will you stop lighting fires, please. The authorities might make us stop and all that sort of thing. So be cool about it, stop lighting fires, and we'll*

carry on playing.' Anyway we went on for about 20 or 30 minutes. Every time they'd stand up for an encore there'd be loads of smoke. What it really was, as it turned out, was the police firing tear gas into the crowd. We didn't know at the time, we just kept saying repeatedly 'Would you stop lighting fires'. Twits you know."

At this point John Paul Jones interjects, *"The eyes were stinging a bit by then. We kept on playing though."*

Page, *"Anyway, we were playing and then we said 'blow this, it's got into tear gas let's cut it really short'. So we did one more number then we went into 'Whole Lotta Love', and they all jumped up. At this point there had been 40 or 50 minutes of tear gas coming in and out lofting about, and somebody threw a bottle up at the police. It was to be expected since the crowd had been bombarded for no reason, for no reason at all. And of course as soon as the bottle went up, that's what they'd been waiting for. Whoooosh there it went, all over the grounds, 30 or 40 canisters of tear gas all going at once. This tunnel that we had to escape through was filled with the stuff. It wasn't done purposely. It's just the way that things went. It was on another level and we had to run straight through this tear gas to get to the other side which was a catwalk of rooms. We didn't know even then if we were going to find chaos on the other side, people panicking and running. We got in there and people were carried off in stretchers, into our room, probably thinking it was immune from the gas."*

Jones, *"The roadies were carried off on stretchers, trying to save the gear. You see they'd cordoned all the audience right around the back. There was a big line of police holding them there, and the only way they could go was forward, onto the stage. They forced something like*

10,000 people up on to the stage."
      Page, *"And our roadies were running around trying to save our instruments. (Italy) is a word never mentioned in my hearing. It causes a big argument, or nervous breakdown."*
      Jones, *"It was a war."*
      Page, *"Right it was a war. And to top it all off, after all this a reporter came back, a guy who'd seen the whole thing and knew exactly what happened and knew that the police had started it. He had the cheek to come into the bar where we were resting, we were completely shattered emotionally, he came in and said, 'What's your comments about that?' Of course we just tore him apart saying, 'C'mon you saw it, now you write it up. Don't ask our opinion. You've got your own.' But he kept saying he wanted a comment from us. He almost got a bottle smashed over his head."*

9 **New Musical Express reports....** Led Zeppelin may be playing a three day outdoor festival in Studley Warwickshire next August.... **Record Mirror reports....** Led Zeppelin II is #40...

16 **New Musical Express reports....** Led Zeppelin were honoured in the city of Hiroshima...the band played to a full house and donated all the proceeds to a charity for the bombing victims and survivors.... they were given a medal of appreciation by the mayor of the city.... **Record Mirror reports....** Led Zeppelin II is #33...

23 **Record Mirror reports....** Led Zeppelin II is #47...

30 **Record Mirror reports....** Led Zeppelin II is #44...**Disc and Music Echo reports....** Win the complete Led Zeppelin album collection...contest featuring a Led Zeppelin crossword puzzle....

Music Life reports.... Multi-page article outlining the band's history in detail concluding with a US tour itinerary. Vancouver Aug 19 Coliseum, Los Angeles Aug 21 Forum, Fort Worth Aug 23 Will Rogers Auditorium, Dallas Aug 24 Memorial Auditorium, Houston Aug 25 Sam Houston Coliseum, San Antonio Aug 26 Hemisphere Arena, New Orleans Aug 29 Municipal Auditorium, Orlando Aug 31 Civic Auditorium, Miami Sept 1 Jai Alai Fon Ton, New York Sept 3 Madison Square Gardens, Toronto Sept 4 Maple Leaf Gardens, Chicago Sept 5 Amphitheater, Boston Sept 7 Boston Gardens, Hampton Rhodes Sept 9 Coliseum, Syracuse Sept 10 War Memorial, Rochester Sept 11 War Memorial, San Francisco Sept 13 and 14 Berkeley Community Theater, Honolulu Sept 16 and 17 Civic Auditorium....

November 1971

6 **Melody Maker reports....** Zeppelin tour.. cover story.... Led Zeppelin are set for a series of British dates during November including a special concert at the Empire Pool Wembley before an estimated crowd of 9,500.... show will be presented by Rikki Farr and Peter Grant.... tickets will be on sale at Harlequin records at 11am tomorrow (Friday).... other dates include.... Newcastle City Hall (11), Locarno Sunderland (12, Caird Hall Dundee (13), St. Matthews Baths Ipswich (16), Kinetic Circus Birmingham (17), Sheffield University (18) and Free Trade Hall Manchester (24).... Farr, *"Wembley is an excellent opportunity for a highly*

New Led Zeppelin Album
Now Available

original production incorporating circus acts. There may well be animals on stage too.".... Acoustic amplifiers which are made in Los Angeles are now being distributed in the UK.... Top groups using Acoustic include Led Zeppelin.... **New Musical Express reports....** Zep Nov. Tour.... cover story.... announcing the tour dates there is also mention of the show being scheduled to last over five hours.... Zeppelin's new album will be released on November 19th to coincide with the tour.... **Disc and Music Echo reports....** cover story.... Led Zeppelin surprise gigs; fourth album at last.... Led Zeppelin do a series of British concerts starting next week. The new album will be released to coincide with the tour. Manager Peter Grant, *"The decision to do some shows here again was taken while we were in Japan several weeks ago. There are eight concerts set so far; we'll try to do more if we can find the halls to take us. Newcastle sold out before word was officially out. The manager found so many people waiting outside the hall that he was forced to sell tickets on the spot."* At the band's show at Wembley there are expected to be other name bands. Zeppelin will feature material from their new album. The album has no title but the cover has instead four Icelandic runes each representing a member of the group. The idea came from Jimmy Page. In Germany the album has garnered 85,000 advance orders. These shows will be Zeppelin's first since the "Back To The Clubs" tour in March.... **Sounds reports....** Cover story Led Zeppelin to Tour Britain.... LED ZEPPELIN are back on the road in Britain this month. They are set to play eight dates including Wembley's Empire Pool on November 20, where they will be heading a five-hour concert which is being produced by Rikki Farr for Buffalo Concert

Presentation Limited in association with Peter Grant. The show will also feature other artists to be announced later, as well as Surprise" acts taken from the world of vaudeville and circus. Said Rikki Farr: 'This is a unique opportunity for us to present a highly original Production of Led Zeppelin to a large London audience—In fact an audience that's not had the opportunity of seeing the boys for well over a year.' The price of the tickets will be 75p for all seats and the Policy will be first come first served, Farr explained. No one person will be able to buy more than five tickets—and this is designed to eliminate fans having to pay high prices to ticket touts. Tickets will be on sale at all branches of Harlequin Records from 11 a.m. on November 5. Zeppelin will also be playing concerts at the following venues: Newcastle City Hall, November 11, Locarno, Sunderland 12, Caird Hall, Dundee 13, St. Matthews Baths, Ipswich 16, Kinetic Circus. Birmingham 17, Sheffield University 18, and Free Trade Hall, Manchester 24. It is expected that further dates will be announced later. No date or title has yet been set for Zeppelin's new album.... **Billboard reports....** Cover page advert for the new album plus teasers running the four symbols throughout the issue.... Advert reads — Ask Led Zeppelin About Mike. Led Zeppelin uses Shure Unispheres to get themselves together for some of the heaviest sounds anywhere. Now music-stoned audiences from coast to coast hear Led Zeppelin as they really sound, naturally!.... Kinney are preparing a big push on the new Led Zeppelin LP....

13 **Melody Maker reports....** Zeppelin Fever.... cover story.... The great Zeppelin rush is on. Fans up and down the country snapped up tickets for Led Zeppelin con-

certs in double quick time.... a second show has been added at the Empire Pool Wembley on November 21.... the first show sold out in 54 minutes.... other dates added are, Preston Town Hall (23), Leicester University (25) and Bournemouth Starkers (Dec. 2).... Zeppelin's fourth album will be in the shops by Christmas.... Solved The Great Zeppelin Mystery.... feature article, album review and interview with John Bonham.... Bonham on the subject of the Far East, *"It was a fantastic place to play. Rock music has only just started to happen there in the last two years but it is now the second biggest market in the world for rock records. The people were so friendly and we had the best rock promoter in the world there looking after us. It turned out that Immigrant Song is one of our biggest songs in Japan and it's the number with which we always open the act. So the audiences went potty! It's a strange scene there. A lot of big groups are going in now, but they don't have a rock station on the radio. There's only the US forces stuff.*

"The American tour we did was good in actual fact. It was quite strange because we hadn't been to America for almost a year. To be perfectly honest, I was scared. But we played really well and had some great things happen. The Los Angeles Forum sold out in one day so we did another concert there and we really didn't expect such a demand. I think I enjoyed it more than any other tour of America.

"You see we had a lot of time at home to think, and we grew a lot closer together. We kept seeing stories, 'Zeppelin are breaking up'. But really we have never been closer together. We all came out of ourselves and everybody played well and we are really happy! These

breaking up rumours are always cropping up. I don't know their source, but they are forever saying that so-and-so is leaving. There was an unbelievable one about a year ago. They said I was leaving to join George Harrison. Well, I've never even met the guy. That's how much I know him. I'd like to meet him.

"We did three tours last year and finished off feeling 'We've just about had enough'. We had done so much in such a short space of time, we were drained. We had offers to go everywhere, France, America, and we could have done them. But what would be the point? We were tired. We had worked hard and Peter had probably worked harder than any of us. We enjoyed working but we needed the break before we got stale. We spent the time, six months, at home and writing songs. Then we said 'Right, we're ready let's go.'

"During the break we did a lot of recording and wrote a lot and improved. We didn't do any gigs, but there was absolutely no inclination to split up and I'm not bullshitting. We've all got ideas and things we want to do. John Paul Jones is incredible. He comes along to the studio and he's always got a new instrument he wants to play. I don't do much writing myself, but I appreciate what they write and I can enjoy playing it. I'm not governed by them in what I play. They ask me how a drum thing should be played and that's how we all work.

"I've never tried consciously to be one of the best drummers and I don't want to be. A lot of kids come up to me and say, 'There's a lot better drummers than you,' or something. But I enjoy playing to the best of my ability and that's why I'm here doing it. I don't claim to be more exciting than Buddy Rich. But I don't play what I don't like. I'm a simple straight

ahead drummer and I don't try to pretend to be anything better than I am. I love playing the drums and I practice a bit. There is always something another drummer can play that will knock me out. I watch all the drummers in groups and I always learn from them."

Interviewer Chris Welch then asks about the new LP, *"Ah ha the new LP. The cover means whatever people want to read into it. For me it means, 'I'd rather live in an old house than a block of flats.' My personal view is that the album is the best thing we've ever done. But that's strictly my personal view, I love it. It's the fourth album and it's the stage we were in at the time of the recording. All the albums have been different and to my mind this is the best, and that's not trying to be big headed or flash. The playing is some of the best we have done and Jimmy is like.... mint!*

"The runes are symbols that simply apply to each of us, I wouldn't like to state what they mean. We each picked one. The printer had problems. But it's an album we can honestly say we are proud of. All the guys are looking forward to the tour. A lot of kids have called us an American group or even a Japanese group. But we are going to do four gigs a week here until the end of January. I hate it when they start slagging us."

And the future? Bonham, *"Bloody hard to say. I can't say what we are going to sound like in the future and I don't really want to know. If I could tell you what we're going to sound like in two years time, it would ruin it anyway. We might be on top next year, or I might be back on the buildings."*.... Exclusive preview of Zeppelin's new LP.... "It is their fourth and not their best or worst. It is a fine new album by a group who can now take a step outside the environment of controversy that expands like a conurbation around the newly successful.... the sound of Zeppelin in full cry is most satisfying."...centre spread two page ad for Wembley...**New Musical Express reports....** Zeppelin add extra tour dates Preston on Nov. 23, Leicester on the 25th, Bournemouth on December 2nd, and a second show at Manchester Belle Vue on November 30th.... **Disc and Music Echo reports....** cover story.... Led Zeppelin's Robert Plant champions the under 30's.... interview with Caroline Boucher conducted in a Wimpy Burger joint in Oxford Street. He has just returned from touring the Far East with Page and tour manager Richard Cole where he claims to have spent all of his earnings from the tour of Japan. Boucher asks about the new album, *"I'm pleased with it, but I'm disgusted at the amount of time it's taken to get it off. We recorded it around April and it was virtually ready then except for the mixing. Jimmy took all the material over to Sunset Sound in Los Angeles with a very famous producer who said it was THE studio, and did the mixes. We finished recording in February and the idea was to mix it there and get it out in March. But he brought the tapes back and they sounded terrible, so we had to start mixing all over again. We were disgusted at the amount of time it had taken to get the album finished. The sound of the mixing room that Andy Johns took Jimmy to was really duff . . .The whole story of the fourth album reads like a nightmare. The sound had to be remixed again in this country, then a master tape of one track 'Four Sticks' was lost. With every cover we've had before, what we've asked for hasn't been what we've got. We wanted a cover with no writing on it, not the Atlantic symbol or the 'uptight and outa sight' bit."*

Boucher then points out that Plant is venturing to play guitar on the new album, specifically the 'Battle Of Evermore'. She asks him about the abuse his vocal cords take on tour, *"You get off a plane that's air-conditioned into staggering heat, then into an air-conditioned car, then into the heat, and into an air-conditioned hotel room and so on to the gig, and that affects my voice. Especially in dry places like Arizona and Texas and in the moist atmosphere like New Orleans and I'm back to normal and I don't have to coax it but just be prepared. I nearly did get nodes on my vocal cords in Texas, but what can you do? You can't walk on stage and say, 'OK chaps you'll have to change the key tonight, I can't cope.'"* Apparently at this point Plant was in the middle of purchasing a 500 acre farm on the West coast of Scotland and his wife was expecting his second child. .... **Record Mirror reports....** Led Zeppelin II is #50...Zep sell-out - Extra Gig at Pool.... Led Zeppelin's shows at Wembley sold out all 9,500 tickets within an hour!.... a second show has been added ...the new album has Icelandic runes for a title.... other dates for Zeppelin include, Newcastle City Hall (11), Locarno Sunderland (12), Caird Hall Dundee (13), St. Matthews Baths Ipswich (16), Kinetic Circus Birmingham (17), Sheffield University (18) and Free Trade Hall Manchester (24).... more dates may be added.... **Sounds reports....** Cover story.... LED ZEPPELIN will play an extra concert at Wembley Empire Pool—on November 21—due to the incredible demand for tickets. Rikki Farr, of Buffalo Concert Presentations, who are staging the Zeppelin concert with their manager Peter Grant, told SOUNDS on Monday that all 9,500 tickets for the concert on Saturday, November 20, sold out in 54

minutes. 'We have never known such an amazing demand for tickets and that includes the Isle of Wight concerts; it is a sure sign of the huge following Zeppelin have in Britain,' he said. 'Because of this, we've decided to stage a second concert at Wembley.' Tickets for November 21 (all at 75p) will be on sale from all branches of Harlequin Records, from November 12. Orders by post should be addressed to Harlequin Records (tickets), 67 Great Richfield Street, London, W1, and enclose a postal order and stamped addressed envelopes. Ray Moss, general manager of Harlequin, told SOUNDS that people had queued for tickets from his shop all night. 'Their behaviour was quite incredible, even those who could not get tickets behaved perfectly.' Tickets will be limited to a maximum of five for each person who applies.... **Billboard reports....** Back cover full page advert for Led Zeppelin's fourth album....

20 **New Musical Express reports....** An extra date is added to the UK tour for November 29th at Liverpool Stadium.... review of Led Zeppelin's new album ᛉ⚡☉①.... "a guaranteed million seller well before it's release.... this new album consolidates their expanding maturity" after a very positive track by track review Roy Carr concludes *"Once again, Led Zeppelin is airborne and the flight course seems very favourable."*.... The Led Mystique...article on the upcoming shows at Wembley by Roy Carr, outlining the band's knack for maintaining their mystique.... weekend gig guide picture of Plant with headline "Zep Wembley Sell Out".... **Melody Maker reports....** extra date at Liverpool on November 29th.... Led Zeppelin's show in Belfast will probably go down in history as the last rock show there.... full page advert for Led

Zeppelin IV.... **Sounds reports....** four page teaser advert for Led Zeppelin IV...full page advert for Led Zeppelin IV.... Review of the fourth album by Billy Walker.... LED ZEPPELIN (ATLANTIC 240 1012) SIDE ONE of this, Zeppelin's fourth album contains perhaps the band's best recorded material to date. For me it smashes everything Zeppelin have done before into the ground it's more innovative and driving than 'Black Mountain Side' 'Whole Lotta Love', 'HeartBreaker' or 'Gallows Pole'. The last album was a very positive move away from what we'd come to expect from the band, but this one gives you the best of both worlds— the excitement of the rock and rolling Zeppelin: and the beauty of the acoustical side which they are more and more into. 'Old Style Zep' is represented by the opening track 'Black Dog'. Bonham crashing and exploding around his drum kit, while Page and Paul Jones lay down the added drive which prods and pushes Plant into those lung-splitting screeches. To cap it all they've included some thrusting breaks between his vocals which typified a lot of their earlier work. 'Rock And Roll' continues the pace but 'The Battle of Evermore' completely breaks the spell. Sandy Denny joins Robert in a really fine song. The band play around it delicately. Plant comes out of it very well, using much more control and poise than most people would give him credit for. But just when you begin to feel that the best must have gone. They move into 'Stairway To Heaven', the best track on the album. which opens slowly— building in speed verse by verse. The lyrics and musicianship are really beautiful and it's Bonham that really starts to move it into an up-tempo tune, kicking it along until the final verse, when Jimmy Page takes an electric guitar solo, showing the verve and

flair we know he possesses but it's Plant's powering, bludgeoning vocals that finally see the track out.

Side two. Whilst not up to the same standard, contains 'Going To California' (a slowish acoustic tune with Plant doing country vocals) and 'When The Levee Breaks' and two other tracks, but despite 'Levee's' punch and commanding strength there's a strong urge to quickly get back to the first side again.... **Disc and Music Echo reports....** cover story.... Zeppelin more shows.... Led Zeppelin are now in line for further British concerts in addition to the dates already announced. A second show at London's Wembley Empire Pool is set for this Sunday November 21 and a second Manchester concert in addition to Free Trade Hall November 24 is Bellevue on the 30th. Other new dates are Preston Town Hall (23), Leicester University (25), Liverpool Stadium (29), Bournemouth Starkers (December 2) and Salisbury (15).... Alexis Korner interview, *"Jimmy Page's been a good guitar player for a long time. I remember him doing an audition with Cyril Davis in 1962 with the Lord Sutch team.... I can understand what it is with Led Zeppelin, I can view it subjectively about why they're successful...I can admire them."....* album review.... After such a long wait one began to get a little worried about Led Zeppelin's fourth album. What had gone wrong? After such a time lag and mounting expectancy, could it still be good? The answer is yes, it is brilliant. It is by far their best album to date, and has a depth and maturity to it which can only result from recording and performing experience. It has many moods and many styles and seems far more emotionally loaded than any of their other albums, they seem to convey a wisdom through experience into their music now.

It rushes headlong into itself with the first number, "Black Dog" which is a driving blues number, with Jimmy Page double tracking the guitar in thirds, and a good guitar break at the end. Then into "Rock and Roll" a splendid send up which must have been fun to do because it's fun to listen to. "Battle Of Evermore" is the first example of the new Zeppelin depths. It's a madrigal type song with a beautiful duet by Robert Plant and Sandy Denny, whose voices really blend together very well; Robert plays beautiful guitar (sic). "Stairway To Heaven" is a beautiful gentle number, whose lyrics are printed on the inside sleeve, with sensitive Page guitar work and the gentlest of voice from Plant. Side two starts off with "Misty Mountain Hop" an off beat syncopated number with sturdy bass line. "Four Sticks" features John Paul Jones on synthesiser to a repetitive bass line with bass and drums working well together. California seems to inspire most people to write dewy-eyed songs; "Going To California" is no exception, gently acoustic with good lyrics. The album ends with "When The Levee Breaks", I don't know what a levee is but it has the sound of surf to it and so does the song.

After all the fuss about the mix on the album, the result is very good, crystal clear and well balanced so no one particular instrument or voice is to the fore. It's a thoughtful well done album with a lovely cover (they won their battle and it hasn't got a single word written on it) with "The Hermit" a tarot card, reprinted on the inside. ****.... Zeppelin good, bad or indifferent.... review of Newcastle.... The months of frustration and impatient waiting were over, Led Zeppelin were back at Newcastle's City Hall last Thursday. And the group that has brought the rock back to rock and roll were, for me at least awful. A young audience cried for more after two and a quarter hour performance. And they got it to the tune of a lengthy encore. They gave us "Immigration Song" (sic) "Heartbreaker" and Robert Plant immediately sank to rock bottom in my estimation. Maybe it was the hall, maybe it was the mike...The tragedy of it all was this band can play, and Plant can sing to rival any group in the world. They proved this with one track from the new LP "Stairway To Heaven". But alas the euphoria was not to last. The mediocrity of the gig could easily be seen in the band's performance of "Celebration Day". I tried desperately to think back to Zeppelin's first mind-shattering explosion on the British music scene and to convince myself that it was the notorious City Hall acoustics that daunted Plant. I've hardly mentioned Jimmy Page, you say? True enough he did some amazing things with that guitar but only spasmodically. This is the start of the great British tour. They should make sure they get a bigger hall and a better presentation than a packed City Hall got Thursday night.... **Billboard reports....** Review of Led Zeppelin's new album says, '...offers all the play and sales potency of the other three smash hit packages.'....

27 **Melody Maker reports....** cover story.... Demand for the new album is so high that the record company are experiencing distribution difficulties.... enough ticket applications for a third show were sent back from Wembley's box office.... review of the Empire Pool Wembley show.... Zapped by Zep.... Roy Hollingworth writes a prosaic and emotional review of the first night at Wembley. The atmosphere almost leaps off the page.... Led Zeppelin performed to

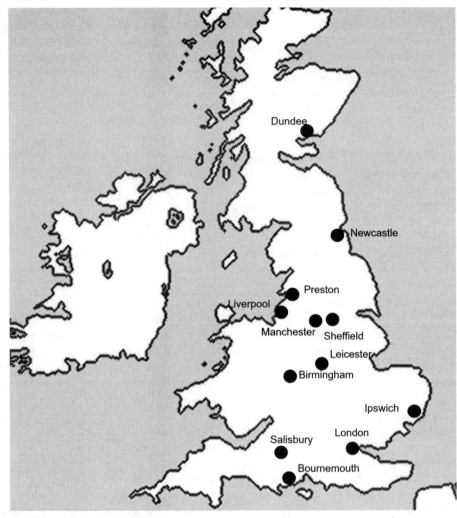

UK Tour Winter 1971

November 11th, 1971 Newcastle City Hall
November 12th, 1971 Newcastle Mecca Ballroom
November 13th, 1971 Dundee Caird Hall
November 16th, 1971 Ipswitch St Matthew's Baths
November 17th, 1971 Birmingham Kinetic Circus
November 18th, 1971 Sheffield University
November 20th & 21st 1971 London Wembley Empire Pool
November 23rd, 1971 Preston Town Hall
November 24th, 1971 Manchester Free Trade Hall
November 25th, 1971 Leicester University
November 29th, 1971 Liverpool University
November 30th, 1971 Manchester Kings Hall Belle Vue
December 2nd, 1971 Bournemouth Starkers
December 9th, 1971 Coventry Locarno
December 15h, 1971 Salisbury

the people on Friday night and 9,000 of them put their hands above their heads and got their Saturday night rocks off.... there's a market set up inside the arena selling T-shirts and incense and a poster for only 30 pence.... the weather is bitter outside but the audience is warmed up by opening act Stone The Crows.... Zep's set includes Immigrant Song, 59th Street Bridge Song, Black Dog, Since I've Been Loving You, Rock And Roll, Dazed & Confused, Going to California, Celebration Day, Moby Dick, Whole Lotta Love and Mary Lou.... Hollingworth criticises Plant's voice in a back-handed sort of way but generally is stupefied by the sheer presence of the band.... **New Musical Express reports....** On stage at Empire Pool Wembley.... front row review...Zeppelin circus roars into town.... once again Roy Carr gives the band a very favourable review for their performances at Wembley.... "The band played at the end of a six hour circus-like evening with a 167 minute set."...songs featured included Communication Breakdown, Since I've Been Loving You, Black Dog, Rock And Roll, Going To California, Stairway To Heaven, Whole Lotta Love, Hello Mary Lou, Mess Of Blues.... Carr concludes, "What the true essence of rock and roll is about.".... **Record Mirror reports....** Led Zeppelin IV is #10...review of the album.... "Heavier than Zep 3.... the album's title is unpronounceable. Just ask for the new Led Zeppelin LP.".... **Disc and Music Echo reports....** review of Wembley.... There's one thing that Zeppelin has always been good at and that's giving their fans their money's worth. At Wembley's Empire Pool on Saturday, packed to the ceiling, they played for two and a half hours, almost twice as long as other big named groups stay on for. And

they provided fans with a little circus entertainment. There were trapeze artists whizzing about and two performing pigs who didn't. "But they were good in rehearsal" said their trainer prodding the luckless beasts. Stone the Crows and Maggie Bell got a much deserved ovation. Zeppelin played their hearts out with a selection of old and new, lots of acoustic things, and lots of rock. Old favourites like "Whole Lotta Love" and "Communication Breakdown" causing near havoc.... **Sounds reports....** Billy Walker reviews the show at Wembley.... The nine and a half thousand spectators seated in the almost endless acres of the Wembley Empire Pool's vast interior certainly got their seventy-five pence worth on Saturday, with a five hour-plus show that included aerobatics, saucer jugglers and performing pigs (which didn't perform) as well as Bronco, Stone The Crows and the reason for the whole show, Led Zeppelin.

The mini-marathon opened at around five o'clock with Bronco having the really rotten task of warming up the half-empty stadium. "The bit of circus" that the audience was promised turned out to be two large performing sows dressed shamelessly in huge ruffs which hung round their necks like absurd cravats. They refused to do anything except put their front trotters up on the ring apron and were bemused at the assortment of bodies in the audience. Everyone hoped Led Zeppelin would do better. The trapeze artists and trampoline experts didn't create too much of a stir either. No doubt they're very exciting in the right atmosphere but in the middle of a rock spectacular it didn't click unless of course you are a real circus freak or just a plain ol' pig lover. Zeppelin followed at long last and they did turn out better than the pigs, much better.

They received the thunderous shouts and applause like real veteran performers, it's their right and they know it, they've earned it over the years of slog and they're going to enjoy it. 'Heartbreaker' broke the wonder spell and all the old Zep memories flooded through the thousands of onlookers. Plant going on stage, mane of hair thrown defiantly back, embroidered waistcoat and see through vest, tight, faded jeans and sneakers—the epitome of the rock idol. But when Plant performs he's really one of the world's great rock vocalists, but there's more to his vocals than many give him credit for. It's granted that his style is suitable to the likes of 'Heartbreaker', 'Black Dog', 'Rock And Roll' and 'Since I've Been Loving You', — the real shouters — but listen to 'Stairway To Heaven' and 'Going To California', they were performed beautifully and dispelled the claims that Zep are a one-legged band. The question of warming up the audience was overcome by Zeppelin's initial impact, a set of storming, fast numbers which through their power alone appeared to pin the fans to their seats, stunned almost unable to move and then, when the job was done, they leveled off into a smoother, slower vein — but only for a while. Choosing any real standout throughout the two-hour plus set would be almost impossible but 'Stairway To Heaven' from the new album must be a fair choice. This terrific number builds verse by verse from quite a soft lilting song until Bonham's drums give it a huge kick up the bum. Plant picks up the pace and Page too. Using twin neck guitar Jimmy employed 12 string for the basic rhythms but split to the 6-string neck for a fantastic solo run towards the end Plant soared in to finish the number, one really excellent line which sticks in

my mind "to be a rock and not to roll" being phrased and delivered perfectly. The amplification level ceased to be of any bother as the set wore its way on through the first hour and Zeppelin seemed to be coping effortlessly. They might only go out on rare occasions but when they do they really work. Apart from those titles already mentioned they included 'Moby Dick', 'Tangerine', 'That's The Way', 'Celebration Day', etc. Whether you prefer your Zeppelin soft or hard there couldn't have been many disappointed faces in the 9,000 odd who attended the concert. They got one of the best performances they could see from one of the world's leading rock bands, plus, don't forget performing pigs et al.

December 1971

4 **Record Mirror reports....** Led Zeppelin IV is #1...Robert Plant thanks "Home" the support band on stage at Wembley.... **Sounds reports....** Two letters to the editor accompanied by a picture of Page, "It looks as if Led Zeppelin have done it again. Their latest album is tremendous. It's got to be the best album released this year. By far the most exceptional track on this glorious sound of music is 'Stairway To Heaven' Plant's lyrics on this number really hit you and Page's guitar work combines well." —Bill Gilbert, Bingham, Notts....

"I was disgusted at the Led Zeppelin gig here in Birmingham last night, by the way the audience showed absolutely no consideration for the band at all. During such acoustic numbers as Stairway To Heaven, Tangerine, and That's The Way, some members of the audience decided that it was an opportune moment to chat, thus the finer parts of those beautiful pieces were inaudible. It's time some people learned to appreciate the finer points of progressive music." — Eric Partridge Birmingham....**Melody Maker reports....** Review of the band's concert at Liverpool University which was attended by 1900 fans. Apparently the audience responded hysterically to the band's set which included 'Mess Of Blues', 'It'll Be Me' and Gallow's Pole'....

9 **Rolling Stone reports....** full page advert reads.... 𝓩☽⚶☊⦶ New Led Zeppelin Album Now Available On Atlantic Records And Tapes....

11 **Record Mirror reports....** Led Zeppelin IV is #1...

18 **Sounds reports....** free poster inside.... **Record Mirror reports....** Led Zeppelin IV is #3...

25 **New Musical Express reports....** Four

new bootlegs will soon be in the shops including one called California by Led Zeppelin.... it will be a 2LP set rumoured to sell for £4 featuring the following tracks, Immigrant Song, Heartbreaker, Since I've Been Loving You, Black Dog, Dazed & Confused, Stairway To Heaven, That's The Way, Going To California, Whole Lotta Love and various twelve bar improvisations including Hello Mary Lou....

Muziek Expres reports.... Cover story. Review of 𝓩☽⚶☊⦶ in Dutch. The album is given three and a half stars out of a possible five. It calls 'Black Dog' a typical Zeppelin number and compares 'Rock And Roll' to the Beatles! It goes on to say that 'Stairway' shows that Plant is one of the best rock singers. It concludes that 'Misty Mountain Hop' and 'When The Levee Breaks' are the album's best tracks....

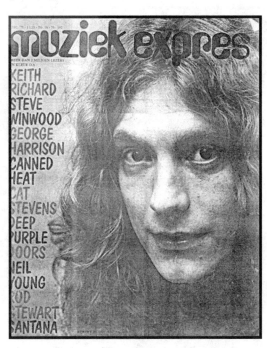

1972

January 1972

15 Disc and Music Echo reports.... Led Zeppelin IV is #2....

22 Disc and Music Echo reports.... Led Zeppelin IV is #3.... **Melody Maker reports....** Article states that Peter Grant will soon be managing Emerson, Lake and Palmer....

29 Disc and Music Echo reports.... Led Zeppelin IV is #5....

February 1972

5 Disc and Music Echo reports.... Led Zeppelin IV is #7....

12 Disc and Music Echo reports.... Led Zeppelin IV is #7.... Zeppelin Rising To New Heights.... Caroline Boucher files a report on the state of the band.... she mentions that the band are off to Australia via India and that their plans to visit Singapore were cut short by their hair length being unacceptable to the authorities there. She also points out that the band have once again been voted best international group by Disc readers. She speculates that the band's success is due partly to Page having had the experience at the top with the Yardbirds and also attributes it to their communal good sense and realistic attitudes towards the fame etc....

19 Disc and Music Echo reports.... Led Zeppelin IV is #9.... **Adelaide Advertiser reports....** Led Zeppelin Show Off Until Tonight. Article detailing the postponement of the show at Adelaide's Memorial Drive due to rain complications. The band had brought 11,800 pounds of equipment with them which had caused the stage to buckle under the weight causing an electrical hazard. The show had been originally scheduled for February 18th and was rescheduled for the 19th....

21 Adelaide Advertiser reports.... Led Zeppelin Is Shattering Rock Experience. Review of the show at Memorial Drive. Journalist Richard Mitchell says the band were 'a shattering experience of controlled violence'. Over 8,000 people attended the show which was sponsored by radio station 5AD and Channel Seven TV. Mitchell goes on to say that Bonham performed a solo which many drummers would find impossible while Page's guitar work was extraordinary. Plant, who was suffering from a virus in his throat 'came into his own on Black Dog, Stairway To The Stars (sic) and Let's Have A Party'. Both Zeppelin and CCR (who were in town the same night) performed the most successful shows ever in Adelaide....

26 Disc and Music Echo reports.... Led Zeppelin IV is #10....

Creem reports.... Review of ᛉᛟ♁♆⊙ by Lester Bangs. He begins the review with his frustration at what to call the album pointing out that Atlantic supplied the Icelandic runes for Creem to reprint. He goes on to say that, 'Led Zeppelin have taken the best aspects of the Yardbirds style and British flash blues tradition and inflated them into a mighty war machine.' He goes on to compare the album to their previous efforts calling it 'far from their best'. He says 'Stairway' is 'as lush as a Kleenex forest'. Bangs suggests that 'When the Levee Breaks' is a 'great groaning, oozing piece of sheer program music, one of the best things ever done by this group' even though he complains it goes on too long although he prefers that to the 'thicket of misbegotten mush' that is Stairway. He concludes that Zeppelin can do little wrong by him and he suggests the reader not pay any attention to the smart asses who suggest the album is just Zo-so....

March 1972

1 **Planet reports....** Review of the band's Australian dates, including a great on-stage picture of the band with an expansive audience in front of them. Plant, apparently upset with the local law enforcement in Melbourne, leaves the stage with, *"We'll be back in a couple of years when you get your screws together."....*

4 **Disc and Music Echo reports....** Led Zeppelin IV is #14.... **Go-Set reports....** Ian Meldrum interviews Robert Plant at the Southern Cross in Melbourne where the band are being presented a gold record award. The band had just come second in the magazine's poll and over 14,000 people had just seen the band's concert in Melbourne at the Kooyong Stadium.... Meldrum starts off with how Plant liked the local audience. Plant, *"I thought they were about the warmest thing I've felt in Australia yet —warmer even than the climate. Really good."*

Meldrum then asks about Perth and the troubles at the concert, *"Well nothing really happened I think it's what they call 'all in the mind'. There was a concert, a very successful concert. At the same time there was the usual element of people who are part of every corner of society who decided they'd bring wire cutters and cut their way in, and I also found that the police over here haven't really sorted out ways of handling situations like this I don't know whether they can even be handled.*

"But anyway, so the whole thing. Although we were playing we didn't even know it was happening. There were people coming over the fences and all that and there were people phoning the Mayor and saying this is too much. There were 8000 inside, 4000 outside and I suppose there were probably two dozen phone calls to the Mayor. So it was about two dozen to 12,000 in odds. Somewhere someone along the line is worried that these things can take place. I'm worried about the fact that they can be abused because the basic idea is to have a wonderful time and see everyone glow really glow."

"But I don't like violence and I never advocate that people should abuse authority when it comes to the fact that they lay open a place, a sports arena or something like that — it's not fair to do it. For people to bash the place about. But at the same time it's not fair for the authorities to get so paranoid that they have to come to deductions and follow the usual run-of-the-mill. Well you know what it is (right) and that part we can't even talk about because we don't even know what goes through the minds of people who retaliate in the way that they did."

What about Adelaide? *"Well. Adelaide was err err Adelaide (pause). Well it was a bit like a sort of mid-west cow-town in America. It's a shame really, because my voice was a bit rough. We'd been traveling a lot and not sleeping and everything like that and I went on — there were people shrieking and shouting and fights ten feet from the stage and I was getting really upset because this is the last thing any of us in the group like to see.*

Because we're pretty intent in what we're doing, especially as we've got a good following here. And there was all that going on in front of us, and no organised security. Well, there was a little guy of about 80 with a flash-lamp and that was about it."

"Every time you call to the cops over here 'Get a barrier line so we can get off' or make sure everything's OK. Everybody turns their heads and ignores you."

Meldrum asks him when he first realised he had so much power in his voice. "It was this group that did it. Before I was singing blues and things like that but it wasn't until the four of us knitted together so perfectly — the catalyst was the unity — it wasn't until that happened that we all suddenly realised that each of us had, not superpowers, but had the ability to come over the top of things—over the top of everything. So really it's been knocked out with what goes on around you 'cause I've sung with a lot of people since, just playing and jamming and it doesn't mean a thing, a lot of the time it don't mean a thing at all. There's so much there in this group, and there's always a smile on their faces as well."

Meldrum asks how the band manages to change so much from album to album and does Plant notice it, "I don't know. I don't really know at all. Oh, you do when it's finished but on the way through it you don't really know how it's going to be at all. You know when you start writing that it's going to be different—you become wiser you know? Your whole horizon gets wider and wider and it's experiences like the ones we've had recently that broaden it one way or the other. You either get a chip on your shoulder or you just laugh 23 hours a day (laughs).

"It's all these different experiences, like when we went to Milan and we started playing and there were 250 riot police I mean. I'm not a social deviant I know you can't change the world without taking 90% of the people with you and I don't intend to try it, or even be a party to anything that does try it if it's not going to consider everybody. But at the same time we're roped in, you see, so experiences create a state of mind. Now like on the fourth album things like Stairway and Going to California they're all different corners of my brain, you know?"

Meldrum observes that the band seem to be content with each other.

"It's because of the different approach each time we play, you see. Like Dazed and Confused has never been like Dazed and Confused was today. Sometimes it's longer and more extended in one part than another. The same even with Immigrant Song and the phrasing of the drums and the bass. You can bring movements into phase with the instruments and different sounds like that. So it's just like one of those magic coloring books that you just add water to. You turn the page and you're still adding water to the coloring book but it's different colors. But we play like that when we're not playing in front of anybody."

Meldrum points out the band's knack for putting on a good show unlike many American performers such as James Taylor who had apparently spent much of his concert tuning up.

"Thanks, but as for Taylor I really don't know because I've never seen him. The only solo artist concert I've been to recently was the Neil Young one and I really dug that because I like a plaintive voice —Neil Young. Joni Mitchell and people like that I really dig. But I'm not going to bother whether they take half an

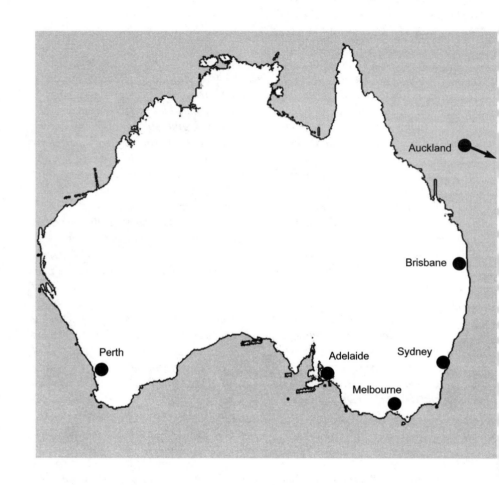

Australia & New Zealand Tour Summer 1972

February 16th, 1972 Perth Subiaco Oval
February 19th, 1972 Adelaide Memorial Drive
February 20th, 1972 Melbourne Kooyong Tennis Courts
February 24th, 1972 Auckland Western Spring Stadium
February 27th, 1972 Sydney Showgrounds
February 29th, 1972 Brisbane Festival Hall

hour to tune up or not, just as long as by the time they're finished I'm full. When I've watched them I'm full and I can say. 'Well that's an experience'."

The subject shifts to the band's acoustic material.

"Yeah. A lot of people said you shouldn't do that, you shouldn't. You should keep to the heavy stuff and all that, but it's an integral part. Very important part. Today was OK. But Perth I think was the best we've played yet - we'd just landed and we were full of Bombay and Singapore and full of traveling, but nevertheless. Well, today was warmer. You could see the people and you could see the colors. Everybody was grooving and everybody was smiling. Even the elements (meaning the rain) couldn't hold it back.

"That was about the first outdoor afternoon concert we've done for two years. Since Atlanta Georgia. When it was about 110 degrees. ohhhhhhg! It was just about the right temperature (today). Yet everyone in the audience was putting blankets over them funny Australian lot. No. It was a good day."

He is asked whether he worries about the new album not being accepted by the critics.

"Well, you know you're going to get the same old criticism 'oh well. oh well' 'cause every critic has got a different opinion of how they expect you to be— long-term."

Does he take much notice of the British critics? "Bugger all, really. They're a bunch of old queens, you know. Well they're not ALL. There must be at least two exceptions somewhere along the line. Oh dear. oh well. I never speak to them at all. Let's say it was 'F' dash dash all I don't really know England has got into a state of errrr I was trying to talk about the sub society, the sub culture and

all that and how it's suddenly got itself its own class system sort of thing like San Francisco and now it's rubbing off onto England a bit. There's a lot of paranoia amongst the kids there everyone's suddenly become a critic and all that. But a critic can only relate what he saw not how good it was on his standards because there's thousands of millions of people who are going to read that. I mean, I've met so many people who've read things in the Beat Beat who've said 'Well what a load of bulldust'. They're just not relating what they saw. I've been to concerts like Crosby, Stills, Nash and Young and things and they haven't been particularly fine musically. But the electric setting was a bit too crowded and things like that. But nevertheless what they gave was the seed and that was the fire that people really had to have. It's sort of like going away and going pphhhh at the end of it. It's an experience and I should imagine especially in Australia those experiences are lacking because the people here seem to have just a few more inhibitions than the English because of this business with Mother England."

How does the group as a whole want the public to accept their songs?

"Well Ian once again it's almost like a cop-out — however they wish to interpret them. A thing like Stairway To Heaven can take on so many different meanings 'cause really it has no direct meaning. With a thing like that if it had a direct meaning you'd have lost half the vibe of it whereas Going To California is pretty straight-forward really."

Does he like touring America?

"Yes and no. Some of the concerts can be very moving I mean, they can bring tears to your eyes sometimes. At other times you just wish that there hadn't been so many wooden ships going over there. See America's in a really different state to us. Over there, the people think the time is now — but the time really ain't now it rubs off on concerts it rubs off on the streets it rubs off with the press the whole thing I mean we really must relax, we really must take things for exactly what they are. To sit down and go pphhew and get up and go pphhew and go away and be really pleased or happy or warm. Instead of all this mumbo jumbo.

"I once read a thing and I think it was in Rolling Stone where they were talking to Lennon about No 9, and all these things and he was really making a mockery of all these peoples interpretations. I mean, at the time when you write something like that, you're half here and half there — you're not really aware of what the public are going to think about it. You're thinking about your next album, you're sitting there and you're trying to create something."

How much significance does he place on the charts?

"None at all. Well, I don't know really I mean to say I've spent six years not being in the charts and that was six years of playing pretty good sounds with Bonzo that people just totally ignored laughed at and that upset me. We had a dedicated following but everyone turned around and said 'Oh, it's not for us man' and it wasn't until the Americans brought it over until San Francisco's revitalization, the pulse of life if you like and then it suddenly meant something to the people it became a valid thing so I really don't think the charts mean much, except that it's nice to be there—because you extend what you're doing to more people."

What does he think of the BBC TV show Top Of The Pops?

"Well you should really go to Top of the Pops in London man. Well the people it's going back to know what it's all about anyway. You can't really relate what you're all about on a half hour program when you're surrounded by Jack the Lad and Fred the Hed and all them other folk. It's a very archaic way of presenting an artist or artists in that medium, they can't go too far either way. If they recorded a concert properly if they could even find the right equipment to record a concert properly. I'm sure they must have it somewhere — after all, it's a government run thing, they must be able to afford it but they can't or won't. We did a live studio recording and it was on a two-track machine installed in 1948. So I mean just where do you start and where do you stop?

"I think it really just lies with doing concerts and having a blow I mean, today was good it was one of the few times we've played in an afternoon and been able to see so many faces. You can fix yourself on one face and watch that face all the way through and it glows and does many different things."

What does he think of English audiences?

"Well I wish they'd come here and check it out and go home. They're OK they're alright I mean it's just individuals isn't it? You can't really say it depends on how they feel and how much brainwashing they've had it's like San Francisco's bell-hatted beatniks. After a while you get fed up with being told what you like and what you don't like, and suddenly you become an individual with long hair.

"See the fact that we're rich people or the fact that we're happy people or the fact that we're not frustrated musicians with so much to say but can't get it out we have the people to thank and if I can get through to them and show them exactly how we are that's far better - the truth. You've got to let them know I spend about 18 months posing and I still pose sometimes now — I mean I'm thinking about some sequins under the eyes. But the public —I luv 'em I'm going to have a really hollow feeling when the day comes that I have to say no more no more and just spend my time driving out into the desert in a Land Rover."

Does he resent the press?

"Well I just alter the answers according to our way of thinking. That's what it's all about you know? You can get so much out of a person and you can get the most out of me just by watching and listening."

Does he listen to the Zeppelin albums?

"Yeah well yeah I do. I don't listen to them all the time at all. What I listen to most is the third album. That seems to be the one that no one else listens to as much as me. I listen to all sorts of things. The early Incredible String Band tracks, I really used to like. But I'm not a softy at all. Anything that really catches you and grabs you by the smalls and says this is it whether it be loud or soft - that's the point I was trying to put over about our acoustic thing — it might be acoustic instrumentation but it's the venom or the bite or the drive or it's the life or it's just what comes from behind. Things like Friends could never be done electrically with so much balls. You know, so, I think we're quite a good band. It grows and grows Bonzo and myself have been playing together since we were 15 and we've had fights and shouting and all of that."

What made them come to Australia?

"It certainly wasn't the money. Look let's put it this way. There are five people in this, there's four musicians and there's Peter and if we just sit down and say 'Right we either want three months sleep or do we want to go somewhere or somewhere else. We wanted to go to Italy and Yugoslavia but when we got there I got really upset I cried for days I did. But one reason we came here was that it would be another return trip to Bombay."

Does he like Bombay? "Yes very much, and sometimes I think I'd like to live there. The first time that Jimmy, Richard and I went there we were coming back from Japan. We didn't know anybody at all. We just dropped off the plane and got into a taxi and halfway from the airport to the hotel the guy said 'Aahh, you change money, you change money? and we said 'No no no'—we just didn't know what was going on. Then he said 'Right I'll stop now and transfer you into the other car' and behind us there was this other car with about five Punjabi's in it armed to the teeth.

"So Richard sort of floated out of the car and got into the front and put his arms around this guy's neck and said 'Hotel, hotel' and I swear this was the only way we got to the hotel alive. You know, if you've ever gone from Santa Crusa Airport to Marine Drive in Bombay you'll know what it's like. But this time we went back and took Peter and John Paul and Bonzo -- the entourage — all the lads and it was just amazing. What with the cups of tea you have and all the offers from the people it's fantastic. Everything's as cheap as can be it's really good.

"I find it really relaxing and I find it very near to the right way to live. It's the right atmosphere. The only unfortunate thing is to be white because you can't understand it - the poverty etc. You learn that when people have nothing absolutely nothing all they can share with each other was themselves and the unity

over there is incredible."
How does he feel about England and his heritage in general? *"I don't really know about all that I just know that England became a great country for several reasons. Some of them have been pretty devious and some of them have been pretty positive and every country that is going to succeed has got to take the people with it. And at one time the people of England were behind the leaders of England. They must have been somewhere along the line even if it goes back to King Arthur. They had faith in the people who led them, and now there's no national conscience. People don't care it's like the 'I'm alright Jack attitude' I think it must come with the type of society we create. The feeling that you get in Australia compared with the feeling you get in India is totally different. Even to the people in the street. If you look wrong you're no good. Whereas in India the Sadu's have got as much respect, other than their crazy holy men, they've got as much respect as Yogis and everyone else. Everyone is taken exactly as they are.*

"I once saw an Incredible String Band concert where they said 'Right shake hands with the people on each side.' If the English did that, and went out into their gardens and said 'Well I don't care if your car costs more than mine — you're pretty groovy' and all that. If everybody realised what it's all about — you can't fart about anymore. There's too many mouths to feed too many consequences. Decisions should be come by as quick as possible and as fairly as possible. The great fear today is inflation and if inflation goes too far then the whole system will just crumble, and when it crumbles it won't be a particularly better thing that will take its place it will be whatever is the strongest thing at the time. It's like going

back to India. You've only got to go over there and see all the political jargon strewn everywhere all over the walls and everywhere. They're badly in need of either a ruling class or somebody to lead them through their troubles. And if man can recognize these people and tally onto them and give them all the support they can get, then hey presto, you've got a successful country.

"Albion would have been a good place to be but that was England before it got messed up. You can live in a fairyland if you read enough books and if you're interested in as much history as I am you know, the Dark Ages and all that. They had one or two home truths that we seem to have lost now 'love thy neighbour' is a Christian saying but it applies to everyone.

"Appreciation of your neighbor and all that is a very important thing. There are so many things but I don't think any one mind can completely cover the subject and be able to give any answer that would give any light to anybody else because everyone has their own point of view. It's like these stupid antics. It's like a drop in the ocean really to say 'Oh, I think this and I think that,'because day by day depending on how you feel the day you get up, you feel differently about it. Some days I get up and I think, England, the master country, the fantastic country keep out of everybody else's way."

The following is a review of the concert in Perth. Following the show the band were accosted by the local Drug enforcement crew.... Led Zeppelin's recent visit to Perth could not be called uneventful. At Subiaco Oval they were swamped at the end of their performance by 100 eager fans while police were just finishing their fight with over 300 would be non payers. Next morning they were awoken in their Scarborough hotel while the Drug Squad made a swoop search. Guitarist and group leader Jimmy Page believes that the raid "was some sort of a rebuff" for the disturbance during their concert. Chief of the CIB Superintendent W H Nielson says that the D S. "was acting on formation received" and that their action was completely divorced from any incidents which occurred at Subiaco Oval. The trouble at the gates started when several thousand people crowded around the entrance and several hundred commenced to ram the gates. Local papers reported that the crowd was not allowed entrance into the oval but promoters deny this. One organiser described the melee which followed as organised trouble.

"A certain section of the group came with one intention, and that was to get in for nothing. They had wire cutters, steel ladders and phosphorous bombs."

Hundreds cut the fence wire and pulled gates from their hinges in an effort to jam the already 8,000 people at the ground. Once through many returned to the entrance to egg the others on. By the end of the night police reinforcements had boosted the number from 24 on duty to well over 70. About four uniformed police were stationed near the stage while another 20 'plainclothes' circulated in the crowd. Prior to the show they had been briefed not to allow anyone over the barrier fence onto the grass in front of the stage not even photographers were allowed within 20 feet. It took only one young girl who dashed forward to take a photo to start the whole crowd going as Led Zeppelin finished their performance. Scores surged forward and many started dancing on stage. Robert Plant seemed in complete control of the situation and asked everyone 'to sit quietly', they did

but only for seconds as Zeppelin went into their last number.

On finishing, managers and roadies formed a tunnel for the group to reach their awaiting cars. It wasn't successful enough though to stop many fans from souveniering pieces of Plant's black flimsy shirt.

After a breather. the group spent some time at a local night club jamming while Robert Plant sang songs like Buddy Holly's 'Teddy Bear'. The crowd adored it while their Australian recording manager shouted 'champagne' and 'get them off the stage' not knowing that the guys had a date with the Drug Squad. It would seem that the whole of Perth is both indignant and embarrassed about the raid. And there's more than one rumor that the local government would be looking into the episode.... The following is a review from the Melbourne show.... Before the Sunday of the Melbourne Zeppelin concert, everyone was thinking that perhaps outdoor venues weren't that good — mainly because there was a possibility of a repeat performance of the three inches of rain in half an hour. The day itself was good, relatively clear skies and even sun. The promoters sigh of relief could be heard all over Melbourne.

By 2 o'clock over half the stadium was full, and there was a steady stream of cars and people arriving. By 3 o'clock the place was packed, and the crowd was wondering what was going to happen, because no one was announcing anything. Where the hell was Zeppelin. Five minutes past three and on they walked. It took the crowd a second or two to realise they were coming on to play unannounced.

"Good afternoon," said Plant, and the crowd roared back. "I can't hear you". So the reply came louder, and then

Jimmy Page started into the first number. They started off with recent album numbers like Black Dog, trying to get instant build-up. Unfortunately, the acoustics of the stadium were against them, and the wind blowing over the stage threw a lot of the sound out into the street to the crowd.

Towards the end of their acoustic set. Zeppelin had the sound licked, and from then, there was nothing but build up. Page's guitar work became faultless, as he strutted and walked around the stage, and for some reason, reminded me of Chuck Berry, when he used to goose walk across stage, with his guitar slung low. Jimmy Page also changed guitars regularly for almost every number, now electric, now acoustic and for one number a double necked job with one neck six string and one neck twelve string. John Bonham and John Paul Jones must also rate mentions as far as the music goes, because they were an integral part of the sound. Page and Plant, however dominate the visual thing, so it's these two you remember when you leave.

I must mention the group's acoustic set which is unlike the Zeppelin I expected to hear and therefore came as a pleasant surprise. By the time the acoustic set was finished the place was packed, at least 13,000 to 14,000 people, with all the aisles packed with people who couldn't get a seat. Until the sound problem was overcome the crowd was inattentive, and along with the acoustics echo, there was a general murmur from people talking. In fact, Plant told the crowd twice to shut up. By halfway through the two hours the group played, the audience was hooked, and by the end of the concert when you looked around all you saw was a moving sea of bodies and bodies jumping up and down against the sky. Plant kept up a continual banter between numbers, commenting on everything from the weather to what individual people were doing in the audience. The group stopped playing for about ten minutes towards the end of the concert, when it started to rain lightly. But they came back on promising to go off again at the first shock (or up in smoke more like!) The last two numbers after this break were probably the best of the day. A great concert that ended with the crowd going wild....

11 Disc and Music Echo reports.... Led Zeppelin IV is #18.... **Melody Maker reports....** review of New Age Of Atlantic it calls 'Hey Hey What Can I Do' a pleasant group composition with Zeppelin swinging in their best non heavy groove....

18 Disc and Music Echo reports.... Led Zeppelin IV is #20....

25 Disc and Music Echo reports.... Led Zeppelin IV is #19....

April 1972

1 Disc and Music Echo reports.... Led Zeppelin's offices are being redecorated....

4 New Musical Express reports.... Interview with Robert Plant by Roy Carr, Plant, *"Whenever possible I really like to get out there with the kids. Only in that way can I get to know what the record buyers want. That's how I make up my mind — from how the public makes up its mind. For me, in fact, the most successful concert is the one when everyone is up on their feet, smiling, yelling and getting into the music.*

"Personally I don't like things to

be too straight-faced. The idea of people just sitting down and getting turned on without showing any signs of response— it's just too melodramatic. The fact is, we don't flog Zep to death. Just like John Lennon once said: 'If you're on the road too long it becomes painful'."

"Speaking for myself I've always got the motivation to work. But like the rest of the band I don't want to charge around the country every night. What's the point? We only tour and bring out an album when we want to. But as most people realise we're always popping up all over the world to do concerts. Whenever possible we always return to those places.

"We were the first band to take over and play the Empire Pool Wembley and present non-rock side features like circus acts— although the pigs didn't quite manage to get it on. A lot of people draw their conclusions without seeing enough of the band. If we came over to them as being just a raw body well then it's OK.

"Music is very much like a kaleidoscope. And I feel that particular album (the fourth) was just a case of us stretching out. It was a very natural development for us. I like people to lay down the truth. No bullshit. That's what the feather in the circle was all about. A lot of the tracks on that album came from various moods where we just got-together and started to contribute to various basic ideas.

"In the case of 'Battle' I had been reading a book on the Scottish Wars immediately before. It was really more of a play-lette than a song, and after I wrote the lyrics I realised I needed another completely different voice, as well as my own, to give that song its full impact. So I asked Sandy Denny along to sing on that track. I found it very satisfying to sing

with someone who has an entirely different style to my own. While I sang about the events of the song. Sandy answered back as if she was the pulse of the people on the battlements. Sandy was the town-crier— urging the people to throw down their weapons. 'Stairway To-Heaven' was the result of an evening when Jimmy and I just sat down in front of the fire. We came up with a song which was later developed by the rest of the band in the studio.

As for the song writing process, "They're really attuned to all those time skips (the band). These things aren't intentional. Just little whims which we'll no doubt expand on the next album. When they're doing these kind of time skip riffs in the studio. Jimmy, John and Bonzo suddenly come up with something like that passage on 'Black Dog', play it. Fall about all over the place for about 10 minutes in fits of laughter: play it again: burst into laughter, then preserve it on tape. It's as simple as that. You know, we've recorded ourselves at the Farm on just an ordinary Revox and achieved a far better sound."

22 **Disc and Music Echo reports....** cover story.... Jimmy Page on magic.... "I'm 27- John Paul Jones is the same age. Robert and John Bonham are both 23. I joined the Yardbirds in 1966 straight from session work. I'd been at Art School and done G.C.E.'s in Sutton and Croydon. I lived in a van for a while and got quite ill from that.

"The good thing about the guitar was that they didn't teach it at school. Teaching myself was the first and most important part of my education I hope they keep it out of the schools. I knew Jeff Beck and I enjoyed music. I couldn't read music, I taught myself that too. I can write it down at my own pace. The Yardbirds eventually folded. We had one hit: 'Over Under Sideways Down' in 1966 and we did the film Blow-Up with Antonioni. I wanted a band. John Paul Jones phoned up to ask if I'd be interested in using him. I jumped at the chance. Musically he's the best musician of us all. He had a proper training and he has quite brilliant ideas. I heard Robert and Bonham and there was just no question about it. Musically, it jelled immediately. It's very hard getting groups together, and the characters become very important particularly on the road. But we seem to get on better and better. Perhaps we're just lucky. We like to take our music off into different tangents. We always have done that. Even now with Dazed And Confused, say. When we first did it in the studio we did it live, setting aside one section of the bow and so forth. We released the second take.

"Album two was insane. We'd put down a rhythm track in London, add the voice in New York, put in harmonica in Vancouver, then come back to New York to do the mixing. Now, on the last record, the sleeve has a lot of meaning. The old man carrying the wood is in harmony with nature. He takes from nature and he goes back to the land. It's a natural cycle—it's right. His old cottage gets pulled down and they put him in these urban slums old slums; terrible places. The hermit as painted by a friend of mine - Barrington Colby—he's holding out the light of truth and enlightenment to the young man at the foot of the hill. No, those aren't Robert's goats they're just goats. Do you know the Tarot cards? Then you know what the hermit means.

"My house used to belong to Aleister Crowley. I knew that when I moved in. Magic is very important if people can go through it. I think Crowley's completely relevant to today. We're still seeking for truth; the search goes on.

"Crowley didn't have a very high opinion of women — I don't think he was wrong. Playing music is a very sexual act; an emotional release and the sexual drive comes in along with all the other impulses. But once you earn money people start assuming things about you and your whole life is changed. Your friends change; you get involved in high finance. You can't try and programme it. It just happens.

"At least as musicians we aren't doing any environmental or moral damage. In fact the musicians can ask some of the ugly questions that politicians don't want to answer. We're not trying to indoctrinate anybody. Why should people automatically assume that they have to fall in with this man-made cycle; go to work and manufacture stuff so that you can get a bit of money to buy manufactured goods. It's only rebels who ever get anything done. Most people in high office are complete idiots. Take Loch Ness. The Hydro Board wanted to put pylons along the edge of the loch to save £55,000 in a scheme that has been costed at £12 million. We have to make sure that natural amenities like Loch Ness are respected. They are irreplaceable. I'm interested in the Loch Ness Phenomena Investigation Bureau. I have a place up there I love it. It's really beautiful. How can these faceless men wreck it for a piddling amount of money? The whole decision rests with one man and that's really wrong. If I wasn't into rock I would be living in somewhere like Wales in a commune."

May 1972

4 The Village Voice reports.... Advert

reads — Concerts East & Ron Delsener Presents Led Zeppelin. June 14 & 15 at 8:00 PM. Very few groups can create vibrations like Led Zeppelin. They've captured it on records and in concert, they bring the art of audience involvement to new heights. It's been a year since they've been in the States. Don't miss their only New York concert. Tickets on sale May 8 For information Ticketron. Nassau Coliseum....

20 **New Musical Express reports....** In the studios with Zeppelin, reporter Ritchie Yorke is invited to attend the recording sessions for Houses Of The Holy at Olympic Studios in London. While Yorke is at the studio, Slade are recording an album in the next room. He describes the relatively innocuous atmosphere. He mentions that Page has shaved off the beard and has also cut off most of his hair. Page, *"Robert's just had a baby. He's up in the wilds of Worcestershire, now with his old lady. We're coming over to North America later in the summer. Probably in July. We won't be playing Toronto this time, but we are doing Montreal and Vancouver. We just got back from a tour of Australia and Japan. It was incredible. Huge crowds, and they really seemed to enjoy the shows. We really enjoyed the tour. We hope to have the album ready for release just before the tour."* Yorke then mentions that he gets a brief preview of Dancing Days and another unfinished track called 'Slush', which many suspect turned out to be Song Remains The Same....

27 **Disc and Music Echo reports....** Are the Osmonds as heavy as Led Zeppelin? Yes according to Donny .... **Billboard reports....** Article details how many British bands come to America simply

because England lacks the large venues capable of paying them adequately. It goes on to say that Led Zeppelin has played at the 8,000 seat Wembley Empire Pool and at the Bath Festival in 1970....

June 1972

15 **The Village Voice reports....** Full page advert reads— Welcome Back ⌇ 🜨🜁🜨⑦ - Led Zeppelin On Tour - 6 June - Cobo Hall Detroit, 7 June - Montreal Forum Montreal, 9 June - Coliseum Charlotte, 10 June-Memorial Auditorium Buffalo, 11 June-Civic Centre Baltimore, 14-15 June Nassau County Coliseum Hempstead N.Y., 17 June - Memorial Coliseum Portland Oregon, 18 June - Coliseum Vancouver, 19 June - Coliseum Seattle, 21 June - Coliseum Denver, 22 June - Swing Auditorium San Bernadino California, 23 June - Sports Arena San Diego California, 25 June L.A. Forum Los Angeles, 27 June - Arena Long Beach California, 28 June - Community Center Tucson....

24 **Melody Maker reports....** Article by Roy Hollingworth in the USA...he says Led Zeppelin are selling out across the country and recently broke the house record in Buffalo New York which had been held by Elvis Presley.... it goes on to say they played to 32,000 people in Nassau Coliseum Long Island....

July 1972

1 **Melody Maker reports....** Cover story.... Reporter Roy Hollingworth follows the band to their performance at the Long Island Coliseum in New York. The article consists of his observations, with

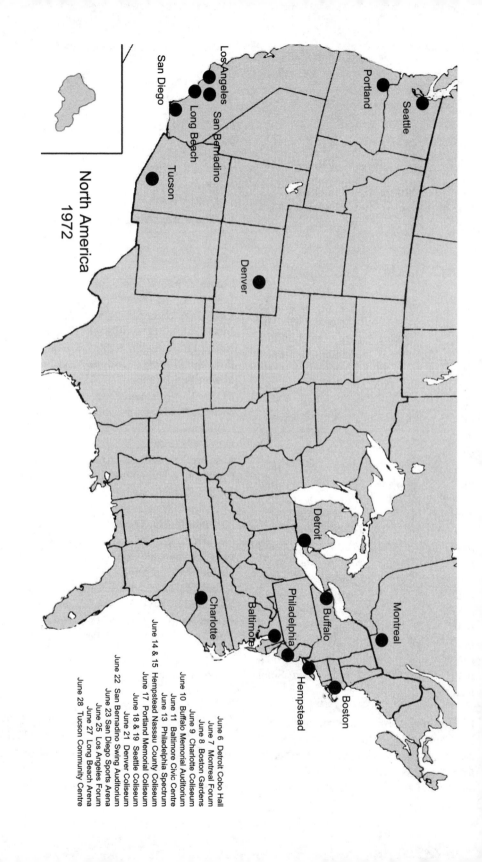

North America
1972

Portland
Seattle
Los Angeles
San Diego
Long Beach
San Bernadino
Tucson
Denver
Detroit
Charlotte
Baltimore
Philadelphia
Hempstead
Buffalo
Boston
Montreal

June 6 Detroit Cobo Hall
June 7 Montreal Forum
June 8 Boston Gardens
June 9 Charlotte Coliseum
June 10 Buffalo Memorial Auditorium
June 11 Baltimore Civic Centre
June 13 Philadelphia Spectrum
June 14 & 15 Hempstead Nassau County Coliseum
June 17 Portland Memorial Coliseum
June 18 & 19 Seattle Coliseum
June 21 Denver Coliseum
June 22 San Bernadino Swing Auditorium
June 23 San Diego Sports Arena
June 25 Los Angeles Forum
June 27 Long Beach Arena
June 28 Tucson Community Centre

interjections by the band. He begins with Plant and Jones complaining about the press ignoring them back in England.

Plant, *"Our egos have been hurt, they really have. For some reason English critics have never told the truth about us. For some reason they've been out to get us a bit. So things are clouded over, and nobody gets to know what's really happening. There's been so much bullshit printed, it's just untrue."*

Jones, *"We read pages on some band - name not mentioned - saying just how big they are here. You ask the people here just how big they are. We know. You see it makes the English press look ridiculous. It's so annoying. Here we are slaving away, and getting consistently incredible reactions and nobody back home can care anything about us. It's just not right."*

Plant, *"Maybe if we were as big in England as we are here, I wouldn't be able to walk down a bloody street without being stopped. Don't know if I'd like that or not. Something has really happened this time. Something has really clicked. It's fantastic, the spirit within the band is just fantastic. They'd never believe how good it is here back home. They'd just never believe what happened tonight."*

Jones, *"They say Jethro Tull are brilliant on stage, well they do the same bloody thing every night, the same gags, everything the same. Each of our gigs is treated differently, we don't have any set, religiously rehearsed thing. And what you've seen tonight has been happening for years here."*

Hollingworth asks manager Peter Grant why the band aren't playing Madison Square Gardens, *"Because it cost 5,300 dollars to book that place and that's just absurd. This is a great place, and this is where the kids live. Shame*

there aren't places like this in England. It's getting absurd over there now. There's nowhere to play. But we're going to be playing somewhere in England at Christmas. I think it will be good. I can't tell you where it is yet, but I think it will be good. You know I wanted to put the band on at Waterloo Station. You know, that massive area before the platforms. I thought it was a great idea - you know we could have Led Zeppelin specials coming in on the platforms, it was going to work, but the station authorities said there was one late train that would get in the way. Shame, it would have been great, imagine Led Zep playing Waterloo Station - a completely covered hall, and very good acoustics."

As the show is about to commence John Bonham arrives. Bonzo, *"I got stopped backstage somewhere you know, and they wouldn't believe I was with the band. They said, 'Where's your stage clothes', I said 'Where's the what?' Someone once asked me what technicalities I applied to my playing, I said, 'Technicalities, what the hell are you going on about?' I said 'This is my technicality', and raised my hand into the air, and let it fall. Hand to drum, that's what it is, hand to drum. I'm not trying to be any superstar. I just do my bit as one quarter of Led Zeppelin. When I have a solo I don't ever imagine drummers around watching me. I don't try to impress people who play the drums. I play for people. I don't try and perform the most amazing changes in tempo, or make people watch me. I just couldn't do that - it would take away the essence of Jimmy's guitar, and Robert's voice. John Paul and myself lay down a thick back-drop, that's what we do."*.... **Montreal la Presse reports....** Advert reads — The Forum Presents Led Zeppelin Wednesday June

7th 8 pm Montreal Forum.... **Billboard reports....** New anti-bootlegging law is passed in the UK....

15 **Melody Maker reports....** Article states that Led Zeppelin's new album may be a double LP set containing live material recorded recently on the West Coast of the USA....

August 1972

12 **New Musical Express reports....** Interview with John Bonham by Roy Carr. Bonham is asked what would happen if any of Zeppelin started an ego trip, *"They'd probably get their bleedin' gear torn off their backs, thrown into the sea or something equally unpleasant. You couldn't do that kinda thing in this group even if you wanted to. For the simple reason that you'd have no chance of getting away with it. For instance, if Robert is more high-spirited than usual during a gig and starts rabbiting on a bit, we'll start yelling 'Wheeeeenrrrrr' and 'Come off it', at him. It would be ridiculous for anyone to try it in the first place. You can't fool anybody in this group and if you did, you'd bloody well suffer for it.*

"You've only got to be in a bit of a mood one day and immediately you'll get ripped to shreds by the rest of the lads. That's the way we are, and that's probably one of the reasons why we work so well and stay together. We're not like some bands—who are worlds apart.

"One danger is when group members start spending most of their time playing with other musicians. Sure, it's O.K. occasionally, but when a guy prefers to play with other musicians it's best to forget the whole thing. You see, all his creative ideas go to other people— and the group eventually suffers. That has never occurred in this group and, I can't ever see it happening. On our recent tour of America, there was a really great atmosphere between everybody in the group. We seemed very close, and you could feel it in the playing. I think we all played much better than we have for a long time . . . the tour was a tremendous success all round.

"There are some bands who do this kinda thing, with the result that the kids go along for the sake of going to a concert and not because it's an event. Before long, your prestige goes and you burn yourself out. You must create your own demand.

"We find we're always getting fresh faces in the audience. Sure, anyone can say that when you don't know your audience personally, but I know it's true. Some of the younger members of the audience may come along for the first time on the strength of having bought our fourth album. They like what they see and hear and as a result go out next day and buy our other albums.

"For instance, our second album is still a strong seller. This seems to happen mainly in the States, where the kids are starting to back track on all our albums.

"In the beginning, nobody could say a bad word about us, but now it appears that everybody is looking for a way in which to knock us.

"You get all these letters in the music papers saying that Led Zeppelin aren't playing and recording anymore because they're too busy buying country mansions and Rolls Royces y'know, for a start there ain't one person in this band who owns a Rolls, it must all stem from false information people have read in articles written by people who assume that's what we're doing.

"I'm still living in the same bloody house as I was when we first started, so's Robert. Nobody's changed that much.

"What most people don't understand is that we're always working, even if we don't choose to spread it all over the place. Everyone thinks we're just laying around relaxing, when in fact we are constantly rehearsing and recording. So that puts paid to all that crap, doesn't it? I remember reading a letter in which the writer moaned that we were neglecting British audiences and not playing the clubs. Then when we did the clubs - and remember we were the only big band to ever go back to the small clubs, people moaned because they couldn't get in.

"Look, we've just toured the States and done as well if not better than the Stones but there was hardly anything about it in the British press. All we read was, the Stones this and the Stones that, and it pissed us off made us feel what the hell, here we are flogging our guts out and for all the notice that's being given to us we might as well be playing in bloody Ceylon, because the kids in England didn't even know we were touring the States it comes across as though we're neglecting the kids when we're not.".... **Melody Maker reports....** Letter to the editor from Hollywood California saying thanks for the article about Zep in New York and stating that they had immediate sell-outs in LA despite recent appearances by Tull and the Stones....

September 1972

1 **Tokyo Asahi reports....** Led Zeppelin Tickets go on sale today!! Tickets will be sold in Tokyo and Yokohama at all "Play Guide" outlets The Shows will be held on 10/2 & 3 in Budokan Big Hall...Tickets are 3000 to 1500 Yen...Contact Udo 400 6536....

22 **Tokyo Asahi reports....** Led Zeppelin Tickets nearly sold out!! Tickets will be sold in Tokyo and Yokohama at all "Play Guide" outlets. The Shows will be held on 10/2 & 3 in Budokan Big Hall. Tickets are 3000 to 1500 Yen.

30 **Tokyo Asahi reports....** Led Zeppelin Japan Tour- 2 years in a row. Rock group Led Zeppelin will tour Japan for the second time in 2 years. Led Zeppelin played explosive shows in Japan during their last tour including 'Immigrant Song', 'Moby Dick' and 'Whole Lotta Love'. Led Zeppelin also left a huge impression in Japan by playing a charity show in Hiroshima. There are four members in Led Zeppelin including Jimmy Page and

John Bonham. Led Zeppelin will play the Budokan on October 2nd & 3rd....

October 1972

14 Disc and Music Echo reports.... Hawkwind break Led Zeppelin's attendance record at the Liverpool Stadium....

21 Disc and Music Echo reports.... Led Zeppelin returned from Japan and went straight into the studio....

November 1972

4 New Musical Express reports.... Led Zeppelin will probably be conducting a short tour of the UK in the next few weeks...the tour will likely include at least two nights at the Manchester Hardrock.... **Melody Maker reports....** Led The Good Times Roll review of the band's concerts in Montreux Switzerland by Chris Charlesworth. Apparently 4,000 fans descended on the small town from all over Europe. Charlesworth, "Zep knocked spots of their many rivals with the ease of true professionals." The sets included Rock And Roll, Black Dog, Over The Hills And Far Away, Misty Mountain Hop, Since I've Been Loving You, Dancing Days, Bron-y-Aur, Dazed & Confused, Stairway To Heaven, Whole Lotta Love, Heartbreaker, and Heartbreak Hotel. Considering that the following week was when Charlesworth makes his prediction that the band will probably not sell out, he is remarkably enthusiastic concluding, "they will reshape your values about what is genuine and what isn't. They just have to be the best heavy band this country has produced."...

11 New Musical Express reports.... Zeppelin Dates.... cover story.... Longest tour ever. Led Zeppelin begin a major British concert tour at the end of this month.... it will be the band's longest tour ever.... A total of 24 dates is set and the tour opens at Newcastle City Hall on November 30. The schedule includes two days at the Manchester Hard Rock. Led Zeppelin have chosen the Alexandra Palace as their London venue for two days during the weekend immediately before Christmas. After a ten day holiday break the itinerary continues until the end of January.... tickets for all shows will be £1 and go on sale tomorrow (Friday).... it is estimated that they will play to a total of 110,000 people...dates are Newcastle Nov. 30 and Dec. 1, Glasgow Green's Playhouse Dec. 3 and 4, Manchester Hardrock Dec. 7 and 8, Cardiff Capitol Dec. 11 and 12, Birmingham Odeon 16 and 17, Brighton Dome 20 and Alexandra Palace 22 and 23. The schedule continues at Sheffield City Hall Jan. 2, Preston Guild Hall 3, Bradford St. George's Hall 4, Oxford New Theatre 7, Liverpool Empire 14, Stoke Trentham Gardens 15, Aberystwyth King's Hall 16, Southampton Gaumont 21, Aberdeen Music Hall 25, Dundee Caird Hall 27 and Edinburgh King's Theatre 28.... **Disc and Music Echo reports....** Zeppelin set for biggest ever UK tour.... Led Zeppelin are expected to play to over 110,000 people when they play an unprecedented 24 dates. In London they play to the 6,000 people at the Alexandra Palace immediately before Christmas on December 22nd and 23rd. The tour also takes in five dates in Scotland. Shows are as follows Newcastle City Hall Nov. 30 and Dec. 1, Glasgow Green's Playhouse Dec. 3 and 4, Manchester Hard Rock Dec. 7 and 8, Cardiff Capitol Dec. 11 and 12,

Birmingham Odeon Dec. 16 and 18, Brighton Dome Dec. 20, London Alexandra Palace Dec. 22 and 23, Sheffield City Hall Jan 2, Preston Guild Hall Jan 3, Bradford St. George's Hall Jan 4, Oxford New Theatre Jan 7, Liverpool Empire Jan 14, Stoke Trentham Gardens Jan 15, Aberystwyth King's Hall Jan 16, Southampton Gaumont Jan 21, Aberdeen Music Hall Jan 25, Dundee Caird Hall Jan 27, and Edinburgh King's Theatre Jan 28. At Zeppelin's request ticket prices will be limited to £1 except for Manchester £1.25, Seats go on sale Friday November 10 at all box offices on a first come first served basis. Tickets are also available at Harlequin record stores in London's Regent Street, Oxford Street, Dean Street and Haymarket.... **Melody Maker reports....** full double page ad for British tour.... all tickets £1.... Chris Charlesworth interviews Plant backstage at their concert in Montreux Switzerland. He begins with the topic of the day which seems to have been, why don't Zep play the UK much? Plant, *"I believe we did something towards the beginning of this year at Wembley."* He is corrected by Charlesworth who points out it was last year. *"Well, it was towards the beginning of this one. From there we had a little break, and went to Australia. We came back and had about three weeks off and then went to America, and we've been recording over a period of time all the time. In between gigs we have always got studio time booked so the albums become a continuous thing. If we keep going in to recording studios a wider spectrum of stuff comes out of it. Already there's enough material recorded for the next Zeppelin album, but problems with the sleeve have held things up. Now it looks as though January will see its release.*

"We can record as often as we want to, and Jimmy has a set-up at his place so the music is far more varied than it used to be. We will rehearse for a tour and get as many as four new numbers off in one day. It's just riffs coming out that we remember, like 'Black Dog' which was a riff. I'd like to think that each album is different from the last. If you imagine two lines on a tangent going outwards and getting wider, that's what we want our music to be. In about four years we will have covered all sorts of ground. There's a track on this new album called 'The Crunge' and it's really funny. It's something we would never have imagined doing. Numbers like this are really good because if you carry on on just one plane you just repeat yourself."

Charlesworth asks if he is worried about Zeppelin getting stale, *"No, people have identified us with the riffy numbers immediately because they are the most easily recognisable things. I think we should be known more for 'Stairway to Heaven' than 'Whole Lotta Love'. There is definitely a pace that is apparent in England that is nothing to do with creativity. If you want to do it, you can keep up with everybody else and get your name in the papers as often as you can. That's done initially because artists like Elton John or T. Rex have something that is good and people have to be made aware of it. In England we could be around every week. It wouldn't be very hard to play once a month and it wouldn't be very hard to get our names in the papers if we went about it the right way by throwing our doors open to everybody in the press. 'Do come up to the farm and see Robert Plant milking his goats' would get us in, but we've got a lot of places to visit and we like sightseeing. We don't want to have to keep up to that pace. People will soon remember us when they*

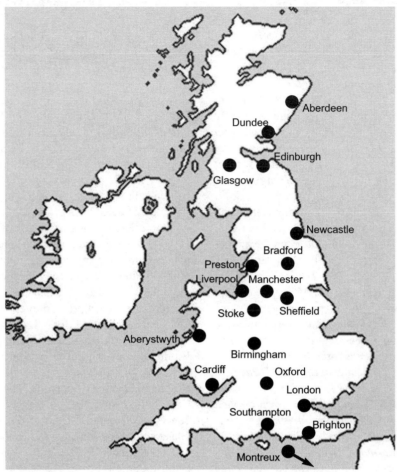

UK Tour Winter 1972 - 1973

October 27th & 28th 1972 Montreux The Pavilion (Switzerland)
November 30th & December 1st 1972 Newcastle City Hall
December 3rd & 4th 1972 Glasgow Green's Playhouse
December 7th & 8th 1972 Manchester Hardrock
December 11th & 12th 1972 Cardiff Capitol
December 16th & 17th 1972 Birmingham Odeon
December 20th, 1972 Brighton Dome
December 22nd & 23rd 1972 London Alexandra Palace
January 2nd, 1973 Sheffield City Hall
January 7th, 1973 Oxford New Theatre
January 14th, 1973 Liverpool Empire
January 15th, 1973 Stoke Trentham Gardens
January 16th, 1973 Aberystwyth King's Hall
January 18th, 1973 Bradford St George's Hall
January 20th, 1973 Southampton University
January 21st, 1973 Southampton Gaumont
January 25th, 1973 Aberdeen Music Hall
January 27th, 1973 Dundee Caird Hall
January 28th, 1973 Edinburgh King's Theatre
January 30th, 1973 Preston Guild Hall

come and see us. We will be doing some gigs in England sooner or later, unless we happen to be playing in Basutoland or Zanzibar around Christmas.

"We've really got into going to places that most bands don't go to. We were among the first to go to Japan and the kids there show their appreciation in the most basic manner which is what it used to be like over here. Hong Kong is another place we want to play."

Charlesworth mentions the band have acquired a mellotron for John Paul Jones but they will still retain the excitement of their rock and roll medleys.

"We do it everywhere but it comes spontaneously. After the opening sequence I just start a song and hope everybody will catch on. I did 'Let's Jump The Broomstick' once, but we often put in 'Party', which is a really good one.

"When we did LA Forum we made some recordings of the rehearsal, and we did about an hour's run-through which ended up getting an echo set going. I think we played every number on 'Elvis's Golden Discs Volume One'. it's amazing that you can stir yourself enough to get all the lyrics from that far back in time, and Jimmy managed to do all the right solos as well. It was all completely spontaneous.

"We were fiddling around once and we wrote a reggae number which will be on the next album, but I would like to have it out as a single."

Plant mentions that he had stopped in Bangkok on the way back from their Australian tour and he would like to play there, "Whether we could play there or not, I don't know because there are all sorts of political things happening like in Italy where there was tear-gas everywhere after the show. But you must move around and play to people who live in the outback as well as in America and England. I don't think we play England any less than America - it just seems that way at the moment. Some performers get very uptight about the press and a lot of groups get affected by this and won't play. And it's the kids who suffer as a result."....

Sounds reports.... Cover story, Zeppelin: Huge British Tour.... LED ZEPPELIN are to make their biggest ever concert tour of Britain at the end of this month. The band will play 24 dates over a two month period before an estimated audience of over 100,000. Zeppelin will play two consecutive dates at some venues— including the 6000 seater Alexandra Palace on December 22 and 23. The band have stipulated that all ticket prices throughout the tour will stand at £1 for all seats—the only exception being at Manchester Hardrock where all tickets will be £1.25. The tour — the band's largest either in Britain or America — opens at Newcastle City Hall on November 30 with a further concert on December 1. Other dates are: Glasgow Greens Playhouse December 3 and 4 Manchester Hardrock 7 and 8 Cardiff Capitol 11 and 12 Birmingham Odeon 16 and 17 Alexandra Palace 22 and 23 Sheffield City Hall January 2 Preston Guildhall 3 Bradford St. George's 4 Oxford New Theatre 7 Liverpool Empire 14 Stoke Trentham Gardens 15 Aberystwyth Kings Hall 16 Southampton Gaumont 21 Aberdeen Musical Hall 25 Dundee Caird Hall 27. Edinburgh Kings Theatre 28. Tickets will go on sale throughout Britain on November 10 at 9 a.m. from all local theatre box offices. The only exception will be tickets for Alexandra Palace. These will be on sale at the same time on November 10 but available only from Harlequin record shops in Oxford Street Dean Street and the Haymarket.

18 **Melody Maker reports....** Full page advert announcing the entire UK tour is sold out pointing out MM journalist Chris Charlesworth's monumental blunder of the previous week that, "Their popularity has undoubtedly waned.".... Article states Whoosh Zep sell out and outlines the speed at which the entire tour was sold.... 110,000 tickets in four hours with fans sleeping on the street in freezing conditions. Page, "When I heard the news about the tickets, I felt very humble.".... **New Musical Express reports....** 100,000 Led Zeppelin seats sold in a day.... Demand for tickets for the upcoming Led Zeppelin tour of the UK is "Incredible". The entire tour sold out within four hours. The band are scheduled to play 24 concerts, a spokesman for the promoters told the NME, "We believe this to be a record for a lengthy tour of this nature, more especially as the final date on the itinerary is two and a half months away."....

25 **Disc and Music Echo reports....** cover story.... Interview with Jimmy Page by Andrew Tyler. A general state of things interview with Page, revealing information about the band's changing live set and studio directions. Page talks about his need to perform, *"As far as the British tour goes I didn't worry about it too much, whether it would sell or not, because that didn't really bother me. What we've got together now is pretty good. It doesn't really matter if there were only 50 people out there. It's just gonna be really good to play. People give these places a miss. A British tour to some groups comprises a few dates around England, you know, a few key dates. But we're going to Wales and Scotland, Edinburgh, Glasgow, Dundee. We wanted to play Ayr Ice Rink, which I remember playing years back, but we couldn't get it. We did Aberdeen, or* was it Dundee, on the last tour and that was phenomenal . . . fantastic. Aberystwyth holds about 900 or even less and it's going to be so good to do.

"We've had to be quite mercenary. The last American tour just got silly. There were something like 28 dates in 30 days we were playing on an average of three hours every night, sometimes more than that and it was really doing us in. So we had to make some radical cuts and changes. But now what we've got are things from every LP from Dazed & Confused through to Stairway To Heaven, Black Dog, Rock and Roll, Misty Mountain Hop. All the more important ones you know. It's really difficult because we really wanted to do it all, just adding new bits on and keep it going, but it's impossible time-wise. But there are four maybe five new numbers.

"Round about the third LP it started mellowing out and more than anything else the lyrics got much better. Robert started to concentrate on the lyrics a lot more and he really put everything he had into them. But then we'll still get together after a long time span, like a month or something, and a riff will just happen and a number will be written. I mean a prime example of this sort of thing is when we did 'Rock And Roll.' We had all the equipment set up because we were doing a mobile recording at the time and Bonzo just started playing an opening which is in fact the opening of the song, and the riff just started.

"We did about 30 seconds. It sounded good and we went into the truck to hear it and within 15 minutes the whole framework for the rest had been written and recorded. That's quite raw and those sort of things are happening all the time. Whenever we get together we come up with something.

"We always seem to be going in and out of the studios and doing something. Right now there's this tremendous backlog of numbers which could have easily made up a double LP but then if you're going to put out a double I think it shouldn't be done just because you've got a surplus of tracks which is a thing that happens a lot. If we ever put out a double album it would be nice to really plan it so that it wouldn't appear to be a bunch of old rubbish stuck together."

Page then talks about his wanderings in the Far East, *"You'd be surprised where they'd really like to hear you but you can't go to a place like India. We stopped in on the way back from Japan and the reaction of the people was.... well, they just wanted to see some music. They just wanted to see a group that could go over and cause a bit of a fuss, that could open up the music scene over there. We heard one guitarist who was really good. I mean he would have held up very easily over here. He played sitar for six years, and he's adapted from that. But it wasn't like raga rock more like the Mahavishnu, yeah, it was very good indeed, a very competent musician, He frightened me to death by saying, 'Oh I practice for at least eight hours everyday,' and you could see that he did too. He played sort of classical guitar too, but not Bach, things that were like Bach Structures but his own inventions. But he was getting no market whatsoever because they didn't understand. They just needed someone to go over and open it up.*

"It would be really nice to do dates in places like Hong Kong, Thailand and all these places through the East. The sort of groups that do those sort of places are Marmalade, Tremeloes and Bee Gees but they haven't had anybody to go over and sort of really rock it up."

When asked whether his leanings have anything in common with George Harrison's efforts, *"It's got nothing whatsoever to do with that because what he took from there were things that were written purely around raga scales and this thing is just totally different. But there are all these projects which could be coming off in the future, like recording far afield and bringing it here on to a track and seeing how it goes. Morocco would be an ideal place to go and record . . . anywhere really that has good folk musicians."*

Page elaborates on his latest equipment which includes the Pye Mobile's mixing desk, *"I've also got things like a mellotron and synthesizer. I'm getting much more involved in instruments that I've never tried before and it's really therapy for myself. I've never played keyboards ever and I've sort of come to grips with that a bit and with the synthesiser and mellotron. Well they have such a good sound you can't help but get something good out of it."*.... **New Musical Express reports....** Interview with Page by Keith Altham, *"I know Clapton went through a sort of Press paranoia, and so did I. I don't think some of those so-called critics realise just how much they can hurt or affect an artist. It's only quite recently I have been able to get a better perspective on their relative significance. No one would dispute the power of the Press en masse but it's those few individuals trying to make a name for themselves, with trite and caustic comments, who get through on a personal level.*

"I've realised now, though, that one or two exceptionally offensive remarks won't harm a group or a career. It'd only be serious if the general consensus of opinion was against us.

"I used to get incensed by some of those so-called readers letters in a paper which had perhaps not been written by readers, but were deliberately contrived by people on the paper to drum up controversy. Then there were those who came along to see us and got on that same silly bandwagon about Robert moving about on stage . . . as if you should stand to attention for rock music. Not just our concerts, either. I remember going to a Crosby and Nash concert which was really good — everyone went away afterwards with that good glow you get from seeing a real good performance.

"When I read one of the reviews in the paper in the morning, I couldn't believe it. It said they were tragically bad and needed Steve Stills 'but obviously not Neil Young' What a thing to say, man—I felt like I must have been to another concert again.

"I don't really want to talk about critics, but they're a sore subject with me. If they want to get their teeth into something, why don't they attack some of the appallingly bad situations there are within Mass Media —like the BBC Radio 1. For example I live in Berkshire, Sussex, and Radio 1 which is supposed to be so 'Wonderful' fades out around 5.30 p.m. each night, just as palatable music starts to be played and the signal sounds like it was being produced by John Cage— everything fading in and out. We pay for the service through our taxes. When it's that bad it's just inexcusable.

"Those are the kind of things which should be attacked by the music Press, and not the musicians, who are usually trying to do their best. There are so few people like John Peel in this business, genuinely trying to help along the new talent and not crush a young artist because they may not be comparable to

the established groups.

"One of the best campaigns run by a musical paper was in the New Musical Express, and their attack on the 'Night Assemblies Act', and there are still plenty of other injustices you could turn your attention toward."

Altham raises the question of whether Led Zeppelin was contrived, *"It was never that controlled. We spent almost a year in England, being totally ignored, before we made ground in America with the eventual backlash in England. In fact I never wanted the Yardbirds to break up at all —it was me who was trying hardest of all to keep them together. Keith Relf had other ideas.*

"It's just not possible for me to be objective about the group's success and how it happened. You can't compute or calculate for a situation like that or the chemistry that arises —the only people with a similar musical approach at the time were Cream, but I always felt their improvised passages used to go on and on. We tried to inject more light and shade into our spontaneous pieces and some sense of the dramatic. If there was a key to our musical success, it was in that.

"The one thing that has remained constant in Led Zeppelin has been a sort of virility that runs through the music— no don't write that down—oh I see you have, never mind. The point is that we are continually changing shape, and each album has been different and slagged for being different. We've never been content to remain in one musical bag.

"The only label people ever tried to tie on us was 'heavy', and if you examine our acoustic and light rock content, even that fails to stand up. What we convey are usually emotions. And I can't convey emotions with the spoken or written

word. All I've ever claimed to be is a musician.

"We've never been a band to stand still—every album has been different every album has been slagged by one or more critics because of it. We play things like Whole Lotta Love on stage, still, because it's not become sterile, and we still enjoy it as much as the audience. It's never the same from one night to the next and it provides the basic framework for us to create some new spontaneous music. You can't disappoint your audience by not playing any of the songs they expect to hear. I think it's selfish to play all new material and expect them to identify with it.

"Joe Cocker made that mistake recently. You just can't do it. We still do 'Black Dog' 'Stairway to Heaven' 'Rock and Roll' and 'Since I've Been Loving You', because they're what we've been; what we are, and what people have the right to expect. One of Zeppelin's strengths has always been that our material is so varied, and we seem to absorb other influences —it really annoys me when I see the band categorized as 'heavy' and put into bags with people like Grand Funk, which actually happened in the States.

"The people who I personally most admire are those fusing the styles of all kinds of music . . . musicians like Zappa and more recently John McLaughlin and the Mahavishnu group. They are going to be huge, because they've pulled so many styles together and come out with something unique."

Altham asks why did they decide on such a lengthy U.K. tour?

"To begin with we hoped that by spreading the venues out this time, we might prevent a huge concentrated rush in one area and give more people the chance

to see us. As it's worked out it seems we are even more popular than we thought. I'm personally a bit disappointed we can't play somewhere like the Royal Albert Hall, because I think it's an ideal place for a rock group— the atmosphere is so great. It's just a pity the place is falling to bits so badly.

"I must admit I was a bit confused when I heard we were playing Alexandra Palace—I thought it was that place with the lake."

Altham points out that Page plays an antique Les Paul guitar, *"There's no doubt that these old guitars between 1952-60 were made by the last of the post-war craftsmen. They're more responsive to the player's touch. Clapton was probably the first to realise and popularize the use of the 'Stratocaster' with two pickups but my favourite was an old Fender-Telecaster. Unfortunately it fed-back on stage and now I only use it on sessions. The Les Paul I have was probably originally sold for about £180, but today people are paying as much as £600 for them. Now you have to be careful you don't pick up a fake, because the Japanese and some of the original manufacturers are remaking the old models. . . but without the individual craftsmanship that counted."*

In conclusion Altham asks how he expects the critics to treat the upcoming tour, *"I just hope that they can go to see with the idea of being entertained by good music. I would like them to capture some of the spirit of the occasion without committing musical lobotomy."*

December 1972

2 **New Musical Express reports....** Led Zeppelin's tour takes off this week with the first show being in Newcastle this

Thursday.... **Sounds reports....** cover story...Jimmy Page and John Bonham will play on Maggie Bell's new album.... **Disc and Music Echo reports....** Newcastle sold out....

9 New Musical Express reports.... Review of the opening night in Newcastle.... Page, *"I can tell you we were really nervous tonight. When you haven't played England for some time, not only do you want things to be spot on, but you always get a little frightened that you'll somehow disappoint the kids. For a first night the reaction was just tremendous. We've got some nice things going, but just wait until we've been on the road for a week. Then we'll really fall into place. It should be exciting 'Ya know? Even though you can get things going when you're playing to 20,000 kids in the States, there's still something about playing in much smaller halls and clubs.*

"The trouble is, you can't seem to please everyone. When we play large stadiums they complain, and when we play small clubs they moan about not being able to get in. You just can't win. It would be even nicer if you just had rails upstairs and around the sides with a large space down front where the kids could leap about or just wander freely."

On stage Plant introduces Black Dog with, *"Good evening, this one's called 'My Brain Hurts'."* He then compares Misty Mountain Hop to My Ding-A-Ling, *"The vice squad should have checked out this one before it was released."*

Other comments on stage include, *"The new album should have come out in August but it'll be out in January. But I went to bed in July and didn't get up until October. Had it come out when we intended, this next number*

'Dancing Days' would have been just right for that time of the year." and, *"Bron-y-Aur Stomp was inspired during a holiday in an amazing cottage in Bron-y-Aur (South Snowdonia), and is dedicated to my dog."*

Bonham, *"We enjoy playing. Every gig is important to us. In this business it doesn't matter how big you are you can't afford to become complacent. If you adopt that attitude then you're dead. That'll never happen to us."*

In reference to a comment in the press Peter Grant states, *"So their popularity has undoubtedly waned, that's a bleedin' laugh."*.... Led Zeppelin's publicist B.P. Fallon was severely beaten by angry fans in Glasgow when they were refused access to the concert due to counterfeit ticket problems.... **Sounds reports....** Led Zeppelin on the road.... cover story.... Interview by Steve Peacock with Jimmy Page. Peacock asks about the latest tour, *"We just seemed to keep adding numbers and adding more numbers, so that what started out as an hour just grew into three hours. We got really fatigued by it, what with all the traveling as well, every night after the gig. We'd decided to commute from a base just outside New York, so we'd fly back every night —it was a good idea in theory, saves living off the top layer of your suitcase, but I got back from that and for a week I just didn't know where I was. The set we're doing now still lasts over two hours. but somehow it feels a lot shorter."*

Were the band cutting back on live work? *"No, if anything we're going to start increasing again, at least that's the way it looks from the way we've been talking. I know we're working in every month right up until August .... on stage it's the spontaneity that's really exciting, and the electricity that builds up between* us and the audience, the rapport that's building up all night. Obviously that's really stimulating. In the studio it's much more of a challenge."

Peacock asks whether he was satisfied with the way things were working out for him. *"I'll never be satisfied with myself —I mean I've set myself certain goals in life and I just haven't reached them yet, not by any means. Having a studio has helped a lot, mind you; I've been working on a film track (for Kenneth Anger's film "Lucifer Rising"), which was another challenge because I wanted it to sound timeless in a way, not to sound dated by anything. I used a synthesiser on it but I tried to use it in such a way that it didn't sound like a synthesiser, just that all the instruments didn't quite sound like what they ought to sound. You don't quite know what it is at any point. It's not synthesiser all the way through, but overall you have to think wait a minute, what's that?', and when you've got six things going on at the same time, it gets quite a good effect."*

Of his time as a session man, he says: *"You just didn't know where you were, and it was really frustrating because you never said anything musically the whole way through it. There was no communication between us and the artist at any point. We were just a bunch of cogs, and that's why I got out of it. It was just nowhere, nowhere at all. I suppose it was useful in that it helped a lot on discipline, coming to terms with being able to read music and so on, being able to in all those different situations. It was good background. But I didn't know any musician who was happy doing it, and yet most of them are still there. And a lot of them were better musicians than I was Jim Sullivan for instance — there's somebody who should have said 'right, that's*

it, I'm going to have a go', but he never did."*

Was Led Zeppelin his band at the start? *"Yeah, because at the time there had to be somebody saying 'let's do this and let's do that', so I suppose at that stage I was really at the helm. But now everybody's got a free hand in everything — if someone comes up with a number, he has a go, it's as easy as that. It's a co-op band. On stage it's the spontaneity that's really exciting and the electricity that builds up all evening, the rapport that builds between us and the audience."*

Peacock asks whether the band has the scope to fulfill Page's musical ideas, *"Sure. That's why it's always changing I suppose. For a start, there are four minds at work, not just one, everybody's coming up with ideas all the time and we can all handle anything so there's no reason why we shouldn't tackle anything. We do like to do everything ourselves, if possible. So rather than use a big string section of people we don't know and who probably don't know us. It's more convenient to use a mellotron. We can do it all ourselves — that hasn't been a hard and fast rule in the past, but we certainly want to in the future, and John Paul can play anything."*

The song writing process, *"Usually we just play and a number comes out — I don't know how or why it's just one of those things a fusion of four people. They develop a lot more as you play them on stage. Obviously as you get to know something better it's going to grow, and as you become more confident with something you can start to take more chances with it, and you start to see all different angles. The actual structure of the numbers changes they can move off at any tangent really, and again, out of those new territories, new numbers often grow.*

"No, I don't think we've got a fixed classified image at all. I know in the past it used to be Led Zeppelin—Heavy Band, full stop. In the Press especially. But I think the essence of change was there even on the first album — there was a wide enough scope—and certainly by the time of the third and fourth albums you could see it wasn't just Heavy Band, full stop. Not by any means. But it has taken some people a long time to realise that and accept it. In the States, "Stairway To Heaven" was the one that really broke all the barriers down for us and I know it still gets a lot of airplay. I don't care about it — as long as those people out there see you and it's a good show. That's all that matters. because if it's a good show they'll remember. All the old crap in the Press isn't going to help if it's not going to work on stage. I'm trying to get better all the time, trying to improve as a musician. The critics can have an orgy over it, and they usually do, but I know where I'm going, and I think everyone else knows where they're going too, which is why it really doesn't matter what's going on anywhere else.".... **Disc and Music Echo reports**.... Big news of the week is the Led Zeppelin tour.... review of the opening show at Newcastle City Hall.... *"I tell you we were as nervous as hell before going out there."* Robert Plant confident looking sleeker than he's done for ages, talks backstage after the opening night of Zeppelin's first British tour for, well it's hard to remember that far back. It's nearly a full thirty minutes since the final encore, their fourth which the audience had simply screamed clapped stood and begged for. Honestly the scenes after John Paul Jones, Jimmy Page, John Bonham and Robert Plant left the stage were amazing. The crowd was like starving rats who'd have done any-

thing for another slice of rock. And even as Plant was talking fans were still pounding away at the stage door. No Britain hasn't forgotten what the real heavy metal actually feels like. Those thudding brain wrenching riffs when "Whole Lotta Love" bursts between the eyes. A lot of people were doing it during the concert cause that's how Zeppelin get you. Simply gripping the inside of the elbow hard with the palm of one hand then bringing the forearm up dead straight. So it was warm up night getting into stride before British audiences again for Zeppelin. All you can say is Aberystwyth City Hall and Stoke Trentham Gardens had better look to their guns. For four years Led Zeppelin have been playing America and the 50,000 dollar band always knock the place out. Now at long last they're back and they truly do shake you down.

Plant now is in more control of his vocals; much of the wild excesses have been ironed out. Page pulled guitar tricks throughout the concert until you thought he'd never stop. John Paul Jones just stood and laid it down. And John Bonham crashed and bashed the night away. Zeppelin have trimmed down their act now, it's tighter and somehow more thorough. And always they work so damned hard at every number as though their whole career depended on it. Yes they're massive but no well-oiled machine going through those old old motions. The concert lasted well over two hours, there was no supporting act and the band delivered right from the beginning. Breaking in with Rock and Roll from their last album and then a new rough edged rocker titled "Over The Hills And Far Away" from their next album due out in January. The latter soared into what's perhaps one their finest songs, "Since I've Been

Loving You" with Plant's voice riding mature and forceful and Page filling in with some beautiful light phrases. By the end of the number the atmosphere had grown electric and the crowd were literally stunned into applause. Another number off the forthcoming album followed "Dancing Days" starting with some intricate guitar from Page and developing into a wondrous climax. After Zep had launched through "Dazed & Confused" then the tender "Stairway To Heaven" you simply knew you were seeing a completely ultimate band. The songs, and they really are powerful, along with their anthem, "Whole Lotta Love" extended out to include snatches of "Boogie Chillun" and "Everybody Needs Someone To Love" did most of the damage. The audience felt it. Zep were superb....

16 **New Musical Express reports....** The new Led Zeppelin album should be out around January 12th.... letter to the editor, fan is disgusted with Led Zeppelin's show in Glasgow due to the band playing no encore and Plant's shameless plugging of the new album.... **Disc and Music Echo reports....** Robert Plant poster free....

23 **New Musical Express reports....** cover story.... A Whole Lotta Rock 'N Roll by Nick Kent reporting from the Angel Hotel in Cardiff. He reviews the show from the Cardiff Capitol.— "Tonight's show has been average, no more, no less, which means the band got the colossal response they've registered as a customary reaction over the last few years." The show apparently lasted for the usual two and a half hours concluding with the Whole Lotta Love Medley. Kent gets into his own interpretation of why the band are so successful and leads into a

brief treatise on Plant's musical tastes. Plant, *"Forever Changes. Now there was a great album. Have you heard 'White Dog' on Vindicator (by Arthur Lee)? Lee dedicated that for me y'know? He just couldn't believe that I dug his stuff, so much so that he wrote the song. Those first two albums (by Bob Dylan), I reckon it was these that brought me round to marijuana."*

For some unknown reason Plant then starts to reminisce about his tour of the red light district in Thailand. *"We were taken by this guy who spoke strictly Queen's English, and it seemed to be the policy to show all visiting rock bands the brothels. I mean it was interesting and that, but they couldn't understand why we didn't do anything. The guy kept saying that all the other bands he'd taken round had enjoyed themselves. Eventually we were labeled as undesirables or something because we hadn't got involved. Anyway it's illegal to have long hair in that country."*

At this point he turns his attention to the evangelists of middle America, specifically Texas, *"It was unbelievably heavy. I mean they never give up. The first thing they actually said was, 'We got Jeremy Spencer'."*

Back to music, *"It's a shame that the whole solo singer-songwriter concept had to degenerate into that James Taylor thing of taking things so seriously. Actually there are a lot of good ideas going around now. Actually this'll probably sound strange but ultimately I can envisage Pagey and myself ending up doing a whole Incredible String Band type thing together. Very gentle stuff."*

Kent then turns to Page and raises the ongoing battle between the band and Rolling Stone magazine, Page, *"Well, the situation we found ourselves in with*

Rolling Stone was purely political and stemmed from their side all along. The reasons are basically so trivial that it's really not worth going into."

After dismissing questions about his early career Page is asked about the evolution of Zeppelin in the studio. Page, "The changes from album to album were roughly these. The first record was made in roughly 30 hours. We went in with some riffs and worked out a set of tracks which were functional as to the sound we were looking for, things we could get off on playing live. The second was recorded in between gigs we were playing in the States and so obviously the album was affected by this. The third album was again affected by a change of pace in that we wrote some of the songs in Wales and there were all sorts of developments then. And the fourth was generally more laid back in the way that it was recorded. It's quite pointless saying, 'Oh yeah this is the Led Zeppelin Acoustic Album' and 'this is the Heavy Led Zeppelin Album' because there have been elements in our music all along and we've never swamped an album with one particular style. People claimed that the fourth album was traditionally influenced, but then 'Babe I'm Gonna Leave You' is a traditional song and that was on the first album. It's complete rubbish that we concentrate our attentions on the States. If people could be bothered to examine just how much time we spend in one country at a time you find that we measure out our touring schedule to take in as many countries as we can. This tour of Britain is no less than the tour we did of the States this year. We tried to play around as many countries as possible and everyone ended up saying 'Oh they're ignoring us' which is rubbish."..... John Cann of Atomic Rooster slams Led Zeppelin for their disgustingly

high ticket prices.... **Melody Maker reports....** Letter to the editor headlined Led Poisoning...The letter complains about the band's recent appearance at the Hardrock in Manchester calling them the world's most overrated band. He goes on to say Robert Plant's vocals were unintelligible, Page's guitaring a blur of super fuzzed notes, Jones bass a dull lifeless thudding and Bonham's drumming bashing away at leather suitcases and dustbin lids....

30 **New Musical Express reports....** Hail Hail Rock N' Roll part two from Cardiff by Nick Kent. Page, "There have been two or three truly magic gigs, Bath was one of them. That was quite incredible because everything seemed to be right for us. The energy was quite phenomenal. Our gigs usually work out to last around 2½ hours. I think the longest we ever played was 4½ hours which was another of those magic occasions. It was never really a conscious thing that we'd play for so long. It was a gradual process of building up material. Someone would want to play this and someone else would throw in a suggestion and eventually we had all this material, both electric and acoustic. And then there were the numbers like Dazed & Confused and Whole Lotta Love which come out different every time."

Kent goes on to describe the band's opening numbers before concluding, "It's around this time that you realise that the Zeps are the ace heavy band."

The band go on to play Song Remains The Same which will not be released for some months. Kent comments, "The song sounds almost like Yes in construction, with the emphasis on the dexterity of rock and roll..." The songs include, Rock and Roll, Black Dog, Rain Song, Bron-y-Aur Stomp, Misty

Mountain Hop, Since I've Been Loving You, Dancing Days, Stairway To Heaven, before the band close with Whole Lotta Love which Kent calls "classic punk rock". (No wonder he apologised for this review a few years later when punk rock had exploded and it's exponents, including Kent, were doing their best to dismiss Zeppelin). During Whole Lotta Love the band throw in a medley of old hits such as Let's Have A Party and Bee Bop A Lula before they end with the Ocean....

Extra reports.... Pierre Grandjean interviews Jimmy Page in Montreux. He begins with the new album and what is it's title. *"I really can't tell you for the simple reason that there isn't a name yet. But the album is finished the recordings are done, the mixing is done and the cover should be done by next week. The problem is the title which we haven't figured out yet. This type of problem is not new its happened with each of our previous albums. It's the reason that none of our other albums have a title. This one will have a title.*

"It's difficult to explain in detail the direction of this album. What I can tell you is that there will be important differences. There'll be much less acoustic than we've done in the past.

"When we decided to make a new album without even thinking about it we decided it would be electric. Because we thought we would give more of our best. That's really the reason."

Grandjean asks if the touring distracted from the recording. *"A record for us and for me is not made in as regular a fashion as you might imagine. It's not really one continuous session. We've been working on this record for months and months when we were touring and not. It's not really the tours that slow us*

but the difficulty is inserting a recording session between concerts. For example it's been three months that we've been wanting to record a few songs and all we could get was three recording sessions because they're all really booked night and day. That's the real problem is trying to get a studio at the time when we need them."

What about the studio at his house? *"But it's only eight tracks and we record in sixteen tracks and I can't even mix what we record."*

Grandjean asks how he feels the various audiences in Japan, the USA and Europe differ. *"That's always surprised me. The reaction in Japan. Even though there's the language barrier that's ten times worse than we're used to in Europe. What I don't like is the interest that they have in the West. That makes them lose their traditions and I think that's tragic in the musical sense. As for the concerts, it could be Tokyo, Munich or Montreux each place stimulates each of us."*

How does he explain the magic on stage at a Led Zeppelin concert? *"I don't know I can't explain it. If there was a magic formula then every group would use it. Maybe it's because our fans really don't know that much about us, you know, our private lives. They only know us through our music. They don't see us on TV they don't listen to us much on the radio. All of this causes them to create their own story. It's the fans that create the magic not us the musicians."*

Grandjean observes that he is very theatrical on-stage and asks if it is all rehearsed. *"Absolutely not. My conduct is the same as everybody else except it's in reverse. Most people are very calm at work and half hysterical at home, ...more themselves at home. People are more themselves at their house where they*

*spend most of their time. For me the place
I am most often is really in concert halls."*
How did he feel about the recent concert in Montreux?

*"It wasn't the worst it wasn't the
best either. It was a good concert and
that's it. We hadn't played in quite a
while."*

What's lined up for Zeppelin?
*"The record which we hope will come out
a bit after Christmas, and probably some
new recordings which we have enough
material for a double album. And then
we'll go back on tour and there'll be a
surprise."*

1973

January 1973

6 Melody Maker reports.... Caught in the act, review of the band's show at the Alexandra Palace Chris Charlesworth points out that the venue is in a pretty dilapidated state but fully 12,000 fans showed up to see the band over two nights. He states that the venue was poorly suited to a concert with dismal acoustics and a cold atmosphere, however he is enthusiastic about the band calling them, 'about as perfect a band as you could hope to hear.' He says that the set included Black Dog, Whole Lotta Love, Stairway to Heaven and Since I've Been Loving You. He concludes, 'Catch them if you can.'....

13 New Musical Express reports.... Led Zeppelin's concerts in Preston and Bradford have been canceled due to illness in the band...Robert Plant is reported to have the flu...the rescheduled dates are now Bradford on January 18th and Preston on January 30th.... John Paul Jones is producing an album by Tony Brimm.... **Melody Maker reports....** Zepp Off....article outlining Plant succumbing to the flu. The article is very confusing saying that Plant and Bonham were on their way to Sheffield when their Bentley broke down and they had to hitch a ride to the gig. It then says that two shows had to be canceled in Preston and *Sheffield* and were then rescheduled as Preston on January 30th and *Bradford* on January 18th. It says that 71,000 people will attend the shows throughout the tour....

19 Sounds reports.... John Bonham's car broke down on the way to a gig in Sheffield he and Robert Plant had to hitchhike to the show and Plant caught the flu.... two dates have been canceled and rescheduled....

23 New Musical Express reports.... Blackfoot claim that Robert Plant used to jam with them and that he used to say that one day they would be his backing band....

27 Melody Maker reports.... Advert reads — Save 30p when you buy Led Zeppelin 5 from Opus Record Shops. This is a very early ad for this album presumably before anyone knew it's title....

February 1973

3 Sounds reports.... Review of the band's performance in Edinburgh by John Anderson.... Any thoughts of Led Zeppelin's stamina giving out at the King's Theatre Edinburgh, on Sunday, on what was the second last gig of their exhausting two months British tour, were promptly dispelled before a full and running - over fanatical crowd of 1,472. The band flexed their muscles with "Black Dog" and two and a half hours later were still bombarding their audience with 'Heartbreaker' and 'Thank You' for encores. Most of the stuff was familiar. Nothing from Jimmy Page was more dynamic then "Dazed And Confused" where his bowed work held the faithful spellbound. "Stairway To Heaven" was one of Robert Plant's frequent triumphs and John Bonham's percussive heroics throughout held everything beautifully in place. The tastes of things to come on the band's fifth album were 'The Song Remains The Same', 'The Rain Song' and 'Dancing Days'. John Paul Jones keyboard work provided an effective symphonic background to 'Rain' but for total impact with this audience nothing topped Page's athletics on guitar—even when he sat down to it for 'Bron Y Aur Stomp' shared country style with Plant and sounding almost naive compared with the mind-blowing volume of the rest of the programme....

24 **New Musical Express reports....** Interview with John Paul Jones by Nick Kent about his early career and his reasons for joining Zeppelin. Jones, *"By the time Jimmy came along with the idea for Led Zeppelin, I was in a position as top fee session arranger where I was completely snowed under with work.*

"Being a session arranger is literally a 24-hour job—working out individual scores for horns and strings the night before, handing them out the next day and knocking the finished product out whenever. That's how all the Tamla Motown arrangers work — I mean, the things they do for the string parts are quite unbelievable. But eventually I became quite satiated by the work which coincided nicely with Zeppelin. I left when I was on top though, which was good.

"But I've worked on some quite ludicrous sessions. Things like Alma Cogan's last work after she had died. I came into the studio and all the musicians were in tears, having to put the backing tracks on. I couldn't believe it.

"And then there was another which had Mike Leander and this grandiose scheme of bringing a huge orchestra something like 12 guitarists and seven established musicians. And Decca decided to scrap the project after they'd heard the tapes.

"My reasons for joining up with Zeppelin were purely musical. Led

Zeppelin have really only ever existed for the music —I can't really see anything image-wise that one can attach to the band.

"I suppose that's why we've stayed together—each of us fulfills a function. Also, we have very strong management— I mean, Peter's been with us on almost . . . well, actually, every gig we've ever played.

"As far as I'm concerned, the key Led Zeppelin gig— the one that just put everything into focus—was one that we played on our first American tour at the Boston Tea Party. We'd played our usual one hour set, using all the material from the first album and Page's 'White Summer' guitar piece and, by the end, the audience just wouldn't let us off the stage. It was in such a state that we had to start throwing ideas around — just thinking of songs that we might all know or that some of us knew a part of, and work it from there.

So we'd go back on and play things like 'I Saw Her Standing There' and 'Please Please Me'—old Beatles favourites. I mean, just anything that would come into our head, and the response was quite amazing. There were kids actually bashing their heads against the stage—I've never seen that at a gig before or since, and when we finally left the stage we'd played for 4+ hours.

"Peter (Grant) was absolutely ecstatic. He was crying—if you can imagine that — and hugging us all. You know with this huge grizzly bear hug. I suppose it was then that we realised just what Led Zeppelin was going to become.

"America has always been very good for us. I can't really recall a place that hasn't accepted us, in the sense that we're absolutely loathed in that area.

"I remember reading in what I

suppose would be termed the Underground Press some very derogatory remarks on our so-called 'capitalist rip-off' tactics, which I find highly offensive simply because I've always thought that we give an audience its money's worth in playing time, while keeping an eye on ticket prices.

"There was a time when it was us, the Rolling Stones . . . I think . . . Deep Purple who got this thing thrown at them. Compared to the way the Stones operate as a touring entity, we're very different. Unfortunately the band found itself appearing at gigs in the States that the Stones had played some two weeks before, and it was just total devastation.

"We always keep down the entourage to a minimum, simply because it's easier to transport a small number of people around. One has to either go completely crazy or else work very strategically at touring."

Kent points out that Jones is working on an album with Madeline Bell and that he would like to score the movie 'Stranger In A Strange Land' the conversation then concludes with his thoughts on the contemporary scene, *"I'm really not over-enthusiastic about anything currently going on in music. People seem to expect me to say something grand, but there's no-one who really moves me to any heights of ecstasy. I used to quite like the Pink Floyd, but then they somehow started to go off. My influences as a bass player? Actually I was asked this some time ago on KSAN radio and I answered Mozart which seemed to put the interviewer off so much so that he never really recovered. I think I also said that I like Tamla Motown bass-players as well which seemed to disgust him even more."*

March 1973

4 Sweden's Daily News reports.... Hardrock Tops. Article states that the band are conducting a rare tour of Europe which brings them from Copenhagen to Göteborg and then Stockholm's tennis Arena on the Tuesday. It also points out that there are still tickets left for the show....

5 Göteborg Tioningen reports.... Led Zeppelin An Ice Cold Show. Håkan Sandblad reports from the Göteborg Scandinavium Arena that Zeppelin drew 500 people more than Jethro Tull the previous week for a total of audience of 4,500. The band played for two hours ending the set with Whole Lotta Love. Sandblad says, "It was an ice-cold show, hard and calculated. Not one ounce of spontaneity." He goes on to mention how the band lay down a wall of sound but Plant's voice is lost in the echoing auditorium. He also mentions that Bonham has an advert for marijuana on his gong. He concludes, "Led Zeppelin were once four guys who seemed to like what they did. Today they are stars who are stuck in clichés."....

12 Bravo reports.... Bravo Tour, Quick interview with Jimmy Page.... Led Zeppelin are here! Two days before their big German tour Bravo spoke with Led Zeppelin's leader Jimmy Page by telephone.

Page is asked why this German tour is so long and will there be any surprises, Page, *"I think we owe it to our fans after such a long time we would like to see as many people as possible. If you are thinking of a show like Alice Cooper our singer Robert Plant makes the show and that is enough. We don't need any fancy surprises. Our music is hard enough. Of course we have a beautiful light show with us."* He is then asked about the set list, *"This is a tough question. It depends on our mood and especially on the mood of our audience but we will include pieces like Whole Lotta Love, Stairway To Heaven, Dazed & Confused, Black Dog, Rock and Roll and Misty Mountain Hop. We'd rather play new songs but if we are on stage we are there for our fans so we play what they expect. We don't want to disappoint anybody but nevertheless we will have some musical surprises, this is the first time that John Paul Jones will play mellotron on stage. This is a type of synthesiser which sounds like any instrument."*

He is then asked to explain the delays with the new album, *"We have enough songs, if we went by that we could bring out a new album every month but we want to put out only good stuff. Every LP is supposed to be a work of art with which we, and the fans too, are satisfied for at least a year. We don't want to put our success into jeopardy by luring the money out of our fans pockets with cheap garbage. So we only try and put out good work.*

"This time we had problems with the LP cover it was supposed to be a work of art, and for the first time we have a name for the LP which is 'Houses Of The Holy'."

Bravo's interviewer then asks about the albums style, *"Because we were in Japan and India last year, we mixed their music with ours we even have one piece with reggae sounds included. In other words it will be something really new."*

Finally Page is asked whether he is excited and how long the band will play each night, *"Of course we are otherwise we wouldn't come. We only perform if it makes us happy and we enjoy it. Every concert we do is very serious it doesn't matter if there are fifty or ten thousand* people there. *If we were to see our concerts as part of some job then we would be out of business really fast. The fans would turn their backs on us. We are really excited about coming to Germany just as excited as the fans who are waiting for us.*

"That also depends on the audience. We're thinking about two hours, with a fifteen minute rock and roll medley at the end but we already had concerts lasting up to four hours and if the fans really get us going then we will play all night."

16 **Melody Maker reports....** Report from the Frankfurt Trade Fair states that Coloursound's new Ring Modulator Pedal has already been shipped to Hawkwind, Atomic Rooster, Led Zeppelin and Marc Bolan....

24 **Melody Maker reports....** Led Zeppelin.... review of the show in Vienna.... The historic city of Vienna...played host on Friday Night to Led Zeppelin.... introduced as the 'Rock sensation of the year'...the band ripped into 'Good Times Bad Times'.... also in the set, Black Dog, Misty Mountain Hop, Bron-y-Aur Stomp (the only acoustic song), The Song Remains The Same, Stairway To Heaven and Whole Lotta Love.... John Paul Jones played well despite being ill....

27 **Popmusic Maxipop reports....** Advert reads — RTL présente Led Zeppelin - Nancy 27 March, Marseille 29 March, Lille 31st March, Paris-St Ouen 1st and 2nd April.... The ad is accompanied by an article covering the band's early career, with mentions of the deleted Live Yardbirds album....

31 **Melody Maker reports....** Zep V At Last.... Led Zeppelin released their fifth album this week.... orders are over a mil-

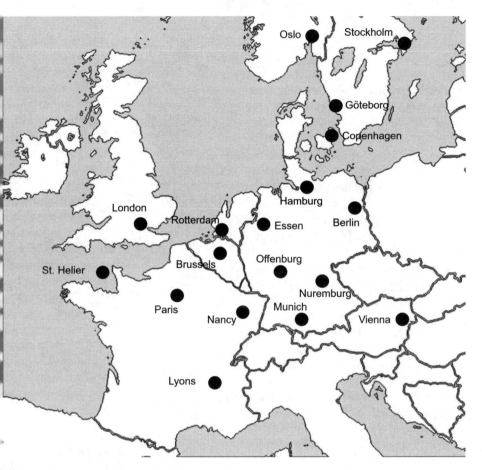

European Tour Spring 1973

March 2nd, 1973 Copenhagen K.B. Hallen
March 4th, 1973 Göteborg Scandinavium Arena
March 6th & 7th 1973 Stockholm Royal Tennis Arena
March 10th, 1973 Oslo
March 11th, 1973 Rotterdam
March 12th, 1973 Brussels
March 14th, 1973 Nuremburg Messehalle
March 16th, 1973 Vienna Concert House
March 17th, 1973 Munich Olympiahalle
March 19th, 1973 Berlin Deutschlandhalle
March 21st, 1973 Hamburg Musichalle
March 22nd, 1973 Essen Grughalle
March 24th, 1973 Offenburg Orthenau Halle
March 26th, 1973 Lyons
March 27th, 1973 Nancy
April 1st & 2nd 1973 Paris Palais De Sports

European Concerts 1975

January 11th, 1975
Rotterdam Ahoy

January 12th, 1975
Brussels Forest Nationale

May 17th, 18th, 23rd, 24th & 25th,
1975 London Earl's Court

October 10th, 1975
St Helier Jersey Behan West Park

lion units worldwide.... the album was delayed for two months by sleeve design problems.... Phil Carson, *"Although most of the advance orders come from the States, the reaction has been fantastic everywhere. In Germany, for example, the album has already been awarded a gold disc for 100,000 sales. This is the biggest advance order for any of the Zeppelin albums, although all of them are steady sellers all the time."*

John Paul Jones plays synthesiser for the first time, Zeppelin are currently half way through a European tour.... full page advert reads — Led Zeppelin Houses Of the Holy The Effect Is Shattering.... review by Chris Welch who is finally disappointed with the band's efforts.... Zeppelin Lose Their Way.... When Led Zeppelin are roaring on stage there is hardly another band in the world to beat them.... thus it grieves me very much when they allow their tremendously high standards to slip.... After the initial brilliance of The Song Remains The Same a malaise began to creep in reaching a nadir in the sadly indulgent D'yer Mak'er.... there is not one song with the exception of "The Song Remains The Same" that has any buzz of excitement.... Perhaps a cool appraisal of this album will spur them on to greater efforts. They have it in their power to stun us all.... article states, the new Monty Python film 'The Holy Grail' will be financed in part by Led Zeppelin, Pink Floyd and Island records.... **Sounds reports....** full page advert for Houses Of The Holy "The Effect is Shattering".... **Disc and Music Echo reports....** review of Houses Of The Holy.... More problems with the sleeve design hence the delay. They've again refused to acknowledge themselves anywhere on the cover and instead settle for a slip over paper band with the album title. It is in fact a superb sleeve by Hipgnosis,

showing unclothed blonde kids scampering and crawling up the craggy face of the Giant's Causeway. Inside is a moss covered castle built on a hill-top with rear view of a bald gentleman holding a blonde girl above his head. What takes place inside is much less pleasing. Much was expected of this their fifth album since they appeared to have cleared the last awkward hurdle from format rock band to something finer. But since album three with magnificent tracks like Gallow's Pole and Since I've Been Loving You, you could sense their energy flagging. There were very definite signs of this at their recent Alexandra Palace concert. On Houses of The Holy both Robert Plant and Jimmy Page are strangely sluggish and vacant, exploding only occasionally on tracks like the Rain Song, Over The Hills And Far Away and Dancing Days. And they seem to have run out of good melody lines as witnessed by the Crunge a straight jam that barrels along on a couple of chords and ends with Plant crying for someone to "take it take it" and "has anyone seen the bridge?" It cuts out without them ever finding it. D'yer Mak'er is another fill track. A not very amusing parody on a 50's boy loses girl and weeps teen ballad. Bass and Drums help build some power and Plant's guitar (sic) is a wicked send up of that age but the track still misses by several yards. "The Ocean" is another track that fizzles to an inconclusive ending. Now for the good news. "The Rain Song" is well up to scratch and definitely a song that needs several hearings. It begins lazily with acoustic guitar and tremolo electric noises squeezing through. Then a surprise burst on mellotron and a French cigarette commercial break. You have to scratch around for the melody but it's there and it shows itself bit by bit. "No Quarter" is a powerfully restful piece with superb warbling synthesiser and a brilliant guitar break from Mr. Page. Perhaps the album's best track "Dancing Days" is also strong for the very real sense of tension it gives off. Perhaps I'll grow to like the others and might even see the joke in "D'yer Mak'er" but on two or three hearings it comes over as an incredibly inconsistent piece of work.... **New Musical Express reports....** Roy Carr reviews Houses Of The Holy with good humour. On Rain Song he says, "Very pastoral and beefed up towards the end, with some well timed dynamics." On the Crunge, "Brother Bobby shows James Brown where it's at." The song which most often caused upset amongst the critics was D'yer Mak'er, but Murray loves it, "Own up. Like everything they attempt it's a bloody great track with a fine workout from Bonzo. See what a diet of bananas and best bitter can do." No Quarter is, "Another faultless track which I'm sure points a direction for things to come."

Murray's comments culminate with, "The greatest live-in-the-studio sound I've heard in yonks. 'So good' yells out Bobby, a built in do-it-yourself review. So who am I to argue.'"...

April 1973

4 **Atlantic press release....**
FOR IMMEDIATE RELEASE FROM: BRIAN VAN DER HORST
LED ZEPPELIN'S "HOUSES OF THE HOLY" SHIPS GOLD: PLANS FOR 1973 TOUR REVEALED
Dave Glew, Vice President in charge of Marketing at Atlantic Records Announced this week that Houses of the Holy, the new album from the English Rock group, Led Zeppelin, was shipped to retailers last week in response to a demand far in excess of sales necessary to qualify for a gold record. Additionally it was revealed that the top-drawing band will also embark on their 1973 American Tour beginning on May 4.

"The demand for Zeppelin's new album has been absolutely fantastic," commented Glew every one of their LPs has been a gold record, and this one is already number five. Led Zeppelin's 1973 tour will encompass 30 cities beginning May 4 in Atlanta and will sweep across the southern United States during May and June, returning via the Northern Border States in July and will culminate in New York on July 27 and 28. The following is a list of planned dates and cities which comprise Zeppelin's summer itinerary.

1973		
May 4	Friday	Atlanta Stadium
May 5	Saturday	Tampa Stadium
May 6	Sunday	Off
May 7	Monday	Jacksonville
May 8	Tuesday	Off
May 9	Wednesday	Off
May 10	Thursday	U. of Alabama
May 11	Friday	St. Louis
May 12	Saturday	Off
May 13	Sunday	Mobile
May 14	Monday	New Orleans
May 15	Tuesday	Off
May 16	Wednesday	Houston
May 17	Thursday	Off
May 18	Friday	Dallas
May 19	Saturday	Fort Worth
May 20	Sunday	Off
May 21	Monday	Off
May 22	Tuesday	San Antonio
May 23	Wednesday	U. of New Mexico
May 24	Thursday	Off
May 25	Friday	Denver
May 26	Saturday	Salt Lake City
May 27	Sunday	Off
May 28	Monday	San Diego

May 29 Tuesday Off
May 30 Wednesday Los Angeles
May 31 Thursday Los Angeles
June 1 or 2 Friday or Saturday
San Francisco

Total of 17 concerts at 16 venues

July 6 & 7 Chicago
July 8   Off
July 9   St. Paul
July 10   Milwaukee
July 11   Off
July 12 & 13   Detroit
July 14   Off
July 15   Buffalo
July 16   Syracuse
July 17   Off
July 18   New Haven
July 19   Off
July 20   Boston
July 21   Providence
July 22   Off
July 23   Baltimore
July 24   Pittsburgh
July 25   Off (Rain Date)
July 26   Off
July 27 & 28   New York

7 **Sounds reports....** full page advert for Houses Of The Holy "Does Things To People".... Wot Zep Gone Soft? Review of Houses Of The Holy. For an album of it's importance this one's surfaced with the minimum of fuss and from the cover alone, and what a superb job it is too, you'd never know who or what was inside. Now Zeppelin albums have a habit of releasing new things to you the more you play them so it's with a little trepidation that I tackle Houses Of The Holy after the most meager of plays but the overall impression is that once again Zep have moved ahead and that in itself is a mixed blessing.

If you're looking for the heaviest of rock with which Zep first blasted your ears you'd be disappointed but if it's a continuance of their last album you're after. OK it's that without the heavies like 'Black Dog'. It does show though what a superb guitarist Jimmy Page is as well as highlighting the expansion of Robert Plant's vocal talents. They both shine throughout the album, almost obliterating the talents of John Bonham on drums and John Paul Jones on bass/keyboards and a variety of modern electronics. And it's these that perhaps sets the scene for Houses, heavily synthesised in places but in those tracks, 'The Rain Song' and 'No Quarter' that come off best, as major works in fact, but a lot of listeners might expect this sort of stuff more from the ranks of the Floyd. From such a perfunctory hearing I'm a little disappointed that Zep haven't come on just a little heavy in places but from an advancement point of view this is a fine album. Plant manages to bend and contort his vocals on several tracks, sounding almost like an instrument himself and for those who might of felt he's just a harsh old rock and roller think again. No Zeppelin album would be complete without the driving force of John Bonham's percussion and although he's sunk a bit by some of the lightish surroundings, make no mistake when it starts to move, as it does, thank heavens, on 'Over The Hills & Far Away' and 'The Ocean' (what a feast from Page on 'Over' too) he's at home. At no time could you mistake this for anyone else but Led Zeppelin and they've proved again, as they have through the years, that they can still demand the highest respect and again put out a recording of real importance, even if it is one a year.... **Disc and Music Echo reports....** Houses Of The Holy is #20.... **Melody Maker reports....** Vive Le

Zeppelin.... Reporter Roy Hollingworth catches Robert Plant at the band's gig in Paris. *"I'm back on me fab farm like and I sit there and I think what the hell am I doing? I think what the bloody hell is a singer if he's not singing?*

"So there's some buggers as don't like the album. Well, God bless them. I like it and there's a few thousand other buggers like it too. I know I'm bragging like buggery but I honestly think we're playing better than we've ever played before. It's working that does it. The British tour three weeks off, and then a solid blow over here. It's so easy to get stale, you know. There's a lot of bands do it. You know they reach a peak and think that that's it. The old country house bit. A year off and all that. Well, it doesn't work that way. There's only one way a band can function and that's on the bloody stage. I think we're going to play more dates this year than we've ever played in our lives. Why? Well, because we damn well want to. I remember a few weeks back, sat on me farm. Well, it came to me, I thought 'Plantey, what's a good lad like you doing sat here contemplating the day like an old goat?' I thought why the .... ain't I out singing. I got so worked up about it that I picked up a spade and dug the whole bloody garden. I have to work, we all have to! When I hear that roar I just roar back. I can't describe how high we get off people. We have reached a high and we ain't going to lose it. And no lousy album review is going to change a thing!".... full page advert reads — Led Zeppelin Houses Of The Holy does things to people....

14 **Disc and Music Echo reports....** Houses Of The Holy is #6.... **Melody Maker reports....** Letters to the editor Led Zep Holy Smoke! Several readers express their disappointment with the new Zeppelin album. *'I must say I'm very disappointed in hearing this album.'* Austin Feeney, Galway. *'Inspiration has been lost.'* S.W. Lomas, Hitchin and one positive letter from Robert Chibbett Newcastle, *'Zep have lost their way have they? Well I'm real glad I got lost with them.'....*

21 **Disc and Music Echo reports....** Houses Of The Holy is #3.... Led All The Way, interview with Robert Plant by Caroline Boucher. First question. Were Zeppelin deliberately passing on the UK as they toured the world? Plant, *"We don't stay away deliberately, it's because we're engrossed in a lot of different things. As well as playing in Japan and playing in the far reaches of the world . . . a thing that a lot of groups are doing now. If you ask any band —a year from January one to the end of December is such a short time because you get involved in the recordings . . . which stretch out, and the actual creation of the songs. And we record a lot of stuff, out of which we actually deliver probably half. So when you get out somewhere like Japan—Page and I have got this terrible lure for the less western parts of the world—we go tooting off if we can, to places that have been starved of rock music. A lot of the people there are more English than we are . . . right down to drinking Tetley's Tea.*

"We stopped in Bombay and we ended up playing in an old dive there for a bottle of Scotch. It was superb, I was singing through a Fender cabinet which is the size of a 12 inch telly and Pagey was playing a guitar which must have had piano strings on it and the people were so happy because they'd never ever witnessed anybody just passing through tak-

LED·ZEPPELIN·HOUSES ⋄ THE·HOLY

DOES THINGS TO PEOPLE...

ATLANTIC

K50014 STEREO

ing the trouble to stop and play. We did some recording in India . . . yes, they have got studios there just about. It turned out to be experimental recording, but it needn't have been. Unfortunately, the Indian Government have got a lot of trouble with the black market, so there is no lawful importation of modern equipment. What's left are remnants of everything that has been brought in."

Boucher then turns Plant to the subject of the group generally avoiding the media, *"When we've got something to say . . . then we say it ! The way I look at it is that when I'm busy writing lyrics, then all I want to do is concentrate on writing lyrics and I don't really want to be bothered by going down to London and talking to somebody else. The reason for this is because I'm involved in what I'm doing, that's my first love, so I'd rather put first things first . . . there's no point in me throwing myself at the general public.*

"I must admit it does annoy me I must have an ego, because I have to go on stage partially to satisfy it . . . that's the same thing with everybody who must step on a stage. I think; it's just a case of the fact that they have space to use up. You can compare it with a successful author. If he writes a book and it's a fantastic success —then he's not expected to follow it up immediately with something else to keep in the public eye, because that makes him a slave to the wrong thing . . . it has to be presented to the people when he's ready to do it. It's the same with us."

Plant then elaborates on the press reaction to the third album, *"I've seen so many headlines about Zeppelin on the letters pages and the only reason that they're headlines is because they're silly . . . like 'Led Zeppelin III is Plant's ego trip' that was one thing that really amazed me because (a) it was no more my*

ego trip than anybody else's, but (b) because, at the time that we made the third album, I thought it was the sun, moon and stars, and that the vibe coming off the album was a really fine one . . . then somebody writes that it's 'Plant's ego trip' and I thought 'How ridiculous,' when I'd really worked hard on it and worked hard on the lyrics and loved it.

"The fourth album opened more doors for me. I always gauge it by how well I'm doing and whether I'm improving or not. It's unfortunate that these silly little statements are put into print because really we could sit in the room now and discuss groups and discuss artists and give our opinions but they're not worth a light."

To conclude Boucher asks whether Led Zeppelin are likely to go the way of other bands, fragmenting into solo recording artists and delivering songs to Top Of The Pops, Plant, *"It's not really a good idea because if I made a solo album it would be very 12 bar, it'd be three chords all the way through. Even if I sang a melody that involved so many other chords, it would have to be three chords, because that's all I can play to. The idea doesn't strike me, because Jimmy and I have developed a sort of sympathy between his acoustic-playing and my lyrics and melodies, and I just couldn't even imagine doing anything without him being there. A lot of groups have done it. C. S. N and Y are beautiful, but if you take the Garcia and Delaney and Bonnie things, then I think that the tangents that they took, they didn't take far enough . . . they didn't peak. Once you've done a 'Stairway,' and you've listened to it after you've recorded it, you've reached a point where you can't really play with anybody else. I don't really want to play with anybody else, permanently . . . I'll get up and* have a blow sometimes but, when you've done that together, you know darn well that you've found what you're looking for. I don't think it will happen. Every day is another day . . . we might eventually have a quadruple album.

"I really would like to put across something in songs that I can't put into words, and that's endeavor, that constant motion of the search for that that man knows little of . . . it's a wide, wide world and when you think about all these cats way down through history, and even today, who are out sussing things out, I mean, I might even get into being a botanist in the end, new doors are opening all the time.

"History is a big pull on me so in 'Immigrant Song' I was wondering about the ancient characters from whence we stemmed, and what they were like, and what they thought about, and how they sung their song . . . whether they sat down and thought: 'Well, we've got to top the last one'.

"Another reason why I'd rather avoid talking to the Press is because, as soon as anything new comes along it's like everybody throws everything up in the air and goes: 'Ali-Baba here we are, saved by James Taylor.' I'm against everybody being made to believe that the new trend that happens to be happening is going to supersede everything else, quality-wise.

"It's quality, you see, everybody jumped on the James Taylor wagon and, unfortunately, his first two albums were as repetitive as 'Iron Butterfly'."

"I really would like to put a single out, there's a track on the new album that I'd have loved to have been a single. In true Zeppelin style, do it as a single, put it out, and then never touch singles again . . . leave everybody saying: What

are they doing? Come on you're due for a follow-up.' If I could get the other three people to agree, but I can see it would be a hard job.

"I couldn't do 'Top Of The Pops' man, because I've been to the 'Top of The Pops' set and I know what it's all about, and I really just couldn't do it. Actually, we could make a record and call it a new group. Then we could have it all set-up to appear on 'Top Of The Pops' and, as the new group were playing, the scenery would collapse to reveal a very embarrassed looking Zep playing behind it."....

New Musical Express reports.... Interview with Jimmy Page by James Johnson.... Page mentions that the band are planning on having a better stage show. "It's nothing phenomenal. It's just that we never had any lights before, so we thought it might be fun and add a little extra atmosphere. Everybody else has been doing it for years but before we always let the music speak for itself."

He is asked about the harsh reviews which met the release of Houses of The Holy, "I don't really care. It doesn't really make any difference. I'm deaf to the album now because we made it such a long time ago, but I know there's some good stuff there. You can't dismiss something like No Quarter or the Rain Song out of hand. Maybe you could attack The Crunge or 'D'yer Maker' for being a bit self indulgent. But they're just a giggle. They're just two send-ups. If people can't even SUSS that out, on that superficial a level then obviously you can't expect them to understand anything else on the album. It beats me but I really don't give a damn.

"There's been a general maturity that was showing by the third album which a lot of people haven't been able to come to terms with. For me the third album was very, very good and still had *more of an attack than anything before.*

"But obviously people have this preconceived notion of what to expect and when a band is constantly in a state of change and that doesn't mean a lack of direction but a natural change, then they can't come to terms with it because each album is different from the last.

"How they should approach our albums is to forget they ever heard of a band called Led Zeppelin forget about what they expect to hear and just listen to what's on that particular record. That's all we ask but we don't get it.

"The rock and roll is in all four of us and on stage that's what comes through. In fact we had two tracks one called 'The Rover' and another unnamed that we were going to use both of which were really hard rock.

"We'll probably use them next time. Possibly re-writing one of them but still keeping the essence. When we went into the studio we had no set ideas on how we wanted the album to turn out. We just recorded the ideas we had at that particular time. We just got together and let it come out. There are never ever any shortages or stagnant periods. I write a lot at home and I'm fortunate having a studio set up where I can try things out. I've been experimenting with chords a lot more and have tried a few unusual voicings. There are several ways material can come to the band, but it's always there. If I find a number coming that I know wouldn't be suitable. I scrap it. I stop working on it from that moment on."

Interviewer James Johnson asks if Page ever sees himself playing with another band, "Nothing else would gel together so nicely. I know it would be a mistake to break it up because you see it happening to other bands. They split and what comes after doesn't work nearly as

well. The chemistry isn't there. And if it's there in the beginning then it's criminal to break it up."

The topic is shifted to the Yardbirds, "Basically the Yardbirds are for me, a mixture of good and bad memories. There were certainly some magic moments and it was a real treat to be playing with new material coming to the public's ears.

"It was great when we had two lead guitars with Jeff Beck. But there was little evidence of it left on record. There was 'Happenings Ten Years Time' which I feel went over a lot of heads in Britain although it perpetuates the Yardbirds reputation in America. They were always into the more lyrical side of what we were doing. Also there was one horrible live album that was going to be released which was recorded by a man who spent most of his time recording stuff like Manuel's Music of The Mountains. I remember he put just one microphone over the drums and that was over the top so there was no bass drum at all which showed how much he knew about it. Obviously the album had to be stopped. It was unfortunate though that no live stuff was ever recorded properly."

Finally he talks about his influences and the craft of learning the guitar, "Simply because of the mechanics of the guitars. I don't personally think the finger style works on an electric guitar. You just get overtones and harmonics coming out. It doesn't sound right at all.

"Then again an electric guitar can work for you. It can start singing on it's own through the electronics which you can't engineer on an acoustic guitar. They're two totally different fields. Personally I find them both equally as fascinating. Probably my greatest influence on acoustic guitar is Bert Jansch who was

a real dream-weaver. He was incredibly original when he first appeared and I wish now that he'd gone back to things like Jack Orion once again. His first album had a great effect on me. Undoubtedly my affection and fascination for the guitar is just as strong as it's ever been. After all everyone's approach to the instrument is so totally different. There are so many styles of playing to listen to and to get off on. You can't help but be totally involved with it. I'm still coming to terms with the instrument even now."....
Sounds reports.... Jimmy Page is interviewed by reporter Rob Mackie.... the interview begins with a question about how the band's music seems to reflect their new found lifestyle as country squires, Page, "Yes. Robert wrote all the lyrics on the last one. It's true, there are a lot of reflections of that, but there are a lot of other subjects employed as well. Like touring round the world. "The Song Remains The Same" there's many different influences on that."

Mackie asks about the apparently reggae influence of D'yer Mak'er, "It's not really reggae is it? I personally see it more like a Fifties thing —it started off like that for a laugh. It's true the drums are like that but I don't think it ended up with the feel of proper reggae, I love the feel of that, but I don't think the end product was. That single that McCartney did was definitely out for that. Not that it sounded like proper reggae to me I think you've got to live it all the time. You can't just do it.

Mackie observes that the early Zeppelin seemed to be more straightforward, "I don't know whether it ever was. Probably on the second album there was more of that, because of the time it was written when we were working on the road and just going to the studio when we

could get in. The feeling of playing all the time was there. On a lot of the following albums. We've been off the road and had time to sit down and think about it."

Page is asked whether he thinks the new album is more diverse than previous efforts, "Mmm. possibly. The previous, album wasn't done like that to have a rock one and a folky one, and so on. It wasn't done like that — you'd have to have been there at the time and experienced what was going on. We were staying in a house and the numbers were just flowing out. We had a mobile truck there and they were just coming out. That particular track that you referred to. 'The Battle of Evermore' .... um. I forget whether people had gone to bed early or what, but it just came out then. I picked up the mandolin, which was actually John Paul Jones' mandolin and those chords just came out. It was my first experiment with a mandolin. I suppose all mandolin players would have a great laugh 'cos it must be the standard thing to play those chords, you know, but possibly not the same approach. Anyway it was just one of those things where I was governed by the limitations of the instrument. Possibly, afterwards, it sounded like a dance around the may pole number I must admit, but it wasn't purposely like that — 'Let's do a folky number'. There are so many things that get done and just for time reasons you can only squeeze 20 minutes on a side. So they don't get used."

He is asked whether the band consciously limit their output, "No. it's not that at all. I think the main problem really is because we're working so much. I'm sure people aren't aware of this—I'm sure they think we sit on our arses all day long, but we don't. All I know is I haven't stopped for three years. If it gives you any indication. I haven't had a holiday ever since the group started. There's just so much going on, as far as studio work, or rehearsing or touring. Then again, there's song writing to do as well. But the main reason is that we've been working abroad. Last year we did just about everywhere. Japan, Australia and America. There's two opinions, people either think we don't work at all, do nothing. Or else they think we're in America all the time which just isn't true. The idea has always been to put out a cross section of what we're doing at the time. So you will be getting acoustic numbers and so on.

What about a double album? "We very well may do. Yesterday actually I was playing some tracks I haven't heard for years, and sometimes the track's that haven't gone on are better than the ones that have, sometimes you think. 'Well that bit's right but that bit isn't. Why don't we rewrite it and shuffle it around.'"

And does Page listen to the Zeppelin albums, "No. By the time the LPs come out I'm deaf. It's nearly always six months behind. This record was finished by Christmas. But by the time you've been through all this bloody nonsense (picking up a proof for the sleeve of the new album). They just couldn't do it. The colours are just so different. It was a photograph in a collage. Then it was hand painted, took a long, long time. Probably a week of work, maybe even more. In the end we just had to settle for a compromise. There should be many more colours here, but to get those colours out you'd find funny things happening to (a) the sky and (b) the children. So that in the end you had to compromise because the sky started to look like an advert for Max Factor lipstick, and the children looked as if they'd turned purple from the cold.

Mackie observes that the cover reminds him of the mood set in 'No

Quarter', "Yeah. it's a sort of dawn and dusk, this feeling of expectancy. The children crawling to the top and what they're going to find. Bags of pollution and shit probably."

Page is asked whether he ever thought of being a solo acoustic artist, "I wasn't good enough. No. I've always been a rocker. And my approach on the acoustic guitar shows that. But I've always been very interested in the acoustic. At one point I had some lessons not for very long, but just to see what the approach was. There are three different styles of actually picking. At one period when I was absolutely obsessed with Bert Jansch. When I first heard that LP (Needle Of Death) I couldn't believe it. It was so far ahead of what anyone else was doing. I mean, there was just nothing anybody else was doing — no one in America could touch that. The best they could come up with was a few Blind Boy Fuller rags and things like that, ragtime guitar. His concept was way beyond that. That was what got me into playing acoustic. I've been playing acoustic quite a lot, but when you go on stage you can make things work with the volume that just wouldn't work on an acoustic —just the total mechanics. But what I'm saying is when you're at home, obviously, you're not going to set up a big stack and play it on your own. So really the thing is to pick up an acoustic. There was acoustic stuff on the first LP. So that shows you how far back it goes. But for the third LP Robert and I and some of the roadies went off to a cottage in Wales which is history now I know. But there was no electricity or anything like that, so we played acoustic guitars. That was why there was more acoustic and that.

Mackie asks whether Page thinks anyone has advanced the art of electric guitar recently, *"Well that depends who you're listening to."* How about John McLaughlin? *"Well he's in a different .... he was always a brilliant jazz guitarist. I'd probably go as far as to say that he was the best jazz guitarist 15 years ago. I don't know. Maybe 15 years is stretching it — 10 years ago he was playing with Graham Bond, and he was just phenomenal. Now he's not playing that stuff at all. If you relate it to art, you'd have someone who goes through ...all the conventional channels during his original studies and ends up doing abstract painting or whatever. I suppose one can only relate it to that, but he was always really brilliant. O.K. that's one you've singled out but what else?"*

He is asked whether he feels anyone can advance the use of the instrument in the way that Clapton, Hendrix and he had, *"Well Hendrix certainly, he'd really worked out and was working out all the possibilities of what you could do with the actual sound of a guitar. But we've had since then the advent of the country feel that came in, the great leaning towards Poco and that sort of band at a certain period. I don't mean now, and thank God, the rise of the pedal steel guitar. I think it's gone more towards clarity and precision. Maybe a lot of guitarists are thinking that way at the moment in the wake of that."*

He is asked why he doesn't record as many fast solos. *"Maybe not on the last record maybe not on the record before that, I don't know. Black Dog was. It depends you see, how long the solo is. On stage the numbers really stretch out. I'm really confident there's going to be a lot more music on the next record as such. There's been this epic acoustic number which is probably about twenty minutes long. I've had it written for a long while*

but it's a case of nerves. I used to do this song 'White Summer' on stage, and it grew out of that. There's a lot of new melodies and things now. All the time I was testing myself and pushing it on. When I attempted it once in the studio I made a huge great muck-up and I thought 'blow it' and discarded it completely, but I really mean to try that again. It's very hard to play, but it's good. It's just a matter of coming to terms. Certainly that would have to be (part of a double album). It's far too self indulgent otherwise. As yet it's only the structure though.

Mackie asks about the singles scene and whether Zeppelin have any plans for single releases, *"I don't know. I don't think so really. Nothing on the album is really right for a single. Nothing was done with that in mind. Of course we've had singles out in America, but that happened because the radio would make something number three or number five on their charts when it isn't even a single. And all this pressure will start coming on to Atlantic. So they'll put it on to us, saying 'Please let us release it', you know. That's how every single has gone out, and it's really down to them. You see the FM stations have changed quite radically since the first conception of the underground or whatever you call it. Now you've got the AM stations playing the singles and the FM station playing the follow-up single that hasn't yet been released. The whole concept of esoteric programs I'm afraid has gone —you know what's going to come on the FMs as much as the AMs.*

"Yes (it's better than the BBC). Purely because there's freedom of choice in every place, I'm totally disgusted with the BBC's coverage of this sort of music. After all you're paying for a license, so why can't you get what you bloody want.

They're happy enough to capitalize on pop music .. when you think what Peel did for music, and he was always being put down, but for why? All this stupidity that goes on in the press. Putting people down. He did a fantastic job, and Bernie Andrews. It's just not on.

Mackie switches over to the subject of big band's playing small venues, "We got attacked for doing that from everyone who couldn't get in. It would be healthier, except that you get so many people coming from such a long way to see you and getting quite understandably bitter about it. That's what happened on that club tour. It was chaotic because of that. There's no really good gigs to do in England. When we did Wembley, nobody had done that for years. Now we're talking about the really big ones. The Albert Hall I used to like. The sound was a bit dreadful, but the atmosphere was there — everyone was really enjoying themselves. I agreed with Lou Reisner when he said 'Ban The Albert Hall'. I reckon we should. Because if the Musician's Union, who are constantly taking dues off people, if they can stop people doing this, that, and the other, like the exchange rate that goes on, musician for musician, and all that crap. And if they're so conscious of taking work away from musicians, then why don't they put an overall ban on the Albert Hall, for taking work away from musicians. Because that's a comfortable size, and after that you've got nothing up to Wembley size. We opened Wembley up. T. Rex and some others did it after us, but for us it was a disaster, sound-wise. It was terrible, 'cos it was going so well on stage, it was so tight, and if you were more than 20 rows back, I gather you couldn't hear anything —it just went into this huge reverberation. It was a tragedy, it should have been a really momentous

gig, and it wasn't. It's highly probable we'll do some gigs at the end of the year, but considering we've been working solidly from October last, and we'll be going through to July solidly without a break. O.K.. there might be three or four days off, but that's not really a break. After that we'll probably have some time off plus we'll have another LP to think about. But quite possibly we will fit some gigs in. I'd like to. I enjoy playing here and up to Scotland and Wales.

Page is asked whether there is any fun left in the music business. "Oh. God, if it became that clear-cut. Just a business. I'd give it up. I really would and everybody else would too. It's just great to be a part of it hoping that the music and the vibes that you give out speaks for itself, and that whatever's said in the press is just stirring up controversy and bullshit and that can be seen for what it is.

Does Page think that Zeppelin are taking their audience with them through their various musical changes? "There hasn't been much of a compromise really, and a lot of people don't like that — they want you to fit in with something preconceived, and if you don't, they don't like it. If that isn't a reflection of society, I don't know what is. No. We'll always be in a state of change, and the best we can do is to try and make sure it's good. We'll always put out something different. You've talked about the sales being good. That's neither here nor there really. O.K. it's a healthy response to know that people appreciate the fact that you're changing and not stagnating. But, I'm not attacking you personally or your paper, but there are certain people who just have found it fashionable if that's the word .... well, their ears are closed — seeds upon stony ground. The people are the ones who are going to go out and buy a record, and they're the ones that are really going to get into it more than a bloke who just reviews an LP and has already made up his mind anyway, before he puts it on the turntable nine times out of ten.

Has he opted out of the ego trip that plagues so many stars? *"Yeah. I suppose I have really. For me personally. the music's more important. I'm such a different person on stage and off stage. I think it's the spontaneity, really for me. Going out there and something comes out of the guitar that never came out before. You don't know where it comes from but it's there. Every time we get together something comes out. We might get together to have what is termed a rehearsal, and in most cases. I suppose a rehearsal is going through your numbers and wiping the dust off. We'll always end up writing loads of new material. It comes out as easy as that. I know how much trouble it is for a lot of people —so I've heard, anyway.*

Mackie points out that it must be difficult to write on the road, *"Well. It's a good time to write on the road, because you start getting into this pace, especially if you're really condensing tours like we do. We'll do three weeks with only a few days off, air flights every day. Sometimes two in a day. If you put that same pace into writing, obviously you're going to get a totally different pace. That urgency which obviously you're not going to get at other times when the mellower things come out at home. So it is good to get both.*

Will he take a vacation soon, *"Yeah, maybe. Everyone else goes. It's just that I've recently become aware of the fact that I haven't. I certainly am going to go on one when we've come back from the States. Going to get one of those .... is it airstream or airflow caravan —* like a cigar tube on wheels. Go over on the ferry and just see what comes up."

How important is money to him? *"I think it has more importance for the tax man really. The only thing that I've really started spending on is studio equipment I've got a small studio now. It's very primitive, eight track. But it's great for getting ideas and building them all up."*

Will he be producing anyone else? *"I always say it's the time element that stops me, but I don't know. That's certainly part of it. Certain things have been suggested. But I'm more involved with just doing what I'm doing and trying to get it better and better and better. Which I think it is. The sort of changes in direction that are happening now are quite exciting."*

In conclusion Mackie asks whether Page thinks the band becomes like one individual when they come together, *"Yes. We're all entirely different personalities. But something like that you just don't want to break. You've just got to go 'F-k it all...what does it matter' to all the rest of it. The most important thing is what the four of you do off stage or on, you get to know your capabilities. We're a very unlikely set. Normally, when someone forms a group. They already know each other pretty well. It took us three years to get to know each other, but then the bond was even tighter."* ....**Melody Maker reports....** Zep, Slade In US...article states that House Of The Holy is #3 in the MM charts and that the band will tour America in May through July. It says they will visit 30 cities beginning in Atlanta on May 4th and culminating in New York on July 27 and 28....

28 **New Musical Express reports....** Led Zeppelin are slated for two tours of the USA.... Houses of The Holy has gone

gold in the USA.... the tours begin in May and July...no UK dates are currently scheduled.... **Sounds reports**.... several letters to the editor condemning the paper's slagging of Houses Of The Holy.... **Disc and Music Echo reports....** Houses Of The Holy is #1....

May 1973

5 **Disc and Music Echo reports....** Houses Of The Holy is #2.... Led Zeppelin spent last week at Shepperton studios rehearsing before leaving for their latest American tour.... the tour begins in Atlanta on May 4th.... line up for Roy Harper's new single "Male Chauvinist Pig" is Jimmy Page guitar, Archie Legget bass and Tony Carr drums it will be released in May.... **Atlanta Constitution reports....** Stadium Rocks Led Zeppelin plays to 50,000. Review of the opening show by Cathy Yarbrough and Barry Henderson. The front cover shows the band and crowd in full swing. Police had a field day towing hundreds of illegally parked cars.... pictures show huge runways stretching out into the crowd similar to those favoured by Mick Jagger and the Stones but unusual for Zeppelin....

8 **Atlantic press release....**
FOR IMMEDIATE RELEASE
FROM: BOB ROLONTZ
LED ZEPPELIN TOUR ROCKETS OFF

The Led Zeppelin's first U.S. tour in almost a year opened like a house afire last week. Group opened in Atlanta on Friday (4) on the first leg of a tour that will keep the group busy performing at U.S. venues until June 2. The second leg of the tour is now being set for July.

Group's Atlanta date was a complete sell-out at the Atlanta Braves Stadium, and marked one of the biggest crowds ever to attend a rock concert in that Southern City. The Zeppelin's Tampa date on Saturday (5) at the Tampa stadium, broke all records for the huge arena, with the group outdrawing every other rock act ever to play the Florida West Coast City. Led Zeppelin continue their tour with dates in Jacksonville, St. Louis, Mobile, New Orleans, Houston, Dallas, Fort Worth, Albuquerque, Denver, Salt Lake City, San Diego, Los Angeles, San Francisco
The group's new Atlantic album, Houses Of The Holy, is now No 1 on all best selling charts.

July 5 & 7,	Stadium	
	Chicago	
July 9	Civic Center	
	St. Paul, Minnesota	
July 10	Arena	
	Milwaukee, Wisconsin	
July 12 & 13	Cobo Hall	
	Detroit, Michigan	
July 15	Memorial Auditorium	
	Buffalo, New York	
July 17	Coliseum	
	Seattle Washington	
July 18	Coliseum	
	Vancouver, B . C.	
July 20	Boston Gardens	
	Boston, Massachusetts	
July 21	Civic Center	
	Providence, RI	
July 23	Civic Center	
	Baltimore, Maryland	
July 24	Three Rivers Stadium	
	Pittsburgh, Pa.	
July 27-28-29	Madison Square Gardens	
	New York, New York	

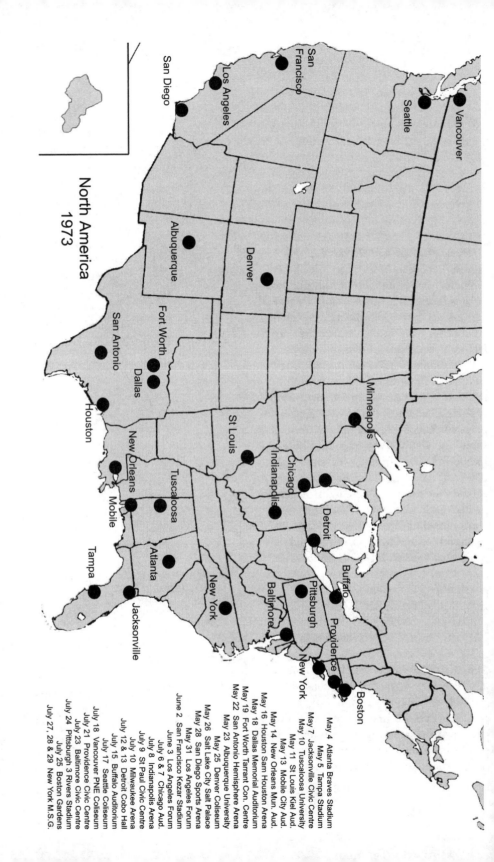

North America
1973

May 4   Atlanta Braves Stadium
May 5   Tampa Stadium
May 7   Jacksonville Civic Centre
May 10 Tuscaloosa University
May 11 St Louis Kiel Aud.
May 13 Mobile City Aud.
May 14 New Orleans Mun. Aud.
May 16 Houston Sam Houston Arena
May 18 Dallas Memorial Auditorium
May 19 Fort Worth Tarrant Con. Centre
May 22 San Antonio Hemisphere Arena
May 23 Albuquerque University
May 25 Denver Coliseum
May 26 Salt Lake City Salt Palace
May 28 San Diego Sports Arena
May 31 Los Angeles Forum
June 2 San Francisco Kezar Stadium
June 3 Los Angeles Forum
July 6 & 7 Chicago Aud.
July 8 Indianapolis Arena
July 9 St Paul Civic Centre
July 10 Milwaukee Arena
July 12 & 13 Detroit Cobo Hall
July 15 Buffalo Auditorium
July 17 Seattle Coliseum
July 18 Vancouver PNE Coliseum
July 21 Providence Civic Centre
July 23 Baltimore Civic Centre
July 24 Pittsburgh 3 Rivers Stadium
July 25 Boston Gardens
July 27, 28 & 29 New York M.S.G.

12 **Disc and Music Echo reports....** Houses Of The Holy is #3.... Lisa Robinson reports from the USA that a Texas style party is being thrown for Led Zeppelin at Gordon McLendon's ranch. McLendon was a business partner of President Lyndon Johnson....

13 **Houston Post reports....** The English Rock Foursome known as Led Zeppelin will be here for a performance in the Coliseum Wednesday at 8 pm (Sold Out)....

15 **New Orleans Times-Picayune reports....** Rock band Led Zeppelin is fire of supergroups. Review of the New Orleans gig by Bill Shearman. "The band is the class of English heavy rock supergroups." He goes on to mention that the band have rented a house in the French quarter of town which seems to please him suggesting that they might permanently move there. After dissecting each song and generally raving Shearman concludes, "You knew you had been entertained, well.... thanks England for letting us borrow them for a while."....

19 **Disc and Music Echo reports....** Houses Of The Holy is #7.... Maggie Bell met up with Led Zeppelin in Florida...rumour has it that she might sing on-stage with the Zep at their upcoming gig in Tampa Florida.... Zeppelin are blowing apart concert attendance records around the USA.... the band grossed £120,000 at one show with 56,800 fans.... this beats the Beatles attendance record set in 1965 at Shea Stadium in New York but is expected to be surpassed at a show later this month in San Francisco...Lisa Robinson files a rave review of the band's show in Jacksonville Florida.... Robinson is almost at a loss for words she is so impressed, *"Where have they been all my life? To rationally explain how goddamn good they were...well words don't come easily."* Apparently 13,000 people turned out for the show, *"It was impossible to be a part of that experience and not watch and listen with total awe. God bless them!"*.... **New Musical Express reports....** Zep in U.S. Biggest ever crowd. Report from Tampa stadium where the band broke the long-standing Beatles attendance record from Shea Stadium in 1965. Total fans at the show were 56,800 grossing $309,000. Other attendance numbers are quoted as 49,236 at Atlanta Braves Stadium (gross $246,000). Apparently the band utilised a large video system which must have been one of the earliest uses for such equipment....

24 **Rolling Stone reports....** full page advert reads — Led Zeppelin Houses Of The Holy Does things to People.... **Zooworld reports....** Cover story and review of Houses Of The Holy. A prosaic and positive review of the album which concludes 'Any more raves about HOTH or LZ and this review might start sounding more like a eulogy than an acclamation....'

26 **Disc and Music Echo reports....** Houses Of The Holy is #7.... **New Musical Express reports....** Ritchie Yorke reports from the band's gig in Atlanta. Yorke staunchly defends the band against the critics. "This is the world's top rock and roll band. Not Alice Cooper, nor the Stones or the Who could come close to sinking Zep." The band's album has topped the US charts within five weeks of release despite the new Beatles and Floyd records. He closes with, "Led Zeppelin reign supreme, and it's high time many

more members of the media realised it."....

27 San Francisco Chronicle reports.... Advert reads — Bill Graham Presents Saturday June 2 Kezar Stadium Led Zeppelin, Supporting acts to be announced. Gates open 10 am, Led Zeppelin plays at 2 pm....

June 1973

2 Disc and Music Echo reports.... Houses Of The Holy is #7.... Zapping With Zep.... Lisa Robinson reports from the band's tour of the USA beginning at the Royal Orleans hotel in New Orleans.... Plant, *"We want to go a lot further than we've got now, musically. And we talk about something that would be as notable as Beethoven's Fifth. Something that would be respected throughout the realms of everything, y'know? And really be wholesome and good. It's not just a dream to write something that's a classic, and when I say a classic I don't mean 'Rockin' Pneumonia and The Boogie Woogie Flu'. I mean 'Whole Lotta Love' is a classic, but I'm talking about something that stretches right out. I feel that we have the capabilities to do that, we just need the right place to bring it out. I'm proud of my writing, but there's a lot of subtlety that I've developed. Mind you I was only 19 when I joined the group. 'The Song Remains The Same' is right to me. It's a statement of right now. As long as there's a face looking up at me in the midst of the sea, or the ocean, as you may have detected from the last album. As long as there's a face that knows what I'm doing it could never be boring. It's the ability to make people smile or just to turn them on one way or another for that dura-*

tion of time. And for it to have some effect later on. I like to think that people go away knowing that we're pretty raunchy and we really do do a lot of things that people say we do, but at the same time this is what we're getting over. It's goodness, it ain't 'stand-up-put-your-fist-in-the-air, we-want-power-revolution', it's not that. I like them to go away feeling the way you do at the end of a good chick, satisfied and exhausted. I mean there's no holds barred. It takes so many colours to make a prism.".... Robinson then reviews the concert in New Orleans concluding, *"It may be only May, but I'm sorry m'dears, the best concert of the year has already happened."* The band's set includes Rock And Roll, Black Dog, Celebration Day, Misty Mountain Hop, Since I've Been Loving You, No Quarter, Song Remains The Same, Rain Song, Dazed & Confused, Moby Dick, Stairway To Heaven, Heartbreaker, Whole Lotta Love and an encore of Communication Breakdown....

9 New Musical Express reports.... Led Zeppelin have been offered £10,000 by promoter Tony Lyne to play at Lincoln Festival.... **Disc and Music Echo reports....** Houses Of The Holy is #7.... Whole Lotta Led In The Deep South, Lisa Robinson reports from the USA and interviews Page. *"I still get very ill being on the road. It's probably called malnutrition . . . I haven't eaten for about three days. You know when you're fasting, after about three or four days you get these pains, and I had one on-stage last night—bang. It wouldn't go away . . . I'll probably eat today. I'm getting petrified of flying. Lately . . . See, in the past we, and I, have had a lot of funny experiences. Like looking out of the windows and seeing fuel pouring out of the wings and crash land-*

ings and all . . . and, well, in those days I thought: 'Well, I've come out of this unscathed, the law of averages and all—I'm doing very well.' But we haven't had any incidents for about two and a half or three years and I'm starting to wonder if the powers-that-be are looking after me or not."

Lisa Robinson asks him whether he is ever intimidated by the size of the audience, *"I must admit that when I went to the first gig—it wasn't the biggest, it was about 50,000 or something—but we got to Atlanta, and we went down to view the place, and there was all this equipment — more than at Woodstock. All this equipment, and this huge great stage and back-cloth mirrored thing with the revolving balls and I was looking around . . . the huge great arena, and I thought: 'My God, there's only four of us, and that's it. And they're all coming down just to see us. And you're bound to get a bit nervy when you think that they're coming down there with a hypercritical attitude—well, I shouldn't have said that actually because they didn't there, but they do in some places. They did in Aberystwyth, in Wales. In Atlanta, they were really warm, and we obviously react to the warmth of the audience. Sometimes the audience is better than the group . . . we get off on them. There, one really had nothing to worry about. In fact, the whole tour has had this sort of warmth about it. You go out and they're giving you so much that you have to give it back to them. (In Aberystwyth) it was the funniest gig. I really have to explain that. We spent a lot of time song writing in Wales, and Aberystwyth was the nearest large town. It's a seaside resort, but it isn't high-rises or anything like that: it probably hasn't changed in 200 years as far as the main structure goes. And we felt quite warm vibes about the*

whole place and so, when we set up our last tour we said, wouldn't it be a gas if we did Aberystwyth. Like a nostalgic thing. So we did it, but I don't think they could believe we were there because it was a really tiny place, it only had about 800 people and it was a real folly to do it . . . and they were just aghast. They were all sitting down, it was a corporation-type place. If the audience had been allowed to stand up it would have been okay, but they were just sort of regimented in these rows, and thinking: 'My god, what are we doing here?' And after a while we were thinking the same thing too! That's what I mean about an audience being really uptight about a situation. It's never happened to us anywhere else, this is the only time. It was quite funny, but we really needed something like that. When it always goes down really well, it does you good to have one that's a bit strange and unnervy.

"With us we're always changing every night. We never get two guitar breaks that are the same, all those riffs appear out of nowhere — every night. And, because of that, because one's mind is constantly working, when it comes to doing an LP —a lot of water's gone under the bridge, you see. That's why every LP's been so different. I have a theory that if we were the sort of group that went out and played exactly the same every night like—well, I'm not going to name anybody, but obviously there are groups that play every guitar note exactly the same way it is on the record — then everything would become so predictable that it would be a thorough bore. No matter how efficient they are musically, I think once you know what's coming—and that relates to anything you get into —it becomes a bore. And if we were like that, our LPs would have all stuck in the same sort of groove, more or less. But as all our

269

minds are alive and still working, that's why we go through these changes."

Robinson asks him why he decided to meet the media on this tour of the USA, *"I just wanted to do interviews this time because I mainly was curious about what sort of questions people would ask me. Sorry if that sounds supercilious, but I really was curious to see what people would come up with after five years. Luckily, they don't pull too many skeletons out of the closet."*

The conversation then turns to a less obvious topic, the problem with maintaining his equipment in the touring environment. *"It's a drag because you're working on something and your ideas start going on a solo and a string breaks. It's really like reaching a climax and not making it. It's just like that really, it feels horrible. It's so frustrating because you have to rethink it. I seem to be having a run of broken strings lately."*

How does he feel about trotting out the old numbers, *"Dazed And Confused changes every night, so it's a vehicle really for exploring and getting off, for me personally. And if we didn't feel we enjoyed doing a number then we'd drop it. That's all there is to it. If somebody in the group said: 'God, we can't ever play "Whole Lotta Love" again'— we just wouldn't play it. The same with 'Stairway'—whatever, if it came to the point where someone didn't want to play it, it would have to go."*

How does he feel about employing another guitarist in the band, an often asked question, *"Sometimes I have felt that it would be nice working with another guitarist but it would have to be somebody really capable, not just a rhythm guitarist, because that wouldn't be any good at all. It would be nice to get somebody that you could work out double lead*

passages with. When I was with the Yardbirds, Jeff and I used two guitars—doing leads. I think that was the first band to use two guitars and since then it's been an obvious progression. There are so many groups that pull it off really well now. Also, the concept of two lead guitars is a really nice one. But then again, I don't think it would be right, because it's more of a challenge to try and get it with just what we've got. That's the thing, really, if we can keep it together ourselves, and just play—like John Paul Jones has got a really good command of other instruments— we should be able to orchestrate anything on our own."

Splitting up?? *"We'll be together certainly until one of us punts out. Perhaps it wouldn't be so intense. We'd only play a few dates. But my dream is to go around like some sort of motorised caravan, with a small unit—just go to Morocco and record musicians —go through the East recording. You see, you get this kind of music on British radio, on Radio Three, the BBC have these huge archives, and you hear some of this music coming out and it's so enthralling that it must be quite an experience to be there and record street musicians.*

"I've done some of this—but the problem is that when they see you, it's a show, and you're the rich European. It doesn't matter if you're dressed in rags, you still stand out as a European the way an American does in London. And bang— they'll come over for the money and you might as well forget about your recording. That's the art of it really—to get them to forget about that and loosen up."

Page then comments on Zeppelin's stage show, *"We don't get bored on-stage because there's always something new to look forward to. You never know what's going to come out, it's like embarking on a mysterious adventure every night. The only annoying thing is when you hit on some good things, they're lost in time. It goes into the other dimension, you've lost it. They only come once and they're gone. But then again it's exciting because you know that something's gone but then something new is going to come."*.... After the interview the band retire to Cosimo's in New Orleans for a party in their honor thrown by Ahmet Ertegun. The band watch performances by The Meters and Snooks Eaglin and at one point John Paul Jones joins the on stage festivities playing the organ....

16 **New Musical Express reports....** cover story.... Zep in the USA. Charles Shaar Murray reports from Los Angeles. The show he reviews is the legendary Bonzo's Birthday Party gig. Murray distinguishes himself by writing one of the most positive reviews to ever appear in the pages of the illustrious old NME. He observes from the wings the 20,000 fans at the forum and states, "Now, I always knew Zeppelin were good, but it had been three years since I'd last seen them and no way was I prepared for this.... the pure clean power of Zeppelin's performance and sound is even more extraordinary than it might otherwise appear.... it's simply good traditional British craftsmanship." He follows the band back to Bonham's party in Laurel Canyon where apparently almost everyone eventually ended up in the swimming pool and George Harrison crowned Bonzo with his own cake. After being chaperoned back to his hotel, the next day he follows the band to San Francisco to watch their gig at Kezar Stadium. "How can I tell you about that show? Led Zeppelin and 50,000 San Francisco people got together to provide one of the finest musical events I've ever

had the privilege to attend." He even admits that he hates drum solos but that Bonham's Moby Dick "broke that prejudice". "All hail Led Zep." he concludes.... **Disc and Music Echo reports....** Houses Of The Holy is #13.... **Melody Maker reports....** Full page Advert reads — 56,800 people came to see Led Zeppelin in Tampa Florida on May 5th 1973. The largest audience for a single artist performance in history. Congratulations from Concerts West and Atlantic Records....

23 **Disc and Music Echo reports....** Houses Of The Holy is #20.... **New Musical Express reports....** An interview by Charles Shaar Murray with Robert Plant at the band's hotel in Los Angeles, *"This is a very close, tightly knit, sensitive group, one member to the next. We've got a very strong bond and so working is a pleasure. What happened was that after we made the third album Jimmy and I were in Wales and we were fed up with going to America. We'd been going twice a year, and at that time America was really a trial, an effort.*

"Anyway, we didn't work for a year and we said: 'Look, this is terrible. Let's get going, let's move', so in the past year we've played every single market that a band in our position could possibly play.

"This is the finest property we possess—without it, the group would be a bore. Not naming names there are a lot of groups in England who still rely on riff after riff after riff. Some audiences can shake and bang their heads on the stage to riffs all night long, but subtlety is an art that must be mastered if you're to be remembered. In this band we're very lucky that everybody is more enthusiastic as time goes on. There is no fatigue or boredom musically at all. There's a bit of

boredom when you're stuck in Mobile, Alabama, or places like that. A few lamp standards may fall out of the windows — things like that—but we move on and we keep playing that music.

"It's just this rapport that we've got between ourselves. It's a good buzz. Man, I mean I've learned how to feel an audience now, and that's my success. I can feel them, they can feel me. If you can't you're not doing anything at all.

"There are a lot of groups who come over here and play very loud and very monotonously and get people off.... but, the other way, it's almost like putting your hands out and touching everybody. That's probably why we're coming back here in three weeks.

"You see, my little boy's just started to walk. and I haven't seen him bloomin' walk yet. Those are the things that upset you about being on the road. The very fact that you miss fantastic occasions like that. I mean, the kid just stands up and starts strolling around —and here I am in Tuscaloosa or wherever."

Murray asks whether Plant is tempted to take his family on the road, *"Oh it'd be chaotic for a young kid. I don't like taking Maureen either really. As much as I love her. When you're on the road you are nomads, you know. There was an album called 'Rock n' Roll Gypsies' and that's it — you've gotta travel on.*

"Robert Johnson once said: 'Woke up this morning got the rain off my shoes my woman left me got the walking blues.'It's just great to move on and set up in another town and see the people there smiling.

"I think I've got one of the finest ladies in the world and it wouldn't do her any good because she's not up there on that stage. So she'd get tired and want to

know why we weren't doing this and that, and the very fact that I've just woken up and it's three o'clock in the afternoon and the shops shut at six, and there's no shopping to be done today and all that sort of thing . . . It isn't practical."

Murray then asks about Plant's Celtic influences, *"That was present really from the second album onwards. It was something that we did well and was pointing in a specific direction. Then there was 'Ramble On', 'Thank You', 'Going To California', 'The Battle of Evermore', 'The Rain Song' — on the new album too—even 'The Song Remains The Same'. Every time I sing that, I just picture the fact that I've been round and round the world and at the root of it all there's a common denominator for everybody. The common denominator is what makes it good or bad. Whether it's a Led Zeppelin or an Alice Cooper. The lyrics I'm proud of. Somebody pushed my pen for me, I think. There are a lot of catalysts which really bring out those sort of things: working with the group. Living where I live having the friends I've got, my children, the animals. There's also the fact that people have finally come to terms with the fact that, three years ago, we made a classic record with 'Whole Lotta Love', and they realise that it's just one colour of the rainbow of what we do and what we are intending to do in the future.*

"I think we've got a lot of friends in England. I remember Bradford on the last tour. When the audience were superb. 'Stairway To Heaven' gets the best reaction of any number we do. But the raunchiness is in everybody; that below the-belt surge that everybody gets at some time or another. Everybody gets their rocks off, I suppose and we supply a little bit of music to that end."

"In the last eight months

Zeppelin have been working solid. We were going back and forward to America, and then to Japan, Hong Kong and Bangkok. Jimmy and I did some recording in India with the Bombay Symphony Orchestra. It was an experiment, and we know what we want to do next time. (Will the tracks be released?) Not those, no. We were just checking out. Just sussing how easy it would be to transpose the ideas that we've got into the musicians- minds. It's very hard for them to cope with the Western approach to music with their counting of everything, their times and so on. Where we count four beats to the bar, their bars just carry on and on. They'll be counting up to 99 or 100, and on the 120th boomph you change instead of on the 18th bar or something like that. But anyway, we found that what we want to play we can do successfully in time to come. We moved on from there and played Switzerland, Scandinavia, Germany and France, which was absolutely chaotic. Promotion people are absolutely nuts over there, and the kids are more interested in using a concert as an excuse to be leery, most of the time. I don't really like that, I don't consider that I've gained anything or given anybody anything when I see that there's a lot of fools fighting. The gig you saw last night was a magic one because the people were so relaxed. It was as if I'd known them years. The vibe that we give out could never advocate violence. A fight in there would have been totally contradictory to the whole vibe of the place and everybody would have been totally disgusted. I mention that at big gigs, particularly in New York. I'm always in mortal terror of an outbreak of violence. You've got to have a rapport for the people and that rapport must eradicate any feelings like that. Alice Cooper's weirdness must really make the kids feel violent. These kids are like my sister. Young people of 14 or so who've come to enjoy themselves. So you put things like that in front of them and I don't think it's right. My idea is that I should go out on stage and be completely normal. And it pays. It pays immensely because I get that vibe right back. That's the thesis really. That's the reason for our success here."

Finally Murray asks if Plant thinks it's the band's chemistry which is responsible for their success, "Yeah. it's the desire to really want to lay something down for ever and ever and ever. I would like to create something now and be part of the creation of something now that would be valid for years and years to come. Not so much in the way that Chuck Berry will be valid in 50 years time, which he will but something like a mammoth stairway which takes in a lot of the mood of the group. It's my ambition to write something really superb. I listen to people like Mendelsohn— Fingal's Cave and that sort of thing — and it's absolutely superb. You can picture exactly where that guy was. You can picture the whole thing and I'd like it to be the same way for us in time to come. I should think that we've got it under our belt to get something like that together. I mean we've started. Last night when all those lights were there that was a spiritual allegiance. You walk out there and they're going. 'Yea, we know you can do it'— and with that sort or thing tucked inside your belt you can only go from strength to strength. Somebody once described me as the original hippie and that's because of the flowery lyrics, you know and also because of the buzz we give out."

30 **New Musical Express reports....** short article slagging Led Zeppelin's choice not to issue singles.... **Disc and**

Music Echo reports.... Houses Of The Holy is #21....

Creem reports.... Lester Bangs returns to review Houses Of The Holy. He begins by contradicting his review of the previous album by referring back to it as 'a true masterpiece'. He then does a song by song breakdown calling the album's highlights, Song Remains The Same, Dancing Days, No Quarter and Over The Hills. He goes on to call The Crunge and D'yer Mak'er both fun but foolish. He expresses his amazement that four musicians can make such a huge sound and after criticising Plant's lyrics he concludes with, 'I know that at least Song and Dancing Days are gonna be with me long after they finally get around to releasing their next one.'....

July 1973

7 New Musical Express reports.... lyrics to Stairway To Heaven reprinted....

16 Buffalo Evening News reports.... Led Zeppelin Kneads Crowd to Silly Putty. Review of the Buffalo show by Dale Anderson. "Led Zeppelin doesn't give concerts, they perform physical transformations. They kneaded the full house into Silly Putty with two hours and forty minutes of massive sensory massage."

19 Rolling Stone reports.... Advert reads — Missing guitar. Reward for return of British rock musician's lost or stolen black Gibson guitar Les Paul Custom with Bigsby arm No. 06130 with extra switches. Missing in U.S. for about one year. No questions asked. Contact Ted Rosenblatt, 444 Madison Ave. NY, NY 10022 (212) 752-1330....

25 Pittsburgh Valley News Dispatch reports.... Led Zeppelin draws 40,000 in Three Rivers.... review of Pittsburgh show.... One of the largest crowds, 40,000 to attend a concert in Pittsburgh's Three Rivers Stadium saw Britain's premier rock group, Led Zeppelin perform a three hour continuous show there last night.... there were some minor incidents involving a small percentage of the throng including an unsuccessful attempt at gatecrashing.... the show started on time and continued almost to midnight.... Led Zeppelin earned $119,763 for their efforts last night. Patrons paid $4.65 to $6.65 for tickets....

30 New York Daily News reports.... Headline.... Led Zeppelin Robbed Of 203G - Rock Group's Hotel Box Rifled - Led Zeppelin In Big Loss.... article reporting the notorious theft of the band's concert takings from their hotel deposit box at the Drake Hotel in New York. Tour Manager Richard Cole, *"I'm still in shock about the whole thing."* Cole had one of two keys to the box which contained $180,000, he agreed to take a lie-detector test, *"I had nothing to fear and I think it was the right thing to do,"* he said. The theft was discovered at 7.15 on the Sunday morning by Cole. The band's manager Peter Grant was being questioned regarding a possible assault on a photographer.... Honolulu Star Bulletin reports.... The Drake's manager Michael Stiller said he had no idea what was in the box, police estimate it was between $203,800 and $220,000....

August 1973

4 Melody Maker reports.... In The House Of The Holy, Loraine Alterman

interviews Robert Plant in New York.... The interview is conducted on the evening of 28th July the night that the bulk of the movie was filmed. They start with the effect of playing New York, *"It does have a sort of psychological impression on me. Despite the fact that we can play for 18,000 people in Chicago, it is more important to do better in New York. I think it's only psychological really, New York people are no different to people anywhere. Last night at the Garden was superb. The only place that I get any nerves at all is when I play the Royal Albert Hall in London. Playing London always gets me nervy. London was always the place that I seemed to think had to be A1. But now I have such a good time strutting about I don't think any place is any different to any other. There's so many individuals in front of you."*

Alterman asks if he changes on stage, *"I wouldn't say that I become different at all because I'm not trying too hard. I mean if I was over-trying then that would be the case, but I'm not. But there are a lot more people so you tend to be a bit more flashy. But so long as I'm smiling it must be real. I wouldn't get too serious. It's a bit like amyl nitrate, it's a rush you're not ready for. I didn't know how many people were going to be there (Tampa 56,800). I had no idea what it would look like. There was nobody else but Led Zeppelin, the four of us and all those people as far as the eye could see. But the minute we walked out there, there were so many little matches held up that the whole place was glowing and that is a start. When you get that sort of a reception at the start then you know the medium is set. People were on the roof tops a mile away. I don't really contemplate the size or the enormousness of a city. I look at a few people and as long as the smile is*

coming back at me it could be ten million. It could be three people. We tried an English tour where we were playing small places. We've got a lot of equipment now and dare I say it, we're good. We're so good you need a big place to get it off. You can feel it bouncing off the walls and everything. We played places where there were like 300 people. It worked but there were 3,000 outside going, 'You bastards why are you playing to 300 people?'."

Alterman points out that the band are now using stage lighting. Plant, *"We decided that the denim jeans trip has been there for a long time. Let's just see how far we can take what we want to take so we just started going out on a limb. We've got some amazing ideas that if they come off we might even vanish into space! But the thing is that they fit perfectly with the mood of the new songs and the excitement of the old ones. It's very refreshing because with a number like Dazed & Confused which we've been playing for five years is never the same twice. It goes right off on a limb now because we've got effects going along with it and everybody's waiting for this. And that sort of augments the effects with even more musical stimulus."*

Alterman raises the question of how he finds time to write. Plant, *"I suppose the time is there but after a gig you just want to collapse and watch television. If the tour was less hectic I would get into it. I scribble down a few bits of verbal now and again but as far as amassing the whole lot of lyrics, no. Sometimes we have backing tapes and tracks worked out and somebody goes, 'Well we got no bloody lyrics'. Sometimes it's quite immediate like 'Black Dog'. Things are there instantly like 'Got to roll can't stand still' all that sort of 'Watching the ladies honey drip' and things come instantly to me, I'm not* sure if it's a gift writing about watching ladies honey drip or whether it comes from the blues close to that, The Raunch. 'Stairway To Heaven' was basically conceived on the spot lyrically. Then sometimes we do some backing tapes and they get quite intricate where I couldn't sing along instantly. I had to really listen to what was going on, on my own. And then someone goes, 'I ain't got no bloody lyrics' and a week later I'd come back with 'Over The Hills & Far Away' or 'The Crunge' on Houses Of The Holy. That was amazing because Bonzo and I were going to just go into the studio and talk Black Country through the whole thing you know, 'Ah bloody hell how you doin' you all right mate', and it just evolved there and then at the end of my tether. It came out. 'The Rain Song' was a sort of little infatuation I had. The next morning I'd scribble it out. If I'd done it the day after it'd have been no good."

Alterman then asks about the band hiring a press agent for the first time, "The only way we could get through after so much silence was to get a liaison who would say 'Look they're ready to talk now. They're not going to throw you out the window. The reason is because we really warrant it you know, and we've been so complacent for so long about publicity. We know what we've done. We can look back on all the platinum and gold discs and the fantastic nights we've had but it's time everybody at least knew what we were doing whether they appreciated it or not. And dear old England they've hung on desperately through those years of silence. There's just so many good people in England who, when you do a tour, show up with as much fervour as I've got for what we do. They know that we are busy and not a lot of recluses or a bunch of paranoid guys who don't want to talk to

anybody. Now everybody finds out that we are quite active. I'd love to do the same in England on this scale."....

5 **Honolulu Advertiser reports....** Led Zeppelin's latest tour netted them a cool $4 million....

11 **New Musical Express reports....** Correspondent Ritchie Yorke follows the band to New York for their sell out gigs at Madison Square Gardens. In fact Yorke can be seen boarding a limo with the band in the movie The Song Remains The Same. He interviews Page at the band's hotel and then Plant after the show. He observes that 25,000 people "burst into standing ovations after nearly every song".

Page, *"It's been an incredible tour, but we're all terribly worn out. I went past the point of no return physically quite a while back but now I've gone past the mental point. I've only kept going by functioning automatically. Someone asked me the other day what songs we were doing on stage and you know, I couldn't remember. I really couldn't. We've kept up a ridiculous pace. We're going to take it easy for about two months and then I expect we'll start work on a new album. It seems like so long since we had a break . . . in fact. I cannot remember when we were not working."*

Yorke asks whether Page had considered taking an extended hiatus, *"No, after a couple of months I'd get itchy feet again. What worries me the most is losing what I've gained playing over the last 12 months. You know, I always worry that if I stop playing for a long period I'd have to start all over again. I really do worry about that. Getting better at what I do means a great deal to me. Before this tour started, I had all that trouble with the tendon in my right hand. I was only able to play for ten minutes a day and even then it wasn't improving. I was terrified that I wouldn't be able to get it together for the tour. It was touch and go right up until the last minute."*

Yorke asks how the band's success has changed his personal life, *"Not a bit really. I know that it has done a bit of damage to some musicians on the scene but I think we've all remained sane, whatever that means. There's really only two things that I've acquired—claustrophobia and vertigo. I've become afraid of small places and of heights. I didn't use to be like that. I suppose I've also become a little bit paranoid of the motives of other people. You tend to get a bit suspicious but basically I'm still the same person. I suppose we should be grateful for that."*

Page mentions that he has taken to gardening at home, *"This summer we grew all of the vegetables we needed and also enough to freeze for the winter. It's nice to have everything fresh out of the garden you never know what you're getting at the supermarket."*

After the gig at the gardens Plant is interviewed, *"We've got a bunch of new songs written and we can't wait to record them. It certainly has been an incredible tour but so were all the others. We'll just have to wait and see if we can top this one. Rock n' Roll. It's quite an ego trip. But where else could you have so much fun earning a living? Life in this band is like a 24-hour a day riot."*

Barry Taylor reviews the concert from out front and is not as impressed with the band as the audience apparently were. He describes how the Zeppelin vibe had hit the city days in advance and that copies of the bootleg album 'Live On Blueberry Hill' are being sold on the street outside the arena. Taylor credits the

band as "looking more like they did four years ago" having lost the beards. He describes how by the third song "Page was sometimes getting his fingers caught in his strings" and how Plant had "lost his voice or he was tired". He does credit Jones and Bonham as being "as indestructible a rhythm machine as ever". Taylor notices that there are cameramen on stage "filming it for posterity". By the time the band reach Misty Mountain Hop and it's medley companion Since I've Been Loving You he acknowledges that the band now seem to be on form. In conclusion Taylor comments, "With all due respect, Led Zeppelin played a great set, at times it was sloppy, but always entertaining, yet I can't help but wonder if they would make it today if they were just starting out."

September 1973

1 New Musical Express reports.... Nick Kent once again interviews Jimmy Page. This time he manages to drag a few stories out about his early career, *"God knows what the others must think when I start talking about my old days. They must say 'Oh Christ, he's off again on his Yardbirds stories'. The thing is, these days, nobody even knows about those old things anymore, and a lot of that really ancient stuff, I'm sure nobody gives a toss about anyway. The Kinks' tracks and things like that are a bit more interesting, credibility-wise or whatever. Or the Who's first single 'I Can't Explain', that I played rhythm guitar on —actually I wasn't really needed, but I was fortunate enough to find myself there. Just strengthening up riffs, that's all—just two guitars doing it instead of one. Concerning the Kinks work, my presence there was to* enable—I gather, looking at it in retrospect — Ray Davies to walk around and virtually control everything without having to be down in the studio all the time, because he was really producing those things as much as Shel Talmy. A lot more so, actually, because he was directing it and everything. At one point there were even three guitars playing the same riff."

"I joined Neil Christian's Crusaders when I first left school and I was just sort of gigging with the band— driving round the country and getting glandular fever and everything. I remember one night walking outside a gig, and the next point waking up and I was laying on the floor in some sort of dressing room. I just collapsed and couldn't keep going, and it was just fatigue and exhaustion. I was remembering the other day all those breakdowns on the M1 which were great in their own way but after a while it starts knocking you out. I was getting ill, and I really thought 'I just can't carry on'.

"I was doing a lot of painting and drawing in what free time I had, and so I thought I'd go to Art college, because a number of my friends had gone to Art college anyway, and I thought . . . maybe this is it, maybe this is my vocation. So I went — but of course I couldn't stop tinkering around with my guitar and I was still playing- at the Marquee in a sort of interval band.

"I was involved in the old Richmond and Eel Pie Island sets—well, I used to play at those jazz clubs where the Kinks played and I'd always been in groups around the Kingston area. Kingston and Richmond were the two key places, really, but by that time I was well into the Marquee. It was a good scene then because everyone had this same upbringing and had been locked away with their records, and there was some-

thing really new to offer. It just exploded from there."

Kent asks about his first session, "It was a nothing song, but the record was a minor hit. They started using me quite a bit after that and then suddenly I became a new name y'know, appearing on what was then a very very tight session scene. Big Jim Sullivan was carrying the whole weight on his shoulders -- he was the only other young face there. Well, at that particular point all the sessions that I was being invited to were really good ones and I was doing the solos — really constructive work —and it wasn't too hard a decision to make. Then about two years later when guitars were almost becoming out of vogue and people were always trying to do something new --- using sax sections and all that -- and we used to play just fuck-all on guitar, I thought it was time to get out."

He is asked about his solo single, "There's nothing to be said for that record except it was very tongue in-cheek at the time. I played all the instruments on it except for the drums and sang on it too, which is quite, uh . . . unique. 'She Just Satisfies', that's what it was called. It's better forgotten."

The Yardbirds? "Well, you see this is all very touchy. Beck would probably say a lot of things. I could tell you a whole story about that but it's not really on the cards. What actually was going on was all cloak and-dagger stuff, and I didn't want to be part of it at all really. And I just don't want it to be printed. You know, Jeff (Beck) must wince every time he reads any of this, but I've never put him down. I've always said that he's a brilliant musician and I defy anyone to show me anything I've said against him in the press. I can certainly think of a lot of times when he's put me down—but he's the one who's *probably a bit paranoid about that. I don't care. Actually, there was a possibility that he and I were going to get to see each other again but. Things like the Beck's Bolero disputes for instance, which he'd claim was his own, which is just not right. Certain parts of it, like the steel part, that was his work over the chords which I worked out in the studio. He put the other parts on afterwards. Again those sort of things look like you're bitching in the press so in a way it's better to leave them out. Nicky Hopkins was another one who said something about some Immediate tapes—some 'grievance against Jimmy Page' thing which again wasn't on at all. Things just get printed and people seem to latch onto them and they don't know the full circumstances."*

"Beck and I had known each other for ages. I'd gone to see quite a few of their gigs because they were a good band to go and see, and there was this great night when (Keith) Relf was thoroughly pissed. I forget whether it was at an Oxford or Cambridge Union dance. but he was shouting "fuck" at the audience and eventually fell back into the drum-kit. Instead of everybody seeing the humour of it, as three of the group and myself did, Paul Samwell-Smith (who was then the Yardbirds' bassist) just blew up and said 'I can't stand this anymore. I'm going to leave the group -—and if I was you Keith, I'd do the same thing'. And that was when he left. They were stuck, of course, so I said 'well I'll play'. I started out at the Marquee playing bass— an instrument I'd never played before, and that was how it came about."

"It was good. Unfortunately there is very little of it that was recorded but for the amount of time that it was working it was really fabulous. It could have led to so many good things except

that there was a personality conflict within the group that wasn't coming from Beck and me, and that's why things started to bubble up. There were a lot of incidents that led to the final break up, something that had been there long before I joined the group, but while it worked it was good. Like on the Rolling Stones '66 tour which was more or less it's debut. I can remember one great gig at the Fillmore, but really there's so little of it left. 'Stroll On' from the soundtrack of 'Blow Up' was one thing. It was funny because it had dual lead guitars and I think I was playing bass in the film. The single we made 'Happenings Ten Years Time Ago' failed miserably in England."

Kent asks about the only album by the Yardbirds to feature Page the Mickie Most produced Little Games, *"We weren't even allowed to hear playbacks. Mickie was far more into a commercial singles consciousness then, right up to the point where he was recording Beck and Rod—when his whole attitude obviously changed."*

Another album was released by Epic in the United States only to be withdrawn it was recorded live at the Anderson Theatre in New York, *"We had the right to state all along whether it be released or not, and the whole thing was that it had been recorded by Epic at a particularly bad gig, engineered by some character who was strictly into Muzak and the concert itself was bad. So the guv said "Listen, wonders can be done in the studio" and he worked on the live tape for three days or more.*

"We came down to hear it and found he'd over-dubbed bull-fight cheers and stuff. There was one number where there was supposed to be utter silence in the audience and there was clinking cocktail glasses, and sort of mumbling like a

club atmosphere which destroyed the whole thing. Every time you took a solo you got a sort of 'rraaaah' coming at you."

As far as his other early work, *"Well, maybe they don't know what I've done and maybe it's as well that they don't. I didn't really do anything of great importance that they could package anything out of. Only a fool would re-issue "She Just Satisfies".*

The subject turns to the formation of Zeppelin and John Paul Jones, *"He seemed to appear on that scene some time after I did. I remember seeing him but we never really knew each other. We just used to bump into each other and say hello— so he joined on bass."*

"He (Terry Reid) was the only vocalist I knew, but he'd just signed up with Mickie Most so he was out of the question. He did suggest Robert Plant— said he lived in Birmingham and that we should try and track him down. So we went to see him at a college gig and I had a chat with him and said I was trying to get something together and would he be interested to come down and have a chat?

"He came down and stayed for a couple of nights and it just went on from there. We had all the songs thoroughly rehearsed at that point and it was just a case of getting our stage act down in the studio.

"I can't really comment on just why we broke so big in the States. I can only think that we were aware of dynamics at a time when everyone was into that drawn out West Coast style of playing. I can tell you when I knew we'd broken through, which was at San Francisco. There were other gigs, like the Boston Tea Party and the Kinetic Circus in Chicago which have unfortunately disappeared as venues, where the response was so incred-

ible we knew we'd made our impression— but after the San Francisco gig it was just— bang!

"I think we're just lucky in that we've always remained a very tight unit. I think it's incredibly sad to see good bands break up and splinter off into vastly inferior projects."

Kent mentions that the Stones still seem to get all the attention. *"That's probably because we didn't have a press agent at the time. But the thing is the press have always been into images rather than music, I mean, who wants to know that Led Zeppelin broke an attendance record at such-and-such a place when Mick Jagger's hanging around with Truman Capote?*

"Anyway, for this tour, we thought we'd bring in some of the press just so the media would be informed of our goings-on. Most of the journalists present seemed so shocked that we'd done this at all. One of them said: "My first question to you, Mr. Page, is—why are you giving me this interview in the first place?"

His reaction to the huge success of the last tour, *"Oh, everyone went over the top a few times. I know I did and, to be honest with you, I don't really remember much of what happened. The thing is that even when we were totally fucked we'd somehow be able to perform on stage. It was just all down to natural adrenaline. We've done a lot of live recording—the Madison Square tapes are really good and could well materialise on an album in future. Also Ian Knight came along and worked on the visuals, filming the concerts. I've seen some of the footage which is great and again something could easily be done with that.*

"We've got so many profession- ally recorded live tapes: from the second

Albert Hall gig onwards. We just seem to get involved in a studio album. I mean right now we've written a number of new songs, and October and November are set aside for recording."

When asked about the theft of the money at the end of the tour he replies, *"It had reached that point where we really couldn't care too much. I mean, if the tour had been a bummer, then that would have been the last straw, but it wasn't. I remember when I heard the news that it had happened: it was just before we were to go on-stage. I seem to remember we played a very good gig that night. I've had to deal with far worse situations than that on the road. Like, In Los Angeles I cut my hand in that area which is crucial for playing the guitar. It was in fact a tendon that was strained—such a stupid thing, really—and in five gigs I fucked it up for five weeks. And I had all manner of treatment and injections.*

"Now think about it this way— you've played gigs for a month solid and then suddenly you can't touch the guitar for a whole month. I didn't know what the first gig after that would be like. The sensation in my hand was still there actually two days before we left— I didn't know if I could co-ordinate or even think straight while playing. Fortunately God was on my side or whatever— and it somehow fell together again. But that was just a totally horrifying experience.

"In the same way I was once informed that someone was set on killing me while I was in the States. Actually it was a lot more serious than I thought— the guy was a real crazy and had all these photographs on the wall with circles around them. It was a real Manson situation and he was sending out waves of this absurd paranoia which a friend of mine got mixed up with. I got to hear of it

through him and actually hired a security guard along for that American tour. It was actually a lot worse than everyone at first believed — this all happened a year ago on that last tour —and eventually this guy was tracked down and got carted away to hospital. He would have definitely had a try though. It's things like that that tend to lessen the effect of having £80,000 ripped off at the end of a successful tour."

Creem reports.... Journalist Lisa Robinson follows the band on their trek across America. She begins with a quote from Robert Plant who is pool-side at the Royal Orleans Hotel in New Orleans, *"I think I realized what Led Zeppelin really was about around the end of our very first American tour. We started off not even on the bill in Denver, and by the time we got to New York City we were second to Iron Butterfly and they didn't want to go on! And I just started getting this little light glowing inside, and I began wiggling me hips and realizing that it was all a fantastic trip, y'know? I'm not even really sure what it is that I've got to do, but I'm doing it. . . I guess it is magic in a way and I'm just glad that I possess it. I suppose I didn't always possess it - possibly it was rough and raw, but it was always there, I'd always give everything I have to give. As far as I'm concerned we don't need no gimmicks. We are us, and there's nobody else who's us.*"

Robinson quotes an abundance of statistics about the tour. In San Francisco they drew 49,304 people to Kezar Stadium, in Tampa 56,800 people, 49,236 in Atlanta. Other concerts she mentions are Jacksonville, Tuscaloosa, St. Louis, Mobile, and New Orleans.

She relates anecdotes about the band's off stage antics, including their frequent trips into the New Orleans nightlife where they apparently frequented such clubs as the Deja Vu, and the Gateway where again she talks to Plant, *"I felt so nervous tonight, it was like playing in me home town. We've been here for a week, I feel that I know all the kids and everything."*

At one point the owner of the restaurant asks Peter Grant if the band would put their hands in concrete outside the restaurant (á la Graumans in Hollywood). Grant suggests they should get Plant to make an imprint with another piece of his anatomy but Plant suggests he doesn't think it would leave a mark.

Plant, *"But since about eight months ago we decided we wanted to work like hell and have been doing that for months. I really wanted it to be like it was in The Band of Joy. I wanted to go out and really work hard and at the end of the day be really finished, really zapped, and then wake up the next day and rock on, y'know? And that is exactly what we did and how I wish I'd never done it!*

"It's really the ability to make people smile, or just to turn them one way or another for that duration of time, and for it to have some effect later on. I don't really think it's power.... I like to think that people go away knowing that we're pretty raunchy and we really do a lot of the things people say we do, but at the same time - this is what we're getting over, it's goodness. It's not power, revolution; put your fists in the air. I like them to go away feeling the way you do at the end of a good chick, satisfied and exhausted. I don't know about riots - that's all gone. And if there's anybody who wishes to create them in this business, he should be electrocuted on-stage in his own chair. That's really negative.

"I could never be bored because

I know that I could have easily been a chartered accountant, that was what I set out to do. As long as there's a face looking up at me in the middle of the ocean that knows what I'm doing, it could never be boring. Some nights I just look out there and want to fuck the whole first row..."

The subject turns to the bad reviews that the new album received especially D'yer Mak'er, *"Do you know how much that song is hated in the English press? They're really adept at writing things like WILL DESMOND DECKER JOIN LED ZEPPELIN. That's the trouble in England, y'see...you've got Emerson, Lake and Palmer who, aside from being a bunch of old queens - people think are okay. Emerson, Lake and Palmer must be great because they're good musicians, they've got capability. But where is the magic? Where is the transmission of something apart from what everybody expects? I'm not worried about press really. I mean you saw it. I saw it, 50,000 people saw it in one town, and it's the relation of it to the people who don't see it and the cacophony of bullshit. If it was related properly, if they wrote down what they saw, that would be cool. But too many people - when it comes to us, say 'Oh well, Zeppelin were fantastic, they've always been fantastic,' and that's it. Full stop. And the thing is it's constantly changing and improving and taking on different filters or color and intensity which they don't even see and if they do they don't write it down.*

"Every paper in England was full of things like 'Well - Zeppelin was the greatest group in the world, that's it - what shall we have next.' And Melody Maker had it's big center spread that said our next LP would be crucial. Christ our next album will be cosmic . . it will be ter-

restrial!! We're just going along different lines than those people, y'know, I don't know what they expect from us, but they ain't gonna get what they want."

The interview then turns to Jimmy Page and begins with the question, why is he doing this interview? "Well, apart from the fact that nobody knew who I was I thought it was time to say something. There was a time when I didn't do any interviews for about eighteen months because I was just so thoroughly sick of that aspect of the business and didn't want to be a part of it. More so in England, because it seemed to be losing the essence of what was important and that was music, purely. They seemed to be having orgies on other issues that didn't have anything to do with it. Well, they do, don't they? Wallow in rubbish. And you know. I'm not that much of a masochist well, I might be a masochist in other regions, but I'm certainly not to that extent that I'm going to pay money to tear myself to bits - reading.

"I've asked all the reporters I've been doing interviews with this time around 'when was the last time you saw the group' - purely out of curiosity, and it's quite surprising. For many it's been two or three years and they've made pre-conceived judgments. See with us, we're always changing on-stage every night, we never get two guitar breaks that are the same. All these riffs appear out of nowhere every night. And I have a theory that if we were the sort of a group that went out and played exactly the same each night ... well, I'm not going to name anybody, but obviously there are groups that play every guitar note exactly the same as it is on the record and everything is so predictable that it becomes a total bore. If we were like that, the albums would have all stuck in the same groove

more or less. But as all our minds are alive and still working, we go through these changes. Dazed and Confused changes every night so it's a vehicle for exploring and getting off, for me personally. And if we felt that we didn't enjoy doing a number we'd drop it. That's all there is to it. If somebody in the group said 'God, we can't ever play 'Whole Lotta Love' again', we wouldn't play it. And the same with - 'Stairway,' whatever, if someone couldn't play it, it would have to go."

He is asked about the Yardbirds, "I did an interview with ZigZag magazine in London and as far as I'm concerned, that was the final interview on the Yardbirds. It explained it totally in terms of chronology without going into information that wasn't for other people's ears. There are things about that band that are purely for people who were involved in that situation; I know there are other people who were with the group who have been indiscreet, but that's up to them. Sometimes I've thought it would be nice to have another guitarist on-stage, but it would have to be somebody--really capable, not just a rhythm guitarist because that wouldn't be any good at all. It would be nice to get somebody you could work out double lead passages with. When I was with the Yardbirds and Jeff and myself used two guitars, doing leads, I think that was the first band to use two guitars. Since then it's been an obvious progression, there are so many groups who pull it off well now. Also, the concept of two lead guitars is a nice one. But then again, I don't think it would be right, because it's more of a challenge to try and get it with just what we've got. That's the thing really if we can just keep it together ourselves, and just play. And John Paul Jones has a really good command of instruments - we *should be able to orchestrate anything on our own."*

Robinson comments on the size of the tour, *"Primarily because we couldn't get fully around last time. We came here for about three weeks and we did something like 19 dates in 22 days, and with all the jet commuting it did us in totally. After that, I just slept for about a week, I was so exhausted. You know we were playing for about three hours then and it takes everything out of you. We've cut it down a bit now, to about 2½ hours and this time we decided it would be better to come here for four weeks, then go home and return for four weeks and get right around. It's quite an experience really; I mean to think that we've only been here twice in the last two years...I must admit that when I went to the first gig it was a bit nervy. It wasn't the biggest, about 50,000 or something, but we went down there - in Atlanta. When we got there - to view the place, and there was all this equipment, there it was, more equipment than was at Woodstock. And power, there were four big speakers which in fact was what it needed, so even though it was a ridiculous amount of equipment, it was right. Anyway there was all this equipment and this huge great stage and backcloth mirrored thing with the revolving balls, and I was looking around this huge great arena and I thought, my god - there's only the four of us, and that's it, they're coming down to see us. And you're bound to get a bit nervy when you think that they might be coming there with a hypercritical attitude... Well, actually I shouldn't have said that because they didn't there. In Atlanta they were really warm and naturally you react to the warmth of the audience. Sometimes the audience, is better than the group, and we really get off on them. At that particular gig one had*

nothing to worry about and in fact, this whole tour has had this sort of warmth about it. You go out and they're giving you so much that you have to give it back to them."

Plant, *"It's like light a candle. I think they realize that we give so much, and they want to give it right back... I think if concrete could propel itself, we could all go over the hills and far away right into the land of good times, y'know?"*

October 1973

27 **New Musical Express reports....** The story of the week.... BP Fallon Led Zeppelin's tour press agent was recently sharing a hotel room with a chicken, goat, sheep and assorted smoke bombs courtesy of Led Zeppelin....

November 1973

10 **New Musical Express reports....** Led Zeppelin's tour of the USA earned them more than £800,000....

December 1973

23 **Advertiser reports....** Led Zeppelin used a converted Boeing 727 on their last tour of the USA, it costs $5 a mile and offers three hostesses, a steward, a bar, and a bedroom. It is owned by Howard Sylvester Jr. business manager for pop vocalist Bobby Sherman....

1974

March 1974

23 Melody Maker reports.... Jimmy Page: The power and the glory by Chris Welch. Full page article covering the band's and Page's career up to that point, with several quotes reprinted from earlier Welch articles. Welch concludes, 'Jimmy Page has contributed much to rock, provided inspiration to younger players and fans for many years, and has yet to realise his full potential as a musician.'....

May 1974

25 Melody Maker reports.... Cover story, Together for just one show Zeppelin, Allmans! Announcement that Zeppelin will play Knebworth Festival (the first one) on July 20th. The article is thin on details but because of this report nearly 100,000 tickets were sold for the show before it was proven to be inaccurate....

26 New York Daily News reports.... Interview with Robert Plant. *"Listen, I'm a fun loving guy. A great philosopher once said 'them dreams are only in your head'. Don't get me wrong, I haven't quieted down or anything. I've just found more intricate ways of enjoying myself. There's more to me than just those stories, and I'd like to think people pick up more on that side of me than the image of a pop brawling, street fighting kind of image. I'm not exactly a sensible, thoughtful person, but I do love the feeling of being together with people. I love my work, communication on a vast level. My lyrics are more me than anything you've heard about me from the waist down. I mean, we have good times. That's why I have the* curtains drawn, just in case I fancy pushing you out the window."....

June 1974

8 Melody Maker reports.... Led Zeppelin turn down Knebworth. Article outlines how the band rejected the offer to play the festival due to prior film and recording commitments....

15 Melody Maker reports.... Irate fans start to write in to MM complaining about the band neglecting the UK.

22 Melody Maker reports.... Michael Watts interviews manager Peter Grant. Most of the details revealed are expanded on by Watts, but Grant is unusually candid. The interview begins with his notorious reputation which is bolstered by his enormous physical presence.

Grant, *"So then there was this time when some sailors were having a go at Jimmy and Jeff Beck. The three of us were flying down to Miami, and I turn round and hear these blokes. One of 'em looked like a little touch, so I lifted him up under the arm and said, 'OK what's your trouble, Popeye?' The other one ran.*

"There was a lovely description of me in an American magazine, they called me 'the ex-rock errand boy.' It was fucking great. Fantastic. (But) if I'm out at a concert and somebody is gonna do something that's snide to one of my artists, then I'll fucking tread on 'em without thinking about it."

Grant comments about his relationship with the moguls of the business calling Hugh Hefner 'boring', *"But quite honestly, I wouldn't know what to talk to all those people about, anyway. When we were in America recently, launching Swan*

Song a woman from the Hollywood Reporter came up and said, 'I know you're very busy now, but I must call you at the hotel. I'm gonna definitely call you tomorrow to get some interesting facts.' And I said, just as a throwaway, 'call me at 12 noon and I'll tell you something boring.'And she swept out of the reception in a great long evening dress. I though it was fucking great, I mean, I know some of those bigshots at the record company cringe when they're with me, 'cause I don't even own a suit, just two pairs of jeans. But I know they have to do it because of what you represent. Which is great."

He is asked whether he would like to manage any of the new wave of glitter rock bands, "I'd be like a fish out of water; it just wouldn't be me. I'd feel uncomfortable, and I would probably fuck up for them. I don't understand music very much, but it's a feel thing: it gives you a tingle, and you know."

He then reminisces about his days with the Yardbirds. The band's ex-manager Simon Napier-Bell gave Grant some advice. "He came to see me, and one of the first things he said was, 'It's a good band but you need to find a guitarist. He's a real troublemaker that Jimmy Page.' I said, 'Oh, why's that?' And he said, 'Well, he's just a stirrer in the band.' So then I met the band and I said to Jimmy, 'I hear I have to give you the bullet 'cause you're a troublemaker.' 'Troublemaker!' he said. 'You're dead right! We did 'Blow Up', four weeks in America and a Rolling Stones UK tour, and we got just 118 quid each.' I took them on. All I know, is that if I 'adn't been a fucking stagehand at the Croydon Empire for 15 bob a show, and if I 'adn't done all the things I have, like being a film extra and on the road with Gene

Vincent and the rest, there's no way I could've coped with the events of the past five or six years."

Grant continues with the band's relationship with radio. "I suppose the bottom line is, none of us is prepared to suck arse just to get bloody good music on state controlled radio. We just decided not to put singles out because of that trip you have to go through, or had to at that time. It was always such an El Greaso job! You had to go and wine and dine these people and all that crap, and they weren't keen on anything that didn't sound poppy. As long as the people want to see you you're all right, and that's the way it should be shouldn't it? If musicians are talented and good, should they have to grease job the media?

"(The BBC) have misrepresented that scene. I mean there's a lot of good bands that haven't made it because their records weren't played."

The subject switches to his notorious encounter with bootlegger Jeffrey Collins. Apparently Grant had gone into Collins London shop and destroyed the Zeppelin bootlegs.

"Mmm, I think we did confiscate them. The funny thing was he rang me up the next day and said Polydor had sent these people down and it was really disgusting how they'd treated him; he'd been terrified. He said one of the men was six feet three, weighed 18 and a half stone, had a beard, and was really vicious. 'It just shows you what the Industry's coming to,' I said. He didn't know who I was when I was in the shop I told him 'I think that's really disgusting of Polydor'. And he said, 'I knew you wouldn't approve of it.' Then the next day he rang back and said, 'Oh all right I know you've made a cunt out of me.'Well we did have a laugh.' I said, 'because we recorded you on the *phone.' We hadn't but it was a parting shot."*

Continuing on the subject of bootlegs, *"Well, they've got legislation together now, but before, all the record companies were doing was moaning to the press, never doing anything about it. Quite honestly, it was a con on the kids, because those albums were really crappy; they wore out quickly and were six quid each. It was a liberty, and when my information found out where the source was I decided to go and do something about it myself."*

At the Bath festival he had thrown a bucket of water into a videotape machine, *"It was like a Will Hay thing Whoosh! It made a horrible smell as it melted. But if somebody is doing something wrong, or being shit to an artist that you manage.... I mean that's what they hire you for. I don't believe in pussyfooting around if it's my artist.*

"I think all that got exaggerated, didn't it? But as far as I'm concerned as an archetypal heavy, most of those incidents have been on the spot situations, not sitting around in Oxford St. and hiring a great crew of heavies to go round."

Grant is apparently equally disenchanted with the legit record labels. *"As soon as they've got the record it isn't Led Zeppelin, Bad Company or Maggie Bell — it becomes matrix number so and so, and the marketing lads take over."*

In conclusion he talks about the newly formed label Swan Song. *"We just want four or five acts that we could all add something to."*

He reminisces about his early days when both managers and artists were treated like dirt by their peers.

"If you're a manager and you don't have a hot act, you don't get in to see those people. They ain't even got the

time of day for you. And I said to myself that if I ever became a manager I should never be like that. That's the main thing, doing the best you can and staying by people, whatever happens."

September 1974

14   New Musical Express reports.... cover story.... Mick Jagger hanging out in New York with Jimmy Page and Ron Wood.... article on Page playing with Bad Company in New York.... Lisa Robinson reports from Bad Company's gig in New York where Page showed up and jammed.... at both the New York and Austin Texas shows Page played 'Rock Me Baby' with the band. Page, *"You know there really is a comparison to be made with this band and Zeppelin. Paul and Simon played together before, like Bonzo and Robert did, and all of them came together from other bands like we did. And the combined fusion of all the musical forces just has worked out so well. And it's such good strong virile music.*

"I've been working really hard on the LP and a bit on the film. The album should be out around October hopefully, then I'll be able to really work and finish up the film. There's just so much to do with that movie, editing all the parts together, working the music in with it, finishing up my little bits. I've been waiting for the autumn to finish up my stuff. I did a few things last winter it's all outside no restrictions.

"It was great playing in Austin though. I mean I wouldn't have wanted to do it as an ego thing, or if the band hadn't asked me to. But I must admit it was so great to get on a stage again. I mean I really enjoy working on the album but that's a head thing really you do need to

get in front of audiences and feel that feedback, that energy."

Robinson continues the conversation with the subject of the British taxes and their effect on Page, *"I wouldn't leave even if I had to live in a cottage. There's just the thing about England the tradition of thousands of years and the beauty of the countryside. it's so gorgeous there. I wouldn't want to be without that. The whole tax thing is ridiculous anyway. Hopefully it'll change. It would be one thing if they took 61% in taxes that's fair if you're making a lot of money, and gave it for home mortgages or such, but of course they don't do that."*

She then asks him about his home in Scotland and his involvement with the conservation going on there, *"It was really amazing to get involved with the town council and politics and all. You really can get something done if you try. I just was so upset that they wanted to put pylons in this magnificent countryside and I really got involved, doing up petitions and all that. Of course at first they didn't know who I was, then later they made a bigger thing out of it. It did do some good, although they ended up doing what they wanted anyway, basically. But you can get things done on that level if you are really willing to get involved, it was a very good experience for me. I feel very strongly about preserving that countryside."....*

October 1974

12 New Musical Express reports.... cover story contest to win Jimmy Page's guitar.... Nick Kent interviews Page about guitars, *"It's strange really. In the early Richmond days we used to all play together, more or less. Everyone had the same*

influences and made the best of them really. It was like a melting-pot and . . . I'm sure, say Beck would agree here . . . that from all that common ground one just picked up one's own ideas and carried straight on from there.

"My own thing has been to keep every style . . . and obviously there are so many ways of playing the guitar it's not true . . . and work on them as parts of a whole as opposed to just getting stuck with one thing. I mean, being a guitarist, well it all depends on the person involved in the first place— how they actually approach the instrument aesthetically. I mean, you could even approach it as just a block of wood, couldn't you. After all it's just a piece of wood with strings."

Page had donated a Gretsch guitar to a competition in NME, Kent asks where he got it, *"About two years ago. It cost about £200 at a place called GTR, in Nashville. They do a whole list of rare instruments and I asked them to look out for one marked with the branded 'G'. Acoustics are their main speciality. They've got 1935 Martins and that sort of thing. When I say £200, it came to that with the customs etc., but it originally cost 450 dollars. Very reasonable really. Les Pauls can cost 1500 dollars there. Eddie Cochran had one very similar to this. I think he customised it, though some people say it was made specially for him. It had an old block Gibson pick up by the neck and a branded G . . . an earlier version. I think it's a Chet Atkins Hollowbody. A bloke who really knows about these things told me there's another one in existence the same as Eddie Cochran's made up by Gretsch. It's somewhere in Tooting, I think."*

Kent asks why he bought it, and what was his first guitar, *"Well, if you're an Eddie Cochran guitar fan you'll know why. It's a good all-rounder with good acoustics when it's strung up properly. My first guitar worth talking about was a Stratocaster. Then I had something called a Grazzioso—don't know where it came from. It was probably a Czechoslovakian version of Fender, that's what it looked like anyway. Then I got a Fender Strat, then something very similar to that but a later model. The company were making patented pickups at that time though I had that for five years. I played that with The Crusaders. God, The Crusaders —another great rock legend.*

"Then I got a Les Paul Custom which I stayed with until it was nicked in the States during the first 18 months of Zeppelin — the second or third tour. Usually I never took that on the road, because it was so precious. But things were going so well for us that I eventually took it over and it suddenly went. It had a big tremolo arm and Joe Jammer custom-wired it for me. I was starting to use it more than anything else. It got nicked off the truck at the airport— we were on our way to Canada. Somewhere there was a flight change and it disappeared. It just never arrived at the other end. I advertised for it in Rolling Stone. Just a photograph—no name—and a reward. No luck though, even though it was very recognisable for all the custom work done on it."

Apparently this was the guitar he used for his session work and the Yardbirds. Kent speculates that he must have got it in 64-65, *"No earlier than that—about 62. It cost £185 which was a lot of money. I got it on the old HP special."*

Kent asks about the sound of the time especially the Rickenbacker 12 strings. *"That was much later. That was in 65, must have been. Yeah, the whole Byrds sound. Christ. I'd been doing sessions for*

three years before that I remember seeing The Byrds in Ciro's before 'Mr. Tambourine Man'. Actually at that time I think it was mainly Telecasters and things. Strats too. And then there was a dramatic switch over to Les Pauls around the time when the blues thing started . . .when Eric Clapton was with John Mayall. You see, there was the flat sound you got from those Humbucking pickups, 'cos you can get a really nice sharp sound from them. It's just totally different. When Marshall amps came out the combination of the two was really fantastic. That's when finger tremolos started. Hendrix was the one who brought (The tremolo arm) back in. He started using it sensibly again."

Kent asks if it was Page who played the solo on Dave Berry's 'The Crying Game', *"Strange that. It was weird because it was all my equipment — but I didn't do that one. I did the next one, 'My Baby Left Me'."*

Page is asked how the Kinks got the guitar sound on 'You Really Got Me', *"Dave Davies used an Epiphone when I was there—that was the Kinks guitar. It certainly wasn't a Gretsch. But the sound was really a combination of things— valve amps and valve mixing units . . . everything sparkled then, sound-wise. It's a matter of taste but I prefer valves. They seem more punchy. Transistors apparently sound better for-bass."*

When asked what guitar he used on stage with the Yardbirds, *"A Telecaster. I started on bass of course, then it came to the twin guitars with Jeff (Beck) and it was a Telecaster. He was using the Gibson and the Les Paul, so it was two different sounds.*
I used the Telecaster right through to the early Zeppelin period. Then I swapped to a Les Paul on the second Zep LP, and I've

been using it ever since. But often I've done solos on a Telecaster—the solo on 'Stairway To Heaven'for example."

Kent asks if he used any other guitars for live work back then, "Yeah, well I used one of those two pickup Dan-Electros which cost 30 or 40 quid then. Actually they were great. That was the time when I used to do a long instrumental called 'White Summer'in strange tunings. It went on for about 20 minutes—'til everyone fell asleep. Then we'd play a bit of rock n'roll.

"At that time I just used one guitar, but later, like when we did "Stairway", I couldn't do all the parts—and that's when I had to get a double necked guitar. Mine had to be specially made up by Gibson. They were really good about that — because they weren't making them anymore."

Kent asks if he had played twelve string before. "Yeah, electric 12-string with The Yardbirds. Maybe you haven't heard stuff like 'Puzzles' and all those weird things. They were all electric 12-string — fast runs and things on a Vox, actually. But most of those were just issued in the States."

Pursuing the subject of the twelve string, "Earl Hooker played the first one I saw. After that I always wanted one—but you just couldn't get them. That bloke in Family had one though, John Whitney.

"You can do so much with a 12-string. If you switch on both necks and turn them up full, when you just play on the six string neck all the other strings start ringing in sympathy .... like the strings on a sitar. That sort of thing adds another dimension to the sound. It can sound like a harp." As for tunings, "I've worked with different tunings all the way through. A lot of the songs we've done

are just weird tunings when I've altered the strings until they sounded right. 'Friends' is one —nobody would ever be able to work that out. 'Rain Song'another. They're just two tunings which I shouldn't think anyone's ever used before, because I just kept altering the strings until it sounded right. They're not open chords even."

"(Whole Lotta Love) that's just standard tuning. The only thing on tuning (on the first album) is 'Black Mountain Side'. It was all standard tuning otherwise. I used to do a lot of acoustic stuff with The Yardbirds and that's when it really works—they don't sound so good on electric really. You know the old standard blues tunings of D and G - you know, the old bottleneck ones like Keith Richards uses—they're the favourites. But then all the more unusual ones don't always sound so good. The one on 'Rain Song' sounds all right on electric, curiously enough. But the one on 'Friends'-sounds better on acoustic. So you've really got to engineer the numbers round the tunings, and guitars round the numbers."

He is asked how many guitars he owns. "I've got a Les Paul and a spare in case a string breaks and a double-neck. I used to have an acoustic guitar as well when we were doing the acoustic numbers. But of late that's all I've been using. Well you see, this is the whole thing. We use so many different tunings that Raymond the road manager spends most of his time re-tuning the guitars—the double neck, for instance, goes into a number of tunings and that's 18 strings on a double neck. So we've bought one of those Strob-o-tuners, because we haven't time for all that. It means you have to work out the way that you plan your numbers, to give you enough time to tune up. 'Stairway' is standard tuning. By the *way."*

Page is asked about his earliest influences, *"Well 'Baby Let's Play House', that was the first thing I ever started playing. Then I went through the early rock 'n' roll efforts, learning the solos. Mainly solos. Most of the chords were pretty straight forward. Old Ricky Nelson things, James Burton that sort of stuff. Just learning from solos, getting a groundwork really. You see I was fortunate, because this friend, who was a really avid blues collector, lived down the road. I was an avid rock collector so I used to send over to him to get all the Sun singles and things like that, and he used to get all the blues ones like B. B. King from me. So between the two of us we got a sort of coverage of all the different sounds. I was doing a bit of everything in the early days. In fact, that's why I jacked it in in the first place.*

"We were doing Berry stuff, would you believe, which some people really liked, but most of them wanted to hear neatly balanced Top Ten numbers. And I was getting ill... probably as a result of knowing I wasn't getting anywhere. I'm not talking about big ambitions, but it was just disheartening to go up to, say Rushden or somewhere like that, and find ten people having a punch-up. In the end, it just didn't appear to be going anywhere, so I jacked it in. The Stones weren't going in those days. Anyway, I was still sort of playing at home, even though I was at art college. And then it all started happening. The Diddley and Berry thing started to come through—in the south anyway. I used to go down the Marquee and jam. All these groups were performing—like The Yardbirds—and suddenly the whole thing started coming through big, and that's why, I guess, as a session guitarist . . .

that's why I suppose I was lucky, because I'd had prior ground-work and I knew what was going on. A lot of the other session guitarists had never even heard of any of these R'n'B people."

Kent asks if he ever played jazz or just sticks to rock, *"I did as it went on. That's when I really had to start working as a guitarist. I really had to learn every sort of style. I was even doing Tubby Hayes' sessions. But in the early days it was mainly rock. I never really got into too many of the jazz musicians. Django Rheinhardt, sure, and Tal Farlowe. Johnny Smith was great for chords . . .I practiced probably six hours a day. When I was at school probably eight.*

"I didn't go into acoustic 'till much later when I got into the whole sitar thing. Dylan was there as well. Bert Jansch just turned my head right around with acoustic. Oh yeah, far more than Renbourne or Davey Graham—Jansch was definitely the one.

"By the way, I'm missing out a whole section here where I got interested in learning classical guitar, which I was for a time. During the session days, this was. By that time I'd had to learn how to read music so I thought I'd combine the two."

Did he take lessons? *"I did, yeah, but I'm not saying where because it was a con and I wouldn't want to mislead anyone into thinking, 'Well, yeah, if he went there then it must be good.' Recently I heard a record put out by 'Showbud' on how to play pedal-steel guitar and Christ, you'd only have to learn that record inside out and you'd be an ace steel-player. I can dabble about but it's strange I met Jerry Garcia recently and I've always liked his pedal steel playing, far more in fact than his six string stuff. I told him so and he just replied that he'd given it all up*

because he said in effect, playing both was just too much to handle. As I said I can dabble but dabbling's no good when there are too many ace players around already."
    What did he think of the psychedelic stuff that he had helped pioneer? *"All I remember with that is that we were the first group to use backing tapes. Y'know bombs dropping and news reels —musician's concrete—as a back-drop to the music. I wasn't so much into that feedback stuff. I thought a lot of what was coming out of San Francisco was laughable. Yeah there was this one group called Kaleidoscope who were the best band - I've ever seen."*
    Inevitably the subject turns to the violin bowing of the guitar. *"I've done that for ages. I picked it up on a session once when a musician told me that if I played the bow over guitar strings it would make this certain sound. I said it wouldn't but in fact when I came to try it out, it worked. Actually I did that a lot with The Yardbirds on the Vox 12 string. (It requires a lot of rosin) because of the shape of the strings and their density."*
    Kent suggests that the old guitar's are better than contemporary models, *"Well it's true. Simple as that. Because the copper that was used on those early Humbucking pick-ups was of a higher quality and had more windings too, I believe. So when America went through the Korean War they had to use all their resources, naturally and that's what made the difference to the copper wiring. Fenders got screwed up when they started making 'em in Japan, of course. Well there aren't many (dependable new models), are there?"*
    Kent observes that the Dan Armstrong Plexiglass guitar is a good instrument, *"Yeah, that was okay —*

they're restocking those in fact. Actually there was a guy at Gibson's who really cared about quality. He was a director, I think, and he got out all those limited editions Of Flying Arrows and Firebirds. He did a pretty good job, I think. Guitars aren't cheap at the best of times so it's ridiculous to be palmed off with some piece of insubstantial rubbish."
    Does he have any recommendations for an instrument? *"Well, as I say, I'm not that well acquainted with the newer models so I'd naturally advise someone to pick up on an older model, should they come across one. That would do for electric. With acoustic models . . . well I could probably contradict myself here but it's true that out of all those Yamaha guitars on the market you could probably find one that would beat a duff £800 Martin — if you were lucky that is. The Dan-Electro model I used to have was very good value. I've got a Harmony myself which I'm well pleased with, plus a Martin I purchased recently. (As for practice amps) a Champ. They're quite expensive now though. About £50 or £60."*
    To conclude Kent asks him whether he has any advice for upcoming guitarists, taking note that Page had taught Joe Jammer 'a lot of tricks', *"A good ear helps. I mean, if you hear something properly then there's no reason why you can't learn to play it. I mean (Joe) already knew how to play so he did it by listening and watching all the time. That's the trick, really. You should always check out someone who already has the rudiments down pat. I mean, there's always someone who knows how to play a guitar even if they live in the next village."*

26 **New Musical Express reports....** Led Zeppelin's new album is due soon, Jimmy Page calls it a summary.... Jimmy Page

and John Paul Jones were spotted at the Charisma Kempton Park Rock and Racing Meet.... apparently Page reports things going bump at Crowley's house in Scotland....

Rock Scene reports.... Cover story, Led Zep Party. Picture article of the Swan Song Label launch party. The pictures reveal in attendance, the band and Grant, Richard Cole, David Geffen, Bill Wyman, Clive Colson, Paul Rodgers, Maggie Bell, Groucho Marx, Ahmet Ertegun, Danny Goldberg and Lisa Robinson.

November 1974

2 **New Musical Express reports....** Led Zeppelin are throwing a Halloween bash at an out of town venue, it is expected to be the party of the year.... Jimmy Page will appear on Maggie Bell's new album Suicide Sal....

9 **Melody Maker reports....** Article mentions the band's reception at Chislehurst for the launching of their own record label Swan Song. It states that naked or half naked women were lining the dark recesses of the caves, and the celebrities that attended included Zeppelin, Bad Company, Jeff Beck, Maggie Bell, as well as several record company executives. Apparently a food fight broke out which was triggered by something to do with a naked woman in a coffin....

13 **Swan Song press release....** From: Danny Goldberg
LED ZEPPELIN TO TOUR AMERICA BEGINNING IN MID-JANUARY COAST TO COAST TOUR IS SUPER-GROUP'S FIRST IN EIGHTEEN MONTHS

Peter Grant, manager of Led Zeppelin and President of their record label Swan Song, has announced a major American tour for the group beginning in mid-January, and extending -with a break in the middle -- until the end of March.

This is Led Zeppelin's first tour since their historic 1973 American tour in which they broke several concert attendance records that had been set years before by the Beatles. The most outstanding record set that year still stands: Led Zeppelin attracted the largest paid attendance ever for one act on May 5. 1973 when 56,800 paid to see them at Tampa stadium in Tampa, Florida. Led Zeppelin consists of Robert Plant, lead singer, Jimmy Page, lead guitar, John Paul Jones, bass and keyboards, and John Bonham, drums.

Shortly before the tour begins, Led Zeppelin will release their sixth album, 'Physical Graffiti' on their recently formed record label, Swan Song. The album is a twin record set of all new material and it is expected to "ship gold," vital advance orders are well over a million dollars. Led Zeppelin's five previous albums have all been "platinum," which means more than a million units sold, and their last two albums, "Houses Of The Holy," and "Led Zeppelin," each stayed on the charts for well over a year and continue to be major catalogue sellers world wide. In fact, Led Zeppelin is the best selling group in the history of Atlantic Records, for whom their first five albums were recorded. Atlantic distributes Swan Song.

Grant announced details of the first half of Zeppelin's tour as follows: Minneapolis Sports Centre, January 18, Chicago Stadium (20,21,22) Cleveland Coliseum (24), Indianapolis Arena (25),

St. Louis, Missouri Arena (27), Greensboro, N. Carolina Coliseum (28), Detroit, Michigan Olympia Stadium (31), Pittsburgh, PA. Arena, February (1), New York's Madison Square Garden (3), Boston, Mass. Gardens (4), Montreal, Canada Forum (6); New York Madison Square Garden (7), Philadelphia, Pa. Spectrum (8), Washington, DC Capitol Centre (10), New York's Madison Square Garden (12), Nassau Coliseum Long Island NY (13,14)

The second half will begin in early March. As is their custom. Led Zeppelin will perform approximately a two and a half show. They will have no opening act.

16 **New Musical Express reports....** Zep massive U.S. tour & new album.... Led Zeppelin will tour America from January to March.... the tour will be split into two legs and will feature songs from the band's new album.... British dates have not been ruled out....

23 **New Musical Express reports....** delay in announcing the winner of Page's guitar due to postal strike....

December 1974

7 **New Musical Express reports....** Cover story....This article reveals many details about the band's plans. Zep: Spring Gigs Here.... Jimmy Page revealed this week that Led Zeppelin will be playing concerts in the UK in the spring. The dates are to follow after the band's American tour in January.... the band are also planning five shows in Europe and they will take place in Belgium and Holland prior to the band leaving for America.... the band have been working on their new album and on a film

of their last US concert tour. It is expected to include some fantasy sequences and it is because of these commitments that the band had to withdraw from the Knebworth Park show this summer. The band's new album Physical Graffiti will be released by Atlantic in the new year.... Nick Kent gets a chance to review Physical Graffiti with only one hearing.... "Quintessential doyens of the kamikaze dizzbuster game" (now tell me with a headline like that, that these journalists have no ego. RG).... With the benefit of twenty years hindsight it is easy to point a finger and say, 'You idiot, are you nuts putting your name to a review of Physical Graffiti after only hearing it once?' However, Kent manages to give a good accounting of himself. He recognises Kashmir as one of the album's highlights calling it, "Most impressive", and he doesn't miss the sheer frenetic pace set by Bonham during In My Time Of Dying. All in all a lucid and generally positive review despite his one main blunder of dismissing Trampled Underfoot as "no way vital Zep". He concludes with, "Led Zeppelin are still absolutely the best mainstream metal band around."....

Interview with Page conducted on 26th November during the band's rehearsals at Liveware an old theatre in Ealing (a London suburb).... apparently the band played for seven hours through until 10 p.m. the songs rehearsed include, Trampled Underfoot, In My Time Of Dying, When The Levee Breaks, Sick Again, Custard Pie, Don't Be Cruel, and Hound Dog. Page is taken back to his early musical adventures when the subject of the band's name is raised. Apparently John Entwistle had been recently claiming to have coined the name and conceived the design for the cover of Led Zeppelin I (not Keith Moon as is commonly believed), Page, *"Well, I don't know about that at all, to start with the thing about the cover is completely wrong. We did that quite separately. The other, Keith Moon gave us the name. We've always credited him for that. I mean originally there was going to be a band formed from the session for 'Beck's Bolero', Jeff, myself, Nicky Hopkins, Aynsley Dunbar and yes, John Paul Jones was in by that time. Maybe John Entwistle did think of the name and told it to Keith Moon in which case I suppose he might have cause to be a bit angry."*

The course of conversation turns to the upcoming movie, Page, *"Well to start with the film is nearing completion,* (hard to believe it didn't make it out for nearly another two years -R.G.) *though we don't have a title or a distributor yet. I've yet to mix the soundtrack and the final editing hasn't been completed. We've finally got a distinct framework. For a start the fantasy scenes do relate to individual numbers the band play. Like Robert's bit comes in 'Song Remains The Same' and 'Rain Song' and Bonzo's is in his drum solo 'Moby Dick', John's is 'No Quarter' and mine comes in 'Dazed & Confused'. Mine's a bit weird actually, well so is everyone's really. They just happened that way."*

Moving on the inevitable references to road fever are raised and the sordid innuendoes about the LA groupie scene, Page, *"I just view it all with amusement. Like the whole Rodney's scene thing, which is just ridiculous. I mean you walk in and the next thing you know there are cameras everywhere and you're ducking under the bar to get away. Roy Harper has this photograph of me on the point of sticking a pork-pie in a girl's face. The last time I was in LA there was this incredible groupie feud which was*

getting down to razor-blade sandwiches. The competition thing out there is incredible and you've got to keep out of the middle of it or else it gets to you too. There's a new song on the album called 'Sick Again' that about sums it up."

Page then goes on to mention how life on the road tends to disrupt his diet and destroy his stamina. He points out that he intends to be more careful this time. The conversation then moves on to Crowley and Page's interest in the occult. The interviewer points out that Page is opening a shop in Kensington's Holland Street to sell books on the occult, the shop is to be called 'The Equinox', the title of a magazine published at the turn of the century by Aleister Crowley. Page, *"I don't want to do a huge job on Crowley or anything, that doesn't interest me in the least. It goes without saying that Crowley was grossly misunderstood. I began being interested in him in school after having read this ridiculous book called 'The Beast' where the author hadn't the faintest idea of what Crowley was all about and was totally condescending so I took it from there. But I mean, how can anyone call Crowley the world's most evil man, and that even carried over to the thirties when Hitler was about? For a start he was the only Edwardian to really embrace, not even the New Age so much as simply the 20th century. Who else would state something like his theory that there would eventually be equality of the sexes, which is where we're at right now. It's like there's this incredible body of literature, there's a diamond there to be found at the end and it involves a life's study."*

Finally the interview concludes with Page's thoughts on the film he has just scored for filmmaker Kenneth Anger, 'Lucifer Rising'. Page, *"I've always got*

on very well with Anger. He's a good friend. He's never been as awe-inspiring and unap-
proachable to me as some would probably tell you. It's just one day he asked me to toss
some ideas around for a sound-track and I went away feeling something but never being
able to really express it, until one day when it all sort of poured out and I got it down
immediately to recording it. Actually I saw him recently and he was playing my sound-
track against some of the rushes and it came together really nicely."

14 **New Musical Express reports....** Jimmy Page and Robert Plant are spotted at Eric
Clapton's second night at the Hammersmith Odeon....

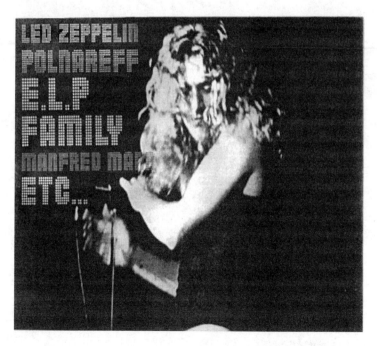

1975

January 1975

4 **New Musical Express reports....** All the tickets for Led Zeppelin's three shows in Chicago were sold out in five hours....

11 **New Musical Express reports....** Contest to win Jimmy Page's guitar...Page is recording this week with Keith Richards and Ron Wood....

Hit Parader reports.... Jimmy Page talks about Swan Song Talent.... cover story.... interview.... Page, *"I see this label as something that could be really good because of the kind of people we have- I mean Paul Rodgers and Maggie are very far apart really. Like Maggie Bell; it's a funny thing - in England she's won all the polls but didn't sell records. And Roy Harper he's had about 6 or 7 LPs out and none of them were released in this country. And we've got The Pretty Things as well - so in all of these cases the record companies totally ignored them, and they're great talents - every one of them. They just haven't come across the right way and I really put that on the record companies. With Swan Song we have a situation where it won't happen, it's a place where people who have talent will be able to be heard; for we can put ourselves behind it and try and pull it off. Of course if they aren't happy they can split and go elsewhere.*

"So far everyone on the label is being produced by their own producer - and I've been working since last Christmas on our stuff and I don't know how I could squeeze in a minute. But I would love to try something different, I just don't know if I can.

"I've been following the Pretty Things for some time and I have a good idea of what they're into...as far as Maggie is concerned, I don't know about that .... certainly there are people and other things I would like to get into, but I just am 100% committed to Zeppelin now.

"I also feel that it's a different kind of record company than some others that groups have formed because it isn't just involved with one group. That's something that time will tell - and let's hope people won't be saying, 'oh, - Zeppelin is on that label' .... but that they'll be saying 'Bad Company and Maggie are on that label.' I mean we're just as much a part of it as they are. It's really a family thing. Not like Rolling Stones Records which is really an ego thing right from the start. I mean we aren't Zeppelin Records or Stairway Records .... it's all together."

On the subject of the name Swan Song, *"Well, it was very odd, really. I had this long acoustic guitar instrumental with just sparse vocal sections - the song was about 20 minutes and the vocal was about 6 minutes, and the whole thing was quite epic really. Almost semi-classical I suppose, and I did have bits of it and we were recording with the truck and there was no title for it and someone shouted out 'what's it going to be called and I shouted out 'Swan Song!' and the whole thing stopped and we said what a great name for the LP, and all the vibes started and suddenly it was out of the LP and onto the record label. I think that Swan Song is a good name for a record label because if you don't have a hit on Swan Song .... well, then you shouldn't have signed up with them ...*

"I'm not personally involved with the business side of it because I'm so involved with the production of the records that I just can't and don't have time to worry about the business side of it

- or even to take a look at it. I mean there are finite points where the two cross and I get involved then - but apart from that I don't really pay much attention to what's going on behind the scenes."

The future is raised, *"I'm ready for performing; but I really won't be ready for it until the film is finished and this LP is finished. There's time for each, but I never really know until it's about to happen.*

"I know that by the time of the end of the last tour all I could relate to was getting on-stage. The adrenaline did its job and I was okay, but after that .... When I was in New York I didn't know whether I was coming or going. It took me about 6 weeks to get over that last tour."

Finally he discusses the soundtrack score, *"I did some film music once for Kenneth Anger - "Lucifer Rising", and that had some very strange sounds on it. They had a show at the Museum of Modern Art where they showed that film, and I saw that the music wasn't synched up to the film, so when I came here to see Maggie, I brought the film music with me, and now I know he's got it synched up right. He showed it in Berkeley and apparently the reaction was pretty good. That was a challenge because I had never done any film music before but for the "Blow Up" music with the Yardbirds and that was great, I really enjoyed it. I saw that recently by the way, and I really got off on it, thought it was very good actually.*

"It has all the instruments on an 8-track recording system which I mix down onto small cassette - well, I haven't got drum but I do all the rest. I mean I don't go to them like a dictator like let's do it this way or no way, I play it for them and they say 'What do you think?', and then everybody takes their own stand.

Otherwise there wouldn't be much of a group identity, would there."

14 **Swan Song press release**.... From: Danny Goldberg

STATEMENT RE: LED ZEPPELIN BOSTON CANCELLATION

Steve Weiss, spokesman for Led Zeppelin, has made the following statement regarding the Led Zeppelin Boston concert. "It has been widely reported today that Boston officials will be announcing shortly the cancellation of the Boston Gardens Led Zeppelin concert that was scheduled for February 4th. If so, this is a matter of great disappointment to the members of the group and to Swan Song.

In seven years of touring America, Led Zeppelin has never had a concert canceled, nor has there ever been a serious incident at one of their concerts. It is unfortunate that the officials in Boston have so little confidence in the young people of Boston - I do not think there would be any problems if the concert was held.

Boston has a special significance for Led Zeppelin, since it was the first city in America where the group played when they first were formed in 1968. We are investigating the possibility of replacing the Boston Gardens date with another concert within driving distance.

All Led Zeppelin concerts for the first half of their tour have sold out, more than 300,000 tickets, not including Boston. The tour is being promoted by Swan Song in association with Jerry Weintraub/ Concerts West . Tour schedule as follows...

January 18 Metropolitan Sports Center Minneapolis Minnesota

January 20, 21 & 22 Stadium Chicago, Illinois

January 24 Arena Cleveland, Ohio

January 25 Arena Indianapolis, Indiana

January 29 Coliseum Greensboro, North Carolina

January 31 Olympic Stadium Detroit, Michigan

February 1 Arena Pittsburgh, Pennsylvania

February 3 Madison Square Garden New York, New York

February 6 Forum Montreal, Canada

February 7 Madison Square Garden New York, New York

February 8 Spectrum Philadelphia, Pennsylvania

February 10 Capitol Center Washington, DC

February 12 Madison Square Garden New York, New York

February 13 & 14 Nassau Coliseum Hempstead, New York

February 16 Missouri Arena St. Louis, Missouri

February 27 Coliseum Houston, Texas

February 28 L.S.U. Assembly Center Baton Rouge, Louisiana

March 3 Tarrant Convention Center Fort Worth, Texas

March 4 & 5 Memorial Auditorium Dallas Texas

March 10 Sports Arena San Diego, California

March 11 & 12 Arena Long Beach California

March 17 Coliseum Seattle, Washington

March 19 & 20 Coliseum Vancouver, BC

March 21 Coliseum Seattle, Washington

March 24, 25 & 27 Forum Inglewood, California

18 **New Musical Express reports....** Dubliner Charles Reid wins Jimmy Page's hollow body orange Gretsch guitar, Page is glad it's going to a good home.... £30,000 damage was caused by bottle throwing vandals in a concert ticket queue in Boston.... Madison Square Gardens in New York reports the biggest demand ever for tickets.... Zeppelin's management are planning the band's biggest gig ever at the West Palm Beach Raceway on March 8th. The venue is expected to hold 150,000 people and the staging will be by Showco of Texas who will provide 70,000 watts of sound and several large video monitors. Over 310,000 watts of lighting will be used. In New York the box office opened a day early when 15,000 fans were camped out waiting for tickets.... **Melody Maker reports....** Zeppelin fans in tickets riot.

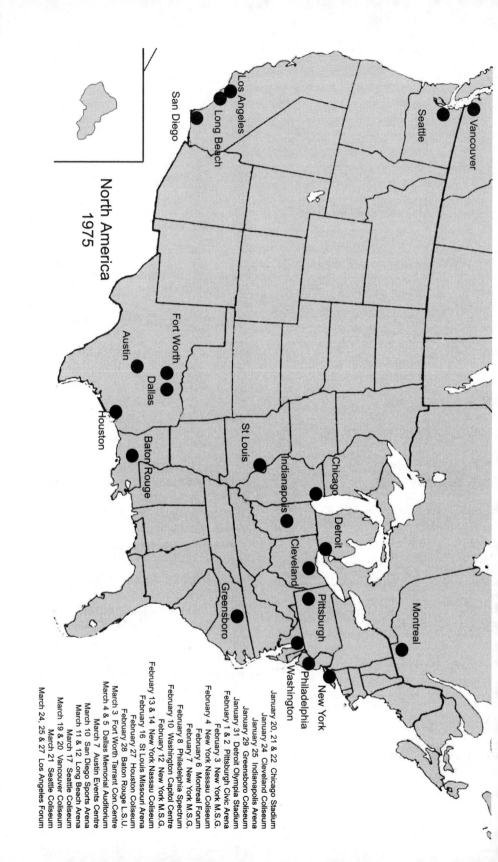

North America
1975

San Diego
Long Beach
Los Angeles

Seattle
Vancouver

Fort Worth
Austin
Dallas
Houston
Baton Rouge

St Louis
Indianapolis
Chicago
Detroit
Cleveland
Pittsburgh
Greensboro
Washington
Philadelphia
New York
Montreal

January 20, 21 & 22 Chicago Stadium
January 24 Cleveland Coliseum
January 25 Indianapolis Arena
January 29 Greensboro Coliseum
January 31 Detroit Olympia Stadium
February 1 & 2 Pittsburgh Civic Arena
February 3 New York M.S.G.
February 4 New York Nassau Coliseum
February 6 Montreal Forum
February 7 New York M.S.G.
February 8 Philadelphia Spectrum
February 10 Washington Capitol Centre
February 12 New York M.S.G.
February 13 & 14 New York Nassau Coliseum
February 16 St Louis Missouri Arena
February 27 Houston Coliseum
February 28 Baton Rouge L.S.U.
March 3 Fort Worth Tarrant Con.Centre
March 4 & 5 Dallas Memorial Auditorium
March 7 Austin Events Centre
March 10 San Diego Sports Arena
March 11 & 12 Long Beach Arena
March 17 Seattle Coliseum
March 19 & 20 Vancouver Coliseum
March 21 Seattle Coliseum
March 24, 25 & 27 Los Angeles Forum

Article outlining the riots in New York when tickets for the Madison square Gardens shows went on sale. Tickets were supposed to go on sale on the Monday but fans were waiting in freezing conditions on the Friday night. The box office opened early on the Saturday and over 50,000 seats were sold by Sunday. The remaining 10,000 tickets were then dispersed to ticket agencies around New York to take the strain off the one ticket office. Another 40,000 tickets were sold for the band's gig at Nassau Coliseum....it goes on to say that the Boston council are considering canceling the band's show in Boston due to rioting....

25 Sounds reports.... LED ZEPPELIN have been banned in Boston. Mayor Kevin White banned the group from appearing there after some 3,000 Zep fans ran wild at Boston Garden last Tuesday. The fans were allowed to stay overnight in the Garden to keep them out of the cold while waiting to buy tickets for Zep's concert to go on sale. The fans ran wild and did some 30,000 dollars worth of damage to the inside of the Garden building. As a result the mayor canceled their concert. Meanwhile an outdoor Zeppelin concert is set for March 4 at Florida's West Palm Beach Raceway which can hold up to 150,000 fans.

February 1975

1 Sounds reports.... Cover story Flu and Fractured fingers don't stop 'em anyhow. Don Heyland does a review of the band's shows in Chicago.... LED ZEPPELIN was alive, but not well in Chicago. Robert Plant's flu-ridden voice hurt the band in its first of three concerts in the Chicago stadium, the second stop on its tour.

Jimmy Page was nursing a broken finger, too, although that didn't make itself evident in any way, except perhaps choice of material. What was worst of all was the old bugaboo of rock and roll a goblin that seems to attack everyone from the most insignificant local band to the mighty supergroups: defective sound equipment. In Led Zeppelin's case it's understandable that the group wouldn't want to be burdened with maintaining its own sound system if it only tours every year and a half. But they're the ones who rented the system being used on the tour. So they must be held responsible. Perhaps the audience sitting to the right side of the stage was luckier. But from a position fairly close up and directly in front of the PA speakers on the left side of the main floor, what was audible was mostly bass and drums, with a bit of guitar squeaking through.

One thing was sure: neither John Paul Jones nor John Bonzo Bonham was under the weather. Jones's bass' lines sounded quite tasty all by themselves, and Bonham roared mightily at the drums. On 'The Song Remains The Same' Jones actually duetted with Page and very nicely. As For Plant he must have felt the irony of singing one of the five new songs, 'Sick Again' which suffered too much from mixing problems to be absorbed. Plant did manage to marshal his strength for 'Trampled Underfoot' a grinding new rocker in the best Zeppelin tradition.

The best of the new songs, 'Kashmir', did not tax his voice too much and even Page's guitar came through enough on it to show that it will be a classic. 'In My Time of Dying', the old folk standard also receives the Zeppelin treatment, and takes to it very well even though the words sometimes don't match the ripping attack by Page on slide and the booming rhythm. 'St. Peter at the gates of Heaven won't you let me in.' pleads Plant, knowing very well that the song is knocking down at those other gates.

The last new number 'Wanton Song' is another rocker. It didn't make much of an impression, but that could be because Page broke a guitar string at the start of it. Other highlights of the concert were 'Over The Hills And Far Away' with Page's fine fragile guitar work at the beginning and end contrasting with fiery playing in the middle and 'When The Levee Breaks' with Jimmy doing some marvelous slide work that I wish I could have heard better.

But of course the finale of 'Stairway To Heaven' was the highlight of the concert. It's funny that this majestic lyric number is, in the end, the song that stands for Led Zeppelin. A band associated with raunchy high decibel riffs and screaming vocals, but it definitely represents the group at its height.... **New Musical Express reports....** Lisa Robinson reports from the band's tour of the USA beginning at the Chicago Stadium gig. She manages to catch Plant in typical expansive mood. Plant, *"The Guess Who are great. Really. They're my favourite group right now. I mean, that guy who used to be the singer — we-e-ell, I just thought he was doing Robert Plant imitations. But the one now is terrific. What happened to the other guy? Randy who? BTO? Oh yeah? Are they a big group here?*

"I'll tell you, at that Chislehurst Caves function I realised I really missed the unity of the four of us. I realised that above everything else, above record companies, above films, we were Led Zeppelin -— above everything. From that moment on we started rehearsing, and getting into *full gear. Some of the new tracks already sound better than they do on the album. They're really building. So once again we recorded at just the right time—because everybody felt the same way. We worked really hard, we worked ourselves almost into the ground. I mean despite the fact that we don't see each other every day and that Bonzo lives right down the road and half the time he's at Hereford Market selling bulls, it still seems that at the right time we got together and we write something that keeps us all satisfied —musically. . . . I love the album. There are some real humdinger, roarings tracks on it— and then there are some others that are going to take a while . . . and then people will see.*

"Some of the lyrics are a bit more groinal if we can start using that phrase. We're really playing well now we're quite mature, you know. We can play stuff like 'Black Dog'— which is the Zeppelin that comes out of our ears, but we can also alter the mood with things like 'Kashmir' or 'The Song Remains The Same' or 'No Quarter' where the mood changes so beautifully. In a big auditorium that's fabulous to take the mood and change the whole thing. I was really nervous before the first gig. We're always so nervous. I dunno why, I think it's because we're so self critical. As we walked up to the stage that night Jimmy turned to me and said 'This is really deja vu, you know?', we have been here before as the heart went, into the mouth. Of course, if Jimmy gets sick or anything goes wrong with him it affects me too."

Robinson asks what he is looking forward to, *"Oh dear. Well. I've already had the biggest turn-on I could imagine, and that was going to watch Buddy Guy and Hound Dog Taylor last night. I mean, really—the blues isn't* dead. *Al Green is great, but underneath all the shim-shim, there's a town called Chicago . . . and Buddy Guy is still fantastic. You know you're getting to where the music is when that FBI guy in the front seat locks his car door . . . You can just sit there and literally shiver listening to that man, and he's playing a café and his amplifier is on top of a pinball machine.*

"You know, you're talking to The New Robert Plant. My perspective has changed on a lot of things. I've been through so many tours that now I see that there are ways and means of making it more enjoyable without having to rush into anything or burning yourself out. If there's any raping or looting about . . . well, it's done with good taste I suppose. We still manage to entertain ourselves like a right young bunch of executives."

At this point Robinson moves on to the gig and is confronted by Bonzo about the latest Playboy magazine poll results, Bonham, *"I'd like to have it publicised that I came in after Karen Carpenter in the Playboy drummer poll! She couldn't last ten minutes with a Zeppelin number."*

During the gig someone throws a roll of toilet paper on-stage and Peter Grant says *"Uh-oh. That doesn't mean Bonzo shit himself, does it?"*

The next day after a better second concert in Chicago Robinson interviews Page. He had recently broken his finger *"I'm having to develop a three-finger style. But it's a drag. It happened when I was on a train in England — on my way to rehearsal. I was at the front of the train planning to rush off and grab a taxi, when the train stopped abruptly. I must have grabbed at something, and the finger got caught in the hinge of the door. I was just totally numb— numb with shock. I just looked at it and said 'oh, no'*

. . . . I mean it's the most important finger for a guitarist: third finger, left hand. The wedding ring finger . . . It's the one that does all the leverage, and most of the work and it really came as a blow because I just couldn't play with it, I'm still not really playing with it. Last night I used it on a couple of chord changes but it still hurts. I'm starting to master a three-fingered technique though. I may start to work at this at home—work out three and two-finger techniques so that whenever there's another accident—which I'm bound to have, at the beginning of an important tour! I'll be ready for it."

Page comments about the harsh realities of touring for weeks on end, *"This time I'm going to get some Afghani hangings and my rooms are going to look like, well, like mosques. You get loads of carpets and lay them on top of each other and have everything candlelit. My home's like that, you see, and I'd like to bring my home on tour. But I can't—so I have to try this. The situation with the house now is that when people come to the door, if they've got anything worthwhile saying, they're allowed in. If they're idiots, or cranks or fanatics, they're welcome to walk around the grounds. You'd be surprised though. Some people really have a lot to say."*

Page shifts to the subject of his recently acquired book shop in London, *"The reason I got the book shop together was because there was not one book shop in London with a good collection of occult books and I was so pissed off at not being able to get the books I wanted. And whereas I can't ever see that shop making money, there'll be a bit of publishing there, astrology books and things like that."*

He then turns his attention to the upcoming movie, *"Mine's a fantasy* sequence of The Hermit—The Hermit tarot card that's on the fourth LP. Lots of laboratory work— aging faces and things like that. I was exhausted at the end of it because I had to stand up all the time . . absolutely rigid my eyes unblinking, totally constant. I really had to bring out all my yoga training for that. The hardest bit was when I had to hold the lantern out.

"Anyway, it's an interpretation of The Hermit card and when people see it, they'll understand what it's all about. It all ties in with the violin part of 'Dazed And Confused'. The movies a musical. It starts in England, shows the total tranquillity of England with just natural sounds, and then goes to the last U.S. tour. The way that it changes is really amazing, the whole pace of the tour really comes in.

"I imagine it'll come out by the summer. We haven't got much to finish — just mixing the soundtrack. I feel that there's so much to do in such a short time, you know. I've had that feeling closing in on me for the last few years. I realize that I've been playing for ten years — I don't know if people realize that. I think some of them think I'm just starting! I've enjoyed it, though. I'd like to play for another twenty years. But I don't know, I just can't see it happening. I don't know why. I can't explain it in words. It's just a funny feeling .... A foreboding . . . Vultures."

After getting only a one line sarcastic retort from John Paul Jones, Robinson is able to secure manager Peter Grant's attention for a rare interview, Grant, "There is something planned (for the UK) but it's not finalised.. It's not an outdoor festival. I can tell you that. It is a big place, in London — and will be over several nights. If everything goes fine it will be in May. I'm not being secretive, it's just that it's not finalized yet. We real-

ly don't get much flak about Zeppelin neglecting Britain in favour, of the States. Because we haven't been here so long. In the beginning there was some of that but you have to realize that when the band started (and I know it was the same for the Beck band and Ten Years After as well) the British promoters weren't really interested. They'd rather put on a reggae disco. So you had to come over here to get to people. When Zeppelin came to the States and started doing really well it suddenly dawned on them that something good was happening. But we will do three or four days in London. An indoor site."

Page, "We've wanted to play a really good gig in England for some years. The problem has always been the site. Like with that Knebworth Park thing, it was never finalized and they put us in a situation where they tried to force us to do it, and that was unforgivable. So the kids felt that we'd let them down and I suppose in a way we did let them down— but we didn't mean to.".... **Melody Maker reports....** Cover story Zeppelin Crazy. Article states that the band have started their American tour and that Physical Graffiti will be released next week retailing for £4.49. Chris Charlesworth reviews the band's show in Chicago. On the way to the show Danny Goldberg of Swan Song talks to Charlesworth, "It's amazing. The FM radio stations in New York have done a poll on what is the most requested track and for two years it's been Stairway. Nothing else comes close to it. They're always playing it." Page talks about his injury which occurred on a train in London, "I can't play any blues at all, can't bend notes either. It's the most important finger for a guitarist, so I'm having to modify my playing to suit the situation. A shame but it can't be helped. We've had to cut Dazed & Confused from *the set and substitute How Many More Times, which we haven't played in four years. I'm still doing the violin bow routine but we've had to alter even that and I can't do it as well as I'd like to. I can tell it's not as good as it usually is, but the audiences don't seem to notice. We almost canceled the tour, but we couldn't as we'd sold all the tickets and a postponement would have meant chaos. It couldn't have happened at a worse time either."* Charlesworth details the specifics of the show which included Rock and Roll, Sick Again, In My Time Of Dying, Over The Hills, Song Remains The Same, Rain Song, Kashmir, Wanton Song, No Quarter, Trampled Underfoot, Moby Dick, How Many More Times, and Stairway. He then mentions that the band are now using their own jet called the Starship, and are using Chicago as a base of operations....

3 **Pittsburgh Valley News Dispatch reports....** A cold flaws Zeppelin but legend lives on, review of the show by Rex Rutkoski.... "When Page and Plant are in top form, the music of Led Zeppelin possesses an awesome power." The show lasted two and a half hours and drew 15,000 people, but apparently Plant was suffering from throat problems due to a cold. Despite Plant's problems Rutkowski offers, "(Zeppelin) is such a fine band that even less than best is still awfully good." The set includes Rock And Roll, Sick Again, In My Time Of Dying, Stairway To Heaven, Kashmir, Moby Dick Whole Lotta Love, Black Dog, Over The Hills And Far Away, and Kashmir....

8 **New Musical Express reports....** cover story.... Robert Plant voted number one singer in the world.... Led Zeppelin the #1 group.... **Melody Maker reports....** Two

articles one chronicling the tour and one an interview with Plant. Zeppelin on tour: illness and riots. Plant is sick in a Chicago hotel room and the band have had to cancel their show in St. Louis, meanwhile the rest of the band go to Los Angeles while he recuperates. By the Wednesday Plant was fit enough to do the show in Greensboro North Carolina. Apparently 500 people stormed the back of the building with clubs and bottles and attacked the band's limousines. In a moment of panic Peter Grant was forced to take the wheel of the car and then drove at over 70 mph away from the venue with a police escort. Grant, *"I didn't care what happened so long as I got the boys out OK. That car I was driving was out of tune otherwise I'd have driven faster still."* It goes on to say that a third gig at the Nassau Coliseum was added to accommodate the ticket holders from Boston who had seen their show canceled by the city officials.... Chris Charlesworth interviews Robert Plant..... **Billboard reports....** Shoot Down Zeppelin's Boston Date. Article details the cancellation of the band's concert at the Boston Gardens due to a riot by 3,000 people waiting to buy tickets. It says it is the first Zeppelin show ever canceled and that the band have sold 330,000 tickets for a gross of $2.5 million on the whole tour....

10 **People Weekly reports....** Interview with Jimmy Page, *"Let's just say I'm like a ship passing through storms, resting in ports now and then until it's time to continue the journey. I once told a friend that I'm just looking for an angel with a broken wing, one that couldn't fly away."*....

11 **Washington Post reports....** 20 arrested in melee.... At least 20 people were arrested and eight injured during a gate

crashing attempt at a Led Zeppelin concert at the Capitol Centre....

15 **New Musical Express reports....** cover story.... A Skirmish Not For Squeamish On Starship One.... Lisa Robinson once more files a report from the band's tour of the USA. She begins with John Paul Jones, *"It seems as though the whole business is getting older. It used to be that everyone was around twenty now everyone seems to be veering around thirty. Wonder what the energy level will be like in twenty years from now. It's amazing really, because when I think about it. I'm doing exactly what my father used to do. He was a musician, played in a lot of big bands traveled on the road, strange hotel rooms all the time."* The band are en route from New York to play in Detroit. Robinson muses over the luxurious trappings of the band's private jet with it's TV's and fur covered beds. She then observes a verbal battle between Page and a mainstream journalist. Page is furious stating, *"Can you imagine, that man referred to my guitar playing as a trade! I didn't go to vocational school."* After trailing the band to Detroit and relating a series of amusing anecdotes Robinson moves on to the band's gig in New York where they revive 'Dazed & Confused' for the first time in the tour due to Page having been injured. The band then retire to a post concert party at the Penn Plaza Club where they are joined by Keith Moon, and Andy Warhol amongst others.... At a Slade concert last year in Texas, members of Led Zeppelin sitting in the balcony threw assorted vegetables at the band...at one point someone threw a boot which bounced off Noddy Holder's head.... **Melody Maker reports....** Six show Zeppelin Blast Off. Article states that Zeppelin will be playing six shows,

three at the Madison Square Gardens and three at Nassau Coliseum. Chris Charlesworth mentions that the band have now begun to include Dazed & Confused in the set as Page's finger is now healing....

22 **New Musical Express reports....** Apparently Jimmy Page was once with Mickey Finn and The Bluemen....

28 **Swan Song press release....**

LED ZEPPELIN EXPRESSES DISAPPOINTMENT OVER CANCELLATION OF "FLORIDA ROCK" FESTIVAL

The members of Led Zeppelin, who returned today for the resumption of their 1975 American tour, expressed disappointment over the cancellation of the "Florida Rock" festival which the group had been scheduled to headline on March 8th.

Florida Rock was canceled last week by David Rupp owner of the West Palm Beach Speedway where the event was supposed to take place. Rupp gave as his reason for cancellation, the failure of the promoters, Connecticut Concerts Corporation, to begin the improvements on the property he considered necessary for a successful event. Primary among these was paving of parking space for the anticipated 60,000 cars the event was expected to have attracted.

Danny Goldberg, vice-president of Swan Song, Led Zeppelin's record company, commented following the cancellation: *"The group and their manager Peter Grant are very disappointed that they will be unable to play Florida on this tour due to circumstances utterly beyond their control. I know that they have a very special feeling for Florida, due in part to the fact that the biggest concert they ever played was in Tampa, Florida at the Stadium there in 1973."* (The Tampa Stadium concert on May 5, 1973 in fact stands as the record for the largest paid attendance ever to see a musical act perform: 56,800.) Following the cancellation of the West Palm Beach festival, a variety of ideas for other dates for Zeppelin to play in Florida were reported in the Florida press. It was reported that the Mayor's office in Miami was attempting to make the Orange Bowl available for a proposed concert by Zeppelin which would benefit the Pediatric Center in Florida. No firm proposal however was ever received by Steven H. Weiss, who is the Attorney and Administrator for Led Zeppelin and for Swan Song. On February 26th, Weiss sent the following telegram to Frank Cobo, Assistant to the Mayor of Miami, explaining that the time was now too late to logistically put together a Led Zeppelin concert in Florida. The text of his telegram was as follows:

"Mr. Frank Cobo Assistant to the Mayor of Miami City of Miami City Hall Denner Key Miami, Florida 33133

Dear Mr. Cobo:
No definite proposal for Led Zeppelin to play Orange Bowl on March 8 or any other date has been received either from Pediatric Center or any other party and therefore there is not even anything for me to submit to President of Swan Song and group manager for his consideration. Efforts of Miami Mayor to make Orange Bowl available for Led Zeppelin concert are much appreciated and the charity is undoubtedly a worthy one. However, since nothing concrete has been submitted for consideration of Swan Song President and group manager it is now no

longer feasible from time point of view to put together a proper and artistic concert for March 8 even if a firm offer was now received. Further there is no other feasible open time period available on remainder of 1975 tour to play Orange Bowl so therefore any consideration of Led Zeppelin playing Orange Bowl this tour no longer feasible. Hope that the Orange Bowl will be made available for next tour. Florida is a very special place for the Led Zeppelin and they like playing Florida very much. I believe they would be most interested in a charity concert at the Orange Bowl on their next tour.

Sincerely,
Steven H. Weiss
Attorney for Swan Song and Led Zeppelin

Creem reports.... Cover story - Jimmy Page tongues his axe. Reprint of Nick Kent's interview in New Musical Express October 12th 1974....

Circus reports.... Brief interview with Robert Plant, *"I'm just a fun loving guy, I don't know whether all those stories are true. I mean we have good times. I've got the curtains drawn just in case I fancy throwing a journalist out the window!*
    "I've found more intricate ways to enjoy myself. At the tender age of 25, I've done so many things and I've had so many fantastic times. Oh, I know I'm a bubbly character. Especially when the sun shines.
    He is asked what interests him at the moment, *"Swan Song, our record company. A lot of groups have formed labels in the last two years and a lot of companies have been prepared to distribute them, even though there's only one group on that label, which is a bit of an*

ego trip. It doesn't really fulfill the station of owning one's own label.

"I didn't start Swan Song to make more bread. I mean, what are we going to do with any more bread? I live in a modest way. I live on the borders of Wales with people I've known for years. I'm sentimental. I'd like to think that people pick up more on that side of me than the image of a street-fighting, chop-a-baby's-head-off-once-a-day and take four quaaludes after each meal image.

"Plant is a Welsh word that means a group of people, a family. I'm not a sensible thoughtful person, but I love the feeling of togetherness with people, I love my work, which is communication on a vast level. Like how good it feels in an auditorium when the vibes are good. My lyrics are more to me than anything you've heard about me from the waist below.

"Rock and roll is big business, there are lousy groups that have made it and there always will be. Some companies will spend millions of dollars on Dick and his Two Swingers and they'll be a big group too. But that kind of stuff doesn't suit me. It's not fair to lay that on the audiences, to hype bad people, and brain-wash the record buying public. You must have a moral code, like me."

Rock & Folk reports.... Cover story. This French magazine gives a brief review of the band's warm-up concert in Rotterdam which was attended by 5,000 or 6,000 'pretty cool old hippies and students'. They were treated to a concert of perfect hard rock although the reviewer says the band needs more heart....Review of Physical Graffiti a re-print of the Nick Kent article from the previous December in NME. In an interview with Robert Plant he reveals a few details about the band's concerts in France and their new label Swan Song. The first thing he is asked is whether he will be producing the albums? *"No we envision a collaboration we are very straight with our artists. It may be that I may sing, or Jimmy might play or Bonzo or John Paul but we will basically let them do their thing."*

He is then asked whether he will be recording any solo albums. *"None of us have any desire to do any solo project we are very occupied with Led Zeppelin and as for me I don't know who else I could record with other than Jimmy Page."*

He is asked who they have signed, *"The Pretty Things, Roy Harper and Bad Co."*

Interviewer Jacques Chabiron comments about how big Bad Co. is in America, *"And in England but they're not very big in this country. Whatever, it's great for them and for us because Swan Song is rapidly becoming known and that's before our own album comes out. I like Paul Rodgers very much. I'm happy with the success he's had with this group. And I think that their next LP, which is coming out soon will have the advantage of being the follow-up to a very successful album.*

"The Pretty Things have always been one of my favorite groups. But they've never had the success that they deserve. Even if all groups have highs and lows, you know they've been around a long long time. I think they've just needed a label that can offer them help, that will understand them and help them in a rational and positive way."

Chabiron comments that Roy Harper is practically an unknown. *"Yes that's true and we don't miss any chance to talk about it. It's a difficult case, because well, he is sure of his own talent.*

He is a strange man you know, he does not want to make any concessions absolutely no concessions. It upsets us to see a man so talented....by the way have you heard his latest album on Harvest? Anyway it upsets us that he's not as well known as he should be."

He is then asked whether he expects to make a lot of money out of Swan Song. *"Certainly not. that's not the reason for the label. If that were the case we would have signed groups that sell a lot more albums. Bad Company, well we didn't know anything, we didn't know what was going to happen. That was just good luck. Even if everybody thought they were good. The Pretty Things, I don't think there'll be any problem, but Roy Harper, I really don't know. As for the other artists. Well I'm sure they're not the type that are going to make us millions of dollars. Many (other groups) have been contacted.*

"I don't think that the Rolling Stones make a lot of money with Rolling Stones Records. If that's what they had wanted from the beginning then I think they wouldn't have done it. Apart from the Stones there is nothing else on that label, and they don't look like they'll be signing any other artists. And even more so now that they're not working with Jimmy Miller any more. Apple was a very different matter. That was created from the beginning as a commercial enterprise. That would not only deal with Beatle records and their productions but also other things that have nothing to do with music. The boutiques etc. Things that existed only because of the Beatles fame. Everything went badly because there was no more consensus between them and it was badly managed. They weren't businessmen and neither are we. We certainly wouldn't do anything similar to the

Beatles. We're certainly not after that. We'll stay in the music and very close to the music."

Chabiron then asks how Zeppelin is doing, *"We're doing very well. We're almost finished our double album, the mixing is done except if Jimmy decides to re-mix this one song. But I don't think so. But now what is delaying the album is the cover. Jimmy has an idea and I have another and we really can't agree. Normally this double album should come out in January. But people know when LZ says January it could also mean the end of December or the beginning of March. It's an album that will surprise people, because it's full of new things that we've never tried. But I think that's normal. Where would the interest be if there was never any surprises?"*

Will they tour? *"We're speaking vaguely about a world tour but there's nothing set as of yet."*

Does he remember the last European tour? *"In France a lot of different things happened. We started our last trip in France then we went to Germany, then Switzerland, then Belgium, then again to Germany which was crazy. Plus we took the wrong route as well. We had our fill of customs, and there was always problems with what we were bringing from each country especially at the border after our concert in Lyons."*

There were fights in Lyons, right? *"It was very unpleasant. Fights during the concert....especially when you want to concentrate on the music, and then when everything became quiet then the fans started to fight with the security."*

Is it possible that your music incites violence? *"No. No. Of course it depends what you mean by violence. If you look closely our music is quite far from what you would call violent. I'd say myself our music is quite positive. I think that the lyrics represent pretty well the essence of man. The energy that is spent from a man walking, you know? One foot in front of the other, very simply. Anyway something like that I've seen happen quite often. Every time a rock group plays there are always some types who think it's OK to come in break some windows, hit a few fans, leave by breaking some more windows, come back and cause more damage, over and over again. So this time I found that Stairway To Heaven didn't make much sense but apart from that it's a nice calm city. So I thought that all of this happened because everyone was anxious to see us.*

"Anyway we weren't feeling that great on the road to Nancy and when we arrived we saw that the concert was in a big hall that could hold 8,000 people and the building was completely enclosed with these big metal fences that we had to get through. We looked for the promoter but he disappeared. Just forgetting all of his responsibilities. He left us this caravan behind the stage. It was a really comfortable caravan but we couldn't get to it because it was behind these big metal fences that were locked and nobody could open them. So our manager told us to lie down on the floor of our car to avoid broken glass and we went... bang...right through the fence. That's really too bad because anything could have happened that night and it wasn't possible to ensure the safety of the 8,000 spectators that were there, but all in all we played very well.

"I think we were a little violent, justifiably so, that night. But afterward we were completely discouraged because the promoter had disappeared and so we left the first chance we could. Usually we would decide when we start and stop

playing, our tours are usually very well organized and we have a reputation for arriving on time and doing our job, which I think is pretty rare in the annals of rock groups but this time it was too much and we left."

Does he think that by touring so infrequently they may lose their fan base? *"Maybe, maybe not. I think we have to take the time to change our direction not only collectively but individually. The group acts like an individual who, within him, has different tendencies that have to be expressed differently. The last time we toured France and Germany it was two years non-stop that we were touring with only two weeks of rest. Two weeks in two years! So we thought it was time to rest up and take it easy. So we went to the USA and we rested for about a year.*

"During that year, when you thought our popularity went down, we were very busy doing other things. I think that we still create interest in ourselves as much as when we played, because the time that we were not on tour was utilized to develop new directions for our music, and the interest that our fans bring to us continues, because they know we are coming out with a double album and that our popularity is as big as it ever was.

"Maybe I said that for my own ego....because it's not really apparent. I see other proof though. Everybody that I meet seems to be very excited by this double album, they're waiting for something and they're waiting for something different."

Chabiron points out that the band never act like rock stars. And that their silence doesn't help them defend themselves when their albums are criticised by the media. *"I think they'll understand one day. Critics should never be in a hurry to talk about an album. It takes a long time to understand and get a good idea what it's all about. That's what happened with us with our third and fourth albums. We have no reason to predict how an album's going to go and to explain it. It's what we were like at the time that's really how it works. Why should we make efforts that we couldn't justify?"*

But what if the audience is caught off guard by their changes in direction? *"You may be right. Maybe not. For us it's simple. We choose what we like best and put it on the record. We like to surprise and we think that it's a bad idea to always follow the same formula. We want to do things that excite us."*....

March 1975

1 **Sounds reports**.... Full page advert on the back cover for Physical Graffiti.... **New Musical Express reports**.... full page advert on the back cover for Physical Graffiti.... review of Physical Graffiti by Steve Clarke.... Kiss Your Skull Goodbye.... "Physical Graffiti is confirmation that the group have lost none of their inspiration or ability....".... Clarke does a track by track analysis before concluding, "Hard rock lives, and how."…. **Melody Maker reports**.... Review of Physical Graffiti by Michael Oldfield. Headline reads, Led Zeppelin: pure genius. Oldfield starts out with how the band take a lot of flak for not working often enough. He then calls Physical Graffiti 'a work of genius'. He praises the band for taking the time to deliver a work of real quality. After a complete song by song breakdown he concludes, 'They can take as long as they like with the next album: Physical Graffiti will last 18 months or 18 years and then some.'....full page advert for Physical Graffiti....

2 **Baton Rouge Sunday Advocate reports**.... Review of the show with headline Zeppelin Decibel Rate Deafening. "Led Zeppelin, reportedly the most popular rock band in the world, tried to destroy the LSU Assembly Center with sound Friday night....The group displayed an uninspiring range of diversity....despite these shortcomings the group received a favourable response from the audience. The concert was delayed for 20 minutes because of the crowd's pushing toward the front."....

8 **Sounds reports**.... two page advert for Earl's Court concerts.... Writing On the Wall, Steve Peacock reviews Physical Graffiti. Sounds reporter Peacock shows that it takes all kinds, when he swiftly dismisses sides one and two of the album (and thus Kashmir, Trampled Underfoot, In My Time Of Dying) in one swift stroke of the critics pen. He calls 'In My Time Of Dying' "acutely tiresome" and Kashmir one of the album's weaknesses "where riffing strings become irritatingly overplayed". While he does acknowledge the band's individual talents he swiftly comes back with an example where he thinks they don't use them, "I find him (Page) a rather too calculating guitar player, particularly as a soloist, but interesting nonetheless. I like Robert Plant best when he is disciplined in form, paradoxically he seems awfully stylised when given his head on long improvised things like In My Time Of Dying."…. **New Musical Express reports**.... Mick Jagger and Ron Wood were spotted at Led Zeppelin's post concert party in New York.... Physical Graffiti is #8 in the UK....

13 **Los Angeles Times reports**.... Led Zeppelin Clichés and all.... scathing

review of the Long Beach show by music critic Robert Hilburn, "The Tuesday night show was a numbing combination of intense, tenacious music and hopelessly limited imagination." Hilburn goes on to acknowledge that the audience response was, "quite strong in spots," he goes on, "the band's limitations .... were simply too obvious to ignore..." He does condescend to recognising Page's skills with the guitar but then offers, "the music end's up as an empty exercise in sound." ....

15 **Sounds reports....** Cover Story.... Zeppelin 3 Days At Earl's Court.... As Sounds was the first to report last week Led Zeppelin are to play three concerts at Earl's Court on May 23- 25. Tickets will be £2.50 to £1.00. Tickets go on sale on Saturday March 15 at 10 am around the country. There will be no support act and the show will begin at 8 pm each night. In order to counteract the problems with the size of the Earl's Court arena the band will bring over their American stage equipment and the stage will be 8' high reducing the number of seats available each night to 17,000. .... **New Musical Express reports....** cover story.... El Zep three gigs for May 25 to 27 at Earl's Court in London.... announcement of the impending dates at Earl's Court on May 23-25. The article outlines that they are the only European dates on the band's schedule and that they are being promoted by Mel Bush. The band will begin each night at 8 pm and will feature material from Physical Graffiti. Tickets are priced from £1 to £2.50 and box offices will open on the following Saturday. A spokesman for Swan Song announced, "Earl's Court was chosen for two reasons. Firstly it enables the largest number of people to see Zeppelin in an enclosed venue, a total of over 50,000 will attend

during the three days. And secondly, it is the most central of all London venues, particularly for those traveling from the provinces. It doesn't matter where they are coming from, Liverpool, Newcastle, Glasgow, Cardiff or Bournemouth, they can go straight into the Tube on arriving at their London terminus, and catch a train direct to Earl's Court. There's a very good service from all key provincial cities, even those traveling from Glasgow won't need to leave until noon on the day of the concert. And a final point is that no one need worry about attending the Sunday concert, because they won't have to work the following day, it's Spring Bank holiday.".... two page advert.... Physical Graffiti is #3 in the UK.... **Melody Maker reports....** Cover Story, Zeppelin's May Daze! Article outlining the band's upcoming shows at Earl's Court. Promoter Mel Bush says, "If we'd played say, a 20 date tour, playing at all the normal venues, only 40,000 or so people would've been able to see the band. But this way, Led Zeppelin will be able to present their full American show, in front of more people." It goes on to say that Physical Graffiti is now #9 in the MM charts and then incorrectly states that it is their first shows in Britain since their appearances at Wembley's Empire Pool two years before....full page reads Mel Bush In Association With Peter Grant Led Zeppelin Earl's Court Fri 23rd Sat 24th Sun 25th Doors open 6 pm....

22 **New Musical Express reports....** Earl's Court is a complete sell-out.... Zepmania in London. Article describes the huge lines outside Earl's Court which began on the Thursday night (the day the shows were announced in the press). By Saturday the line was nearly a mile long. Apparently everyone queuing managed to

get a ticket by late afternoon. All the other ticket offices up and down the country were also sold out and the mail order had to return tens of thousands of applications.... Physical Graffiti is #2 in the UK.... **Sounds reports....** Led Zeppelin Score Gold and Platinum.... On it's first day in release Physical Graffiti was awarded gold and platinum status in the USA. The album which entered the UK charts at #1 and the US charts at #3 shipped a million copies on it's first day of release. It is the sixth Led Zeppelin album to go platinum but it is a double album with a retail price of $11.98 and thus initial orders exceed $10 million. Jerry Wexler President of Atlantic Records stated, *"No album in Atlantic history has generated so many immediate sales."* Meanwhile Led Zeppelin have expressed considerable disappointment at the cancellation of their proposed one day concert at the West Palm Beach Speedway in Florida. The cancellation was due to the Promoters Connecticut Concerts Corporation failure to pave the parking lot to hold the expected 60,000 cars. Consequently it is now too late for Led Zeppelin to arrange another concert in Florida.... **Billboard reports....** No Paving No Zeppelin In Florida. Article detailing the cancellation of the band's gig at the Florida Speedway. Apparently promoters Shelly Finkel and Jim Koplik did not do upgrades to the parking lot to accommodate the influx of cars expected and so the owner of the facility canceled the concert leaving the promoters $200,000 out of pocket in an advance to Zeppelin and another $50,000 in advertising. 25,000 tickets were sold in advance. The article goes on to mention that Physical Graffiti is number one and that the band have ruled out a substitute Florida date at the Orange Bowl due to

the bathrooms being refurbished....

Extra Encyclorock reports.... Review of Physical Graffiti and the two concerts in Rotterdam and Brussels. All the more important because the review covers the first gigs of 1975 with the early set list.... "We've been waiting all summer and almost two years since the release of the album Houses Of The Holy for the release of Physical Graffiti. The first pressing of Led Zeppelin on their own label Swan Song. It contains two records which approximate the sound of their first and fourth albums. The cover art which contributed to the delay of the album represents a facade of an apartment building where the windows are cut out to show people within the dust jacket with the possibility of animating it like a strip tease sequence. After examining the packaging there's nothing to do except listen to the four sides by Jimmy Page, John Paul Jones, John Bonham and Robert Plant. Custard Pie starts the album off in a style of savage rock of pure Led Zeppelin style. The Rover continues the theme of the first song and the side ends in a paroxysm of rhythmic power lasting eleven minutes with In My Time Of Dying where John Bonham, John Paul Jones, Jimmy Page and Robert Plant explode with energy.

The second side starts less ferocious with Houses Of The Holy which has nothing to do with the album of the same name, and the memory erases itself after listening to Physical Graffiti. The next song Zep leaves their regular style to try some soul music with Trampled Underfoot before entering a type of exotic oriental music with Kashmir where the harmonies between the guitars of Jimmy Page and the mellotron of John Paul Jones is very successful.

With the second disc Led

315

LED ZEPPELIN.
"PHYSICAL GRAFFITI."

Zeppelin with In The Light takes a bit of spirit of the preceding cut in the intro. and multiplies the variations with numerous breaks before starting Bron-y-Aur an instrumental based on multi-tracked acoustic guitar. This is a technique that Zeppelin uses often, principally for Page but also for Plant. Down By The Seaside is treated in a similar manner but with the support of voices until the bridge. The side ends with Ten Years Gone a strong soothing ballad. I must say that we need some soothing because we start the fourth side a little bit like the first side with a very catchy aggressive rock song called Night Flight followed by The Wanton Song in the same style. Boogie With Stu, the next song, is a boogie, as the name indicates, with the participation of Ian Stewart the Stones pianist. After Black Country Woman an acoustic composition in a folk-blues vein we close off the album with a beautiful song called Sick Again a fantastic R&R of the best kind. Physical Graffiti no more and no less than Led Zeppelin at it's best....

The two concerts by Led Zeppelin in Rotterdam on the 11th of January and Brussels on the 12th were basically rehearsals before an important American tour. It was a pretext for Jimmy Page, John Paul Jones, John Bonham and Robert Plant to go on stage before their public and finally work out the songs of their new double album and to include them in their repertoire. The crowd seemed to be surprised by the new compositions by Plant and Page but they still longed for the classics such as a rock medley of Whole Lotta Love or even Heartbreaker but they didn't play them. Success was important at this show. The approximately 6,000 spectators at the Forest National, were too aware of being at an event, the return of Zeppelin, to real-ly feel let down. You could tell that Plant and Page had a simple plan, to show their enthusiasm for their new music. They did How Many More Times and Communication Breakdown although at this concert the musicians did not look at ease which might be explained by their long absence from the stage. There was no surprises to this show other than the new music.

Led Zeppelin needs to create a new empathy for each other and there is no doubt they will succeed and that the four musicians will come back from their American tour with a show as convincing as those of the past. After an absence of close to two years Led Zeppelin seems destined to be as important this year as in other years."....

24 **Swan Song press release....** LED ZEPPELIN "PHYSICAL GRAFFITI" LP NUMBER ONE AFTER TWO WEEKS. ALL FIVE PREVIOUS ZEPPELIN ALBUMS RETURN TO BILLBOARD CHART WITH BULLETS IN HISTORY MAKING OCCURRENCE!

Led Zeppelin's new album, "Physical Graffiti," is number one in all three music trades, Billboard, Cashbox and Record World, as well as in England, Australia, and several other countries around the world.

In an even more extraordinary development, all five previous Led Zeppelin albums, Led Zeppelin, Led Zeppelin II, Led Zeppelin III, Led Zeppelin (the group's fourth album) and "Houses Of The Holy" all went back on the Billboard charts with bullets this week at the following positions: Led Zeppelin I - #83, Led Zeppelin II - #104, Led Zeppelin III - #124, Led Zeppelin (IV)- #116, Houses Of The Holy - #92.

No other artist in history has ever had six albums on the charts at the same time.

Furthermore, two weeks is the fastest that any album has ever gone to number one. Both Billboard (where the album went to number three the first week) and Record World (where it had a debut at number five) announced that "Physical Graffiti" had the highest first-week chart number in their history. "Physical Graffiti's" chart performance is all the more extraordinary because it is a two record set with a retail price of $11.98.

Zeppelin completes their 1975 American tour this week with three concerts at the L.A. Forum on March 24, 25 and 27th. All 35 concerts on the tour -- which began on January 18th have been sold out.

"Physical Graffiti" is on Zeppelin's own label, Swan Song. That label is currently one of the hottest in the business. In addition to the Zeppelin album, Swan Song has three other albums on the charts, The Pretty Things "Silk Torpedo," Maggie Bell's "Suicide Sal," and Bad Company's "Bad Co." A new Bad Company album, "Straight Shooter," is scheduled for release later this month. It is believed that no other label started by a rock group has ever had four albums on the charts at the same time. Combined with the Zeppelin albums -- this makes nine albums on the charts for the young Swan Song organisation. Swan Song is owned by the members of Led Zeppelin and their manager Peter Grant. In the United States it is run by vice-president Danny Goldberg and Attorney and Administrator Steve Weiss.

27 **Rolling Stone reports....** Full page advert for Physical Graffiti.... Jim Miller reviews Physical Graffiti and acknowl-

edges that it is, "a tour-de-force. The band's Beggar's Banquet and Sergeant Pepper rolled into one." From Rolling Stone this is a RAVE review. He doesn't follow through with much detail about the album but wallows trying to explain the band's popularity, still this IS Rolling Stone....

29 **New Musical Express reports....** Physical Graffiti is #1 in the UK.... Robert Plant and Jimmy Page were spotted at the Troubadour in Los Angeles with Al Kooper.... Led Zeppelin, J Geils and Bachman Turner Overdrive are slated for the Florida Rock Festival....

April 1975

5 **New Musical Express reports....** Physical Graffiti is #1 in the UK....

12 **New Musical Express reports....** Physical Graffiti is #1 in the UK.... **Melody Maker reports....** Article headline reads, Zep Tickets 'We were fair'....The article states that Melody Maker have received a lot of complaints about the lack of tickets out side London, the lack of gigs outside of London and the lack of security at the ticket office. It says that only 10,000 of the possible 51,000 tickets were available outside of London while 11,000 were held back to deal with mail-order responses. Apparently over 100,000 applications were received in the mail. In the ticket lines there was a lot of shoving due to a lack of security. Mel Bush the promoter, *"There was a bit of shoving in the first hour when people were getting excited after the box-office opened. This was because people were pushing forward and those who had got their tickets couldn't get out. When you*

*have a queue that long you're liable to get a chain reaction of panic, people can't see how they'll ever get a ticket. So I went along that queue with a loud-hailer personally assuring everybody in the queue that they would get a ticket. After that everything went smoothly, we sold 30,000 tickets in six hours. The problem is that whenever the demand exceeds the supply, as in this case, you'll always get complaints. There's no way you can avoid it. If you queue for five hours and don't get a ticket, you'll think that some kind of postal lottery system is better, but if you do get a ticket, then there won't be too many complaints."....*Article reviewing the band's shows in Los Angeles which mentions that the band had grown since their first appearance there at the Whisky in 1969. Although reviewer Justin Pierce doesn't think much of Physical Graffiti or the band's lengthy solos he does conclude that, 'It was a convincing and sometimes outstanding performance that reaffirms Zeppelin's status.'....

19 New Musical Express reports.... Physical Graffiti is #5 in the UK.... Zeppelin add two more gigs at Earl's Court.... due to the unprecedented response Led Zeppelin have added a further two shows at Earl's Court. Over 100,000 mail order applications have been returned due to the huge demand. Promoter Mel Bush, *"We intended to see that everyone who queues for tickets at Earl's Court will be accommodated. I am fully aware of complaints regarding the lack of tickets but if you're a real ardent Zeppelin fan and are prepared to queue then you should be given the facility of getting a good seat. If we sold by mail order only, it would mean that anyone could get seats and the real Zeppelin fan might not be the lucky ones drawn. We feel that our method is the fairest way, even though I realise that there will still be complaints from those who don't get a ticket. I am sorry that those who have had their money refunded have now got to start all over again, but these two concerts were not premeditated. Once Zeppelin had agreed to do them we had to panic to get new tickets printed at a rush cost of £1,000."* Zeppelin will now play to over 85,000 people over the five nights.... picture of Jimmy Page with William Burroughs.... Burt Sugarman producer of Midnight Special in the USA has been told he can have Led Zeppelin on his show if he finds Jimmy Page a Martin B-1 guitar of which only six were made.... full page advert for two extra gigs in London.... **Sounds reports....** Cover story.... Extra Dates For Zep.... Led Zeppelin are to play two extra concerts at Earl's Court on May 17 and 18 in addition to the three dates announced for May 23, 24, 25. A further 34,000 people will attend bringing the total to 85,000. Tickets have been rush printed to be at agencies by Saturday April 19 at 10 am. Only four tickets will be available per person.... **Melody Maker reports....** Cover Story, Extra Zep....article with details of the two extra shows added for Earl's Court on May 17th and 18th. Tickets were slated to go on sale that week with better security due to the complaints the previous month....full page Advert reads — Due to Unprecedented Demand in the history of rock music Extra Concerts Sat May 17 and Sun May 18....

26 New Musical Express reports.... Physical Graffiti is #8 in the UK....

May 1975

3 New Musical Express reports.... Physical Graffiti is #9 in the UK.... ticket contest....

10 New Musical Express reports.... Physical Graffiti is #15 in the UK.... **Melody Maker reports....** The Led Zeppelin Story, part one in a huge two week retrospective of the band's career by Chris Welch. Welch covers the details of the band's career from 1968 and 1969. The article features many more eye-openers for the fact starved British Zeppelin fan.

17 New Musical Express reports.... Physical Graffiti is #17 in the UK.... cover story.... Everything you ever wanted to know about Led Zeppelin.... double page article compiled by Howard Mylett and Roy Carr. Probably the first really in depth article covering neat trivia of the band's beginnings. In this article you are introduced to John Bonham riding his motorcycle through the lobby of the Hyatt in LA, John Paul Jones real name (Baldwin) Page's early production credits, the band's birthdays and places of birth, the costs of wrecking dressing rooms, and the fee earned in a bar in Bombay (a bottle of scotch). It is packed with insights many of which have gone on to be the stuff of legend. It also includes a reprint from **Record Mirror** of their article on Robert Plant from 1967, it pictures Plant as an aspiring 18 year old singer which reads, "Gent with the beard, the solemn expression and the beads is Robert Plant, recently out with a CBS release 'Long Time Coming'. So happens I specially liked this record and checked into his background. He's 18,

Birmingham born, grammar school educated, with A levels in English, history, civics and maths. Started singing two years ago with a group called Listen. First disc solo was 'Our Song', recognised by Robert as a gigantic flop. He plays violin (!), piano, organ and guitar. Now he works, all over the country with his backing group 'The Band Of Joy'. Already his disc has hit the Birmingham Top Twenty which is at least Plant-ing the seeds of his talent." .... Another gem dug up by Carr and Mylett is the review of John Paul Jones solo single from April 17th 1964, which reads, "John Paul Jones, bass guitarist from the Tony Meehan Combo, offers a beaty instrumental with novelty tambourine effects. Weak melody, but compelling rhythm. Main gimmick of 'A Foggy Day In Vietnam' lies in it's title, sounds like the chords of a beat ballad without the vocal." .... **Melody Maker reports....** Cover story Zeppelin Lift-Off, announcement of the impending concerts at Earl's Court which will include 17,000 people per night, 340,000 watts of lighting a 24 by 30 foot video screen and a 24,000 watt P.A.... The Led Zeppelin Story, part two by Chris Welch. Welch covers the details of the band's career from 1970 to 1975. His most daring revelation being to actually picture the bootleg "Live On Blueberry Hill" which must have not sat too well with Grant.

24 Sounds reports.... cover story...This Gig Is Scarred On My Brain For Life by Pete Makowski. "In six and a half years Led Zeppelin are THE biggest and judging by the excellence of their performance at Earl's Court last Sunday, one of, if not the most exciting live acts in the world." Makowski is unabashed with his gushing praise, (I can't blame him it was a HELL of a show). He runs through the show song by song describing every nuance before concluding, "The audience left shattered and satisfied. Those who weren't obviously expected miracles. The show had the dynamism, excitement and sheer professionalism that some people say represents the ultimate in rock. Somehow I find it difficult to argue with that.".... **New Musical Express reports....** Physical Graffiti is #23 in the UK.... cover story.... Earl's Court report.... Charles Shaar Murray reviews the show. Murray falls victim to the trend of comparing the band to the Who. Something which seems to become more commonplace as the band's career progressed. He comments, "Led Zeppelin are so English that if they weren't they'd have to be German." He continues, "Page's guitar playing ...blazes with inhuman energy. John Bonham's drumming represents an enormous amount of raging energy channeled into specific areas. John Paul Jones contributions are so goddamn self-effacing...he's as much the archetype of the Stolid Anchor Man bassist as any rock and roll ideologue could desire. But the man who gives Zeppelin their real wildness is Robert Plant. (His) siren howl and primping strut make Zeppelin undoubtedly the world's champion male chauvinist fantasy band." Murray seems disturbed by the band's efficiency complaining that they are an exercise in contradictions, "How can you be a controlled berserker?" he asks. His conclusion, "They're like a vibrator. It can get you off something ridiculous, but it can't kiss you goodnight.".... Led Zeppelin issue secret single. Article reveals the band's intentions to release Trampled Underfoot backed with Black Country Woman in the UK. Only 5,000 copies were pressed, each one being given out free when a store owner bought a five album package of Zeppelin

albums.... **Melody Maker reports....** Cover story, superb cover photo of Plant and Page on stage at Earl's Court with the headline "Front Page".... Article outlines 34,000 people attended the three hour performances.... article by Edward Jones about the rising inflation on concert tickets. On asking Earl's Court promoter Mel Bush whether Zeppelin are ripping off the public with a top ticket price of £2.50, Bush, "*Zeppelin are not going to make any money out of Earl's Court on five shows. This is a fact. All the equipment's coming in from America, and they've got to fly it in. Work out what it costs to hire an airplane from Dallas Texas. Any band that sells a lot of records in a country has a moral responsibility to play. We could have charged £3 or £4 a ticket and we'd still have got the people in there you know?*".... Chris Welch reviews the Saturday 17th performance, "Led Zeppelin came among us like avenging angels at the weekend." At the show Plant became something of a raconteur between songs and Welch quotes many of the sound-bytes which for some reason have become extremely familiar due to the miracle of bootlegging. "That was the first time that we've had four part harmony on stage with Led Zeppelin," he boasts after Tangerine. Yes even Bonham sang. After admitting Robert Johnson's Terraplane Blues was the source of inspiration for Trampled Underfoot, at which point Bonham accuses him of stealing the lyrics, the band rip into the song, Welch, "This was the band firing on all cylinders, at their absolute best." After suggesting that the sheer size of the event overwhelmed many British fans, he concludes, "It was a splendid return, proof that Zeppelin have their strength and imagination intact." ...The Ultimate Trip, review of the Sunday show by Michael

Oldfield. "...before Led Zeppelin had got far into their set...it became obvious this was the definitive rock performance...it's inconceivable that another band could do as well." Oldfield then philosophises about the band's no-nonsense approach. "Plant and Page pose and strut proud as peacocks, lords of the jungle. Jones hugs the shadows wearing a look of quiet intensity while Bonham is grim-faced as he piles on the pressure, the stoker of the Zeppelin express." He concludes that the audience cheered for at least ten minutes for an encore (as they did the previous night), "We came, we saw, they conquered."

31 New Musical Express reports.... Physical Graffiti is #20 in the UK.... three young students were busted in Seattle for ripping off their teacher's rare guitar and giving it to Jimmy Page.... **Sounds reports....** Letter to the editor.... a punter complains about the seats at Earl's Court. "We paid £2.50 to Mel Bush Productions, promoters for the Zeppelin concerts at Earl's Court and what we saw was a gantry of lights and stacks of amplifiers. What would we have seen if we'd paid only £1? For £2.50 we couldn't even see the screen." The editor replies by stating that Mel Bush had foreseen the problem and had put aside 400 seats for people who may have had an obstructed view once the equipment was installed. However instead of the people with genuine grievances getting the unobstructed seats people from the cheap seats quickly cashed in and moved into the more expensive seating.... **Melody Maker reports....** Dazed & Confused, review of the band's show the previous Saturday at Earl's Court by Steve Lake. In what has to be one of the most unlikely reviews ever, Lake knocks the stuffing out of the band.

He calls Moby Dick, '...so much the archetypal duff rock drum solo that it was hard to believe....20 minutes of stultifying indulgence crowned with laughable electronic stereo effects. John Bonham has no musical intelligence at all.' He then targets Jones as being 'too intelligent' for being over-fussy and distracting. He then has a go at the choice of material suggesting the band have no faith in the new songs. He does at least recognise that Plant is 'genuinely inventive' and Page he says 'played pretty much magnificently'. He concludes that 'they still do it better than most even if the competition is mounting,' before finally (and somewhat hypocritically) complaining that they only did one encore....

Creem reports.... Jaan Uhelszki reviews Physical Graffiti. She begins by suggesting that the album is better than all of their previous works, and calls Kashmir the best cut on the album. She calls Trampled Underfoot a 'basic drunken boogie' and says that Page's guitar work could only be improved upon by a machine. She says Custard Pie and Boogie With Stu are 'macho masterpieces'. 'Led Zeppelin moves in strange ways. Sure they're gutsy, ballsy and flamboyantly aggressive, but they're also cerebral, by way of the glands.' Using equally flamboyant prose Uhelszki concludes that, 'Zeppelin are avatars in a cultural vacuum.'....

June 1975

7 New Musical Express reports.... Physical Graffiti is #20 in the UK.... the post concert party at Earl's Court included Jeff Beck, Marianne Faithful, Jon Anderson, Chris Squire.... Dr. Feelgood provided the music, Robert Plant commented they were the best band in the world next to Led Zeppelin.... Jimmy Page may join the Rolling Stones.... Robert Plant was spotted at Wembley with Mel Bush and David Essex.... Jimmy Page is on the Stones new Metamorphosis album.... Page was spotted buying a rocket shaped juke box....

14 **New Musical Express reports....** Physical Graffiti is #12 in the UK.... John Bonham actually ordered live octopus to his hotel room during the band's last tour of the USA.... **Melody Maker reports....** Several letters to the editor tear strips off reporter Steve Lake's Earl's Court review....'Steve Lake's review of Led Zeppelin's penultimate concert seemed to me to reflect not so much a critical review, rather the usual diatribe reserved for big bands from the bored "I've seen it all before" blasé rock reviewers in-crowd.' Sam Summers, Cambridge....'I think it's time Steve Lake stayed home and reviewed records not concerts.' Jack Haynes, Manchester....

21 **Melody Maker reports....** Bonham: over the hills and far away.... Chris Welch interviews Bonham at his farm.... *"I was never into farming at all. I wasn't even looking for a farm, just a house with some land. But when I saw this place, something clicked, and I bought it back in 72."*

Showing off his car collection, *"This is the hot car shop, that one is a 67 Corvette with a seven litre engine. This one is a 1954 two door Ford with an eight litre engine. You get guys coming past in a sports car who think it's an old banger, until I put my foot down. It's an amazing car, look at all the chrome inside. She'd only done 10,000 when I bought her."* John then discusses the Rolls Royce he

used to have. *"It was a white one. I went to a wedding reception in Birmingham. When I came out it looked like a bomb had hit it. All these skinheads had jumped on it. They kicked in the windscreen, smashed everything. If it had been any other car they would have left it alone."*

"This used to be just a three bedroomed house. My father did all the wood paneling, and I did a lot of the work with my brother and sub-contractors. If you have builders in they'll make excuse after excuse about delays during the summer so that they can have work inside during the bad weather. I know, because when I left school I went into the trade with my dad. He had a building business and I used to like it. But drumming was the only thing I was any good at, and I stuck at that for three or four years. If things got bad I could always go back to building.

"I had a group with Nicky James, an incredible lead singer. But we had so much of the equipment on hire purchase, we'd get stopped at night on the way back from a gig and they'd take back all the PA. Nicky had a big following then, and he could sing any style, but he couldn't write his own material. We used to have so many clubs we could play around Birmingham in those days. Lots of ballrooms too. All those places have gone to the dogs — or bingo.

"I was so keen to play when I quit school I'd have played for nothing. In fact I did for a long time. But my parents stuck by me. I never had any drum lessons. But I remember Carl went (Carl Palmer), he had a lot of lessons. I just played the way I wanted, and got blacklisted in Birmingham. ' You're too loud!' they used to say. 'There's no future in it.'

"But nowadays you can't play loud enough. I just wish there was a way

of wiring a drum kit to get the natural sound through the PA. I've tried so many different ways, but when you're playing with a band like ours you get so many problems with sound.

"With Jimmy and John Paul on either side playing lead, they can leak into the drum mikes, and if you have too many monitors you start to get feedback. I never get it the way I want.

"I enjoyed those concerts (Earl's Court) I thought they were the best shows that we've ever put on in England. I always get tense before a show, and we were expecting trouble with such a huge audience. But everything went really well and although we couldn't have the laser beams at full power, I thought the video screen was well worth doing. It cost a lot of bread, but you could see close-ups you'd never be able to see normally at a concert. It was worth every penny."

Did they rehearse much? *"Nah, three days. Mind you, it was only a few weeks before we got back from the States. We just needed a bit of rust remover. We had already done a lot of planning for that States tour, because we like to change the show each year. There's nothing worse than playing the old numbers over and over again. You've got to keep in some of the old songs or course. I don't know what would happen if we didn't play 'Stairway To Heaven,' because it's become one of the biggest things we've ever done. When Jimmy plays the first chord in the States, it's like instant bedlam, until Robert comes in with the first line. And we always play 'Whole Lotta Love' because people want to hear it, and I still get a great kick out of 'Dazed And Confused'. I always enjoy the number because we never play it the same. With the other stuff, we'll put one in, or take one out. On the last night at Earls Court*

we played 'Heartbreaker,' 'Black Dog,' and a bit from 'Out On The Tiles'. With the songs from 'Physical Graffiti' we've got such a wide range of material. "It wasn't done on purpose. It's just that we went through a stage where we were very conscious of everything we played. We felt it had to be a certain kind of thing for Zeppelin. Now we record every thing that comes up and, of course, in the States they play it on the radio so the people know what we're doing. In Britain we never get any airplay except from John Peel and Alan Freeman. In the States they'll play 'Trampled Under Foot,' all day.

"When we first ran through it, John Paul and Jimmy started off the riff, but then we thought it was a bit souly for us. Then we changed it around a bit. It's great for me. Great rhythm for a drummer. It's just at the right pace and you can do a lot of fills. But compare that to 'Dazed And Confused.' The speed of the thing! While we're playing, I think 'Christ if I drop one, knit one and purl one — that's it.' You've gotta be fit to play that one, and if I don't feel too good, it's very hard. We keep tapes of every show, and it's very useful afterwards, especially for my drum solo, because then I can hear what works best.

"I've got worse (with age)— terribly bad nerves all the time. Once we start into 'Rock And Roll' I'm fine. I just can't stand sitting around, and I worry about playing badly, and if I do then I'm really pissed off. If I play well, I feel great. Everybody in the band is the same, and each has some little thing they do before we go on, just like pacing about, or lighting a cigarette. It used to be worse at festivals. You might have to sit around for a whole day and you daren't drink, because you'd get tired out and blow it. So you sit drinking tea in a caravan with everybody

saying 'Far out man.'We don't do festivals much now because of the amount of equipment we have. There's all the P.A. and lights and the black floor for the stage. Imagine the changeover between us and the Floyd it would take hours! The Bath festivals were the only ones we ever played here, and they went really well."

Did he use a synthesiser during his drum solos? "No, it was just phasing on the pedal tymps. I was using them in '73. It's just a different sound. Not everybody likes or understands a drum solo, so I like to bring in effects and sounds to keep them interested. I've been doing the hand drum solo for a long time long before I joined Zeppelin. I remember playing solo on 'Caravan'when I was 16. Sometimes you take a chunk out of your knuckles on the hi-hat or you can catch your hand on the tension rods.

"I try to play something different every night on the solo, but the basic plan's the same, from sticks hands and then the timpani and the final build up. It would be really boring to play on straight kit all the time. The last States tour I was really chuffed when I got some good reviews from people who don't even like drum solos. I usually play twenty minutes and the longest I've even done was just under thirty. It's a long time but when I'm playing it seems to fly by. Sometimes you come against a blank and think 'how am I going to get out of this one?' Sometimes you go into a blank and you know halfway through it's going to be disastrous. There have been times when I've blundered, and got the dreaded look from the lads, but that's a good sign. It shows you're attempting something you've not tried before.

"I'm losing strength. I'm more tired after a solo than I used to get in the old days. Of course we used to have a

break for acoustic numbers then. But it was so cold at Earls Courts we had to have an electric fire in the dressing room.".... **New Musical Express reports**.... Physical Graffiti is #25 in the UK.... Plant takes time trip in Zep movie.... Zeppelin's new movie directed by Peter Clifton is nearly complete. Clifton, "Jimmy Page recently finished dubbing the music at New York's Electric Ladyland studios and only some quadraphonic dubbing remains to be done. It's more of a modern musical, extending the band's music into something visual and really trying to say something. It's a real film that has a beginning, a middle and an end, and it's been shot by some of the finest cameramen in the business. What we have tried to do is to extend Zeppelin's musical feelings and re-enact their fantasies, for instance in one part of the film we have Robert Plant living in 14th century Wales. No plans have yet been made about distributing the completed product. We're waiting for Jimmy Page to return from Morocco before any further decisions are taken."....

28 **Sounds reports**.... The long awaited two hour Zeppelin movie is nearly finished it features Robert Plant in 14th century Wales.... **New Musical Express reports**.... Physical Graffiti is #21 in the UK....

Hit Parader reports.... Cover story - Journalist Lisa Robinson re-writes her tour report from the 1973 American Tour. She originally wrote these observations for Creem in September 1973, but original included a lengthy interview. She goes on to add that following the original interview in New Orleans, the band had gone on to a party thrown for them by Atlantic boss Ahmet Ertegun. The music for the party was provided by The Meters, Ernie Doe, and Professor Longhair. Afterwards a jam session ensued with Phil Carson, Jerry Greenberg and John Paul Jones.... Full page advert reads — Led Zeppelin Physical Graffiti Swan Song distributed by Atlantic records....

July 1975

7 **Swan Song press release....** From: Fran Fiman

LED ZEPPELIN TO RETURN TO U.S.A. IN AUGUST
OAKLAND STADIUM CONCERTS AUGUST 23-24 ARE FIRST TO BE ANNOUNCED

Led Zeppelin, who sold out 33 concerts at the beginning of the year, and who hold attendance records in most major cities, are returning to the United States to play in areas of the country that their winter tour missed.

The first dates to be announced are Saturday and Sunday, August 23-24 at Oakland Stadium. 55,000 seats will be sold to each of the two concerts at $10.00, making a $1.1 million gross potential for the two days. The concerts will be in the afternoon, and The Pretty Things (who record for Zeppelin's Swan Song label) and Joe Walsh will also be on the bill. Bill Graham is the promoter of the concerts at the Oakland Stadium, which is normally used as the baseball field for the World Champion Oakland A' s.

Further Led Zeppelin concerts will be announced shortly, according to Zeppelin attorney Steve Weiss.

Led Zeppelin, for the past several years, has been the biggest grossing and top record selling rock act in the world. Recently they had all six of their albums on the Billboard chart at the same time -- an unprecedented feat. All of their albums have been "platinum", signifying more than a million units sold and the highest accolade the record industry can bestow.

Their most recent "Physical Graffiti" is still on all charts after more than five months, and has retailed more than $13 million!

Led Zeppelin consists of Robert Plant, lead vocalist, Jimmy Page, lead guitarist, John Paul Jones, bass and keyboards and John Bonham, drums. Zeppelin is managed by Peter Grant and in partnership with him, they have their own record label, Swan Song. In one year of existence, Swan Song has released five albums, including three gold albums. All five have been on the charts, and total sales have been more than $27 million. This is by far the most successful label ever started by a rock group. Besides Led Zeppelin, Swan Song's roster includes Bad Company, Maggie Bell and the Pretty Things.

12 **New Musical Express reports....** Physical Graffiti is #18 in the UK....

19 **New Musical Express reports....** Physical Graffiti is #25 in the UK.... Jimmy Page, John Paul Jones, and Robert Plant are currently tax exiles in Montreux Switzerland....

26 **New Musical Express reports....** Physical Graffiti is #26 in the UK.... Led Zeppelin will be doing shows in the USA starting in Oakland California on August 23rd and 24th with a possibility of South American dates.... Zeppelin are still exiled in Montreux....

August 1975

2 New Musical Express reports....
Physical Graffiti is #28 in the UK....

8 Swan Song press release.... IMMEDI-
ATE RELEASE/ AUGUST 8, 1975

LED ZEPPELIN AUGUST-SEPTEM-
BER TOUR POSTPONED FOLLOW-
ING AUTO ACCIDENT OF LEAD
SINGER ROBERT PLANT AND HIS
FAMILY ON GREEK ISLAND.
From: Danny Goldberg
The August-September tour of English
supergroup, Led Zeppelin, has been post-
poned following an auto accident on the
small Greek island of Rhodes in which
Zeppelin lead singer Robert Plant and
members of his family were injured.

The accident took place on
Monday afternoon, August 4th. Due to the
nature and extent of the injuries sustained
by Plant and his family, and the inadequate medical facilities in Rhodes, a
member of the London staff of Swan
Song, Led Zeppelin's record company,
flew to Rhodes in a chartered jet equipped
with stretchers, blood plasma, and two
doctors from Harley St., England's finest
medical center.

Plant and his family are currently under intensive care in a London hospital. Earlier today, physicians there diag-
nosed his injuries as multiple fractures of
ankle, bones supporting the foot, and
elbow. Following this diagnosis, it was
announced by Led Zeppelin manager,
Peter Grant, and Zeppelin attorney, Steve
Weiss, that the August September
American tour was postponed, as was the
October tour that had been scheduled for
the Far East. Additionally, there is the
possibility that the scheduled November
tour of Europe and December tour of
Japan may also have to be postponed.

Within the next couple of weeks,
doctors expect to have a better idea of
when Plant will be recovered and able to
perform again.

Plant's wife, Maureen, also in
the car, suffered a lengthy period of con-
cussions, and has broken her leg in several places. She has four fractures of the
pelvis and facial lacerations. Plant's son,
Karac 4, suffered a fractured leg and multiple cuts and bruises. His daughter,
Carmen 7, has a broken wrist, cuts and
bruises.

The band was due to begin
rehearsals for their forthcoming U.S. tour,
in Paris on August 14. 110,000 tickets to
two shows at the Oakland Stadium were
completely sold out at $10 apiece. Among
the other concerts which were postponed
were those in Los Angeles at the Rose
Bowl, Kansas City, Louisville, New
Orleans, Tempe Arizona, Denver, and
Atlanta.

Danny Goldberg, vice-president
of Swan Song in the U.S.A., said that any
fans or well wishers who wish to write to
Plant or his family can write care of Swan
Song, 484 Kings Road, London S.W.10
OLF, England.

Led Zeppelin has been called the
biggest group in rock and roll. They hold
the record for the largest attendance ever
drawn by a single act: 56,800 who paid to
see them at Tampa Stadium in Florida on
May 5, 1973, toppling a seven year old
Beatles record. Their six albums have
sold in excess of 15 million copies worldwide, and their most recent tour of
America last winter broke records all over
the country. Besides Plant, the group consists of Jimmy Page, Lead guitar, John
Paul Jones, bass and keyboards, and John
Bonham, drummer. Their manager is

Peter Grant who is also president of Swan Song.

9 **Sounds reports....** Led Zeppelin are set to play the USA again.... **New Musical Express reports....** Physical Graffiti is #26 in the UK.... **Melody Maker reports....** Letter to the editor suggesting that readers should write to the Prime Minister to cut back the super-tax rate that Led Zeppelin are subjected to. The point being, it is better to have 50% of something than 83% of nothing....

16 **New Musical Express reports....** Plant badly hurt.... Lead singer for Led Zeppelin Robert Plant was badly hurt in a car crash on the Greek island of Rhodes.... **Melody Maker reports....** Plant Injured, article details the cancellation of the band's upcoming American tour. It goes on to say that his wife and children were also hurt in the accident. They were airlifted to a Harley Street surgeon and are now recuperating in a London hospital....

September 1975

6 **Melody Maker reports....** Further article stating that the tour has been canceled in the USA. A spokesman said, *"Robert is recovering but we still don't know how fit he will be until the doctors take the plaster cast off in six weeks time. So the tour, which was planned for the autumn, is off until next year, there's no question of it starting any earlier. We just don't know when he'll be back in action."....*

13 **New Musical Express reports....** Robert Plant is getting around in Hollywood with the aid of crutches....

20 **Melody Maker reports....** Cover

Story, Yes It's Zeppelin...Article details how Zeppelin swept the Melody Maker reader's poll with seven first places. Best Vocalist, best guitarist, Best album, best live act, and Trampled Underfoot was voted second best single even though it was a limited edition. The band also placed in nine further categories....

27 **Melody Maker reports....** At the Melody Maker Poll Awards luncheon at the Carlton Hotel on the 24th. Page had flown in directly from Los Angeles to accept the awards and was in attendance with his daughter Scarlet and John Bonham. Comedian Billy Connolly hosts the event and calls Zeppelin's achievement staggering. Page, *"If it was staggering for Billy to read out the awards, it was more staggering for us to receive them, and I really wish we could all have been here to receive them but I'm sure you'll understand."....*

October 1975

11 **New Musical Express reports....** Led Zeppelin are currently living in Malibu California...they attended a Donovan concert at the Santa Monica Civic centre, Robert Plant in a wheelchair.... Plant and Bonham were also spotted at a Toots and the Maytals show at the Roxy on Sunset in West Hollywood.... the band are currently rehearsing in Los Angeles....

18 **New Musical Express reports....** Led Zeppelin will begin a new LP soon in the USA....

November 1975

1 **New Musical Express reports....** Led

Zeppelin's new album is due out in February....

December 1975

French Magazine reports.... Article reviewing surprise gig in the town of St. Helier on the Channel Island of Jersey.... It was in total secrecy that Led Zeppelin appeared on stage last month. Not completely recovered from his period of convalescence, Robert Plant chose the small English island of Jersey for his recovery. It was in Jersey that John Paul Jones, and John Bonham spent a weekend at the beginning of December at the house of Norman Hale, rock pianist. Having promised to return to the island to give a concert it was a great surprise for a crowd of approximately 350 people who were gathered around a stage in West Park near Behan where the complete Led Zeppelin performed a 45 minute set, which included their own material as well as some old classic rock and roll such as Blue Suede Shoes and Jail House Rock. Robert Plant who is still recovering from an injury to his leg as a result of an automobile accident this past summer, sang sitting on a stool for the whole length of the short show.

Jimmy Page flies to the USA during the Christmas holidays to direct the editing of the film and soundtrack filmed during their last American tour. This soundtrack will be the basis of an album which will be released two or three months after the release of their new LP which was recorded in Munich and should be out by February. We can then envision a European tour which will start next Spring in England and will pass near us before Summer.... Jackie De Shannon who signed a contract with CBS recently, says she had a young session man perform on one of her albums in 1964 called Jimmy Page ....

20 New Musical Express reports.... John Bonham apparently needed 13 stitches after an altercation at the Rainbow in Hollywood, he has been banned from several other Hollywood night spots....

27 New Musical Express reports.... Robert Plant's injuries are severe enough to keep him off the stage until at least next summer.... Surprise live act by Zep in Jersey...Led Zeppelin performed for 350 people at Behan's West Park on the island of Jersey last week. Their set included "Blue Suede Shoes" as well as several of their own songs. Robert Plant sat on a stool for the duration of the set and moved around with the aid of crutches. He commented that the reunion had been fantastic. The band have been in Jersey since August they are expected to return home for Christmas with the exception of Page who heads to the USA to master and mix the soundtrack for the upcoming film of the band. The soundtrack album will be released next year but the new studio album recorded in Munich is due first....

1976

January 1976

7 Melody Maker reports.... Article states that the new Led Zeppelin album will be called 'Obelisk' and is to be released on February 20th....Jimmy Page is pictured at the British Music Festival....

10 New Musical Express reports.... Led Zeppelin's new album "Presence" will be released next month, apparently it was recorded quicker than any album since Led Zeppelin I....

Circus reports.... Interview with Robert Plant.... Plant is interviewed in his hotel room during a stay in America.... He is asked whether the first tour of America was hard work.... Plant, *"No, because Atlantic had done a good job with the white label copies of the first album, getting them out to the FM stations a couple of days before we got to town. The reaction was very good. We weren't even billed the majority of the time. I remember the marquee that read 'Vanilla Fudge, Taj Mahal plus Supporting Act.' I didn't care; I'd been playing for years and I'd never seen my name up there so it meant nothing to me. But the reception that we got was something else again, and that was especially surprising because in some of those towns the albums had not yet reached the stores. Even so, after about the third number you could feel that the buzz coming back to us from the audience was different than what they'd given the other bands. The first gig was the day after Christmas in Denver and then we came back here to the Whisky, where Jimmy and I were both chronically ill and only played one gig out of three we were supposed to have played. And I saw the GTO's and I saw everything buzzing* around me. I saw the Plaster Casters, and I saw rows and rows and rows of possibilities, you know? And I said, "Man, there's no end." The day will never come when I stop looking at—what did Joni Mitchell call her album, Miles of Aisles? Just as long as you can look out there and get a twinkle. So that was it, that was the first tour. By the time we got to the East Coast, it was really hot. It was really surprising; it just devastated me. The antics, the tricks and just the whole world that I'd slipped into, after having to struggle back in the midlands of England just to play. And suddenly we were in places like Steve Paul's Scene, where the mini-Mafia would be kicking the tables over and chicks would be sleazing up to you and everything like that I mean, why stop ever?"*

Circus then asks him when he started really writing songs for Zeppelin. Plant, *"It was with the second album, when I got into doing "Ramble On," which a lot of people say is a sort of Lord of The Rings type of thing. By then I had developed a wanderlust and that song was really just a reflection of myself.*

"I wrote one song with the Band of Joy called "Memory Lane." It was really quite funny, something about a chick on the back of a motorbike with a chrome horse between her legs. I suppose it was an early version of "The Wanton Song." But I've never considered writing to be a problem; I've always looked forward to it, it's just that sometimes it becomes a challenge. I usually just leave the phone off the hook, send the flesh on its way and shut the door tightly. "The Song Remains The Same" is possibly one of the few songs that I don't think I really did justice to."

The subject turns to the short time spent recording Presence a mere 18 days, Plant, *"It was really like a cry of survival. I didn't know whether I was going to be able to work with the band again; I didn't know if my leg would heal. We had planned to do a world tour, but obviously that was nipped in the ankle, so to speak. I was stuck in Malibu for a long while, and I said "Please, let me do something to do with music; let me do something or otherwise I'm gonna go balmy." We already had some ammunition from our trip to Morocco—Jimmy and I had put together some epic sort of material— but every time that we started listening and thinking about the ideas that we already had put together, we shied away. We hadn't been back to England in nine or ten months, and consequently l don't think that we were in one of our more mentally stable periods, not in a condition that enabled us to come to grips with what would be a huge accomplishment in our eyes. So we went to S.I.R. [Studio Instrument Rentals —a complex of rehearsal facilities] to work on some things. And it was hard in the beginning; I had to sit in an arm chair with my leg up in the air while the band was on the stage. And I'd go into another room where Detective were playing and Michael Des Barres was singing, aping all of my movements and looking in the mirror at the same time.*

"We figured that if I don't go out on the road again, we'd just change his name quickly and send him out as me. But anyway, slowly and painfully we began working on the album and it gradually came together. And then we went straight to Germany; that was where we did the 18-day shuffle. We worked pretty much straight through. We didn't—or at least I didn't—go out at all at night. Normally after hard work we always take our rewards; but that time there were no rewards for Robert."

He is asked about Presence as an achievement, Plant, *"Well, there won't be another album like it, put it like that. It was an album of circumstances; it was a cry from the depths, the only thing that we could do. I honestly didn't know what was going to happen and neither did anybody else. If it had been six, seven or eight years ago, it would probably have been a good deal more raw. It was taken from the balls, you know; that was where it was coming from."*

The subject turns to the movie The Song Remains The Same, Plant, *"We knew exactly how we wanted it, I mean, we knew the material so we knew just what should be illuminated at what point of the film. So all of us were equally involved with it—there was no other way to do it, because we couldn't leave it to anybody else. It was a big thing for us to do, and I don't think you do it more than once.*

"Film people really puzzle me. I believe that music is the master; that is, it can bring you elation and sadness and satisfaction while the visual part of film is just the diversion. The attitude and antics of the people involved with film, the way they follow their own odd trips are really beyond my comprehension altogether. I could never imagine being involved in movies by myself. If I had to repeat the work on that film again, I would refuse to do it.

"I don't premeditate how I act or react or motivate myself on-stage. I know what to do, but I don't know when to switch what on; it's just a case of how I'm driven on by the people who are with me. If I weren't with the other three gentlemen in the band, I probably wouldn't be worth interviewing. Whereas the idea of the solitary man standing in front of the camera

repeating himself time and time again to some irate lunatic sitting in a chair with "Director" written in back —yecch, no thanks."

On the subject of traveling in North Africa, Plant, "Well, I'd been there before with my wife Maureen and I'd started to touch beyond the usual clip-cloppity "This way mister, this way mister" kinds of places. I went back with Maureen directly after the Earl's Court gigs, which were the last gigs before the accident. I went straight off the beaten track. I'd had three days lying in the sun in a glossy hotel and then we just took a car and went. I had one friend in Morocco; he was a friend of the infamous Harold, who hangs around with us and a few other bands occasionally. As it happened, this Moroccan guy had spent 11 years learning the Koran to be a holy man but he turned out to be a hustler instead. He'd been to London and so he was a big deal locally, and he'd do things like get hold of a telephone in the Hilton hotel, cut the cord, and put it in his ear—so he'd be driving around Marrakesh pretending that he was talking on the telephone. A real sassy guy, always trying to sell you things even though he was your friend. It was with him that we went down to the Sahara."

The interviewer mentions that Page was along on the Morocco excursion, he asks Plant whether he thinks Morocco might have affected Page's music. Plant, "I'd imagine so. It doesn't manifest itself as a direct emulation of their music, but when you've seen it and felt it, it has an effect on you, just like a car accident has its effects too. Everything washes off on you, although some things aren't so immediately apparent as other things. But I don't think Morocco is the most inspiring place that I

shall ever go to. It's my ambition to go to Kashmir, and I'm saving that as the last trek. What I want to do is to travel north from India, but not singing Hari Krishna or anything like that. My old lady comes from India, and her uncle was chief of the Calcutta mounted police during the '40s. He can speak about ten different dialects and he's a really great guy. In fact one of the times that I worked before the Zeppelin days, I had a job as a production control manager in a factory that he ran. I got the sack because I ordered enough steel to keep three factories going for about a year, but I managed to remain his friend and one day I'd like to take him with me and go right up through Kashmir and then stop. Then I'd like to just disappear for about four or five years. It's not a Marco Polo trip, it's just that I know that you can mingle; I know people who have lived in those places for a long time. Of course it's not wine and roses or even the spiritual aspects of life there that I'm interested in. It's day to day experiences, and you have to work because as you work you become a part of society. There's so much to learn there, so much that we here in the West have lost.

"I have a lot of friends in England who have done a lot of traveling over there. A guy who currently works for me escaped the police by virtually walking to Bombay from England; he just hitched and went and went and went. He'd take buses here and there and catch rides wherever he was able. He slept in caves in Hindu -Kush, came out covered with these big flies and had to jump in a ditch full of shit to get the flies off him. I mean, he just had the most amazing time, life and death in the palm of his hand. He had to play games with the guards on the borders of India and Pakistan, where the borders close at six o'clock and there's *nobody who's going to take any responsibility for your safety when you go through. There's that excitement, a little less of the expected if you compare it to going to Philadelphia, for example, and getting your rocks off. It's just my ambition to see if I can do it, to see if I've got it inside me to live with those people. I noticed when I was in India that just because we admired the people there, they looked upon us as idiots. Because they're scratching to get into Western society, and we were just trying to touch upon the pulse of the very things they were trying to leave behind. But I shall still go to the Roxy tonight, I haven't yet given up that part of my life. But the time will come when I will do that. And without a four-wheel drive vehicle, too. And no stimulants."*

He is asked whether he would find it difficult to do without the trappings of Western life, Plant, *"I'll not give them up forever; I'll just soak it in and come back. Everybody will think I'm a complete loony by the time I return. I've already declared myself this week as the Billy Graham of rock; I'm trying to clean up rock & roll for a week. But who knows what could happen up there after four years in the wilderness."*

What are his plans on his return from trips into the hinterland... *"Become a Mormon."*

31 **Melody Maker reports....** Interview with Lord Sutch who says he was performing at Thee Image Club in Los Angeles when he talked to Jimmy Page about playing on an album. He says Page was so keen he offered to co-produce and write some songs....

February 1976

7 **Melody Maker reports....** Cover story announces an interview with Robert Plant next week....

14 **New Musical Express reports....** cover story.... Sensitive Plant Pines For British Soil.... Interview by Lisa Robinson with Plant.... reminiscing about his recent close call in his car accident, Plant, *"I remember talking to Mick (Jagger) at the Plaza one night about the sort of separatism or lack of communication between one rock band and another. You know in the old days there was a constant sort of jousting for position, a definite ego number that was apparent all the way up to a certain point. I guess I realised talking to him that there isn't all this clanship and unity between bands in this rock and roll scene. Then when this accident happened, there was a giant rally round from a lot of people who I never think of that often. Wishes and regards sent to Maureen, to us both. From people on all levels of the business, you know."*

Robinson turns the topic to Plant's self-imposed tax exile status, Plant, *"I really can't believe the criticism that I've had hurled against me, the remarks made by people about leaving my wife when she was in hospital...all that. It's a very sad situation you know, to have to leave one's own country for the sake of money. The government in England is almost saying, 'Well, never mind, they'll come back you know, they're English and they'll come home.' And they're damn right the number of times we have come so close to getting on a plane and going home. The spirit of Albion is really embedded in everybody's soul."*

The conversation next turns to the impromptu performance that the band gave at Behan's in Jersey the previous fall. Plant, *"You see the possibility of playing and who can avoid it? It was like a dance hall that was like some place ten years gone by, in the best old English tradition. Guys with dickey bows and evening jackets ready to bang your head against a wall if you stepped out of line, and chairs and tables lined up in escalation. Chicks wearing suspenders and stockings and a lot of rock and roll. Bonzo said, 'C'mon man, let's plan on going.' and I said, 'I can't even walk for God's sake, don't embarrass me. I can't hobble across the dance floor and onto the stage.' He said we'd go through the side door and then up the back steps. And with amazing grace that's what I did and I found myself plunked on a stool. Every time I went to hit a note, I stood up. Not putting any weight on my foot, but just sort of standing. Oh there were some great photos. I gave this guy a free hand to shoot like crazy, you know, shoot all these shots of Led Zeppelin in this antiquated ballroom, backing this pianist. Of course I made sure that I sat almost behind Bonzo wedged between the piano and the drums, but then I found myself edging forward just a little bit. Then after the third number I was wiggling the stool past the drums and further out. It was great really good. Except we wouldn't stop playing. They kept flashing the lights inside the place and really like, 'Get them off the stage now they've done enough.'"*

He talks about the recording of Presence. Plant, *"I moved to Sunset Strip because the trek to rehearsals from Malibu was a bit long. And I got bored with the Hyatt in a shorter time than it normally takes, so I knew I must be getting better. Then I hopped on a plane and went to Germany. After getting used to it, the studio turned out to be OK, and as soon as we came to an understanding with the machinery and the equipment we were off. I think we only went out twice, we were really too tired to do anything but put our heads down. It was like 14 hours a night, eighteen days. Jimmy worked like a Trojan, no two ways about it. It's his energy that got this album together so quick. I mean I was not in any physical condition to hop around with gusto inspiring the situation greatly, although I was surprised the vocals were so good. The lyrics were coming thick and fast, presenting no problems at all. I had no second thoughts about the lyrics, they were all reflections on the time near and before the accident and that time afterwards, that contemplative thing, so I was very determined lyrically and vocally, but Jimmy put his energy into it. He worked so hard, and the guitar playing on this album surpasses anything I've heard for ages and ages. Brilliant, so much life in it. It's like hallelujah and we're back. There's one song called Achilles Last Stand, you know immortal but for the heel, or being a heel, I don't know which. No I mustn't joke about it, because I am very proud of it. There's one song I wrote when I was very sad and missing Maureen in Malibu, and it's very personal. You know times go very slowly when you get up every day and you can't even kick a ball, run and kick a roadie, even kick your drummer. So time has been the teacher and I've been the pupil. I mean I believe that we could start another album right now. Three weeks is amazing to record and mix and walk away."....* Robinson then briefly broaches the subject of Plant starring in film's like Roger Daltrey which Plant quickly dismisses. He then concludes that the band have no

immediate plans to return to the UK....
poll results, Led Zeppelin #1 band, Robert
Plant #1 singer, Jimmy Page #1 guitarist,
Physical Graffiti #1 album.... **Melody
Maker reports....** Robert Plant vents his
rage at the socialist British government's
tax practices which prevent him from
playing the UK. He also predicts the
wrath of the punters in later letter writing
to MM's Mailbag. *"You can't just sit
down and write a song that you're prepared to put out, because you'll be taxed
to the hilt. Why the hell should you put out
something and come out of it with tup-
pence? It aggravates me that people have
worked for something for a long time and
they've had to leave because of these tax
laws. New York grey as it may be, is full of
some of the finest English talent, not just
music but sports personalities and actors,
and anybody who has a flair for something. We all want to go home but there's
an outrageous state of affairs taking place
in England, an outrageous mishandling of
the country's affairs in general. It's a very
pitiful situation where a lot of the more
established musicians have to flee. You
only have to go from here, and four sky-
scrapers down the street there's Mick
Jagger. He'd echo the same thing. We're
all holed up in little boxes here, looking
over Central Park. It's very very sad.
Now, I can just imagine the letters to
Mailbag, saying, 'fuck the money and
come home.' but you have to live with
reality.*

*"It's one thing to forget the
money, but there's a moral aspect which is
ludicrous. Rock and roll is a very lucrative form of making money easily, and just
because the government has loused up all
the way round, they shouldn't just turn to
music or any form of entertainment. If it
weren't for this tax, we'd be doing an
English tour at least once a year for sure,*

*but even when we did Earl's Court we
didn't come out with anything."*....In an
interview with Chris Charlesworth Plant
reveals how he dealt with his car accident
and the subsequent self-inflicted pres-
sures of recording Presence. Plant, *"The
memory is very vivid, but it's like spilt
milk and there's no time to cry over it
when there's another bottle around the
corner, you know what I mean? I had the
normal instant reaction of anybody and
that was for my family who were in the
car with me. I didn't know what the impli-
cations and the final outcome of the
wounds or whatever would turn out to be,
but they were of minimal importance at
the time. I didn't think about the possible
consequences for the band as I had plenty of time to lie back, not even sit back, I
started gaining a new perspective on the
situation.*

*"After I'd been pieced back
together I had to think about it all
because I didn't really know whether
things were going to be the same as they
were before...uh, physically. I had to, not
so much grow up very quickly, as be prepared to face odds that I never thought I
would come up against. I haven't come
out of it too scared, either physically and
mentally, and, in fact, once I knew
Maureen and the kids were OK I really
threw myself back into my work. By
engrossing myself more and more in the
work we had on hand, the time passed by
quicker. If I stop and brood, which is a
very bad thing to do, then time moves with
a lead weight around it, but the time between August 4 and now has gone by
quickly because I applied myself to what I
do best. I mean...I can do 99 percent of
what I could do before, so we sat down
and had a meeting.*

*"We obviously couldn't tour, so
we decided to make an album which*

wouldn't have happened if it hadn't been for me. It was quite remarkable that I found myself sitting in an arm-chair facing the band with my leg in the air. We were planning to tour right around the world and back to England, playing possibly in South America, Hawaii, Japan and Asia Minor and ending up doing dates in Europe, especially Scandinavia, before dropping anchor in Albion.

"I was idly researching the possibility of recording various ethnic groups of different tribes in Morocco, just checking out how hard it would be, not so much the actual recording, but cutting through the ridiculous bureaucracy in Morocco. They were governed by the French for so long that they have a lot of the French traits on efficiency which, of course, are absolutely nil. The Moroccan version of that is even sillier.

"On the Monday morning after the last gig at Earl's Court I was on my way to Agadir with Maureen, and three weeks later Jimmy flew out to meet me in Marrakesh where we spent several nights at the folk festival. That gave us a little peep into the colour of Moroccan music and the music of the hill tribes. Once you get off the normal tourist path and have the right vehicle, so long as you know a little bit of Arabic, which I do, then you discover they are quite fine people. They're very warm people and they're overjoyed when they find you have taken the trouble to learn their language.

"One day we had lunch with a local police chief and received his blessing before traveling on, and we showed him on an old map where we wanted to go. He called round one of his friends who was a tourist guide and the guide told me and Jimmy he had been that route once in his life but wouldn't go again because he was a married man. We still

went, driving for hours and hours and the further south we went, the more it seemed like a different country. Gone are the people who can take the back pocket off your Levi's without you knowing it and you're into a land of nice, honest people who find a Range Rover with Bob Marley music very strange.

"We tried to get down as far as the Spanish Sahara at the time when the war was just breaking out. There was a distinct possibly that we could have got very, very lost going round in circles and taking ages to get out. It's such a vast country with no landmarks and no people apart from the odd tent and a camel.

"We kept reaching these army road blocks where we'd get machine guns pointed at us and we'd have to wave our passports furiously and say we were going to bathe at the next beach. Then we'd go on thirty miles to another road block and claim we were going along to the next beach again. We wanted to get down to a place called Tafia which is not very far from the border of the Spanish Sahara. We got as far as we could but eventually the road got so bad we had to turn back.

"It was devastating leaving behind Morocco and suddenly finding ourselves in Europe. For two months I'd lived at a Moroccan speed which is no speed at all, and then suddenly I was in Spain being frisked.

"We saw the jazz festival in Montreux, living on top of a mountain in a total extreme of climate from what we'd had for the past two months. After a while I started pining for the sun again, not just the sun but the happy, haphazard way of life that goes with it, and Rhodes seemed a good idea. I knew Phil May was going

to be there so down we went. Jimmy came down with me but he left to go to Italy the morning before the accident, and we started rehearsing. Then there was the accident and well, we were just stopped in our tracks.

"I had to share a room with a drunken soldier who had fallen over and banged his head and as he was coming around he kept focusing on me, uttering my name. I was lying there in some pain trying to get cockroaches off the bed and he started singing The Ocean from Houses Of The Holy. I can remember a doctor working on us for 36 hours non-stop because there was no one else there. My brother-in-law and Maureen's sister were there, so he managed to get things together pretty fast. As soon as the news got through I was whisked out of there quick. The doctor in London told me I wouldn't walk for at least six months and he gave me some odds of various possibilities about the future, so we had another group meeting, canceled all the tour plans and decided to make an album instead. We've always taken so much time making albums, but we thought that this time we'd take a totally different attitude and cut one as quickly as possible.

"It's so adamantly positive, so affirmative for us. Everybody was aware that there was a crisis in the band so we got together and went forward as if nothing had happened, like turning into a storm instead of running from it. In LA we just rehearsed and rehearsed. It was so strange for me the first time because, as I said, I was sitting in an armchair, singing, and I found myself wiggling inside my cast. The whole band really wanted to play and had wanted to do that tour, so the same effort was put into the album. It was a unique situation where we rehearsed for three weeks - on and off in

true Zeppelin style because we're not the greatest band for rehearsing. We've always felt that too much rehearsing on a song can spoil it for us, sort of take the edge off the excitement, but this time it worked in the opposite way because the enthusiasm was contained in such a small space of time. Then we went to Munich to record and it took us just 18 days to finish it. That's ridiculous for us because we usually take an eternity to finish an album.

"Now I can play soccer all day and run and swim and I still love to be very alive, but here I was hobbling around in the middle of this great track when suddenly my enthusiasm got the better of me. I was running to the vocal booth with this orthopedic crutch when down I went, right on the bad foot. There was an almighty crack and a great flash of light and pain and I folded up in agony. I'd never known Jimmy to move so quickly. He was out of the mixing booth and holding me up, fragile as he might be, within a second. He became quite Germanic in his organization of things and instantly I was rushed off to hospital again in case I'd re-opened the fracture, and if I had I would never have walked properly again. It was a bit rash of me to bop around but, well, the track is brilliant.

"Already I've surprised the doctors by recovering as much as I have in such a short time. They've called me a model patient and that surprises me because hospitals are really not my cup of tea. I mean, I was faced with a situation that dented every single thing I had going for me. My usual...er...sort of leonine arrogance was instantly punctured by having to hobble around, so I'm having to take my time. I don't want to rush. Every day I walk more and more without the stick and I'm going to need physiotherapy

so I should think it'll be the beginning of the next soccer season before I'm running about again.

"There have been so many amazing things, things that were once beyond my wildest dreams. I mean, basically I wanted to sing, and sing and sing. I mean heavens, how could I ever have envisaged anything like this? Me and Bonzo had just come down from the Midlands to join a band. Jimmy was the experienced man and he'd been over here on the Dick Clark show or whatever, so he knew we would end up at least on that level. I don't think Jonesy had been to the States before, but Bonzo and I had no idea. We even got lost in London. I remember when we played the Fillmore West in San Francisco, Bonzo and I looked at each other during the set and thought 'Christ, we've got something'. That was the first time we realised that Led Zeppelin might mean something; there was so much intimacy with the audience, and if you could crack San Francisco at the height of the Airplane, Grateful Dead period then it meant something. Mind you, we went on with Country Joe and the Fish so we didn't have that much of a problem.. how could we fail? But we knew the chemistry was there when we recorded the first album."

In conclusion he talks about his lyric writing, *"You've got to live with them so it's a very personal thing. I did some of the lyrics on 'Whole Lotta Love' and some of the broader things like 'Ramble On', but it wasn't until later that I really worked hard on them; I think that songs, like 'Kashmir' and 'Stairway' are far more relevant to the band now than songs like 'Whole Lotta Love' which we don't really do now. Ever since it came out 'Stairway' has been the most requested track on FM radio here in America*

which is amazing because it's so old now. That song was astoundingly well accepted and personally I'm very proud of it, but I think 'Kashmir's' as good and so is the one that I fell over on when we recorded this new album.

Charlesworth points out that Led Zeppelin simply couldn't do without their manager Peter Grant, *"Yes, but the thing is there's no shit with this management. There's no hoodwinking. Everybody knows exactly what's going on. If anybody played rhythm guitar in this group, it would have to be Peter. The fact that we're still together after all these years has a lot to do with him, and the fact that we've come to terms with everything along every step of the way is because of Peter.*

"Peter is ultra-important, the fifth member of the group, and as such we have a highly conscientious attitude about the material that we put out, so too has Peter with the responsibility on his shoulders. He's never run us, he's always put things to us for joint decisions. I know what the alternatives in management can be, even nowadays, and they're far, far removed from our joyous little relationship."

Charlesworth now switches the topic to the subject of the new film, *"We're as happy with it as we possibly could be. It's been mixed in quad, but I'm not sure whether the Futurist Cinema in Birmingham is going to be able to handle that, but I would say it will be released about the same time as the opening of next soccer season, probably in August.*

"The film features more than just us on stage. It has a few tastes of spice from everybody's imagination, sort of humourous in parts. It ain't all music, anyway, it touches on some of the things that make up the personalities in the

group, Peter included, and Richard Cole too. *Richard deserves a feather in his hat, if we're going to wear them, because he's been a great part of Zeppelin too. He's such a rock on the road, such a unique man. He went off to work for Eric Clapton for a while, but he was too much for them. Ricardo knows what he's doing all the time, at least during the time he's supposed to: after that who knows?"*

Finally Charlesworth asks about the possibilities of solo efforts, *"I think to want to do that, you've obviously got to be dissatisfied with the set-up as it stands. If you can't bring out everything that comes to mind musically with the group you are working with, then to go away and do a solo album and then come back, is an admission that what you really want to do is not play with your band. If you have to depart from the unit to satisfy your soul, then why go back afterwards? I know I couldn't find anybody as musically imaginative as Jimmy, anybody who could play the drums as hard as Bonzo and anybody who could play as steadily as Jonesy. It's as simple as that."...*

21 **Melody Maker reports....** Letter to the editor says Good Riddance to tax exiles like Robert Plant....

26 **New Musical Express reports....** Plant is recovering from his recent injuries by training with the Wolverhampton Wanderers soccer team.... Led Zeppelin will play an "extended run" of concerts at New York's Madison Square Gardens....

28 **Melody Maker reports....** Letter to the editor says Plant should belt up and stop complaining about taxes. In a lengthy diatribe the writer pulls no punches claiming that Plant's assertion of pay-ing 98% tax is completely erroneous and that he should be careful to distinguish between 'artist' and 'entertainer'. He does make one blunder saying that he doubts if Physical Graffiti will still be selling in twenty years!....Article states that Presence will be released on March 19th and will feature seven tracks, Achilles Last Stand, For Your Life, Royal Orleans, Nobody's Fault But Mine, Candy Store Rock, Hots On For Nowhere and Tea For One....

March 1976

6 **New Musical Express reports....** Presence will be released March 19th the Old Grey Whistle Test will preview the album on Tuesday.... **Melody Maker reports....** Lengthy article discusses the differences between British and American pop music. The journalist says that since the Beatles and Led Zeppelin the American's have been running to catch up....

13 **Sounds reports....** Interview with Jimmy Page touching on various occult subjects. *"I feel Aleister Crowley is a misunderstood genius of the 20th century. Because his whole thing was liberation of the person, of the entity, and that restriction would foul you up, lead to frustration which leads to violence, crime, mental breakdown, depending on what sort of makeup you have underneath. The further this age we're in gets into technology and alienation, a lot of the points he's made seem to manifest themselves all down the line.*

"I don't want to get too dippy about all this. If you take the view of the scientist and everything is in a state of vibration, then every note is a vibration,

which has a certain frequency, and you know that if you put 40 beats into a frequency it's going to be the same note every time. You take that into infra sound and people can be made to be sick, actually killed. Taking it the other way, not to be too depressing, what about euphoria etc. and what about consciousness being totally....no, I won't go into that one. Time warps.

"There's a man in Morocco, in fact a holy man, but he'll invite you for mint tea, and while he's standing there, mint grows up around his feet and he picks it, makes tea and a small animal eats the stalks and it's gone. I haven't seen that but the person who had and told me had no reason to lie. I've witnessed other things which I don't care to discuss. I think if a person's into it, they're the kind of things he'll experience himself rather than having it related to him.

"I'm obsessed, not just interested, obsessed with folk music, street music, the parallels between a country's street music and it's so-called classical and intellectual music, the way certain scales have traveled right across the globe. All this ethnological and musical interaction fascinates me. Have you heard any trance music? That's the thing."....

20 **Melody Maker reports....** Cover story - Interview with Jimmy Page. The article says that Led Zeppelin will be releasing two albums this year, Presence in April and a live album in October. Interview with Page by Harry Doherty. They start off with Robert Plant's health. *"I don't want to make too much hoo-hah about that, about the mending process. No I wouldn't really. I've got very superstitious after that. It was just strange that it happened within a week of rehearsals. It was just like something saying 'no you're*

not going to do it.' It's personal that's why I don't want to talk about it. Well, it was bloody unpleasant. I know you're going to bloody print it or I'd tell you the truth. It was just touch and go, I don't think those things should come out in print. Far be it from me, or you, to start delving into that. It's a very personal thing. It was really touch and go."

Doherty asks whether the cover on 'Presence' has anything to do with the music. *"Well, it does in a way. There is a link between the artwork and the music. The artwork is such that you could look at it and put your own interpretation to it. It's one of those. I'd rather that people saw it for themselves and see what they make of it, because it's not a cut and dried situation. You can put a number of interpretations on it, so it's best to leave it as an open book situation as far as people seeing it goes.*

"It could either be viewed as past or present. If you look at it, it could be the Forties and it could be the Seventies. It's got to be viewed in it's entirety, otherwise the whole point would be lost. I'm sorry to be elusive on it, but I don't think I should say that it's this, that and the other, because it's an ambiguous thing. Photographically it's an ambitious statement, so it's not the right thing to lay down an impression because somebody might have a more illuminating one."

Page talks about 'Presence' and the speed with which it was recorded. *"It was a bit of a gamble really, to just set down an amount of time and say that it was going to be finished by such and such. We had kicked over the tracks so we had a starting ground. Robert was still working on lyrics, and I hadn't thought about too many of the overdubs, but one was pretty confident that we could do it. It was just a sort of a test, really. We could* have come dreadfully unstuck. (It was) a gamble to see whether we could meet the deadline or not. Fortunately we did. We worked practically every minute of the day. It was really great to be able to do it like that. At no other time apart from the first LP have we had that stretch in the studio. We usually recorded on the road, and it was spread over such a long time.

"There is a lot of urgency about it. There's a lot of attack to the music. I think that's reflecting a state of mind of actually being constantly on the move. You know no base, because of the situation then. That definitely is reflected. I know it's talking in a pretty nebulous fashion, but I think people will know what I mean when they hear it. I don't think it was missing in any of the earlier ones, because I think each LP has an identity of it's own and it's different from the previous one. I wouldn't say it was better or worse than any of the other records. It was very uplifting to actually tackle a situation like on the new LP and find that things were really coming out and being fresh all the time, as opposed to being sort of cliched, because you were concentrating on one particular period of time.

"The only way you can get cliched is if you just follow a particular pattern to what you know is successful along your particular line, but I don't think, well, I know that we haven't done that. We've been quite the opposite without consciously doing it."

Doherty proposes that the fans are pleased with Zeppelin's return to hard-rock after the diversity of 'Houses Of The Holy'. "Well, I don't know. Let me put it this way. When the third LP came out after, for instance, the second one.....I should really explain how the things are done. The first LP really had material that had been played on stage before it was

recorded. Then we felt at home. The second LP was recorded basically on the road when everybody could get in the studio, so that's got that very sort of rock and roll orientation. Now following that you had got the third LP, where a lot of that was written in the cottage, Bron-y-Aur, and it's got, you know, the writing is far more narrow in approach.

"But there was an outcry about doing this, that and the other acoustic. In fact, there were acoustic numbers on the first LP. It's just that the mood was different. It was more dramatic and laid-back. I would say about this particular LP that we're playing as a group. It's very controlled. There's no blowing out or whatever. There's a great level of control on the new one, and sympathy within the four."

Doherty asks an interesting question, how does he see 'Presence' as advance on previous work? "A bit subjective this. Well as far as laying down, I suppose the word is orchestration, guitar harmonies and stuff. I've usually immersed myself in it, laid down things and there'd be room to amplify it with extra harmonies or whatever. With this one it came straight up. There's a hell of a lot of spontaneity about it. I think that's the element really. That aspect of it has to be when you start talking about the actual development of it, because that's the whole key to the theme of it, the level of spontaneity.

"You see in the past when it came to the point where we were getting an album together, there were always a number of frameworks that you would toy with at home. At this particular point in time there were no sort of complete frameworks just little bits kicking around. There have been sort of phrases, melodies, rhythms that have been picked up on the travels through Morocco and *places like that, which all get consumed. You take it all in and it comes out in the music."*

Page says he attaches a lot of significance to the influences of his traveling. *"One is always open to new influences and different concepts and approaches. I couldn't say that there was a number built around a Moroccan rhythm on the new LP, but I definitely learned a lot from Morocco which I can relate to on songs. The whole thing that goes on in Morocco is incredible. It's trance music, basically, and when you see the sort of things that are done by the power of music as such, one couldn't help but sort of reassess what one thought one knew already."*

Doherty suggests that the band may have a future limited by what their fans expect. *"There's an unmistakable identity about the music and whatever the piece is, you naturally say 'that's them'. I don't mean cliched writing by that, but certainly, as far as development goes there's more intense writing, unusual chord patterns.*

"One wants to improve, and the only way that you can feel satisfied is by setting up certain milestones along the way as far as the writing goes. A lot of that has to do with the construction of songs. All I know is that we're really critical of our own stuff, probably over-critical as far as writing goes. If something starts to sound similar to something we've done before, it immediately gets rubbed out. It doesn't get used. But that's no problem within itself, because we never seem to be at a loss for coming out with new stuff, new ideas, new rhythms. I'm not relating this to anything else that's going on because we only take up half a degree of a 360 degree circle of what's going on, but never the less, it's all exploratory to us.

"Obviously there's an essence within the group, and obviously there was a certain intensity on the first LP, and I would say that it grew from that and stretched this way and that.

"As far as the rock elements go, they veered over one way, and the acoustic ones again another way, and there's the blues side of it. I think that there are enough elements within that to keep a changing face. It just comes out that way. It's not as though it's definitely planned or calculated."

Doherty asks if he thinks there is room in Zeppelin for that much growth and development. *"Yeah. Definitely. If the content was being difficult, if it was hard to write and we sat in LA and nothing came out apart from a couple of numbers, then I would start to question it, but when everything is coming out so fluently and there're no problems coming up with new ideas, I feel pretty confident. As far as the playing side of it goes, I know that we can have a go at anything. Don't forget John Paul Jones was an arranger, and both of us worked on sessions. You never knew when you went into a session what was coming. They didn't inform you that you were going to do such and such a thing. You just walked in there and it could be, you know, a huge orchestra or a rock and roll session or jazz, so you really had to be able to weather any storm. I guess that sort of background helped us."*

Page is asked whether there is much left for Zeppelin to do. *"Crikey yeah. I mean we're only scratching the surface if you start relating it to classical work, it depends how far you want to take it. There's such a wealth. There are no horizons as to what could be done. It just takes a lot of work, writing and recording. You can bet your life that in the next five or ten years, there'll be some amazing things happening with musicians coming up.*

"For instance, we got most of our influences from the blues players and the early rock players. Well the musicians that are coming through now have got such a great textbook to take it all from, that you just know and feel that there's going to be some new and great music coming up. I wouldn't accept in any way that music is going to become stagnant. People say 'Oh well it's just going to keep blossoming out'."

After that highly optimistic comment Doherty suggests that things *are* stagnating, *"No, it's only people that are — and I don't mean to insult you — people that have got to try and keep it ticking over on a weekly basis. Obviously you can't have a new trend coming out every week. Things take months and years to come out, then you get a really strong thing, say like the Beatles or Hendrix or something like that, you know? People who could just tie up all the loose ends and really come forging through. But there are still a lot of healthy aspects in British music, I would say, in relation to American music. I know there's a feeling that the American music has got a lot stronger, but I still believe that the British musicians have it, you know? They just had to fight a lot harder to get it going and come through. They didn't have it really cushy to begin with, and I think that with every struggle there's always a lot of sense to come through.*

"What I mean is that I've always felt that there's far more conviction, especially in rock anyway, in people behind British music than there is in American.

"I don't know about new fans. It's hard to say. I think when you're talking about new folk you usually get those

from singles, I think. By that I mean to say that you've got more of a pushing power through the medium of radio and television, which we normally don't exploit in that sort of way. We're more into touring, doing dates, and coming across more with the environmental thing. Then the name gets spread by word of mouth. That's certainly what happened in the beginning. We don't write single material. It's got to sort of be within that three minute time schedule. When we're writing things together, it's just a number that develops and is worked on and becomes a statement at that time, and then they get grouped together on an LP. It's not ever thought of as single material, and it would be a bit of a drag to have to start thinking that way."

Doherty cites 10cc as an example of an albums band who pick LP tracks for release as singles. *"With 10cc, I'm sure it's like a singles oriented group. I would say so. I don't think they'd be pissed off if somebody said that. I'm sure they do think that way. If you get accustomed to bringing out a record, going on television, doing a spot there, getting airplay, you keep fulfilling that role, surely?"*

And his views on television? *"It's a shame in a way that there isn't a programme that just goes into that area of bands who don't necessarily concentrate on singles. The Old Grey Whistle test is the only one as we well know."*

Finally Doherty asks about the prospects of a series of British dates. *"But we can't. As far as criticism goes, we can't win over here. When we started doing bigger places, there was an outcry about Zeppelin deserting the Marquees, the Nottingham Boathouses etc. So we did a tour of those and then it was 'How selfish can they be to play in small pubs when people can't get in to see them,' I mean*

you just can't win.
"We've done a lot of construc-
tive work in the period off the road. It's
not as if we've retired."

27 **Melody Maker reports....** Article says Foghat recently beat Led Zeppelin's attendance record at the Pittsburgh Civic Centre by 3,000 people. The comparison is made to an upset win by a fourth division soccer team over the league champions....

April 1976

10 **New Musical Express reports....** Presence is reviewed.... How A Stampede Of Rogue Elephants Missed Me By Inches.... renowned journalist Charles Shaar Murray begins, *"Zep albums are like Sherman tanks or platoons of charging elephants; stand in front of one of those, baby, and you best believe you'll know that something's just run over you."* Murray compares the band to an ex-Commando taking out a street-fighter in four seconds flat. His enthusiasm for the album is contagious and the review is packed with entertaining metaphors, *"Page, is as near to absolute storm centre as you can get.... "*. After noting that the album is flat out solid from start to finish he also points out that there are no real contenders for adding to the Zeppelin-song hall of fame. He concludes, *"Zeppelin are rock and roll's greatest ground to ground tactical nuclear missile.... if the Russkies start any hoohah, we'll just beam this mutha at Moscow.... "*.... **Sounds reports....** Cover story showing David Bowie watching the Presence object on several televisions. John Ingham reviews the album. He grants it a full five stars and calls it their best album yet. "After this platter spun incessantly for

an afternoon on the office phonogram I asked a non-Zep fan what he thought, 'Oh it's OK I guess. They're just the best at what they do.' Well of course. But what they do is also the best." He compares the band to the best of Elvis and Gene Vincent and claims, "The rumours were right, this album is unadulterated rock and roll. It's fabulous. The real star of the show is Bonzo, who is dynamite. He's everywhere bulldozing songs along mercilessly." Ingham's enthusiasm is so contagious it makes you want to go and listen to the album! He's a great advert for potential customers breaking down each song and bubbling with passion for each song. He concludes with, "It sounds best really loud with your head really close to the speakers.".... **Melody Maker reports....** Cover story.... Led Zeppelin Storm Back.... Article reports that Presence will be released tomorrow (Friday) and that it is assured of gold status immediately. Dave Dee general manager of Atlantic records comments, *"This Zeppelin album is going to be a monster. It will be the biggest Zeppelin album in this country ever. We were prepared for this one. We'd heard the tapes of the album some time ago and knew demand would be enormous. Everyone here is very enthusiastic about it."* .... Chris Welch reviews the album enthusiastically, *"This album has certainly caught Zeppelin with their atomic particles flying."*.... Double page advert reads — Led Zeppelin Presence. The New Album Available Now On Swan Song Records And Tapes. Distributed by WEA Records Limited.....

17 **New Musical Express reports....** Presence is #15 in the UK.... **Melody Maker reports....** Presence enters the MM charts at #30....

LED ZEPPELIN
PRESENCE

THE NEW ALBUM AVAILABLE NOW
ON SWANSONG RECORDS AND TAPES

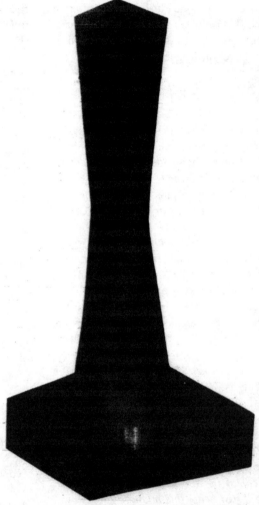

24 **New Musical Express reports....** Presence is #7 in the UK.... Bad Company are signed to Swan Song. **Melody Maker reports....** Letters to the editor expressing disappointment with Presence....

May 1976

1 **New Musical Express reports....** Presence is #2 in the UK.... **Street Life reports....** Interview with Page.... Journalist Steve Peacock asks about how and where Page would like to record and why does it lead to so much procrastination by the band, Page, *"Well, we never would procrastinate exactly, but I can think of certain places where your attention is brought away from what you want to do. Like when we want to spend four weeks concentrating, making the album . . . I can imagine some places where that wouldn't happen. Like LA. But LA's a great place and you can feed off another sort of vibe, but there's only that one that's to be offered there. What we want to do is be a little more adventurous rather than do it all the accepted way. For obvious reasons our plans didn't happen last year, but that's not to say they won't this year."*

He is then asked whether he'd prefer to travel alone, *"Whichever. I'd prefer it to be as a group, but it can be done on as casual or permanent a basis as each person wants. If some of us fancy it for a couple of weeks and others for a couple of months, OK — meet up in a couple of months. See who's got what out of where."*

Page often refers to rock and roll as being a form of folk music he elaborates, *"I don't immediately think of people in beards and fisherman's pullovers singing sea shanties to acoustic guitars. What I was . . .Environmental music. If you think of rock'n'roll from its earliest inception, what was being sung about. I don't want to get too pompous about it, but things like Chuck Berry, 'Back In The USA,' I really thought that was like an anthem when I first heard that. But rock 'n 'roll has got so far away from that. There's only so far it can go before it hits its boundaries. I know there shouldn't be boundaries really, but as far as the statements go you've still got to own up that most of the people that are playing are self-taught people, even though there have been some that have come from a classical training.*

"And then again if you want to relate it to music on a complete scale, relating it to the really serious composers in terms of the ideas and the textures they're laying down, then you're really going to start getting into deep water if somebody's saying that it's got that far, because I don't think it has. I have my ideas about what's going to come, but at this stage that's how I see it anyway. That it's really just reflected some sort of sociological change, that it's documented it through the lyrics . . ."

He is asked about the financial rewards, *"Well . . . the money thing is .... when you start playing, that doesn't come into it at all. Then when you get a hit record, it still doesn't come into it, but for the fact that there's a snowball building up somewhere of royalties and so on. But most of the people I know aren't even thinking about that, they're thinking about how things are shaping up with their playing, how things are shaping up artistically. In fact, most people get totally out of touch with that other end of it and really resent the fact that suddenly a whole*

THE ALBERTOS GIVE
IT TO YOU STRAIGHT

SUBJECT YOURSELF TO THE OBJECTIONABLE DEBUT ALBUM
FROM ALBERTO Y LOST TRIOS PARANOIAS ON WHICH THEY
PULL THE FEET FROM UNDER THE WORLD'S LEADING ROCK
BANDS AND LEAVE THEM FLAT ON THEIR FAECES

ALSO, IF YOU'RE IN THE VICINITY OF LONDON VICTORIA PALACE
ON SUNDAY 9th MAY OR MANCHESTER PALACE THEATRE
ON FRIDAY 21st MAY YOU'LL SEE THE ALBERTOS PERFORM THEIR
UNNATURAL ACT ALL OVER THE STAGE

AVAILABLE NOW ON TRANSATLANTIC RECORDS
TRA 316

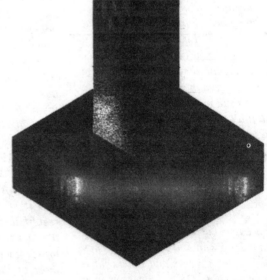

DISRUPTED BY WEE WEE RECORDS

THE THING ⓒ 1976 TRANSATLANTIC RECORDS LTD.

team of professionals—accountants, tax lawyers - comes into their lives. That's that side of it; as far as the living of it goes, the actual lifestyles . . . well look at the old blues singers, their attitudes. It's a perfect parallel in its own way with, say, the Stones' lifestyles in this age. You know. Involvement with booze and . . . oh come on, you can't push it, can you? It's . . . actually it's a real devil may - care attitude. They don't really give a shit, I know they don't.

"People can select or reject quite positively as far as groups like us go, because we're not on a massive radio or TV campaign, it's only really by word of mouth—there's that aspect of it if you're going to start talking about street philosophy. I suppose what you're really saying is that on the general scale, if you start talking about groups like Yes, shall we say . . .

Peacock asks if there is a danger of becoming detached from the audience.

"Obviously that's something that one's very aware of, that you are detached. As regards friends you'd known before, if they were true friends they'd still be your friends after, unless you'd become some kind of monster. I guess once you've sorted out your set of values, which is usually quite early on in your life, you usually stick more or less to them.

"I relate much more to the actual communication with those people at the gig, which to me is more like the vibe of what it's all about than driving back through streets at six in the morning. If the audience is vibing you up and you're vibing them, you can get this gigantic feedback which can become quite magical. I relate far more to that, the communication between us and the people coming to see us. From the start, rock'n'roll as such had this incredible communica-

tive effect, and I think the thread of what was being communicated has carried through, no matter what else has come into the music."

Peacock turns the conversation to Page's quitting from session work in the early sixties, Page, "I got out of it because I became too aware of just being a cog. I hadn't gone into it with that sort of attitude. I'd gone into it because there was only one other guitarist working those sessions who was able to come up with those riffs and ideas, and that was Jim Sullivan. And he couldn't be everywhere at once. But whereas there was bags of guitar work being played to begin with, I ended up well, I might just as well have been playing tambourine in the corner. Then when it came to having to play and invent, I found I was getting fogged under. It really was like a kind of cancerous growth. I thought I'd got to get out, otherwise I'd lose everything I ever had. You see, once the element of spontaneity went out of the session playing, all you were doing was interpreting somebody else's stuff. That's all well and good, and I'm not pig-headed enough to say I didn't want to do that, especially when someone was giving me a fee to do it, but there were people in that session field who were better than me at doing that—especially reading. Some people are really cut out for all that, but I'm not.

"On a busy day I was doing 12 or more hours, and I think with anyone who's working that hard, doing something that goes against the grain, it begins to show in strange ways. I was getting mystery illnesses, starting to feel uncomfortable . . . all these things were going on. But fortunately I was able to recognise what was happening, and even more fortunately I managed to find a remedy (The Yardbirds)."

Peacock points out that he was getting mystery illnesses and all those symptoms before, at the end of his time on the road with Neil Christian, *"Yes, but for different reasons. That was jumping in at the deep end and not being prepared for it."*

Peacock quotes Lisa Robinson of Melody Maker, "The Beatles battled the Stones in a parking lot, and Led Zeppelin won." Page, *"What? That's her talking is it? Oh, thank God I didn't say anything as pretentious as that. Everybody's got a part to play and a statement to make, and I don't see how it can ever get to those proportions, that one person can permanently be better — covering all the aspects of music today—than anybody else. I just don't see it. I did an interview with Lisa Robinson once, and I didn't know I'd done it. When I read it there were things like: "Is your music your salvation?" "No, it's my crucifixion." No turning back from that one."*

Peacock asks Page's reaction to the strange stuff written about the band, *"It's very hard to figure out what it is that's addictive about it really, on that scale. There's a lot of people puzzled and always will be puzzled, but none more so than me. Whatever's written about us, I think people appreciate that when it comes down to the nitty, when we go out there, we're going to give of our best. Whether its good or bad, it'll be our best. I suppose "Ever Onward" is our motto - not that it's ever said."*

Peacock asks about the band's reputation as the King of the Heavy Bands, *"But we weren't. I think the early stuff has a very dramatic quality about it, especially as far as the light and shade is concerned. The heavy bands that instantly come to mind, the riff kings, didn't*

always employ that, especially as far as improvisation was concerned. They more or less just kept going on one level, whereas we'd be shooting off in all directions. And we were definitely not note - for - note the same every night either—lots of spontaneity involved."

Page says that he was never really aware of the band's preeminent status in the rock world, *"Not until we did Atlanta and Tampa and all that sort of thing, where it was just you at the festival, and there were 58,000 people who'd come to see you in Tampa, Florida. I was really shocked, the first two dates on the tour to walk into huge great audiences like that. We never had any publicists. There was always a feeling of we were being blown out at home, and then we were breaking records and playing to all these people and doing well and everyone was still ignoring you. That's how it appeared anyway. Obviously it was disappointing. It would piss anybody off. But not for long. After that we got a publicist, and then it was all right. Which just goes to show."*

Peacock points out that Page had once claimed he needed the seclusion of a mental hospital or a monastery, *"That's how I felt - I was thinking 'What the hell am I going to do?' because it was like the adrenaline tap wouldn't switch off. Doing those concerts to that many people, there was so much energy being .... stored up. I felt like a kettle with a cork in the top. I'd stay up for five nights on the trot. It didn't seem to affect my playing, but I'd come off stage and I just was not leveling off at all, not turning off the adrenaline, I couldn't. I felt I needed to go somewhere where there was a padded cell so I could switch off and go loony if I wanted to, or find somewhere where there was solitude, but still with people around. I was quite serious about it.*

"(I wasn't) out of control, because if I did that I wouldn't be able to play. It was more not being able to sleep, writing, fiddling about with tape recorders and TV sets, never settling: it was a feeling that somehow you'd touched the source of whatever creative drive you had, and you didn't dare lose it, you wanted to get as much out of it as you could before it finally went off, which inevitably it would two or three weeks after the tour. I built up to such a pitch that I couldn't see myself ever coming down again.

"When you're actually on a tour and you look at it, you think you're never going to be able to get through it; but then after a couple of days of staying up all night, your body gets used to it, and your subconscious takes you on to this total thing, an assault upon the whole tour. You see part of yourself which doesn't appear at any other time. It doesn't seem at all weird.

"It all goes along with what you said about us living in a bubble, but it only happens to you in a particular period, it isn't always there. And it's got so much to do with the whole business of pacing, and waiting too—the waiting before a concert, where there's nothing to do, but you can't quite relax because there's this thing coming up in a few hours . . ."

Does he miss it when he's not out on the road? *"Sometimes, but not just to achieve an absurd mental state; I like the whole feedback that you get. Because you never know what's coming next when you go out on stage, you can always be really surprised. But the thing of sitting down at a hotel at 3.00 in the afternoon waiting for 8.00 to come . . . there's only a certain number of things you can do in that situation. You are living in a vacuum,* but only because you're physically being put into a position where you have to live in a vacuum."

In conclusion Peacock asks Page if he is surprised to be 32 years old and does he expect to reach 35, *"Well, I don't think we're going to dry up as a creative force. I never really thought we would, but there was always the chance that somebody might say "That's it, I've had enough." I don't think that's likely to happen now. One can only be optimistic about the future especially having come out of Munich."*.... **Melody Maker reports....** Cover story says win 200 albums including Led Zeppelin....Robert Plant was seen at the Hope & Anchor in London last week watching the band Little Acre....Old Grey Whistle Test producer says he was given two different visuals for the airing of a Led Zeppelin track. He chooses a combination of a French film from 1910 and an American film from the 20's....

8 **New Musical Express reports....** Presence is #3 in the UK.... **Melody Maker reports....** Ian Anderson of Jethro Tull rebuts Robert Plant's position on his tax exile status. The story makes the cover of MM again and causes a storm of letters and rebuttals over the following weeks. It needs to be said that there didn't seem to be much sympathy for Plant's position at the time, but with the perspective of the nineties I think most people would agree that 98 per cent even on unearned income is ludicrous. Anderson, *"I'm not prepared to go over to America for the sake of having an extra 10 or 20 percent of my money as opposed to paying it in tax. Ron Wood suggested he pays 98 per cent tax. But he couldn't pay 98 per cent tax if he tried. Living in Britain Ron Wood could pay no more than about 53 per cent. And some-*

one should tell Robert Plant that he's wrong. It's really sad that people go around spouting this out in public, because those ridiculous figures just don't exist. You pay 98 per cent on non-earned income, but ours is earned income. The public believe people like me when we say we're paying 98 per cent tax, but it's simply not true. I would say that overall one can pay between 70 and 75 per cent of all your income. Whether it's earned abroad or in Britain, whether it's from concerts, you shouldn't have to pay more than that, unless you're silly enough to conduct your life that way.

"No way under the sun can you be paying 98 per cent. And it's time somebody got up and said B—— Ron Wood. Don't give me that, I don't want to know because you're talking up your ****. And he is. So is Robert Plant.

"So I have to believe that Robert Plant is saying it in a moment of fury because his favourite football team lost that weekend or something, so he's decided he hates England. Or maybe he's homesick and can't come to grips with it so he pretends he doesn't want to live in England anyway by saying how bad it is. Sure the tax is a lot of bread. But it isn't what you have they believe. That's the truth. The English people are being misinformed. They should be given the facts. People are actually starting to hate pop stars for making money and running away. Twenty five per cent of what people like me earn is still a lot of money. I earn as much as a brick-layer who works really hard, and that's a lot of money. That's about my level of income and that's all I need to live comfortably."......Advert reads — full page parody advert of Presence by Albertos Y Lost Trios Paranoias....

15 New Musical Express reports.... Presence is #4 in the UK.... A major Led Zeppelin appearance is planned for the summer.... **Melody Maker reports....** Letter to the editor defending Presence as a good step by the band into the 80's....

22 New Musical Express reports.... Presence is #4 in the UK.... **Melody Maker reports....** Keith Relf the original lead singer with the Yardbirds has died. He was found slumped over a live guitar at his home.....

29 Melody Maker reports.... Cover story - Zep Men In Jam. Article covering Plant and Page's jam on stage at the LA forum with Bad Company. Arriving at the forum Plant couldn't resist the opportunity to stick his head out of the roof of his limo to the surprise of all around him. He states that he is jealous that he is not performing tonight but he does manage to get on stage with Page for the encore of 'I Just Want To Make Love To You'. He takes his opportunity to get a shot back at Ian Anderson of Jethro Tull who had spoken out against Plant in the MM saying he only needed to earn as much as a bricklayer. Plant, *"So he only earns as much as a brick-layer does he? Well he writes songs like a bricklayer too, as far as I'm concerned."* Bonham is also in attendance at the show but his arm is in a cast and so he says he can't contribute to the jam properly.... **New Musical Express reports....** Presence is #5 in the UK....

Creem reports.... Cover story - Reprint of Chris Charlesworth's interview with Robert Plant from Melody Maker February 14th....

June 1976

5 Melody Maker reports.... A rumour of Led Zeppelin appearing at the Marquee Club in London caused chaos last week. Rumour had it that the band would appear with the Pretty Things. Only John Paul Jones showed and played with the Pretties during their encore of Route 66.... **New Musical Express reports....** Presence is #6 in the UK.... Wembley gig offered Zeppelin On Stage Soon...Led Zeppelin have been offered to play one of three dates available this summer at Wembley Stadium, July 3, July 31, or August 21.... a spokesman from Swan Song records said, *"Zeppelin would love to get back on stage, and there is an imminent possibility of their doing so, especially now that Robert Plant is almost back to full fitness. But I have no knowledge of any specific date or venue. When they're good and ready they'll announce something."*...the national press story last week that the band had moved to America was denied by Abe Hoch of Swan Song, *"They've been here all the time. They had just slipped over to the States to see Bad Company and tie up some business. And now they'll be completing work on their film and soundtrack album, both of which will hopefully be released later in the year."*.... rumours have been persisting that Zeppelin would appear with the Pretty Things at the Marquee in London last Thursday. A national daily printed the story as fact and so John Paul Jones sat in as a gesture.... the rest of band apologised for the disappointment but said they had no idea how the rumours got started....

12 New Musical Express reports.... Presence is #10 in the UK....

19 Melody Maker reports.... Letter to the editor criticising Plant's attack on Jethro Tull's Ian Anderson. It quotes the lyrics from D'Yer Mak'er as examples of Plant's lyrics.... **New Musical Express reports....** Presence is #12 in the UK.... Led Zeppelin's new movie will be called "The Song Remains The Same"....

26 New Musical Express reports.... Presence is #28 in the UK.... Robert Plant was spotted at the Cardiff Rock Festival to see the Pretty Things....

Hit Parader reports.... Noted journalist Lisa Robinson secures in interview with Robert Plant in particularly introspective mood. He has just recovered from his car accident in Greece. Plant, *"Well, I know it's a punk thing to say but I really am glad just to be alive. And ... as people o.d. or fall around left and right, I'm sort of standing there shouting, 'wait a minute ... hold on,' you know?*

"This has been the longest, most pensive period of my life. A lot of time to think, and a lot of time to wonder if I'd ever be doing what I do again. Really. I had no choice but to question it because I didn't know how everything was going to turn out. It was a little bit heavy at the beginning, and all I could do was put my mind behind putting it all back together again. And it's worked.

"The very fact that I can enjoy the fact that I'm here, in this syndrome again ... talking to Lisa syndrome, magazine syndrome, everything's okay again, virtually.

"That whole accident left me, well it gave me - I suppose you take something good from it, it gave me a fresh appreciation of things. Which, apart from all the posing and laughing and joking, sort of gave me a true perspective of what

it is that I'm doing, why I'm doing it and everything. An eye opener, although a painful one.

"I've had the time to see. Before I was bowled along with the sheer impetuousness of everything we did, we are, and what was created around it. That was knocked off course the fulcrum was tilted a little. I just really did not know what would be happening six months later. So therefore I had to just sort of think everything anew, instead of just being allowed to sort of go along with the rampaging, the hustle and bustle of what we are about. And in a very, very strange way— being carted out to Malibu, even the way I got there ... lying on my back for thirteen hours in first class! I couldn't put my leg straight ... I had recovered a bit in Jersey until I started going loony, because it can be rather boring, y'know. Even in my impoverished state, the mind was already ticking on far away places, the worst had past. I was ready to fight back, with the help of Benjie ... of course there were times I thought 'Oh my god will I forever be like this', hopping around on one leg, seen in the L.A.nightspots on one leg. Like a flamingo ... not a pink flamingo, but a flamingo.

"So I got to Malibu, and I felt right, if I'm going to win this battle it's time for a real close look at yourself rather than go along with everybody saying yeah, this is great, this is it. I sat looking at the ocean until the beach got washed up ... and we had a tour planned, in no way could I have done it. So we said 'What are we going to do?' and we decided to do an album. My mind, which had been taken up with repairing the physical, was taken up with the musical. So, with all the contemplation that the accident had given me time for, and the fact that we agreed to sit down and do an album

together, it was quite an eye - opening period. Because not only was I writing lyrics for an album, but just sitting in a chair and singing ... all that strange sort of thing I had never done before. Sitting in an armchair singing ... usually I sit in a high stool, or I stand there and move around a little bit. So then I had the case of having to get myself physically back to normal again, and also make an album.

"And it turns out that the lyrics really came from that period of contemplation where I was wondering Christ, is it all through, is it ended and as such, the album is so full of energy because of that primal sort of fight within me to get back again, to get better, to be whole again There is so much adamance and determination on that album, fist - banging on the table."

Robinson points out that Presence was recorded extremely quickly, only eighteen days, "Well that's it. What were we going to do, you know? Sit around and mope for a member of the band or get on with what we can do best so everybody said right, and as much as we hate rehearsing, we rehearsed in L.A. Well it was like a flash of white light.

"I have no career. It's basically a wanderlust and an ego - satisfier, you know? And I can satisfy my ego as could any man or woman, in so many ways, I should think. You do find that those lights do act as sort of a magnet so I knew that I just must fight, there was no talk of re-thinking things. Although it did sort of keep coming past me as a recorded message ... what are you going to do, what are you going to do ... The fight was returning and step by step taking on everything that I had taken on before, except for the flesh ... which I thought would draw too much from my vitamin sources ... calcium deposits ... You know, when you've got a stick, people think you can't do anything, you know...

"Well, it was a flash of light, like a flash of white light. It was very important at the time to be back, even at the Rainbow in L. A., every step made me sincerely appreciate the very essence of life. I see around me so many advertisements for people who have had too much of everything ... success, and everything that goes with it, they don't quite realize the fact that you're alive and you can enjoy on any level, what a city's got to give ... in response for what you've given a city ... so the Rainbow was the first flash of white light, the first step up the ladder again, or the first branch on the tree.

"It's part of me to get off on those moments where ... well, what people would call attention. Obviously that isn't the be-all and end-all of life, but ... at the states of creativity that I've reached well, it helps the lyrics along a little bit.

"But it's nice to sit here with a mouthful of onion bagel, you know? It's nice to go in there and be part of it for a moment in time. Now I know the way, I can see my own destiny for the next few years ... sitting at a stool with an overcoat over my shoulders, hat over my eyes, with a cup of coffee, singing The Tender Trap."

Robinson asks how much sympathy the rest of the band had for his plight, "Well, there was obviously a sympathetic vibe, but it's like you can't be sympathetic with somebody else's toothache, you know? You can be aware of pain, but my pain was not all physical ... it was a contemplative thing as well. It was like I was going through something that I don't know if anybody else had gone through around me. Obviously people have, just repairing oneself after a great trauma like that, but there were several times that I felt really alone. But I

had to draw my strength from those periods, that was like getting to know myself again. Because very seldom in the past had I stopped to think - which way left or right, you know what I mean?

"The time on my own in between tours used to be sort of coming back down to earth. That's the very early stages of it you come to terms with your position. I now think that my life at home is as exhilarating on its own level as the life that I've led with Zeppelin, and it is that way. Benjie, who was responsible for making me sound brilliant onstage but hardly really knew me before all this, went up to the farm while I was away and saw it for himself ... what a great thing it is there.

"And that's the sort of thing a lot of rock and rollers go through when they get home ... the sort of stallion dragging his foot in the dust, not knowing where to move next. That hasn't happened at all, I'm quite at peace with myself, especially now. The very fact that I'm talking to you today is yet another flash of white light.

"It's all like new days for me, very new days. And as for Maureen, I've heard all these stories about the horrible things that supposedly happened to her as a result of the accident. But it's just not true. She's as pretty as ever, and we're both improving. It'll still take quite awhile for the both of us, it's taken quite awhile already. But I'd like to think that she's come out with it with as much freshness as I have from it.

"I defy you to find me, I defy you to hear me do anything ... even fart in the United States for twelve months after that (his return to the UK in February). Well, I guess people thought that by January, that would be five months after the thing happened, and I'd be okay again. There was talk of 'Well, if he's better, we'll do it.' But—I didn't start taking steps until

January 1st. I was in Paris, drunk, and it was a new year so l took a step. One small step for man, one giant step for six nights at Madison Square Garden."

July 1976

3 New Musical Express reports.... Presence is #23 in the UK....

10 New Musical Express reports.... President Jimmy Carter says he likes Led Zeppelin....

Creem reports.... James Wolcott reviews Presence. He begins by suggesting that even though Page and Plant are showing some wear around the edges 'Zeppelin has such command of heavy-metal weaponry that even their modest efforts have scorched earth capability.' He continues with Presence, in it's best moments still manages to rattle the window-panes.' He thinks Achilles is too long and that in For Your Life, Plant is boring with a sound like 'his vocal cords are in his testicles'. He concludes that Hots On For Nowhere is the album's highlight and that he resents the fact that Zeppelin are too difficult to write about because they are so damned perfect providing 'no sauce for us young dogs to lap up'.

August 1976

28 Melody Maker reports.... Radio Luxembourg will air a two hour special on Led Zeppelin in it's Rocktober radio series....

Rolling Stone reports.... Interview with Jimmy Page, *"I do not worship the devil. But magic does intrigue me. Magic of all*

kinds. I bought Crowley's house to go up and write in. The thing is, I just never get up that way. Friends live there now."....

September 1976

11 New Musical Express reports.... rumour has it that a live Led Zeppelin album is imminent...

18 New Musical Express reports.... The Old Grey Whistle Test airs an extract from the new Led Zeppelin movie on October 5th....

25 Melody Maker reports.... MM Poll results - Robert Plant #1 singer, Led Zeppelin #2 band, Presence #2 album, Jimmy Page #1 producer and #2 guitarist, John Bonham #2 drummer, John Paul Jones #3 bass player..Led Zeppelin's engineer Keith Harwood was killed last week in a car accident....Article states Led Zeppelin will soon release a double live album. The album features a 27 minute version of Dazed & Confused. The movie will open in November....

October 1976

9 Melody Maker reports.... Cover story - Led Zeppelin Screened. Announcement that the movie will be playing in London's West End on November 4th. The movie will only be shown in theatres equipped with 4-track stereo....Michael Oldfield reviews the soundtrack album saying, *"This album is a magical experience."*....Advert reads — John Paul Jones Led Zeppelin Professional Users Of Rotosound Swing Bass Strings.....

16 Melody Maker reports.... Advert

reads — Led Zeppelin The Song Remains The Same (A) Film Opens Nov 4th at Warners West End 2 and ABC Shaftesbury Avenue....Article states that due to ticket demand the new Led Zeppelin movie will now run in two London theatres.....News flash states that John Bonham has just completed his first solo album in Montreux Switzerland. The album is produced and recorded by Jimmy Page who also plays guitar and electronics on some tracks....

23 **Melody Maker reports....** Double page advert reads — The Soundtrack Album Led Zeppelin The Song Remains The Same. Available on Swan Song Records & Tapes....Article states that the long awaited Led Zeppelin movie will premiere at Cinema 1 in New York next week. All proceeds will go to the Save The Children Foundation. A few tickets will be available to the public and all of the band are expected to attend. It goes on to say that the movie will then open in LA, San Francisco, Dallas, Boston, Toronto and Atlanta....

30 **Melody Maker reports....** Cover story. Zeppelin Movie: honest, heavy and hot. Review of the movie premier by Chris Charlesworth in New York. He reports that the band received a standing ovation at the movie theatre in New York. He concludes that, *"It's been three years in the making but The Song Remains The Same is a classy and surely enormously successful film."*.... **New Musical Express reports....** The Song Remains The Same is #15 in the UK.... cover story Zep Trash Globe in 77.... Led Zeppelin are slated to begin a world tour in February.... the band have been kept dormant since singer Robert Plant sustained injuries in a car crash last year. Plant is

still suffering some problems with his foot.... British dates are expected to be extensive and may take place early in the tour. The band's movie The Song Remains the Same is expected to premier on November 4th...the BBC will air an extract on the Old Grey Whistle Test on Tuesday the second.... Check your speakers the Zeppelin way.... review of the soundtrack album by journalist Angie Ferrigo.... in a moment of characteristic tabloid journalism Led Zeppelin are compared to a religion, with all that is implied by that. Ferrigo re-iterates much of the contemporary waffling about the machine-like quality of the band's management, she also does a track by track analysis of the album and concludes, *"This soundtrack is an experience more than an album.... some of the most staggering moments that can be felt in rock."*....

November 1976

6 **Melody Maker reports....** Full page advert reads — Led Zeppelin The Song Remains The Same (A) Presented in 4-Track Magnetic Stereo. NOW! Warners West End 2 and ABC Shaftesbury Avenue....The soundtrack album entered the American charts at #5.... **New Musical Express reports....** The Song Remains The Same is #14 in the UK....

13 **Melody Maker reports....** Article says the band held a party at the Floral Hall in Covent Garden after the movie premier. The event was attended by the band as well as Rick Wakeman, Boz Burrell and Wings. There is also a review of the party at the Hollywood Bistro attended by Page, Cole, Grant, Ron Wood, Linda Ronstadt, Tony Kaye and Danny Bonaducci.... **New Musical Express reports....** The Song Remains The Same is #5 in the UK.... full page ad for the movie.... review of the movie.... Zep Blow It.... reporter Nick Kent absolutely savages the Song Remains the Same beginning his appraisal with the line *"This is one dumb movie."* After a whole page of typical British tabloid cynicism (punk was afoot as could be seen by Kent's ludicrous self indulgent portrait attached to the article) he then qualifies, *"I like Led Zeppelin. That's why I'm so pissed at them making a big thing about this movie."*

18 **Rolling Stone reports....** Full page advert for The Soundtrack Album The Song Remains The Same....

20 **New Musical Express reports....** The Song Remains The Same is #6 in the UK.... cover story.... interview with Jimmy Page - The Roaring Silence by

Nick Kent.... after Kent's debilitating review of the band's movie the previous week he still somehow manages to gain access to Page for an interview about same.... Kent starts off by apologising for his "well meaning" positive reviews of the band from 1972, and states flatly how much he disliked them personally. He then qualifies this by saying that he has since come to appreciate them on a personal level. It seems that he can't quite bring himself to say what he really wants to say for fear that he might be forever cast out from his highly lucrative position of having access to the band. Kent begins by mentioning the live album, Page, *"Well that's just one of those unfortunate things, because if you start picking that apart, well first and foremost it's a soundtrack album and such simply has to be available. As for an actual live album, well my idea, prior to Robert's accident which dictated virtually everything we've done since was to do a chronological affair with tracks dating back to 1970...and going though the various incarnations right up to tracks we'll be doing on the next tour for Presence."*

On the film itself, Page, *"As regards the gig, well it's not a terribly good night and it's not terribly bad. Certainly not a magic one but not tragic. It's just a reasonably honest statement of where we were at that particular time."*

On the subject of Plant's recovery, Page, *"Well let's say he's playing football again. I mean after all the physiotherapy, well that's the green light as far as I'm concerned."*

Kent then turns the topic to the Kenneth Anger film "Lucifer Rising" which Page was scoring for the notorious filmmaker. At the time Anger was creating quite a stir by accusing Page of letting him down and not delivering the music in time. Page, *"I must start by saying that I've lost a hell of a lot of respect for him...at one point he was writing silly little letters to everybody he thought I knew so that they would naturally bring it up in conversation when they saw me. Hell, you* (Kent) *know that I did the film music....* (Kent saw a screening with Page's music in LA) *Well he's implying that he received nothing from me, which is totally untrue. Anger's time was all that was needed to finish that film."* In conclusion Page notes, *"Something epic is going to happen musically anyway. That's what I feel. This next tour, you'll see."....* **Melody Maker reports....** Chris Welch interviews Jimmy Page. *"We had two premieres in America, one in New York and in LA. They held them apart by a few days so we could check the cinemas out. It's not as easy a job as you'd think, getting the sound right for cinemas. I remember seeing Woodstock and they had towers of speakers.*

"Well the first time in New York it was great — the first time one had sat in a real audience. Every time I had seen the film before was with technicians, people with a really critical eye. Then the film lived for the first time and you could see people getting off on things, applauding and laughing at the right times, generally vibing. Although this project spanned three years, obviously we hadn't worked on it every week for three years. When you've been on something for that amount of time, there is always that slight reservation: have we gone over the top?

"When you have committed yourself to something and there's a high standard to compete with, like Woodstock and all those other rock films you realise that there is no mucking about, no half measures. Curiously enough I hadn't seen many of the other rock films, except

Monterey and Woodstock. *I don't know what Slade's film was like, they say it was a rock and roll feature film. This one was just a musical really, the gig, with fantasy sequences, part-documentary. It's one sequence frozen in celluloid.*

"Obviously there were things that weren't quite the way one wanted them. It's a massive compromise making films. You can just go on spending a fortune, there's no two ways about that. The fantasy sequences were introduced because we knew we had gaps in the film of the performance, and you can't really cut the soundtrack because so much of our stuff is improvised. So we thought let's do it that way and curiously enough, it's fair to say it built very much like a Zeppelin song or track. 'Achilles Last Stand' grew and built in the studio, and the same with the fantasy sequences in the film as ideas were added. We had complete control of the film which was made during our non-residency period. We categorically stipulated what we wanted and it was pretty much done that way."

He is asked how they arrived at the various fantasy sequences, *"It was like when we each chose a symbol for the fourth album. We each went away and came up with an idea. It gave insight into each personality, whether it be tongue-in-cheek or deadly serious.*

"Yeah it was a bit hairy actually. It wasn't done in one take - that was the trouble. It was a very steep climb, at this place in Scotland, and it didn't occur to me I'd have to go and do it again! The crew said, 'Back down there' and believe me, it's very steep, and I've got a great fear of heights.

"I wanted to get a full moon in the shot and it came up in December. I thought it would be great in snow so there would be a luminescent quality. Curiously

LED·ZEPPELIN
THE·SONG·REMAINS·THE·SAME Ⓐ

JOHN BONHAM   JOHN PAUL JONES · JIMMY PAGE · ROBERT PLANT

MUSICAL SEQUENCES RECORDED AT MADISON SQUARE GARDEN

SOUNDTRACK ALBUM AVAILABLE NEXT WEEK ON **SWANSONG** RECORDS AND TAPES DISTRIBUTED BY ATLANTIC RECORDS A WARNER COMMUNICATIONS COMPANY TECHNICOLOR

FROM WARNER BROS Ⓦ A WARNER COMMUNICATIONS COMPANY RELEASED BY COLUMBIA WARNER DISTRIBUTORS

Tickets on sale Now from:

BOX OFFICE Warner West End 2. **HARLEQUIN RECORDS** 158 Oxford Street W.1. 201 Oxford Street W.1.
Haymarket W.1. 5 Coventry Street W.1. Shaftesbury Avenue W.1. 60 Dean Street W.1. 97/99 Dean Street W.1.
Cranbourne Street W.C.2. Liverpool Street E.C.4. 76 Cheapside E.C.2.
THE VIRGIN WAREHOUSE New Oxford Street W.1. **VIRGIN RECORDS** Marble Arch W.1. Notting Hill Gate W.2.

Film opens Nov 4th at Warner West End 2 and ABC Shaftesbury Avenue.

enough, the night we arrived was a full moon and blow me if there wasn't snow on the mountain. But they didn't get the camera up in time and the snow had melted by the next night. It wouldn't have worked anyway. You need so much floodlighting to get that luminescent quality. It would have been nice, though.

"You need a good range of frequencies to be able to hear what's going on in groups like ours, and you can do that now with stereo radio broadcasts along with TV sound. The film soundtrack was going to be in Quint, by the way, which is a form of Quad. Take stereo, for example, in the cinema, stereo isn't two tracks - it's three. This was all new to me. When they refer to Quad they have an extra track which makes it Quint. We started to work to that system, but we found that Tommy went around the out of-town cinemas, they had the music coming from four speakers and the voices coming out of the fifth speaker behind the screen, and at a lot of points in the cinema you couldn't get a complete sound picture. They were getting a strangled sound with the voices, so we took all this into account and settled on four track stereo, three at the front and one at the back. It works out to give you a circle of sound. It's by no means an easy job to get the sound right in every venue. Cinema managers don't like it if you say 'Your equipment isn't quite what we need, you know, the low end the driving bass lines.' They look down their noses at you especially if they think their stuff is tip-top.

"There's no standard, you know, about the reflective quality of the screen, some have very bright images, some are very dull, same again with the speakers and amplifiers. There's just no standard. It really shocked me. One would have thought a chain of cinemas would have

standard equipment, but no! It was a whole new world to me! Slightly frustrating, but some cinemas have put in special speakers for Tommy, Lizstomania and Earthquake.

"(It was) an incredible challenge because we're not a bunch of chaps that compromise easily. When things went out of synch, for example, it just went right against the grain. Having got over the hurdle of making it, it's exhilarating to feel the response. New York was incredible. It's a great relief that it's out.

"We didn't just want the film to be an in-concert type of thing. It had to have bigger dimensions. In America they have a lot of stereo broadcasts linked with TV concerts, so with the film we had to have more than just the sound to capture the imagination."

Welch asks if they think they might now have to live up to the film. "No, not really. The film ends up with 'Whole Lotta Love' which we only play a couple of bars of now. It means nothing here anyway, it's the Top Of The Pops signature tune now! People who have beamed in on us at a later date would think, what's that load of rubbish? On the last tour we did of America, we in fact only played eight bars of 'Whole Lotta Love' without any vocal, it was just a link and we were ending with 'Stairway', so you see we've moved on from there. We've had two albums out since that concert was filmed, there's a wealth of new stuff. We have already started rehearsals and are pacing ourselves towards touring. And I'm really looking forward to it. We have so many more epics to get into! The tour of the world we were going to embark on was going to include places like Cairo, but that didn't come together. We'd still like to do that one day, because you've gotta have change, you can't stand *still. We're rehearsing now and will start a tour in February. It'll be the States to begin with. I don't know when we'll be back to England. Obviously next year sometime, but I don't know exactly when. The main thing is we're bursting to get back on the road, as you may well imagine.*

"That Presence album really did so much good. When you've been together that long and embark upon an LP, whatever we've got ready, we say, 'Forget about that, we'll go straight in.' And the spontaneity of rehearsals in the studio brings out the best in us. To come up with all that stuff after a frustrating and emotional period, and to find it was all there was marvelous.

"You see we were only a week or so away from the first date when the accident happened, and suddenly we were.... let down, not knowing at all what was coming in the future. There was a great amount of uncertainty. Now the group is very tight. Nobody went off to do sessions or anything like that. There is a great feeling in the band, you know? We'll be going on for years!

"The good feelings are still there. Before our rehearsals for the last album began, we had no idea a thing like 'Achilles' would come out, and it was so exhilarating. You never know what is going to come around the corner next, and that's the whole magic of it.

"Obviously we were committed to putting this album out although it wasn't necessarily the best live stuff we have. I've been working on a lot at home. I've got a couple of long pieces that would make good albums. We've got six live concerts on tape which were good nights. With a computerised desk you can put your mix down, leave it in a box, put it on two years later and it's exactly as you

originally planned it. And you can build up gradually and make a lot of dramatic changes within the space of a four-minute track. We've got some ancient stuff, live at the Royal Albert Hall in 1970, and it's very interesting to listen to now. You can compare different versions of tunes as they span a couple of years. A chronological compilation is the thing I've always been keen on, but the soundtrack came instead, so that can be shelved for a while."

Welch asks whether they had considered more footage of the behind the scenes work of manager Peter Grant, *"Well we were rather dubious about putting something like that down. The scene featuring Peter was pretty honest I thought. I suppose you noticed the silences, did you? I don't know if you saw that link-up broadcast to the States when they had Peter Cook on and they played part of 'Derek & Clive Live' and they had the bleeps in? If you can lip read, it was a bit like 'Derek & Clive'. Possibly we could have had more of that, but the thing we wanted most was the pace to build. The film could have been another concept altogether, and we were trying to keep the music going as much as possible. We didn't want interviews with each member of the group. We were going to leave out the New York hotel robbery, but it was a documentary, it was all true, it happened. It was a montage wasn't it? That was the challenge, to keep it from just being a concert, and I think it's a fair old balance. It could be interesting to do a full documentary on that side of the group, you know, what goes down. But it's a taster. Get your imagination working!"....*

27 Melody Maker reports.... John Bonham, BP Fallon, Roger Chapman went and jammed together at the

Speakeasy after the Thin Lizzy party following Lizzies three night stint at Hammersmith Odeon.... **New Musical Express reports....** The Song Remains The Same is #5 in the UK....

December 1976

4 **Melody Maker reports....** Full page advert reads — Look Forward To Lucifer Rising Kenneth Anger's Vision. Music By Bobby Beausoleil. A supernatural thriller based on Aleister Crowley's "Hymn To Lucifer" from the Book Of Oaths. A Puck Production starring Marianne Faithful as Lilith, introducing Leslie Huggins as Lucifer, Kenneth Anger as Magus, Miriam Gibril as Isis, Donald Cammell as Osiris, Nicky Lane as Scarlet Woman, Haydn Coots as Mithras, Mohammed Jamir as Iblis, Hon. Michael Portman as Junkie, Sir Francis Rose as Chaos, Jimmy Page as Scapegoat. Music by Bobby Beausoleil conducting the Freedom Orchestra recorded live inside Tracy Prison (California). Soundtrack album on Glow-Worm Records. Coming in 1977. Worth waiting for....Apparently Anger wrote a nasty letter about Page to the MM who didn't print it.... **New Musical Express reports....** The Song Remains The Same is #6 in the UK....

11 **New Musical Express reports....** The Song Remains The Same is #11 in the UK....

18 **New Musical Express reports....** The Song Remains The Same is #18 in the UK....

20 **People Weekly reports....** Cover story with headline, "Robert Plant of Led Zeppelin, his songs spin heavy metal into platinum." Feature article in a major mainstream publication. Interview by Jim Jerome with Plant littered with statistics and pictures. Band have sold 24 million albums all eight having gone platinum. $15 million in concert grosses, their movie is in 80 theatres and will gross $3 million by Christmas. It also quotes the Rolling Stone review of the movie which called it, "a tribute to their rapaciousness and inconsideration." Plant then comments about the band, "*We ebb and flow to soothe, then explode as we do in Stairway To Heaven. We have always stood alone in that regard, and critics have allowed our name to be linked with that horrendous boring period of music, heavy metal. I hate the term.*" He then talks of his extracurricular interests, "*I can find my way from 500 AD through to 1066 pretty well as an amateur historian.*" He then talks of the band's on tour antics, "*I was a voyeur, watching it all happen. To rock isn't necessarily to cavort. I still like to get carried away but passively.*" He describes his home with a typically lewd analogy, "*(The farm is) Plunk on the side of a conical Welsh mountain tucked away in the fold of a good skirt, where we should all be. No, no I didn't mean that. It's much easier to live that settled life when you know there's the other too. They augment each other. I dare say one good concert justifies a week of satisfaction at home. Kids are very stabilizing. Carmen used to think she had two fathers, the one whose singing she heard through the speakers and the one on whose knee she was sitting. They love it when I come back to tell them tales.*" ....

25 **Melody Maker reports....** Cover Story.... Zep Men 3 shows.... Article outlining Plant and Bonham's intentions to re-join the Band of Joy for three charity

shows in aid of the relatives of Birmingham band The Possessed who apparently were victims of a car crash. One show will be at Birmingham's Barbarellas and the other at Wolverhampton's Civic Hall.... Robert Plant tried to speak to Allan Jones editor at MM but the switchboard wouldn't put him through, apparently the girl didn't believe he was who he said he was.... **New Musical Express reports....** The Song Remains The Same is #22 in the UK....

1977

January 1977

1 **New Musical Express reports....** The Song Remains The Same is #22 in the UK....

8 **Melody Maker reports....** Letter asks where you can buy Led Zeppelin albums at which point the reply is that they can be bought anywhere, however if they are bootlegs they should be reported to the BPI. Another reader asks what the band's birthdays are, JP 9/1/44, RP 20/8/48, JPJ 3/1/46, JB 31/5/48. And finally someone asks what equipment Jones and Bonham use. Jones uses a Clavinet, a Fender Rhodes Electric Piano and a Steinway Grand Piano. John Bonham uses Ludwig drums and Paiste cymbals....Feature article on Zeppelin publicist B.P. Fallon. Fallon, *"I don't know why but G said that we should get together for a chat. We did and I said, 'Look I love their music but if this is going to work out they've got to dig me and I've got to dig them.' So they flew me over to Switzerland so that I could check them out. They didn't know me. I remember they were doing a sound check and I went onto the stage, and I was sitting on an amp. Then I suddenly realised that I wasn't sitting on an amp. I was sitting on the floor. I'd fallen asleep and fallen off the amp. In the middle of this noise I'd passed out. So they must have thought I was a bit curious. Then we had to get back to the hotel to change for the gig, and I put on my blue velvet cloak and me eye make-up and I'm introduced to the band. And they're all looking at me and Bonzo, particularly is so obviously thinking, 'F—— hell! What have we got here?' But we got on tremendously well and went into business for the British tour, and it was all hunky-dory. I used to play with* them on stage during 'Whole Lotta Love'. I just used to whack out on tambourine. After one concert G came up to me and got me in a corner and said very quietly, 'Beep, there's four members of this band: Remember?' I never played with them after that."

Apparently Fallon then had a severe bout of depression and attempted suicide. He had been badly beaten in Glasgow when he confronted some ticket scalpers outside the show. *"I walked up to some people who were doing a ticket scam and there were all these forged tickets and I said, 'Excuse me, there seems to be some confusion about the tickets you're selling.' And they all jumped on me.*

"I decided to do meself in. I saw this bottle of pills. I don't know if you've ever tried swallowing a bottle of pills, but it's really hard work getting them all in, you know? But I managed it, and I lay down on the bed with my arms crossed over my chest, because I wanted to look like one of those knights in Westminster Abbey. And I decided that when they found me they'd find me with a smile on my face so that they could say, 'Oh great, Beep went out grooving.' So I'm laying there and I thought, 'Fuck I really need a shit. Oh come on Beep, this is no time to be thinking of things like that. Steady on, you've got a more important task in hand.' So I'm still laying there trying to keep the grin together, but it was no good. I really needed a shit.

"I ran to the bathroom whacked down my trousers and it was like Squirter City. A real squirter vibe. There was steam everywhere. And I got hold of the bottle and found that I'd eaten a whole bottle of laxatives. I don't know how they got there, but I remember sitting on the toilet with steam and stench everywhere, with tears rolling down my cheeks and

realised how stupid it all was. Because I'd only have come back as a two legged spider or something. And that would have been a major hang-up."

Fallon then says he has written a book about his on tour antics with Zeppelin called 'Over The Top'. *"Jimmy just used to sit there sometimes looking pretty whacked, and he's really a fragile geezer, and suddenly he'd be on his feet shouting, 'Right, Over the top!' And it would start all over again. The book really is the best rock and roll book I've ever read. It's mostly about Zeppelin, but there's all kinds of sideshoots. Like being with Robert in Chicago and this is the great thing about Zeppelin, they're all still great fans. And Robert wanted to go and see Bobby Bland in a club on the South Side, and everybody told us to keep well out of that one. So we went. So Robert and I are sitting in this dressing room after the gig, and Robert is really gushing to Bobby Bland because he adores this geezer. And there's Bobby Bland sitting at this table counting his money from the gig with a fucking great gun in front of him.*

"I got the book typed out by some dear old lady who didn't know, thank God, what it was all about. I read it a month after she'd finished working on it and I thought, 'Fuck me, I can't put this out.' I made the mistake of just writing down everything that happened, And that's a good way to lose friends. I tried changing it and leaving bits out, but it wasn't as good. I spent eleven months on that book. But I couldn't have published it. It's in a bank in Amsterdam at the moment. Some years really need to elapse before it comes out, because in a way it's about a peak in rock and roll that'll never be surpassed. Just the scale of the tour and the availability of every toy, every

pleasure or perversion. All encapsulated in an experience that lasted like two months.

"None of the band have seen it, and I won't show them. I daren't show it to them. There's friendships that have to be considered too. I mean I can see pound notes hovering in the air, but I won't sell it. It's like a good offer to do a gossip column. Good money was involved and I could've done it under a pseudonym, and I could have said who was sleeping with who and who's whacking what up their nose. But I wasn't interested because I don't want to betray the confidence that people have in me."....**New Musical Express reports....** The Song Remains The Same is #22 in the UK....

15 **New Musical Express reports....** Radio Luxembourg will air a two hour two part series called Led Zeppelin The Way They Were on Monday And Tuesday this week, it is hosted by Tony Prince and Roy Carr.... **National Rock Star reports....** Cover story. Led Zeppelin Back In Action. Article states that Led Zeppelin may play British dates in 1977. The band are reported to have just begun intensive rehearsals at the Fulham studios - Cabin in West London. The band are preparing for their upcoming American tour. It goes on to report that they are looking for luxury flats in Belgravia and Mayfair for the duration of the rehearsals....

22 **Melody Maker reports....** Following MM interview with Zep publicist BP Fallon, Peter Grant has expressed some concern about Fallon's tell-all book. Fallon says the book is in a bank vault in Amsterdam at which point Grant said, "It's certainly safe there. I own the bank!"....

stage, and screen.

Led Zeppelin have sold over 25 million records worldwide. Their fourth LP, according to Billboard magazine is the biggest selling rock album ever! In concert they have broken attendance records around the world - most notably in 1973 at Tampa Stadium in Florida when they broke the Beatles seven year old record for the largest paid audience for a single artist performance in history. On screen, their recently released feature film, "The Song Remains The Same", remained among the top ten grossing films in Variety's charts for over a month. Led Zeppelin are managed by Peter Grant who is also president of their record label, Swan Song.

25 **Swan Song press release....** From: Janine Safer - Sam Aizer

LED ZEPPELIN TO TOUR U.S. FIRST LIVE PERFORMANCES IN TWO YEARS

On February 27, 1977, Led Zeppelin will return to the concert stage for the first time in two years. The itinerary for the first part of the tour is as follows: Feb. 27 - Ft. Worth, Texas (Tarrant County Convention centre); Feb. 28 - Houston (The Summit); March 1 - Baton Rouge (Louisiana State University Assembly Hall); March 3 - Oklahoma City (The Myriad); March 4 - Dallas (Memorial Auditorium); March 6 - Tempe (Arizona St. University Activities Center); March 8 - San Diego (Sports Arena); March 9,12,13 - Los Angeles (The Forum) .
Eight years ago Led Zeppelin exploded onto the music scene with their first LP, creating a new genre of progressive music. Eight platinum albums later, they continue to break new ground on record,

29 **Melody Maker reports....** Robert Plant was seen with Mitch Mitchell at a Tom Robinson concert at the Golden Lion in Fulham last week. It goes on to say that Plant and other Zeps went to see The Damned at the Roxy in Covent Garden..... Israeli radio says Led Zeppelin's Presence is one of their albums of the year.... **New Musical Express reports....** Led Zeppelin start their US tour in February...British dates may happen in the summer.... The Song Remains The Same is #22 in the UK....

February 1977

2 **Swan Song press release....** FROM: Janine Safer - Sam Aizer
LED ZEPPELIN CONCERTS SELL OUT IN RECORD TIME RECORDS SMASHED IN EIGHT CITIES

In an unprecedented feat, Led Zeppelin the British rock and roll powerhouse, sold out every show on the first part of their upcoming U.S. tour in record time. In San Diego (The Sports Arena - capacity 14,000) tickets were sold out in one and a half hours. Tickets in Houston (The Summit - capacity 17,000) were gone in three hours. In Dallas (Memorial Auditorium - capacity 10,000), where people had camped out the previous night in twelve degree weather, the show was sold out in three and a half hours. The Fort Worth (Tarrant County Convention Centre - capacity 14,500) tickets were gone in three and a half hours. The Baton Rouge seats (L.S.U. Assembly Hall - capacity 14,500) were gone in five hours. The Tempe show (Arizona State University Activities Center - capacity 13,500) was sold out in a day and a half and the tickets in Oklahoma City (The Myriad - capacity 14,000) vanished in four hours.

In Los Angeles where tickets for three shows went on sale Monday morning, January 31 (The Forum - capacity 18,000), people were lining up as early as the previous Wednesday. Tickets were sold out in two hours. A fourth show was added immediately as there were over 5,000 people still waiting to purchase tickets.

These concerts will be Led Zeppelin's first performances in two years. The group has been unable to tour due to injuries sustained by vocalist Robert Plant in an auto accident in August, 1975. Plant, now fully recovered promises that the tour will be "adamantly Zeppelin . . . blood thunder and the hammer of the gods." Zeppelin are managed by Peter Grant. Richard Cole is their tour manager.

5 **Melody Maker reports....** Zeppelin To Tour says Chris Charlesworth from New York. he goes on to say the tour will start February 27th in Fort Worth Texas and eleven other shows have been booked on the West Coast including three nights in Los Angeles....

19 **Melody Maker reports....** Zeppelin Men Still Plan Band Of Joy Reunion. Article states that because Zeppelin had shifted their tour dates the charity concert had been rescheduled. It goes on to say that the Band Of Joy will reunite during Zeppelin's tour break in March and they will play two shows with Bonham and Plant at Birmingham Barbarellas and the Wolverhampton Civic Hall. It says they have already concluded rehearsals. Proceeds from the concert are for the families of Birmingham band The Possessed who were recently killed in an automobile accident....

26 **Melody Maker reports....** Robert Plant was on hand to witness Mike Heron's new band at the Wolverhampton Civic before taking Heron on a pub crawl of the area..... **New Musical Express reports....** Cover story, Led Zeppelin Fab Pix Hot Poop, after winning a landslide in the NME music poll the band are interviewed.... Page, *"It only goes to prove that Led Zeppelin are not a nostalgia band."*

Plant, *"The very essence of why you're talking to Zeppelin as four people all in the same room is because we still excite each other. It's not a stagnant situation whereby we're just going through the paces."*

Page, *"I think that if you've got a set that's so cut and dried, so well-rehearsed that you've no other option but to play it note-for-note each night, then it's bound to get stagnant. We've always structured things so that there's an element in which we can suddenly shoot off* on something entirely different and see what's happening. Personally speaking, for me, that's where the element of change and surprise comes in in the possibilities of having that kind of freedom, should you suddenly require it, right in the middle of a number.

"You never quite know what's waiting around the corner. The last time, it was 'Presence'. For that album we all agreed that we'd go right back to square one. Start with nothing, just a few basic structures and the minimum of rehearsal. We completed the album in less than two weeks. That's why 'Presence' was a testament .... if you like, two fingers to all the kinds of things that destroy other bands. We needed to do that album in so much as we had been together a long time and that we required the challenge of working fast and simply."

Plant, "We've never never reached a stage when we've turned to each other in despair and said where do we go from here? But when we recorded 'Presence' we were fighting to survive. I feel that in some ways we have fulfilled our Destiny. But by the same reckoning, there's absolutely no end to that fulfillment. The Doors of Creation are always open.

"'Presence was our stand against everything. Our stand against The Elements, against Chance. We were liter-

ally fighting against Existence itself. We'd left home for 12 months and it seemed that everything was about to crumble. We all knew that maybe it wouldn't come together—but there's absolutely no doubt about it, that album helped pull me through at a time where I just couldn't have taken any more. There's no getting away from the fact that we had our backs up against the wall, but we were determined that nothing was going to stop us. Once we got into the studio, it just happened spontaneously.

"If ever there was a time to quit that was it, because before we went into Musicland, we didn't actually know if we'd ever play together again or, if we did stop, just how long we'd have to wait—and whether or not it would ever be the same should we get back together again. That's why, alone of all the albums we've recorded, 'Presence' relates specifically to a point in time. 'Presence' isn't a précis on aspects of Life in General, but aspects of hurt. That's what songs like 'Tea For One' and 'Hots On For Nowhere' are all about. I was questioning everything."

The suggestion is made about recording solo albums. Plant, "Well, who are we gonna make solo albums with? There's nobody better than this band to play with and nobody better to help you. Sure, one's imagination is a great thing

but it isn't nearly as good as bouncing ideas off one another. You can really only achieve a personal peak after being around certain people for any length of time."

Bonham, *"You've been listening to those interviews George Harrison's been doing on the radio!"*

Plant, *"I think The Beatles were fools to split."*

Page, *"It's all down to the question of the importance of being happy and content within the framework of the group you're a member of. Sufficiently happy enough not to feel the need to go off and make a solo album. Now for quite some time, The Beatles had that kind of mutual contentment. I was in New York, and I can remember McCartney telling me at the time he was cutting his second solo album that it was difficult for him to play with other musicians. McCartney felt that, on his own, it was an uphill struggle. He didn't know the musicians and apart from his reputation as a Beatle, they didn't know him. He didn't realise the immense difficulties until he was suddenly confronted with that specific problem."*

The subject of conversation turns to the Who and the possibility that they might use each other on solo projects, Page, *"Well it's taken them long*

enough to reach that conclusion but isn't that because, in terms of virtually everything The Who undertake, Townshend plays Fuehrer?"

The movie the Song Remains The Same had just been released and the band were having difficulty getting the film shown in theatres that were prepared to present it correctly.

Page, *"Apart from that, it really has proved to be a hard battle against the cinema circuits and their managers. Obviously, one tries to be idealistic about such things, but it's not possible to do what you want on the regular cinema circuits in Britain."*

Plant, *"It's almost the same as when we announce a tour. If Zeppelin play small places like the Nottingham Boat Club, people complain about the size of the place and the sound in the same way as when we put a show on in the biggest indoor arena in the country. In the end, you can't be too discriminating, otherwise you'd end up with a hernia. A lot of people want to see 'The Song Remains The Same' and so we have to leave it up to their better judgment and that of the cinema that's screening it. It's either that or not show it at all!"*

Finally the subject of Plant's health is raised in view of his recent injuries in a car crash in Rhodes, Plant, *"I wouldn't be risking the use of my leg and going out on such a lengthy tour if I felt that it really wasn't worth it. If I and the rest of the band didn't honestly feel that there was something to achieve we'd stay at home. You have to understand, it now goes far beyond how much one can gross on the gate. The bread doesn't come into it any more. Never mind the prissy things—that's something 'Presence' taught us. No matter what some people may think we still care enough to go plonking off around the world yet again."*

Creem reports.... Kevin Doyle reviews The Song Remains The Same. Doyle begins by calling the album 'a boring collection of heavy rock' before qualifying with 'It's also a really good Druid folk-rock album with solid performances.' He suggests that the band have outgrown the need to play the same old stuff and asks the question, how can Page look in the mirror after playing the same riffs for eight years. Doyle then points out that if the album had included White Summer and Ramble On it would have been great, before concluding that if Page and Plant would take to the road with an acoustic show they may achieve the ultimate Zeppelin concert. (A particularly interesting conclusion in light of the Unplugged triumph in 1995. R.G.)....

March 1977

3 **Swan Song official press release....** ALL POSTPONED LED ZEPPELIN CONCERTS NOW RESCHEDULED - All the Led Zeppelin concerts postponed due to the illness of lead singer Robert Plant have now been rescheduled. The Baton Rouge concert is now set for May 19th, The Houston concert has been rescheduled for May 21. Led Zeppelin will now play Ft. Worth on May 22 and Tempe, Arizona on July 20.

This tour will commence in Dallas on April 1, followed by the new Oklahoma City date on April 3rd. Due to the priority of rescheduling the already sold-out shows in the Southwestern United States, several dates have been rearranged. The concert in Atlanta originally set for May 21st will now be April 23. The May 23 Greensboro, North Carolina show has been reset for May 31st. The concert in Birmingham, Alabama has been changed from May 20 to May 18th. The shows in Toronto and Montreal (originally set for April 1, 3-4, respectively) and the Dayton, Ohio date (originally April 22) will be rescheduled later in the tour.
From: Canine Safer - Sam Aizer

5 **Melody Maker reports....** Led Zeppelin's American tour is delayed due to Plant suffering from tonsillitis. The tour will now begin April 1st in Toronto.... **New Musical Express reports....** Led Zeppelin's US tour has been postponed for four weeks due to Robert Plant suffering from tonsillitis....

12 **New Musical Express reports....** Zep

comeback.... Led Zeppelin's manager Peter Grant announced that the band would be playing 41 concerts between April and July. They will appear at the Los Angeles Inglewood Forum and the New York Madison Square Gardens for six nights each. The tour was to have opened in March but was delayed as Robert Plant was suffering from tonsillitis.... the new dates begin in Toronto on April 1st.... because of the delays any chance of UK gigs has been pushed further into the future....

19 **Melody Maker reports....** Chris Welch interviews Plant for a series of ongoing articles on the great singers from Britain.

Plant, *"To start at the beginning, I had been surrounded by English rock way back in the early Sixties. Some of it was very ballsy, but the majority of it was half-baked, and didn't seem to be coming from any place in particular.*

"I'd listen to, say, the Fenmen when they came to the town hall, but I didn't know that 'Money' was a Barrett Strong thing. You always heard these things in the context of English rock.

"Then I'd start to find the originals on the London-American label and a lot of obscure labels that they didn't even know much about in America

"But stuff from Chris Kenner on the Minit label was coming out of New Orleans. The pop music in America was coming direct from local roots I started going back to listen to Snooks Eaglin, and then I heard Robert Johnson for the first time when I was 15.

"One of the things I picked up from Robert Johnson when I started singing was the liaison between the guitar playing and his voice. It was so sympathetic, it almost seemed as if the guitar was his vocal cords

"There was a tremendous amount of emotional content in the guitar and the vocals. It was the most amazing thing I'd ever heard I think Muddy Waters took a lot from his style and later on came Son House and Skip James

"I didn't really relate to their lifestyles as traveling singers. They had a lot of torment in their life, but life can be a torment for anybody. And as far as

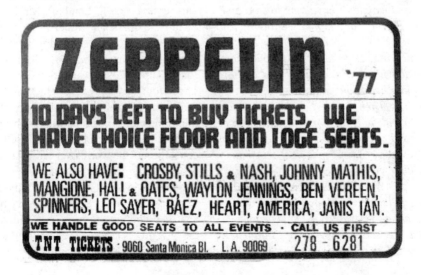

lifestyle goes, I wouldn't have liked to live as some of the blues singers did.

"But they are all the people I listened to around 1960 and by 1965 I was listening to Ray Charles and the more contemporary blues style; and his songs like 'Drown In My Own Tears'.

"On the first Zeppelin LP we did, there was nothing at all to stop me— vocally — from doing what I wanted. Of course, I didn't want to end up like Screaming Jay Hawkins, and the funny thing is that when you finally get the freedom you've been looking for, you don't know what to do with it. At first I didn't know what restraint meant, but then I wanted to use my range more effectively. I never consciously had the idea of mirroring the guitar with my voice but I remembered Robert Johnson had done it, and when I started singing with Jimmy, it just seemed natural.

"I wasn't trying to scat sing but the voice was imitating the guitar. There were no spoken instructions about it for that first album, but we broke into it on 'You Shook Me' and we all broke into smiles.

"Nothing was planned in those days and we didn't have time to stop and think. By the third album we didn't just want to be known as the band that played 'Whole Lotta Love' and 'Communication Breakdown' but of course we had lots of wobbling heads out front.

"Then Deep Purple took that kind of music, that horrible phrase you just used which I refuse to mention (he meant 'heavy-metal'), *took it much further than we ever intended.*

"We always had a much wider range of music we wanted to play. By the third album we wanted to show people we could play something else. Yes, I do listen to the albums mostly from the fourth

onwards but each album has its own importance to me 'Physical Graffiti' I play a bit."

In conclusion Welch asks him if he would like to record a solo album, *"No. Not at all. It wouldn't make any sense. Everything I want to do, I can do with the band."*

Swan Song press release.... LED ZEPPELIN

As the years go by and we watch rock and roll bands reach peaks, fall from those same peaks, break up, glue themselves back together again or just plain re-cycle.. Led Zeppelin continues to be. As with all the great 'superstar' rock bands, Led Zeppelin continues to produce the kind of visceral spirit, gripping music that is always an instantaneous success with an audience that transcends age categorization. A lot of people get off on it, prima facie success rule of rock that Zep has lived up to with full heart and mind since its inception back in late '68.

At that time there was a small London rehearsal hall that housed Mr. Jimmy Page (late of the Yardbirds and numero uno session man in London), Mr. Robert Plant (late of Alexis Korner Blues Band), Mr. John "Bonzo" Bonham (a rising young drummer), and Mr. John Paul Jones (super session man, and arranger). These four men played together and created some of the best contemporary blues rock music ever heard earning eight gold multi million seller LPs, constant sell-out concert tours the world over with standing ovations as normal procedure. Led Zeppelin is in the contemporary pantheon of rock which includes only the very best, and they continue to grow and evolve in the best professional sense, assuring us of years of great music to come.

The scene is London mid-winter 1968. A small rehearsal hall with four musicians who are about to play together for the first time. Jimmy Page, former Yardbird and leading session guitarist in England had jammed with John Paul Jones (ace keyboard session man, bass player and arranger.) They were pleased with the results and now were thinking about projecting that jam into a total 'band concept'. With the fortuitous addition of Robert Plant (ex Alexis Korner Blues Band singer) and John 'Bonzo' Bonham on drums that projection was to take form in a group named Led Zeppelin. A group that was to be the totally successful prototype for the super heavy English blues-rock bands of the sixties.

The very distinctive sound that Zep developed was built on powerful, mesmerising guitar riffs by Mr. Page and a mammoth rock bottom bass-drum sound with Plant's vocals pushing the general energy level along. Added to this were some incredible solo instrumentals, a stunning use of electronic technology to supplement the sound and a dynamic visual stage presentation that brought standing ovations on their very first tours. In each of these areas, Zeppelin established precedent setting modes that became Standard Operating Procedure for many bands that followed. They were the first group to take high volume and distortion, make it a distinct, creative entity and key it directly to the emotional thrust of each song. Jimmy Page combined the virtues of precision and innovation from his session days with the unbridled power and soaring emotionalism that typifies rock and roll at its best. The rest of the group contributed in equal parts that welded the group into a total fusion of electronic excitement.

The public was quick to recognise all of the inherent virtues in Led Zeppelin and have consequently made the group a world leader in contemporary music. Each of the group's eight albums has been a certified gold-million seller while Zeppelin continues to get SRO audiences in concert halls and arenas in Europe, Japan, England and America. They have won just about every music poll and their albums get continuous and extensive play on radio stations throughout the world. One of the reasons for Zep's solid continuity in music is their regenerative ability to grow and change without lessening in overall power or effectiveness. Their individual talents as musicians; arrangers; songs writers; producers and 'sound creators' assures them a continuing position in the vanguard of modern music.

DISCOGRAPHY:

LED ZEPPELIN
LED ZEPPELIN 2
LED ZEPPELIN 3
LED ZEPPELIN (FOUR SYMBOLS)
HOUSES OF THE HOLY
PHYSICAL GRAFFITI
PRESENCE
SOUNDTRACK OF THE FILM "THE SONG REMAINS THE SAME"

THE PLAYERS:
JIMMY PAGE - Lead guitar. Equipment on stage: choice of three Gibson Les Pauls (vintage models) 1 Gibson SG Double neck, 1 Dan Electro, 1 Fender Stratocaster. Thirty two year old Jimmy Page, together with Peter Grant founded Led Zeppelin and produced all their recordings, he began playing guitar in his

early teens taking his roots from blues, Chuck Berry, and early Elvis Presley recordings. Originally from Feltham, near London's Heathrow airport, he began touring with small groups but later decided to go to Art College. Page spent some time in college, but continued to play clubs in and around London, never losing his interest in music. He moved onto studio work, and by the time he was twenty had become a successful session guitarist, recording with, among others, the Kinks, the Who, Van Morrison and Joe Cocker.

In 1966 Page joined the legendary Yardbirds as bass player and shortly thereafter the band re-organised and Page was playing dual lead with Jeff Beck. Page remained after Beck left in 1967, taking the band to new heights and achieving lasting respect and critical acclaim.

With the folding of the Yardbirds, Page decided to form his own band, christened by Keith Moon - Led Zeppelin.

ROBERT PLANT - Vocals. Growing up in the Black Country of Birmingham, twenty eight year old Robert Plant's intentions and training were directed towards being a chartered accountant, but his great love was always music. He played in a succession of Birmingham blues bands, among them The Crawling King Snakes, Black Snake Moan, Alexis Korner Blues Band and the Band of Joy. Earning a reputation of "The Wild Man of Blues from the Black Country", Plant found little recognition in Birmingham so he moved to London where he stayed until Jimmy Page asked him to join Led Zeppelin.

JOHN PAUL JONES - Bass and Keyboards. Equipment on stage: Fender Fretless Bass, Fender Jazz Bass, 1 Fender Set Bass Pedals, 2 W Dunne Bass Pedals, Mellotron, Clavinet Fender Rhodes Electric Piano, 8 String Bass guitar, Steinway Grand Piano (tuned to Concert pitch with electric pick ups).

It was John Paul Jones' father, an accomplished pianist with the famous Ambrose Orchestra in the Big Band Era who insisted that John learn to read music so at the age of six he began to study Piano. While at school in Christ College, Blackheath he formed his own group, and subsequently played several American Bases in the area. He also worked on the road with his parents as part of a trio, John playing bass and his father on piano.

In London John Paul Jones began to do session work, especially arrangements, contributing to the Rolling Stones 'Their Satanic Majesties Request' LP and to tunes by Donovan and Dusty Springfield. Jones was the arranger of Donovan's 'Sunshine Superman' and 'Mellow Yellow' and while working on the singer-songwriter's 'Hurdy Gurdy Man' he met Jimmy Page. When Jones heard that Page was putting a band together, they renewed their acquaintance and Jones became a member of Led Zeppelin. John is thirty.

JOHN BONHAM - Drums. Equipment on stage: Ludwig Drum Kit, 2 Timpani, Dinner gong and effects. Raised in the Birmingham area, John Bonham never had any formal music training. He played in clubs around his home town but was unpopular because he played too loudly. One time he was drummer with Robert Plant in the Band of Joy. With drums the only spot to be filled with the new Led Zeppelin, Plant suggested Bonham, who was at the time working with Tim Rose. It took a good deal of convincing, but finally Bonham agreed to join the group, completing the band. An avid auto enthusiast, twenty eight year old Bonham is also an active farmer in Worcestershire.

PETER GRANT - Manager. As much a member of the band as the four musicians, Peter has combined a rare mixture of hard business sense with close personal friendship with each member of Zeppelin. As Executive Producer he has worked on all eight albums, and far prefers to be on the road, traveling to each of the group's gigs around the world than puffing a fat cigar in an office complex. Peter's initial involvement was with Jimmy in the Yardbirds days - a relationship which flourished into the formation of Led Zeppelin in 1968. There is no disputing the fact that along with one of the finest bands in the world, Peter Grant is undoubtedly the finest manager.

Sixth Revision....
LED ZEPPELIN 1977 TOUR DATES
First Leg of Tour

April 1 Memorial Aud. Dallas, Texas
April 2 Off
April 3 The Myriad Oklahoma City,OK
April 4 Off
April 5 Off
April 6 Stadium Chicago, Illinois
April 7 Stadium Chicago, Illinois
April 8 Off
April 9 Stadium Chicago, Illinois
April 10 Stadium Chicago, Illinois
April 11 Off
April 12 Metropolitan Sports Center Minneapolis, Minnesota
April 13 Civic Center St. Paul, Minnesota
April 14 Off
April 15 Blues Arena St. Louis, Missouri

April 16 Off
April 17 Market Square Arena Indianapolis, Indiana
April 18 Off
April 19 Riverfront Coliseum Cincinnati, Ohio
April 20 Riverfront Coliseum Cincinnati, Ohio
April 21 Off
April 22 Off
April 23 OMNI Atlanta, Georgia
April 24 Off
April 25 Kentucky Fairgrounds & Exposition Center Louisville, Kentucky
April 26 Off
April 27 Coliseum Richfield, Ohio (Cleveland)
April 28 Coliseum Richfield, Ohio (Cleveland)
April 29 Off
April 30 Silverdome Pontiac, Michigan (Detroit)
May 1 to May 17 Off

Second Leg of Tour

May 18 Coliseum Birmingham, Alabama
May 19 L.S.H. Assembly Hall Baton Rouge, LA.
May 20 Off
May 21 The Summit Houston, Texas
May 22 Warrant County Convention Center Ft. Worth, Texas
May 23 Off
May 24 Off
May 25 Capitol Center Largo, Maryland (Washington, DC)
May 26 Capitol Center Largo, Maryland
May 27 Off
May 28 Capitol Center Largo, Maryland
May 29 Off
May 30 Capitol Center (Subject to P.G. decision) Largo, Maryland
May 31 Coliseum Greensboro, North

Carolina
June 1 Off
June 2 Off
June 3 Stadium Tampa, Florida
June 4 Off (Raindate-Tampa)
June 5 Off
June 6 Off

Second Leg of Tour

June 7 Madison Square Garden New York, New York
June 8 Madison Square Garden New York, New York
June 9 Off
June 10 Madison Square Garden New York, New York
June 11 Madison Square Garden New York, New York
June 12 Off
June 13 Madison Square Garden New York, New York
June 14 Madison Square Garden New York, New York
June 15 Off
June 16 Off
June 17 Off
June 18 Off
June 19 Sports Arena San Diego, CA
June 20 Off
June 21 The Forum Los Angeles, CA
June 22 The Forum Los Angeles, CA
June 23 The Forum Los Angeles, CA
June 24 Off
June 25 The Forum Los Angeles, CA
June 26 The Forum Los Angeles, CA
June 27 The Forum Los Angeles, CA
June 28 to July 16   Off
July 17 Kingdome Seattle, Washington
July 18 Off
July 19 Off
July 20 Arizona State University Activities Center Tempe, Arizona
July 21 Off
July 22 Off

July 23 Oakland Stadium Oakland, CA
July 24 Oakland Stadium Oakland, CA
July 25 Off
July 26 Off
July 27 Off
July 28 Off
July 29 Off
July 30 The Superdome New Orleans, Louisiana

April 1977

16 **Melody Maker reports....** Dave Gilmour of Pink Floyd calls the MM to correct them. He says Floyd used lasers long before Led Zeppelin....

29 **Plain Dealer reports....**Zeppelin Goes Over Big. Review of the show in Cleveland. Tickets were being scalped for over $100. Apparently 19,000 fans gave the band a two minute standing ovation before they played a note. Journalist Jane Scott says that 'Page proved once again that he is the world's top blues guitarist.' The show ran for three hours and included Page's Star Spangled Banner which Scott says was the first performance of that number. She goes on to say that the song list was the same as at the Indianapolis show last week except they did two encores for the Cleveland audience....

Creem reports.... Cover story reprinting Nick Kent's interview with Jimmy Page in New Musical Express on November 20th 1976....

May 1977

14 **Melody Maker reports....** Review of the show in St. Louis. Zep: No Messing.

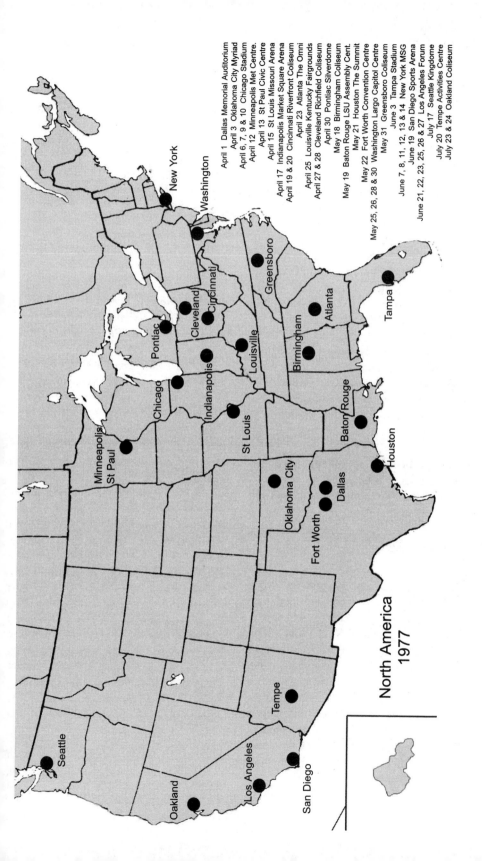

North America
1977

April 1   Dallas Memorial Auditorium
April 3   Oklahoma City Myriad
April 6, 7, 9 & 10 Chicago Stadium
April 12 Minneapolis Met Centre.
April 13 St Paul Civic Centre
April 15 St Louis Missouri Arena
April 17 Indianapolis Market Square Arena
April 19 & 20 Cincinnati Riverfront Coliseum
April 23 Atlanta The Omni
April 25 Louisville Kentucky Fairgrounds
April 27 & 28 Cleveland Richfield Coliseum
April 30 Pontiac Silverdome
May 18 Birmingham Coliseum
May 19 Baton Rouge LSU Assembly Cent.
May 21 Houston The Summit
May 22 Fort Worth Convention Centre
May 25, 26, 28 & 30 Washington Largo Capitol Centre
May 31 Greensboro Coliseum
June 3 Tampa Stadium
June 7, 8, 11, 12, 13 & 14 New York MSG
June 19 San Diego Sports Arena
June 21, 22, 23, 25, 26 & 27 Los Angeles Forum
July 17 Seattle Kingdome
July 20 Tempe Activities Centre
July 23 & 24 Oakland Coliseum

New York
Washington
Greensboro
Cincinnati
Cleveland
Atlanta
Tampa
Pontiac
Louisville
Birmingham
Chicago
Indianapolis
Baton Rouge
St Louis
Minneapolis
St Paul
Houston
Oklahoma City
Dallas
Fort Worth
Tempe
Seattle
Los Angeles
Oakland
San Diego

Patti Dewing notes that the band are in the mood to reclaim their title after Plant's physical ordeal. She concludes, *"There was absolutely nothing to deny their purposefulness: no smugness, no sloppiness, and no more holding back. Just an apparent all out effort on the part of each man to make Led Zeppelin the best and most significant rock band in the world."*....

21 **Melody Maker reports....** Article states the band were presented with Ivor Novello Awards last week for their contributions to British Music. Only John Bonham was not in attendance. The awards were presented by John Inman star of 'Are You Being Served'.... **New Musical Express reports....** Jimmy Page will be flying to Cairo on vacation.... apparently due to his frail condition he has a doctor on hand at all times.... promoters are actively chasing the band for UK dates....

28 **New Musical Express reports....** Led Zeppelin have been asked to play at a Festival in Wrotham Park Barnet on August 20th....

June 1977

4 **New Musical Express reports....** Mick Ralphs of Bad Company joined Led Zeppelin on stage at their recent show in Fort Worth Texas....**New York Post reports....** 50 injured in Fla. Rock riot. 19 arrested as Led Zeppelin is rained out. The article goes on to detail that when a thunderstorm struck five minutes into the band's Tampa show. The concert was called to a halt which was the beginning of a riot amongst the 70,000 fans who were then subdued by the local riot police armed with clubs....

9 **Circus reports....** Interview with Jimmy Page shortly after canceling the show early in Chicago due to illness, *"They think it was food poisoning. The Doctor says no solids. It's the first time we've ever stopped a gig like that. We always have a go, really, because we're not a rip-off band. But the pain was unbearable if I hadn't sat down I would've fallen over. Anyway, we'll make it up to them. We'll do an all-request show.*

"It's so embarrassing, because I've been jumping across the stage, really moving. I'm sorry you missed my Psycho Strut. I'm too vain. But we've all got our pride, haven't we?"

He addresses the subject of a recent bad review, *"You can't sum up nine years of total commitment in one day. I always take a chance, I can't just play safe. Dancing on the edge of the precipice; you've gotta live like that. Better to live one day as a lion than a thousand years as a lamb, y'know?*

"I think Presence was a highly under rated record. Presence was pure anxiety and emotion. I mean, we didn't know whether we'd ever be able to play in the same way, again. It might have been a very dramatic change, if the worst had happened to Robert. Presence is our best in terms of uninterrupted emotion. The whole thing took three weeks and a bit did you know that?

"The last day of rehearsal was pure magic, and I thought, 'Right. We're going to have a go. We've got the stamina to play ten straight hours.' And then suddenly Robert got tonsillitis."

Apparently the band's equipment had already been shipped to America for the tour when Plant was struck down with tonsillitis.

"All I had was a dulcimer. After the postponement, I didn't touch a guitar for four weeks. It was a bit unnerving, really. (I was) pacing around like a caged lion and I'm not even a Leo. Climbing the walls. Sleepless nights, you bet your life. You hear that you've been selling out stadiums in twenty four hours, and you think, 'Christ.' When we finally did our first date in Dallas, it was a vast emotional release.

"Our acoustic set is a bit of a breather, but 'Going to California' is our only relaxed number. Even 'Battle of Evermore' is taxing to play. I was just a rock 'n roller with the Yardbirds. I still am just a rock 'n roller but more obnoxious really."

He is asked why he doesn't include Dazed & Confused in the set, *"I'm not really dazed and confused any more, I got over the wall and broke through the boundaries about a year ago. I've been having a bit of fun. A bit of outrage at clubs and things, dancing with all the couples, going generally mad and doing football chants. The old ultra violence, y'know? 'I've got a pint of bitter. Now I'm feeling better cause I'm out on the tiles.' It's good out on the tiles, away from home. It's a stag party that never ends. And it's been great to get back on the road after all the trials and tribulations that have been a hazard for over a year. It's great to see the smiles.*

"This is no last tour. We're here, and we'll always come back. It would be a criminal act to break up this band."....

11 **New Musical Express reports....** This Man Destroys Hotels.... an in depth article reviewing the band's tour of the USA by Creem Magazine's Jaan Uhelski.... the well known US pulp magazine follows the tour and reporter Uhelski scatters news reports of the rioting amidst her edi-

torial to give the maximum shock effect. Apparently riots ensued in Cincinnati when 1,000 people tried to gate crash the show, 100 arrests were made. In Oklahoma City fans camped out for three days and set fires to beat back the weather, while in Houston the police used water cannons to control over three thousand fans who tried to stampede a Warehouse Records ticket outlet. In Chicago thirty arrests were made at the ticket windows. In Miami nearly 1,000 fans broke into the Orange Bowl and began to vandalise the area, while in Poughkeepsie New York when ticket demand couldn't be met the punters resorted to sending plastic explosives to the ticket agency. God Bless America....

Meanwhile Uhelski does manage to get good access to the band and manages to open a few windows to the besieged Zeppelin camp.... Plant is confronted about the band's penchant for destroying hotels, *"It's not any release you know, all that shit about road fever is just bullshit. We only do what we do because it's fun. The lifestyle of rock n' roll is to live well and to take a good woman."*

When she meets up with Page there is a brief discussion about the previous nights show in Minneapolis, Page, *"I think there were some tremendous moments last night, it was very intense.... we were tight, yet loose. Loosely tight. You know someday I'd like to call an album that, 'Loosely Tight'."*

Uhelski reveals that the tour is expected to gross something like $10 M in 40 cities with 700,000 tickets sold. She then asks Plant what they would do if the tickets hadn't sold, *"We'd just do the tour and become our own best advertisement. I mean our music may change so much in times to come that our audience does diminish. Because I know we won't become passé, we might take things beyond what people are prepared to accept from us. For example, our third album wasn't immediately accepted, but it was a signpost for the continuity of the internal stimulus of the band. It had to be. It was the next step and people didn't take to it too quickly. They were more interested in where's Whole Lotta Love? Had we not done that, we would probably have stayed together for only one more album. When you think you've reached a dead end you have to get off the horse."*

One of the things dogging the band are the reports of violence at the shows and the throwing of firecrackers. Plant, *"Well one thing that does upset me I see a lot of craziness around us. Somehow we generate it and we revile it. This is an aspect since I've been away from it which made me contemplate whether we are doing more harm than we are good. That's very important to me. I'm not doing a Peter Green or anything. What I mean is, what we are trying to put across is positive and wholesome; the essence of a survival band, and almost a symbol of the phoenix if you will; and people react in such an excitable manner that they miss the meaning of it, and that makes me lose my calm and I get angry. I don't know why the fans toss firecrackers. I think it's horrible. That's the element that makes you wonder whether it's better to be half way up a tree in Wales. The thing is I look into so many eyes every night, and when I initially look those eyes are sort of sealed cause they don't think I'm real, but bit by bit I work on just those pairs of eyes until they glow with warmth, and then it makes it worthwhile, and wooooosh, the firecrackers dim down."....* Plant then concludes by expressing a desire to go to Kashmir to grow up....

18 **Melody Maker reports....** Harvey Goldsmith says he is trying to get Led Zeppelin for the Barnet Festival this summer.....

23 **Los Angeles Times reports....** Music critic Robert Hilburn dusts off his 1975 review of the band and re-iterates many of the same points, "The tunes mostly are exercises in style rather than substance." He then offers that the other great British outfits such as the Stones, Who and Kings (?? presumably he means the Kinks and not the Canadian "Switchin To Glide" combo) are more satisfying. He does however acknowledge that the first 45 minutes were, "...tenacious and well paced leaving little doubt about the quartets ability to deliver on stage." He complains that the shows at three and a half hours are, "too long by at least a third." A point which no doubt most of those in attendance would probably not agree with. He maintains that all three solos are uneventful and detract from the overall pace of the show, and neglects to point out that the audience expects them.

25 **Melody Maker reports....** Under the banner 'Biggest Of Them All' this article speculates that the band will play in front of 1,338,729 people during their current US tour. It also reports that the band's own attendance record was beaten at the Pontiac Silverdome when they played in front of 76,229 with a gross take of £467,000. It goes on to mention the abrupt ending at the Tampa concert on June 3rd when rain stopped play after 20 minutes. After the audience rioted the rain date was canceled by local authorities.... Ray Coleman interviews Robert Plant. It may well be the best interview Plant gave from the era, covering all manner of

things such as his perceptions of Punk rock, his use of 'star power' etc. Coleman begins the interview touching on the subject of Plant's injury, Plant, *"So I was really at home with the idea of playing. The only thing I didn't know about was whether I was going to be able to pace myself out, with my foot problems. For the first two or three gigs I was really measuring every move I made, to find if I'd gone too far or whatever. The first gig in Dallas, Texas, I was petrified. Since Earl's Court in London, all this horrendous physical hoo-ha had taken place and for the ten minutes before I walked up those steps in Dallas I was cold with fright. Supposing I couldn't move around the stage properly, because my right foot is permanently enlarged now. Well, it was killing for the first two gigs. I had to be virtually carried back on one foot. But once I'd got it used to the concussive knocks of stage work, it was OK and now I've paced myself so I can work without anyone, hopefully, realising that I have this thing to live with. The thing is, I don't really know what I'm doing with my body when I'm playing and I just throw myself around the stage instinctively. But Dallas was the worry: I thought about what would happen if the foot wouldn't take it. Yet when I walked up the steps to the stage, all the premonitions and anxieties just loved being back up there - and I was a looney again!"*

The band had recently re-introduced the acoustic set, Plant, *"To begin with, people were a little bit restless. They didn't know what the hell was going on. Kept looking at us, presumably thinking: Are they really THAT old? But because of the way in which we've taken the challenge of re-working some of our old material and introducing some unlikely aspects of it into stage work, that way*

we've gone a stage farther again. Suddenly it burst through after six gigs, so that by the time we got to places like St. Louis, it had taken on another level of control, rather than merely trotting out the old favourites - for example, John Paul Jones is getting far more involved now, he's the sort of man-of-the-match! I've won the battle up to now. It's a great feeling, I can tell you."

Coleman continues, asking about Plant's perception of the band's future, *"We took off with so much invigorating energy in '68, and then we curbed that energy so that the whole dynamics of the band would ebb and flow, so that we wouldn't burn ourselves out musically by taking the opportunity to go hair-raisingly mad and fade a whole-lotta-loving into the sunset! By sitting down and taking up the challenge and realising that we were, are, and will be, capable of expanding, that can be the only hope for the future, and that's how we want to make our impression and be remembered...for constantly trying to ride the winds of change. And how good we were at it in the end, when it's all over, will be up to the individual to judge. I personally think we've done all right. I'd say we have a lot of people there from the beginning or people who look as if they were! Then again, I looked behind the stage tonight, in the seats that are not readily sought after, and found a whole new breed coming up. Kids who've got a pirate Zeppelin T-shirt on that's much too big for them. And then I smile. And I see our children, and kids a few steps behind them digging it, and in the end I come round to thinking that it's funny it took such a long time to bridge so many gaps, musically, y'know. There was, I mean, that period when there was us, alone, with so many other bands of good quality and calibre - the 'under-*

ground music'thing. Now, it doesn't mean a light, just an old cliché. Now the whole scene's wide open, and it's a matter purely of how good you are, whatever your style."

Coleman points out that Plant has been listening to Bulgarian folk music, *"They use quarter-tones but at the same time in their harmonies, instead of firsts, thirds, fifths and sevenths and all the conventional Western European styles of harmony, they use firsts and seconds. And I've never been trained to do anything in my life and I find it difficult to harmonise with myself on record. But I find it very inspiring to listen to stuff, like that, on the Nonsuch label from the Elektra catalogue. It comes straight out of the hills - it's what you might call mass singing, like village singing when a village gets together at various times of the year when they hope for this, that and the other to happen all that we in Britain have almost lost. Otherwise, I'm never too far away from Robert Johnson. There's no way on this earth that I could ever find his work tiring. And then there are several things which have come up very nicely - Fleetwood Mac have taken a nice turn. Obviously it's not musically new, but I do like that kick-in-the-air California-sand music when it's played really well. A lot of it went sour, but Fleetwood Mac have brought something good out of it. You can never get too far away from Mick Fleetwood's drums, which is just like it used to be, the way he uses tom-toms. Little Feat have always intrigued me. They've never really got their just deserts for what they don't play, rather than for what they do play. I'd like to see which way Mike Heron goes next, because that album with the Reputation was good, but the Heron album was much better. He seemed a little rigid and I think*

he'll loosen up a little bit.

"Lots of varying styles appeal to me. There's one track over here by a group called Kansas that hasn't even come out in England, which is a big hit single here. If they have a good record company in England you should be hearing it soon and it's a good 'un - I think they're probably a bit like bands like Boston, who seem to have one good song on every album! And without blowing our own trumpet too much - Dave Edmunds is great. Bit of a looney, but he's really, really good."

Plant denies any competitiveness with the other giant rock bands, *"In the early days, I guess we were in competition a little, when Beck and Ronnie Wood and Rod Stewart and Mickey Waller and Nicky Hopkins were on the road, because Jeff Beck had come out of the Yardbirds and Jimmy had, and there was that interplay.*

"But Jimmy's my mate, and I can tell you none of this competitiveness came from him, even though it seemed to make all the going-out- together for pleasure with other musicians an uncomfortable thing. But once we started going off, musically, on our own things settled down and we could mix easily with anyone because there's no competition. I don't mean that to sound how it probably does, big headed, but with all good individual acts, like say the Stones, we are on our own. It's only on a musical level that we think of ourselves anyway. It's not who can pull the biggest crowds, 'cos we leave that to Elton, God bless him!"

Coleman points out that the Punk bands think that by playing in huge stadiums there is no longer any contact between the band's and the audience. *"It was like playing in a living room tonight at Madison Square Garden. You could easily walk to the side of the stage, just* catch somebody's eye and work to that person, like in any club. Okay, so there were 20,000 people there, but I'm willing to bet that nearly every one of them left that place happy at what they'd seen. It certainly sounded like it to me, anyway, judging from the reception they gave us. Let's face it, if Johnny multi-vocabulary Rotten gets his act together he'll have to take it elsewhere, leave Nottingham Boat Club behind, because they'll be too many people to get into that size of place and he'll have more people being unhappy at his lack of foresight. He'll just have to open it up bigger than that. He'll also have to change his act soon. It's getting a bit tiring, all that, because the dinosaur bands are still dancing."

Apparently Plant had seen the Sex Pistols at The Roxy. His comments about Johnny Rotten, *"Kim Fowley's the closest I've ever seen to him, but Kim Fowley's old enough to be Johnny's dad, and Johnny's as old as me. Kim Fowley's great, one of the great innovators of all time, but he's so permanently weirded out on such a nice level, freaky but great...anyway, I went to the Roxy and got frightened to death, but, at the same time, stood my ground for all we dinosaurs, and I saw the Damned. I found them very exciting, thrilling. Rat Scabies is a great drummer. He's no spring chicken either, and when I look at those eyes - well, I know that those leapers do terrible things to your eyes, but I can read the sands of time as well! But they're good, the Damned. If they didn't have the paint and clothing or whatever and just came along and did it, they'd probably be twice as big as they are now. But they've had to throw off the robes of the punk thing, and in doing so it's cost them time. They did that T. Rex tour, so they've obviously broken out of that melee...but anyway, they were*

very good.

"Other bands? I saw the group - what's that one with the 15-year-old drummer? Eater! Well, a lot of people need to go home and do their homework. I mean, I play guitar on four tracks on our albums but I wouldn't dare play on stage. When all the shouting's over and it's just down to music and pulling people in who are going to sit through it, then I'll be there to see it. As a basic movement. . .it's good, but I wish the music was more original and was moving on a stage. The Stranglers, for example, sound like an English Doors pre- 'LA Woman.' So that doesn't do much for me or anyone else, really. The intensity and the excitement I do like, because I never forget the first time I saw the Small Faces and the Who, when I was at school. It was that very thing that made me go: 'YEAH' - and I rushed to the barber's and got a French crew or whatever they were called, the right mod haircut. So I know what all that's about, rushing around getting a parka and immediately getting chrome side panels for your scooter, and belonging again, 'cos I was just a bit too young for the drape jackets. I understand all that. Everyone needs something to hang on to a little bit, on some level of mass entertainment 'when-the-work-is-done-what-are-we-gonna-do?' As long as everybody doesn't go overdosing on leapers again, it's fine.

"But I go to a lot of soccer and I see another element of youth and that really frightens me. We have to make sure that the music doesn't dance hand in hand with the shed boys, because if the two elements got together, that music would do just as much harm as Chelsea losing 3-1. So provided the music really has got some content so that the kids really get off on it, and they wait for certain numbers to come

and they really enjoy 'em - then it's worked, and it's the next step. Then it'll be only a matter of time before you're asking them, after a nine-year career, what they think of this and that. But you'll only be asking these punk rock bands or new wave bands, or whatever, if they vary what they're doing because there's no staying power in staying the same."

Coleman asks him about the supposed expectations of being blatantly sexual as a rock singer, *"I suppose that when I wear a Wolverhampton Wanderers football shirt, that's hardly sexual, but I still read a lot of things saying I'm sexually doing this and sexually looking that on the stage. If any of my movements appear sexual, then they are really just accessories to the music at that point in time. I get quite heatedly involved with what's going on musically, and invariably I'm right in front of John Paul's equipment or Jimmy's. I'm concentrating on what I'm listening to and I move accordingly. There are movements I do all the time, regularly, but if I was going to start consciously thinking about how I was going to appear, I might begin to take myself a little too seriously in the wrong direction."*

Does he think of himself as a star? *"Oh god no. I'm a member of a band. I remember reading once something John Entwistle said about 'there go Zeppelin again, saying how they're one big happy family and they'll never break up and we've heard all this before.' But all those critics should realise that I have no vocal accelerations or any vocal movements. They are all inspired by the music around me and the knowledge that I can do it anyway and want to push it a bit farther. And that can only come by playing with people who surprise you. Like Jimmy's solo tonight in 'No Quarter' - it was just fantastic, very well-constructed*

in such a manner different from before, so that I can't help but respond differently to that. So that I can never see myself projecting myself as the one who does the vocals while the other three play the music. I can't see it changing dramatically either. I'm the guy who puts the words in. No part of my job is to overshadow the music. I'm not a symbol or anything. The only reason that could change it is if character-wise, we started drifting apart, and then to keep things together, I'd have to look elsewhere for stimulation."

Coleman asks if the band are in danger of splitting, *"Oh no, no. Bonzo and I are getting on better now than we ever have done. We've only had one fight on this tour!"*

Did he have any inspiration from contemporary singers such as Steve Marriott? *"I could never be compared with Steve Marriott because he's too good, unfortunately! He has got the best white voice, for sheer bravado and balls. How he applies it to his career is neither here nor there, but he is the master of white contemporary blues. He came down to some of our rehearsals in London before this tour and to me, the two of us singing Muddy Waters songs was almost as hair-raising as our first gig. That's the dynamism of my vocalism which I do touch on occasionally. It's only one aspect, although Steve is the best at what he does. On the more mellow side, there are a lot of people who can control their voices in such a way that makes it pleasurable to the ear. At one point, Jesse Colin Young had that ability, when the Youngbloods were at their best, on 'Elephant Mountain' and things like that. Lowell George I do like, and when he sings in a subdued manner he's very good."*

Coleman asks a very perceptive

and interesting question, whether due to the band's blues roots they are perceived differently by the American audiences, *"Right now, America is getting a rebirth from us, like the capital letter of the first sentence of a new paragraph. Nobody comes up and taps you on the shoulder to involve you in anything that isn't related to work when you're on the road in America. This is solely work. No side effects. Whereas if you're traveling from home to a gig in England, you tend to come out differently on stage, maybe you're more relaxed - but whatever, you're not wound up for work like in America, where you're in a hotel and there's all this security around us and you can definitely feel a kind of tension. So you get out on that stage knowing that that's the only release you can possibly have, 'cos you're here to work and WHOOSH! And after the gig, no jingle jangles or going anywhere, just back to the hotel, put on the Elmore Jones albums, and unwind that way. Whereas in England, working from a set base and doing a gig, going home again, it's different. Of course, if we did just an acoustic set back in England it would probably be our finest hour! Nice and mellow and gentle. But there's a kind of an excitement in an American audience that belongs only to an American audience, and events during the concert which you can pick up on tend to make your reactions to them, through the music, that much more adamant.*

"There's a lot of mishandling of kids, for instance, by the authorities, and there are a lot of kids without manners who don't contemplate their neighbour at all - so there is all this interplay which you're very aware of. Whereas at an English concert it usually goes on the way it starts off. The enthusiasm builds, but it's

always retained inside that composure. There are some towns in the Midwest where they have what's called 'festival seating', which means no seating, the first come-first-served effect. So you get people who've been queuing up all afternoon and they're the first in. By the third number, say by the time we reach 'Nobody's Fault But Mine,' there's this great milling of people and it's a bit chaotic. I have to spend about thirty minutes trying to convince these folk that it would be much better both for us and them if they had some semblance of order.

"Worst of all is the realisation that if the mob scenes continue, and people are milling around in a crush, somebody is going to get hurt and hit the deck."

Coleman pursues his intelligent line of questioning with one about whether Plant is tempted to use his celebrity stature as an ego trip, *"I got over that power thing about seven years ago. Everybody goes through that 'where do I stand in all this?' scene when their audiences build up from clubs to concerts to gigantic arenas and you wonder how far you should go. My own feeling is that you should play it very cool. A lot hangs on the balance struck, the relationship between the guy at the front of that microphone and 20,000 people, and I've learned to soft pedal very carefully. In the beginning you tend to try to channel their enthusiasm and build it the right way; you tend to manipulate the crowd a little bit - but it's a positive manipulation. It's not a case of let's have a riot, and f - the cops.' You have to go the reverse, gentle way: try to take it this way, folks, because this is the best way to enjoy it. No, the feeling of power is a big NO in the rule book. Anyway, on stage we rely on each other so much and if that was to come out of any* one of us, the other three of us would jump on the one and say: come on, you might kid two people but you aren't kidding three!"

Coleman is led to a different tack and is reluctant to let Plant off the hook so easily. He pushes the awkward subject of who is the band's leader, *"Mick might be the Stones' leader, so you could ask him that one, but ours is er...well, more of a co-operative band. Does that answer the question? Well that's all you're gonna get! What else shall we discuss?"*

Did Plant feel that the band weren't hungry any more and as such might grow complacent? *"I don't accept that at all. On every level, our fans seduce us to bring out the best work we can produce, and as for getting blasé just because we've made money - like the punk rock people say we have become unreachable - this isn't true, and no genuine musician who began in the clubs could get like that if his origins were pure. If you'd felt the magic of my mind when I first got back on that stage in Dallas six weeks back, or the magic I'm gonna feel when the next album comes out and it's the best we can do and we like it...no, we haven't got lazy or anything. Like I said, the only way we could have problems in this band is if our characters shape differently over the next few years and none of us has total control over the directions our individual personalities will take. But right from the time Jimmy Page came up to see me in the Midlands and said he was gonna form this band, way back in '68, he and I have known that we're such different characters that we're good for each other. We're totally different individuals. So no, we're not ever gonna take easy ways out."*

Coleman asks if Plant expected Led Zeppelin to be so big. *"I didn't know what this big was! I mean, the Band of Joy*

was a little baby band and it's way back in the past, but that was always enjoyable as well. There are so many connotations to being big. I don't think I can yet properly relate to the magnitude of the band, although I guess it's nearly as big as sliced bread. It's been said that these shows are events rather than concerts, and I suppose that's true. But what's the option? I guess we must carry a little bit of a legend with us, and you don't have to over-try, or it will come over clinical, clear-cut and jumpy. We have to bring out our very best all the time, because kids have a right to expect that, but we don't have to produce it in a stiff-upper-lip way or it comes out the wrong kind of tight. It's got to be Tight But Loose. That's probably the title of the next album."*

Finally Coleman asks when the new record will be ready? *"We haven't even started thinking about it constructively yet. We're hoping to do a summer show and make a mark on England and maybe we'll be working on the album in the autumn. Then again, after this marathon American tour we might all want to go home and lie horizontal for a whiles or lean against the apple tree."*

July 1977

2 New Musical Express reports.... Led Zeppelin and Bad Company were sharing a hotel in Fort Worth, the promoter commented it was akin to a nuclear holocaust....

9 Melody Maker reports.... Harvey Kubernik reports from Los Angeles that Keith Moon jammed with Led Zeppelin during their concert at the Inglewood Forum. On stage Moon says, *"I'll be back at the forum later this year with my back-*

up group!" After the show the band retired to a party at a Stone Canyon home. The party was attended by, Rod Stewart, Moon, Detective, Dave Clark, Dennis Wilson and more....

15 Seattle Post Intelligencer reports.... Cover story. What's Heavy Metal And Floats On A Sea Of Screams? In The Kingdome Sunday, The Answer is Led Zeppelin. Article by George Arthur detailing the specifics of Zeppelin's upcoming concert at the Seattle Kingdome. The show is scheduled to begin at 7.30 and 57,000 people have bought tickets at $10 each. Arthur goes on to speculate that many people will have come from around the country, perhaps attending all of the shows. Although many recent shows have had difficulty with the acoustics at the Kingdome he says that Showco (the people staging the concert) have as good a chance as any of pulling it off....

24 San Francisco Chronicle reports.... Led Zeppelin comes back with a big but boring sound.... review of the first day at Oakland Coliseum by Phil Elwood. 55,000 fans packed the stadium for a rare daylight appearance by the band who were preceded by Rick Derringer's new band and Judas Priest. He accuses the band of being, "largely boring and guilty of excessiveness." He mentions that Bill Graham had over 200 security on hand and that the stage was decorated like Stonehenge (shades of Spinal Tap). The band's set included Ten Years Gone, Nobody's Fault But Mine, Stairway To Heaven, and Whole Lotta Love. The show lasted a full eight hours and the audience were apparently exhausted by the final encore Black Dog.

25 San Francisco Chronicle reports....

Led Zeppelin Drummer Arrested For Assault. Ignominious article with a very sullen picture of Bonham chosen to make him look like some kind of psychopath. The article reports that Bonham, the band's manager, road manager and security chief were all arrested. Bonham and Grant were each charged with one count of assault. Cole, two charges for assault and likewise for John Bindon. The arrests took place at the San Francisco Hilton.

26 San Francisco Chronicle reports.... Three employees of Bill Graham have filed a $2 million law suit against the band.

27 San Francisco Chronicle reports.... Led Zeppelin the Aftermath. Reporter John Wasserman details the events which led up to the conflict back stage at the Oakland Coliseum. The general indication being that Peter Grant's son wanted to take a sign from a dressing room door and was accosted for it by a security guard in Graham's employ. Grant then stepped in with the assistance of John Bonham and John Bindon and reputedly beat the security guard and then refused to play the concert until Graham signed a note saying he wouldn't sue them. As much as most Zeppelin fans would like to think that this is untrue and one-sided it seems like it may be the nearest thing printed to the truth. Bill Graham's statement, *"There were ten years of ongoing respectful relationship between members of the Led Zeppelin organisation and myself. However the incident in question that took place on Saturday afternoon encroached on moral boundaries. Relating to two of the three incidents in question, I can only go by the facts as they were given me by the employees involved, who I consider honest and trustworthy. I* *was not present at these incidents. As for the third incident, I was directly involved and feel justification in the action taken. Now that I've seen the horror of seeing two men, whose total weight exceeds 500 pounds wreak physical havoc on one man weighing around 200 pounds. I cannot help but wonder how much of this did in fact go on in the past with these people. One of these gentlemen involved was Mr. Peter Grant, manager of Led Zeppelin. He had given me his word, based on our ten years relationship, that he simply wished to speak to this man (Matzorkis). I took him at his word, and I must now live with the consequences. I think in time all the facts will be a matter of public record. I am truly sorry that this sort of incident occurred. No producer wants this type of action on his premises, however, in a way, if it were to happen at all, then let it happen here, where there are people of strong moral fibre, like the victims in this series of incidents, who are willing to stand up and defend their human rights."...*

28 **Daily Express reports....** cover story Pop millionaire mourns his son. In typical tabloid fashion London's Daily Express puts the glummest picture they can find of Plant on the cover and just *has* to point out that he's a millionaire as though this is somehow relevant to the moment. After outlining the tragic details of Robert's loss of his son Karac the paper manages to track down Plant's father for a quote, *"All this success and fame, what is it worth? It doesn't mean very much when you compare it to the love of a family. They are heartbroken. Karac was the apple of my son's eye. He was a strong child, mischievous, bright and full of life. he had never been ill before. His death seems so unreal and unnecessary."* It goes on to relate that the family had retired to

Plant's farm in Blakeshall Worcestershire after Plant had returned from New Orleans where he was informed of his son's illness.

30 **Melody Maker reports....** In one of the first slams by the punk movement. Joey Ramones asks the question, 'Who wants to listen to Led Zeppelin?'....

Creem reports.... Cover story reprinting the article by Jaan Uhelszki in New Musical Express on June 11th....

Guitar Player reports.... Journalist Steve Rosen manages to capture a rare interview with John Paul Jones in which he talks about his early career and the technical side of his playing. Jones, *"I used to play piano when I was younger, and there was a rock and roll band forming at school when I was fourteen, but they didn't want a piano player all they wanted was drums or bass. I thought. 'I can't get the drums on the bus.' Bass looked easy four strings, no chords, easy, so I took it up. And it was easy, it wasn't too bad at all. I took it up before guitar, which I suppose is sort of interesting. Before I got a real 4 string, my father had a ukulele banjo, a little one, and I had that strung up like a bass. But it didn't quite have the bottom that was required. Actually my father didn't want to have to sign a guarantor to back me in the payments for a bass; he said, 'Don't bother with it: take up the tenor saxophone. In two years the bass guitar will never be heard of again.' I said, 'No Dad, I really want one; there's work for me.' He said, 'Ah. there's work.' And I got a bass right away.*

"(My first bass) was a pig; it had a neck like a tree trunk. It was a solid body Dallas bass guitar with a single cutaway. It sounded all right though, and it

was good for me because I developed very strong fingers. I had no idea about setting instruments up then, so I just took it home from the shop. I had an amplifier with a 10" speaker oh, it was awful. It made all kinds of farting noises. And then I had a converted television, you know, one of those big old standup televisions with the amp in the bottom and a speaker where the screen should be. I ended up giving myself double hernias. Bass players had the hardest time because they always had to cope with the biggest piece of equipment. It never occurred to me when I was deciding between that and drums that I'd have to lug a bass amp."

He is asked what kind of music he played in his first band.

"Shadows, Little Richard, Jerry Lee Lewis stuff. I started doubling on piano. We didn't have a drummer at first because we never could find one. That happened to another bass player. Larry Graham, Sly Stone's bass player. He started off in a band with no drummer which is how he got that percussive style. You've got a lot to make up for once the lead guitar takes a solo because there's only you left. You've got to make a lot of noise. We got a drummer after a while whom I taught, would you believe. I've never played drums in my life. I suppose it must have (influenced my playing). I don't like bass players that go boppity boppity bop all over the neck; you should stay around the bottom and provide that end of the group. I work very closely with the drummer; it's very important."

"I found a band with a drummer. This band also came along with really nice looking guitars, and I thought, 'Oh, they must be great.' They had Burns guitars so I got myself one too, the one with the three pickups and a Tru-Voice amplifier. We all had purple band jackets and white shoes, and I thought 'This is it, this is the big time.' But as soon as I got out of school I played at American Air Force bases, which was good training plus they always had great records in the jukebox. That was my introduction to the black music scene, when very heavy gentlemen would come up insisting on 'Night Train' eight times an hour.

(My first professional gig) was with Jet Harris and Tony Meehan, that was when I was seventeen, I suppose. And those were the days when they used to scream all the way through the show. It was just like now, really, where you have to make a dash for the limos at the end of the night, make a sort of terrible gauntlet. In the days before roadies you'd have to drag around your own gear, so we all invested in a roadie. We thought we owed it to ourselves, and this bloke was marvelous. He did everything: he drove the wagon, he lugged the gear, he did the lights—the whole thing. I got my first Fender then. I lusted after this Jazz bass in Lewisham, and it cost me about $250 I think. It was the new one. They'd just changed the controls, and I used that bass up until the last tour, and then she had to go. She was getting unreliable and rattling a lot. and I had to leave her home this time."

After his time with Jet Harris? "I got into sessions. I thought, 'I've had enough of the road', bought myself a dog, and didn't work for six months. Then I did start up again, I played in other silly bands I remember that Jet Harris and Tony Meehan band. John McLaughlin joined on rhythm guitar. It was the first time I'd met him, and it was hilarious. Here he was sitting there all night going Dm to G to Am. That was my first introduction to jazz when he came along, because we'd all get to the gig early and have a blow. Oh, that was something, first meeting him. And then I joined a couple of other bands with him for a, while, rhythm and blues bands."

Does he remember his first session, "No, I don't think so; it was in Decca Number 2. I was late, and I suddenly realized how bad my reading was. There was another bass player there, a stand-up bass, and I was just there to provide the click. It was nearly my last session."

What other sessions does he remember? "All kinds of silly people; used to do calls with Tom Jones, Cathy Kirby, Dusty Springfield. The Rolling Stones and Donovan, too. I only did one Stones session, really. I just did the strings—they already had the track down. It was 'She's a Rainbow'. And then the great Donovan session was a shambles, it was awful. It was 'Sunshine Superman'. and the arranger had got it all wrong, so I thought, being the opportunist that I was, 'I can do better than that' and actually went up to the producer. He came around and said 'Is there anything we can do to sort of save the sessions', and I piped up, 'Well, look, how about if I play straight'—because I had a part which went sort of ooowooooo every now and again, and the other bass player sort of did woooooo down below, and then there was some funny congas that were in and out of time. And I said, 'How about if we just sort of play it straight; get the drummer to do this and that.'

"The session came off, and I was immediately hired as the arranger by Mickie Most whom I loved working with; he was a clever man. I used to do Herman's Hermits and all that. I mean they were never there; you could do a whole album in a day. And it was great fun and a lot of laughs. I did all of Lulu's

stuff and all his artists. I did one Jeff Back single, and he's never spoken to me since. It was 'Hi Ho Silver Lining', I did the arrangement for it and played bass. Then we had 'Mellow Yellow' for Donovan which we argued about for hours because they didn't like my arrangement at all, not at all. Mickie stood by me he said, 'I like the arrangements I think it's good'. It wasn't Donovan—he didn't mind either—but he had so many people around him saying, 'Hey, this isn't you'. But he sold a couple of million on it, didn't he?

"On most of the sessions I played the Fender Jazz bass. It was a '61 because it was new the year I bought it. Amps were murder: amps were always murder. We were all right with Jet Harris and Tony Meehan because we used Vox amps, and I had the big T-60 which was, in fact, a forerunner of all these things we use nowadays with that big reflex cabinet and a little transistor top. It sounded great, but we had to have an arrangement with Vox to replace them every couple of weeks because they would not last any longer. Suddenly there'd be a horrible noise, and the thing would just sit there looking at you, so you'd just wheel another one on. Basically the problems haven't stopped, I find an amp that I love, and they stopped making it. I can't win."

Rosen asks if he first met Page at Donovan's Hurdy Gurdy Man session, "No, I'd met Jimmy on sessions before. It was always big Jim and little Jim—Big Jim Sullivan and little Jim and myself and the drummer. Apart from group sessions where he'd play solos and stuff like that. Page always ended up on rhythm guitar because he couldn't read too well. He could read chord symbols and stuff, but he'd have to do anything they'd ask when he walked into a session. But I used to see a lot of him just sitting there with an acoustic guitar sort of raking out chords. I always thought the bass player's life was much more interesting in those days, because nobody knew how to write for bass, so they used to say, 'We'll give you the chord sheet and get on with it.' So even on the worst sessions you could have a little run-around. But that was good: I would have hated to have sat there on acoustic guitar.

"I did sessions for three or four years, on and off. Then I thought I was going to get into arranging because it seemed that sessions and running about was much too silly. I started running about and arranging about forty or fifty things a month. I ended up just putting a blank piece of score paper in front of me and just sitting there and staring at it. Then I joined Led Zeppelin, I suppose, after my missus said to me, 'Will you stop moping around the house: why don't you join a band or something?' And I said, 'There's no bands I want to join, what are you talking about?' And she said, well, look, I think it was in Disc, 'Jimmy Page is forming a group.'—he'd just left the Yardbirds,—'Why don't you give him a ring?' So I rang him up and said, 'Jim, how you doing? Have you got a group yet?' He said, 'I haven't got anybody yet.' And I said, 'Well, if you want a bass player give me a ring.' And he said, 'All right. I'm going up to see this singer Terry Reid told me about, and he might know a drummer as well, I'll call you when I've seen what they're like.' He went up there, saw Robert Plant, and said, 'This guy is really something.' We started under the name the New Yardbirds because nobody would book us under anything else. We rehearsed an act, an album, and a tour in about three weeks, and it took off. The first time we all met in this little room just to see if we could even stand each other. It

was wall-to-wall amplifiers and terrible, all old. Robert had heard I was a session man, and he was wondering what was going to turn up—some old bloke with a pipe? So Jimmy said, 'Well, we're all here, what are we going to play?' And I said, 'I don't know, what do you know?' And Jimmy said, 'Do you know a number called The Train Kept A-Rollin?' I told him 'No.' And he said, 'It's easy, just G to A.' He counted it out, and the room just exploded, and we said 'Right, we're on, this is it, this is going to work!' And we just sort of built it up from there 'Dazed and Confused' came in because Jimmy knew that. But I could never get the sequence right for years; it kept changing all the time with different parts, and I was never used to that: I'm used to having the music there. I could never remember—in fact, I'm still the worst in the band remembering anything. And the group jokes about it: 'Jonesy always gets the titles wrong and the sequences wrong.' Even now I have a piece of paper I've stuck on top of the mellotron which says- 'Kashmir— remember the coda!' "

Rosen asks about his amplifier set up in his early days, "I've used everything from a lousy made-up job, to a great huge top valve amp. We started off in a deal with Rickenbacker where we had these awful awful Rickenbacker amps; they were so bad. Our first tour was a shambles. For about a year I never even heard the bass. They said, 'We've designed this speaker cabinet for you' and I said, 'Let me see it, what's it got in it?' It had one 30" speaker! I said 'All right, stand it up there alongside whatever else I've got, and I'll use it I plugged it in, and in a matter of five seconds I blew it up. I thought the bloke was having me on; I said, there's no such thing as a 30" speaker! And I had to take the back-off because

I couldn't believe it. Then we met the guy from Univox, and he came up with a bass stack which unfortunately didn't last the night. But while it was going, it was the most unbelievable sound I've ever heard. It was at the Nassau Coliseum in New York. I remember and the bass filled the hall. It was so big, it couldn't have lasted. I don't think I'll come across anything that sounded like that. But as I said, three numbers and wheel the Acoustics out again. I used two or three 360 standard Acoustics for quite a long time; they served me well."

Rosen asks about his choice of bass guitar, *"Oh, I got a hold of a very nice old Gibson violin bass pictured in the little cutout wheel on the cover of Led Zeppelin 3. That was nice, too: it's not stage-worthy, but it gives a beautiful warm sound. I don't like Gibson basses generally because they feel all rubbery; I like something you can get your teeth into. But the violin bass was the only Gibson that was as heavy as a Fender to play, but still had that fine Gibson sound. I used it on Led Zeppelin 3 and I've used it every now and again, usually when I'm tracking a bass after I've done keyboards for the main track. The one I have went through Little Richard's band and then through James Brown's band, and it arrived in England. In fact, I saw it on an old movie clip of Little Richard. It was probably about a 48 or 50 or something like that: it was the original one. Actually, I've also got an old '52 Telecaster bass. I used that onstage for a while for 'Black Dog' and things like that. Rick Turner of Alembic made me an Alembic bass and it's beautiful. It has standard Alembic circuitry and is extremely versatile: two pickups, and there's a hum canceling system in it. It runs from a power supply; it's power assisted somehow with a pre-amp, which*

fits into the guitar. I've got LEDs all up the side—I love those and it's got a full two-octave neck. In a shop, I came across an 8-string before this one and when I found out it was Alembic, I rang up the bloke and said, 'Look, what else do you do?' I think I'll get him to make me a fretless next. Last I heard he was working on some idea with a stainless-steel fingerboard.

"(The two full octaves) gives you so much more room, and there isn't any position on the instrument that sounds off—you can use it all. I'm finding out all sorts of things: you could never get up there with a Fender. It's much more fun, and there's a lot more to do on it. When your intonation is true on all four strings all the way up, you suddenly realize you can play chords, and the notes are clear. It's a whole different way of playing. It definitely has changed my technique. I can now get above the 5th fret which always has been somewhat of a mystery. I still use the Fender fretless because I need a fretless onstage. I don't particularly like the instrument, but it's better than any of the other ones they have."

Rosen asks whether he found using a fretless difficult? *"No, you think it's going to be, but it's not. I also use a stand-up electric bass onstage, I think it's an Arco. There was a spate of them came out in the middle Sixties—Italian made basses, and I bought it for fun. It's nowhere near accurate enough (to play on record), and it's too hard to play, you can't do anything with it. Since I've got a bit more power back in my fingers now, I can begin to go a little bit further up the neck. You couldn't use it for more than one number.*

"The amp I use they don't make anymore. GMT 600B which has since been replaced by the 400B which bears no

resemblance at all. But I'm going to ring them up, too, and ask if they'll please make me another of the old type, because it is excellent. It has a curious kind of shelving on the filter system; I think they call it Contour. It's very ballsy for a transistorized amp; maybe the Alembic is a little too hot for it, but I might be able to work something out. This is just the head; I use Cerwin-Vega cabinets which are excellent. I use just the one top and two cabinets, each of which I think has one 15" and one 10" speaker. It's loud, right? There's a lot of power, proper power.

"I find solid state a bit tighter than valve amps, really. I don't think they're so good for guitar. The sound tends to spread a lot, and you don't get the definition. I prefer more of a recorded sound onstage. In the studio I like to mix direct and amp. With the Fender, the direct was never that good but the Alembic can go direct, and it sounds really good."

Rosen asks what setting he uses, "I usually set the amp in the middle; we have to run it a little lower than I like because as I say, the Alembic is a bit hot. But that guitar is going to be more fun to record with as far as settings are concerned because there's a lot of variations in tone and all sorts of things you can do. I haven't used the Alembic for recording yet. I used the 8-string on Presence but the 4 string was made after that. I'm still using the Fender on the live album."

Does he use a pick? "Yes, when the situation demands it; on the 8-string it's awful messy with your fingers. On 'The Song Remains The Same' I use a pick to get that snap out of the instrument. It's fun, you play different. If I was just playing straight bass, I'd use fingers. When I first started, I always used my fingers. (I use) Herco gray and Rotosound wire-wounds, I got into them with the Alembic because I never used to like the round-wound strings; on the Fender I used Rotosound, but they were flat-wound, and I've never liked the string noise. But the Alembic just demands you use something a bit brighter, otherwise you're doing the instrument a disservice. I first put round-wound strings on the Telecaster bass because it demanded that, and I tried flat-wounds on the Alembic, and sort of lost half the instrument. Plus the wire-wounds seem to fill out better if Jimmy's soloing: they make more of a guitar sound on the Alembic than a bass sound. But the Alembic's got enough lows on it enough low end, it fills out the spectrum. I think it's going to be all right.

"I never have (used a booster or pedals), what can you do with the bass anyway? You can go wah-wah wah. or you can phase it and make it sound even muddier than it usually does. I think I'm more into the musical side of things; I don't use synthesizers because they always sound like synthesizers."

Rosen asks how playing with Page has affected his style, "That's hard; I play a lot looser than I used to. For instance, somebody like John Entwistle is more of a lead instrument man than I am. I tend to work closer with Bonzo I think. But then again I don't play that bass on stage anymore what with the pianos and the Mellotron. I'll always say I'm a bass player though.

"You put in what is correct and what's necessary. I always did like a good tune in the bass. For an example, listen to 'What Is and What Should Never Be'. The role of a bassist is hard to define. You can't play chords, so you have a harmonic role, picking and timing notes. You'll suggest a melodic or a harmonic pattern, but I seem to be changing anyway toward more of a lead style. The Alembic is doing it. I play differently on it. But I try to never forget my role as a bass player: to play the bass and not mess around too much up at the top all the time. You've got to have somebody down there, and that's the most important thing. The numbers must sound right, they must work right, they must be balanced."

Does he practice? "No, in a word. I fool around on piano but bass I never practice. Although again with the Alembic. I'm beginning to feel 'Wouldn't it be nice to have it in the room?' it really makes you want to play more which is fantastic.

"I don't (listen to much). I used to listen to a lot of jazz bass players once, but jazz has changed so much now it's hardly recognizable. I listened to a lot of tenor sax players: Sonny Rollins, John Coltrane and all those people. Bass players? Scott La Faro, who died; he used to be with Bill Evans. Excellent player. I liked the late jazz bassist Paul Chambers, and Ray Brown, and Charlie Mingus of course. I'm not too keen on the lead bass style of some players. Paul McCartney I've always respected; he puts the notes in the right place at the right time. He knows what he's about."

His future ambitions? "I always get the feeling I'd like to write a symphony. I like all music I like classical music a lot—Ravel, Bach, of course, Mozart I could never stand though to play it on the piano is great fun. If Bach had ever come across the bass guitar he would have loved it. Rock and roll is the only music left where you can improvise. I don't know what's happened to jazz; it has really disappointed me. I guess they started playing rock and roll."

In conclusion Rosen asks whether he feels he is continually expand-

ing his talents within Led Zeppelin, "Yes, absolutely. I wouldn't be without Zeppelin for the world."

In the same remarkable issue Rosen also interviews Page in expansive mood. For once he is prepared to talk about his early session work and various technical aspects to his performance techniques. Page, "I got really stimulated by hearing early rock and roll; knowing that something was going on that was being suppressed by the media. Which it really was at the time. You had to stick by the radio and listen to overseas radio to even hear good rock records, Little Richard and things like that. The record that made me want to play guitar was 'Baby, Let's Play House' by Elvis Presley. I just sort of heard two guitars and bass and thought, 'Yeah, I want to be part of this.' There was just so much vitality and energy coming out of it.

"When I was about fourteen (I got my first guitar). It was all a matter of trying to pick up tips and stuff. There weren't many method books, really, apart from jazz which had no bearing on rock and roll whatsoever at that time. But that first guitar was a Grazzioso which was like a copy of a Stratocaster; then I got a real Stratocaster; then one of those Gibson 'Black Beauties' which stayed with me for a long time until some thieving magpie took it to his nest. That's the guitar I did all the Sixties sessions on."

Rosen asks if he came from a musically inclined family, "No, not at all. But they didn't mind me getting into it; I think they were quite relieved to see something being done instead of art work, which they thought was a loser's game.

" (When I first started) I wasn't really playing anything properly. I just knew a few bits of solos and things, not much. I just kept getting records and *learning that way. It was the obvious influences at the beginning, Scotty Moore, James Burton, Cliff Gallup - he was Gene Vincent's guitarist, Johnny Weeks, later, and those seemed to be the most sustaining influences until I began to hear blues guitarists Elmore James, B.B. King, and people like that. Basically, that was the start: a mixture between rock and blues. Then I stretched out a lot more, and I started doing studio work. I had to branch out, and I did. I might do three sessions a day, a film session in the morning, and then there'd be something like a rock band, and then maybe a folk one in the evening. I didn't know what was coming! But it was a really good disciplinary area to work in, the studio. And it also gave me a chance to develop on all of the different styles."*

Rosen asks if he remembers his first band and what sort of stuff did he play with the Crusaders, *"Just friends and things. I played in a lot of different small bands around, but nothing you could ever get any records of. This was before the Stones happened, so we were doing Chuck Berry, Gene Vincent, and Bo Diddley things mainly. At the time, public taste was more engineered towards Top 10 records, so it was a bit of a struggle. But there'd always be a small section of the audience into what we were doing.*

"I stopped playing and went to art college for about two years, while concentrating more on blues playing on my own. And then from art college to the Marquee Club in London. I used to go up and jam on a Thursday night with the interlude band. One night somebody came up and said, 'Would you like to play on a record?' and I said, 'Yeah, why not?' It did quite well, and that was it after that. I can't remember the title of it now. From that point I started suddenly getting all

this studio work. There was a crossroads: is it an art career or is it going to be music? Well anyway, I had to stop going to the art college because I was really getting into music. Big Jim Sullivan, who was really brilliant, and I were the only guitarists doing those sessions. Then a point came where Stax Records started influencing music to have more brass and orchestral stuff. The guitar started to take a back trend with just the occasional riff. I didn't realize how rusty I was going to get until a rock and roll session turned up from France, and I could hardly play. I thought it was time to get out, and I did.

For a while I just worked on my stuff alone, and then I went to a Yardbirds concert at Oxford, and they were all walking around in their penguin suits. Keith Relf got really drunk and was saying 'Fuck you' right into the mike and falling into the drums. I thought it was a great anarchistic night, and I went back into the dressing room and said, 'What a brilliant show!' There was this great argument going on; Paul Samwell-Smith saying 'Well, I'm leaving the group, and if I was you, Keith, I'd do the very same thing.' So he left the group, and Keith didn't. But they were stuck, you see, because they had commitments and dates, so I said, 'I'll play the bass if you like.' And then it worked out that we did the dual lead guitar thing as soon as Chris Dreja could get it together with the bass, which happened, though not for long. But then came the question of discipline. If you're going to do dual lead guitars riffs and patterns, then you've got to be playing the same things. Jeff Beck had discipline occasionally, but he was an inconsistent player in that when he's on, he's probably the best there is, but at that time, and for a period afterwards, he had no respect whatsoever for audiences."

Rosen asks if he ever used acoustic in his session days and whether he used the Les Paul, *"Yes, I had to do it on studio work. And you come to grips with it very quickly too, very quickly, because it's what is expected. There was a lot of busking in the earlier days, but as I say. I had to come to grips with it, and it was a good schooling. (Yeah) The Gibson 'Black Beauty' Les Paul Custom. I was one of the first people in England to have one, but I didn't know that then. I just saw it on the wall, had a go with it, and it was good. I traded a Gretsch Chet Atkins I'd had before for the Les Paul.*

"(I used) A small Supro (amp), which I used until someone, I don't know who, smashed it up for me I'm going to try to get another one. It's like a Harmony amp, I think, and all of the first album was done on that.

"One thing is (with the Yardbirds) *it was chaotic in recording. I mean we did one tune and didn't really know what it was. We had Ian Stewart from the Stones on piano, and we'd just finished the take, and without even hearing it Mickie Most said, 'Next.' I said, 'I've never worked like this in my life,' and he said, 'Don't worry about it.' It was all done very quickly, as it sounds. It was things like that that really led to the general state of mind and depression of Relf and Jim McCarty that broke the group up. I tried to keep it together, but there was no chance; they just wouldn't have it. In fact Relf said the magic of the band disappeared when Clapton left. I was really keen on doing anything, though, probably because of having had all that studio work and variety beforehand. So it didn't matter what way they wanted to go; they were definitely talented people, but they couldn't really see the woods for the trees at that time.*

"Giorgio Gomelsky was good for him (Beck) *because he got him thinking and attempting new things. That's when they started all sorts of departures. Apparently Simon Napier-Bell sang the guitar riff of 'Over Under Sideways Down' to Jeff to demonstrate what he wanted, but I don't know whether that's true or not. I never spoke to him about it. I know the idea of the record was to sort of emulate the sound of the old 'Rock Around The Clock' type record; that bass and backbeat thing. But it wouldn't be evident at all; every now and again he'd say, 'Let's make a record around such and such,' and no one would ever know what the example was at the end of the song.*

"Sometimes it worked really great, and sometimes it didn't. There were a lot of harmonies that I don't think anyone else had really done, not like we did. The Stones were the only ones who got into two guitars going at the same time from old Muddy Waters records. But we were more into solos rather than a rhythm thing. The point is, you've got to have the parts worked out, and I'd find that I was doing what I was supposed to, while something totally different would be coming from Jeff. That was all right for the areas of improvisation, but there were other parts where it just did not work. You've got to understand that Beck and I came from the same sort of roots. If you've got things you enjoy, then you want to do them to the horrifying point where we'd done our first LP with 'You Shook Me,' and then I heard he'd done 'You Shook Me'. I was terrified because I thought they'd be the same. But I hadn't even known he'd done it, and he hadn't known that we had."

Rosen asks if Beck played bass on 'Over Under Sideways Down', *"No; in fact for that LP they just got him in to* do the solos because they'd had a lot of trouble with him. But then when I joined the band, he supposedly wasn't going to walk off anymore. Well, he did a couple of times. It's strange: if he'd had a bad day, he'd take it out on the audience. I don't know whether he's the same now; his playing sounds far more consistent on records. You see, on the 'Beck's Bolero' thing I was working with that, the track was done, and then the producer just disappeared. He was never seen again; he simply didn't come back. Napier-Bell, he just sort of left me and Jeff to it. Jeff was playing, and I was in the box. And even though he says he wrote it, I wrote it. I'm playing the electric 12 string on it. Beck's doing the slide bits, and I'm basically playing around the chords. The idea was built around Maurice Ravel's 'Bolero.' It's got a lot of drama to it; it came off right. It was a good lineup too, with Keith Moon and everything."

Rosen points out that it was the beginnings of Led Zeppelin, "It was, yeah. Not Led Zeppelin as a name; the name came afterwards. But it was said afterwards that that's what it could have been called. Because Moony wanted to get out of the Who and so did John Entwistle, but when it came down to getting hold of a singer, it was either going to be Steve Winwood or Steve Marriott. Finally it came down to Marriott. He was contacted, and the reply came back from his manager's office: 'How would you like to have a group with no fingers, boys?' Or words to that effect. So the group was dropped because of Marriott's other commitment, to Small Faces. But I think it would have been the first of all those bands sort of like the Cream and everything. Instead, it didn't happen-apart from the 'Bolero.' That's the closest it got. John Paul Jones is on that too; so's Nicky

Hopkins."

Page is asked what he did with Beck, " 'Happenings Ten Years Time Ago', 'Stroll On' , 'The Train Kept A-Rollin'', and 'Psycho Daisies' 'Bolero', and a few other things. None of them were with the Yardbirds but earlier on just some studio things, unreleased songs: 'Louie Louie' and things like that; really good though, really great."

At this point Rosen switches to the technical side of his recordings beginning with the question of whether he used any boosters, "Fuzztone which I'd virtually regurgitated from what I heard on '2000 Pound Bee' by the Ventures. They had a Fuzztone. It was nothing like the one this guy, Roger Mayer, made for me; he worked for the Admiralty in the electronics division. He did all the fuzz pedals for Jimi Hendrix later; all those octave doublers and things like that. He made this one for me, but that was all during the studio period, you see. I think Jeff had one too then, but I was the one who got the effect going again. That accounted for quite a lot of the boost and that sort of sustain in the music."

Feedback? "You know 'I Need You,' by the Kinks? I think I did that bit there in the beginning I don't know who really did feedback first; it just sort of happened. I don't think anybody consciously nicked it from anybody else; it was just going on. But Pete Townshend obviously was the one, through the music of his group, who made the use of feedback more his style, and so it's related to him. Whereas the other players like Jeff and myself were playing more single notes and things than chords."

He is asked about whether he used his Danelectro guitar which he later used for Kashmir, "Yes, but not with Beck. I did use it in the latter days. I used it

onstage for 'White Summer'. I used a special tuning for that; the low string down
to B then A, D, G, A, and D. It's like a
modal tuning; a sitar tuning in fact. I
wasn't totally original on that (Black
Mountain Side). It had been done in the
folk clubs a lot; Annie Briggs was the first
one that I heard do that riff. I was playing
it as well, and then there was Bert
Jansch's version. He's the one who crys-
tallised all the acoustic playing as far as
I'm concerned. Those first few albums of
his were absolutely brilliant. And the tuning on 'Black Mountain Side' is the same
as 'White Summer.' It's taken a bit of a
battering, that Danelectro guitar, I'm
afraid. I played them on that guitar before
so I'd thought I'd do it again. But I might
change it around to something else, since
my whole amp situation is different now
from what it used to be; now it's
Marshall, then it was Vox tops and different cabinets-kind of a hodge-podge but it
worked."

Apparently he used a Vox twelve
string in the Yardbirds, "That's right. I
can't remember the titles now; the Mickie
Most things, some of the B sides. I remember there was one with an electric 12-
string solo on the end of it which was all
right. I don't have copies of them now,
and I don't know what they're called. I've
got Little Games. but that's about it.

"(I used Vox) AC-30 (amps).
They've held up consistently well. Even
the new ones are pretty good. I tried
some; I got four in and tried them out, and
they were all reasonably good. I was
going to build up a big bank of four of
them, but Bonzo's kit is so loud that they
just don't come over the top of it properly."

He denies that he ever customised his Vox amps, "You could get
these ones with special treble boosters on

the back which is what I had. No, I didn't
do that much customizing apart from
making sure of all the points, soldering
contacts, and things were solid. The
Telecasters changed rapidly, you could
tell because you could split the pickups,
you know that split sound you can get and
again you could get an out of phase
sound, and then suddenly they didn't do it
anymore. So they obviously changed the
electronics. And there didn't seem to be
any way of getting it back. I tried to fiddle
around with the wiring but it didn't work
so I just went back to the old one again."

He choice of guitar for Led
Zeppelin One? "A Telecaster. I used the
Les Paul with the Yardbirds on about two
numbers and a Fender for the rest. You see
the Les Paul Custom had a central setting,
a kind of out-of-phase pickup sound
which Jeff couldn't get on his Les Paul, so
I used mine for that."

He is asked whether Beck gave
him the Telecaster, "Yes. There was work
done on it but only afterwards. I painted
it; everyone painted their guitars in those
days. And I had reflective plastic sheeting
underneath the pick guard that gives rainbow colors. You see. I could get a lot of
tones out of the guitar which you normally couldn't. This confusion goes back to
those early sessions again with the Les
Paul. Those might not sound like a Les
Paul, but that's what I used. It's just different amps, mike placings, and all different things. Also, if you just crank it up to
distortion point so you can sustain notes
it's bound to sound like a Les Paul. I was
using the Supro amp for the first album
and still do. The 'Stairway to Heaven'
solo was done when I pulled out the
Telecaster, which I hadn't used for a long
time, plugged it into the Supro and away
it went again. That's a different sound
entirely from any of the rest of the first

album. It was a good versatile setup. I'm using a Leslie on the solo on 'Good Times Bad Times'. It was wired up for an organ thing then."

The guitar used on Black Mountain Side and Babe I'm Gonna Leave You? "That was a Gibson J-200 which wasn't mine; I borrowed it. It was a beautiful guitar, really great. I've never found a guitar of that quality anywhere since. I could play so easily on it, get a really thick sound; it had heavy-gauge strings on it, but it just didn't seem to feel like it.

"I used fingerpicks once, but I find them too spikey; they're too sharp. You can't get the tone or response that you would get, say; the way classical players approach gut string instruments. The way they pick, the whole thing is the tonal response of the string It seems important. I don't know, really; my style's a cross between fingerstyle and flatpicking. There's a guy in England called Davey Graham and he never used any fingerpicks or anything. He used a thumbpick every now and again, but I prefer just a flatpick and fingers because then it's easier to get around from guitar to guitar. Well it is for me anyway. But apparently he's got calouses on the left hand and all over the right as well; he can get so much attack on his strings, and he's really good."

Rosen asks how he arrived at the sound on 'Communication Breakdown', "I put it in a small room. A little tiny vocal booth-type thing and miked it from a distance. You see, there's a very old recording maxim which goes, 'Distance makes depth.' I've used that a hell of a lot on recording techniques with the band generally, not just me. You always used to get them close-miking amps, just putting the microphone in front, but I'd have a mike

right out the back as well, and then balance the two, and get rid of all the phasing problems; because really, you shouldn't have to use an EQ in the studio if the instruments sound right. It should all be done with the microphones. But see, everyone has gotten so carried away with EQ pots that they have forgotten the whole science of microphone placement. There aren't too many guys who know it. I'm sure Les Paul knows a lot; obviously, he must have been well into that, well into it, as were all those who produced the early rock records where there were only one or two mikes in the studio."

Rosen mentions how much he likes the inventiveness of the solo in 'I Can't Quit You', "There are mistakes in it, but it doesn't make any difference. I'll always leave the mistakes in. I can't help it. The timing bits on the A and Bb parts are right, though it might sound wrong. The timing just sounds off. But there are some wrong notes. You've got to be reasonably honest about it. It's like the filmtrack album there's no editing really on that. It wasn't the best concert playing-wise at all, but it was the only one with celluloid footage so, there it was. It was all right; it was just one 'as-it-is' performance. It wasn't one of those real magic nights but then again it wasn't a terrible night. So, for all its mistakes and everything else, it's a very honest filmtrack. Rather than just trailing around through a tour with a recording mobile truck waiting for the magic night, it was just, 'There you are take it or leave it.' I've got a lot of live recorded stuff going back to '69."

Rosen then asks about Whole Lotta Love, "I had it worked out already, that one, before entering the studio. I had rehearsed it. And then all that other stuff, sonic wave sound and all that, I built it up in the studio, and put effects on it and things; treatments. (The descending riff is done) *with a metal slide and backwards echo. I think I came up with that first before anybody. I know it's been used a lot now but not at the time. I thought of it on this Mickie Most thing. In fact some of the things that might sound a bit odd have, in fact, backwards echo involved in them is well."*

On Ramble On, *"If I can remember correctly, it's like harmony feedback and then it changes. To be more specific, most of the tracks just start off bass, drums, and guitar, and once you've done the drum and bass, you just build everything up afterwards. It's like a starting point, and you start constructing from square one. I don't like anybody else in the studio when I'm putting on the guitar parts. I usually just limber up for a while and then maybe do three solos and take the best of the three."*

Rosen asks if there is a twelve string on Thank You, *"Yes. I think it's a Fender or Rickenbacker."*

How about Out On The Tiles? *"Now that is exactly what I was talking about, close miking and distance miking; that's ambient sound. Getting the distance of the time lag from one end of the room to the other and putting that in as well. The whole idea, the way I see recording, is to try and capture the sound of the room live and the emotion of the whole moment and try to convey that across. That's the very essence of it. And so, consequently, you've got to capture as much of the room sound as possible."*

Rosen asks if he used a pedal steel on Tangerine, *"I did, and on the first LP there's a pedal steel. I had never played steel before, but I just picked it up. There's a lot of things I do first time around that I haven't done before. In fact, I hadn't touched a pedal steel from the*

first album to the third. It's a bit of a pinch really from the things that Chuck Berry did. But never the less it fits. I use pedal steel on 'Your Time Is Gonna Come.' It sounds like a slide or something. It's more out of tune on the first album because I hadn't got a kit to put it together."

As for other instruments he's played on record, *"Gallows Pole, was the first time for banjo and on 'The Battle of Evermore,' a mandolin was lying around. It wasn't mine, it was Jonesy's. I just picked it up, got the chords, and it sort of started happening I did it more or less straight off. But you see that's fingerpicking again, going on back to the studio days and developing a certain amount of technique. At least enough to be adapted and used. My fingerpicking is a sort of cross between Pete Seeger, Earl Scruggs, and total incompetence.*

"I didn't use a double neck on that (the fourth album), *but I had to get one afterwards to play 'Stairway to Heaven'. I did all those guitars on it; I just built them up. That was the beginning of my building up harmonised guitars. 'Ten Years Gone' was an extension of that, and then 'Achilles Last Stand' is like the essential flow of it really, because there was no time to think the things out; I just had to more or less lay it down on the first track and harmonise on the second track. It was really fast working on Presence. And I did all the guitar overdubs on that LP in one night. There were only two sequences. The rest of the band, not Robert, but the rest of them I don't think really could see it to begin with. They didn't know what the hell I was going to do with it. But I wanted to give each section its own identity and I think it came off really good. I didn't think I'd be able to do it in one night; I thought I'd have to do*

it in the course of three different nights to get the individual sections. But I was so into it that my mind was working properly for a change. It sort of crystallized and everything was just pouring out. I was very happy with the guitar on that whole album as far as the maturity of the playing goes."

Page agrees that he needed to learn a new approach when he started using the double neck, "The main thing is, there's an effect you can get where you leave the twelve string neck open as far as the sound goes and play on the six string neck, and you get the twelve strings vibrating in sympathy. It's like an Indian sitar, and I've worked on that a little bit. I use it on 'Stairway' like that; not on the album but on the soundtrack and film. It's surprising; it doesn't vibrate as heavily as a sitar would, but nonetheless it does add to the overall tonal quality."

Rosen asks whether he thinks that the fourth album is the best example of his talents, "Without a doubt. As far as consistency goes and as far as the quality of playing on a whole album, I would say yes. But I don't know what the best solo I've ever done is, I have no idea. My vocation is more in composition really than in anything else. Building up harmonies. Using the guitar, orchestrating the guitar like an army, a guitar army. I think that's where it's at, really, for me. I'm talking about actual orchestration in the same way you'd orchestrate a classical piece of music. Instead of using brass and violins you treat the guitars with synthesizers or other devices; give them different treatments so that they have enough frequency range and scope and everything to keep the listener as totally committed to it as the player is. It's a difficult project, but it's one that I've got to do."

He cites the following songs as examples of what he is talking about. "'Stairway to Heaven,' 'Ten Years Gone,' and 'Achilles Last Stand,' the way the guitar is building I can see certain milestones along the way like 'Four Sticks' in the middle section of that. The sound of those guitars; that's where I'm going. I've got long pieces written; I've got one really long one written that's harder to play than anything. It's sort of classical, but then it goes through changes from that mood to really laid-back rock, and then to really intensified stuff, with a few laser notes thrown in, we might be all right."

Rosen ask him what he uses for amps and how he sets them currently, "Onstage? Marshall 100s which are customised in New York so they've got 200 watts. I've got four unstacked cabinets, and I've got a wah-wah pedal and an MXR unit. Everything else is total flash. I've got a harmonizer, a theremin, violin bow, and an Echoplex echo unit. Depending on the acoustics of the place; the volume is up to about three, and the rest is pretty standard."

Rosen asks about his use of the violin bow on the guitar, "The first time I recorded with it was with the Yardbirds. But the idea was put to me by a classical string player when I was doing studio work. One of us tried to bow the guitar, then we tried it between us, and it worked. At that point I was just bowing it, but the other effects I've obviously come up with on my own-using wah-wah, and echo. You have to put rosin on the bow, and the rosin sticks to the string and makes it vibrate."

Rosen asks what other details he can give him about his gear, "Herco heavy-gauge nylon picks and Ernie Ball Super Slinky strings. God, this is really hard, there are so many. My Les Paul, the usual one, and I've got a spare one of those if anything goes wrong. I've got a double-neck; and one of those Fender string benders that was made for me by Gene Parsons. I've cut it back from what I was going to use on tour. I have with me a Martin guitar and a Gibson A4 mandolin. The Martin is one of the cheap ones; it's not the one with the herringbone back or anything like that. It's probably a D-18, it's got those nice Grovers on it. I've got a Gibson Everly Brothers which was given to me by Ronnie Wood. That's like the current favorite, but I don't take it out on the road because it's a really personal guitar. I keep it with me in the room. It's a beauty; it's fantastic. There's only a few of those around; Ron's got one, and Keith Richard's got one, and I've got one as well. So it's really nice. I haven't had a chance to use it on record yet, but I will because it's got such a nice sound. Let's see, what else have we got? I know when I come onstage it looks like a guitar shop, the way they're all standing up there. But I sold off all of my guitars before I left for America; there was a lot of old stuff hanging around which I didn't need. It's no point having things if you don't need them. When all the equipment came over here, we had done our rehearsals, and we were really on top, really in top form, Then Robert caught laryngitis, and we had to postpone a lot of dates and reshuffle them and I didn't touch a guitar for five weeks. I got a bit panicky about that after two years off the road that's a lot to think about. And I'm still only warming up; I still can't coordinate a lot of the things I need to be doing. Getting by, but it's not right; I don't feel 100% right yet."

His legendary Les Paul is a... "'59. It's been rescraped, but that's all gone now because it chipped off. Joe Walsh got it for me." He agrees that his

playing changed when he switched guitars, "It's more of a fight with a Telecaster, but there are rewards. The Gibson's got stereotyped sound maybe, I don't know. But it's got a beautiful sustain to it, and I like sustain because it relates to bowed instruments and everything; this whole area that everyone's been pushing and experimenting in. When you think about it, it's mainly sustain."

He admits he uses special tunings on his electric guitars, "All the time; they're my own that I've worked out, so I'd rather keep those to myself really. But they're never open tunings; I have used those, but most of the things I've written have not been open tunings, so you can get more chords into them."

Rosen asks whether he ever met any of his folk guitar heroes, "No, and the most terrifying thing of all happened about a few months ago. Jansch's playing appeared as if it was going down or something, and it turns out he's got arthritis. I really think he's one of the best. He was, without any doubt, the one who crystallized so many things. As much as Hendrix had done on electric, I think he's done on the acoustic. He was really way, way ahead. And for something like that to happen is such a tragedy, with a mind as brilliant as that. There you go. Another player whose physical handicap didn't stop him is Django Reinhardt. For his last LP they pulled him out of retirement to do it; it's on Barclay Records in France. He'd been retired for years, and it's fantastic. You know the story about him in the caravan and losing fingers and such. But the record is just fantastic. He must have been playing all the time to be that good—it's horrifyingly good. Horrifying. But it's always good to hear perennial players like that; like Les Paul and people like that. Have you ever heard 'It's Been a

Long, Long Time'? You ought to hear that. He does everything on that, everything in one go. And it's just one guitar it's basically one guitar even though they've tracked on rhythms and stuff. But my goodness his introductory chords and everything are fantastic. He sets the whole tone, and then he goes into this solo which is fantastic. Now that's where I heard feedback first—from Les Paul. Also vibratos and things. Even before B.B. King, you know, I've traced a hell of a lot of rock and roll, little riffs, and things back to Les Paul, Chuck Berry, Cliff Gallup and all those—it's all there. But then Les Paul was influenced by Reinhardt, wasn't he? Very much so. I can't get my hands on the records of Les Paul, the Les Paul Trio, and all that stuff. But I've got all the Capitol LPs and things. I mean he's the father of it all, multi-tracking and everything else. If it hadn't been for him there wouldn't have been anything really."

Page apparently lays the Les Paul sound at Eric Clapton's door, *"Yeah, without a doubt. when he was with the Bluesbreakers, it was just a magic combination; he got one of the Marshall amps, and away he went. It just happened. I thought he played brilliantly then, really brilliantly. That was very stirring stuff."*

What, if any, guitar sounds does he attribute to himself, *"The guitar parts in Trampled Underfoot, this guy Nick Kent, he came out with this idea about how he thought that was a really revolutionary sound. And I hadn't realized that anyone would think it was, but I can explain exactly how it's done. Again it's sort of backwards echo and wah-wah. I don't know how responsible I was for new sounds because there were so many good things happening around that point, around the release of the first Zeppelin*

album, like Hendrix and Clapton. The trouble is keeping a separation between sounds, so you don't have the same guitar effect all the time. And that's where that orchestration thing comes in; it's so easy, I've already planned it, it's already there; all the groundwork has been done now. And the dream has been accomplished by the computerized mixing console. The sort of struggle to achieve so many things is over. As I said, I've got two things written; but I'll be working on more. You can hear what I mean on Lucifer Rising. You see, I didn't play any guitar on that, apart from one point. That was all other instruments, all synthesizers. Every instrument was given a process so it didn't sound like what it really was, the voices, drones, mantras, and even tabla drums. When you've got a collage of, say, four of these sounds together, people will be drawn right in because there will be sounds they hadn't heard before. That's basically what I'm into, collages and tissues of sound with emotional intensity and melody and all that. But you know there are so many good people around like John McLaughlin and people like that. It's a totally different thing than what I'm doing. He's always had that technique right from when I first knew him when he was working in a guitar shop. I would say he was the best jazz guitarist in England then, in the traditional mode of Johnny Smith and Tal Farlow; a combination of those two is exactly what he sounded like. He was easily the best guitarist in England, and he was working in a guitar shop. And that's what I say you hear so many good people around under those conditions. I'll tell you one thing, I don't know one musician who's stuck to his guns, who was good in the early days that hasn't come through now with recognition from everybody. Albert Lee and all these

people that seem to be like white elephants got recognition. I think he's really
good, bloody brilliant. He's got one of
those string benders, too, but I haven't
heard him in ages. But I know that every
time I've heard him, he's bloody better
and better.

"I've got two different approach-
es, like a schizophrenic guitarist, really. I
mean onstage is totally different than the
way that I approach it in the studio.
Presence and my control over all the contributing factors to that LP, the fact that it
was done in three weeks, and all the rest
of it, is so good for me. It was just good
for everything really, even though it was a
very anxious point, and the anxiety shows
group-wise you know, 'Is Robert going to
walk again' from his auto accident in
Greece and all this sort of thing. But I
guess the solo in 'Achilles Last Stand' on
Presence is in the same tradition as the

solo from 'Stairway to Heaven' on the
fourth LP. It is on that level to me."....

August 1977

6 **Melody Maker reports....** Article covering the loss of Robert Plant's son. The
article mentions that Plant had flown back
from New Orleans to be with his wife and
daughter and that further concerts in New
Orleans, Chicago, Buffalo, Pittsburgh and
Philadelphia had been canceled. The article also covers the Oakland altercation
and a spokesman says that all of the
charges have been dropped except against
one security guard (presumably John
Bindon). Journalist Chris Welch extends
his and the Melody Maker's sincere con-
dolences to Plant and his family. Atlantic
exec Phil Carson says, "*We have received
a mountain of letters and telegrams.*"....
New Musical Express reports.... Plant's
Tragedy.... story recounting the accidental
death of Robert Plant's young son
Karac.... a Swan Song spokesperson said
that Plant's son had become ill with a
mild stomach bug which had given rise to
complications. The child's temperature
had risen on Tuesday and he suffered con-
vulsions. Despite the arrival of an ambu-
lance the child was pronounced dead on
arrival at Kidderminster hospital. Plant
and drummer John Bonham had flown
back from the USA and all the band's
shows in the USA are on hold. Swan
Song's spokesman stated, "*Obviously all
the band are going to heed whatever
Robert's wishes are, and give him time to
decide what to do. It will be a week or two
before Robert knows what his plans will
be. I don't know which way he'll go.*" The
band's tour was in jeopardy after assault
charges were laid in San Francisco following an incident backstage at the band's

shows in Oakland. Swan Song confirmed both Peter Grant and John Bonham were charged but that the offense was like a parking ticket.... there is still some speculation that Zeppelin might play a date in the UK before Christmas....

Pittsburgh Valley News Dispatch reports.... 30,000 tickets sold, Zeppelin concerts canceled at Arena.... Civic arena spokesman says all the tickets for the upcoming shows on August 9th and 10th will be refunded. The shows have been canceled due to the death of singer Robert Plant's 5 year old son....

13 **New Musical Express reports....** Led Zeppelin have canceled the rest of their US tour....

20 **New Musical Express reports....** Jimmy Page and Ron Wood played a recent charity gig in Plumpton in front of 140 people.... **Melody Maker reports....** Tony Hills owner of the Half Moon in Plumpton says, *"Down here, Jimmy Page is God."* Page and Ron Wood had been appearing at a charity event at the venue.... John Bonham is reported to be in hospital with two broken ribs after being in a car crash near his home in Kidderminster....

September 1977

10 **New Musical Express reports....** Led Zeppelin have been banned from the Plaza hotel...guests thought the hotel was under attack by Puerto Rican terrorists....

24 **New Musical Express reports....** The Song Remains The Same But Does It?.... Article speculating on the future of Led Zeppelin.... apparently the BBC radio ran

a story outlining the band's imminent demise on it's show Rock On. One of the rumours that abounds is that Jimmy Page has offered his services to the Rolling Stones should Keith Richards be unable to continue to perform with the band due to his being charged for drugs in Canada.... both Zeppelin's manager Peter Grant and tour manager Richard Cole vigorously deny any rumours of a split in the Zeppelin camp. Aside from the obvious problems caused by the death of Plant's son Karac, the band is also embroiled in a controversy after battery charges were laid in San Francisco following the band's two shows at the Oakland Coliseum. Both

Grant and drummer John Bonham were charged with assault after an altercation between them and some of promoter Bill Graham's road crew. Graham has said that in good conscience he couldn't book the Zeppelin in the USA again....

Rock Scene reports.... Cover story - Led Zep On Tour. Four page photo article with pictures by Neal Preston of the American tour. No editorial....

November 1977

5 **New Musical Express reports....** cover story.... Jimmy Page stomps rumours of Led Zeppelin splitting up.... *"All that was really tasteless. I think it was in bad taste because obviously after the tragedy Robert experienced he needs time alone with his family, and Zeppelin's so close no one in the band would think twice about that situation."....* **Melody Maker reports....** Once again Chris Welch interviews Jimmy Page. *"So much rubbish has been written about us recently. There was one thing about me joining the Stones, and it even got to the point of them asking Mick Jagger if Robert was joining. I thought this is getting silly. There were rumours that the group was breaking up, and all this sort of crap, and for some reason I don't understand, it just keeps going on.*

"In fact I've been very busy for the past few months, but unless you're being monitored all the time people think you are doing nothing.

"I've got a studio at home finally. It's taken me fifteen years to turn it into a reality. It's all together and last weekend was the first playback of the tape. The console was installed last January and it's taken all this time to sort out the acoustics. *I've been listening to lots of live tapes of the band going back to the Royal Albert Hall in 1969. I know that 'Song Remains The Same' was a live album, but it WASN'T the best performances, it was just one that happened to have celluloid with it. And there are loads of howling guitar mistakes on it. Normally one would be inclined to cut them out, but you can't when it's a sound-track.*

"It's an honest album in it's own way, but a chronologically live album is something I've always fancied, and now I've got the facilities at home to play back the hundreds of hours of tape, it's definitely on. There's great stuff there, and it takes us right up to this year."

Apparently Page had just acquired a guitar synthesizer, *"It's really phenomenal, a Roland synthesizer, and it's a knock-out. There are three guitar synthesizers available at the moment, and I guess you know there is this problem with getting polyphonic sound. Well the other two only play one note at a time and you can get harmonies with the oscillators, but this one plays chords. It's just a whole new world. I haven't used it on stage yet, but we were trying to get it together just before the end of the American tour. It's definitely something to use on stage. So while I've been totally self-indulgent and knocking myself out with new things, there has been all this stuff going on in the press. So I thought it was a good idea to speak."*

Welch asks about the incessant break-up rumours. *"Definitely not. I've got to say to you right now there are areas that are bloody touchy. You see I've never known a family to have such bad luck as Robert's and it's really awful."*

Apparently perturbed by the

subject Page switches back to, *"As well as listening to old tapes, I'm preparing material for the new LP, which I'll pace along with the live stuff. But I'd like the new studio album out first. I think I've spoken to you before about a long piece I'd written which was to have gone on 'Presence'. I had it all planned out and arranged, but it was too dangerous to rely on because of the time factor.*

"I knew how much time would be needed for the overdubs, and it wasn't the sort of thing John Paul Jones and I could do together. I wanted to orchestrate the guitar and put it through various treatments, which with the guitar synthesizer will be even easier now.

"I once worked on a guitar epic when I was doing studio work with Mike Leander. It was a classical thing rocked up. All the guitars were playing in unison and it didn't work. But I know now the whole thing can work, and from the trial runs I've laid down it does work. Think if Django Reinhardt, Les Paul and Jimi Hendrix, all as tonally different as chalk from cheese, and imagine them blocked together! That's what I'm seriously involved with right now, and another long piece."

Welch asks if this will be a solo project. *"No, no, no — with the rest of the guys. But it's basically an instrumental. The original idea was to have four sections for the vocals, coming back to the same theme each time. But there would be four separate melody lines dealing with the four seasons. Robert would be doing the lyrics for it, but right now it's difficult to tell if the lyrics would deal with the seasons. We're used to doing complete demos of songs and it's a bloody nuisance actually, because I've lost two and a half years work. The cassette briefcase...it's gone. My luggage was being brought back*

through customs by somebody else, and it's just gone. You get so used to working with cassettes you don't bother to learn it. Once it's on the tape you feel safe and that's the record of a particular idea. There were loads of orchestrated sections. It's a damn nuisance. Fortunately the excitement of having the new studio transcends the grief of losing all those demos, and I'll be coming up with new stuff anyway."*

Was his studio in Scotland? *"No, Plumpton, not Scotland. I've got a house there but I don't spend nearly as much time there as I'd like to. The worst thing is not being able to do anything, a feeling of helplessness really. The studio console arriving now has helped me to get on with something.*

"There's a winning version of 'No Quarter' from the Earl's Court concert, and from the Albert Hall there's 'I Can't Quit You Baby'. The 'How Many More Times' is pretty good. It's great hearing them again, numbers that we'll probably never play again. We've got numbers from Southampton University and some small clubs."

Welch asks about bootlegs and his feelings on the subject. *"I'm furious about them. The quality and the pricing of them. When you think about the overheads that the bootleggers have, pretty much nil, and they charge more than the price of a regular album. And they're re-recorded on tiny cassette players. None of the one's I've heard actually came from the mixing board. I remember going into a shop in Chicago which had a wall completely full of bootleg albums, which came as a shock as I thought the legislation had stopped them.*

"There was one called 'The Genius Of Pete Townsend' which was all his home demos. I don't know how they

got hold of them. They can be very interesting, but the main thing about bootlegs is the quality. I had one of us live in Japan, and it's slow. It's a tone and a half down, and that was selling."

Page shifts his attentions to the new wave, specifically The Damned, *"They are a knockout. I had heard so many derogatory statements about punk, as it was called then, and I was really curious to see what it was all about, and they were the best initiation one could have had. So powerful and tight. Exactly what rock and roll is all about, sheer adrenaline music. I think the new wave is the most important thing that's happened since Hendrix. But the ones that are good will last, like XTC, who seem to have a lot going for them — nice arrangements and chord changes, really interesting. And the Pistols, a couple of tracks are really great. There is a lot of energy there and I hope it becomes more positive, because one detects the negative vibe going on which is really silly.*

"The thing about Hendrix was that he had so many ideas linked to energy that were streets ahead of his contemporaries. Now there is a new energy statement being made, and love it or hate it, it's definitely there."

Page is asked about his future ambitions. *"We had a great plan to spend our non British residence period soaking up the musical vibe in places like Morocco. We went there after Earl's Court and spent quite a lot of time driving around there. We got turned back on our way to the Sahara because there was a lot of mobilization of troops going on. But we heard a lot of local music and I was really influenced by them in tunes like 'Achilles Last Stand'. The week of Robert's accident we had planned to go to Japan and Australia and then work our*

way back slowly through the East. And we wanted to record in Bangkok, Delhi and Cairo, and soak up the vibes, as we had done in Morocco.

"We didn't want to sound like a half-baked imitation but to use the acoustic qualities of their music. It was an interesting challenge to attempt. That would have been a milestone in our career, an aim fulfilled, but for circumstances. At that time we had considered shelving the film to film the forthcoming American Tour. We had learnt a lot and wanted to re-do the film. But then after Robert's accident, we had to fill the gap and go ahead with the film."

The press had recently considered that the band were reaping bad karma due to their inordinate stretch of bad luck. *"It's just the wrong term to ever use and how somebody could write that down, knowing the full facts about what has happened. I don't know. It shocks me. The whole concept of the band is entertainment. I don't see any link between that and karma, and yet I've seen it written a few times about us, like 'yet another incident in Zeppelin's karma — John Paul Jones has a broken hand'. It's nonsense, that was years back. It's all crap."*

He is asked if he thinks the band have made any enemies. *"No I don't think so... there was only the thing with Bill Graham, and that was just a case of manhandling going on at the back of the stage, people getting pulled over the barriers and being given whacks. But I didn't know anything about that. I didn't see what happened. I know that heavy vibe thing has surrounded us, but it's more like...well when Peter did his scene in the film, it was really tongue-in-cheek. You couldn't find a gentler man, but people totally misunderstood him. And that thing about karma really bothers me. Where's the clue? I'm putting it to you to supply the answer. Why are they using that term? It's a horrible tasteless thing to say. We can take constructive criticisms and attacks, and one comes to terms with that and laugh it off and...I'm only thinking out loud really. We shouldn't even discuss it. Just say that Jimmy Page is perplexed by the use of the word 'karma'. I just don't know what's going on."*

December 1977

3 **Melody Maker reports....** Angie Errigo interviews Page about the future of the band. Page, *"There's no question of the thing splitting up. I know Robert wants to work again."*

Errigo brings up the rumour that all of the band's seeming misfortunes are the result of the band reaping bad karma, one suggestion being that filmmaker Kenneth Anger had somehow cursed them, *"What do you mean by karma? It's not karma at all, I don't see how the band would merit a karmic attack. All I or we have attempted to do is to go out and really have a good time and please people at the same time. I always thought I was very fortunate through that, 'cause I can't think of anything better than doing what you really want to do and seeing just a mass of smiles. That's Utopia. If everybody in the band is really determined to do the best for themselves and the people who've followed us up to now without bullshitting around. I just don't see how there could be a bad karma or whatever. I think it's just bad coincidence. Okay, one may say there's no such thing as coincidence, but I really feel that. It just really upset me, that, because I really did think that he (Anger) was an avatar at one point. Sure enough, he really is good*

when it comes down to his statement on celluloid. But you can never know, I mean, it's like Blake, Einstein, any of these people, you never really know what they're going through. Some of the things that manifested on his personal life just totally perplexed me. I can't account for the lunatic fringe."

The subject switches to the infamous fracas in Oakland at the end of the last American tour. Page, *"I'll tell you, there was a whole team of guys there with sand in their gloves. It was a very, very hairy scene. I've had brushes with Bill Graham in the past. I'll give you an example. It was the Fillmore East where we really broke, and the whole name and news of the group spread like wildfire through the States from there. Obviously, on the return we were excited to be back and really wanted to do our best. Now, when we got there it was in the afternoon and I went in with the road manager 'cause we wanted to cart the gear in then, and Graham was playing basketball. I remember going up to him - he didn't seem to be doing anything at the time, he seemed like the referee - and I said, 'Hi Bill, it's really good to see you. Can we bring the gear in now?' And he said, 'Don't you fucking get in here, you mother-fuckers' and all this real abuse. It was just like he exploded. I was really brought down because we really built ourselves up to going back. Then later he apologised. What I mean is, he's a pendulum."*

Ludicrous rumours had been circulating that someone had been killed during the incident, *"That's nonsense! Listen, if we'd killed anybody we'd be bloody in prison. It's ridiculous. It was just a civil case. If somebody hits you and you hit them back it's self-defence, innit? It's just another thing that got blown up. I don't want to say too much about it."*

411

Another product of the rumour-mill was that he had been inspired to visit Egypt by a sighting of UFO's. Page, *"That's because somebody didn't really read what I'd said, and they were just being bloody stupid. I was going to go to Cairo on the tour break and I was tossing up whether or not to go. And there was this TV programme hosted by Omar Sharif about the mysteries of the pyramids. And they showed this old footage of the pyramids with a zeppelin flying in and I thought, 'That's it! I'll definitely go.' It seemed to be such a strange coincidence that that bit of footage should be there on the day I was thinking about it. But UFOs, that's just the usual sort of nonsense that goes on."*

How about the flak that the band's label Swan Song was taking? *"The only criticisms that have gone down about Swan Song are from Jake Riviera, who seems to be using anything as a springboard to get his name out. I don't really understand all that thing with Nick Lowe. Lowe is as sweet as apple pie to your face; that's all I really need to say about him. Well, there is one awkward situation with the label, which is that a lot of folk come along and seem to think that Peter Grant is going to be able to do everything for them. It's just one of those unfortunate things that he's there and they respect him, but he just doesn't want to know. He's got too much on his plate. We've had a bit of a shake-up in the record department. After having gone through two label managers we've found out we can do it better ourselves."*

How about the band? *"I do feel it's time to do some really major, meaty work. I get such a charge from playing with everybody. It became so apparent on the last tour that it was something which I really needed. If we hadn't had the awful*

end on this last tour everyone would have been in the frame of mind to bring over everything that we had in America because we were so knocked out with the show and the presentation.

"It was a great relief and release to be able to get back on stage and work. Obviously the first five gigs were rusty, but the audience just acted like 'Whoo, great to see you back'. I must admit I didn't know whether I was capable of playing for three-and-a-half hours. You could bullshit for an hour, but you can't bullshit for three-and-a-half hours or people are going to get bored. And they didn't - the enthusiasm was building all the time. We had a good programme which covered everything, and we had worked very hard on the environmental aspect of it. You could see the effects like the laser pyramid from a mile away. In the really massive places we used videos, which is only fair, really. Because I remember going to Wembley to see Crosby, Stills, Nash and Young and I thought it was the roadies on stage at first. When we did Earl's Court we were so determined to do the same sort of show and more than what we'd been doing in America that in the end; we came out of it with just a few hundred pounds over the five days; but it didn't matter because the vibe was so electrifying."

Page shifts the subject to his work at home. *"I've been setting up a studio at home which is so advanced that there's one bit which is still in the laboratories having tests made on it. Basically it's a computerised desk with a memory bank. There are automated desks around now which just do the volume and the level, but this does every single thing on the board. I've been learning how to use it. It's taken a bloody long time; the structural part of it was started before last Christmas and the wiring-up's been two* solid months. But anyway, it's playing back now and I've started attempting to do a bit of recording on it. I dreamed of having a studio years and years back, before the group even started. But I always wanted to have one which wouldn't go out of date in a year. Now this thing should last until they do digital recording. I don't want to get too technical, but what it does is, as you build up your mix track by track and you get your balance and equalisation and all the rest of it, it's logging it all the time and playing it back exactly as you've programmed it. When you finally build up the mix, if you find that the voice wasn't loud enough or something like that, you can just put the track into Rewrite and nothing else changes. It stays constant while you make your alterations. And you can put down six or eight alternative mixes and then go into those and take the best bits if you want to. The possibilities are immense. It allows you to work on your own without an engineer, and anyone who's familiar with 24-track knows how many hands are usually needed to get it right."

It is suggested that he is working on a chronological live Led Zeppelin album. This is one of the few early references to this project. "I'm working on it slowly because I get into that and it's really good academic practice. Then I'll get sidetracked and want to write something."

Page mentions his use of an early Roland guitar synthesiser (which he ended up endorsing for Roland). "It takes over from the keyboard; it's just programmed by the guitar, and it also plays chords. I've been working on all these things - new ideas and sounds. And I've got like two and-a-half years of demo stuff to merge in with all this new work. It's all very good at the moment, because as I

say, it's like the pre-Zeppelin dream. So there's all that - apart from all these things like holidays people keep going on about."

How about punk and the new wave music? "When I heard it it seemed like adrenaline music, so high-powered, and I thought it was amazing, especially The Damned. It was very much like mantra music; they weren't altering the tempo at all, just keeping it really, really intense. But the ones who want to stick to the original format are probably getting a bit hackneyed now. It'll be interesting to see how they do develop, keeping that raw earthiness."

Apparently he expresses his concern that there are no geniuses being spawned by the rock culture. "That's what really upsets me about rock. All the barriers are opened up, all the classification is gone really, and you find people amalgamating this, that and the other music together, and yet there doesn't seem to be anything that's really important without being pretentious. All those really strong melodies like Wagner's - there just isn't anybody. So maybe it's just destined to be street music and social comment. Which makes it art, because an artist is somebody who, ideally, reflects his environment."

Page backtracks to the subject of his work at home, "There are two pieces which are heavily orchestrated. One thing might sound odd, but the guitars are doing everything, taking over the string part and the brass part. They are heavily treated with synthesisers and effects. I've done a few bits of orchestration on the records up to now, but nothing really long or substantial. This is something entirely different. One thing I'm doing is like a cross between flamenco and modern classical on the acoustic with electric parts

that keep coming in and fading out again,
so that there are four totally different, but
related, sections coming in. It's not quite
the same as symphonic stuff. I don't keep
going back to a theme, but it's got that
sort of thickness to it. There are lots of
counter melodies and things.

"Now when you start talking like
that a lot of people I know go, 'Oh dear,
well that's not what's really happening'.
But I was very interested to notice that
when The Damned split Rat Scabies was
saying, 'We were trying to stretch out'.
That's it, it's a matter of change. A lot of
people can't handle that, they just want to
fit you into one bag and hope that you're
going to stay there all the time."

"I've always had a little plan of
what I'd like to do, and it's materialising
a lot slower than the way I initially
intended. But it still goes hand-in-hand
with the band. Whatever I'm going to do,
it's only going to be a fourth of that. I'm
totally committed to music. There's no
point in trying to deny it within myself.
It's the only thing I'm any good at. And
I'm not a natural player or anything like
that. It's all down to work. But I really
enjoy the recorded sound and messing
around getting unusual combinations.
Most people would find it very boring, but
I get as much buzz out of that as a motor-
cyclist gets out of his motorcycle.

"I'd never ever be happy. The
only time I felt, oh no, I won't say the only
time - but you know I get very enthusias-
tic and excited over something that's
being written out of nowhere. Obviously
there are a lot of things one has to come
up against which you really hate. But I
could never retire because it's so fasci-
nating; you never know what's coming
next. It's a challenge, a mystery. It's like
dancing on the edge of a precipice..."

1978

January 1978

14 New Musical Express reports.... Old Grey Whistle Test declares 1977 the year of Led Zeppelin....

February 1978

Creem reports.... Cover story - Led Zeppelin fly again! reprint of Angie Errigo's article in Melody Maker December 3rd 1977....

April 1978

8 New Musical Express reports.... Robert Plant's old band The Band Of Joy are reuniting at Plant's suggestion to perform a concert in aid of the dependents of a previous member of the band who had been recently killed in a car accident. Members of the band to reunite include Paul Lockey, Kevin Gammond and John Pasternak...

June 1978

6 Melody Maker reports.... Zeppelin back — album and tour. Article which mentions the band's first time reunited since Plant's death. It goes on to mention that they are rehearsing at Clearwell Castle in the Forest Of Dean. An Atlantic spokesman said, *"I don't know what will come of the rehearsals, an album, a tour or what, but I expect things will be clarified in the next few weeks."* Further details imply that Page may record a solo guitar album....

July 1978

29 New Musical Express reports.... Rumour has it that Led Zeppelin may play a series of pub gigs under what will probably be an assumed name.... Zep were all set to open for Maggie Bell last Sunday at the Royal Festival Hall but they backed out at the last minute.... no confirmation from Swan Song.

September 1978

16 Sounds reports.... Geoff Barton and Dave Lewis begin a four week series of indepth articles about the band....

23 New Musical Express reports.... Robert Plant jammed with Dave Edmunds and his band last Saturday, Edmunds introduced him as Robert Palmer. Plant was also a guest at Simon Kirke's wedding on Friday at which he sang two songs including My Baby Left Me.... **Sounds reports....** Geoff Barton and Dave Lewis continue their four week special on Led Zeppelin. This week is a breakdown of the band's itinerary from 1968 to 1980 covering the highlights. Some of the more interesting points include, the final Yardbirds date was at Luton Technical College, the band's rehearsals in August 1968 are mentioned, the band's fee at the Marquee was £150, Bath Pavilion £75, Exeter City Hall £125. They then repeat a common error for the time listing the band's first gig in the USA as the Boston Tea Party also mentioning Chicago and Detroit as having been played in 1968 (both wrong). In reference to the band's gig opening for Iron Butterfly in New York manager Peter Grant says, *"My instructions were to go out there and really blast them out, make* *each performance something to remember. They certainly did that."* Many of the facts related by Lewis and Barton are specifics about concert dates (as one would expect).

30 **Sounds reports....** Geoff Barton and Dave Lewis continue their four week special on Led Zeppelin. This week the concentration is on the Led Zeppelin discography. This ranks as probably one of the first of many done of the band, (including a few by yours truly). In what was almost certainly a daring move for the day (no doubt incurring the wrath of Peter Grant) they print a rudimentary guide to the bootlegs available of the band complete with illustrations.

October 1978

7 **Sounds reports....** Geoff Barton and Dave Lewis conclude their four week special on Led Zeppelin. It concentrates on the balance of the information missed from the previous three weeks. Radio appearances, TV appearances, Books, Films etc. All in all an excellent four week synopsis of the band's career to that point...

November 1978

11 **New Musical Express reports....** Robert Plant played in a charity five-a-side soccer game organised by The Sun for Goaldiggers.... Plant's team lost to Hugh Cornwall's team of boys from Finchley....

25 **New Musical Express reports....** Warner records will make a series of albums available at Christmas on coloured vinyl including Led Zeppelin IV....

December 1978

9 **New Musical Express reports....** T-Zers gets Itself Together In A Studio In Stockholm. Column accompanied by picture of Plant and Page reporting that the band are in Abba's Polar Studios in Stockholm Sweden recording their new album....

16 **New Musical Express reports....** Led Zeppelin finished recording their new album last week, however the album has yet to be mixed....

1979

February 1979

24 **New Musical Express reports....** Led Zeppelin's new album should be released within a month....

May 1979

12 **New Musical Express reports....** Robert Plant was spotted at Dave Edmund's wedding at the Marylebone registry office....

19 **New Musical Express reports....** Jimmy's good deed. Article outlining Page's involvement in a small town's attempts to resurrect their harbour from a catastrophic storm which devastated the local economy. Page was moved enough by the plight of the people of Phillip's Harbour in Scotland that he volunteered to open the new harbour and did just that. Page, *"My craft is my music, and all the way along I've kept hammering away at it to try and achieve excellence. You chaps involved in this project have also striven for excellence and have done a really worthwhile job."*....

26 **New Musical Express reports....** Zep Are Back.... Announcement of the impending dates at Knebworth. The shows are expected to be Zeppelin's only shows anywhere in the world this year. The band's new album is expected to be released to coincide with the show on August 4th. Despite Knebworth's previous track record as Britain's biggest festival drawing from talents such as The Rolling Stones and Pink Floyd the promoter, Frederick Bannister, expects this to be the biggest ever with the band performing their full American stage show.

The show is expected to begin at 11 am and will run for about twelve hours. Bannister, *"Everyone has been extremely co-operative. The police are pulling out all the stops to ensure a better traffic flow. British Rail are laying on a better than usual train service from King's Cross to Stevenage and return. And National Coaches are organising a number of all-in trips from various areas."* Apparently Bannister had been negotiating with the Eagles to headline but couldn't accept their terms. Bannister called this *"the greatest scoop of my career."* Tickets are expected to go on sale on Monday June 3rd and 4th around the country....

June 1979

2 **New Musical Express reports....** 2 page advert for Led Zeppelin at Knebworth.... Zep Ticket Mania. Apparently the response to Led Zeppelin's announcement to play Knebworth has been "phenomenal". Both Harlequin and Virgin records have been inundated with calls for tickets. Promoter Frederick Bannister says, *"A certain number of tickets have been set aside for postal applicants. The rest have been distributed as fairly as possible to the various personal sales points."* The support acts for Knebworth are expected to be announced next week....

16 **New Musical Express reports....** Zepmania Continued. Article stating that all tickets for Knebworth are sold out. Promoter Frederick Bannister is concerned that some of the mail order bookings may be left unfulfilled but he has hired more staff to deal with the crush of mail....

July 1979

7 **New Musical Express reports....** Zep Knebworth 2 On August 11 is confirmed. The second show is agreed to by Zeppelin after the huge demand for tickets over the last six weeks. August 4th is completely sold out. The admission for Knebworth 2 will remain at £7.50 even though the UK government has hiked the taxes in the interim. Zeppelin have agreed to absorb the tax increase....

14 **New Musical Express reports....** Zep At Knebworth. Support acts for the Zeppelin Knebworth shows will include, Chas & Dave, Marshall Tucker Band, Southside Johnny & The Asbury Dukes and Todd Rungren's Utopia. Promoter Frederick Bannister is trying to keep both dates the same with the same attractions which means most of the American bands have exclusive UK performance contracts for Knebworth, Bannister, *"They'll either have a holiday at our expense, or pop over to the Continent to do some midweek dates."* Although the second date on August 11th is not expected to sell out as fast as the first show ticket sales are reportedly going well and ticket offices have been opened in many foreign countries....

August 1979

4 **New Musical Express reports....** cover story...Tory Rocker speaks out.... In an unusual interview with Chris Salewicz Page is confronted by the skepticism of the new wave of British journalists. Punk rock is at it's apex and Led Zeppelin are at an all time low in the eyes of the media. Salewicz manages to fill four huge pages with small print, insisting on bringing politics into the interview. For the most part his observations are about as jaded and representative of the general mood of punk rock. However, it makes for interesting reading to see Page in top form very cautiously and for the most part successfully parrying Salewicz efforts to bait him. The interview goes under the banner of 'Smiling Men With Bad Reputations'. Knowing full well that his readers will be reading this in a field at Knebworth Salewicz takes half a page grumbling about Page's efforts to begin with the upcoming mammoth concert.

Page, *"Well, I'm looking forward to .... to Knebworth, actually. We've done a lot of rehearsing and checked things out. We've actually been down there and worked things out relative to the actual site. But then again it's like a natural amphitheatre so I should imagine it's actually quite a good gig to be at. I went to Blackbushe, but that was a bit of a sea of bodies. But it was great to see Dylan."*

At this point Salewicz suggests that he would rather talk about Dylan (rather than Zeppelin) and mentions the Dylan concert in Nuremberg Germany, the site of the infamous Nazi war trials.

Page, *"I couldn't believe him doing that. They passed the place where they had all the big rallies. He must have come out of there feeling very strange I know I would and I'm not even Jewish. We met his mum once, actually, it was about the third tour and we were in Miami, and this typical Miami woman comes up with the spectacles and tinted hair bit and she says 'Oh, I hear you're a group. My son's a singer. You've probably heard of him— Bobby Dylan. He's a good lad,' she said.*

"The strangest thing she said of all was that he always goes back to his .... You know, the school turn-out when they

got their degrees and things. He always goes back to that .... Which is obviously a side of Dylan that many people would be actually shocked about. He's probably very orthodox in some areas where you expect him to be very bizarre and anarchistic."

Apparently the gig where Dylan met Salewicz was a reggae concert and this leads them into the subject of the Rastafarians. Salewicz is seemingly surprised by Page's knowledge of the subject.

"Yeah, it's very interesting: the lost Tribe of Israel and all that. It was at the time when Haile Selassie died that I wondered, 'What's going to happen now?' because there is this big thing that he's invincible and that he would never die but obviously, he could give up his bodily form if he wanted to—that was the loophole. But it is fascinating."

Salewicz mentions Page's trip's to Egypt, *"I didn't want to come home. It was so good. I didn't go for long enough, though. I went at the end of an American tour and with every day I was there family ties in England were pulling, more strongly. I just thought, 'oh, I'll be back soon' and haven't made it yet. I'd certainly like to see The Valley of The Kings near Luxor. I haven't been to many Arab countries, but I've been to Morocco and there and in other hot countries there's this constant hub-bub, but in Egypt it's just so tranquil. It really is quite an experience. Let alone the pyramids."*

This in turn leads to Page's book shop in Kensington which had recently closed down. *"It obviously wasn't going to run the way it should without some drastic business changes and I didn't really want to have to agree to all that. I basically just wanted the shop to be the nucleus, that's all."*

For some completely obscure reason, at this point Salewicz brings up the whole theory that Mussolini had invaded Ethiopia with the Vatican's blessing, ostensibly to make sure that Catholicism remained the preeminent Christian church.

Page, *"I know the Pope definitely blessed the bombers going to Ethiopia, that's a fact. My lady went to the Vatican. She said it's like Fort Knox, a completely separate state. A highly guarded treasury. And they have all these links with suspect organisations .... The whole image of the Pope being borne around St. Peter's on a throne doesn't even bear thinking about. They had some programme on TV about the Vatican and they got through to one of the heads of the business division. And he was asked if it wouldn't be an act of faith to give all this wealth away—if your faith was sufficiently high and strong then obviously this wouldn't really affect the church. But he was dumb struck. So obviously, he didn't have the faith."*

At this juncture Salewicz switches to local politics and Page's recent involvement in a small civil revolt near his home in Scotland. Page, *"I just got up and said I'm not here for any political reasons whatsoever but just from my own endeavours as an untrained musician. And it's just sheer, determination that's been employed here against a good eighty per cent of the council who wished them to have no encouragement whatsoever. The Hydro board in Scotland were putting in this scheme which wasn't of benefit to anyone except for a small percentage of local labourers, although, in fact, most of them were being brought in from places like Manchester and Liverpool. What it was going to do was pump power at peak times to the South. It wasn't going to benefit the Scots at all.*

And for this they were going to put pylons up all over the place and mess up the loch. There were no pylons there whatsoever before and I just didn't think it was on. For them of course it was purely a financial investment it was really a revelation to see how these things go on. So corrupt. But we managed to force a public inquiry whereby it was put under the Secretary of State. They really put you through it at those things. It's like a court of law. They try and throw so much mud at you. Although it does seem that in London these days if they're pulling down buildings to put up new ones they are trying to keep the old facade and it makes it much more palatable. At least you don't get things like that too much. But so often people just get apathetic and think there's nothing they can do. At least sometimes you can uncover a bit of unsavoury business that's going on I do really care about those things I don't particularly go around doing a load of public campaigning, but both those things were there on my doorstep on the other hand it can help if it was on your doorstep because it gives your protest much more credibility."

Salewicz now turns his attentions to mainstream politics. No doubt the theory being that punk rockers were intent on unleashing their anarchistic views on the world then surely Page and his generation must be in league with the 'enemy'. Page admits to voting Conservative in the last election but seems understandably reluctant to be drawn in to this particular debate. Page, *"(I voted Tory) not just for lighter taxes—I just couldn't vote Labour. They actually stated that they wanted to nationalize the media—so what possible criticism of them would you be able to have. I voted Conservative then because I believed in Heath and I still believe that Edward Heath was a very honest man. He*

was too honest to be a politician, in fact Wilson was very slippery, but a good politician. But I suppose that's politics."

Salewicz clings to the subject of politics as it relates to music and standing up for what you believe. Roy Harper is mentioned, *"Harper's 'Stormcock' was a fabulous album which didn't sell anything. Also, they wouldn't release his albums in America for quite a long time. For that I just thought, Well 'hats off to you'. As far as I'm concerned, though hats off to anybody who does what they think is right and refuses to sell out."*

As punk's primary dictum seems to have been anarchy he is asked what he thinks, *"Well, anarchy's all right if you can see where you're going afterwards. Although I don't see any point in destroying things just for the sake of it. It's the easiest, way out. It's hard to have an optimistic goal and strive towards it, that's really hard work. But, yes, anarchy can certainly be an answer to a situation if there's no other answer. It's difficult at the time when Hitler came into power in Germany during the '30s, he appeared to be stabilising the economy and giving people more work and was emerging as a very patriarchal figure. The Germans felt that everything was going to be all right. Yet underneath was this fundamental plan— be it evil or whatever. And at the time when Hitler came in there'd been a form of anarchy existing so, yes, you just have to see at the end of the day what's really gone down."*

At this point Salewicz gets on to Page's impressions of punk and new wave. He seems to think that this is what his readers have been waiting for (probably partially true). He starts with Ian Dury, Page, *"He really imparts such a great feeling, doesn't he? Makes you feel so good. That was certainly the first thing* that struck me about New Wave music, that it was sheer adrenaline pouring out. Real energy just tearing to get out. We were aware of it but it's not.... I mean, music is like a 360 degree circle from which some people may drop out to let others come in. And there are obvious examples of that say, the feeling that Free generated and which was replaced by Bad Company. Also, the raw blues, going back to the early Fleetwood Mac days. Well, now you have George Thorogood. And Herman's Hermits are replaced by The Bay City Rollers. Bands like us and I hate to say it but, The Floyd, we're off in our own little bits. It's always open for anybody who's really raw and earthy and who makes sheer rock'n'roll music. Even though much of the New Wave had the political content.... I mean, The Damned, I was absolutely amazed by the power that was coming out of them. Though they didn't really fit into the New Wave movement as such.

"Nevertheless, there are categories But it's all relative; anyone who plays good music and is expressing themselves with an instrument or on vocals has got something to say. It just depends whether you can relate to them or not. And that also depends on whether your musical tastes are narrow or very broad. Yes, (I can relate). But I can also relate to classical music—and you wouldn't find them saying that."

In what must have seemed to Salewicz like an ambush he mentions to Page that Zeppelin are almost universally loathed by the new wave fans. "Really???? Well, people write to us you know and a lot of younger people who I'd never have expected to have got into us have said that they got really fired up by the energy of New Wave bands—and they still like New Wave bands—but they got

interested in the actual musical content and wanted to go one step further which is how they discovered bands like us. And uhh I'm not sure whether that's going to last or not but it's quite good if you can keep turning people on."

Page is asked whether he was ever concerned that no one would buy the new album or attend the Knebworth event. "Yeah, but no— because when we'd finished our album I knew at the time that it didn't matter if it didn't come out for nine months afterwards, because I knew that I could rely on the fact that Led Zeppelin hadn't dated—the actual identity of the band is still there. There's a fresh approach which can still give it an edge. I had my reservations at one point about playing a date like Knebworth. But in the end it all went hand-in hand with the LP when that was finished I did actually stop and take a breath and I thought 'No it's alright'. We've moved on sufficiently to be able to see the next horizon. We're not sounding complacent I hope. There's a lot of hard work still to come obviously it's not like we've felt we had to change the music to relate to any of the developments that've been going on. There's no tracks with disco beats or anything. But I think some of the numbers are some of the most immediate we've done anyway. Like I say it's not a new musical form but there is still something very fresh about it."

Salewicz asks if he is still concerned with being respected by the UK fans and was he apprehensive, "No sure we were concerned about it being good. And we were pleased to hear that the actual environmental area of the stage was good. But if the playing hadn't been feeling right I would've worried. But that feels alright so I'm pretty sure it'll be good. We were worrying about too many other things at the time I was worried *more about whether we were still going to gel. Having felt something special towards the band for that amount of time and still wanting that feeling to be there without being quite sure it would be. But then we got together a few times to play and could see that it still was...well it was a very good feeling. The LP really is a bit of a by-product to me Knebworth is far more important. Because people can buy the LP and we won't see how they're reacting to it. But I will at Knebworth. The LP's a frozen statement which can be always referred to but Knebworth's going to be different."*

Despite answering the question in just about every interview, he is asked again about why they don't play smaller gigs. *"We did that—about the third year of the band. And we got fucked for it. Previously we'd played places like Manchester Free Trade Hall and the Albert Hall and we'd had all these letters saying 'Why do they let their fans down? Why don't they play the clubs any more?' So we said 'Yeah let's play clubs.' And it was chaos because people couldn't get in. So the next barrage was why are they so selfish doing small clubs? So the supply-and-demand thing becomes a problem. So from then on we were faced with a sort of dilemma. But then again it became a challenge to see if we could try and make it work on a large scale. Don't get me wrong. I'm the first to admit it can get too large but something like Knebworth can be a challenge because you know it's worked in the past. But we couldn't do that. We tried. When we'd done the LP we were trying to work out where we could get in and play. But then we thought, 'Are we running away from something?' And we weren't. It was almost like denying what you were, and you've got to be true to yourself. I know what you mean but it*

just gets impossible to do unless you play four weeks in the Marquee."

In the days of punk rock, being associated with the corporate nature of the business was definitely a bad idea. In what was surely a rhetorical question Salewicz asks whether Page feels that Zeppelin are part of the corporate structure, *"Obviously. Yeah. But to them you're only a matrix number. We sweat the songs out though. But don't you see that we're only as good as whatever we come up with. Say we didn't put out another LP. Well we've probably done really well for our record company but if we did that, they'd probably come right down on us. I think it's probably really ruthless behind the scenes. It comes down to things like Kinney owning car parks and things."*

Salewicz counters with the charge that by playing the huge gigs Zeppelin are perpetuating the problem, Page, *"I see what you mean—though I'm not sure you see what I mean. The problem is trying to supply the demand of the people who want to see you. You can only gauge that. I mean it is a rather nice feeling deciding on this huge date and not being quite certain that there's enough demand and then finding you can play a second one the same size. Anyway at this point in time we just want to get back into playing music. And we will be doing other dates. I don't know where: not necessarily in England. We've been talking about playing Ibiza just getting in there and playing. Just so we've got a chance of trying out new ideas and new riffs and arrangements and songs."*

Was the idea of making money ever paramount to Zeppelin? *"No. Never. NO because we've been our own worst enemies over that. But you wouldn't see it like that now. But at the time we put out our fourth LP we had the worst reviews of anybody. And to put out an untitled LP at that time was considered professional suicide. It probably doesn't seem it now. But then..."*

Fishing further into the barrel and trying to presumably show up Page, Salewicz asks if he is materialistic, presumably not expecting Page to say, *"Well I dunno. Yeah I suppose I am a bit. But on the other hand even though I have material possessions the most important things are books, studios and records. If I had to get up and run that's what I'd try and take."*

Finally in conclusion he is asked if he is happy. *"Well as happy as the next one. I think I'm pretty fortunate in that I'm able to do what I'm best at. It's a pretty fortunate position to be doing what you really want to do and turning people on. In the end it comes down to playing with the people who I really like to play with."....*

Full page advert for Knebworth II.... Zep LP Surprise. Led Zeppelin's new album will be released worldwide on August 20th. It will be titled In Through The Out Door and was recorded in Polar Studios in Stockholm. Tracks include, In The Evening, South Bound Suarez, Fool In The Rain, Hot Dog, Carouselambra, Hot Dog and I'm Gonna Crawl. The camp site at Knebworth will not open until 10 am on Friday the 3rd but early arrivals will have to pay £1 to park and camp.... Led Zeppelin's new album will have four different covers all in brown paper so you can't tell which is which.... Dazed 'n' Abused article reviewing the band's gigs in Copenhagen by Eric Kornfeldt.... 'Led Zeppelin tested their stage show on 2,200 defenseless fans in Copenhagen.... Let me say that I have never been a Zep hater but the band do bask in the glories of 1974.... The first

hour comprised of agonisingly long guitar solos from Jimmy Page.... other band members also proved shockingly inadequate'. He goes on to call Bonham's drumming 'thunderously insensitive', Jones keyboard work 'redundant pretentious pseudo classical dribblings' he concludes that Plant was wasted as he stands back for so many endless solos by the rest of the band. His final deliberation is, 'They were no more than a quartet of sloppy uninspired old men, a relic from the past.'....

Review of In Through The Out Door by Nick Kent. Kent with usual condescending style admits that, *"I came in off the lam expecting to drive the stake through the heart of an ailing behemoth but In Through The Out Door is no epitaph."* He runs the gamut of how Zeppelin have virtually disappeared since the unexpected loss of Plant's son and inevitably compares them to the Stones and The Who (again), points out that they are the subject of unerring contempt by the Punk movement and points out that they have not really got any support due to the fact that, *"they never really influenced any contemporary bands beyond the reactionary heavy metal combos."* He attacks the band's "empty virtuosity" preferring the "punchy relevance" of the new wave (Translation, if you can play you must be no good). Even though he clearly enjoyed the record he is afraid to say so, *"Fortunately In Through The Out Door isn't the outright turkey that many of us cynics expected."* He goes on to say something positive about every track except 'Hot Dog'. Concluding, "The ensemble has never played better...the doctor orders a period of intense activity." With hindsight this is really a RAVE review considering who wrote it and when, rumour has it that Bonham once threw a drink on

Kent for a bad review, from that point on one has to question his objectivity.... **Melody Maker reports....** Article Zep Album Date.... ITOD will be released August 20. The band were to release a single from the album as a special Knebworth commemorative disc but plans fell through, (It was to have been the song Wearing & Tearing which didn't even make the album but was saved until Coda.) The article then goes on to suggest that the band have no tour plans but will do a few selected gigs including one planned in a bullring in Ibiza one of the Balearic Islands off the coast of Spain.... Under the banner 'Warming up in Denmark: Duckwalks and Lasers' Jon Carlsson reviews the band's shows in Copenhagen....

'Even in an out of town rehearsal they proved that they can still cut it.' Carlsson describes how the light show had failed miserably the first night and due to the long wait the press has dubbed it the "Led Zeppelin Fiasco" which apparently contributed to a low attendance the second night. He describes the second night as progressing from 'good to amazing'. In one highly amusing analogy he refers to playing to the loyal Danish fans as 'like kicking the shit out of a lovable sheep dog'. He observes that the band seemed to be enjoying themselves with Plant at one point prancing about like 'Wild Willy Barrett stung by a wasp.' He describes Page's bow solo (during which Page uses an illuminated bow with a laser attached), 'Page resembled Obe Wan Kenobe on exotic snuff'. .... Reporter Steve Gett interviews Page.... Gett begins the conversation with Page asking about the band's recent rehearsals at Clearwell Castle in the forest of Dean, Page, *"That was basically a period of saying hello to each other musically once again. We had-*

n't played together for so long and Clearwell was the first actual playing we'd done for what seemed like an eternity, although it was only about 20 months. It was really just limbering up."

Page explains why the band chose to use Abba's Polar Studios for the new album, *"It was a case of wanting to try a new approach to a lot of things. The environment was new, and one was practically a prisoner in the studio. It was more of a working project than a recreation ground. We went there with a project in mind, I'm not saying we had a job to do, but we knew what we were doing and felt ready, having had some pretty good weeks of playing."*

The discussion turns to the new album, *"There's a lot more keyboards and synthesiser employed by John Paul. He has one of those Yamaha monster electronic machines that practically sound like a one man orchestra. John had been working with that a lot and one could see it's possibilities."*

Gett asks whether the new album features much in the way of acoustic material, Page, *"There's an acoustic gutstring solo on one number, but it hasn't got any other mellow things. Every LP has always been a summing up of where we are at a particular time. The second album for example was recorded on the road, and then after the first two years of playing virtually night after night we had time off. Robert and I went to that cottage and it was a sort of feeling that came through in the songs of the third album. I think the mood is one of the most important things anyway with recording, actually trying to capture a sort of essence, the sound of the thing and the emotion. The whole key is to capture something."*

Gett points out that Page is reluctant to discuss the album in much detail so he switches the topic to the altercation that took place in Oakland at the end of the band's last US tour. Page, *"People told us that he'd (Bill Graham) been allowing his men to really smash up others with a fist of iron for ages. That's from the other side, and I don't know how true that was, it certainly looked pretty ugly to me, (but) I wasn't there, I honestly wasn't there."*

Promoter Bill Graham had stated at the time that Zeppelin wouldn't play for him again. However the band went on to play the second show, *"Stands to reason, if you think about it. We played the second gig, so he wasn't too bothered about us not performing in the States, was he? When there were a few dollars coming over the counter. There's nothing stopping us playing in the States, in California, or even in San Francisco, except that we wouldn't play for Bill Graham out of personal preference. It seems to me that Bill Graham's whole thing was suddenly shown up for what it was, and he tried to make a big fuss to get licenses for his next concerts. His thing about us never playing in the States again is an example. The sheer fact that we played the second night if anything heavy had gone down he should have had the moral conviction there and then. Not wait until we're gone and start back biting, he's so obvious."*

Having attempted to lay that particular spectre to rest the subject switches to Knebworth, Page, *"Knebworth was suddenly starting to become a bit of a nightmare, because there was a bit of worry about getting licenses. Initially it was put out that another band was going to be headlining, and then it was us. Then all the bands that were going to be on the bill were nowhere to be seen. The line-up we had hoped for was to have included Dire Straits, Joni Mitchell and Little Feat, also Fairport of course. We've tried years back to do smaller venues, but it just can't be done. When the Albert Hall was still a rock venue, we tried to do a tour of the clubs. Obviously the reaction was 'How selfish can they be? We couldn't get in.' It's supply and demand."*

Gett asks about the band's use of video screens to facilitate a better view for people, Page, *"I remember going to see Crosby, Stills, Nash and Young at Wembley, and standing on the terraces. I arrived a bit late — as usual and there was this music coming out which I couldn't determine whether it was the roadies or something. Suddenly I realised that it was the band, and thought that this definitely shouldn't happen to us."*

One of the proposed ideas for Knebworth which didn't appear was a commemorative single of 'Wearing And Tearing', *"Well, we had an idea about putting out a commemorative single for the event, just to be sold there another track that wasn't on the album. But time ran out because of rehearsals and unfortunately we never got around to it."*

At this point for some strange reason Gett switches the clock back three years to the band's movie, Page, *"I think that the film world is fascinating, certainly more on the musical aspect than actually being a character. It hadn't occurred to me, when I was scrambling up the mountain, that I'd have to do about half a dozen takes. Suddenly it hit me that I'd bitten off more than I could chew. In the film it didn't look anywhere near the distance covered—it looked like I was having a promenade!"*

Page explains why the band don't follow trends in the same way as The Stones, *"That doesn't mean to say that we're not aware of what's going on,* but I don't think there's been a case where fashion has affected what we've done. We haven't been faced with the situation of having to do a disco number. There's enough coming through the normal writing channels for us not to have to, we're fortunate enough to always have a surplus. I thought the new wave thing was fantastic but there's two channels the ones who remain true to their ideals and really keep being honest, and those who don't. It takes a lot of guts to go around in the punk uniform. I thought what was going to happen especially around the mid-Seventies, was that there'd be a lot more thinking man's Composition. The time is always right for a rock revival, but I felt that a lot more major works would be coming out. It's surprised me that it hasn't happened already, and it looks like we'll have to wait until the Eighties."

The subject of the band's record label Swan Song is raised, "We want to try and keep it basically a family affair although that's looking at it idealistically. The Pretty Things and Metropolis were really good, but they just couldn't get any work and so they couldn't keep going. All the bands that are signed to the label are a group decision. And, basically, the whole idea is that, as an artist, one can have more control over one's destiny. I wish we had more groups, but we've been spending a lot of time trying to coax on the ones we had."

With the huge event at Knebworth looming on the horizon Page speculates about the band's performing future, "We're talking about doing a bull-ring in Ibiza. Why not? I think that the time has come for us to be working at a sensible pace, not massive slogs across the States. I'm not saying that there won't be any long tours but to do isolated concerts seem to be a wiser way of working.

At the moment, everyone seems to be in that frame of mind. That's again talking idealistically. The first step is to do these gigs. If they come off, it could be a workable situation doing just two or three gigs at a time. It gets a bit heavy doing very big sets, three days on and one day off. You come off these tours not knowing where you are, and have to go through a rehabilitation period before going out again."

Gett concludes the interview by suggesting that Page and Plant are the band's backbone, "Backbone? I would have thought the backbone would be the rhythm section." .... **Sounds reports....** Something Heavy In The State Of Denmark...review of the Copenhagen warm-up gigs. Erik Von Lustbaden states, "Page came off like John McLaughlin on speed, John Bonham was merely competent, and low-key John Paul Jones was undoubtedly the best musician on stage." He goes on to complain about the lights not working before admitting that he left to, "take a piss, and buy a bar of chocolate," while Page played his solo. He concludes, "It can't be easy being Led Zeppelin."..... **Record Mirror reports....** Cover story, Led Zep special. Lengthy article covering the band's history. Quotes from the bio includes, Jimmy Page 'Whether he's in contact with the devil or not is unknown but he plays like a demon', Plant, 'something of a stud on the road, hence his nickname Percy', Jones, 'he might have gone to Westminster Cathedral where he nearly applied for the job of choirmaster', and Bonham, 'his school report said he would either be a dustman or a millionaire'....

5 **The Sunday People reports....** Cover Story The Amazing Zeppelin Spotters .... "More than 200,000 people were at

Knebworth Herts. to pay homage to such blockbusters as Led Zeppelin and a list of top bands. Tented cities sprung up as much as five miles away from the site. (It was) Britain's biggest ever rock festival."

11 New Musical Express reports.... Peter Grant was considering having Led Zeppelin return to the concert stage by performing on the deck of an aircraft carrier or at Waterloo station.... Ghosts Of Progressive Rock Past...review of the first Knebworth date by Paul Morley.... in an indication of how the band had been almost completely ignored by the British music press the biggest concert ever held in the UK since the Isle Of Wight doesn't even make the cover of the weeklies. Morley delivers a predictably trendy review designed to sell papers and ignore the facts. At the time it was not fashionable to give even a passing acknowledgment to the giant groups such as Zeppelin and so we get such staggeringly patronising remarks as, "...the majority of the masterfully produced but erratic and naive music the group recorded has been surpassed many times by the young groups thrown up by punk." One can only wonder exactly which young groups he is referring to. He then goes on to grudgingly acknowledge, "They did more than enough not to embarrass themselves.... playing rock and roll of such stinging insistence and convulsive perseverance it wouldn't have mattered how old or processed it was." He then notes, "Led Zeppelin made the Knebworth hollowness into something that, if pushed, I would call an occasion." In the final triumph of punk journalism over fact he declares, "Kashmir was meticulous and banal," this while he admits he was falling asleep. His conclusions, "After all, they're just four confused naive craftsmen who got

themselves tangled in the ridiculous paradoxes through little fault of their own, idiots more than Gods. I don't care whether they go away for another bunch of years, but over 140,000 people can't be wrong, and neither can I." No ego there.

14 Toronto Star reports.... In Through The Out Door Zeppelin's Best album yet.... Star Music critic Peter Goddard gives the band a glowing review. "Like the great white whale, Led Zeppelin surfaces every so often with a new album scuttling every other band in sight only to sink down into the gloom again, trailing wreckage behind it." He points out that the band are often at odds with the cognoscenti and critics but, "In Through The Out Door will change all that. It's simply the best piece of work the band's ever done."

15 Swan Song official press release.... FOR IMMEDIATE RELEASE FROM: BOB KAUS AUGUST 15, 1979 NEW LED ZEPPELIN ALBUM, "IN THROUGH THE OUT DOOR," SET FOR AUGUST 22 RELEASE "IN THROUGH THE OUT DOOR" (SS 161002), the new album from Swan Song recording group Led Zeppelin, has been set for official national release on August 22 79. The first new studio album in 3 years from the British supergroup, "IN THROUGH THE OUT DOOR" is a single album containing seven new songs written by members of the group. Produced by Jimmy Page, the complete track listing is : Side 1 - IN THE EVENING * SOUTH BOUND SAUREZ * FOOL IN THE RAIN * HOT DOG; Side 2 - CAROUSELAMBRA * ALL MY LOVE * I'M GONNA CRAWL. The album was recorded and mixed at Polar Music Studios in Stockholm, Sweden.

The elaborate packaging concept for "IN THROUGH THE OUT DOOR" was designed by Hipgnosis and it includes the production of six different album sleeves (variations on a theme) which are inserted into a plain brown bag simply stamped with the group name, title and tracks. The whole package is shrink-wrapped, and therefore the buyer is unable to determine which cover variation he or she has until after the purchase has been made.

Coinciding with the completion of the new Led Zeppelin album the group (Jimmy Page, Robert Plant, John Paul Jones, John Bonham) made its first live appearances in two years over the past few weeks. Following two warm-up shows in Copenhagen, Denmark, the band headlined two massive concerts at England's Knebworth Park on August 4 and 11. 1979 marks the tenth Anniversary of the release of the first Led Zeppelin album.

18 **New Musical Express reports....** full two page advert for In Through The Out Door....

27 **People Weekly reports....** Comment from Robert Plant, *"We did nothing for a year and a half. I tinkered on the village piano and grew so obese drinking beer that nobody knew who I was."*

September 1979

1 **New Musical Express reports....** In Through The Out Door is #12 in the UK....

8 **New Musical Express reports....** In Through The Out Door is #15 in the UK.... the album is straight in at #1 in the USA....

11 **Circus reports....** Cover story, article covering the band's return with pictures

from Knebworth. Mostly a retrospective piece but with a couple of great comments from promoter Bill Graham who had problems with a brawl back-stage after the band's last US concert in Oakland, *"Because of that deplorable event I will never allow myself the privilege of working with the band again. But I still tip my hat to them because they have more personal pulling power than anybody since Mahatma Ghandi. Other groups can outsell them in records and get more radio airplay, but nobody can outdraw them on a concert tour."*

15 **New Musical Express reports....** In Through The Out Door is #4 in the UK....

22 **New Musical Express reports....** In Through The Out Door is #2 in the UK.... Frederick Bannister's company has gone bankrupt the attendance at Knebworth was grossly exaggerated and the numbers were more like 98,000 and 48,000 at the second show....

29 **New Musical Express reports....** In Through The Out Door is #3 in the UK....

October 1979

6 **New Musical Express reports....** In Through The Out Door is #6 in the UK.... Advertisement from Frederick Bannister.... *"There have been some misconceptions reported in the press concerning Led Zeppelin and Knebworth, which as the concert promoter I would like to clarify. Firstly, before anyone knew what the total ticket sales for the two concerts would be, at my request, Led Zeppelin voluntarily reduced their guarantee by a substantial amount and were willing to accept an alternative arrangement in order to help ensure the best possible con-*

cert for the patrons and payment to all concerned, in the event there was insufficient funds to pay everyone. Peter Grant, manager of Led Zeppelin, was particularly concerned that all acts appearing at the concert be paid. Unfortunately because of a large increase in production and staffing costs, increased VAT amongst other reasons, this very substantial reduction by Zeppelin, while very helpful and very much appreciated was unfortunately not sufficient. secondly at all times Led Zeppelin, the manager and his staff have been completely cooperative. The group's performance at Knebworth, was in my opinion, really tremendous and their popularity as shown by their album being No 1 throughout the world speaks for itself. Finally it would be a privilege and pleasure for me to promote another Led Zeppelin concert in the future and hope to have the opportunity of so doing." Signed Frederick Bannister Director Tedoar Ltd....

13 New Musical Express reports.... In Through The Out Door is #17 in the UK.... still #1 in the USA....

20 New Musical Express reports.... In Through The Out Door is #12 in the UK.... #2 in the USA...

27 New Musical Express reports.... In Through The Out Door is #14 in the UK.... **Billboard reports....** A feat not attained before and not likely to be paralleled for a long time, Led Zeppelin have every single one of their albums in the Billboard Hot 200 LP and Tape charts, Led Zeppelin III is #189, Presence is #183, Led Zeppelin I is # 174, The Soundtrack to The Song Remains The Same is # 164, Led Zeppelin II is #150, Physical Graffiti is # 130, Led Zeppelin ⚡🪶⊙Ⓘ is # 101, Houses Of The Holy is #91, and In Through The Out

Door is #1.

The New Music reports.... Colin Richardson reports from the second Knebworth show. He briefly touches on the subject of the money problems with a suggestion that because the city council were worried about overcrowding Peter Grant took control of the flow of traffic at the gates and thus the cash flow. Leading to the bands not being paid promptly. This however was rebutted by Frederick Bannister's letters to the music press that month. Richardson concludes that, "Whatever the press reviews said, (the fans) weren't disappointed by Zep in any way. And let's face it that's what counts."....

November 1979

3 New Musical Express reports.... In Through The Out Door is #27 in the UK....

December 1979

Creem reports.... John Swenson reviews In Through The Out Door. He begins by stating 'Led Zeppelin has never made a bad album and In Through The Out Door is no exception....these guys bring home the bacon every time.' He goes on to say that Bonham's drumming is more complex than before but his sound is intact due to Page's deft handiwork on the board. Swenson then tackles each track individually calling Carouselambra the album's centre piece before concluding that it is an album full of 'production dazzle and stunt guitar work.'....

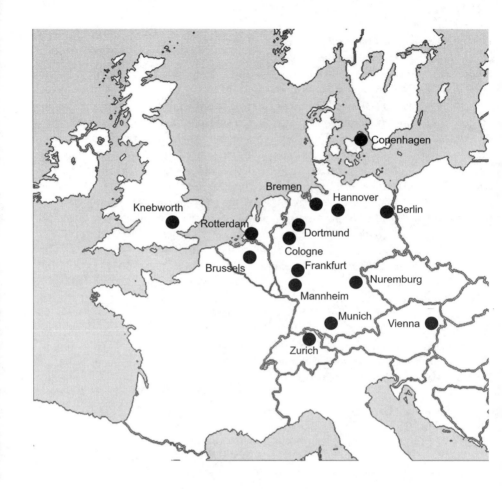

European Concerts 1979 - 1980

July 23rd & 24th 1979 Copenhagen Falkoner Theatre
August 4th & 11th 1979 Knebworth
June 17th, 1980 Dortmund Westfalenhalle
June 18th, 1980 Cologne Sportshalle
June 20th, 1980 Brussels Forest National
June 21st, 1980 Rotterdam Ahoy
June 23rd, 1980 Bremen Stadthalle
June 24th, 1980 Hannover Messehalle
June 26th, 1980 Vienna Stadthalle
June 27th, 1980 Nuremburg Messezentrum Halle
June 29th, 1980 Zurich Hallenstadion
June 30th, 1980 Frankfurt Festhalle
July 2nd & 3rd 1980 Mannheim Eisstadium
July 5th, 1980 Munich Olympichalle
July 7th, 1980 Berlin Eissporthalle

1980

January 1980

5 New Musical Express reports....
Robert Plant sang on Saturday at the Concert for Kampuchea with Dave Edmund's Rockpile performing Little Sister, Paul McCartney's Rockestra then performed featuring John Paul Jones, Plant, and John Bonham as well as a host of others...

July 1980

5 New Musical Express reports....
Jimmy Page narrowly escaped injury when a punter threw a fire-cracker at the stage during Led Zeppelin's gig in Vienna....

12 New Musical Express reports....
Jimmy Page Robert Plant and Toyah Wilcox were seen talking in a club in Nuremberg.... **Melody Maker reports....** Back cover story, Led Zeppelin Uber Alles!....Steve Gett reports from the band's tour in Europe....Gett notes that the German audiences are going off "like volcanoes" at the shows and that the band, especially Page has a rejuvenated air about them. He dismisses the sloppy playing as irrelevant and generally marvels at the band's enthusiasm. Songs included in the set at Munich's Olympic Hall - Train Kept A Rollin, Black Dog, Nobody's Fault But Mine, Rain Song, Hot Dog, All My Love, Achilles Last Stand, White Summer, Black Mountain Side, Stairway To Heaven, Trampled Underfoot, Kashmir, Since I've Been Loving You, Rock And Roll, Whole Lotta Love, and In The Evening. For a review from this era it is remarkably favourable (as it was certainly not fashionable to be generous to

them at this stage), Gett concludes, "It was one of the most enjoyable gigs I have experienced and certainly the best this year."

August 1980

30 Juke reports.... Cover story - Led Zeppelin Storm Clouds Over Europe. Australian magazine Juke manages to get a journalist (Andrew Baroutas) to the band's concert in Munich. He reports that a huddle of fans are braving the cold weather to try and hear the band from outside the arena. Over 35,000 people are squashed into the venue, which offers no seating. He comments that the band show no evidence of being dinosaurs, especially Page who he says was leaping about like a madman.

Baroutas notes the absence of British music journalists who he chastises for slagging the band's performances at Knebworth while conveniently ignoring the huge sea of fans that had attended the shows. He says that since then the band have refused to give interviews to people who are only intent on slagging them. Plant was disappointed with the reviews of 'In Through The Out Door' about which he says, "*I don't think it's a particularly bad album. On reflection there may be a couple of numbers that aren't so hot, but there are some pretty good ones.*"

Baroutas notes that in Vienna recently a firecracker thrown at the stage almost took Page's eye out, and that the only other incident was the early cancellation of the show in Nuremberg after John Bonham collapsed of exhaustion.

At the Munich Hilton (which houses Musicland studios in it's basement) the band come down and sign autographs for the fans. At the show he generally says the band live up to their legend before concluding the night with Simon Kirke of Bad Company filling a second drum seat for 'Whole Lotta Love'. He concludes, *"Excitement, dynamics, a casual sense of professionalism, Led Zeppelin still ruled."*....

Rock & Folk reports.... Cover story Led Zeppelin and Hard Rock. In a feature article about heavy rock. AC/DC are introduced along with Motorhead, UFO and Van Halen as 'Young Heavy', Aerosmith as 'The heavy heart,' Ted Nugent as 'The love of heavy' and Led Zeppelin as 'The Head Heavy'. Journalist Philippe Manoeuvre follows the band to their show in Belgium. At one point he manages to ask Plant why the band is not playing Paris on this tour, *"Paris? Why is the tour not going to Paris? Because there isn't a hall there that can hold ten thousand Led Zeppelin fans three nights in a row. What a stupid question!"*....

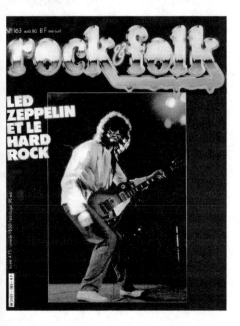

September 1980

Official Swan Song Press release.... Led Zeppelin The 1980's Part One. North American Tour begins October 17th. The itinerary is as follows:

October 17 Montreal Forum
October 19 & 20 Landover Capitol Centre
October 22 Philadelphia Spectrum
October 23 Landover Capitol Centre
October 26 & 27 Cleveland Richfield Coliseum
October 29 & 30 Detroit Joe Louis Stadium
November 1 Buffalo War Memorial Auditorium
November 3 & 4 Philadelphia Spectrum
November 6 & 7 Pittsburgh Civic Arena
November 9 St. Paul Civic Centre
November 10, 12, 13, 15 Chicago Stadium

25 **Chicago Tribune reports....**Full page advert announcing S&L in association with Concerts West presents Led Zeppelin In Concert at Chicago Stadium Monday Nov. 10, Wednesday Nov. 12, Thursday Nov. 13, Saturday Nov. 15, tickets $10 - $15....announcement comes from Swan Song/Atlantic, "John Bonham, drummer with Led Zeppelin, was today found dead at a friend's house in England. There will be no further statement from their manager until after an autopsy which will be held tomorrow."....
Buffalo Evening News reports.... Full page advert announcing S&L in association with Concerts West presents Led Zeppelin In Concert Saturday November 1, 1980 8.00 pm Buffalo Memorial Auditorium tickets $10 - $15....

26 **Buffalo Evening News reports....** An autopsy was ordered today to determine what killed John Bonham the drummer of the rock music group Led Zeppelin who was found dead after a party at which police said he had been drinking heavily. Authorities said the band's bass player discovered Bonham's body Thursday at the Old Mill House the $2 million home of the group's lead guitarist Jimmy Page. Led Zeppelin was scheduled to perform in Buffalo Nov. 1 but that concert was postponed indefinitely as a result of Mr. Bonham's death.

October 1980

4 **New Musical Express reports....** cover story...John Bonham....Zep To Split, Bonham Dead After Drinking Bout.... Stooping to new depths John Bonham's death is covered like a supermarket tabloid. An indication of how badly the quality of journalism had sunk at the NME during the late seventies. The beginning of the suggestions that Bonham's death was somehow linked to Page's interest in the occult occurs here. It is pointed out that because no immediate cause of death was noted then it must surely be the handiwork of the devil. The absolute bottom of the barrel in Zep reporting.... **Melody Maker reports....** John Bonham - The beat behind Zeppelin. Head, Heart and Drums....Chris Charlesworth writes a fitting tribute to the mighty Bonzo which includes an in-depth appraisal of his contributions to the Zeppelin sound. He concludes, *"John Bonham was an integral part of that unit and, like millions of others who caught Led Zeppelin at their very best, I deeply regret his passing."*.... **Billboard**

reports.... Led Zeppelin's Drummer Bonham Dies — Article explains the circumstances of Bonham's accidental death. It also details the cancellation of the upcoming American tour dates in Landover, Phialdelphia, Cleveland, Detroit, Buffalo, Pittsburgh, and Chicago....

December 1980

13 **New Musical Express reports....** World In Action's report on the Rossminster tax avoidance scam, apparently Led Zeppelin are one band who owe the tax man a bundle....Zep Split (or do they)....the statement from Swan Song arrives at the NME offices. *"We wish it to be known that the loss of our dear friend and the deep respect we have for his family together with the sense of undivided harmony felt by ourselves and our manager, have led us to decide we could not continue as we were."* The letter is signed Led Zeppelin and dated December 5th 1980. Rumours had been running around that Bonham was to be replaced by Cozy Powell, Carmine Appice, Paul Thompson, Aynsley Dunbar, Ian Paice, Ringo Starr and Peter Criss. All these were finally put to bed with the above statement. The article then goes on to suggest that Plant may form a Rockpile style band. An extremely incisive piece of reporting or just a damn good guess as the next time anyone heard from Plant was with the Honeydrippers. Considering the speed with which Plant returned to performing and the date of this article it would suggest that Plant may have been considering the Honeydrippers even before Bonzo passed away....

LED-ZEPPELIN

IN THROUGH THE OUT DOOR

Epilogue

November 1995

26 **New York Times reports....** Peter Grant, 60, An Ex-Wrestler Who Managed Led Zeppelin....Obituary for Peter Grant who died the previous Tuesday aged 60 of a heart attack. The article outlines his early career as a professional wrestler, part-time actor and Fleet Street messenger boy. A quote from Phil Everly of the Everly Brothers, *"Without his efforts, musicians had no careers. He was the first to make sure the artists came first and that we got paid and paid properly."*....

LED-ZEPPELIN
TOUR OVER EUROPE 1980

ROTTERDAM
AHOY
JUNE 21ST

BREMEN
STADTHALLE
JUNE 23RD

HANNOVER
MESSEHALLE
JUNE 24TH

BERLIN
EISSPORTHALLE
JULY 7TH & 8TH

BRUSSELS
FOREST NATIONAL
JUNE 20TH

DORTMUND
WESTFALENHALLE
JUNE 17TH

KÖLN
SPORTSHALLE
JUNE 18TH

FRANKFURT
FESTHALLE
JUNE 30TH

MANNHEIM
EISSTADIUM
JULY 2ND & 3RD

NÜRNBERG
MESSEZENTRUM HALLE
JUNE 27TH

MÜNCHEN
OLYMPICHALLE
JULY 5TH

VIENNA
STADTHALLE
JUNE 26TH

ZURICH
HALLENSTADION
JUNE 29TH

ATLANTIC RECORDS · 40 YEARS OF MUSIC

ATLANTIC RECORDS
40TH ANNIVERSARY

"It's Only Rock'n Roll"

MAY 14, 1988 · MADISON SQUARE GARDEN · NEW YORK CITY

ASHFORD & SIMPSON · AVERAGE WHITE BAND · DAN AYKROYD
LAVERN BAKER · BEE GEES · BOOKER 'T' AND THE MG'S · LISA BONET
LAURA BRANIGAN · RUTH BROWN · ACHELE CAPPELLI
THE COASTERS · PHIL COLLINS · STEVE CROPPER BLUES BAND
CROSBY, STILLS & NASH · ROBERTA FLACK · FOREIGNER · BOB GELDOF
GENESIS · DEBBIE GIBSON · ROBERT HAYS · MIKI HOWARD
IRON BUTTERFLY · JOHN PAUL JONES · BEN E. KING
LED ZEPPELIN REUNION · LeVERT · THE MANHATTAN TRANSFER
HERBIE MANN · SAM MOORE · NU SHOOZ · JIMMY PAGE · WILSON PICKETT
ROBERT PLANT · BERNARD PURDIE · THE RASCALS · PAUL RODGERS
MIKE RUTHERFORD · PAUL SHAFFER HOUSE BAND · THE SPINNERS
STACY Q · ROBERT TOWNSEND · VANILLA FUDGE · YES
PLUS SUPER SPECIAL SURPRISE GUESTS!

HBO

Appendix A
The Early Days

January 13th 1968 Yardbirds Chelmsford Corn Exchange
January 19th 1968 Yardbirds Middle Earth Club London
January 26th 1968 Robert Plant's Band Of Joy Middle Earth London (with Bonham)
February 8th 1968 Robert Plant's Band Of Joy Marquee London (with Bonham)
February 23rd 1968 Robert Plant's Band Of Joy Marquee London (with Bonham)
March 2nd 1968 Yardbirds Southampton University
March 8th 1968 Yardbirds Aston Birmingham
March 8th 1968 Robert Plant's Band Of Joy Westfield College Hampstead (with Bonham)
March 9th 1968 Yardbirds on the BBC Saturday Club
March 10th 1968 Yardbirds on the BBC Top Gear
March 16th 1968 Yardbirds Luton
March 23rd 1968 Yardbirds Retford
March 30th 1968 Yardbirds Wolverhampton
April 6th, 1968 Yardbirds BBC Saturday Afternoon Show
April 14th, 1968 Yardbirds Top Gear BBC
May 3rd & 4th, 1968 Yardbirds Detroit Grande Ballroom
May 10th, 1968 Yardbirds Top Gear BBC
May 23rd - 25th Yardbirds Fillmore West
May 31st - June 1st Yardbirds Shrine Auditorium Los Angeles
June 26th 1968 Alexis Korner & Band Hampstead Country Club (possibly with Plant)
June 28th 1968 Tim Rose (with Bonham) Hastings
July 14th 1968 Tim Rose (with Bonham) Blaises London
July 16th 1968 Tim Rose (with Bonham) Marquee London
July 30th 1968 Tim Rose (with Bonham) Fishmongers Arms Wood Green London
July 31st 1968 Tim Rose (with Bonham) Hampstead Country Club
(This last date is possibly the night Page and Bonham met)

The Yardbirds circa 1968 Picture courtesy Capitol Records

Interview by Steve Gett with Robert Plant about his early roots. This originally appeared in a much longer form in a special Sounds magazine released to coincide with Plant's solo tour of 1983. It has been edited down to include just Plant's comments.

"This is one of the songs that first got me going. In fact I can remember when it came out. (Shop Around by The Miracles) What a great number! By the time I was twelve I was pretty well aware of the current trends in pop music and also things that weren't immediately that popular. People were buying stuff that was in the American charts that wasn't particularly breaking out over here, like Ritchie Valens and The Miracles, and I got into all that. There was something infectious about the way a lot of the guys sang in those days that I thought I could do. I just used to ape them, although I never took it particularly seriously until later.

"There was a lot of black American rhythm 'n' blues stuff which opened the doors to the Muddy Waters/ Sonny Boy Williamson type of things that were coming out on Pye. People like Chuck Berry and Bo Diddley sort of paved the way for me listening to the more bluesy kind of material. The more accessible stuff was the sort of thing that people were actually pushing out to sell as hit records here, like Berry, but then you became aware of the Chess Record label, which included artists like Howlin' Wolf. Willie Dixon would be playing bass on a Chuck Berry record one minute and then next you'd hear him on 'Long Distance Call' by Muddy Waters. If you looked to see where it all came from, you'd step back a little bit further. And the great thing was that it never got worse it always got more interesting."

He is asked whether his family were musically inclined, *"Well I think they were to the degree that they might have appreciated Johnny Mathis and people like that, but not Blind Willie Johnson doing 'Nobody's Fault But Mine' or something. Some music kind of threatens the whole social structure.*

"I had a friend at school, whose parents were quite wealthy, and he was in a position to buy quite a few records. There was no taping in those days, but I could borrow them and come back home and play them. And obviously how could anybody in middle-class England relate to them when they were coming from New Orleans and Baton Rouge and out the back of a greengrocer's shop? I mean, what did Slim Harpo have in common with anything people had known before?"

He is asked why he quit his apprenticeship as an accountant, *"Well, what would you do if you were doing that? You'd run as fast as you could. By that time I'd really got the bit in my teeth and all I wanted to do was sing."*

Gett asks him if he remembers his first gig, *"Yes I can, actually. I stood in for some guy who'd got laryngitis and played in Leicester, which was a long way to go in those days! It was quite sort of hair-raising as far as I can recall."*

He is then asked about the other band's that he played for, *"Well the group that I stepped in with for a while was Andy Long and The Original Jurymen and then after that I joined a few, what you might call, folk club blues bands. Most of the blues bands had these semi-acoustic guitars and you used to do a lot of Muddy Waters stuff and that sort of thing. The solid-body guitar was really not for them and most people wore suits and yes, sports jackets, Hush Puppies, and sat on chairs. There was the Delta Blues Band,*

The New Memphis Bluesbreakers, all of whom swapped personnel with other bands who were around. Eventually I realised that I was perhaps a little young to be standing there with a washboard around my neck and some thimbles, singing in that environment. Everyone had long beards and pipes and it wasn't even 'groovy'! Groovy hadn't even come along then!

"So it was time to act my age. There was an intellectual plane, with which that folk music and blues boom fitted and I really wanted to get my rocks off, if I can use that term. I wanted to enjoy myself and I wanted to sing to an audience that actually moved too. It was then that I joined a group called The Black Snake Moan, named after a Blind Lemon Jefferson song - and it would be terribly hard to guess what the old black snake was! That group had about three guitarists, a drummer and a bass player, and I actually even played guitar as well. In fact there was a cameo part where I played some song on my own and sang at the same time. It must have been dreadful I know we had to fight our way out of one gig using saucepans because we were that bad everybody wanted their money back!

"Then there was a group called The Banned, which was OK. It was kind of jazzy blues stuff. And after that came The Crawling King Snakes, which took its name from the John Lee Hooker number. It's a shame really because I was in two bands with snakes in them, but I was never in a band of snakes! I suppose if I'd lived in Henley I might have been!

"Anyway, at the time of The Crawling King Snakes there was another group in the same town called The Shakedown Sound, with Jess Roden singing, and there was quite a hip sort of musical mod/rhythm 'n blues thing going

on then. We'd get a lot of records off the Stax label and do that sort of thing. But that only went as far as the van would take us. And by then my desire and hunger for what I'd already tasted was growing quite a lot.

"I used to play on a circuit of clubs and dance halls, where one night you'd be on with Solomon Burke, the next with Wilson Pickett and then perhaps Dave, Dee, Dozy, Beaky, Mick and Tich. There were all sorts of bands and so I met more and more musicians. And it was at that point that I first met Bonzo, when he joined The Crawling King Snakes for a while.

"There was a really healthy thing going on in these clubs and there'd be two thousand people in, four nights a week. You'd get up and play for twenty minutes and if you were dramatic enough, or idiot enough, you could stop everything and everybody would suddenly stand still and watch what you were doing. And I liked that idea - it was quite a remarkable thing to feel all that.

"It was then that a group called The Tennessee Teens asked me to join them and they were basically, as you can imagine, a three-piece Tamla sort of band. So I joined them as lead singer. We changed the name to 'Listen' and it was in 1966 that I made my first record. I did three singles. There was one with Listen called, 'You Better Run' and two on my own - one called 'Long Time Coming' and one called 'Our Song'. They all came out on CBS. Listen were OK and in fact we did lots of touring and work. I met so many people in those days. Rod Stewart was in The Steampacket with Long John Baldry and The Creation were playing around with Ronnie Wood in the band. By this time the mod scene was happening prickly hair and scooters and the r 'n b and Tamla thing was really strong. You could play three-quarters of the night like that and then you could put in some Muddy Waters and so still really be doing what you wanted to do. It was a very healthy musical thing.

"But all that subsequently faded out. The band had its limitations and that's when The Band Of Joy began. There were various formations and the first one was quite good, but there were all sorts of rucks in the group. We were still doing some obscure soul and stuff like that and had quite a good following but then I got fired! I think it was for being too mouthy or something like that ... some characteristic that's gone! God knows what they'd have done with someone like Lemmy! But there you go.

"So I formed another Band Of Joy and I got everybody to paint their faces and it was like a 1966 version of Adam and the Ants! There were the beginnings of a current influence, in other words the West Coast bands, rather than it all being black, Tamla and soul. That Band Of Joy extinguished itself after a while and then came the one when Bonzo and I teamed back up again. That went on and we played the Middle Earth in London with Ten Years After, Fairport and people like that. We were quite well respected, although the music by then had become pretty inaccessible. The whole soul and blues thing had moved on a peg and the bands were starting to extend the instrumental passages. It was the natural advent of Bonzo and I teaming with Jimmy and Jonesy.

"From The Band Of Joy, Bonzo went with Tim Rose and I played around for a while with Hobbstweedle and it was at that point that Jimmy Page and Peter Grant came up to see me."

JIMMY PAGE

... is the greatest guitarist in Europe. He is the greatest harmonica player in Europe. Jimmy Page is a phenomenon.

At 19 he has already played guitar as a sessions musician for The Kinks, Cliff Richard, Dave Berry, P. J. Proby, Brenda Lee and Jackie de Shannon.

It was at one of her recording sessions that Jimmy first met Jackie de Shannon and she has constantly encouraged and helped his career so far. Jackie persuaded him to make his own record after hearing him doodling with his guitar in a studio. She has written songs with him too.

No stranger to the recording studio, Jimmy Page recently went in to make his first disc himself. The result is...

"SHE JUST SATISFIES"

FONTANA TF 533

THE SESSION MEN
No. 8 John Paul Jones

John Paul Jones is one of the younger members of the session ranks. He was just 20 in January, but such is his musical ability that his future in British show-biz is virtually assured.

John has been signed up by Mickie Most as a Musical Director, and his first two products are "Everything I Touch Turns To Tears" by Barry St. John, and "Land Of 1,000 Dances" by The Cherokees. His big task comes up in April when he flies to the States to take charge of the music for Herman's film. John has developed tremendously in this direction of his career, and along with Mike Vickers of Manfred Mann, seems to be spearheading the "New Breed" of MD's.

But don't get the idea that John is putting sessions aside. This is a very important part of his day-to-day life and he has no intention of stopping his work in the recording studio as bass player.

A PIANO IN THE HOUSE

He can play piano, organ and bass but it's on the latter instrument that he is really in demand by the top stars. And by top stars, we mean people like Kathy Kirby, Lulu, Dave Berry, Paul and Barry Ryan and Shirley Bassey, all of whom John has backed at one time or another. And they are just a few.

John has worked hard to get where he is today. Music was in his blood from the start, as his father was a pianist, arranger and bandleader; and his mother, a singer and dancer.

He lived in Eltham and with a piano in the house, he was influenced musically from an early age. He was taught the basics of the piano

and decided he was more interested in the organ as a keyboard instrument, but found that to learn this instrument properly he needed tuition. He came up to London for lessons and by the age of 14 was playing at the local church.

HE TOOK HIS CHANCE

It was around this time that he began to take an interest in the bass. "I couldn't even play a 6-string acoustic guitar when I started. I was just fascinated by bass work generally. I used to turn up the bass on my records and listen to the runs, and in time I just picked it up. I can also play ordinary guitar now, by the way."

He got hold of a Dallas Tuxedo bass guitar and a made-up amp of "about 10 watts" John recalls. When he was pretty proficient on this instrument, he joined a few local semi-pro groups and gained an entrance into Tin Pan Alley by joining up with a backing group for vocalist Chris Wayne.

The group didn't make any hit records, but were quite well known in London due to appearances on "Saturday Club" and other programmes on radio and TV, and through this John began to get to know quite a few people "inside" show-biz and one day saw his chance of a big break and took it with both hands.

And this, in fact, should serve as an example to all our younger readers of how to brush aside shyness and seize an opportunity when one presents itself.

"I saw Jet Harris walking along Archer Street one day", John told "B.I.". This was just when "Diamonds" was hitting the high-spots. It was

breaking big in the charts, but had happened so quickly that Jet and Tony had made no plans for backing group.

"So I saw my chance and took it", added John. "I went up to Jet and asked him outright if he wanted a bass player! He fixed me up for an audition and I got a job with him and Tony."

John played in Jet and Tony's backing group in concerts and one-night stands all over the country, and on their successful follow-up discs. And this was just the start. All his experience has led up to a very attractive offer from Mickie Most . . . but not even this will tear him away from his role of "Mr. Bassman" in the recording studio.

Appendix B
Concerts
(arranged by City)

Aberdeen Music Hall	Scotland	1973	January 25
Aberystwyth King's Hall	Wales	1973	January 16
Adelaide Memorial Drive	Australia	1972	February 19
Albuquerque University Of New Mexico	USA	1973	May 23
Amsterdam R.A.I.	Holland	1972	May 27
Anaheim Convention Centre	USA	1969	August 9
Asbury Park NJ Convention Hall	USA	1969	August 16
Athens Ohio University	USA	1969	May 17
Atlanta Pop Festival	USA	1969	July 5
Atlanta Braves Stadium	USA	1973	May 4
Atlanta The Omni	USA	1977	April 23
Auckland Western Spring Stadium	New Zealand	1972	February 24
Austin Events Centre	USA	1975	March 7
Baltimore Jazz Festival	USA	1969	July 11
Baltimore Civic Center	USA	1970	April 5
Baltimore Civic Centre	USA	1972	June 11
Baltimore Civic Centre	USA	1973	July 23
Bath Pavilion	England	1968	December 16
Bath Festival	England	1969	June 28
Bath Festival	England	1970	June 28
Bath Pavilion	England	1971	March 13
Baton Rouge LSU Assembly Cent.	USA	1975	February 28
Baton Rouge LSU Assembly Cent.	USA	1977	May 19
Belfast Ulster Hall	Ireland	1971	March 5
Berkeley Community Theatre	USA	1969	August 7
Berkeley Community Theatre	USA	1971	September 13
Berkeley Community Theatre	USA	1971	September 14
Berlin Deutschlandhalle	Germany	1970	July 19
Berlin Deutschlandhalle	Germany	1973	March 19
Berlin Eissporthalle	Germany	1980	July 7
Bewdley Heath Hotel	England	1990	May 12
Birmingham Coliseum	USA	1977	May 18
Birmingham Mother's	England	1969	March 22
Birmingham Town Hall	England	1969	June 13
Birmingham Town Hall	England	1970	January 7
Birmingham Kinetic Circus	England	1971	November 17
Birmingham Odeon	England	1972	December 16
Birmingham Odeon	England	1972	December 17
Bolton	England	1969	March ??
Bombay India Recording Session	India	1972	March ??
Boston Tea Party	USA	1969	January 23
Boston Tea Party	USA	1969	January 24
Boston Tea Party	USA	1969	January 25
Boston Tea Party	USA	1969	January 26
Boston Tea Party	USA	1969	May 27
Boston Tea Party	USA	1969	May 28
Boston Tea Party	USA	1969	May 29
Boston Gardens	USA	1969	October 25
Boston Gardens	USA	1970	September 9
Boston Gardens	USA	1971	September 6
Boston Gardens	USA	1972	June 8
Boston Gardens	USA	1973	July 25
Bournemouth Starkers	England	1971	December 2
Bradford St. George's Hall	England	1973	January 18
Bremen Stadthalle	Germany	1980	June 23
Brighton Dome	England	1972	December 20

Brisbane Festival Hall	Australia	1972	February 29
Bristol Colston Hall	England	1969	June 21
Bristol Colston Hall	England	1970	January 8
Bron-y-Aur Rehearsals	Wales	1970	May ??
Brondby Pop Club Norregard Hallen	Denmark	1968	September 7
Brondby Pop Club Norregard Hallen	Denmark	1969	March 13
Brussels Forest Nationale	Belgium	1972	May 28
Brussels	Belgium	1973	March 12
Brussels Forest Nationale	Belgium	1975	January 12
Brussels Forest Nationale	Belgium	1980	June 20
Buffalo Kleinhan's Music Hall	USA	1969	October 30
Buffalo Memorial Auditorium	USA	1972	June 10
Buffalo Memorial Auditorium	USA	1973	July 15
Canterbury Bridge Country Club	England	1968	December 13
Canterbury University	England	1971	March 10
Cardiff	Wales	1969	March 5
Cardiff Capitol	Wales	1972	December 11
Cardiff Capitol	Wales	1972	December 12
Charleston	USA	1970	April 2
Charlotte	USA	1969	October 26
Charlotte Independence Coliseum	USA	1970	April 7
Charlotte Coliseum	USA	1972	June 9
Chicago Kinetic Playground	USA	1969	February 7
Chicago Kinetic Playground	USA	1969	February 8
Chicago Kinetic Playground	USA	1969	May 23
Chicago Kinetic Playground	USA	1969	May 24
Chicago Kinetic Playground	USA	1969	July 18
Chicago Kinetic Playground	USA	1969	July 19
Chicago Kinetic Playground	USA	1969	October 19
Chicago Amphitheatre	USA	1971	September 5
Chicago Auditorium	USA	1973	July 6
Chicago Auditorium	USA	1973	July 7
Chicago Stadium	USA	1975	January 21
Chicago Stadium	USA	1975	January 22
Chicago Stadium	USA	1977	April 6
Chicago Stadium	USA	1977	April 7
Chicago Stadium	USA	1977	April 9
Chicago Stadium	USA	1977	April 10
Chicago Stadium	USA	1975	January 20
Cincinnati Riverfront Coliseum	USA	1977	April 19
Cincinnati Riverfront Coliseum	USA	1977	April 20
Clearwell Castle Rehearsals	England	1978	May ??
Cleveland Musicarnival	USA	1969	July 20
Cleveland Public Auditorium	USA	1969	October 24
Cleveland Public Hall	USA	1970	August 26
Cleveland Coliseum	USA	1975	January 24
Cleveland Richfield Coliseum	USA	1977	April 27
Cleveland Richfield Coliseum	USA	1977	April 28
Cologne	Germany	1970	July 16
Cologne Sportshalle	Germany	1980	June 18
Columbia Merriweather Post Pavilion	USA	1969	May 25
Copenhagen Tivolis Koncertsal	Denmark	1969	March 16
Copenhagen K.B.Hallen	Denmark	1970	February 28
Copenhagen K.B.Hallen	Denmark	1971	May 3
Copenhagen K.B. Hallen	Denmark	1973	March 2
Copenhagen Falkoner Theatre	Denmark	1979	July 23

Copenhagen Falkoner Theatre	Denmark	1979	July 24
Dagenham Roundhouse	England	1969	April 5
Dallas State Fair Coliseum	USA	1969	August 4
Dallas Pop Festival	USA	1969	August 31
Dallas Memorial Auditorium	USA	1970	March 28
Dallas Memorial Auditorium	USA	1971	August 24
Dallas Memorial Auditorium	USA	1973	May 18
Dallas Memorial Auditorium	USA	1975	March 4
Dallas Memorial Auditorium	USA	1975	March 5
Dallas Memorial Auditorium	USA	1977	April 1
Denver Auditorium	USA	1968	December 26
Denver Coliseum	USA	1970	March 25
Denver Coliseum	USA	1972	June 21
Denver Coliseum	USA	1973	May 25
Derby Locarno	England	1971	December 9
Detroit Grande Ballroom	USA	1969	January 17
Detroit Grande Ballroom	USA	1969	January 18
Detroit Grande Ballroom	USA	1969	January 19
Detroit Grande Ballroom	USA	1969	May 16
Detroit Olympia	USA	1969	October 18
Detroit Olympia	USA	1970	August 28
Detroit Cobo Hall	USA	1972	June 6
Detroit Cobo Hall	USA	1973	July 12
Detroit Cobo Hall	USA	1973	July 13
Detroit Olympia Stadium	USA	1975	January 31
Dortmund Westfalenhalle	Germany	1980	June 17
Dublin Boxing Stadium	Ireland	1971	March 6
Dundee Caird Hall	Scotland	1971	November 13
Dundee Caird Hall	Scotland	1973	January 27
Dusseldorf	Germany	1970	March 11
Edinburgh Usher Hall	Scotland	1970	February 17
Edinburgh King's Theatre	Scotland	1973	January 28
Edmonton Gardens	Canada	1969	May 9
Edmonton Kinsmen Field House	Canada	1969	July 29
Essen	Germany	1970	July 17
Essen Grughalle	Germany	1973	March 22
Eugene	USA	1969	July 31
Evansville Indiana Roberts Stadium	USA	1970	April 16
Exeter City Hall	England	1968	December 19
Fort Worth Tarrant Convention Center	USA	1970	August 22
Fort Worth Tarrant Convention Center	USA	1971	August 23
Fort Worth Tarrant Convention Center	USA	1973	May 19
Fort Worth Tarrant Convention Center	USA	1975	March 3
Fort Worth Tarrant Convention Center	USA	1977	May 22
Framingham MA. Carousel Theatre	USA	1969	August 21
Frankfurt Festhalle	Germany	1970	July 18
Frankfurt Festhalle	Germany	1980	June 30
Göteborg Liseburg Amusement Park	Sweden	1968	September 15
Göteborg	Sweden	1970	February 25
Göteborg	Sweden	1973	March 4
Gladsaxe Teen Clubs Box 45	Denmark	1968	September 7
Gladsaxe TV-Byen	Denmark	1969	March 13
Gladsaxe Teen Clubs Box 45	Denmark	1969	March 15
Glasgow Green's Playhouse	Scotland	1972	December 3
Glasgow Green's Playhouse	Scotland	1972	December 4
Greensboro Coliseum	USA	1975	January 29

Greensboro Coliseum	USA	1977	May 31
Guildford Surrey University	England	1968	October 25
Hamburg Musikhalle	Germany	1970	March 12
Hamburg Musikhalle	Germany	1973	March 21
Hampton Roads Coliseum	USA	1970	August 17
Hampton Roads Coliseum	USA	1971	September 9
Hannover Messehalle	Germany	1980	June 24
Headley Grange Recording Session	England	1970	May ??
Headley Grange Recording Session	England	1971	January ??
Headley Grange Recording Session	England	1973	December ??
Headley Grange Recording Session	England	1974	June ??
Helsinki	Finland	1970	February 24
Hempstead Nassau County Coliseum	USA	1972	June 14
Hempstead Nassau County Coliseum	USA	1972	June 15
Hiroshima Shiei Taiikukan	Japan	1971	September 27
Hollywood Florida Sportatorium	USA	1971	September 1
Honolulu Civic Auditorium	USA	1969	May 13
Honolulu International Center	USA	1970	September 6
Honolulu International Center	USA	1971	September 16
Honolulu International Center	USA	1971	September 17
Houston Music Hall	USA	1969	August 3
Houston Hofheinz Pavilion	USA	1970	March 29
Houston Hofheinz Pavilion	USA	1971	August 25
Houston Sam Houston Arena	USA	1973	May 16
Houston Coliseum	USA	1975	February 27
Houston The Summit	USA	1977	May 21
Indianapolis Arena	USA	1970	April 4
Indianapolis Arena	USA	1973	July 8
Indianapolis Arena	USA	1975	January 25
Indianapolis Market Square Arena	USA	1977	April 17
Iowa City Iowa University	USA	1969	January 15
Ipswich St. Matthew's Baths	England	1971	November 16
Irvine UC Irvine	USA	1969	May 1
Jacksonville Veterans Memorial Coliseum	USA	1969	August 24
Jacksonville Civic Centre	USA	1973	May 7
Kansas City	USA	1969	November 5
Kitchener Memorial Auditorium	Canada	1969	November 4
Knebworth	England	1979	August 4
Knebworth	England	1979	August 11
Kyoto Kaikan #1 Hall	Japan	1972	October 10
Leeds Town Hall	England	1970	January 24
Leeds University	England	1971	March 9
Leicester	England	1969	March 12
Leicester University	England	1971	November 25
Liverpool University	England	1968	October 19
Liverpool University	England	1971	May 10
Liverpool University	England	1971	November 29
Liverpool Empire	England	1973	January 14
London BBC Studio Session	England	1969	March 19
London Alexandra Palace	England	1972	December 22
London Alexandra Palace	England	1972	December 23
London BBC Paris Theatre	England	1971	April 1
London BBC Playhouse Theatre	England	1969	June 27
London Chalk Farm Roundhouse	England	1968	November 9
London Cooks Ferry Inn	England	1969	March 31
London Dave Symonds Show BBC	England	1969	June 16

Location	Country	Year	Date
London Earl's Court	England	1975	May 17
London Earl's Court	England	1975	May 18
London Earl's Court	England	1975	May 23
London Earl's Court	England	1975	May 24
London Earl's Court	England	1975	May 25
London Hampstead Klook's Kleek	England	1969	April 1
London Hornsey Wood Tavern	England	1969	March 7
London How Late It Is BBC TV	England	1969	March 21
London Island Studio Session	England	1972	May ??
London John Peel's Top Gear BBC	England	1969	June 24
London Julie Felix TV Appearance	England	1970	April 26
London Lyceum Ballroom	England	1969	October 12
London Maida Vale BBC Studios	England	1969	March 3
London Marquee	England	1968	October 18
London Marquee	England	1968	December 10
London Marquee	England	1969	March 28
London Marquee	England	1971	March 23
London Morgan Studio Session	England	1969	June ??
London Olympic StudioSession	England	1968	September 27
London Olympic Studio Session	England	1968	October ??
London Olympic Studio Session	England	1969	November ??
London Olympic Studio Session	England	1972	May ??
London Royal Albert Hall	England	1969	June 29
London Royal Albert Hall	England	1970	January 9
London Southall Northcote Arms Farx	England	1969	March 30
London Tolworth Toby Jug	England	1969	April 9
London Victoria Theatre Rehearsal	England	1980	May ??
London Wood Green Fishmongers Hall	England	1968	December 20
Long Beach Arena	USA	1972	June 27
Long Beach Arena	USA	1975	March 11
Long Beach Arena	USA	1975	March 12
Los Angeles Whisky a Go Go	USA	1969	January 2
Los Angeles Whisky a Go Go	USA	1969	January 3
Los Angeles Whisky a Go Go	USA	1969	January 4
Los Angeles Whisky a Go Go	USA	1969	January 5
Los Angeles Mirror Sound Studio Session	USA	1969	May ??
Los Angeles Forum	USA	1970	March 27
Los Angeles Forum	USA	1970	September 4
Los Angeles Forum	USA	1971	August 21
Los Angeles Forum	USA	1971	August 22
Los Angeles Forum	USA	1972	June 25
Los Angeles Forum	USA	1973	May 31
Los Angeles Forum	USA	1973	June 3
Los Angeles Forum	USA	1975	March 24
Los Angeles Forum	USA	1975	March 25
Los Angeles Forum	USA	1975	March 27
Los Angeles Forum	USA	1977	June 21
Los Angeles Forum	USA	1977	June 22
Los Angeles Forum	USA	1977	June 23
Los Angeles Forum	USA	1977	June 25
Los Angeles Forum	USA	1977	June 26
Los Angeles Forum	USA	1977	June 27
Louisville Kentucky Fairgrounds	USA	1977	April 25
Lyons	France	1973	March 26
Macon Coliseum	USA	1970	April 3
Manchester College Of Science	England	1968	November 16

Manchester Free Trade Hall	England	1969	June 15
Manchester University	England	1971	March 19
Manchester Free Trade Hall	England	1971	November 24
Manchester Kings Hall Belle Vue	England	1971	November 30
Manchester Hardrock	England	1972	December 7
Manchester Hardrock	England	1972	December 8
Mannheim Eisstadium	Germany	1980	July 2
Mannheim Eisstadium	Germany	1980	July 3
Melbourne Kooyong Tennis Courts	Australia	1972	February 20
Memphis	USA	1969	February ??
Memphis Mid-South Coliseum	USA	1970	April 17
Miami Thee Image Club	USA	1969	February 14
Miami Thee Image Club	USA	1969	February 15
Miami Beach Dania Pirates World	USA	1969	August 22
Miami Beach Dania Pirates World	USA	1969	August 23
Miami Convention Hall	USA	1970	April 10
Milan Vigorelli Stadium	Italy	1971	July 5
Milwaukee State Fair Park	USA	1969	July 25
Milwaukee Arena	USA	1970	August 31
Milwaukee Arena	USA	1973	July 10
Minneapolis Guthrie Memorial Theatre	USA	1969	May 18
Minneapolis Met Centre	USA	1970	April 12
Minneapolis Met Centre	USA	1975	January 18
Minneapolis Met Centre	USA	1977	April 12
Mobile City Auditorium	USA	1973	May 13
Montreal Forum	Canada	1970	April 13
Montreal Forum	Canada	1972	June 7
Montreal Forum	Canada	1975	February 6
Montreux Casino	Switzerland	1970	March 7
Montreux Casino	Switzerland	1971	August 7
Montreux Casino	Switzerland	1971	August 8
Montreux The Pavilion	Switzerland	1972	October 27
Montreux The Pavilion	Switzerland	1972	October 28
Munich	Germany	1970	March 8
Munich	Germany	1973	March 13
Munich Olympiahalle	Germany	1973	March 17
Munich Musicland Studio Session	Germany	1975	December ??
Munich Olympiahalle	Germany	1980	July 5
Nagoyashi Kokaido	Japan	1972	October 5
Nancy	France	1973	March 27
Nashville	USA	1970	April ??
New Haven Yale	USA	1970	August 15
New Orleans Municipal Auditorium	USA	1971	August 29
New Orleans Municipal Auditorium	USA	1973	May 14
New York Atlantic Studios	USA	1969	May 19-23
New York Carnegie Hall	USA	1969	October 17
New York Central Park	USA	1969	July 21
New York Fillmore East	USA	1969	January 31
New York Fillmore East	USA	1969	February 1
New York Fillmore East	USA	1969	May 30
New York Fillmore East	USA	1969	May 31
New York Madison Square Gardens	USA	1970	September 19
New York Madison Square Gardens	USA	1971	September 3
New York Madison Square Gardens	USA	1973	July 27
New York Madison Square Gardens	USA	1973	July 28
New York Madison Square Gardens	USA	1973	July 29

New York Madison Square Gardens	USA	1975	February 3
New York Madison Square Gardens	USA	1975	February 7
New York Madison Square Gardens	USA	1975	February 12
New York Madison Square Gardens	USA	1977	June 7
New York Madison Square Gardens	USA	1977	June 8
New York Madison Square Gardens	USA	1977	June 11
New York Madison Square Gardens	USA	1977	June 12
New York Madison Square Gardens	USA	1977	June 13
New York Madison Square Gardens	USA	1977	June 14
New York Madison Square Gardens	USA	1988	May 14
New York Nassau Coliseum	USA	1975	February 4
New York Nassau Coliseum	USA	1975	February 13
New York Nassau Coliseum	USA	1975	February 14
New York The Scene	USA	1969	February 3?
New York The Scene	USA	1969	February 4?
New York The Scene	USA	1969	February 5?
New York The Scene	USA	1969	February 6?
New York Singer Bowl	USA	1969	August 29
New York Singer Bowl	USA	1969	August 30
New York Waldorf Astoria	USA	1995	January 15
Newcastle City Hall	England	1969	June 20
Newcastle City Hall	England	1970	January 15
Newcastle Mayfair	England	1971	March 18
Newcastle City Hall	England	1971	November 11
Newcastle Mecca Ballroom	England	1971	November 12
Newcastle City Hall	England	1972	November 30
Newcastle City Hall	England	1972	December 1
Newport Jazz Festival	USA	1969	July 6
Nottingham Rowing Club	England	1971	March 21
Nuremberg Messezentrum Halle	Germany	1973	March 14
Nuremberg Messezentrum Halle	Germany	1980	June 27 Nyköbing
Raventlow Park Falster Island	Denmark	1968	September 8
Oakland Coliseum	USA	1970	September 2
Oakland Coliseum	USA	1977	July 23
Oakland Coliseum	USA	1977	July 24
Odensen Fyns Forum	Denmark	1971	May 4
Offenburg Orthenau Halle	Germany	1973	March 24
Oklahoma City Coliseum Fairgrounds	USA	1970	August 20
Oklahoma City	USA	1971	August 27
Oklahoma City Myriad	USA	1977	April 3
Orlando Civic Auditorium	USA	1971	August 31
Osaka Festival Hall	Japan	1971	September 28
Osaka Festival Hall	Japan	1971	September 29
Osaka Festival Hall	Japan	1972	October 4
Osaka Festival Hall	Japan	1972	October 9
Oslo	Norway	1973	March 10
Ottawa Civic Centre	Canada	1970	April 14
Oxford New Theatre	England	1973	January 7
Paris Olympia	France	1969	March ??
Paris Olympia	France	1969	October 10
Paris Tous En Scene TV Show	France	1969	June 25
Paris Palais De Sports	France	1973	April 1
Paris Palais De Sports	France	1973	April 2
Pasadena Rose Palace	USA	1969	May 2
Pasadena Rose Palace	USA	1969	May 3
Perth Subiaco Oval	Australia	1972	February 16

Philadelphia Jazz Festival	USA	1969	July 12
Philadelphia Spectrum	USA	1970	March 31
Philadelphia Spectrum	USA	1972	June 13
Philadelphia Spectrum	USA	1975	February 8
Philadelphia JFK Stadium(Live Aid)	USA	1985	July 13
Phoenix Arizona Coliseum	USA	1970	April 18
Pittsburgh Civic Arena	USA	1970	March 30
Pittsburgh 3 Rivers Stadium	USA	1973	July 24
Pittsburgh Civic Arena	USA	1975	February 1
Pittsburgh Civic Arena	USA	1975	February 2
Plymouth Van Dyke Club	England	1969	March 1
Pontiac Silverdome	USA	1977	April 30
Portland	USA	1968	December 31
Portland	USA	1969	May ??
Portland Memorial Coliseum	USA	1970	March 23
Portland Memorial Coliseum	USA	1972	June 17
Portsmouth Guild Hall	England	1969	June 26
Portsmouth Guild Hall	England	1970	January 13
Preston Town Hall	England	1971	November 23
Preston Guild Hall	England	1973	January 30
Providence RI Auditorium	USA	1969	October 31
Providence Civic Centre	USA	1973	July 21
Raleigh	USA	1970	April 8
Reykjavik Laugardalsholl Sports Center	Iceland	1970	June 22
Richmond Athletic Club	England	1968	November 29
Rochester	USA	1970	April ??
Rochester Memorial Auditorium	USA	1971	September 11
Roskilde Fjordvilla	Denmark	1968	September 8
Rotterdam	Holland	1973	March 11
Rotterdam Ahoy	Holland	1975	January 11
Rotterdam Ahoy	Holland	1980	June 21
Sacramento Memorial Auditorium	USA	1969	August 6
Salisbury	England	1971	December 15
Salt Lake City Lagoon	USA	1969	July 30
Salt Lake City Salt Palace	USA	1970	March 26
Salt Lake City Salt Palace	USA	1973	May 26
San Antonio Hemisphere Arena	USA	1970	August 23
San Antonio Municipal Auditorium	USA	1971	August 26
San Antonio Hemisphere Arena	USA	1973	May 22
San Bernadino Swing Auditorium	USA	1972	June 22
San Bernadino Swing Auditorium	USA	1969	August 8
San Diego Sports Arena	USA	1969	August 10
San Diego Sports Arena	USA	1970	September 3
San Diego Sports Arena	USA	1972	June 23
San Diego Sports Arena	USA	1973	May 28
San Diego Sports Arena	USA	1975	March 10
San Diego Sports Arena	USA	1977	June 19
San Francisco Fillmore West	USA	1969	January 9
San Francisco Fillmore West	USA	1969	January 10
San Francisco Fillmore West	USA	1969	January 11
San Francisco Fillmore West	USA	1969	January 12
San Francisco Fillmore West	USA	1969	April 24
San Francisco Fillmore West	USA	1969	April 27
San Francisco Fillmore West ?	USA	1969	August 11
San Francisco Winterland	USA	1969	April 25
San Francisco Winterland	USA	1969	April 26

San Francisco Winterland	USA	1969	November 6
San Francisco Winterland	USA	1969	November 7
San Francisco Winterland	USA	1969	November 8
San Francisco Kezar Stadium	USA	1973	June 2
Santa Barbara Fairgrounds	USA	1969	August 1
Santa Clara Fairgrounds	USA	1969	May 23
Seattle Center Arena	USA	1968	December 27
Seattle Green Lake Aquatheatre	USA	1969	May 11
Seattle Center Arena	USA	1970	March 22
Seattle Center Coliseum	USA	1970	September 1
Seattle Center	USA	1971	August 20
Seattle Coliseum	USA	1972	June 18
Seattle Coliseum	USA	1972	June 19
Seattle Coliseum	USA	1973	July 17
Seattle Coliseum	USA	1975	March 17
Seattle Coliseum	USA	1975	March 21
Seattle Kingdome	USA	1977	July 17
Sheffield	England	1968	November 23
Sheffield City Hall	England	1970	January 16
Sheffield University	England	1971	November 18
Sheffield City Hall	England	1973	January 2
Southampton University	England	1971	March 11
Southampton Gaumont	England	1973	January 21
Southampton University	England	1973	January 20
Spokane Gonzaga University	USA	1968	December 30
St. Helier JerseyBehan's Nightclub	Channel Islands	1975	October 10
St. Louis Kiel Auditorium	USA	1970	April 11
St. Louis Arena	USA	1971	August 28
St. Louis Kiel Auditorium	USA	1973	May 11
St. Louis Missouri Arena	USA	1975	February 16
St. Louis Missouri Arena	USA	1977	April 15
St. Paul Civic Centre	USA	1973	July 9
St. Paul Civic Centre	USA	1977	April 13
Staines Movie Session	England	1969	March 25
Stargroves Studio Session	England	1972	May ??
Stockholm Gronalund Tivoli	Sweden	1968	September 12
Stockholm Inside Club	Sweden	1968	September 13
Stockholm Concerthouse	Sweden	1969	March 14
Stockholm Konserthuset	Sweden	1970	February 26
Stockholm Royal Tennis Arena	Sweden	1973	March 6
Stockholm Royal Tennis Arena	Sweden	1973	March 7
Stockholm Polar Studio Session	Sweden	1977	November ??
Stockholm Polar Studio Session	Sweden	1978	December ??
Stoke	England	1969	March ??
Stoke	England	1969	April 14
Stoke Hanley Place	England	1971	March 14
Stoke Trentham Gardens	England	1973	January 15
Sunderland	England	1969	March ??
Sunderland	England	1969	April 17
Sutton Coldfield Belfry	England	1971	March 20
Sydney Showgrounds	Australia	1972	February 27
Syracuse Onadaga War Memorial	USA	1969	November 1
Syracuse Onadaga War Memorial	USA	1971	September 10
Tampa Curtis Hixon Hall	USA	1970	April 9
Tampa Stadium	USA	1973	May 5
Tampa Stadium	USA	1977	June 3

Tempe Activities Centre	USA	1977	July 20
Tokyo Budokan Hall	Japan	1971	September 23
Tokyo Budokan Hall	Japan	1971	September 24
Tokyo Budokan Hall	Japan	1972	October 2
Tokyo Budokan Hall	Japan	1972	October 3
Toronto Rockpile	Canada	1969	February 2
Toronto Rockpile	Canada	1969	August 18
Toronto O'Keefe Centre	Canada	1969	November 2
Toronto Maple Leaf Gardens	Canada	1971	September 4
Tucson Community Centre	USA	1972	June 28
Tulsa	USA	1970	August 21
Tuscaloosa University Of Alabama	USA	1973	May 10
Uppsala University Lecture Hall	Sweden	1969	March 14
Vancouver PNE Agrodome	Canada	1969	May 10
Vancouver PNE Agrodome	Canada	1969	July 26
Vancouver Pacific Coliseum	Canada	1970	March 21
Vancouver Pacific Coliseum	Canada	1971	August 19
Vancouver PNE Agrodome	Canada	1973	July 18
Vancouver Coliseum	Canada	1975	March 19
Vancouver Coliseum	Canada	1975	March 20
Vienna Konserthaus	Austria	1970	March 9
Vienna Concert House	Austria	1973	March 16
Vienna Stadthalle	Austria	1980	June 26
Wallingford Oakdale Theatre	USA	1969	August 17
Washington Capitol Centre	USA	1975	February 10
Washington Largo Capitol Centre	USA	1977	May 25
Washington Largo Capitol Centre	USA	1977	May 26
Washington Largo Capitol Centre	USA	1977	May 28
Washington Largo Capitol Centre	USA	1977	May 30
Welwyn Garden City Cherry Tree	England	1969	April 8
Wembley Empire Pool	England	1971	November 20
Wembley Empire Pool	England	1971	November 21
Winnipeg Arena	Canada	1970	August 29
Woodinville Goldcreek Park	USA	1969	July 27
Zurich Hallenstadion	Switzerland	1980	June 29

Appendix C
Concerts
(arranged by day)

January 2 1969	Los Angeles Whisky a Go Go
January 2 1973	Sheffield City Hall
January 3 1969	Los Angeles Whisky a Go Go
January 4 1969	Los Angeles Whisky a Go Go
January 5 1969	Los Angeles Whisky a Go Go
January 7 1970	Birmingham Town Hall
January 7 1973	Oxford New Theatre
January 8 1970	Bristol Colston Hall
January 9 1969	San Francisco Fillmore West
January 9 1970	London Royal Albert Hall
January 10 1969	San Francisco Fillmore West
January 11 1969	San Francisco Fillmore West
January 11 1975	Rotterdam Ahoy
January 12 1969	San Francisco Fillmore West
January 12 1975	Brussels Forest Nationale
January 13 1970	Portsmouth Guild Hall
January 14 1973	Liverpool Empire
January 15 1969	Iowa City Iowa University
January 15 1970	Newcastle City Hall
January 15 1973	Stoke Trentham Gardens
January 15 1995	New York Waldorf Astoria
January 16 1970	Sheffield City Hall
January 16 1973	Aberystwyth King's Hall
January 17 1969	Detroit Grande Ballroom
January 18 1969	Detroit Grande Ballroom
January 18 1973	Bradford St. George's Hall
January 18 1975	Minneapolis Met Centre
January 19 1969	Detroit Grande Ballroom
January 20 1973	Southampton University
January 20 1975	Chicago Stadium52
January 21 1973	Southampton Gaumont
January 21 1975	Chicago Stadium
January 22 1975	Chicago Stadium
January 23 1969	Boston Tea Party
January 24 1969	Boston Tea Party
January 24 1970	Leeds Town Hall
January 24 1975	Cleveland Coliseum
January 25 1969	Boston Tea Party
January 25 1973	Aberdeen Music Hall
January 25 1975	Indianapolis Arena
January 26 1969	Boston Tea Party
January 27 1973	Dundee Caird Hall
January 28 1973	Edinburgh King's Theatre
January 29 1975	Greensboro Coliseum
January 30 1973	Preston Guild Hall
January 31 1969	New York Fillmore East
January 31 1975	Detroit Olympia Stadium
January ?? 1971	Headley Grange Studio Session
February 1 1969	New York Fillmore East
February 1 1975	Pittsburgh Civic Arena
February 2 1969	Toronto Rockpile
February 2 1975	Pittsburgh Civic Arena
February 3 1969	New York The Scene ?
February 3 1975	New York M.S.G.
February 4 1975	New York Nassau Coliseum
February 4 1969	New York The Scene ?

February 5 1969	New York The Scene ?
February 6 1975	Montreal Forum
February 7 1969	Chicago Kinetic Playground
February 7 1975	New York M.S.G.
February 8 1969	Chicago Kinetic Playground
February 8 1975	Philadelphia Spectrum
February 10 1975	Washington Capitol Centre
February 12 1975	New York M.S.G.
February 13 1975	New York Nassau Coliseum
February 14 1969	Miami Thee Image Club
February 14 1975	New York Nassau Coliseum
February 15 1969	Miami Thee Image Club
February 16 1972	Perth Subiaco Oval
February 16 1975	St. Louis Missouri Arena
February 17 1970	Edinburgh Usher Hall
February 19 1972	Adelaide Memorial Drive
February 20 1972	Melbourne Kooyong Tennis Courts
February 24 1970	Helsinki
February 24 1972	Auckland Western Spring Stadium
February 25 1970	Göteborg
February 26 1970	Stockholm Konserthuset
February 27 1972	Sydney Showgrounds
February 27 1975	Houston Coliseum
February 28 1970	Copenhagen K.B.Hallen
February 28 1975	Baton Rouge L.S.U.
February 29 1972	Brisbane Festival Hall
February ?? 1969	Memphis
March 1 1969	Plymouth Van Dyke Club
March 2 1973	Copenhagen K.B. Hallen
March 3 1969	London Maida Vale BBC Studios
March 3 1975	Fort Worth Tarrant Con.Centre
March 4 1973	Göteborg
March 4 1975	Dallas Memorial Auditorium
March 5 1969	Cardiff
March 5 1971	Belfast Ulster Hall
March 5 1975	Dallas Memorial Auditorium
March 6 1971	Dublin Boxing Stadium
March 6 1973	Stockholm Royal Tennis Arena
March 7 1969	London Hornsey Wood Tavern
March 7 1970	Montreux Casino
March 7 1973	Stockholm Royal Tennis Arena
March 7 1975	Austin Events Centre
March 8 1970	Munich
March 9 1970	Vienna Konserthaus
March 9 1971	Leeds University
March 10 1971	Canterbury University
March 10 1973	Oslo
March 10 1975	San Diego Sports Arena
March 11 1970	Dusseldorf
March 11 1971	Southampton University
March 11 1973	Rotterdam
March 11 1975	Long Beach Arena
March 12 1969	Leicester
March 12 1970	Hamburg Musikhalle
March 12 1973	Brussels
March 12 1975	Long Beach Arena

March 13 1969	Brondby Pop Club Norregard Hallen
March 13 1969	Gladsaxe TV-Byen
March 13 1971	Bath Pavilion
March 13 1973	Munich
March 14 1969	Stockholm Concerthouse
March 14 1969	Uppsala University Lecture Hall
March 14 1971	Stoke Hanley Place
March 14 1973	Nuremberg Messehalle
March 15 1969	Gladsaxe Teen Clubs Box 45
March 16 1969	Copenhagen Tivolis Koncertsal
March 16 1973	Vienna Concert House
March 17 1973	Munich Olympiahalle
March 17 1975	Seattle Coliseum
March 18 1971	Newcastle Mayfair
March 19 1969	London BBC Studio Session
March 19 1971	Manchester University
March 19 1973	Berlin Deutschlandhalle
March 19 1975	Vancouver Coliseum
March 20 1971	Sutton Coldfield Belfry
March 20 1975	Vancouver Coliseum
March 21 1969	London How Late It Is BBC TV
March 21 1970	Vancouver Pacific Coliseum
March 21 1971	Nottingham Rowing Club
March 21 1973	Hamburg Musichalle
March 21 1975	Seattle Coliseum
March 22 1969	Birmingham Mother's
March 22 1970	Seattle Center Arena
March 22 1973	Essen Grughalle
March 23 1970	Portland Memorial Coliseum
March 23 1971	London Marquee
March 24 1973	Offenburg Orthenau Halle
March 24 1975	Los Angeles Forum
March 25 1969	Staines
March 25 1970	Denver Coliseum
March 25 1975	Los Angeles Forum
March 26 1970	Salt Lake City Salt Palace
March 26 1973	Lyons
March 27 1970	Los Angeles Forum
March 27 1973	Nancy
March 27 1975	Los Angeles Forum
March 28 1969	London Marquee
March 28 1970	Dallas Memorial Auditorium
March 29 1970	Houston Hofheinz Pavilion
March 30 1969	London Southall Northcote Arms Farx
March 30 1970	Pittsburgh Civic Centre
March 31 1969	London Cooks Ferry Inn
March 31 1970	Philadelphia Spectrum
March ?? 1969	Bolton
March ?? 1969	Stoke
March ?? 1969	Sunderland
March ?? 1969	Paris Olympia
March ?? 1972	Bombay Session with Orchestra
April 1 1969	London Hampstead Klook's Kleek
April 1 1971	London BBC Paris Theatre
April 1 1973	Paris Palais De Sports
April 1 1977	Dallas Memorial Auditorium

April 2 1973	Paris Palais De Sports
April 2 1970	Charleston
April 3 1970	Macon Coliseum
April 3 1977	Oklahoma City Myriad
April 4 1970	Indianapolis Arena
April 5 1969	Dagenham Roundhouse
April 5 1970	Baltimore Civic Center
April 6 1977	Chicago Stadium
April 7 1970	Charlotte Independence Coliseum
April 7 1977	Chicago Stadium
April 8 1969	Welwyn Garden City Cherry Tree
April 8 1970	Raleigh
April 9 1969	London Tolworth Toby Jug
April 9 1970	Tampa Curtis Hixon Hall
April 9 1977	Chicago Stadium
April 10 1970	Miami Convention Hall
April 10 1977	Chicago Stadium
April 11 1970	St. Louis Kiel Auditorium
April 12 1970	Minneapolis St. Paul
April 12 1977	Minneapolis Met Centre.
April 13 1970	Montreal Forum
April 13 1977	St. Paul Civic Centre
April 14 1969	Stoke ?
April 14 1970	Ottawa Civic Centre
April 15 1977	St. Louis Missouri Arena
April 16 1970	Evansville Indiana Roberts Stadium
April 17 1969	Sunderland ?
April 17 1970	Memphis Mid-South Coliseum
April 17 1977	Indianapolis Market Square Arena
April 18 1970	Phoenix Arizona Coliseum
April 19 1977	Cincinnati Riverfront Coliseum
April 20 1977	Cincinnati Riverfront Coliseum
April 23 1977	Atlanta The Omni
April 24 1969	San Francisco Fillmore West
April 25 1969	San Francisco Winterland
April 25 1977	Louisville Kentucky Fairgrounds
April 26 1969	San Francisco Winterland
April 26 1970	London Julie Felix TV Appearance
April 27 1969	San Francisco Fillmore West
April 27 1977	Cleveland Richfield Coliseum
April 28 1977	Cleveland Richfield Coliseum
April 30 1977	Pontiac Silverdome
April ?? 1970	Nashville
April ?? 1970	Rochester
May 1 1969	Irvine UC Irvine
May 2 1969	Pasadena Rose Palace
May 3 1969	Pasadena Rose Palace
May 3 1971	Copenhagen K.B.Hallen
May 4 1971	Odensen Fyns Forum
May 4 1973	Atlanta Braves Stadium
May 5 1973	Tampa Stadium
May 7 1973	Jacksonville Civic Centre
May 9 1969	Edmonton Gardens
May 10 1969	Vancouver PNE Agrodome
May 10 1971	Liverpool University
May 10 1973	Tuscaloosa University Of Alabama

May 11 1969	Seattle Green Lake Aquatheatre
May 11 1973	St. Louis Kiel Aud.
May 12 1990	Bewdley Heath Hotel
May 13 1969	Honolulu Civic Auditorium
May 13 1973	Mobile City Aud.
May 14 1973	New Orleans Mun. Aud.
May 14 1988	New York Madison Square Garden
May 16 1969	Detroit Grande Ballroom
May 16 1973	Houston Sam Houston Arena
May 17 1969	Athens Ohio University
May 17 1975	London Earl's Court
May 18 1969	Minneapolis Guthrie Memorial Theatre
May 18 1973	Dallas Memorial Auditorium
May 18 1975	London Earl's Court
May 18 1977	Birmingham Coliseum
May 19-23 1969	New York Atlantic Studios
May 19 1973	Fort Worth Tarrant Con. Centre
May 19 1977	Baton Rouge LSU Assembly Cent.
May 21 1977	Houston The Summit
May 22 1973	San Antonio Hemisphere Arena
May 22 1977	Fort Worth Convention Centre
May 23 1969	Chicago Kinetic Playground
May 23 1969	Santa Clara Fairgrounds
May 23 1973	Albuquerque University Of New Mexico
May 23 1975	London Earl's Court
May 24 1969	Chicago Kinetic Playground
May 24 1975	London Earl's Court
May 25 1969	Columbia Merriweather Post Pavilion
May 25 1973	Denver Coliseum
May 25 1975	London Earl's Court
May 25 1977	Washington Largo Capitol Centre
May 26 1973	Salt Lake City Salt Palace
May 26 1977	Washington Largo Capitol Centre
May 27 1969	Boston Tea Party
May 27 1972	Amsterdam R.A.I.
May 28 1969	Boston Tea Party
May 28 1972	Brussels Forest National
May 28 1973	San Diego Sports Arena
May 28 1977	Washington Largo Capitol Centre
May 29 1969	Boston Tea Party
May 30 1969	New York Fillmore East
May 30 1977	Washington Largo Capitol Centre
May 31 1969	New York Fillmore East
May 31 1973	Los Angeles Forum
May 31 1977	Greensboro Coliseum
May ?? 1969	Los Angeles Mirror Sound Studio Session
May ?? 1969	Portland
May ?? 1970	Bron-y-Aur Rehearsals
May ?? 1970	Headley Grange Studio sessions
May ?? 1972	London Olympic Studio Session
May ?? 1972	Stargroves Studio Session
May ?? 1972	London Island Studio Session
May ?? 1978	Clearwell Castle Rehearsals
May ?? 1980	London Victoria Theatre Rehearsal
June 2 1973	San Francisco Kezar Stadium
June 3 1973	Los Angeles Forum

June 3 1977	Tampa Stadium
June 6 1972	Detroit Cobo Hall
June 7 1972	Montreal Forum
June 7 1977	New York Madison Square Gardens
June 8 1972	Boston Gardens
June 8 1977	New York Madison Square Gardens
June 9 1972	Charlotte Coliseum
June 10 1972	Buffalo Memorial Auditorium
June 11 1972	Baltimore Civic Centre
June 11 1977	New York Madison Square Gardens
June 12 1977	New York Madison Square Gardens
June 13 1969	Birmingham Town Hall
June 13 1972	Philadelphia Spectrum
June 13 1977	New York Madison Square Gardens
June 14 1972	Hempstead Nassau County Coliseum
June 14 1977	New York Madison Square Gardens
June 15 1969	Manchester Free Trade Hall
June 15 1972	Hempstead Nassau County Coliseum
June 16 1969	London Dave Symonds Show BBC
June 17 1972	Portland Memorial Coliseum
June 17 1980	Dortmund Westfalenhalle
June 18 1972	Seattle Coliseum
June 18 1980	Cologne Sportshalle
June 19 1972	Seattle Coliseum
June 19 1977	San Diego Sports Arena
June 20 1969	Newcastle City Hall
June 20 1980	Brussels Forest National
June 21 1969	Bristol Colston Hall
June 21 1972	Denver Coliseum
June 21 1977	Los Angeles Forum
June 21 1980	Rotterdam Ahoy
June 22 1970	Reykjavik Laugardalsholl Sports Center
June 22 1972	San Bernadino Swing Auditorium
June 22 1977	Los Angeles Forum
June 23 1972	San Diego Sports Arena
June 23 1977	Los Angeles Forum
June 23 1980	Bremen Stadthalle
June 24 1969	London John Peel's Top Gear BBC
June 24 1980	Hannover Messehalle
June 25 1969	Paris Tous En Scene TV
June 25 1972	Los Angeles Forum
June 25 1977	Los Angeles Forum
June 26 1969	Portsmouth Guild Hall
June 26 1977	Los Angeles Forum
June 26 1980	Vienna Stadthalle
June 27 1969	London BBC Playhouse Theatre
June 27 1972	Long Beach Arena
June 27 1977	Los Angeles Forum
June 27 1980	Nuremberg Messezentrum Halle
June 28 1969	Bath Festival
June 28 1970	Bath Festival
June 28 1972	Tucson Community Centre
June 29 1969	London Royal Albert Hall
June 29 1980	Zurich Hallenstadion
June 30 1980	Frankfurt Festhalle
June ?? 1969	London Morgan Studio Session

June ?? 1974	Headley Grange Session
July 2 1980	Mannheim Eisstadium
July 3 1980	Mannheim Eisstadium
July 5 1969	Atlanta Pop Festival
July 5 1971	Milan Vigorelli Stadium
July 5 1980	Munich Olympiahalle
July 6 1969	Newport Jazz Festival
July 6 1973	Chicago Aud.
July 7 1973	Chicago Aud.
July 7 1980	Berlin Eissporthalle
July 8 1973	Indianapolis Arena
July 9 1973	St. Paul Civic Centre
July 10 1973	Milwaukee Arena
July 11 1969	Baltimore Jazz Festival
July 12 1969	Philadelphia Jazz Festival
July 12 1973	Detroit Cobo Hall
July 13 1973	Detroit Cobo Hall
July 13 1985	Philadelphia JFK Stadium
July 15 1973	Buffalo Auditorium
July 16 1970	Cologne
July 17 1970	Essen
July 17 1973	Seattle Coliseum
July 17 1977	Seattle Kingdome
July 18 1969	Chicago Kinetic Playground
July 18 1970	Frankfurt Festhalle
July 18 1973	Vancouver PNE Coliseum
July 19 1969	Chicago Kinetic Playground
July 19 1970	Berlin Deutschlandhalle
July 20 1969	Cleveland Musicarnival
July 20 1977	Tempe Activities Centre
July 21 1969	New York Central Park
July 21 1973	Providence Civic Centre
July 23 1973	Baltimore Civic Centre
July 23 1977	Oakland Coliseum
July 23 1979	Copenhagen Falkoner Theatre
July 24 1973	Pittsburgh 3 Rivers Stadium
July 24 1977	Oakland Coliseum
July 24 1979	Copenhagen Falkoner Theatre
July 25 1969	Milwaukee State Fair Park
July 25 1973	Boston Gardens
July 26 1969	Vancouver PNE Agrodome
July 27 1969	Woodinville Goldcreek Park
July 27 1973	New York M.S.G.
July 28 1973	New York M.S.G.
July 29 1969	Edmonton Kinsmen Field House
July 29 1973	New York M.S.G.
July 30 1969	Salt Lake City Lagoon
July 31 1969	Eugene
August 1 1969	Santa Barbara Fairgrounds
August 3 1969	Houston Music Hall
August 4 1969	Dallas State Fair Coliseum
August 4 1979	Knebworth
August 6 1969	Sacramento Memorial Auditorium
August 7 1969	Berkeley Community Theatre
August 7 1971	Montreux Casino
August 8 1969	San Bernadino Swing Auditorium

August 8 1971	Montreux Casino
August 9 1969	Anaheim Convention Centre
August 10 1969	San Diego Sports Arena
August 11 1969	San Francisco Fillmore West ?
August 11 1979	Knebworth
August 15 1970	New Haven Yale
August 16 1969	Asbury Park NJ Convention Hall
August 17 1969	Wallingford Oakdale Theatre
August 17 1970	Hampton Roads Coliseum
August 18 1969	Toronto Rockpile
August 19 1971	Vancouver Pacific Coliseum
August 20 1970	Oklahoma City Coliseum Fairgrounds
August 20 1971	Seattle Center
August 21 1969	Framingham MA. Carousel Theatre
August 21 1970	Tulsa
August 21 1971	Los Angeles Forum
August 22 1969	Miami Beach Dania Pirates World
August 22 1970	Fort Worth Tarrant Convention Centre
August 22 1971	Los Angeles Forum
August 23 1969	Miami Beach Dania Pirates World
August 23 1970	San Antonio Hemisphere Arena
August 23 1971	Fort Worth Tarrant Convention Center
August 24 1969	Jacksonville Veterans Memorial Coliseum
August 24 1971	Dallas Memorial Aud
August 25 1971	Houston Hofheinz
August 26 1970	Cleveland Public Hall
August 26 1971	San Antonio Municipal Auditorium
August 27 1971	Oklahoma City
August 28 1970	Detroit Olympia
August 28 1971	St. Louis Arena
August 29 1969	New York Singer Bowl
August 29 1970	Winnipeg Arena
August 29 1971	New Orleans Municipal Auditorium
August 30 1969	New York Singer Bowl
August 31 1969	Dallas Pop Festival
August 31 1970	Milwaukee Arena
August 31 1971	Orlando Civic Auditorium
September 1 1970	Seattle Center Coliseum
September 1 1971	Hollywood Florida Sportatorium
September 2 1970	Oakland Forum
September 3 1970	San Diego Sports Arena
September 3 1971	New York Madison Square Gardens
September 4 1970	Los Angeles Forum
September 4 1971	Toronto Maple Leaf Gardens
September 5 1971	Chicago Amphitheatre
September 6 1970	Honolulu International Center
September 6 1971	Boston Gardens
September 7 1968	Gladsaxe Teen Clubs Box 45 Copenhagen
September 7 1968	Brondby Pop Club Norregard Hallen Copenhagen
September 8 1968	Fjordvilla Roskilde
September 8 1968	Nykøbing Raventlow Park Falster Island
September 9 1970	Boston Gardens
September 9 1971	Hampton Roads Coliseum
September 10 1971	Syracuse Onadaga War Memorial
September 11 1971	Rochester Memorial Auditorium
September 12 1968	Stockholm Gronalund Tivoli

September 13 1968	Stockholm Inside Club
September 13 1971	Berkeley Community Theatre
September 14 1971	Berkeley Community Theatre
September 15 1968	Liseburg Amusement Park Göteborg
September 16 1971	Honolulu International Center
September 17 1971	Honolulu International Center
September 19 1970	New York Madison Square Garden
September 23 1971	Tokyo Budokan Hall
September 24 1971	Tokyo Budokan Hall
September 27 1968	London Olympic Studio
September 27 1971	Hiroshima Shiei Taiikukan
September 28 1971	Osaka Festival Hall
September 29 1971	Osaka Festival Hall
October 2 1972	Tokyo Budokan Hall
October 3 1972	Tokyo Budokan Hall
October 4 1972	Osaka Festival Hall
October 5 1972	Nagoyashi Kokaido
October 9 1972	Osaka Festival Hall
October 10 1969	Paris Olympia
October 10 1972	Kyoto Kaikan #1 Hall
October 10 1975	St. Helier Jersey Behan's Nightclub
October 12 1969	London Lyceum Ballroom
October 17 1969	New York Carnegie Hall
October 18 1968	London Marquee
October 18 1969	Detroit Olympia
October 19 1968	Liverpool University
October 19 1969	Chicago Kinetic Playground
October 24 1969	Cleveland Public Auditorium
October 25 1968	Guildford Surrey University
October 25 1969	Boston Gardens
October 26 1969	Charlotte
October 27 1972	Montreux The Pavilion
October 28 1972	Montreux The Pavilion
October 30 1969	Buffalo Kleinhan's Music Hall
October 31 1969	Providence RI Auditorium
October ?? 1968	London Olympic Studio Sessions
November 1 1969	Syracuse Onadaga War Memorial
November 2 1969	Toronto O'Keefe Centre
November 4 1969	Kitchener Memorial Auditorium
November 5 1969	Kansas City
November 6 1969	San Francisco Winterland
November 7 1969	San Francisco Winterland
November 8 1969	San Francisco Winterland
November 9 1968	London Chalk Farm Roundhouse
November 11 1971	Newcastle City Hall
November 12 1971	Newcastle Mecca Ballroom
November 13 1971	Dundee Caird Hall
November 16 1968	Manchester College Of Science & Technology
November 16 1971	Ipswich St. Matthew's Baths
November 17 1971	Birmingham Kinetic Circus
November 18 1971	Sheffield University
November 20 1971	Wembley Empire Pool
November 21 1971	Wembley Empire Pool
November 23 1968	Sheffield
November 23 1971	Preston Town Hall
November 24 1971	Manchester Free Trade Hall

November 25 1971	Leicester University
November 29 1968	Richmond Athletic Club
November 29 1971	Liverpool University
November 30 1971	Manchester Kings Hall Belle Vue
November 30 1972	Newcastle City Hall
November ?? 1969	London Olympic Studio Session
November ?? 1977	Stockholm Polar Studio Session
December 1 1972	Newcastle City Hall
December 2 1971	Bournemouth Starkers
December 3 1972	Glasgow Green's Playhouse
December 4 1972	Glasgow Green's Playhouse
December 7 1972	Manchester Hardrock
December 8 1972	Manchester Hardrock
December 9 1971	Derby Locarno
December 10 1968	London Marquee
December 11 1972	Cardiff Capitol
December 12 1972	Cardiff Capitol
December 13 1968	Canterbury Bridge Country Club
December 15 1971	Salisbury
December 16 1968	Bath Pavilion
December 16 1972	Birmingham Odeon
December 17 1972	Birmingham Odeon
December 19 1968	Exeter City Hall
December 20 1968	London Wood Green Fishmongers Hall
December 20 1972	Brighton Dome
December 22 1972	London Alexandra Palace
December 23 1972	London Alexandra Palace
December 26 1968	Denver Auditorium
December 27 1968	Seattle Center Arena
December 30 1968	Spokane Gonzaga University
December 31 1968	Portland
December ?? 1973	Headley Grange Session
December ?? 1975	Munich Musicland Studio Session
December ?? 1978	Stockholm Polar Studio Session

Appendix D
Concerts
(arranged by country)

Australia	Adelaide Memorial Drive	1972 February 19
Australia	Brisbane Festival Hall	1972 February 29
Australia	Melbourne Kooyong Tennis Courts	1972 February 20
Australia	Perth Subiaco Oval	1972 February 16
Australia	Sydney Showgrounds	1972 February 27
Austria	Vienna Konserthaus	1970 March 9
Austria	Vienna Concert House	1973 March 16
Austria	Vienna Stadthalle	1980 June 26
Belgium	Brussels Forest Nationale	1972 May 28
Belgium	Brussels	1973 March 12
Belgium	Brussels Forest Nationale	1975 January 12
Belgium	Brussels Forest Nationale	1980 June 20
Canada	Edmonton Gardens	1969 May 9
Canada	Edmonton Kinsmen Field House	1969 July 29
Canada	Kitchener Memorial Auditorium	1969 November 4
Canada	Montreal Forum	1970 April 13
Canada	Montreal Forum	1972 June 7
Canada	Montreal Forum	1975 February 6
Canada	Ottawa Civic Centre	1970 April 14
Canada	Toronto Rockpile	1969 February 2
Canada	Toronto Rockpile	1969 August 18
Canada	Toronto O'Keefe Centre	1969 November 2
Canada	Toronto Maple Leaf Gardens	1971 September 4
Canada	Vancouver PNE Agrodome	1969 May 10
Canada	Vancouver Mirror Sound Studio Sessions	1969 May ??
Canada	Vancouver PNE Agrodome	1969 July 26
Canada	Vancouver Pacific Coliseum	1970 March 21
Canada	Vancouver Pacific Coliseum	1971 August 19
Canada	Vancouver PNE Agrodome	1973 July 18
Canada	Vancouver Coliseum	1975 March 19
Canada	Vancouver Coliseum	1975 March 20
Canada	Winnipeg Arena	1970 August 29
Channel Islands	St. Helier Jersey Behan's	1975 October 10
Denmark	Brondby Pop Club Norregard Hallen	1968 September 7
Denmark	Brondby Pop Club Norregard Hallen	1969 March 13
Denmark	Copenhagen Tivolis Koncertsal	1969 March 16
Denmark	Copenhagen K.B.Hallen	1970 February 28
Denmark	Copenhagen K.B.Hallen	1971 May 3
Denmark	Copenhagen K.B. Hallen	1973 March 2
Denmark	Copenhagen Falkoner Theatre	1979 July 23
Denmark	Copenhagen Falkoner Theatre	1979 July 24
Denmark	Gladsaxe Teen Clubs Box 45	1968 September 7
Denmark	Gladsaxe TV-Byen	1969 March 13
Denmark	Gladsaxe Teen Clubs Box 45	1969 March 15
Denmark	Nykøbing Raventlow Park Falster Island	1968 September 8
Denmark	Odense Fyns Forum	1971 May 4
Denmark	Roskilde Fjordvilla	1968 September 8
England	Bath Pavilion	1968 December 16
England	Bath Festival	1969 June 28
England	Bath Festival	1970 June 28
England	Bath Pavilion	1971 March 13
England	Bewdley Heath Hotel	1990 May 12
England	Birmingham Mother's	1969 March 22
England	Birmingham Town Hall	1969 June 13
England	Birmingham Town Hall	1970 January 7
England	Birmingham Kinetic Circus	1971 November 17

England	Birmingham Odeon	1972 December 16
England	Birmingham Odeon	1972 December 17
England	Bolton	1969 March ??
England	Bournemouth Starkers	1971 December 2
England	Bradford St. George's Hall	1973 January 18
England	Brighton Dome	1972 December 20
England	Bristol Colston Hall	1969 June 21
England	Bristol Colston Hall	1970 January 8
England	Canterbury Bridge Country Club	1968 December 13
England	Canterbury University	1971 March 10
England	Clearwell Castle Rehearsals	1978 May ??
England	Dagenham Roundhouse	1969 April 5
England	Derby Locarno	1971 December 9
England	Exeter City Hall	1968 December 19
England	Guildford Surrey University	1968 October 25
England	Headley Grange Recording Session	1970 May ??
England	Headley Grange Recording Session	1971 January ??
England	Headley Grange Recording Session	1973 December ??
England	Headley Grange Recording Session	1974 June ??
England	Ipswich St. Matthew's Baths	1971 November 16
England	Knebworth	1979 August 4
England	Knebworth	1979 August 11
England	Leeds Town Hall	1970 January 24
England	Leeds University	1971 March 9
England	Leicester	1969 March 12
England	Leicester University	1971 November 25
England	Liverpool University	1968 October 19
England	Liverpool University	1971 May 10
England	Liverpool University	1971 November 29
England	Liverpool Empire	1973 January 14
England	London BBC Studio Session	1969 March 19
England	London Alexandra Palace	1972 December 22
England	London Alexandra Palace	1972 December 23
England	London BBC Paris Theatre	1971 April 1
England	London BBC Playhouse Theatre	1969 June 27
England	London Chalk Farm Roundhouse	1968 November 9
England	London Cooks Ferry Inn	1969 March 31
England	London Dave Symonds Show BBC	1969 June 16
England	London Earl's Court	1975 May 17
England	London Earl's Court	1975 May 18
England	London Earl's Court	1975 May 23
England	London Earl's Court	1975 May 24
England	London Earl's Court	1975 May 25
England	London Hampstead Klook's Kleek	1969 April 1
England	London Hornsey Wood Tavern	1969 March 7
England	London How Late It Is BBC TV	1969 March 21
England	London Island Studio Session	1972 May ??
England	London John Peel's Top Gear BBC	1969 June 24
England	London Julie Felix TV Appearance	1970 April 26
England	London Lyceum Ballroom	1969 October 12
England	London Maida Vale BBC Studios	1969 March 3
England	London Marquee	1968 October 18
England	London Marquee	1968 December 10
England	London Marquee	1969 March 28
England	London Marquee	1971 March 23
England	London Morgan Studio Session	1969 June ??

England	London Olympic StudioSession	1968 September 27
England	London Olympic Studio Session	1968 October ??
England	London Olympic Studio Session	1969 November ??
England	London Olympic Studio Session	1972 May ??
England	London Royal Albert Hall	1969 June 29
England	London Royal Albert Hall	1970 January 9
England	London Southall Northcote Arms Farx	1969 March 30
England	London Tolworth Toby Jug	1969 April 9
England	London Victoria Theatre Rehearsal	1980 May ??
England	London Wood Green Fishmongers Hall	1968 December 20
England	Manchester College Of Science	1968 November 16
England	Manchester Free Trade Hall	1969 June 15
England	Manchester University	1971 March 19
England	Manchester Free Trade Hall	1971 November 24
England	Manchester Kings Hall Belle Vue	1971 November 30
England	Manchester Hardrock	1972 December 7
England	Manchester Hardrock	1972 December 8
England	Newcastle City Hall	1969 June 20
England	Newcastle City Hall	1970 January 15
England	Newcastle Mayfair	1971 March 18
England	Newcastle City Hall	1971 November 11
England	Newcastle Mecca Ballroom	1971 November 12
England	Newcastle City Hall	1972 November 30
England	Newcastle City Hall	1972 December 1
England	Nottingham Rowing Club	1971 March 21
England	Oxford New Theatre	1973 January 7
England	Plymouth Van DykeClub	1969 March 1
England	Portsmouth Guild Hall	1969 June 26
England	Portsmouth Guild Hall	1970 January 13
England	Preston Town Hall	1971 November 23
England	Preston Guild Hall	1973 January 30
England	Richmond Athletic Club	1968 November 29
England	Salisbury	1971 December 15
England	Sheffield	1968 November 23
England	Sheffield City Hall	1970 January 16
England	Sheffield University	1971 November 18
England	Sheffield City Hall	1973 January 2
England	Southampton University	1971 March 11
England	Southampton Gaumont	1973 January 21
England	Southampton University	1973 January 20
England	StainesMovie Session	1969 March 25
England	Stargroves Studio Session	1972 May ??
England	Stoke	1969 March ??
England	Stoke	1969 April 14
England	Stoke Hanley Place	1971 March 14
England	Stoke Trentham Gardens	1973 January 15
England	Sunderland	1969 March ??
England	Sunderland	1969 April 17
England	Sunderland Locarno	1971 November 12
England	Sutton Coldfield Belfry	1971 March 20
England	Welwyn Garden City Cherry Tree	1969 April 8
England	Wembley Empire Pool	1971 November 20
England	Wembley Empire Pool	1971 November 21
Finland	Helsinki	1970 February 24
France	Lyons	1973 March 26
France	Nancy	1973 March 27

France	Paris Olympia	1969 March ??
France	Paris Olympia	1969 October 10
France	Paris Tous En Scene TV Show	1969 June 25
France	Paris Palais De Sports	1973 April 1
France	Paris Palais De Sports	1973 April 2
Germany	Berlin Deutschlandhalle	1970 July 19
Germany	Berlin Deutschlandhalle	1973 March 19
Germany	Berlin Eissporthalle	1980 July 7
Germany	Bremen Stadthalle	1980 June 23
Germany	Cologne	1970 July 16
Germany	Cologne Sportshalle	1980 June 18
Germany	Dortmund Westfalenhalle	1980 June 17
Germany	Dusseldorf	1970 March 11
Germany	Essen	1970 July 17
Germany	Essen Grughalle	1973 March 22
Germany	Frankfurt Festhalle	1970 July 18
Germany	Frankfurt Festhalle	1980 June 30
Germany	Hamburg Musikhalle	1970 March 12
Germany	Hamburg Musikhalle	1973 March 21
Germany	Hannover Messehalle	1980 June 24
Germany	Mannheim Eisstadium	1980 July 2
Germany	Mannheim Eisstadium	1980 July 3
Germany	Munich	1970 March 8
Germany	Munich	1973 March 13
Germany	Munich Olympiahalle	1973 March 17
Germany	Munich Musicland Studio Session	1975 December ??
Germany	Munich Olympiahalle	1980 July 5
Germany	Nuremberg Messezentrum Halle	1973 March 14
Germany	Nuremberg Messezentrum Halle	1980 June 27
Germany	Offenburg Orthenau Halle	1973 March 24
Holland	Amsterdam R.A.I.	1972 May 27
Holland	Rotterdam	1973 March 11
Holland	Rotterdam Ahoy	1975 January 11
Holland	Rotterdam Ahoy	1980 June 21
Iceland	ReykjavikLaugardalsholl Sports Center	1970 June 22
India	Bombay India Recording Session	1972 March ??
Ireland	Belfast Ulster Hall	1971 March 5
Ireland	Dublin Boxing Stadium	1971 March 6
Italy	Milan Vigorelli Stadium	1971 July 5
Japan	Hiroshima Shiei Taiikukan	1971 September 27
Japan	Kyoto Kaikan #1 Hall	1972 October 10
Japan	Nagoyashi Kokaido	1972 October 5
Japan	Osaka Festival Hall	1971 September 28
Japan	Osaka Festival Hall	1971 September 29
Japan	Osaka Festival Hall	1972 October 4
Japan	Osaka Festival Hall	1972 October 9
Japan	Tokyo Budokan Hall	1971 September 23
Japan	Tokyo Budokan Hall	1971 September 24
Japan	Tokyo Budokan Hall	1972 October 2
Japan	Tokyo Budokan Hall	1972 October 3
New Zealand	Auckland Western Spring Stadium	1972 February 24
Norway	Oslo	1973 March 10
Scotland	Aberdeen Music Hall	1973 January 25
Scotland	Dundee Caird Hall	1971 November 13
Scotland	Dundee Caird Hall	1973 January 27
Scotland	Edinburgh Usher Hall	1970 February 17

Scotland	Edinburgh King's Theatre	1973 January 28
Scotland	Glasgow Green's Playhouse	1972 December 3
Scotland	Glasgow Green's Playhouse	1972 December 4
Sweden	Göteborg Liseburg Amusement Park	1968 September 15
Sweden	Göteborg	1970 February 25
Sweden	Göteborg	1973 March 4
Sweden	Stockholm Gronalund Tivoli	1968 September 12
Sweden	Stockholm Inside Club	1968 September 13
Sweden	Stockholm Concerthouse	1969 March 14
Sweden	Stockholm Konserthuset	1970 February 26
Sweden	Stockholm Royal Tennis Arena	1973 March 6
Sweden	Stockholm Royal Tennis Arena	1973 March 7
Sweden	Stockholm Polar Studio Session	1977 November ??
Sweden	Stockholm Polar Studio Session	1978 December ??
Sweden	Uppsala University Lecture Hall	1969 March 14
Switzerland	Montreux Casino	1970 March 7
Switzerland	Montreux Casino	1971 August 7
Switzerland	Montreux Casino	1971 August 8
Switzerland	Montreux The Pavilion	1972 October 27
Switzerland	Montreux The Pavilion	1972 October 28
Switzerland	Zurich Hallenstadion	1980 June 29
USA	Albuquerque University Of New Mexico	1973 May 23
USA	Anaheim Convention Centre	1969 August 9
USA	Asbury Park NJ Convention Hall	1969 August 16
USA	Athens Ohio University	1969 May 17
USA	Atlanta Pop Festival	1969 July 5
USA	Atlanta Braves Stadium	1973 May 4
USA	Atlanta The Omni	1977 April 23
USA	Austin Events Centre	1975 March 7
USA	Baltimore Jazz Festival	1969 July 11
USA	Baltimore Civic Center	1970 April 5
USA	Baltimore Civic Centre	1972 June 11
USA	Baltimore Civic Centre	1973 July 23
USA	Baton Rouge LSU Assembly Cent.	1975 February 28
USA	Baton Rouge LSU Assembly Cent.	1977 May 19
USA	Berkeley Community Theatre	1969 August 7
USA	Berkeley Community Theatre	1971 September 13
USA	Berkeley Community Theatre	1971 September 14
USA	Birmingham Coliseum(USA)	1977 May 18
USA	Boston Tea Party	1969 January 23
USA	Boston Tea Party	1969 January 24
USA	Boston Tea Party	1969 January 25
USA	Boston Tea Party	1969 January 26
USA	Boston Tea Party	1969 May 27
USA	Boston Tea Party	1969 May 28
USA	Boston Tea Party	1969 May 29
USA	Boston Gardens	1969 October 25
USA	Boston Gardens	1970 September 9
USA	Boston Gardens	1971 September 6
USA	Boston Gardens	1972 June 8
USA	Boston Gardens	1973 July 25
USA	Buffalo Kleinhan's Music Hall	1969 October 30
USA	Buffalo Memorial Auditorium	1972 June 10
USA	Buffalo Memorial Auditorium	1973 July 15
USA	Charleston	1970 April 2
USA	Charlotte	1969 October 26

USA	Charlotte Independence Coliseum	1970 April 7
USA	Charlotte Coliseum	1972 June 9
USA	Chicago Kinetic Playground	1969 February 7
USA	Chicago Kinetic Playground	1969 February 8
USA	Chicago Kinetic Playground	1969 May 23
USA	Chicago Kinetic Playground	1969 May 24
USA	Chicago Kinetic Playground	1969 July 18
USA	Chicago Kinetic Playground	1969 July 19
USA	Chicago Kinetic Playground	1969 October 19
USA	Chicago Amphitheatre	1971 September 5
USA	Chicago Auditorium	1973 July 6
USA	Chicago Auditorium	1973 July 7
USA	Chicago Stadium	1975 January 21
USA	Chicago Stadium	1975 January 22
USA	Chicago Stadium	1977 April 6
USA	Chicago Stadium	1977 April 7
USA	Chicago Stadium	1977 April 9
USA	Chicago Stadium	1977 April 10
USA	Chicago Stadium	1975 January 20
USA	Cincinnati Riverfront Coliseum	1977 April 19
USA	Cincinnati Riverfront Coliseum	1977 April 20
USA	Cleveland Musicarnival	1969 July 20
USA	Cleveland Public Auditorium	1969 October 24
USA	Cleveland Public Hall	1970 August 26
USA	Cleveland Coliseum	1975 January 24
USA	Cleveland Richfield Coliseum	1977 April 27
USA	Cleveland Richfield Coliseum	1977 April 28
USA	Columbia Merriweather Post Pavilion	1969 May 25
USA	Dallas State Fair Coliseum	1969 August 4
USA	Dallas Pop Festival	1969 August 31
USA	Dallas Memorial Auditorium	1970 March 28
USA	Dallas Memorial Auditorium	1971 August 24
USA	Dallas Memorial Auditorium	1973 May 18
USA	Dallas Memorial Auditorium	1975 March 4
USA	Dallas Memorial Auditorium	1975 March 5
USA	Dallas Memorial Auditorium	1977 April 1
USA	Denver Auditorium	1968 December 26
USA	Denver Coliseum	1970 March 25
USA	Denver Coliseum	1972 June 21
USA	Denver Coliseum	1973 May 25
USA	Detroit Grande Ballroom	1969 January 17
USA	Detroit Grande Ballroom	1969 January 18
USA	Detroit Grande Ballroom	1969 January 19
USA	Detroit Grande Ballroom	1969 May 16
USA	Detroit Olympia	1969 October 18
USA	Detroit Olympia	1970 August 28
USA	Detroit Cobo Hall	1972 June 6
USA	Detroit Cobo Hall	1973 July 12
USA	Detroit Cobo Hall	1973 July 13
USA	Detroit Olympia Stadium	1975 January 31
USA	Eugene	1969 July 31
USA	Evansville Indiana Roberts Stadium	1970 April 16
USA	Fort Worth Tarrant Convention Center	1970 August 22
USA	Fort Worth Tarrant Convention Center	1971 August 23
USA	Fort Worth Tarrant Convention Center	1973 May 19
USA	Fort Worth Tarrant Convention Center	1975 March 3

USA	Fort Worth Tarrant Convention Center	1977 May 22
USA	Framingham MA. Carousel Theatre	1969 August 21
USA	Greensboro Coliseum	1975 January 29
USA	Greensboro Coliseum	1977 May 31
USA	Hampton Roads Coliseum	1970 August 17
USA	Hampton Roads Coliseum	1971 September 9
USA	Hempstead Nassau County Coliseum	1972 June 14
USA	Hempstead Nassau County Coliseum	1972 June 15
USA	Hollywood Florida Sportatorium	1971 September 1
USA	Honolulu Civic Auditorium	1969 May 13
USA	Honolulu International Center	1970 September 6
USA	Honolulu International Center	1971 September 16
USA	Honolulu International Center	1971 September 17
USA	Houston Music Hall	1969 August 3
USA	Houston Hofheinz Pavilion	1970 March 29
USA	Houston Hofheinz Pavilion	1971 August 25
USA	Houston Sam Houston Arena	1973 May 16
USA	Houston Coliseum	1975 February 27
USA	Houston The Summit	1977 May 21
USA	Indianapolis Arena	1970 April 4
USA	Indianapolis Arena	1973 July 8
USA	Indianapolis Arena	1975 January 25
USA	Indianapolis Market Square Arena	1977 April 17
USA	Iowa City Iowa University	1969 January 15
USA	Irvine UC Irvine	1969 May 1
USA	Jacksonville Veterans Memorial Coliseum	1969 August 24
USA	Jacksonville Civic Centre	1973 May 7
USA	Kansas City	1969 November 5
USA	Long Beach Arena	1972 June 27
USA	Long Beach Arena	1975 March 11
USA	Long Beach Arena	1975 March 12
USA	Los Angeles Whisky a Go Go	1969 January 2
USA	Los Angeles Whisky a Go Go	1969 January 3
USA	Los Angeles Whisky a Go Go	1969 January 4
USA	Los Angeles Whisky a Go Go	1969 January 5
USA	Los Angeles Mirror Sound Studio Session	1969 May ??
USA	Los Angeles Forum	1970 March 27
USA	Los Angeles Forum	1970 September 4
USA	Los Angeles Forum	1971 August 21
USA	Los Angeles Forum	1971 August 22
USA	Los Angeles Forum	1972 June 25
USA	Los Angeles Forum	1973 May 31
USA	Los Angeles Forum	1973 June 3
USA	Los Angeles Forum	1975 March 24
USA	Los Angeles Forum	1975 March 25
USA	Los Angeles Forum	1975 March 27
USA	Los Angeles Forum	1977 June 21
USA	Los Angeles Forum	1977 June 22
USA	Los Angeles Forum	1977 June 23
USA	Los Angeles Forum	1977 June 25
USA	Los Angeles Forum	1977 June 26
USA	Los Angeles Forum	1977 June 27
USA	Louisville Kentucky Fairgrounds	1977 April 25
USA	Macon Coliseum	1970 April 3
USA	Memphis	1969 February ??
USA	Memphis Mid-South Coliseum	1970 April 17

USA	Miami Thee Image Club	1969 February 14
USA	Miami Thee Image Club	1969 February 15
USA	Miami Beach Dania Pirates World	1969 August 22
USA	Miami Beach Dania Pirates World	1969 August 23
USA	Miami Convention Hall	1970 April 10
USA	Milwaukee State Fair Park	1969 July 25
USA	Milwaukee Arena	1970 August 31
USA	Milwaukee Arena	1973 July 10
USA	Minneapolis Guthrie Memorial Theatre	1969 May 18
USA	Minneapolis Met Centre	1970 April 12
USA	Minneapolis Met Centre	1975 January 18
USA	Minneapolis Met Centre	1977 April 12
USA	Mobile City Auditorium	1973 May 13
USA	Nashville	1970 April ??
USA	New Haven Yale	1970 August 15
USA	New Orleans Municipal Auditorium	1971 August 29
USA	New Orleans Municipal Auditorium	1973 May 14
USA	New York Atlantic Studios	1969 May 19-23
USA	New York Carnegie Hall	1969 October 17
USA	New York Central Park	1969 July 21
USA	New York Fillmore East	1969 January 31
USA	New York Fillmore East	1969 February 1
USA	New York The Scene	1969 February 3?
USA	New York The Scene	1969 February 4?
USA	New York The Scene	1969 February 5?
USA	New York The Scene	1969 February 6?
USA	New York Fillmore East	1969 May 30
USA	New York Fillmore East	1969 May 31
USA	New York Madison Square Gardens	1970 September 19
USA	New York Madison Square Gardens	1971 September 3
USA	New York Madison Square Gardens	1973 July 27
USA	New York Madison Square Gardens	1973 July 28
USA	New York Madison Square Gardens	1973 July 29
USA	New York Madison Square Gardens	1975 February 3
USA	New York Madison Square Gardens	1975 February 7
USA	New York Madison Square Gardens	1975 February 12
USA	New York Madison Square Gardens	1977 June 7
USA	New York Madison Square Gardens	1977 June 8
USA	New York Madison Square Gardens	1977 June 11
USA	New York Madison Square Gardens	1977 June 12
USA	New York Madison Square Gardens	1977 June 13
USA	New York Madison Square Gardens	1977 June 14
USA	New York Madison Square Gardens	1988 May 14
USA	New York Nassau Coliseum	1975 February 4
USA	New York Nassau Coliseum	1975 February 13
USA	New York Nassau Coliseum	1975 February 14
USA	New York Singer Bowl	1969 August 29
USA	New York Singer Bowl	1969 August 30
USA	New York Waldorf Astoria	1995 January 15
USA	Newport Jazz Festival	1969 July 6
USA	Oakland Coliseum	1970 September 2
USA	Oakland Coliseum	1977 July 23
USA	Oakland Coliseum	1977 July 24
USA	Oklahoma City Coliseum Fairgrounds	1970 August 20
USA	Oklahoma City	1971 August 27
USA	Oklahoma City Myriad	1977 April 3

USA	Orlando Civic Auditorium	1971 August 31
USA	Pasadena Rose Palace	1969 May 2
USA	Pasadena Rose Palace	1969 May 3
USA	Philadelphia Jazz Festival	1969 July 12
USA	Philadelphia Spectrum	1970 March 31
USA	Philadelphia Spectrum	1972 June 13
USA	Philadelphia Spectrum	1975 February 8
USA	Philadelphia JFK Stadium(Live Aid)	1985 July 13
USA	Phoenix Arizona Coliseum	1970 April 18
USA	Pittsburgh Civic Arena	1970 March 30
USA	Pittsburgh 3 Rivers Stadium	1973 July 24
USA	Pittsburgh Civic Arena	1975 February 1
USA	Pittsburgh Civic Arena	1975 February 2
USA	Pontiac Silverdome	1977 April 30
USA	Portland	1968 December 31
USA	Portland	1969 May ??
USA	Portland Memorial Coliseum	1970 March 23
USA	Portland Memorial Coliseum	1972 June 17
USA	ProvidenceRI Auditorium	1969 October 31
USA	Providence Civic Centre	1973 July 21
USA	Raleigh	1970 April 8
USA	Rochester	1970 April ??
USA	Rochester Memorial Auditorium	1971 September 11
USA	Sacramento Memorial Auditorium	1969 August 6
USA	Salt Lake City Lagoon	1969 July 30
USA	Salt Lake City Salt Palace	1970 March 26
USA	Salt Lake City Salt Palace	1973 May 26
USA	San Antonio Hemisphere Arena	1970 August 23
USA	San Antonio Municipal Auditorium	1971 August 26
USA	San Antonio Hemisphere Arena	1973 May 22
USA	San Bernadino Swing Auditorium	1972 June 22
USA	San Bernadino Swing Auditorium	1969 August 8
USA	San Diego Sports Arena	1969 August 10
USA	San Diego Sports Arena	1970 September 3
USA	San Diego Sports Arena	1972 June 23
USA	San Diego Sports Arena	1973 May 28
USA	San Diego Sports Arena	1975 March 10
USA	San Diego Sports Arena	1977 June 19
USA	San Francisco Fillmore West	1969 January 9
USA	San Francisco Fillmore West	1969 January 10
USA	San Francisco Fillmore West	1969 January 11
USA	San Francisco Fillmore West	1969 January 12
USA	San Francisco Fillmore West	1969 April 24
USA	San Francisco Fillmore West	1969 April 27
USA	San Francisco Fillmore West ?	1969 August 11
USA	San Francisco Winterland	1969 April 25
USA	San Francisco Winterland	1969 April 26
USA	San Francisco Winterland	1969 November 6
USA	San Francisco Winterland	1969 November 7
USA	San Francisco Winterland	1969 November 8
USA	San Francisco Kezar Stadium	1973 June 2
USA	Santa Barbara Fairgrounds	1969 August 1
USA	Santa Clara Fairgrounds	1969 May 23
USA	Seattle Center Arena	1968 December 27
USA	Seattle Green Lake Aquatheatre	1969 May 11
USA	Seattle Center Arena	1970 March 22

USA	Seattle Center Coliseum	1970 September 1
USA	Seattle Center Arena	1971 August 20
USA	Seattle Coliseum	1972 June 18
USA	Seattle Coliseum	1972 June 19
USA	Seattle Coliseum	1973 July 17
USA	Seattle Coliseum	1975 March 17
USA	Seattle Coliseum	1975 March 21
USA	Seattle Kingdome	1977 July 17
USA	Spokane Gonzaga University	1968 December 30
USA	St. Louis Kiel Auditorium	1970 April 11
USA	St. Louis Arena	1971 August 28
USA	St. Louis Kiel Auditorium	1973 May 11
USA	St. Louis Missouri Arena	1975 February 16
USA	St. Louis Missouri Arena	1977 April 15
USA	St. Paul Civic Centre	1973 July 9
USA	St. Paul Civic Centre	1977 April 13
USA	Syracuse Onadaga War Memorial	1969 November 1
USA	Syracuse Onadaga War Memorial	1971 September 10
USA	Tampa Curtis Hixon Hall	1970 April 9
USA	Tampa Stadium	1973 May 5
USA	Tampa Stadium	1977 June 3
USA	Tempe Activities Centre	1977 July 20
USA	Tucson Community Centre	1972 June 28
USA	Tulsa	1970 August 21
USA	Tuscaloosa University Of Alabama	1973 May 10
USA	Wallingford Oakdale Theatre	1969 August 17
USA	Washington Capitol Centre	1975 February 10
USA	Washington Largo Capitol Centre	1977 May 25
USA	Washington Largo Capitol Centre	1977 May 26
USA	Washington Largo Capitol Centre	1977 May 28
USA	Washington Largo Capitol Centre	1977 May 30
USA	Woodinville Goldcreek Park	1969 July 27
Wales	Aberystwyth King's Hall	1973 January 16
Wales	Bron-y-Aur Rehearsals	1970 May ??
Wales	Cardiff	1969 March 5
Wales	Cardiff Capitol	1972 December 11
Wales	Cardiff Capitol	1972 December 12

Appendix E

Bootleg Tapes

9/ 27th	1968	London Olympic Studio
10/ ??	1968	London Olympic Studio Sessions
12/ 30th	1968	Spokane Gonzaga University
1/ 9th	1969	San Francisco Fillmore West
1/ 10th	1969	San Francisco Fillmore West
1/ 11th	1969	San Francisco Fillmore West
1/ 12th	1969	San Francisco Fillmore West
1/ 23rd	1969	Boston Tea Party
1/ 26th	1969	Boston Tea Party
1/ 31st	1969	New York Fillmore East
2/ 1st	1969	New York Fillmore East
2/ 2nd	1969	Toronto Rockpile
2/ 14th	1969	Miami Thee Image Club
2/ 15th	1969	Miami Thee Image Club
3/ 3rd	1969	London Maida Vale BBC Studios
3/ 13th	1969	Brondby Pop Club Norregard Hallen
3/ 13th	1969	Gladsaxe TV-Byen
3/ 15th	1969	Gladsaxe Teen Clubs Box 45
3/ 16th	1969	Copenhagen Tivolis Koncertsal
3/ 19th	1969	London BBC Studio Session
3/ 25th	1969	Staines
4/ 24th	1969	San Francisco Fillmore West
4/ 25th	1969	San Francisco Winterland
4/ 26th	1969	San Francisco Winterland
4/ 27th	1969	San Francisco Fillmore West
5/ ??	1969	Mirror Sound Studio Sessions
5/ 25th	1969	Columbia Merriweather Post Pavilion
5/ 27th	1969	Boston Tea Party
5/ 30th	1969	New York Fillmore East
6/ ??	1969	London Morgan Studio Session
6/ 16th	1969	London Dave Symonds Show BBC
6/ 24th	1969	London John Peel's Top Gear BBC
6/ 25th	1969	Paris Tous En Scene TV
6/ 27th	1969	London BBC Playhouse Theatre
7/ 6th	1969	Newport Jazz Festival
7/ 20th	1969	Cleveland Musicarnival
7/ 21st	1969	New York Central Park
7/ 25th	1969	Milwaukee State Fair Park
8/ 8th	1969	San Bernadino Swing Auditorium
8/ 17th	1969	Wallingford Oakdale Theatre
8/ 18th	1969	Toronto Rockpile
8/ 31st	1969	Dallas Pop Festival
10/ 12th	1969	London Lyceum Ballroom
10/ 30th	1969	Buffalo Kleinhan's Music Hall
11/ 2nd	1969	Toronto O'Keefe Centre
11/ 5th	1969	Kansas City
11/ 6th	1969	San Francisco Winterland
11/ 7th	1969	San Francisco Winterland
11/ ??	1969	London Olympic Studio Session
1/ 8th	1970	Bristol Colston Hall
1/ 9th	1970	London Royal Albert Hall
2/ 24th	1970	Helsinki
2/ 28th	1970	Copenhagen K.B.Hallen
3/ 7th	1970	Montreux Casino
3/ 9th	1970	Vienna Konserthaus
3/ 11th	1970	Dusseldorf
3/ 12th	1970	Hamburg Musikhalle
3/ 21st	1970	Vancouver Pacific Coliseum
3/ 25th	1970	Denver Coliseum
3/ 27th	1970	Los Angeles Forum
3/ 28th	1970	Dallas Memorial Auditorium
3/ 29th	1970	Houston Hofheinz Pavilion
4/ 5th	1970	Baltimore Civic Center
4/ 8th	1970	Raleigh
4/ 9th	1970	Tampa Curtis Hixon Hall
4/ 14th	1970	Ottawa Civic Centre
4/ 17th	1970	Memphis

4/ 26th	1970	London Julie Felix TV Appearance
5/ ??	1970	Bron-y-Aur Rehearsals
5/ ??	1970	Headley Grange Studio sessions
6/ 28th	1970	Bath Festival
7/ 19th	1970	Berlin Deutschlandhalle
8/ 15th	1970	New Haven Yale
8/ 17th	1970	Hampton Roads Coliseum
8/ 21st	1970	Tulsa
9/ 2nd	1970	Los Angeles Forum
9/ 3rd	1970	San Diego Sports Arena
9/ 4th	1970	Los Angeles Forum
9/ 6th	1970	Honolulu International Center
9/ 9th	1970	Boston Gardens
9/ 19th	1970	New York Madison Square Garden
1/ ??	1971	Headley Grange Studio Session
3/ 6th	1971	Dublin Boxing Stadium
4/ 1st	1971	London BBC Paris Theatre
5/ 3rd	1971	Copenhagen K.B.Hallen
7/ 5th	1971	Milan Vigorelli Stadium
8/ 21st	1971	Los Angeles Forum
8/ 22nd	1971	Los Angeles Forum
8/ 31st	1971	Orlando Civic Auditorium
9/ 3rd	1971	New York Madison Square Gardens
9/ 4th	1971	Toronto Maple Leaf Gardens
9/ 6th	1971	Boston Gardens
9/ 9th	1971	Hampton Roads Coliseum
9/ 11th	1971	Rochester Memorial Auditorium
9/ 13th	1971	Berkeley Community Theatre
9/ 14th	1971	Berkeley Community Theatre
9/ 23rd	1971	Tokyo Budokan Hall
9/ 24th	1971	Tokyo Budokan Hall
9/ 27th	1971	Hiroshima Shiei Taiikukan
9/ 28th	1971	Osaka Festival Hall
9/ 29th	1971	Osaka Festival Hall
11/ 20th	1971	Wembley Empire Pool
11/ 24th	1971	Manchester Free Trade Hall
12/ 2nd	1971	Bournemouth Starkers
2/ 19th	1972	Adelaide Memorial Drive
2/ 20th	1972	Melbourne Kooyong Tennis Courts
2/ 27th	1972	Sydney Showgrounds
2/ 29th	1972	Brisbane Festival Hall
3/ ??	1972	Bombay Session with Orchestra
5/ ??	1972	Stargroves Studio Session
5/ 27th	1972	Amsterdam R.A.I.
6/ 7th	1972	Montreal Forum
6/ 9th	1972	Charlotte Coliseum
6/ 11th	1972	Baltimore Civic Centre
6/ 14th	1972	Hempstead Nassau County Coliseum
6/ 15th	1972	Hempstead Nassau County Coliseum
6/ 17th	1972	Portland Memorial Coliseum
6/ 18th	1972	Seattle Coliseum
6/ 19th	1972	Seattle Coliseum
6/ 22nd	1972	San Bernadino Swing Auditorium
6/ 25th	1972	Los Angeles Forum
6/ 27th	1972	Long Beach Arena
10/ 2nd	1972	Tokyo Budokan Hall
10/ 3rd	1972	Tokyo Budokan Hall
10/ 4th	1972	Osaka Festival Hall
10/ 5th	1972	Nagoyashi Kokaido
10/ 9th	1972	Osaka Festival Hall
10/ 10th	1972	Kyoto Kaikan #1 Hall
11/ 30th	1972	Newcastle City Hall
12/ 1st	1972	Newcastle City Hall
12/ 4th	1972	Glasgow Green's Playhouse
12/ 8th	1972	Manchester Hardrock
12/ 12th	1972	Cardiff Capitol
12/ 22nd	1972	London Alexandra Palace

12/ 23rd	1972	London Alexandra Palace
1/ 2nd	1973	Sheffield City Hall
1/ 7th	1973	Oxford New Theatre
1/ 14th	1973	Liverpool Empire
1/ 15th	1973	Stoke Trentham Gardens
1/ 18th	1973	Bradford St George's Hall
1/ 20th	1973	Southampton University
1/ 25th	1973	Aberdeen Music Hall
1/ 27th	1973	Dundee Caird Hall
3/ 6th	1973	Stockholm Royal Tennis Arena
3/ 14th	1973	Nuremburg Messehalle
3/ 16th	1973	Vienna Concert House
3/ 17th	1973	Munich Olympiahalle
3/ 19th	1973	Berlin Deutschlandhalle
3/ 21st	1973	Hamburg Musichalle
3/ 22nd	1973	Essen Grughalle
3/ 24th	1973	Offenburg Orthenau Halle
3/ 26th	1973	Lyons
4/ 1st	1973	Paris Palais De Sports
4/ 2nd	1973	Paris Palais De Sports
5/ 5th	1973	Tampa Stadium
5/ 13th	1973	Mobile City Aud.
5/ 14th	1973	New Orleans Mun. Aud.
5/ 16th	1973	Houston Sam Houston Arena
5/ 18th	1973	Dallas Memorial Auditorium
5/ 19th	1973	Fort Worth Tarrant Con. Centre
5/ 31st	1973	Los Angeles Forum
6/ 2nd	1973	San Francisco Kezar Stadium
6/ 3rd	1973	Los Angeles Forum
7/ 6th	1973	Chicago Aud.
7/ 10th	1973	Milwaukee Arena
7/ 12th	1973	Detroit Cobo Hall
7/ 13th	1973	Detroit Cobo Hall
7/ 17th	1973	Seattle Coliseum
7/ 18th	1973	Vancouver PNEColiseum
7/ 21st	1973	Providence Civic Centre
7/ 23rd	1973	Baltimore Civic Centre
7/ 24th	1973	Pittsburgh 3 Rivers Stadium
7/ 25th	1973	Boston Gardens
7/ 27th	1973	New York M.S.G.
7/ 28th	1973	New York M.S.G.
7/ 29th	1973	New York M.S.G.
12/ ??	1973	Headley Grange Session
6/ ??	1974	Headley Grange Session
1/ 12th	1975	Brussels Forest Nationale
1/ 20th	1975	Chicago Stadium
1/ 21st	1975	Chicago Stadium
1/ 22nd	1975	Chicago Stadium
1/ 24th	1975	Cleveland Coliseum
1/ 25th	1975	Indianapolis Arena
1/ 29th	1975	Greensboro Coliseum
1/ 31st	1975	Detroit Olympia Stadium
2/ 3rd	1975	New York M.S.G.
2/ 4th	1975	New York Nassau Coliseum
2/ 6th	1975	Montreal Forum
2/ 7th	1975	New York M.S.G.
2/ 8th	1975	Philadelphia Spectrum
2/ 12th	1975	New York M.S.G.
2/ 13th	1975	New York Nassau Coliseum
2/ 14th	1975	New York Nassau Coliseum
2/ 28th	1975	Baton Rouge L.S.U.
3/ 4th	1975	Dallas Memorial Auditorium
3/ 5th	1975	Dallas Memorial Auditorium
3/ 10th	1975	San Diego Sports Arena
3/ 11th	1975	Long Beach Arena
3/ 12th	1975	Long Beach Arena
3/ 17th	1975	Seattle Coliseum

3/ 19th	1975	Vancouver Coliseum
3/ 20th	1975	Vancouver Coliseum
3/ 21st	1975	Seattle Coliseum
3/ 24th	1975	Los Angeles Forum
3/ 25th	1975	Los Angeles Forum
3/ 27th	1975	Los Angeles Forum
5/ 17th	1975	London Earl's Court
5/ 18th	1975	London Earl's Court
5/ 23rd	1975	London Earl's Court
5/ 24th	1975	London Earl's Court
5/ 25th	1975	London Earl's Court
4/ 3rd	1977	Oklahoma City Myriad
4/ 6th	1977	Chicago Stadium
4/ 7th	1977	Chicago Stadium
4/ 9th	1977	Chicago Stadium
4/ 10th	1977	Chicago Stadium
4/ 19th	1977	Cincinatti Riverfront Coliseum
4/ 27th	1977	Cleveland Richfield Coliseum
4/ 28th	1977	Cleveland Richfield Coliseum
4/ 30th	1977	Pontiac Silverdome
5/ 18th	1977	Birmingham Coliseum
5/ 22nd	1977	Fort Worth Convention Centre
5/ 25th	1977	Washington Largo Capitol Centre
5/ 26th	1977	Washington Largo Capitol Centre
5/ 28th	1977	Washington Largo Capitol Centre
5/ 30th	1977	Washington Largo Capitol Centre
6/ 3rd	1977	Tampa Stadium
6/ 7th	1977	New York Madison Square Gardens
6/ 8th	1977	New York Madison Square Gardens
6/ 11th	1977	New York Madison Square Gardens
6/ 12th	1977	New York Madison Square Gardens
6/ 13th	1977	New York Madison Square Gardens
6/ 14th	1977	New York Madison Square Gardens
6/ 19th	1977	San Diego Sports Arena
6/ 21st	1977	Los Angeles Forum
6/ 22nd	1977	Los Angeles Forum
6/ 23rd	1977	Los Angeles Forum
6/ 25th	1977	Los Angeles Forum
6/ 26th	1977	Los Angeles Forum
6/ 27th	1977	Los Angeles Forum
7/ 17th	1977	Seattle Kingdome
7/ 20th	1977	Tempe Activities Centre
7/ 23rd	1977	Oakland Coliseum
7/ 24th	1977	Oakland Coliseum
5/ ??	1978	Clearwell Castle Rehearsals
11/ ??	1977	Stockholm Polar Studio Session
12/ ??	1978	Stockholm Polar Studio Session
7/ 23rd	1979	Copenhagen Falkoner Theatre
7/ 24th	1979	Copenhagen Falkoner Theatre
8/ 4th	1979	Knebworth
8/ 11th	1979	Knebworth
6/ 17th	1980	Dortmund Westfalenhalle
6/ 18th	1980	Cologne Sportshalle
6/ 20th	1980	Brussels Forest National
6/ 21st	1980	Rotterdam Ahoy
6/ 23rd	1980	Bremen Stadthalle
6/ 24th	1980	Hannover Messehalle
6/ 26th	1980	Vienna Stadthalle
6/ 27th	1980	Nuremburg Messezentrum Halle
6/ 29th	1980	Zurich Hallenstadion
6/ 30th	1980	Frankfurt Festhalle
7/ 2nd	1980	Mannheim Eisstadium
7/ 3rd	1980	Mannheim Eisstadium
7/ 5th	1980	Munich Olympichalle
7/ 7th	1980	Berlin Eissporthalle
9/ 24th	1980	Windsor Rehearsal
7/ 13th	1985	Philadelphia JFK Stadium
5/ 14th	1988	New York Madison Square Garden
5/ 12th	1990	Bewdley Heath Hotel
1/ 15th	1995	New York Waldorf Astoria

Appendix F

Concert Itinerary
Updates & Corrections

Completing the Led Zeppelin concert dates itinerary has been a favourite pastime of mine for years. For such an enormously popular band it is amazing that their performances were so badly documented. Since the CD ROM edition of my Collector's Guide in December 1995 quite a few new dates have surfaced due to the enthusiasm of the band's fans around the world and their ability to now communicate with one another efficiently through the Internet.

It is always gratifying to have my speculations confirmed with hard proof from around the world. Naturally I am in debt to those same people and also to a list of other publications and their authors. Hugh Jones magazine 'Proximity' is a well produced source of hard-core info. Hugh somehow continues to turn up an abundance of rarities and I never cease to be amazed by his findings. Dave Lewis and Simon Pallett in the UK have recently co-authored a superb volume published by Omnibus Press called 'The Concert File' which I am tempted to say may almost put the final nail in this particular coffin due to it's comprehensive content. It is thanks to Dave and his Tight But Loose magazine that many pieces of the band's history are available to their fans.

Anyway with a tip of the hat to Dave, Simon, Hugh, Rick Barrett, Bob Walker at Hot Wacks and to all those others who I have forgotten, here are the shows which are either new or corrected since my CD ROM, especially included for those who didn't buy Dave's book - both of you!

September 7th, 1968 Gladsaxe Teen Clubs
September 7th, 1968 Brondby Pop Club
September 8th, 1968 Nykøbing Raventlow Park Falster Island
September 8th, 1968 Roskilde Fjordvilla
September 12th, 1968 Gronalund Tivoli Stockholm
September 13th, 1968 Inside Club Stockholm
September 15th, 1968 Liseburg Amusement Park Göteborg
Oddly, after languishing in the history books for nearly thirty years these dates from the first tour were confirmed by at least two different Scandinavian fans almost simultaneously and independently. Complete with adverts and reviews. What happened on 9th - 11th? Could this have been the elusive trip to Norway?

October 26th, 1968 Bristol Boxing Club
An anecdote, taken from a book, quotes Russell Hunter of The Deviants and relates how both the Deviants and Zeppelin were subjected to an assault by the audience, with everything not bolted down being thrown at them. This incident is also mentioned by Page in an interview in Melody Maker (March 22 1969). However Mick Farren insists that this took place at Exeter Town Hall. He comments, "We opened for Zep at a few gigs in the West Country. This was before their first album was out. I remember clearly that the incident took place in Exeter at the town hall. There was no *city* hall. The audience had thrown glasses at us and when we went back to the dressing room Planty and Page were having a real good laugh at us, they said 'You must have been awful.' We just said 'Yeah, you wait.' Anyway they went out and didn't get through one number before the barrage came.

'Afterwards I talked with Planty at the Speakeasy in London. It was a bar we used to hang out at. We were talking about how difficult he was finding it to keep hitting those high notes every night. His voice was taking quite a beating. They were shooting in and out of the studio between one-nighters trying to finish their album. I said I gargled with some stuff the dentist gave me, and that helped. He thought that was a good idea. The night we opened for them at the Marquee I didn't hang around to see them but left after John Lee Hooker finished his set. That first tour that you are referring to wasn't really a tour just a bunch of one-nighters. We shot back and forward from London. I don't think we did any gig in Bath with them.

'You got to remember we knew Planty from doing a bunch of shows with him and his band around Birmingham and the Midlands. We didn't really know Page that much because he hadn't really done that underground club thing. In those days the venues were like Bingo on Thursday, Boxing on Friday and bands on Saturday, so sometimes we would be setting up in the boxing ring but it wasn't a boxing club, you know?'

Mick is now a noted author and journalist. He has written award winning screen plays and a number of books including 'The Hitchhiker's Guide To Elvis', he was also a contributing editor at International Times in the 60's.

February 3rd - 6th, 1969 The Scene, New York
Finally I managed to uncover where they were supposed to be for this four day period. Apparently, according to NME, Bonham had to rush back to England when his son Jason was injured. Due to this the band may have cancelled all four nights at Steve Paul's Scene Club in Manhattan. However in an interview with Robert Plant in Circus in January 1976 he mentions hanging out at this venue. Very little notice was given which probably explains why they never played there again.

February ?, 1969 Memphis
Although I discovered an interview with Page where he mentions this show there still seems to be no documentation. However more evidence has come to light. In an interview in Rock magazine in October 1970 Page talks about his failed efforts to get Zeppelin into Sun studios in Memphis to record, during their *first* tour of America.

March 1st, 1969 Plymouth Van Dyke
For some reason I omitted the venue for this gig in Plymouth, the Van Dyke club.

March, 1969 Scandinavia
This tour has been subjected to much revisal over the years. The latest press clippings to surface suggest that the band may have played the following schedule.
March 13th, 1969 Brondby Pop Club Norregard Hallen
March 13th, 1969 Gladsaxe TV-Byen
March 14th, 1969 Stockholm Concerthouse
March 14th, 1969 Uppsala University Lecture Hall
March 15th, 1969 Gladsaxe Teen Clubs Box 45
March 16th, 1969 Copenhagen Tivolis Koncertsal
One article from Stockholm says that they left some equipment at a TV studio that day. Some have interpreted that to mean that they did the TV broadcast on the 14th in Copenhagen and then went on to do Stockholm in the early evening followed by Uppsala that night. Recent evidence has just surfaced that suggests the band did TWO sets at the Copenhagen TV studio. This begins to stretch common sense. It seems highly unlikely that the band would do FOUR shows in one day especially as they are located 650 km apart. It is possible, but I think the article may be interpreted to mean that they flew out to Stockholm on the morning of the 14th and thereby left their equipment behind 'that day'. One thing is certain the only Swedish dates were both on the 14th, however an interview with Plant at the end of March says that the band were nearly killed in an air

accident flying in from BREMEN in Germany. The only reason I can think that they would choose to return home from Bremen would be that they may have played a concert there. Could this have been whence the mysterious 'Beat Club' footage came from? Also — Hamburg is en route from Copenhagen to Bremen.

March 31st, 1969 London Cooks Ferry Inn
An error in calculation put this gig on the 24th but it was advertised in Melody Maker March 29th as coming up the following week.

May ??, 1969 Los Angeles Thee Experience Club
An article in Cashbox says the band played a charity benefit. Page however says that only he performed, jamming with the Mike Pinero band.

May 13th, 1969 Honolulu Civic Auditorium
Adverts and reviews of this show finally confirm the venue and the date.

May 23rd, 1969 Santa Clara Pop Festival
With the benefit of an anecdote unearthed by Dave Lewis it would seem that this show did take place. Apparently the band were provided with a private jet to get from California back to the Chicago venue that night.

June 25th, 1969 Paris Tous En Scene TV broadcast
Dave Lewis has this date as June 19th. Any actual documentation to confirm this show's date would be nice to see. Over to you Dave...

July 20th, 1969 Cleveland Musicarnival
As I had previously speculated this show was not the 16th due to the story circulating about the band cutting the set down to five songs so people could watch Neil Armstrong's moon walk. Reviews and adverts have since shown up.

July 30th, 1969 Salt Lake City Lagoon
This one is something of a surprise. It throws off the common perception that the band played Oregon. This is clearly plugged in Billboard just four days before the show. Zep share the bill with Vanilla Fudge. This may also throw out the Eugene Oregon date?

August 4th, 1969 Dallas State Fair Festival
A significant amount of documentation has turned up over the years, however Dave Lewis has reported that this show didn't happen.

August 1969 San Antonio Texas
As has been recently pointed out Plant mentions at the Toronto concert on the 18th that the band have just returned from San Antonio. There is a window in the itinerary from the 11th to the 15th when they may have played there.

August 1969. Woodstock weekend.
Two new articles finally explain why the band didn't play the legendary festival. Apparently they were originally approached to appear but decided not to because the contract required that they not play anywhere else in the area. They had several dates booked and those dates paid considerably more money and thus they refused to cancel

them. An interview with an agent from Premier says that they had five shows in the area around that weekend. This suggests there are a few still missing from the itinerary.

August 21st, 1969 Framingham-Natick MA. Carousel Theatre
This one popped up out of nowhere, complete with a review which mentions the first ever public performance of What Is & What Should Never Be.

August 29th, 1969 New York Singer Bowl
A new advert and a Billboard report say they played two nights at the Pavilion. The only other previous proof was an ad which only listed Saturday shows but they also played the Friday.

October, 1969 Holland
In an article on October 18th Record Mirror reports that the band have just returned from a successful tour of Holland. This tour would have coincided with postponed dates in Scandinavia, but there is nothing to suggest that they didn't play Holland.

October 26th, 1969 Charlotte
Two articles in Billboard cover this tour, both in the same issue but they contain some inconsistencies. One article doesn't mention this date, the other does.

February 25th, 1970 Göteborg Concerthouse
The name of the venue is finally confirmed.

March 10th, 1970 Frankfurt
According to an article in NME on February 28th the band's upcoming show in Frankfurt was canceled due to riots the previous week at a Jethro Tull concert. Some have suggested this was shifted to an additional Hamburg date. Disc confirmed in it's March 7th issue that the band added a show in Hamburg 'because of the lines'.

March - April 1970, American tour.
In an article in the Memphis newspaper it says that by the time the band reached Montreal, on this tour, they had played seventeen straight concerts in as many nights. A later article says they played 26 shows. Neither number seems to match the facts as there is now good evidence for more shows than that and there are still unconfirmed dates in Indianapolis, Dayton, Rochester and Nashville.

April, 1970 Boston
In an interview with Jimmy Page with Disc he talks about problems in Boston. He may have been talking about the show the previous October but it is still possible that a Boston date from this Spring tour is eluding the sleuths.

March 25th, 1970 Denver Coliseum
A review of this show in Proximity finally nails this date and venue.

April 2nd, 1970 Charleston West Virginia
A new listing filling out this tour.

April ?, 1970 Indianapolis
This show is mentioned in an article in Billboard but there seems to be no other press locally. However in an interview in Beat in October 1970 Bonham mentions almost getting into a brawl in Indianapolis. Anyone?

April ?, 1970 Nashville
An article in Billboard mentions this show but with no specific date. Page talks about buying a guitar while in Nashville in an interview years later. In a conversation in June 1997 Page says he recalled playing Nashville, 'Right after Memphis'. He said he remembered it well because all through the south they had encountered problems. He says the group had experienced difficulties in Memphis and were looking forward to Nashville only to find that they were threatened again by some thug with an iron bar. This would seem to put Nashville around the 20th April, after what is generally considered to be the final date on the tour, Phoenix, where Plant collapsed of exhaustion.

April 7th, 1970 Charlotte Independence Coliseum
An article for this show appeared in Billboard. After confirming the date, and consequently throwing off Raleigh (presumably to the 8th) I found a review which mentions that the band played a new song called 'When Will Be The Next Time'.

April 12th, 1970 Minneapolis St. Paul
Handbill for another new show courtesy of Merit Adventures.

April 15th, 1970 Toronto
Ritchie Yorke interviewed all four members of the band in Toronto for the NME in England. I am taking a guess that this was probably the day that the interviews took place as there was certainly at least one night while they were in Toronto for Bonham to take a trip to the Penny Farthing night club. This would seem to be the only date when this would make any sense.

April 16th, 1970 Evansville Indiana Roberts Stadium
I had just found this one in Billboard when it appeared and was reviewed in detail in Proximity magazine, an entirely unknown show complete with ticket stub and amazed punter.

April 26th, 1970 Julie Felix TV Show
Dave Lewis has this show on the 26th but the only evidence I have managed to find is an article in DISC putting the show on April 12th. Dave however is rarely wrong and it is almost impossible to be in Minneapolis and London the same day.

May 19th, 1970 Olympic Studios
In an article from Record Mirror it says that the band will begin recording the third album on this date. In an interview published June 6th by Melody Maker Bonham mentions that the band will be recording for the next two weeks.

June 22nd, 1970 Reykjavik Laugardalsholl Sports Center
The name of the venue is confirmed.

August - September, 1970 American Tour
This tour was to have begun on August 5th and parts of it still remain a mystery. If the rumours were correct I knew Cleveland almost certainly had to be in August. The anecdote was that the band had to perform a part of the show acoustically because John Paul Jones had to leave for a flight to England due to his father's death. This story finally led me to the correct date. The review of the Detroit Olympia show on my CD ROM spurred me to continue looking and thanks to the various pieces falling into place during the course of putting this book together I finally found that one also.

The original itinerary was to have included a show in Cincinnati on August 6th. A later press article (dated Aug 8th) said that the tour was to be four weeks long and that it will begin on August 14th. A follow up article (dated Aug 15th) has the band flying out on the Sunday (16th) to begin the tour in Hampton Beach Virginia (17th). Other dates canceled and rescheduled include Boston (from Aug 8th to Sept 9th) and Milwaukee (from Aug 27th to 31st), Quebec (not re-scheduled) and New Orleans, Atlanta and Albuquerque (all of which are still a mystery). The band were slated to take an eleven day holiday after the Hawaiian dates before concluding in New York on the 19th. Instead they played the Boston date and then went back to England to accept some awards before concluding in New York.

August 15th, 1970 New Haven Yale
This date was exhumed by a Proximity reader complete with handbill and ads. This suggests that this was the first show of the tour. All the fuss about the band turning down Yale to do Bath was obviously just a publicity ploy for the benefit of the British public.

August 26th, 1970 Cleveland Public Hall
Finally the details reveal that the show was rescheduled the day before from an 8.30 show to a 5.30 show so Jones could return to England. As the band cancelled the following day's scheduled show in Milwaukee it is safe to assume this was a day off.

August 28th, 1970 Detroit Olympia
This show seems to have survived with it's original scheduling intact and was the first show played after Jones returned from England.

September 2nd, 1970 Oakland Coliseum
Somehow this one got screwed up on the CDROM. It was a typo. We had a few!

Spring 1971 European Tour
An article from the time says that the band will play dates in Holland in early 1971.

March 20th, 1971 Sutton Coldfield Belfry
This date is a bit of a mystery. It seems to have happened the very night that conventional wisdom puts them at Birmingham Mothers. Sutton Coldfield's Belfry was a favoured venue for the lads in the Birmingham area and may well have been played on their first tour of the UK. Either way, the reviews of this show confirm that they definitely were not at Mothers that Saturday night.

November 12th, 1971 Sunderland Locarno
Dave Lewis has produced an anecdote which suggests this show was switched to the Mecca Ballroom in Newcastle at the last minute.

December 9th, 1971 Coventry Locarno
Another new date although one person who attended this show swears it was at the neighbouring Lanchester Polytechnic. Anyone?

December 15th 1971 Salisbury
An article in Disc dated November 20th says the band have added this show but there is no other supporting evidence yet.

1971 American Tour
An article from August says the band will play eighteen concerts beginning on August 19th. By the end of September NME was reporting that the tour would include twenty shows. As the confirmed itinerary already includes more shows than that, the remaining five open dates may yet yield a few surprises.

May 27th, 1972 Oude Rai Amsterdam
Documentation for this show finally gives the name of the venue.

1972 American Tour.
In an interview in 1973 Page says the band played 19 shows in 22 nights in 1972. The itinerary which appeared in my Collector's Guide only showed 15 shows. A further show in Philadelphia showed up bringing the known list to 16. There is a possible three more shows not listed.

March 6th - 7th, 1973 Stockholm Royal Tennis Arena
The name of the venue is finally confirmed.

March 4th, 1973 Göteborg Scandinavium Arena
The name of the venue is finally confirmed.

July 19th 1973 Philadelphia Spectrum
I don't know how this show crept into the itinerary on my CD-ROM collector's guide but there doesn't seem to be any evidence that this one ever happened.

Warm up dates Europe 1975
An article from December 1974 suggests that the band had planned five shows in and around Europe before leaving for the USA. This is almost certainly wrong.

Late Additions

September 1968
4 **Glostrup Handelsbladet reports....** Article covering the band's first ever concert - Now the Brondby-pop starts and the club has booked to this year's opening, among others, the Yardbirds,which consists of Jimmy Page, John Paul Jones, Robert Planto (sic) and John Bonham. As usual the clubowners has booked the best names and bands to entertain. This time they have fail-safely booked the Yardbirds,and even a whole new Yardbirds.The band that is led by Jimmy Page has again reformed. This time more dramatically having three new members. These will be warm-up shows.The band has decided to first play Scandinavia and then play to the picky English audiences. The style is still the same. The Day of Phoenix and a band named "Ham" will also play....
6 **Copenhagen Politiken reports....** Opening for new Yardbirds - Yardbirds with new line-up is this years first special presentation at the Brondby pop-clubs for members. It starts Saturday.The same evening the city celebrates one year-birthday with different festivities. Among others performing are The Eye; with a film show, and the band Day of Phonix which today are considered Denmark's top band. After several successes and after a sensational break-through in America the Yardbirds broke up in July. The band's lead-guitarist Jimmy Page immediately got new members together, and the band continues under the same name. As vocalist, he has chosen the hereto unknown Robert Planto (sic), on drums John Bonham who among others has backed Tim Rose in England, and John Paul Jones as bass-player and organist. Jones has never played in a band before, but being a very well acknowledged and used studio-musician, he has played on Donovan's last LPs and has, among other things, arranged three songs on the Stones not yet released LP and several of Lulu's songs. Other than Brondby pop club, the Yardbirds plays Gladsaxe Teen Club on Saturday. Sunday, the band can be heard in Fjordvilla,Roskilde.....

February 1969
1 **Cashbox reports....** The band pay a visit to Cashbox offices for an interview. The article says that they rehearsed for only six hours before playing their first concert. Someone in the band is quoted about America, *"Everybody here goes wild over drum solos. They can't tell and don't seem to care if it's good or bad as long as it's loud. Solos are nice if someone knows what they're doing."* It goes on to say that reaction to the band on the West Coast has been phenomenal....
8 **Cashbox reports....** "Led Zeppelin to play The Scene New York February 3rd - 6th If the Fillmore is any indication the place should be overflowing."...
15 **Cashbox reports....** Led Zeppelin I is reviewed.
22 **Cashbox reports....** The band's performance at the Fillmore East is reviewed. The reviewer states, "The Led Zeppeplin album is very very good, the group in-person is even better." A further article outlines the details of Led Zeppelin signing with Premier Talent Agency 'covering all fields of the entertainment industry in the United States and Canada.' The deal was negotiated between Peter Grant and Frank Barsalona of Premier....

March 1969
1 **Cashbox reports....** Biography of the band....
22 **Cashbox reports....** The band's second American tour is announced as starting at the

Fillmore West....Good Times Bad Times is reviewed as a 'Newcomer Pick'. 'A blistering single debut.'...
29 **Cashbox reports....** Full page advert reads — The Heavy Hits Are On Atlantic-Atco. Led Zeppelin Good Times Bad Times b/w Communication Breakdown. Atlantic #2613 Produced by Jimmy Page From the Hit Album Led Zeppelin Atlantic SD 8216....(this advert ran again on April 12th)....

May 1969
17 **Cashbox reports....** Review of the band's show at the Rose Palace in Pasadena. The reviewer says that they are, "Instrumentally super tight, led by blazing rock bottom guitar by Jimmy Page. The group's biggest improvement being the dynamic awakening of Robert Plant..."...Article states that the band will be playing on July 12th at the Philadelphia Pop Festival at the Spectrum and at the Laurel Race Course in Laurel Maryland between Baltimore and Washington on July 11th.....
24 **Cashbox reports....** Article outlines how T.I.M.E. drummer Richard Tepp was gunned down in Hollywood and how Eric Burdon, Led Zeppelin and the Mothers Of Invention played a charity concert at Thee Experience in Los Angeles to help cover his hospital bills....

June 1969
14 **Cashbox reports....** Article with picture shows Jimmy Page and sundry industry types at the band's gold record presentation at the Plaza 9 room of the Plaza Hotel in New York on the 26th May....review of the band's return to the Fillmore East. The reviewer concludes that 'Led Zeppelin is real, and their show last week showed them to be better than we had remembered.'...
19 **Cashbox reports....** Article reviewing the string of events that took place at the Newport Jazz festival. Only 12,000 people stayed to see the band after promoter George Wein announced they wouldn't be appearing. The reviewer concludes that "It was 2.00am when we all left and as I walked to the parking lot all I could think was Jimmy Page, Robert Plant, John Paul Jones and John Bonham: you're beautiful."...

August 1969
9 **Cashbox reports....** Review of the band's performance at the Wollman Rink in Central Park New York. "The band practically brought the house down; no kidding. By the end of a four encore musical colossus the beam and erector set framework of the temporary stage were creaking under the strain as performers and audience alike were swept into a rock 'n roll bacchanalia that would have made the most cynical critic wilt."....

October 1969
18 **Cashbox reports....** Article details the band's fourth American tour under the banner "Third Tour Set For Led Zeppelin". It says both Carnegie Hall shows are sold out and that Led Zeppelin II will be released on October 15th to a half million advance orders. The rest of the tour dates are listed as Detroit (18), Chicago (19), Cleveland (24), Boston (25), Buffalo (30), Rhode Island (31), Syracuse (Nov 1), Toronto (2), Kitchener (4), and Kansas City (5)....

February 1970
27 **Sweden's Daily News reports....** Working Victory For Zeppelin. Article about the band's receiving gold records in Sweden and a review of the show at the Stockholm

Concerthouse. Henrik Salander reports, "...the audience thumped on the stage and the rows full of disco-dressed girls looked like the devil had got hold of them. There is no longer any doubt that Led Zeppelin is an extremely professional band with a vibe of their own. Page at his best last night, performed sheer magic. His guitar is like a third arm. John Bonham's solo was actually a musical experience." In the same article is a picture showing the band receiving gold records. A further addition notes th at the band were interviewed by Johan Zachrisson of TV1 for a fifteen minute program to be aired later....

March 1973
7 **Sweden's Daily News reports....** Led Zeppelin a disappointment. Review of the show at the Stockholm Tennis Arena by Christer Lundblad. He points out that the show wasn't sold out and that the band survives purely on Bonham and Page's skills. He says that the band's sound was total chaos and 'an inferno of tones' but does concede that Stairway To Heaven sounded good and that Whole Lotta Love was the best song. He concludes that Deep Purple rate higher on his scale but 'to be fair Led Zeppelin usually sounds better.'

Interview Disc

The disc enclosed represents a segment of an interview conducted in 1977 by journalist Dave Schulps while he was writing for Trouser Press Magazine. It is generally conceded that this is one of the most important interviews ever conducted with Jimmy Page about his career. The full content of the interview was omitted from this book because I knew that it has been reprinted many times before, most recently in Charles Cross and Erik Flannigan's excellent book 'Led Zeppelin - Heaven and Hell' (Random House).

Schulps opportunity to spend several hours with Page produced nearly seven hours of tape and it was extremely difficult to pick only an hour for inclusion.

I made the decision to include a segment of this interview on disc because I felt that it represented that rare moment of insight when someone was actually sitting there asking many of the same questions we all might want to ask. Thanks go to Dave, not only for allowing the inclusion of his tape but for being the right guy in the right place at the right time with the right questions.

English 'underground' group currently making a lot of international noise is Led Zeppelin. Four talented musicians in their own right Jimmy Page (guitar); John Paul Jones (bass/organ); John Bonham (drums) and Robert Plant (vocal) joined forces five months ago and made an immediate impact. They toured America earlier this year where their album "Led Zeppelin" is issued on Atlantic. They are now on their second Stateside tour playing San Francisco, Los Angeles, Seattle, Vancouver, Portland, Detroit, Minneapolis and Baltimore culminating in a concert at New York's Fillmore East May 29/31.

Second Edition Updates.

The last edition of this book concentrated on the years 1968 to 1980. During the course of the research I also turned up quite a bit of information about the band from the years preceding and several readers had asked for some details from those early years — so here it is.

1963

January 25. New Musical Express reports... Jet Harris and Tony Meehan top the charts with their single Diamonds. This single is generally recognized as one of Jimmy Page's earliest sessions.

October 25. New Musical Express reports... Advert for Carter Lewis and the Southerners, "Your Momma's Out of Town" on Oriole Records.

November 1, New Musical Express reports... The front cover advert reads "Congratulations! Carter Lewis and the Southerners, straight into the charts at No. 22 with your great recording of Your Momma's Out of Town on Oriole CB 1868."... an article about Carter Lewis briefly mentions the lineup in the band and reads, "The rest of the lineup consists of 19 year old Jimmy Page (lead guitar and harmonica) who comes from Epsom and is a great R & B fan, and drummer Vic Prince. Jimmy's hobby is sculpture, while Vic's is staying in good class hotels."

1964

May 16. Record Mirror reports... A half page color advert of Mickey Finn and the Bluemen for their single "Pills". The picture shows a very young Jimmy Page.

May 23. Record Mirror Reports...half-page advert which reads, "Don't Forget! Mickey Finn's party. Write today for your free invitation. To Mickey Finn, c/o 72 Wardour Street, London W. 1. Or phone Mickey Finn any Wednesday between 7 and 10 p.m. (Pills-Oriole CB 1927)"

May 30. Record Mirror Reports...half-page advert which reads, "Keep Looking Mickey Finn, c/o Don White agency limited. 72,Wardour street London W. 1. Don't say marvelous say Mickey Finn." Advert also features a photograph of the band with Jimmy Page...advert reads "The Gateway to the Stars the Cellar Club. 22 a High Street Kingston 5856, Sunday, May 31st Mickey Finn and the Bluemen. Monday, June 1st the Yardbirds are back." — By July 4th of that year adverts for the band do not show Page. During that same week this same club had Beck's group the Tridents, Yardbirds with Clapton, Mickey Finn with Page and John Lee Hooker with John Mayall's Bluesbreakers!

1965

February 20. Record Mirror reports... review of Jimmy Page's solo single, "One of the finest guitarists in the business is now in the personal spotlight. Furious beat with vocal touches almost vanishing in a welter of amplified backing. Right for dancing, right for listening, just right."...quarter-page advert reads, "Jimmy Page is the greatest guitarist in Europe. He is the greatest harmonica player in Europe. Jimmy Page is a phenomenon. At 19 he has already played guitar as a session musician for the Kinks, Cliff Richard, Dave Berry, P. J. Proby, Brenda Lee, and Jackie de Shannon. It was at one of her recording sessions that Jimmy first met Jackie de Shannon and she has constantly encouraged and helped his career so far. Jackie persuaded him to make his own record after hearing him doodling with his guitar in a studio. She has written songs with him too. No stranger to the recording studio, Jimmy Page recently went in to make his first disc himself. The result is..."She Just Satisfies" Fontana TF 533."

February 26. New Musical Express reports... Jimmy Page's solo single "She Just Satisfies" is reviewed, this presumably pinpoints the date when the single was released.

March 5. New Musical Express reports... Life lines of the Ivy League. In their weekly series "Life lines", NME looks at the band the Ivy League. As some may already know Jimmy Page recorded with the Ivy League and this article perhaps explains why. The Ivy League consists of John Carter, Ken Lewis, and Perry Ford, previously known as Carter Lewis and the Southerners, a band which featured Jimmy Page briefly. Carter Lewis became an enormously successful songwriting team. Ken Lewis lists Jimmy Page as one of his favorite instrumentalists.

March 6. Record Mirror Reports... Yardbird leaves group. Eric Clapton played his last date as lead guitarist with Yardbirds last night. After a gig at Bristol Corn Exchange, he left the group. Eric's place in Yardbirds is

---

The Gateway,
to the Stars
THE CELLAR
CLUB
22a High Street, Kingston
KINgston 5856

Wednesday, May 27th
R & B with the TRIDENTS
Friday, May 29th
STORMVILLE SHAKERS
Saturday, May 30th
THE KARNELLS
Sunday, May 31st
MICKEY FINN
and the Bluemen
Monday, June 1st
THE YARDBIRDS
ARE BACK
Wednesday, June 3rd
JOHN LEE HOOKER
backed by
JOHN MAYALL
and the Bluesbreakers
plus the exciting PLEBS
Ticket in advance at the door

taken by Jeff Beck of the Tridents. Jeff is also a session man and has worked often with Jimmy Paige (sic).

1966

June 10. New Musical Express Reports...Yardbirds Paris trip. Article mentions that the Yardbirds leave for Paris on June 26 for television and Club appearances. It then goes on to mention several other dates including Page's first with the group at the London Marquee on June 21st followed by a performance at Durham University on the 24th and the Bury Palais on the 25th.

June 11. Record Mirror reports... In an interview Jeff Beck mentions that he has been experimenting with Jimmy Page's sitar.

June 18. Melody Maker reports...advert reads, "Marquee 90 Wardour Street London W. 1. Tuesday June 21st (7.30-11.00) The Yardbirds and the Clayton Squares." This was Jimmy Page's first concert with Yardbirds.

June 24. New Musical Express reports... Samwell-Smith quits Yardbirds. The article goes on to mention that he is replaced by session guitarist Jimmy Page. It also mentions that Page's first appearance with the group was the previous Tuesday at London's Marquee Club, (that makes Page's first date as June 21st 1966.)

June 25. Disc Reports...Paul Samwell-Smith quits Yardbirds! Jimmy Page signed....Paul Samwell-Smith has quit the Yardbirds! He announced his decision on Monday, and is to concentrate on full-time recording activities. Replacement for 23 year old Paul is 20 year old top session guitarist Jimmy Page, who began playing bass with the group this week. Page is an old friend of the Yardbirds, when Eric Clapton left it was he who recommended Jeff Beck as replacement....**Record Mirror Reports**...PaulSamwell-Smith leaves Yardbirds. He is replaced by guitarist Jimmy Paige (sic) who will play bass with the group. Paul left the group on Monday, to concentrate on songwriting and record production. In fact Sam will continue to co-produce the Yardbird's records with their manager Simon Napier Bell. Their current single Over Under Sideways Down was produced by Sam and Simon although all of their previous singles were produced by their former manager Giorgio Gomelsky. His replacement, Jimmy Paige (sic) is one of the most talented and in demand session guitarists in the country.

July 2. Record Mirror reports... Full-color cover with group shot of the Yardbirds including Page....**Disc Reports**...New Yardbird in the Nest. Article about Page joining the Yardbirds....New Yardbird Jimmy Page is the original Mr. Tall dark and handsome. He is 20, has sleepy eyes, long curly dark hair and elegant sideburns more befitting an actor in a Victorian melodrama. He's also reckoned to be one of the best guitarists in the business. But his sudden appearance in Bird brain Paul Samwell-Smith's shoes is a big surprise. Why, stars and session men alike are asking themselves, should Jimmy forsake the regular, immensely remunerative session stool for the exhausting, often cutthroat life of a full-blown pop star? When I finally cornered the elusive Mr. Page he'd been dashing around London fulfilling outstanding session engagements. The night before he'd done his first gig with the Yardbirds at London's Marquee, and was desperately worried about how he'd gone down. *"Frankly,"* he explained, *"I felt I was getting stale doing sessions. I was restricted, and it was beginning to tell. You can let yourself go in a group. Jeff Beck,* (who he's known for years and recommended for the job when Eric Clapton quit) *and I have hundreds of ideas stored away."* Jimmy who taught himself to play guitar, has done studio work with top musicians for two years, he's been in the backing tracks of some of the top pop names record's. *"You name them, I've played with them,"* he grinned self consciously. *"Except the Beatles!"*. He's been to America and he's written songs with Jackie De Shannon for Marianne Faithfull and Barbara Lewis. Strangely enough, joining the Yardbirds won't be his first taste of solo pop though. *"I was pressurized into doing a single of my own once. Nothing fantastic. A song called "She Just Satisfies" which Jackie persuaded me to record. Still, I got a great advance for it and was able to go to the States."* Jimmy will fit into the group nicely. He's known most of the boys since pre-hit days. In fact, when he was first approached to play sessions, he was with Keith Relf at the time, who almost tagged along to play harmonica. His Marquee debut in front of fans had him worried he admitted. *"After playing for two years at muted volume, I was a little uncertain about playing Live and loud. I thought I would fluff it up. I only had a couple of hours rehearsal, and when I got up onstage I just gave everything I had. I got very excited. I expect people will obviously think I've taken a chance. I always felt secure on sessions. But I've got so many ideas going, things I've had tucked away at the back of my mind for ages. Anyway group life is a little more intimate. It appeals to me now."* **Melody Maker reports**...Jimmy, the new Yardbird settles in. Article and interview about

Jimmy Page joining the Yardbirds. The article implies that Jimmy is doing everything backwards by going from session man to band member. *"I've mucked about on a bass guitar for about two minutes but never played one properly. We had about two hours rehearsal last week and then played at the Marquee Club on Tuesday night. I was a bit worried that I said to myself- give it all you've got. As long as it's not too drastic. Fortunately once we started playing everything was all right."* He is asked whether he expects to have his earnings affected, *"Oh no, certainly not in the long run. I lost a lot of spontaneity lately playing sessions. Things weren't flowing out so easily as they were a year ago, and my ideas weren't happening very well. I joined the Yardbirds because I thought it would wake up my mind a bit. Yes, I might still do the occasional session."* When he is asked what he expects to do in the Yardbirds he replies, *"This is something that hasn't been ascertained yet. At the moment I'm playing bass guitar but maybe I'll do a few things with a second guitar. Jeff Beck and I have had a lot of very interesting talks about using two lead guitars. In fact we've even experimented with them ourselves but not with the group. On the free form parts of the numbers, twin lead guitars will be absolutely great. The whole trouble with feedback is that there is never enough power or backing to carry the sound itself. I was using bass guitar feedback the other night which was very good- a whole wall of sound- I got a ridiculous droning sound. On Mr. You're a Better Man, the overall sound was fantastic. We've been cutting some more records this week. Very little is planned with the Yardbirds. They like to go into the studio, pick up their instruments and then take it from there. They've got some very good ideas and Jeff and I have got one or two sounds we'd like to start on. I hope that I can add ideas and techniques to the group."* At this point in the interview it is pointed out that it is unknown whether Jimmy will be replacing Paul Samwell-Smith permanently. *"Everything is very cool at the moment. I have sort of stepped in because Sam has left, but I wouldn't like to say I was exactly on trial. I'm sure they're keeping an eye on me, but it's not like an audition. We're just playing together and seeing which way things go. I'd like to go to America with them in the near future because I want to see what the scene is like. The Yardbirds are a big, big, group over there and they are very interested in what they are doing on the West Coast of America. The Californians are interested in the electronics and all that-whereas the rest of the U.S. aren't quite so keen."*

July 8. New Musical Express Reports... Yardbirds why I left, why I joined. Two articles by Keith Altham featuring interviews with Paul Samwell-Smith and Jimmy Page. *"I'm a bit too old at 23 for all those screaming kids leaping about. I don't really think I'll be missed in the group, no one really noticed me onstage. I might just as well have been the dummy. A robot could have done what was required of me. Keith and Jeff are really the only two faces that matter in the Yardbirds,"* said Paul Samwell-Smith.

"I want to contribute a great deal more to the Yardbirds than just standing there looking glum. Just because you play bass does not mean you have no presence. Look at Bill Wyman in the Stones, he wears all that strange gear onstage and stands there doing nothing, but he does it better than anyone else! Chris Dreja is learning the bass at the moment, and it seems likely that I will take over on guitar at a later date," said Jimmy Page. When asked if he didn't enjoy session work anymore Page replied, *"I was drying up as a guitarist. I played a lot of rhythm guitar, which was very dull and left me no time to practice. Most of the musicians I know think I did the right thing in joining the Yardbirds. I wrote a few songs to which Jackie De Shannon put words, and sure I produced records, but take a look around who hasn't produced a record?"* The article then goes on to mention that Jimmy played with Neil Christian while he was still at school. *"I was only 14 then, and Neil was older! I chucked it in because of the terrible conditions and traveling rough. With the Yardbirds we travel in a Chevrolet, and the instruments follow on behind in a Van. If we have a date like the one in Blackpool at the weekend, we fly, that's not a hardship."* When asked about Jeff Beck, Page comments, *"Jeff and I have known one another since school days, when he tried to sell me a guitar he had made. I was delighted when the offer was made to join the group. The Yardbirds have begun something with their new sounds and unusual techniques which is by no means over, and I would like to contribute and help develop their ideas."* The article then goes on to mention several sessions that Page worked on including the Kinks and the Who.

July 22. New Musical Express reports... Yardbirds are to begin American tour on August 5th in Minneapolis, they will appear on Dick Clark's "Where The Action Is" on August 22nd. The tour will last five weeks and the band fly out on August 2nd to New York, the tour ends in Honolulu on Sept. 4.

July 30. Record Mirror Reports ... U.S. tour for Yardbirds...the Yardbirds fly to America on Tuesday August 2nd for their third U.S. tour. They spend three days in New York on promotional work and making personal appearances. TV and radio work is being lined up for the group and are likely to record during their stay. They kick off their tour dates at Minneapolis and Devenport on August 5, then play Chicago 6, Mentor 7, Fargo 8, Arnold Park 9, Hamilton Beach 10, Monticello 12, Denver 14, Amarillo 15, Lubbock 16, Colorado Springs 17, Tulsa 18, Oklahoma City 19 and 20, Tucson 21, Monterey 24, San Francisco 25, San Leandro 26, Santa

Barbara 27, San Diego 29, San Jose 30, Santa Rosa Sept. 1, Salem 3, and finally Hawaii 4.
August 19. New Musical Express Reports... Yardbirds to Australia. Yardbirds will undertake tour of Australia in the new year followed by three weeks in the Far East. The group returns from America on September 2nd.
September 2. New Musical Express reports... Jeff Beck has had an operation on his tonsils in San Francisco this previous weekend, he is expected to be out of the game for the rest of the tour.
September 9. New Musical Express Reports...front page advert reads "Rolling Stones 66 starring the Rolling Stones, Ike and Tina Turner, the Yardbirds, etc. Friday 23rd September Royal Albert Hall London, Saturday 24th September Odeon Theatre Leeds, Sunday 25th September Empire Theatre Liverpool, Wednesday 28th September ABC Theatre Manchester, Thursday 29th September ABC Theatre Stockton, Friday 30th September Odeon Theatre Glasgow, Saturday 1st October City Hall Newcastle, Sunday 2nd October Gaumont Theatre Ipswich, Thursday 6th October Odeon Theatre Birmingham, Friday 7th October Colston Hall Bristol, Saturday 8th October Capital Theatre Cardiff, Sunday 9th October Gaumont Theatre Southampton.
September 16. New Musical Express Reports... Yardbird out of hospital. Jeff Beck has been released from the San Francisco hospital where his tonsils were removed. He is expected to rejoin the group in time for the tour of England with the Rolling Stones beginning next Friday at London's Albert Hall. Band's latest single Happening' Ten Years Time Ago is scheduled for release on September 30th. The band return to America October 14th and will remain there until November 27th. They play the Paris Locomotive on December 3rd and Bristol University on the 10th.
October 21. New Musical Express Reports... Great Yardbirds but What's It All about? Review of the single Happenings Ten Years Time Ago/Psycho Daisies... "some of the weirdest sounds on disc, its hypnotic wild and different but what's it all about?"
November 19. New Musical Express Reports... Yardbirds split soon? Yardbirds finished their American tour on November 27th at which time they will return to London where it is expected that guitarists Jeff Beck and Jimmy Page will both quit. When the band return to England they are expected to play concerts at Aberystwyth University on December 13 and Hull City Hall 15th, they then return to United States on December 26 for eight days followed by three days in Denmark from January 6, and then two weeks in Australia from January 15.
November 26. New Musical Express Reports... Yardbirds Beck is mentally exhausted. June Harris reports from New York that Jeff Beck is not appearing on the current Yardbirds tour due to mental exhaustion. Jimmy Page is doing a fine job standing in.
December 3. New Musical Express Reports... Yardbird definitely leaving group...Yardbirds manager Simon Napier-Bell confirms that Jeff Beck will be leaving the Yardbirds due to ill health. The future of group member Jimmy Page remains in doubt.
December 31. Record Mirror Reports... Jeff Beck has left Yardbirds, not replaced. With the departure of Jeff Beck from the Yardbirds, the group intend to remain a quartet. Jimmy Page now moves to lead guitar. On Christmas day, the group left for an 8 day concert tour of United States. Before leaving, the Yardbirds recorded tracks for their next single release which is due in late January or early February. On their return to Britain they will be in the Studios again to wax tracks for their forthcoming album which is due to be released in April. On January 15 they leave the country again for a two-week concert tour of Australia, prior to appearing for ten days in the Philippines, Singapore and Hong Kong.

1967

January 21. Melody Maker reports...article on the Yardbirds. An interview with Keith Relf and Jimmy Page. *"We are still going down very well in America. It's still all fresh to them. Over here the scene is in a funny way at the moment,"* said Jimmy Page. *"I've been on three American tours. On the first two there was nothing happening there at all. I was shocked by the groups we played with. Now you find good guitarists and good ideas everywhere - especially on the West Coast. They don't just reproduce Beatles or Stones things anymore. The trouble is we aren't allowed to record in the United States and that means we must do everything in a terrible rush when we are here."* They then go on to discuss psychedelic music. *"It's a pity it's become associated with drugs, the whole idea was to liberate the mind without using drugs."*
March 11. Melody Maker reports... Yardbirds new single is completed.
April 8. **Record Mirror Reports...**review of Robert Plant's solo single. Our Song/Laughing Crying Laughing (CBS 202656). An expressive new voice. The song is tortuous and rambling but there's a stack of inspiration in the phrasing. Good.***
April 15. New Musical Express Reports... Yardbirds first as foursome...review of Little Games/Puzzles. The bands first disc as a four piece. "Gee whiz, what a shattering beat from the Yardbirds."...**Record Mirror Reports...**Review of Little Games/Puzzles. "So okay, the Yardbirds don't always make it. But this is a clever song idea and the arrangement is first straightforward, though with a shove along beat, and there's an instru-

mental spasm of high excitement. A hymn of praise to the big games that big boys play! Flip: not far short of the top deck for commercial quality. Top 50 tip.

April 22. New Musical Express reports... Yardbirds will spend six weeks in United States July 9th to August 20th, with two shows in Canada on July 7th and 8th. They fly to Paris on April 30th to film a TV show. On May the eighth they will appear at the Cannes film Festival in support of the movie "Blow Up".

May 20. Record Mirror Reports...interview with the Yardbirds. Keith Relf, Chris Dreja, and Jimmy Page discuss the fact that the pop world is constantly under attack. Jimmy Page, "*I was walking along the street laughing and joking with some friends and we were stopped by a policeman and searched. Just for laughing and being happy. If you enjoy yourself these days they think you're on a trip! But this sort of thing is happening to hundreds of young people, that's the terrifying thing. Two of my friends were taken to a police station and stripped just because they were out after midnight. All this sort of thing makes it hard on the pop groups who don't do evil things...and look at the amount of pop groups being searched. So few of them have got anything to hide.*" Jimmy pointed out the raid on a recent London club. "*There must have been about a hundred police involved. They raided the club where there must have been over 1000 kids. They put up partitions and stripped and searched everyone. About three people were found with tablets. A small percentage, you'd find that sort of average in any age group. Yet all those police were tied up for over three hours and I shuddered to think how many important crimes were being committed, apart from the vast amount of public money wasted on the raid. Then there were all those hundreds of completely innocent kids, humiliated, their evening ruined, their money wasted and further humiliation of having to wait for their parents to collect them at the police headquarters. Then the club owners must have suffered from loss of business as a result. Yet there doesn't seem to be as much hysteria about the crimes and perversions of the older generation. Look at the West end, some of the seedy things in Soho. The book shops, the filth, the smut that's sold. Look at the really genuine crime in certain parts of London. Look at the wife swapping, the rapes...the perversions. I'll even go so far as to point out the crowds at football matches, the thrown bottles and the wrecked trains. But you must get our point by now.*"

June 17. New Musical Express Reports... Advert reads, "Charity Pop Concert at the Saville Theatre, on Sunday, 18th June, 1967 7.30. Groups appearing, Manfred Mann, The New Vaudeville Band, The Zombies, The Yardbirds, The Settlers, and full supporting groups. Tickets: stalls £ 1.1.0 15/-, dress circle,£ 2.2.0, £ 1.1.0, upper circle, 15/-, 10/-, tickets on sale at the Saville Theatre box office and all ticket agencies.

NITA ANDERSON AGENCY LTD.
Agents for :- ROBERT PLANT & THE BAND OF JOY
HERBIES PEOPLE, C.B.S.
THE TRACTION, THE CHOICE
SCARLET RELIGION
Phone : OWO-73 3356/4080   Day & Night

July 15. Record Mirror Reports...review of Robert Plant's solo single. Long Time Coming: I've Got a Secret (CBS 2858). In some ways (song, performance, style) my record of the week. Rather bluesy, with a neat repeated riff on the title. It swings, but gently. I dug deeply. See?****

July 22. New Musical Express Reports... Nita Anderson Agency Limited, agents for:-Robert Plant And the Band of Joy, Herbies People, CBS, The Traction, The Choice, Scarlet Religion, Phone: OWO-73 3356/4080 Day and Night.

September 2. Record Mirror Reports... Robert Plant is pictured with caption that reads.. Gent with the beard, the solemn expression and the beads is Robert Plant, recently out with a CBS Release "Long Time Coming". So happens I especially liked this record and checked into his background. He's 18, Birmingham born, grammar School educated, with A level's in English, History, Civic's and Maths. Started singing two years ago with a group called Listen. First disc solo was "Our Song", recognized by Robert as a gigantic flop. He plays violin, piano, organ and guitar. Now he works all over the country, with his backing group The Band of Joy. Already his disc has hit the Birmingham top 20 which is at least planting the seeds of his talent.

September 9. Melody Maker reports... The Magnificent Seven. Article highlighting seven of the great rock guitarists including Eric Clapton, Jimi Hendrix, Pete Townshend, Jeff Beck, Stevie Winwood, Peter Green and Jimmy Page. Jimmy is described as the dark horse of the seven. It goes on to say that he is highly rated by his fellow guitar players that he plays the sitar and has a big interest in electronics. It says that he was playing guitar with Neil Christian and the Crusaders.

October 7. New Musical Express reports... The Yardbirds returned from the USA on September 30th. They go back to the USA on October 6th for three weeks. In November they are in the UK for various television and radio appearances, their new album "Little Games" is released on November 3 while the first single is out on November 10th.

1968

January 6. Record Mirror reports... the Yardbirds gear was stolen over Christmas, £2,500 worth. However

the thieves will probably have trouble using it as it is all wired for American power.
January 20. Record Mirror reports...the Yardbirds are offering a reward of £500 cash for information leading to the recovery of equipment stolen from them when their van was broken into on Christmas night. £3,000 worth of equipment was stolen, all of it American and unobtainable in this country, including all Jimmy Page's electronic equipment, five amplifiers, PA gear and a drum kit. Because they are working with inferior equipment they are unable to give good stage performances. They also need the original gear very urgently as they are about to start recording a single and an album.
February 10. Record Mirror reports... Review of the Yardbirds Single Good Night Sweet Josephine....the Yardbirds have a new single out on March first called Good Night Sweet Josephine. On April 1st Yardbirds leave for two-week tour of America they then return for a week before going to Australia for a three-week tour. Negotiations are also underway at the moment for the Yardbirds to appear in the New York Pop festival on May 31st, and June 1st and 2nd.
March 23. New Musical Express reports... The Yardbirds are in the studio in March. On April 6th they leave for an 8 day tour of Scandinavia, on April 17th they leave for America for three weeks.
March 30. Melody Maker reports... Advert reads, " Ewell Technical College Students Union presents Rag Week Dance in aid of multiple sclerosis at the college, Reigate Road, Ewell, Surrey. On Saturday March 30 Herbie Goin's and the Night Timers plus Robert Plant and the Band of Joy admission available at the door starts 8 p.m..
June 22. New Musical Express reports... Yardbirds returned from America last week having grossed $250, 000. They return to America on September 14th...Advert for Woburn Music Festival, July 6 and 7 Featuring Tim Rose (with John Bonham) along with Jimi Hendrix Experience, Fleetwood Mac, John Mayall, Donovan, T. Rex, Alexis Korner, etc.
Another interesting thing that I stumbled across while researching the Press Reports was a series of articles which allowed me to put together the itinerary for Tim Rose's tour of England. This is the tour which featured John Bonham. June 28 Hastings, June 29 Sheffield Students Union, July 2 Ritz Ballroom Bournemouth, July 4 Royal Festival Hall London, July 5 Pavilion in Hemel Hempstead, July 6 Gaiety Ballroom Ramsey, July 7 Woburn Abbey Pop Festival, July 14 Blaize's London, July 15 Wolverhampton, July 16 Marquee Club London, July 18 Liverpool, July 19 Grimsby Jazz club, July 20 Mistral Club Beckenham? - Middle Earth London? – Hatchett's London, July 21 Union Club Nottingham, July 30 Fishmonger's Arms Wood Green, July 31 Hampstead Country Club. — A series of other concerts were scheduled and canceled including a brief tour of Yugoslavia between July 8th and 13th, and a trip to Majorca Spain on July 23rd. Other dates which may have been played include Middlesbrough, the London Revolution, and the Windsor Jazz Festival. The Woburn Abbey Pop Festival also featured an incredible cast of top stars including Donovan, Fleetwood Mac, John Mayall and Jimi Hendrix. July 20th is a bit of a mystery since apparently Tim Rose may have played at three different places that day.
December 27, 1968 Georgia Strait reports... Advert reads Pacific Coliseum Sat. Dec. 28, 8P.M. Vanilla Fudge A Concerts West Production.
December 28, 1968 Vancouver Sun reports... Advert reads — Pacific Coliseum Tonight 8P.M. Concerts West Presents Vanilla Fudge Tickets $4.50, $3.50 $2.50 at the door and at Vancouver Ticket Centre...(Zeppelin were probably on this bill).

1969

January 8. New Musical Express reports... Article reviewing Led Zeppelin 2 mentions that the second track on side 2 is called "Living Loving Wreck."
May 17. Melody Maker reports... The album by the band Cartoone is reviewed. "Jimmy Page as guest artist is a helpful bonus."...**New Musical Express Reports...**June Harris reports from New York that the town of Woodstock, best known in England as the home of Bob Dylan, has announced its first music and art fair. A two-day event to be held August 16th and 17th. Among those scheduled to appear are Blood Sweat and Tears, Canned Heat, Led Zeppelin, Crosby Stills and Nash etc.... Ann Moses reports in from Los Angeles and says that Julie Driscoll and the Trinity and headlining Led Zeppelin brought out two of the largest audiences yet packed into the Pasadena Rose Palace last Friday and Saturday nights.
June 21. New Musical Express Reports...review of Joe Cocker's album With a Little Help from My Friends. "(Joe) injects a great deal of feeling into the number, which features a Jimmy Page guitar solo."
August 2. New Musical Express reports... Article mentions that Led Zeppelin will be appearing at the Bilzen Jazz Festival in Belgium.
August 9. New Musical Express reports... Led Zeppelin sold-out Cleveland Music Carnival... They will appear on the Top Gear radio show on August 10th with the Edgar Broughton band.